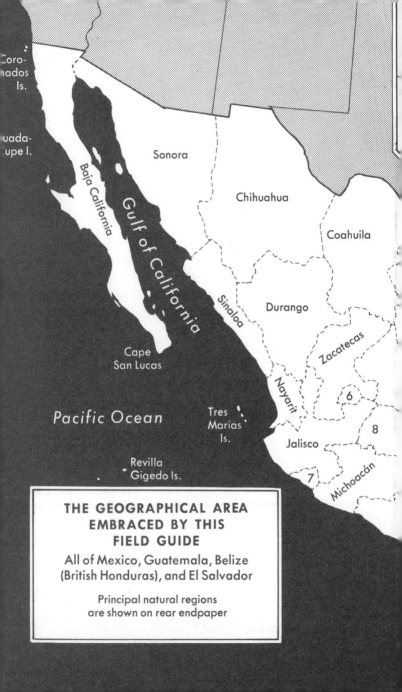

THE GEOGRAPHICAL AREA
EMBRACED BY THIS
FIELD GUIDE

All of Mexico, Guatemala, Belize
(British Honduras), and El Salvador

Principal natural regions
are shown on rear endpaper

THE PETERSON FIELD GUIDE SERIES®

Edited by Roger Tory Peterson

1. Birds (eastern) — *R.T. Peterson*
1A. Bird Songs (eastern) — *Cornell Laboratory of Ornithology*
2. Western Birds — *R.T. Peterson*
2A. Western Bird Songs — *Cornell Laboratory of Ornithology*
3. Shells of the Atlantic and Gulf Coasts, W. Indies — *Morris*
4. Butterflies (eastern) — *Opler and Malikul*
5. Mammals — *Burt and Grossenheider*
6. Pacific Coast Shells (including Hawaii) — *Morris*
7. Rocks and Minerals — *Pough*
8. Birds of Britain and Europe — *Peterson, Mountfort, Hollom*
9. Animal Tracks — *Murie*
10. Ferns (ne. and cen. N. America) — *Cobb*
11. Eastern Trees — *Petrides*
11A. Trees and Shrubs — *Petrides*
12. Reptiles and Amphibians (e. and cen. N. America) — *Conant and Collins*
13. Birds of Texas and Adjacent States — *R.T. Peterson*
14. Rocky Mt. Wildflowers — *Craighead, Craighead, and Davis*
15. Stars and Planets — *Pasachoff and Menzel*
16. Western Reptiles and Amphibians — *Stebbins*
17. Wildflowers (ne. and n.-cen. N. America) — *R.T. Peterson and McKenney*
19. Insects (America north of Mexico) — *Borror and White*
20. Mexican Birds — *R.T. Peterson and Chalif*
21. Birds' Nests (east of Mississippi River) — *Harrison*
22. Pacific States Wildflowers — *Niehaus and Ripper*
23. Edible Wild Plants (e. and cen. N. America) — *L. Peterson*
24. Atlantic Seashore — *Gosner*
25. Western Birds' Nests — *Harrison*
26. Atmosphere — *Schaefer and Day*
27. Coral Reefs (Caribbean and Florida) — *Kaplan*
28. Pacific Coast Fishes — *Eschmeyer, Herald, and Hammann*
29. Beetles — *White*
30. Moths — *Covell*
31. Southwestern and Texas Wildflowers — *Niehaus, Ripper, and Savage*
32. Atlantic Coast Fishes — *Robins, Ray, and Douglass*
33. Western Butterflies — *Tilden and Smith*
34. Mushrooms — *McKnight and McKnight*
35. Hawks — *Clark and Wheeler*
36. Southeastern and Caribbean Seashores — *Kaplan*
37. Ecology of Eastern Forests — *Kricher and Morrison*
39. Birding by Ear: Eastern and Central — *Walton and Lawson*
40. Advanced Birding — *Kaufman*
41. Medicinal Plants — *Foster and Duke*
42. Birding by Ear: Western — *Walton and Lawson*
43. Freshwater Fishes (N. America north of Mexico) — *Page and Burr*
44. Eastern Bird Song — *Walton and Lawson*
45. Western Trees — *Petrides*
46. Ecology of Western Forests — *Kricher and Morrison*

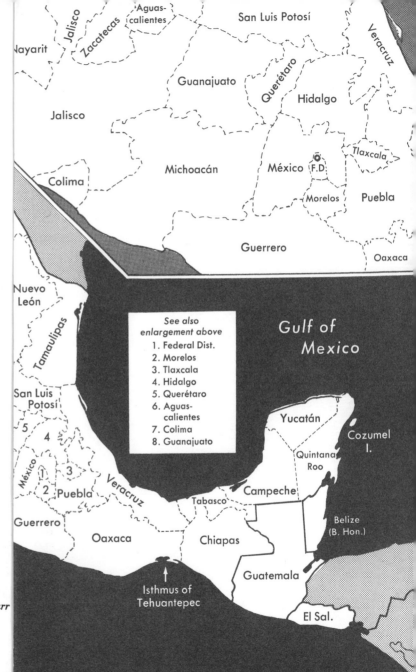

A Field Guide
to Mexican Birds

2
2
23
24
25.
26.
27.
28.
29. B
30. M
31. So

32. Atl
33. We
34. Mu
35. Haw
36. Sout
37. Ecolo
38. Birdi
39. Advar
40. Medic
41. Birdir
42. Freshw
43. Backya
44. Western
45. Ecology

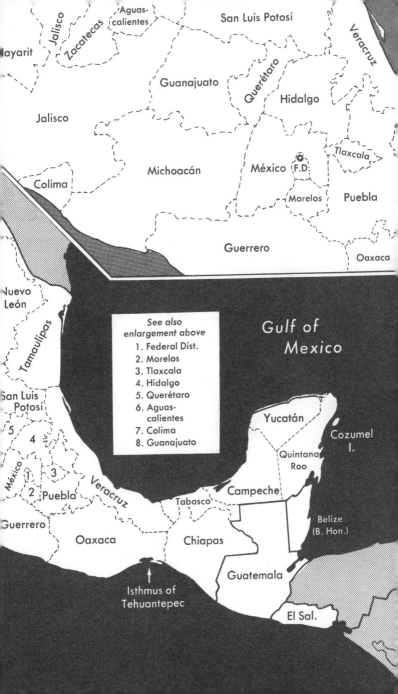

A Field Guide
to Mexican Birds

THE PETERSON FIELD GUIDE SERIES®

Edited by Roger Tory Peterson

1. Birds (eastern) — *R.T. Peterson*
1A. Bird Songs (eastern) — *Cornell Laboratory of Ornithology*
2. Western Birds — *R.T. Peterson*
2A. Western Bird Songs — *Cornell Laboratory of Ornithology*
3. Shells of the Atlantic and Gulf Coasts, W. Indies — *Morris*
4. Butterflies (eastern) — *Opler and Malikul*
5. Mammals — *Burt and Grossenheider*
6. Pacific Coast Shells (including Hawaii) — *Morris*
7. Rocks and Minerals — *Pough*
8. Birds of Britain and Europe — *Peterson, Mountfort, Hollom*
9. Animal Tracks — *Murie*
10. Ferns (ne. and cen. N. America) — *Cobb*
11. Eastern Trees — *Petrides*
11A. Trees and Shrubs — *Petrides*
12. Reptiles and Amphibians (e. and cen. N. America) — *Conant and Collins*
13. Birds of Texas and Adjacent States — *R.T. Peterson*
14. Rocky Mt. Wildflowers — *Craighead, Craighead, and Davis*
15. Stars and Planets — *Pasachoff and Menzel*
16. Western Reptiles and Amphibians — *Stebbins*
17. Wildflowers (ne. and n.-cen. N. America) — *R.T. Peterson and McKenney*
19. Insects (America north of Mexico) — *Borror and White*
20. Mexican Birds — *R.T. Peterson and Chalif*
21. Birds' Nests (east of Mississippi River) — *Harrison*
22. Pacific States Wildflowers — *Niehaus and Ripper*
23. Edible Wild Plants (e. and cen. N. America) — *L. Peterson*
24. Atlantic Seashore — *Gosner*
25. Western Birds' Nests — *Harrison*
26. Atmosphere — *Schaefer and Day*
27. Coral Reefs (Caribbean and Florida) — *Kaplan*
28. Pacific Coast Fishes — *Eschmeyer, Herald, and Hammann*
29. Beetles — *White*
30. Moths — *Covell*
31. Southwestern and Texas Wildflowers — *Niehaus, Ripper, and Savage*
32. Atlantic Coast Fishes — *Robins, Ray, and Douglass*
33. Western Butterflies — *Tilden and Smith*
34. Mushrooms — *McKnight and McKnight*
35. Hawks — *Clark and Wheeler*
36. Southeastern and Caribbean Seashores — *Kaplan*
37. Ecology of Eastern Forests — *Kricher and Morrison*
38. Birding by Ear: Eastern and Central — *Walton and Lawson*
39. Advanced Birding — *Kaufman*
40. Medicinal Plants — *Foster and Duke*
41. Birding by Ear: Western — *Walton and Lawson*
42. Freshwater Fishes (N. America north of Mexico) — *Page and Burr*
43. Backyard Bird Song — *Walton and Lawson*
44. Western Trees — *Petrides*
45. Ecology of Western Forests — *Kricher and Morrison*

A Field Guide to
Mexican Birds

Mexico, Guatemala, Belize, El Salvador

Roger Tory Peterson
and
Edward L. Chalif

Illustrations by
Roger Tory Peterson

Sponsored by the National Audubon Society,
the National Wildlife Federation,
and the Roger Tory Peterson Institute

HOUGHTON MIFFLIN COMPANY
Boston   New York

PETERSON FIELD GUIDES and PETERSON FIELD GUIDE SERIES are registered trademarks of Houghton Mifflin Company.

Library of Congress Cataloging in Publication Data

Peterson, Roger Tory
A field guide to Mexican Birds

(The Peterson field guide Series, 20)
"Sponsored by the National Audubon Society and National Wildlife Federation"
1. Birds — Mexico — Identification. 2. Birds — Central America — Identification. I. Chalif, Edward L., joint author. II. Title
QL686.P47   598.2'972   73-4970
ISBN 0-395-17129-6

Printed in the United States of America

VB 16 15 14 13 12 11 10 9 8

An Appreciation

to our wives

MARGARET CHALIF,
*who encouraged her husband
to put his knowledge of Mexican birds
on record and who often accompanied him
on his Mexican forays,*

and

BARBARA C. PETERSON,
*who undertook the almost
endless task of secretarial work and
saw the manuscript through its
long evolutionary process.*

Preface

IN 1934 my first *Field Guide* was published, covering the birds east of the 100th meridian in North America. This book was designed so that live birds could be run down by their field marks without resorting to the technical details and measurements employed by the old-time collector and systematist. The "Peterson System," as it is now called, is based on patternistic drawings that indicate the key field marks with arrows. These and the comparisons between similar species are the core of the system. This practical method — visual but not always phylogenetic — has enjoyed universal acceptance, not only in North America but also in Europe, where *Field Guides* now exist in twelve languages.

Some years ago, in 1940, just about the time I had put the first edition of *A Field Guide to Western Birds* in my publisher's hands, Edward Chalif, who had birded with me in the West, suggested that a Mexican *Field Guide* was much needed; why not do one together? He had already probed the delights of the neotropical avifauna — I had not.

Our involvement in the Armed Services during the next several years drove out all thoughts of a Mexican bird guide, and it was not until World War II was behind us that we talked about it again. The task of dealing with an avifauna of more than 1000 species seemed overwhelming, and I took the position that I could attempt it only if another artist or two would participate.

Edward Chalif made a number of subsequent expeditions. I took part in some of this preliminary field work to acquaint myself with as many species as possible (I have now had actual field experience with about 850 of the 1000+ species covered in this guide — close to 85 percent). Chalif soon prepared a first draft of the text, but the prospect of painting so many species staggered me. We approached George Sutton, dean of American bird portraitists, who already had much Mexican experience, and he tentatively agreed to take part. Soon afterward, because of an overloaded work schedule he was reluctantly forced to withdraw. We next tried Don Eckelberry, who was becoming increasingly intrigued by the birds of the American tropics and painted them brilliantly. He too said yes, then after some realistic second thoughts, no. It was evident that I would have to do them all myself; hence the long delay in the publication of this book.

In the meantime we drew L. Irby Davis into the picture as a third co-author because of his many years of pioneer work in Mexico, especially with bird vocalizations. This collaboration was

vii

most promising but eventually he too withdrew, to publish his own book with a greater area coverage (all of Middle America), following his own concept of speciation and adopting the vernacular names of his preference.

Inasmuch as so many years had elapsed since Chalif prepared the first draft of the text and so much new information had been published while I was planning the color plates, it fell to me to prepare the subsequent and final text revisions. These were then checked again by Chalif before we submitted them to the fine-tooth comb of several of our colleagues, to whom we express our gratitude. Peter Alden, leader of many excursions to the tropics for the Massachusetts Audubon Society and author of *Finding the Birds in Western Mexico,* examined the entire text and made numerous suggestions. Dr. Raymond A. Paynter, Jr., checked those species occurring in the Yucatán Peninsula, and his publication *The Ornithogeography of the Yucatán Peninsula* was also consulted.

The person who gave the manuscript the most complete and critical going over was Dr. Eugene Eisenmann of the American Museum of Natural History. As Chairman of the A.O.U. Check-List Committee, which plans to include all of Middle America in the next edition of the *Check-List,* he has an impeccable up-to-the-minute knowledge of publications, records, range extensions, taxonomic decisions, etc., as they affect Mexican birds. He also had the specimens of the American Museum at hand to examine when necessary, especially when checking color plates. Many of the voice descriptions were derived from his own field notes made in Panama, except for those of the Crested and the Mottled Owls heard in Venezuela and identified with the aid of Paul Schwartz.

Dr. Kenneth C. Parkes of the Carnegie Museum also examined some of the color plates and made available many of his color notes of soft parts which he had recorded while collecting in Mexico. In addition, he made available certain specimens that we needed when study material at the American Museum proved inadequate. Most of the specimens used for the text and color plates were from the American Museum; a few were from the National Museum (Smithsonian) in Washington and the Peabody Museum of Natural History at Yale University.

Dudley Ross, an avid and well-traveled bird watcher, took it upon himself to analyze the species coverage in other Middle American countries (percentages covered by this guide). These figures are given on page xvii.

I also thank the Western Pennsylvania Conservancy for appointing me "Scholar in Residence" and thereby making available to me the seclusion of Frank Lloyd Wright's "Fallingwater" while I was painting many of the color plates.

Numerous students of Mexican birds other than those mentioned earlier also gave suggestions or other help: Dr. Richard O.

Albert, Dr. John Aldrich, Dr. Arthur A. Allen, Dr. Elsa Allen, Dr. Dean Amadon, Margaret Chalif, L. Irby Davis, Don Eckelberry, Mrs. Bradley Fisk, Ben King, Dr. Wesley Lanyon, Christine Lillie, Dr. George Lowery, Dr. Joe T. Marshall, Jr., Dr. Robert Newmann, Charles O'Brien, Allan O'Connell, Dudley Ross, George Saunders, Dr. Walter Spofford, Alexander Sprunt IV, Dr. George Miksch Sutton, Dr. Josselyn Van Tyne, Dr. Charles Vaurie, Dr. Alexander Wetmore, and Dora Weyer.

In preparing the text we have researched every pertinent published source, including a large number of papers and notes in the ornithological journals, especially *The Auk, The Condor,* and *The Wilson Bulletin.* All important regional publications south to Panamá were also consulted.

A list of major reference works useful to the student is given in a Selected Bibliography on page 261.

Since neither Edward Chalif nor I (R.T.P.) have recorded the voices of all Mexican birds in our notes, we have filled in many gaps with descriptions by the following students of neotropical birds (these are credited by surname after each voice description): Peter Alden, Dean Amadon, Robert F. Andrle, H. G. Anthony, D. H. Baepler, Arthur C. Bent, Emmet Blake, James Bond, Herbert Brandt, F. O. Chapelle, R. Crossin, L. Irby Davis, D. R. Dickey, Ernest Edwards, Eugene Eisenmann, James Fisher, Herbert Friedmann, R. R. Graber, Ludlow Griscom, Shelly Grossman, John William Hardy, C. Hartshorne, F. Haverschmidt, Thomas R. Howell, L. Ingles, Edgar Kincaid, Douglas Lancaster, Hugh C. Land, Wesley Lanyon, R. M. Laughlin, A. Starker Leopold, F. W. Loetscher, Jr., George Lowery, Joe T. Marshall, Jr., C. J. Maynard, Burt L. Monroe, Jr., Robert T. Moore, Theodore Parker, Raymond A. Paynter, Jr., Stephen Russell, Robert K. Selander, Alexander Skutch, Paul Slud, A. P. Smith, W. J. Smith, Frank B. Smithe, B. B. Sturgis, George M. Sutton, R. E. Tashian, A. J. van Rossem, Charles Vaurie, Fred Webster, Alexander Wetmore, Edwin Willis, and Dale Zimmerman. A number of these descriptions were based on vocalizations heard in countries other than Mexico, and may differ. This applies to those credited to Bond (West Indies); Lancaster, Russell, Willis (Belize); Land, Smithe (Guatemala); Monroe (Honduras); Howell (Nicaragua); Skutch, Slud, A. P. Smith (Costa Rica); Chapelle, Eisenmann, Wetmore (Panama); Schwartz (Venezuela); and Haverschmidt (Surinam).

The long, almost endless task of secretarial work fell to Barbara C. Peterson, who took care of a mountain of correspondence and typed and retyped the manuscript several times. To her we express special gratitude. Those of the staff of Houghton Mifflin Company who wrestled with the involved problems of actual publication were Morton H. Baker, Katharine Bernard, Paul Brooks, Virginia Ehrlich, Richard B. McAdoo, Arnold Paine, and especially Helen Phillips, who is a marvel of thoroughness in smoothing out the intricacies of editorial styling.

ROGER TORY PETERSON

Contents

Preface   vii
How to Use This Book   xvii

Tinamous: Tinamidae   1
Loons: Gaviidae   2
Grebes: Podicipedidae   3
Albatrosses: Diomedeidae   4
Shearwaters, Large Petrels, etc.: Procellariidae   5
Storm-Petrels: Hydrobatidae   8
Tropicbirds: Phaethontidae   9
Pelicans: Pelecanidae   10
Gannets and Boobies: Sulidae   10
Cormorants: Phalacrocoracidae   11
Darters (Anhingas): Anhingidae   12
Frigatebirds (Man-o'-War Birds): Fregatidae   13
Herons and Bitterns: Ardeidae   13
Boat-billed Herons: Cochleariidae   16
Storks: Ciconiidae   17
Ibises and Spoonbills: Threskiornithidae   18
Flamingos: Phoenicopteridae   18
Ducks, Swans, and Geese: Anatidae   19
New World Vultures: Cathartidae   25
Ospreys: Pandionidae   26
Kites, Hawks, Harriers, Eagles: Accipitridae   26
Caracaras, Forest-Falcons, and Falcons: Falconidae   36
Chachalacas, Guans, and Curassows: Cracidae   40
Wood-Partridges, Quails, etc.: Phasianidae   43
Turkeys: Meleagrididae   47
Cranes: Gruidae   48
Limpkins: Aramidae   48
Rails, Gallinules, Coots: Rallidae   49

Finfoots: Heliornithidae 52
Sunbitterns: Eurypygidae 52
Jacanas: Jacanidae 53
Oystercatchers: Haematopodidae 53
Plovers, etc.: Charadriidae 54
Sandpipers, Snipe, etc.: Scolopacidae 55
Stilts and Avocets: Recurvirostridae 60
Phalaropes: Phalaropodidae 60
Thick-knees: Burhinidae 61
Jaegers and Skuas: Stercorariidae 61
Gulls and Terns: Laridae 62
Skimmers: Rynchopidae 66
Auks, etc.: Alcidae 66
Pigeons and Doves: Columbidae 67
Macaws, Parakeets, Parrots: Psittacidae 72
Cuckoos, Anis, Roadrunners: Cuculidae 78
Owls: Tytonidae (Barn Owls) and Strigidae (True Owls) 81
Potoos: Nyctibiidae 88
Nightjars (Goatsuckers): Caprimulgidae 89
Swifts: Apodidae 92
Hummingbirds: Trochilidae 94
Trogons: Trogonidae 108
Kingfishers: Alcedinidae 111
Motmots: Momotidae 112
Jacamars: Galbulidae 114
Puffbirds: Bucconidae 115
Toucans: Ramphastidae 115
Woodpeckers: Picidae 117
Woodcreepers (Woodhewers): Dendrocolaptidae 124
Ovenbirds (Horneros) and Allies: Furnariidae 128
Antbirds: Formicariidae 130
Manakins: Pipridae 134
Cotingas: Cotingidae 136
Tyrant Flycatchers: Tyrannidae 140
Larks: Alaudidae 158
Swallows: Hirundinidae 158

Crows and Jays: Corvidae   161
Titmice, Verdins, Bushtits: Paridae   167
Nuthatches: Sittidae   168
Creepers: Certhiidae   169
Wrentits: Chamaeidae   169
Dippers: Cinclidae   169
Wrens: Troglodytidae   170
Thrashers and Mockingbirds: Mimidae   179
Thrushes, Solitaires, Bluebirds: Turdidae   183
Gnatcatchers, Gnatwrens, Kinglets, etc.: Sylviidae   189
Wagtails and Pipits: Motacillidae   191
Waxwings: Bombycillidae   192
Silky-Flycatchers or Silkies: Ptilogonatidae   192
Shrikes: Laniidae   193
Starlings: Sturnidae   193
Peppershrikes: Cyclarhidae   194
Shrike-Vireos: Vireolaniidae   194
Vireos: Vireonidae   195
Honeycreepers: Coerebidae   200
Wood-Warblers: Parulidae   202
Weaver Finches, etc.: Ploceidae   216
Blackbirds, Orioles, Meadowlarks: Icteridae   216
Tanagers: Thraupidae   227
Grosbeaks, Buntings, Sparrows, and Finches: Fringillidae   235

Selected Bibliography   261
Index   263

Illustrations

Line illustrations

Map of Area Covered by This Book (political)   *front endpaper*
Map of Area Covered by This Book (physical)   *rear endpaper*
Topography of a Bird   xxii
Atitlán Grebe   4
Muscovy   23
Distribution of Mexican Chachalacas (map)   41
Olivaceous Piculet   117

Plates (following page 137)

1. Long-legged Wading Birds
2. Birds of Prey: Kites, Accipiters, Black-collared Hawk
3. Birds of Prey: Falcons, Forest-Falcons, Buteonine Hawks
4. Large Birds of Prey
5. Black Birds of Prey Overhead
6. Guans, Curassows, Chachalacas
7. Tinamous, Horned Guan, and Ocellated Turkey
8. Quails and Wood-Partridges
9. Quails
10. Rails, Sunbittern, Sungrebe, Waders, etc.
11. Pigeons and Doves
12. Pigeons and Doves
13. Macaws and Parrots
14. Parakeets and Small Parrots
15. Cuckoos, Nightjars, Potoos
16. Owls
17. Swifts and Swallows
18. Hummingbirds
19. Hummingbirds
20. Hummingbirds
21. Trogons

22. Toucans, Motmots, Puffbirds, Jacamar, Kingfishers
23. Woodpeckers
24. Woodcreepers
25. Antbirds; Ovenbirds and Allies
26. Manakins and Cotingas
27. Flycatchers
28. Flycatchers
29. Flycatchers
30. Jays
31. Jays
32. Wrens
33. Wrens, Gnatcatchers, Gnatwren
34. Mimic-Thrushes, Silky-Flycatchers
35. Thrushes
36. Vireos and Allies
37. Honeycreepers and Warblers
38. Warblers
39. Oropendolas, Caciques, Blackbirds, etc.
40. Orioles
41. Orioles
42. Tanagers
43. Tanagers
44. Tanagers
45. Finches
46. Finches
47. Finches
48. Sparrows

How to Use This Book

IT IS ASSUMED that anyone using this *Field Guide to Mexican Birds* will already be familiar with one of the other Peterson *Field Guides* (East, West, or Texas) and will in a general way know the form. The reader will find it most expeditious in this guide to go directly to the color plates, which are grouped for convenience. In most instances the pictures and their legend pages tell the story without help from the main text. The arrows point to outstanding field marks, briefly explained on the legend page opposite.

However, to encompass more than 1000 species in a book of *Field Guide* size we are forced to make certain constrictions. All Mexican species not already treated in at least one of the three North American *Field Guides* are illustrated in this book (with rare exception), and they are treated fully in the text. On the other hand, most species that are widespread in North America are not illustrated, nor are they treated fully in the text. Their occurrence in Mexico is given briefly, as well as a one-line memorandum of field marks; but for other details the reader is referred to the appropriate North American *Field Guides* by initial, thus: E (East), W (West), or T (Texas). *Note:* General statements in the descriptions and habitats apply only to the area covered in this book.

In this book a total of 1038 species are treated. Of these 1018 have been recorded in Mexico (or 1000 to 1018, depending on taxonomic opinion). This number includes 28 *accidentals* and a number of *casuals* (not quite in the accidental category but to be expected occasionally because their normal range is not far from Mexican boundaries). Five species are established introductions from other lands, 3 occurred formerly, but are no longer found in Mexico, and 4 have become extinct during recent times. Add to the Mexican total of 1018 the 17 species recorded in Guatemala but not yet in Mexico, 3 others from British Honduras, and the grand total is 1038. This total figure does not include subspecies. In an analysis made previous to publication by Dudley Ross, it was determined that about 93 percent of all the birds known to Honduras are also included in this book, 86 percent of those in Nicaragua, 66 percent of those in Costa Rica, and 56½ percent of the birds in Panamá. The student who wishes to know the appearance of the remaining 400± Central American birds not dealt with in this *Field Guide* will find them illustrated in L. Irby Davis's *Field Guide to the Birds of Mexico and Central America*.

Numbers of Birds: The comparative numbers of species in various bird families will interest some students. The world numbers follow the recent appraisal of James Fisher in *The World of Birds* by Fisher and Peterson (2nd edition, 1971).

Subspecies: Subspecies have no definite entity but merely represent subdivisions within the geographic range of a species. These may be *clinal,* with a smooth gradation or blend from one so-called race to another, or they may be more sharply defined in cases of species with interrupted ranges. In most instances, subspecies should play no part in field recognition. Most are determined with accuracy only with a collecting gun. The problem of speciation is very complex in Mexico, and there are frequent disputes among systematists as to whether certain species are valid or worthy only of subspecific distinction. In this book we have seldom expressed a strong opinion in controversial matters of this sort, but have gone along with the most current thinking, based mainly on the checklists of Eugene Eisenmann *(The Species of Middle American Birds)* and R. Meyer de Schauensee *(The Species of Birds of South America)* and modified by recent technical publications. Except in those cases where field distinctions are very obvious, we have ignored subspecies. A breakdown of these can be found in Emmet Blake's *Birds of Mexico.*

Names of Birds: The English names of birds are those selected by Eugene Eisenmann in collaboration with Emmet Blake and Edward Chalif (1955) in an effort to bring about a consistency in the names of Mexican birds, many of which went by a number of confusing vernacular names in the ornithological literature. The Eisenmann names have been in large part accepted as standard by the ornithological fraternity, and with rare exception we use them here. To orient those who may also be using other guides with dissimilar names we have included cross-references in our Index.

We have followed in a general way Eisenmann's systematic order but have modified this order within certain groups of birds to conform to recent revisions by Amadon-Brown (hawks), Amadon-Delacour (cracids), Bourne (petrels), Delacour (waterfowl), Jehl (shorebirds), Marshall (screech-owls), and by Eisenmann himself.

The next A.O.U. *Check-List* will include the birds of Middle America. If the sequence of species in this guide differs at times from the last *Check-List* (1957), it is because of recent decisions by the Check-List Committee.

Range: This book covers all birds found in Mexico, Guatemala, Belize (British Honduras), and El Salvador. In order that the user may have an overall concept of each bird's distribution, we have first given under the heading **Range** a capsule statement of the bird's general range (if widespread) and then, under **Mexico**, described how it fits into the Mexican picture. *Note:* The name British Honduras was changed to Belize in 1973, and the country, which is located on the Caribbean coast of Central America, became independent in 1981. However, "British Honduras" remains in the range accounts because this book was originally printed before the country's name was changed.

Acquaint yourself with the comparative locations of the various states in Mexico (see front endpaper). Know precisely where you are when you are in the field. Study also the rear endpaper, which shows the major faunal areas (very much simplified). Birds from eastern and central North America tend to migrate through eastern Mexico. (When we speak of the Gulf slope we mean Gulf of Mexico, not Gulf of California.) Western birds go down the Pacific slope and through the western mountains and central plateau. Many eastern and western birds mingle in the Isthmus of Tehuantepec and Chiapas. Middle (or Mid.) America, as used in this book is the area from Mexico to and including Panamá; Central (or Cen.) America does not include Mexico, but here encompasses the countries between it and Panamá. Yucatán Peninsula in toto includes the three Mexican states of Campeche, Yucatán, and Quintana Roo, as well as Belize (British Honduras). The latter country has no highlands and therefore many of the birds of the mountains of Mexico and Guatemala do not occur there except as strays.

Habitat: Each bird's preferred environment is indicated briefly under this heading, but do not be surprised if your bird is not always where it is expected, particularly in migration. At coastal points, islands, city parks, and desert oases, birds in passage or strays may often be found in an untypical environment. A bird's preferred habitat may also vary regionally.

The Illustrations: The color plates are grouped in the center of the book for convenience. They are portraits and at the same time somewhat schematic, arranged for quick comparison of the species most resembling each other (and therefore not always in phylogenetic sequence). Arrows point to the key field marks. It is a visual system.

Birds adequately illustrated in the three North American *Field Guides* (East, West, or Texas) are usually not illustrated in the present book. Exceptions are made in the case of certain birds (Green Jay and Kiskadee, for example, which are much more typical of Mexico than the U.S.). Included also are a few widespread North American species when comparisons are useful in dealing with similar Mexican species. We admittedly have been somewhat arbitrary in these inclusions.

Measurements: The lengths of birds are given in inches after the scientific name. When a range of measurement is given, the lesser figure may be closer to the actual size of the bird in life (from tip of beak to end of tail); the larger figure may more accurately represent some museum skins (on back, in tray, neck stretched, etc.).

Definitions of Symbols and Terms: ♂ is the symbol for male; ♀ means female.

Accidentals, as used here, are defined as birds that have not been recorded more than two or three times in Mexico; usually only once, but so far out of normal range that they might not be reasonably expected again. We have not segregated the accidentals in a special appendix as in the other *Field Guides.*

Casual. Casual means very few records, usually of species that might be expected to occur again because Mexico is not far from their normal range.

Question mark: A question mark (?) after a locality means probable, not certain; needs confirmation.

Resident means the same as *permanent resident;* the bird is found throughout the year.

Migrant, breeds, and *winters* are self-evident terms.

Anatomical and plumage terms: See the diagram on page xxii (topography of a bird).

Voice: We have used our own voice descriptions when possible and have supplemented these from other sources, some published, some not. Each voice description is credited; so if it does not sound that way to you, the onus is on the interpreter. In learning bird voices (and some experts do 90 percent of their field work by ear), there is no substitute for actual sounds. Authors often attempt to fit songs into syllables, words, and phrases; musical notations, comparative descriptions, and ingenious systems of symbols are also employed. But with the advent of the tape recorder these techniques have been eclipsed.

Although the songs of many Mexican birds have now been recorded on tape, the only commercial record available is by L. Irby Davis, *Mexican Bird Songs,* produced by the Laboratory of Ornithology at Cornell University and published by Houghton Mifflin Company. This 12-inch LP record gives a representative selection of the voices of 74 Mexican birds and is an excellent introduction.

Guides to Bird Finding: We urge the birder who wishes to get the most from his Mexican travels to obtain copies of the following books, which do for Mexico what Dr. Olin Sewall Pettingill's two guides to *Bird Finding* (East and West) have done for the U.S. The first is *Finding Birds in Mexico* by Ernest P. Edwards, obtainable from the author at Sweet Briar, Virginia 24595. The other is more limited in the area covered but goes into greater detail: *Finding the Birds in Western Mexico* by Peter Alden is published by the University of Arizona Press at Tucson and is indispensable to anyone planning to bird in Sonora, Sinaloa, or Nayarit.

A Selected Bibliography of these and other books will be found on page 261.

A Field Guide
to Mexican Birds

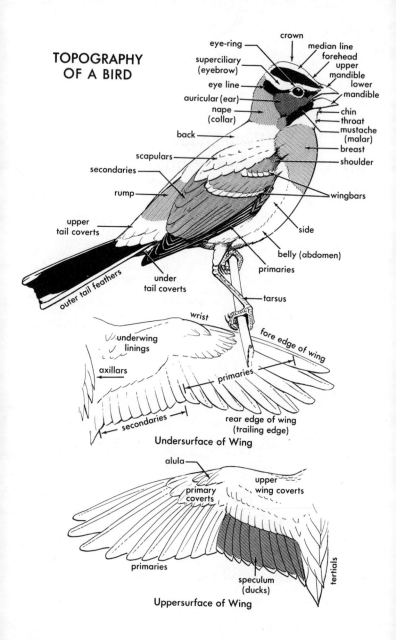

TOPOGRAPHY OF A BIRD

crown
eye-ring
median line
superciliary (eyebrow)
forehead
upper mandible
eye line
lower mandible
auricular (ear)
nape (collar)
chin
throat
back
mustache (malar)
scapulars
breast
secondaries
shoulder
rump
wingbars
upper tail coverts
side
belly (abdomen)
primaries
under tail coverts
outer tail feathers
tarsus

wrist
underwing linings
fore edge of wing
axillars
primaries
secondaries
rear edge of wing (trailing edge)

Undersurface of Wing

alula
upper wing coverts
primary coverts
primaries
tertials
speculum (ducks)

Uppersurface of Wing

Tinamous: Tinamidae

PRIMITIVE fowl-like ground birds of almost tailless aspect; plump, with short legs, slender necks, small heads, and slightly decurved bills. Mexican species are dark with whitish throats. Sexes similar, female larger. All Mexican species inhabit forests and brush; heard more often than seen. Terrestrial, they flush reluctantly on whirring wings. Eggs extremely glossy. **Food:** Fruit, seeds; a few insects. **Range:** Mexico to s. Argentina. **No. of species:** World, 42; Mexico, 4.

GREAT TINAMOU *Tinamus major* 15–18   **Pl. 7**
    Field marks: A shy, olive-brown, fowl-like bird, paler below, with a slender, slightly decurved bill, slender neck, and stub-tailed appearance. Legs *blue-gray*. The largest Mexican tinamou.
    Voice: A melancholy, plaintive call; 3 sets of paired tremolos (Slud). In Panamá, 2 long-drawn tremulous whistles, mainly at dawn and dusk (Eisenmann).
    Range: S. Mexico to Ecuador, cen. Brazil, n. Bolivia. **Mexico:** Se. Puebla, s. Veracruz, and n. Oaxaca east through n. Chiapas, Campeche to Quintana Roo. **Habitat:** Shady humid forests; lowlands to 2500 ft.

LITTLE TINAMOU *Crypturellus soui* 8½–9½   **Pl. 7**
    Field marks: Quail-sized, furtive; the smallest Mexican tinamou. Reddish brown, darker on back and paling to cinnamon on belly. Head *slaty*. Legs *greenish*. No barring (larger Thicket Tinamou has barring).
    Voice: A clear, tremulous whistle of a varying number of notes, rising with a slight change of pitch, then several downward notes ending on a minor key (Chalif). Like dragging the hammer up the upper keys of a xylophone about 7 tones, then starting at original pitch and running down about 5 tones (Friedmann and Smith).
    Range: Mexico to Peru, Bolivia, Brazil. **Mexico:** S. Veracruz, n. Oaxaca, n. Chiapas, Tabasco, Campeche, Quintana Roo. **Habitat:** Humid second-growth forests, woodland thickets; lowlands and lower mt. slopes.

SLATY-BREASTED (BOUCARD'S) TINAMOU   **Pl. 7**
Crypturellus boucardi 10–11
    Field marks: A very dark, almost *blackish* tinamou with

1

bright *orange or red* legs. Very difficult to see in the forest un-
dergrowth; more often heard than seen.
Voice: Call of ♂ a ventriloqual hollow *ah-oowah,* the *oo* slur-
ring down, then returning to pitch (Lancaster).
Range: S. Mexico to n. Costa Rica. **Mexico:** S. Veracruz, n.
Oaxaca, n. Chiapas, s. Tabasco, s. Quintana Roo. **Habitat:**
Floor, undergrowth of humid forests; sea level to 5000 ft.

THICKET (RUFESCENT) TINAMOU   Pl. 7
Crypturellus cinnamomeus   11
Field marks: Note the *conspicuous barring* and *bright red*
legs. Brown above, heavily barred on back, rump, and tail;
cheeks and underparts usually cinnamon, paler on belly. Well-
defined ear coverts. Much geographic variation in color (nw.
Mexican birds are grayish below).
Similar species: (1) Slaty-breasted Tinamou (also red legs) is
slaty. (2) Great Tinamou (larger) has blue-gray legs.
Voice: A plaintive minor whistle, *hoo-oo,* with a slight upward
inflection (RTP).
Range: Mexico to Costa Rica; also Colombia, Venezuela.
Mexico: Pacific slope from s. Sinaloa south; Gulf slope from s.
Tamaulipas through Yucatán Pen., etc. **Habitat:** Inhabits more
arid country than do other tinamous; brushy thickets, dense
second growth, woodland edges; lowlands to 6000 ft.

Loons: Gaviidae

SWIMMING birds with daggerlike bills. Larger than most ducks;
longer-bodied, thicker-necked than grebes. Can dive to 200 ft.;
may dive or merely submerge. Sexes alike. **Food:** Small fish,
other aquatic animals. **Range:** Northern parts of N. Hemisphere.
No. of species: World, 4; Mexico, 3 (+ 1 accidental).

RED-THROATED LOON   *Gavia stellata*   See E, W, or T
Memo: Pale color; slender upturned bill.
Range: Far northern N. America, Eurasia; circumpolar.
Winters south along coasts to Mediterranean, China, Florida,
nw. Mexico. **Mexico:** Straggler to coasts of n. Baja California
and Sonora.

ARCTIC LOON   *Gavia arctica*   See E or W
Memo: Bill slender but not upturned.
Range: N. Eurasia, nw. N. America. Winters along coasts to
Mediterranean, India, nw. Mexico. **Mexico:** Winter visitor to
coasts of Baja California and Sonora; rarely Sinaloa.

COMMON LOON   *Gavia immer*   **See E, W, or T**
   Memo: Stout, straight bill.
   Range: Northern N. America, Greenland, Iceland. Winters chiefly along coasts to Mediterranean, n. Mexico. **Mexico:** Winters along coasts of n. Baja California, Sonora, and n. Sinaloa; also in Gulf of Mexico rarely to n. Tamaulipas.

YELLOW-BILLED LOON   *Gavia adamsii*   **See W**
   Memo: Stout, pale, upturned bill (straight above, angled below).
   Range: Arctic, U.S.S.R., n. Alaska, nw. Canada. Winters to se. Alaska. **Mexico:** Accidental Baja California.

Grebes: Podicipedidae

AQUATIC; expert divers, labored fliers. Known from ducks by thin neck, tailless look, pointed bill (in most species). Toes lobed (flaps). **Food:** Small fish, crustaceans, tadpoles, aquatic insects; also eats feathers (reason?). **Range:** Nearly worldwide. **No. of species:** World, 17 or 18; Mexico, 5 (+ 1 in Guatemala).

LEAST GREBE   *Podiceps dominicus*   **See W or T**
   Memo: Small, dark; dark bill, yellow eye, white wing patch.
   Range: S. Texas through Mid. America to Chile, Argentina; W. Indies. **Mexico:** S. Baja California, n. Sonora, and n. Tamaulipas south through s. Mexico. **Habitat:** Lakes, rivers, ponds mainly at lower altitudes (to 7000 ft.).

HORNED GREBE   *Podiceps auritus*   **See E, W, or T**
   Memo: Whiter neck than in Eared Grebe, cap *above* eye (winter).
   Range: N. Eurasia, n. N. America. Winters to s. Eurasia, s. U.S. **Mexico:** Casual; Baja California, Sonora.

EARED GREBE   *Podiceps nigricollis*   **See E, W, or T**
   Memo: Black neck (summer); dark cap to below eye (winter).
   Range: Western N. America, Colombia, Europe, Asia, Africa. **Mexico:** Nw. Baja California, Chihuahua (local). In winter widespread (except Yucatán Pen.) to Guatemala.

WESTERN GREBE   **See E, W, or T**
Aechmophorus occidentalis
   Memo: Blackish upperparts; long white neck.
   Range: Western N. America to Mexico. **Mexico:** May breed in western highland lakes from Chihuahua to Michoacán. Migrant and winter visitor along western coasts south to Baja California and Jalisco; locally in interior from Chihuahua to Puebla.

PIED-BILLED GREBE   See E, W, or T
Podilymbus podiceps
  Memo: Rounded bill, white "stern"; bill ring in summer.
  Range: Canada locally through Mid. America to Chile, Argentina. **Mexico:** Widespread in winter; local in summer.

ATITLAN GREBE   *Podilymbus gigas*   14–16
  Field marks: Like a large edition of the Pied-billed Grebe. Heavier and darker than Pied-billed; almost black on head and neck, offering little contrast to black throat; bill heavier, white with dark band. Flightless.
  Range: Only on Lake Atitlán, Guatemala. Population 130 in 1969. **Habitat:** Reed beds, open water. *Caution:* Pied-bill is very common in winter on Lake Atitlán.

ATITLAN GREBE

Albatrosses: Diomedeidae

NARROW-WINGED gliding birds of the open sea; much larger than gulls; wings proportionately far longer. Bill large, hooked, sheathed in horny plates; nostrils in 2 tubes. Sexes alike. **Food:** Cuttlefish, fish, small marine animals. **Range:** Mainly oceans of S. Hemisphere; 3 species north of Equator in Pacific. **No. of species:** World, 12; Mexico, 2 (+1 formerly).

SHORT-TAILED ALBATROSS   *Diomedea albatrus*   See W
  Memo: White back, pink bill.
  Range: W. Pacific (off Japan; numbers very small); formerly wandered to Baja California.

BLACK-FOOTED ALBATROSS   *Diomedea nigripes*   See W
  Memo: Nearly all dark; whitish on face; dark bill and feet.
  Range: N.-cen. Pacific; offshore, Alaska to Baja California.

LAYSAN ALBATROSS *Diomedea immutabilis*   **See W**
  Memo: White body, dark back and wings.
  Range: N.-cen. Pacific; wanders to waters off Baja California.

Shearwaters, Large Petrels, etc.: Procellariidae

GLIDING birds of *open sea.* Bills slender (except Fulmar's) with tubelike external nostrils. Wings narrower than gull's, tail smaller, not as fanlike. Sexes alike. Flight several flaps and a stiff-winged glide. Inasmuch as these pelagic birds often wander far out of range, a number of accidentals could turn up on the Pacific Coast of Mexico. Some of these are not covered in the western Peterson *Field Guide,* so we suggest as an excellent reference, Peter Slater's *Field Guide to Australian Birds,* Vol. 1. **Food:** Fish, squid, crustaceans. **Range:** Oceans of world. **No. of species:** World, 47; Mexico, 8 or 9 (+ 7 accidental).

NORTHERN FULMAR *Fulmarus glacialis*   **See E or W**
  Memo: Bull-necked; stubby yellow bill, light wing patch.
  Note: A similar form, Southern (Silver-gray) Fulmar, *F. glacialoides,* of the Antarctic and Subantarctic, has been once recorded off w. Mexico (Mazatlán). Variously regarded as a race or a full species, it is not safely separated in the field from pale phase of Pacific race of Northern Fulmar.
  Range: Northern oceans of N. Hemisphere. Winters to Japan, nw. Mexico, Newfoundland, n. France. **Mexico:** In winter south to n. Baja California; casual Sinaloa.

CAPE (PINTADO) PETREL   **Not illus.**
Daption capense 14
See Slater, *A Field Guide to Australian Birds,* Vol. 1
  Field marks: Boldly spotted above; 2 large roundish white patches on each wing; tail white with black band at tip.
  Range: Breeds in Antarctic; wanders northward. **Mexico:** Accidental; 1 record Acapulco.

PINK-FOOTED SHEARWATER *Puffinus creatopus*   **See W**
  Memo: Dark above, white below; pinkish bill.
  Range: Breeds on islands off Chile; wanders up e. Pacific; rarely to Alaska. **Mexico:** Migrant off west coast.

WEDGE-TAILED SHEARWATER   **See W**
Puffinus pacificus
  Memo: Wedge-shaped tail, flesh-colored feet; dark or white below.

Range: Islands of Indian Ocean and warmer parts of Pacific. **Mexico:** Ranges to islands and seas off western Mexican coast. Breeds on San Benedicto I. in Revilla Gigedo group.

GRAY-BACKED (NEW ZEALAND) SHEARWATER
Puffinus bulleri   See W
Memo: Broad M or W on gray back and wings; black cap.
Range: New Zealand; visits California waters. **Mexico:** Has been observed once off Coronados Is. To be looked for.

SOOTY SHEARWATER   *Puffinus griseus*   See E or W
Memo: Sooty body, whitish wing linings.
Range: Breeds on islands off New Zealand, s. S. America; ranges to N. Pacific and N. Atlantic. **Mexico:** Common off west coast of Baja California; rare Gulf of California; casual Gulf of Mexico. Accidental B. Honduras.

SHORT-TAILED (SLENDER-BILLED) SHEARWATER
Puffinus tenuirostris   See W
Memo: Sooty body, sooty wing linings.
Range: Breeds on islands off s. Australia. Ranges through N. Pacific to Bering Sea. **Mexico:** Rare off w. Baja California.

CHRISTMAS ISLAND SHEARWATER   See W
Puffinus nativitatus
Memo: All blackish, including underwing and feet.
Range: Tropical Pacific; Hawaii, etc. **Mexico:** Accidental; recorded once between Clipperton I. and Mexican coast.

MANX (COMMON) SHEARWATER   See E or W
Puffinus puffinus
Memo: Small; black above, white below; black bill, pink feet.
Note: The specific status of the form of western Mexican waters is uncertain. Although lumped here with *P. puffinus,* it has also been regarded as a race of *P. gavia* (Fluttering Shearwater) of New Zealand and has also been given full rank as *P. opisthomelas* (Black-vented Shearwater).
Range: Breeds on islands in Pacific and N. Atlantic; Mediterranean. **Mexico:** Breeds off w. Baja California (Guadalupe, San Martín, San Benito, Natividad). Recorded off Sonora.

REVILLA GIGEDO (TOWNSEND'S) SHEARWATER
Puffinus auricularis   12–13   Not illus.
Field marks: A small black and white shearwater; very similar to the Manx and regarded by some as a race of that bird, but smaller, more slaty black; flanks white, not black; axillars (wingpits) and underwing coverts clear white without dark mottling.

Similar species: (1) Manx Shearwater, more widespread, has black flanks, mottled axillars. (2) Wedge-tailed Shearwater (light phase) is larger, browner above, with wedge-shaped tail. (3) See also Pink-footed Shearwater.

Range: Breeds on Revilla Gigedo Is. (Clarión, San Benedicto, and Socorro) south of Baja California. Ranges off coast of Baja California and to Clipperton I.

DUSKY-BACKED (AUDUBON'S) SHEARWATER   See E
Puffinus lherminieri

Memo: Similar to Manx Shearwater but feet dark.

Range: Many closely related populations breed locally on islands in tropical Atlantic, Pacific, and Indian Oceans. **Mexico:** Stragglers from Caribbean said to occur rarely off coast of Gulf of Mexico. Substantiation needed.

VARIABLE (KERMADEC) PETREL   Not illus.
Pterodroma neglecta
See Slater, *A Field Guide to Australian Birds,* Vol. 1

Field marks: Dusky underwing with a whitish "window" at base of primaries. Pale phase has an almost white head, whitish body.

Range: Warmer waters of Indian and Pacific Oceans. **Mexico:** Accidental off Revilla Gigedo Is.

DARK-RUMPED PETREL   *Pterodroma phaeopygia*   See W

Memo: White forehead; dark above, clear white below.

Range: Hawaiian and Galápagos Is. **Mexico:** Ranges to Clipperton I. off w. Mexico.

WHITE-NECKED PETREL   Not illus.
Pterodroma externa   17
See Slater, *A Field Guide to Australian Birds,* Vol. 1

Field marks: Underwing almost all white, with small carpal edging of black. Kermadec race has black crown and white nape.

Range: Pacific; Kermadec and Juan Fernández Is. **Mexico:** Casual in vicinity of Clipperton I.

BLUE-FOOTED (COOK'S) PETREL   Not illus.
Pterodroma cookii   12

Field marks: In flight shows a dark inverted W across wings and back. Gray above, white below; face white with black eye patch. Legs and toes blue.

Similar species: Gray-backed (New Zealand) Shearwater (see *A Field Guide to Western Birds*) has a similar wing pattern. It has been seen off Baja California. Larger (16½ in.), with *blackish cap,* wedge-shaped tail; legs and toes whitish.

Range: Pacific. Breeds off New Zealand and Chile. **Mexico:** Regarded as accidental but probably a regular transient off Baja California, where observed in small numbers.

Storm-Petrels: Hydrobatidae

SMALL, dark, swallowlike birds that flit erratically over the *open sea,* skimming the waves and momentarily "dancing" on the water with their webbed feet. Some follow boats. Nostrils in tube on bill, fused. Sexes alike. **Food:** Plankton, crustaceans, small fish. **Range:** Oceans of world (except Arctic). **No. of species:** World, 18; Mexico, 5 (+3 accidental and 1 recently extinct).

WILSON'S STORM-PETREL *Oceanites oceanicus*   See E
    Memo: White rump, square tail; feet project in flight; yellow webs.
    Range: Antarctic, ranging north into Atlantic, Pacific, and Indian Oceans. **Mexico:** Taken off Veracruz in Gulf of Mexico. To be looked for on Pacific side.

LEAST STORM-PETREL *Halocyptena microsoma*   See W
    Memo: All dark; wedge-shaped tail; very small (5½–6 in.)
    Range: Breeds on islands off both coasts of Baja California; wanders north to San Diego and south to Ecuador.

LEACH'S STORM-PETREL   See E or W
Oceanodroma leucorhoa
(including Beal's, Socorro, and San Benito Storm-Petrels)
    Memo: Rump white (or not); tail forked.
    Note: Populations of Leach's Storm-Petrel in the Pacific show a progressive transition from larger white-rumped birds in the north to smaller all-dark birds in the south. Those in Coronados Is., *O. l. willetti,* may or may not have some white on the rump. Those on Guadalupe I., *O. l. socorroensis* (sometimes considered a separate species), show grayish rumps, whereas those of San Benito, *O. l. chapmani,* the darkest race, have uniformly dark rumps. Black Storm-Petrel is larger than the last, with longer wings, more deeply forked tail, more languid flight.

GUADALUPE STORM-PETREL   Not illus.
Oceanodroma macrodactyla
    Field marks: A white-rumped storm-petrel; very similar to the northern race of Leach's Storm-Petrel, but underwing coverts light gray-brown; broad dusky tips to white upper tail coverts. The breeding race of Leach's Storm-Petrel on Guadalupe I. *(O. leucorhoa socorroensis)* has a largely *gray* rump.

Range: Formerly bred on Guadalupe I. off Baja California. Probably extinct. Last record 1912.

ASHY STORM-PETREL *Oceanodroma homochroa* **See W**
  Memo: All dark; forked tail; small (7½ in.).
  Range: Off California (breeds on Farallon and Channel Is.); extreme nw. Mexico. **Mexico:** Coronados Is. off n. Baja California; wanders at sea to cen. Baja California.

WEDGE-RUMPED (GALAPAGOS) STORM-PETREL
Oceanodroma tethys 6½ **Not illus.**
  Field marks: Smaller than Leach's Storm-Petrel and with more fluttery flight. Tail less deeply forked; white rump patch large, wedge-shaped, obscuring much of black tail. No yellow in feet as in Wilson's Storm-Petrel, which has been recorded off California and Pacific Panamá but not yet off w. Mexico.
  Range: Galápagos Is. and islands off Peru; ranges at sea to w. Mexico. **Mexico:** Probably regular between Revilla Gigedo Is. and s. Baja California.

BAND-RUMPED (HARCOURT'S) STORM-PETREL
Oceanodroma castro 7–8 **See W**
  Field marks: Stouter than Leach's Storm-Petrel, with shorter wings; not as bounding a flight. White of rump broad, forming a *straight band* above black tail and extending onto flanks and under tail coverts. Wings not as bicolored as Leach's. Shows much more black in tail than Wedge-rumped Storm-Petrel.
  Range: Islands in e. Atlantic; also Hawaii and Galápagos in Pacific. **Mexico:** Birds apparently of this species have been observed off w. Mexico; unconfirmed.

SOOTY STORM-PETREL *Oceanodroma markhami* **See W**
  Memo: Brown; lighter wing coverts; forked tail; large (11 in.).
  Range: Pacific; Japan to S. America. **Mexico:** Taken off Clipperton I.

BLACK STORM-PETREL *Oceanodroma melania* **See W**
  Memo: Blackish; lighter wing coverts, forked tail; large (9 in.).
  Range: Breeds on islands off both coasts of n. Baja California; ranges north to cen. California.

Tropicbirds: Phaethontidae

TROPICBIRDS, although considered related to pelicans and cormorants, resemble large terns with greatly elongated central tail feathers and stouter, slightly decurved bills. Sexes alike. **Food:** Squids, crustaceans. **Range:** Tropical seas. **No. of species:** World, 3; Mexico, 2 (+ 1 casual Guatemala).

RED-BILLED TROPICBIRD   *Phaethon aethereus*   **See W**
  Memo: 2 long white tail feathers, barred back, red bill.
  Range: Tropical Atlantic (incl. Caribbean), e. Pacific and n.
  Indian Oceans. **Mexico:** Entire Pacific Coast. Breeds locally on
  islands off Baja and in Gulf of California and south. Ranges
  Caribbean coast from Honduras south.

WHITE-TAILED TROPICBIRD   **See E, W, or T**
Phaethon lepturus
  Memo: Long white central tail feathers; yellow or orange bill.
  Range: Tropical Atlantic, cen. Pacific and Indian Oceans; cas-
  ual in Gulf of Mexico close to our area. 1 record Guatemala.

RED-TAILED TROPICBIRD   *Phaethon rubricauda*   **See W**
  Memo: 2 long red tail feathers; no black wing patches.
  Range: Cen. Pacific and Indian Oceans. **Mexico:** Recorded
  near Guadalupe I., Clipperton, etc.

Pelicans: Pelecanidae

HUGE water birds with long flat bills and great throat pouches
(flat when deflated). Neck long, body robust. Sexes alike. **Food:**
Mainly fish, crustaceans. **Range:** N. and S. America, Africa, se.
Europe, s. Asia, E. Indies, Australia. **No. of species:** World, 6;
Mexico, 2.

WHITE PELICAN   **See E, W, or T**
Pelecanus erythrorhynchos
  Memo: Huge, white; black in wings, long yellow bill, pouch.
  Range: W. and cen. N. America. Winters from s. U.S. to Gua-
  temala. **Mexico:** Winters mainly along both coasts.

BROWN PELICAN   *Pelecanus occidentalis*   **See E, W, or T**
  Memo: Huge, dark; long bill with pouch.
  Range: Coasts of s. U.S., W. Indies, Mid. America to n. and w.
  S. America. **Mexico:** Entire length of Pacific Coast (incl. Gulf
  of California), breeding locally on offshore islands. Also entire
  length of east coast (Gulf of Mexico).

Gannets and Boobies: Sulidae

LARGE, somewhat gull-like seabirds with large, rather thick
pointed bills, pointed or wedge-shaped tails. Sexes usually simi-

lar. They dive from the air, headfirst, for fish, squids. Gannets are primarily birds of cold seas; boobies inhabit more tropical seas. **No. of species:** World, 9; Mexico, 5.

NORTHERN GANNET *Morus bassanus*   **See E**
   Memo: White; pointed white tail, black primaries (adult).
   Range: N. Atlantic. Winters to Gulf of Mexico and Mediterranean. **Mexico:** Casual in Gulf of Mexico to Veracruz.

BLUE-FOOTED BOOBY *Sula nebouxii*   **See W**
   Memo: White; dark back, wings, tail; blue feet (adult).
   Range: W. Mexico, w. Honduras, Costa Rica, Panamá to n. Peru. **Mexico:** Most of Pacific Coast, breeding mainly on islands in Gulf of California and south to Nayarit.

MASKED (BLUE-FACED) BOOBY   **See E, W, or T**
Sula dactylatra
   Memo: White; black flight feathers and tail; dark face (adult).
   Range: Pan-tropical oceans. **Mexico:** Breeds locally on islands off Pacific Coast (Clarión and San Benedicto Is.) and off n. Yucatán; casual Tamaulipas, B. Honduras.

RED-FOOTED BOOBY *Sula sula*   **See W**
   Memo: White or pale brown; bright red feet (adult).
   Range: Pan-tropical oceans. **Mexico:** Pacific. Breeds or has bred Revilla Gigedo Is. and islands off Sinaloa and Nayarit (extirpated?). Also breeds in B. Honduras (Half Moon Cay) and Honduras (Little Swan I.). Recorded Quintana Roo.

BROWN BOOBY *Sula leucogaster*   **See E or W**
   Memo: Brown; dark breast against clear white belly (adult).
   Note: Males of the race in w. Mexico have *pale gray* heads.
   Range: Tropical oceans. **Mexico:** Breeds on islands off Baja California and in Gulf of California; ranges thence south along Pacific Coast. Less frequent in Gulf of Mexico, breeding or probably breeding on islands off Campeche (Cayo Arcos), Yucatán (Recife Alacrán), Quintana Roo (Banco Chinchorro), and possibly B. Honduras. Often seen from land.

Cormorants: Phalacrocoracidae

LARGE dark water birds with slender hook-tipped bills; perch upright, often in "spread eagle" pose. Swim low, necks erect. Sexes alike. **Food:** Fish, amphibians, crustaceans. **Range:** Nearly worldwide. **No. of species:** World, 26; Mexico, 4.

DOUBLE-CRESTED CORMORANT   See E, W, or T
Phalacrocorax auritus
   Memo: Black body, yellow-orange throat pouch. See next species.
   Range: Canada to Mexico, B. Honduras, Bahamas, Cuba.
   Mexico: Coastal resident Baja California and Gulf of California; ranges south to Guerrero. In winter also Yucatán Pen. (breeds?) and B. Honduras. Absent from remainder of east coast.

NEOTROPIC (OLIVACEOUS) CORMORANT   See W or T
Phalacrocorax olivaceus
   Field marks: Similar to Double-crest, but slimmer and smaller; thinner-billed, usually with duller yellowish throat pouch. In breeding plumage may show a tuft of white filoplumes on neck and a *white border* on throat pouch.
   Similar species: Double-crest is larger, pouch is more orange. At close range feathers of back are rounded (more pointed in Neotropic).
   Range: Texas, Louisiana, through Mid. and S. America to Tierra del Fuego; also Bahamas, Cuba. **Mexico:** From Sonora in west and Tamaulipas in east through cen. and s. Mexico, including Yucatán Pen. **Habitat:** Coastal waters; also fresh lakes, streams.

BRANDT'S CORMORANT   See W
Phalacrocorax penicillatus
   Memo: Blue throat pouch edged with buff patch.
   Range: Coast from Vancouver I. to tip of Baja California. Breeds locally on islands off w. Baja California and in Gulf of California. Winters to Sinaloa (Mazatlán).

PELAGIC CORMORANT   *Phalacrocorax pelagicus*   See W
   Memo: Dull red face, slim bill, white flank patch (summer).
   Range: Japan to Bering Sea and south along Pacific Coast to nw. Baja California (breeds Coronados Is.).

Darters (Anhingas): Anhingidae

SIMILAR to cormorants, but much more slender, tail longer, bill sharp-pointed. Often soars. **Food:** Fish, other aquatic life. **Range:** Tropical and warm temperate zones of world. **No. of species:** World, 4 (or 1); Mexico, 1.

ANHINGA   *Anhinga anhinga*   See E or T
   Memo: Serpentine neck, long fan-shaped tail.

Range: Se. U.S., Mid. and S. America to ne. Argentina. **Mexico:** Lowlands east and south; in west, north to Sinaloa.

Frigatebirds (Man-o'-War Birds): Fregatidae

TROPICAL seabirds with a greater wingspan in proportion to weight than any other birds. Bill long, strongly hooked. Tail deeply forked. Sexes unlike. **Food:** Fish, jellyfish, squids, crustaceans, young turtles, young birds. Often force other seabirds to disgorge food. **Range:** Islands of pan-tropical oceans. **No. of species:** World, 5; Mexico, 2.

MAGNIFICENT FRIGATEBIRD　　　　　See E, W, or T
Fregata magnificens
　　Memo: Long wings, long forked tail, long hooked bill; largely black. ♀ has white chest; immature has white head and underparts.
　　Range: Both coasts; California to n. Peru, Galápagos Is.; se. U.S. and W. Indies to Brazil; locally off w. Africa. **Mexico:** Both coasts, breeding in colonies on a few wooded coastal islands. May soar well inland at times.

GREAT FRIGATEBIRD　　*Fregata minor*　　　　See W
　　Memo: Light wing coverts in adult ♂. ♀ has white throat, red eye-ring. Immature has rufous tinge on white head and breast.
　　Range: E. and cen. Pacific to w. Indian Ocean; locally, S. Atlantic. **Mexico:** Breeds on Revilla Gigedo Is. Casual elsewhere off Pacific mainland.

Herons and Bitterns: Ardeidae

LARGE wading birds with long necks, long legs, spearlike bills. In flight, heads tucked back in an S. May have plumes when breeding. Sexes similar. **Food:** Fish, frogs, crustaceans, insects. **Range:** Nearly worldwide except in colder regions, some deserts and islands. **No. of species:** World, 63; Mexico, 15 or 16 (+1 hypothetical).

GREAT BLUE HERON　　*Ardea herodias*　　See E, W, or T
　　Memo: Large; blue-gray; yellowish bill.
　　Range: Se. Alaska, Canada to s. Mexico, Galápagos, Cuba. Winters U.S. through Mid. America to n. S. America. **Mexico:** Nearly throughout, but breeds only locally.

GREAT WHITE HERON   *Ardea "occidentalis"*   **See E or T**
Memo: Very large, white; pale yellowish legs.
Range: Mainly s. Florida, Cuba, Caribbean islands. **Mexico:** White herons (with pale legs) of this "form," often regarded as a white race or color phase of the Great Blue, are occasionally observed along coasts of n. Yucatán and Quintana Roo.

GREAT (COMMON) EGRET   **See E, W, or T**
Casmerodius albus
Memo: Large, white; yellow bill, dark legs.
Range: U.S. through Mid. America, W. Indies to s. Argentina.
Mexico: Nearly throughout; mainly lowlands.

SNOWY EGRET   *Egretta (Leucophoyx) thula*   **See E, W, or T**
Memo: Small, white; black bill, yellow feet.
Range: U.S. through Mid. America, W. Indies to Chile, Argentina. **Mexico:** Nearly throughout; mainly lowlands.

LITTLE BLUE HERON   *Florida caerulea*   **See E, W, or T**
Memo: Dark (adult) or white (imm.); dark bill and legs.
Range: E. U.S. through Mid. America to Ecuador, Brazil, Uruguay. **Mexico:** From s. Baja California, s. Sonora, and n. Tamaulipas south; mainly in lowlands.

REDDISH EGRET   *Dichromanassa rufescens*   **See E, W, or T**
Memo: Dark or white; flesh-colored bill.
Range: Coasts of Texas, s. Florida to Guatemala, B. Honduras, El Salvador, W. Indies. Winters to n. Venezuela. **Mexico:** Uncommon, local, on all coasts except nw. Baja California.

TRICOLORED (LOUISIANA) HERON   **See E, W, or T**
Hydranassa tricolor
Memo: Dark; contrasting white belly.
Range: New Jersey through Mid. America, W. Indies to Ecuador, Brazil. **Mexico:** Widespread in lowlands and on coasts; absent in arid interior.

CATTLE EGRET   *Bubulcus ibis*   **See W or T**
Memo: Small, white; yellow bill; yellow, pink, or dark legs.
Range: Africa, s. Europe, Asia, e. and s. N. America, n. S. America, W. Indies, n. Australia, New Zealand. **Mexico:** Mainly lowlands of both coastal slopes; locally in highlands. A recent invader from Old World, rapidly extending range.

CHESTNUT-BELLIED (AGAMI) HERON   **Pl. 1**
Agamia agami   28–30
  Field marks: Note the *bright chestnut* belly. A dark, medium-sized heron suggesting Louisiana Heron except for chest-

nut belly, shorter legs. Deep glossy green to black above; most of head black. May have pearly-gray plumes on crown and shaggy chest. *Immature:* A nondescript dark bird; upperparts greenish black; neck brownish, crown black; underparts buffy white with brownish striping.
Similar species: See tiger-herons (below).
Voice: A piglike bass rattling *krurr* (Slud).
Range: S. Mexico, Cen. America to Bolivia, Brazil. **Mexico:** S. Veracruz, Tabasco, Chiapas, Quintana Roo; very rarely seen.
Habitat: Lowland forest pools, jungle streams.

GREEN HERON *Butorides virescens* See E, W, or T
Memo: Small, dark; short yellowish or orange legs.
Range: Se. Canada, nw. U.S. through Mid. America to cen. Panamá, W. Indies. Winters to n. Colombia, n. Venezuela.
Mexico: Resident except in north-central highlands.

BLACK-CROWNED NIGHT-HERON See E, W, or T
Nycticorax nycticorax
Memo: Whitish underparts; black back and crown (adult).
Range: Eurasia, Africa, N., Mid., and S. America, Pacific islands. **Mexico:** Year-round resident of Baja California and west coast from Sonora to Jalisco; locally along Gulf of Mexico (except Yucatán Pen.); local in interior. More widespread in winter.

YELLOW-CROWNED NIGHT-HERON See E or T
Nyctanassa violacea
Memo: Gray; black head, whitish crown and cheek (adult).
Range: Ne. and cen. U.S. south through Mid. America to coastal Ecuador, Galápagos Is., and Brazil. **Mexico:** Mostly coastal lowlands; in west, from s. Baja Calif., s. Sonora south; in east, from n. Tamaulipas through Yucatán Pen.

RUFESCENT (LINEATED) TIGER-HERON Pl. 1
Tigrisoma lineatum 28–30
Field marks: Note the *chestnut* head and neck. Upperparts very dark, finely barred. White stripe on foreneck and breast; belly striped with brown or rufous. Middle of throat feathered. *Immature:* Tawny, boldly banded or spotted with black; underparts buff. Middle of throat feathered.
Similar species: See immature Bare-throated Tiger-Heron.
Voice: Suggests a night-heron: deep *quok quok quok* (Wetmore).
Range: Honduras to n. Argentina. **Mexico:** Doubtful in our area. Immature reported once in Chiapas but needs confirmation. No records for Guatemala or B. Honduras. **Habitat:** Freshwater swamps, marshes, mudflats.

BARE-THROATED TIGER-HERON (TIGER-BITTERN)
Tigrisoma mexicanum   28–32   **Pl. 1**
  Field marks: Note the *black* crown and *bare greenish-yellow to orange* throat. Neck narrowly barred with black; back dull brown, finely barred, belly tawny. *Immature:* Buffy brown coarsely barred with black; note bare yellow throat.
  Similar species: (1) Rufescent Tiger-Heron (possibly accidental in our area) has chestnut head and neck. Immature lacks bare yellow throat. (2) Pinnated Bittern is buffier than immature of this species; breast broadly *streaked* (not barred).
  Voice: A harsh croaking *wok wok wok*. Also a curious far-carrying snoring sound (Wetmore).
  Range: Mexico, Cen. America to nw. Colombia. **Mexico:** Coastal slopes; s. Sonora and s. Tamaulipas south and east.
  Habitat: Wooded streams, swamps, mangroves, marshes, mudflats.

LEAST BITTERN   *Ixobrychus exilis*   **See E, W, or T**
  Memo: Tiny; back and crown black, wings buff.
  Range: Nw. U.S. and se. Canada through Mid. and S. America to Paraguay. **Mexico:** Locally n. Baja California and Río Grande Valley south. More frequent in migration.

AMERICAN BITTERN   **See E, W, or T**
Botaurus lentiginosus
  Memo: Tawny; black neck stripe bordering white throat.
  Range: Canada to s. U.S. Winters through Mid. America to Panamá. **Mexico:** Winters locally, mainly in lowlands.

PINNATED BITTERN   *Botaurus pinnatus*   30   **Pl. 1**
  Field marks: A buffy, tawny bittern, coarsely barred and streaked with black above; head and neck with *dark bars;* underparts buffy, broadly striped with brown.
  Similar species: (1) American Bittern lacks strong barring on head; a broad black stripe borders white throat. (2) See Barethroated Tiger-Heron (above).
  Range: Se. Mexico, w. Guatemala, se. Nicaragua, Costa Rica; also Colombia to Argentina. **Mexico:** Very local; reported Veracruz, n. Chiapas, Tabasco, Quintana Roo. Casual B. Honduras. **Habitat:** Marshes.

Boat-billed Herons: Cochleariidae

A NOCTURNAL heron, placed in a separate family because of its strange bill. Probably should be included in Ardeidae. **Food:** Fish, mice, crabs, frogs. **No of species:** World, 1; Mexico, 1.

BOAT-BILLED HERON *Cochlearius cochlearius* 20   **Pl. 1**
  Field marks: Suggests Black-crowned Night-Heron but with a
  very broad, slipperlike bill. Crown, crest, and upper back,
  black; rest of upperparts gray. Cheeks and breast pale grayish
  buff, shading to tawny brown on the belly. Flanks *black.* When
  flying overhead wings appear white with black inner linings.
  Immature: Back and wings brown; underparts buffy or tawny.
  May lack light forehead.
  Similar species: Black-crowned Night-Heron has daggerlike
  bill; lacks black sides and tawny underparts.
  Voice: Quawking suggestive of a night-heron. Bill-rattling.
  Range: Mexico through Cen. and S. America to Bolivia, n. Argentina. **Mexico:** Lowlands; north on west slope to Sinaloa;
  east slope to s. Tamaulipas. **Habitat:** Nocturnal visitor to
  swamps and wooded streams; roosts in mangroves, trees near
  water.

Storks: Ciconiidae

LARGE, long-legged, heronlike birds with long bills (straight, recurved, or decurved); some with naked heads. Sexes alike. Fly
with neck extended. **Food:** Frogs, crustaceans, lizards, rodents.
Range: Se. U.S. to Argentina; Eurasia, E. Indies, Australia,
Africa. **No. of species:** World, 17; Mexico, 2.

WOOD STORK (AMERICAN WOOD-IBIS)   **See E, W, or T**
Mycteria americana
  Memo: White; naked gray head, decurved bill; black in wings.
  Range: S. U.S. through Mid. America to Argentina, Cuba,
  Hispaniola. **Mexico:** Wanders along Pacific Coast from
  Chiapas north to Sonora, n. Baja California; also Yucatán Pen.
  to Tamaulipas; mostly coastal, irregular in interior. Colonies
  known in Campeche, Quintana Roo; also coastal B. Honduras.

JABIRU *Jabiru mycteria* 48–57   **Pl. 1**
  Field marks: A very large white stork with no black in wings.
  The outsized black bill is thick and *slightly turned up.* A *broad
  red collar* separates the white body from the bare black skin of
  the head and upper neck. *Immature:* Gray-brown or patched
  with white. Note upturned bill.
  Similar species: Wood Stork has down-curved bill and exten-
  sive black in wings and tail.
  Range: S. Mexico, Cen. America to n. Argentina. **Mexico:**
  Rare visitor to Veracruz, Campeche, Chiapas, Quintana Roo.
  More frequent in B. Honduras (has bred). **Habitat:** Savannas
  with scattered trees and marshes.

Ibises and Spoonbills:
Threskiornithidae

LONG-LEGGED marsh birds that fly with necks outstretched, flapping and gliding. Bills of ibises are sickle-shaped, those of spoonbills spatulate. **Food:** Crustaceans, insects, leeches, small fish, etc. **Range:** U.S. to s. S. America; Eurasia, Africa, Australasia. **No. of species:** World, 30; Mexico, 3.

WHITE IBIS   *Eudocimus albus*   See E or T
  Memo: White; red face, decurved bill.
  Range: Se. U.S., Mid. America to cen. Peru, Venezuela; W. Indies. **Mexico:** West coast from s. Baja California and s. Sonora south; east coast from Tamaulipas to Yucatán Pen.

WHITE-FACED IBIS   *Plegadis chihi*   See W or T
  Memo: Glossy dark plumage, decurved bill. See below.
  Note: Birds in nonbreeding plumage lack the reddish skin before the eye and the broad white line on the face. These birds may be mistaken for the very similar Glossy Ibis *(P. falcinellus)*, migrants of which might be expected to occur in Mexico due to the recent buildup in e. U.S. and W. Indies.
  Range: W. U.S. to Mexico (wintering to Cen. America); also S. America, Peru to Argentina. **Mexico:** Locally common resident and migrant. Absent from most of Baja California and east of Isthmus of Tehuantepec.

ROSEATE SPOONBILL   *Ajaia ajaja*   See E or T
  Memo: Pink wings, spatulate bill.
  Range: S. U.S., Mid. America, W. Indies to cen. Argentina. **Mexico:** Mainly coastal; s. Sonora to Chiapas; Tamaulipas to Yucatán Pen. Straggler n. Baja California.

Flamingos: Phoenicopteridae

EXTREMELY slender, gregarious, pink wading birds that fly with long necks extended. Bill sharply bent; flamingos feed with head in inverted position. **Food:** Algae, diatoms, mollusks, crustaceans, etc. **Range:** Caribbean, S. America, Galápagos Is., Africa, s. Eurasia. **No. of species:** World, 6; Mexico, 1.

AMERICAN FLAMINGO   *Phoenicopterus ruber*   See E
  Memo: Bright pink; very long neck and legs.
  Range: Mainly Bahamas, Caribbean region, Galápagos Is.;

wanders to cen. Florida, coast of n. S. America. **Mexico:** One or two colonies on coast of Yucatán; may wander west to s. Veracruz and east to Quintana Roo.

Ducks, Swans, and Geese: Anatidae

A LARGE family of water birds, divided into several subfamilies. See the Peterson *Field Guides* (East, West, or Texas) for discussions of (1) tree-ducks, (2) swans, (3) geese, (4) surface-feeding ducks, (5) diving ducks, (6) stiff-tailed ducks, (7) mergansers. **Food:** Aquatic plants, seeds, grass, small aquatic animals, insects, fish, mollusks, crustaceans (various waterfowl specialize in their foods). **Range:** Almost worldwide. **No. of species:** World, 147; Mexico, 34 (+5 accidental).

FULVOUS TREE-DUCK   **See E, W, or T**
Dendrocygna bicolor
 Memo: Tawny color, white side stripe.
 Range: S. U.S. to Honduras; locally S. America to Argentina; also India, e. Africa. **Mexico:** Mainly lowlands; in east from Tamaulipas to Campeche; in west, s. Sonora to Oaxaca. Occasional n. Baja California, cen. Mexico, Chiapas, Yucatán.

BLACK-BELLIED TREE-DUCK   **See W or T**
Dendrocygna autumnalis
 Memo: Black belly, white wing patches, pink bill.
 Range: S. Texas, Mid. America to n. Argentina. **Mexico:** Mainly low coastal regions; s. Sonora to Chiapas; Tamaulipas to Yucatán Pen.; occasional in interior.

TRUMPETER SWAN *Cygnus buccinator* **See W**
 Memo: Larger than Whistling Swan; deeper voice, no yellow spot on bill.
 Range: Northwestern N. America. **Mexico:** Accidental. 1 old record (Jan. 1909) at Matamoros, Tamaulipas.

WHISTLING SWAN *Cygnus columbianus* **See E, W, or T**
 Memo: White; long neck, small yellow spot on black bill.
 Range: Arctic Canada. Winters to s. U.S. **Mexico:** Casual visitor to n. Baja California, Chihuahua, Tamaulipas, Guanajuato.

WHITE-FRONTED GOOSE *Anser albifrons* **See E, W, or T**
 Memo: White foreface, blotches on belly.
 Range: Arctic; circumpolar (except ne. Canada). Winters to Gulf states, Mexico, n. Africa, India. **Mexico:** Winter visitor mainly in northern and central portions; occasionally south to

Tabasco on east coast and Chiapas on Pacific Coast. Casual B. Honduras.

SNOW GOOSE
Chen caerulescens ("hyperborea")   See E, W, or T
Memo: White with black primaries.
Range: Ne. Siberia, arctic America. Winters to Japan, Mexico, Gulf states. **Mexico:** In winter to s. Mexico.

BLUE GOOSE *Chen caerulescens*   See E, W, or T
(considered a gray phase of the "Lesser" race of Snow Goose)
Memo: Gray with white head.
Range: Arctic Canada. Winters mainly in Gulf states. **Mexico:** A few migrate with white Snow Geese to eastern lowlands.

ROSS' GOOSE *Chen rossii*   See W or T
Memo: Smaller than Snow Goose, small bill.
Range: Arctic Canada. Winters mainly in California. **Mexico:** Accidental; reported Chihuahua, Tamaulipas.

CANADA GOOSE, etc. *Branta canadensis*   See W
Memo: Black neck stocking, white cheek patch.
Range: Breeds in n. N. America. Winters to n. Mexico. Canada Geese come in various sizes and shades. Inasmuch as 10 or 11 races are involved, the most practical system (if field separation is desired) is to divide wintering Canadas into 3 size categories: (1) large "honkers," (2) medium-sized geese, and (3) duck-sized geese. These can then be subdivided into (a) lighter eastern forms and (b) darker western forms. Thus we offer this breakdown of the 5 forms that reach Mexico:
Large "honkers." A few cross the Mexican border in the Southwest. Banding evidence indicates that they are the **Western Canada Goose,** *B. c. moffitti.*
Medium-sized geese. 2 forms reach Mexico: (1) **Lesser Canada Goose,** *B. c. parvipes,* ne. Mexico (Tamaulipas, Veracruz), and (2) **Tundra Canada Goose,** *B. c. leucopareia,* browner, darker, nw. Mexico.
Small geese. 2 are involved: (1) the light form, **Richardson's Canada Goose,** *B. c. hutchinsii,* ne. Mexico (Tamaulipas, Coahuila; casually Jalisco), and (2) the darker form, **Cackling Goose,** *B. c. minima,* occasional in nw. Mexico (Baja California and probably Sonora). Some recent authors separate these 2 small forms from the larger Canadas as a distinct species — **Cackling Goose,** *Branta hutchinsii* (with 2 subspecies), or as 2 species, Richardson's Goose and Cackling Goose.

BLACK BRANT *Branta nigricans*   See W
Memo: Small, blackish; white neck patch.

Range: Arctic coasts; Siberia, Alaska; nw. Canada. In winter to salt bays of China, Japan, w. U.S., w. Baja California.

MALLARD *Anas platyrhynchos* **See E, W, or T**
Memo: Green head, white neck-ring.
Range: Northern parts of N. Hemisphere. Winters to Mid. America, W. Indies, n. Africa, Malaysia. **Mexico:** Rare winter visitor to northern border states; formerly common to Valley of Mexico.

HAWAIIAN DUCK *Anas wyvilliana* **See W**
Memo: ♂ intermediate in appearance between ♀ and ♂ (in eclipse) of Mallard.
Range: Hawaiian Is. **Mexico:** Accidental, Mazatlán (Sinaloa).

MEXICAN DUCK *Anas diazi* **See W or T**
Memo: Similar to ♀ Mallard but bill all yellow.
Range: New Mexico and w. Texas to cen. Mexico. **Mexico:** Central uplands from Chihuahua south to Puebla.

MOTTLED DUCK *Anas fulvigula* **See E or T**
Memo: Darker than ♀ Mallard; unmarked yellow bill.
Range: Florida; Gulf Coast of Louisiana, Texas, and Tamaulipas. A few winter to San Luis Potosí and Veracruz.

GREEN-WINGED TEAL *Anas crecca* **See E, W, or T**
Memo: ♂ gray with vertical white mark behind chest.
Range: Breeds nw. and n.-cen. N. America. Migrates and winters through Mexico, Guatemala, B. Honduras, Honduras.

GADWALL *Anas strepera* **See E, W, or T**
Memo: Gray body, black rear, white speculum (♂).
Range: Eurasia, sw. Canada, w. and n. U.S. Winters to Mexico, Africa, India. **Mexico:** Winters to Guerrero, Tabasco.

EUROPEAN WIGEON *Anas penelope* **See E, W, or T**
Memo: Rufous head, buff crown (♂).
Range: Iceland, Eurasia. Regular visitor to N. America. **Mexico:** Accidental; recorded n. and s. Baja California.

AMERICAN WIGEON (BALDPATE) **See E, W, or T**
Anas americana
Memo: White crown (♂).
Range: Breeds nw. N. America. Winters to Colombia, W. Indies. **Mexico:** Winters throughout.

NORTHERN PINTAIL *Anas acuta* **See E, W, or T**
Memo: Needle tail, white neck stripe (♂).

Range: Northern parts of N. Hemisphere. Winters to Colombia, n. Africa, India, E. Indies. **Mexico:** Winters throughout.

BLUE-WINGED TEAL *Anas discors* See E, W, or T
Memo: ♂ with white face crescent, bluish wing patch.
Range: Breeds Canada, U.S. Winters to n. S. America. **Mexico:** Widespread migrant and winter visitor.

CINNAMON TEAL *Anas cyanoptera* See E, W, or T
Memo: ♂ deep chestnut; bluish wing patch.
Range: Breeds sw. Canada, w. U.S. to cen. Mexico. Also locally in S. America to s. Argentina. **Mexico:** Breeds locally in Baja California, Tamaulipas, and in cen. Mexico south to Jalisco; in winter elsewhere (except Yucatán Pen.).

NORTHERN SHOVELER *Anas clypeata* See E, W, or T
Memo: Shovel bill, chestnut sides (♂).
Range: Widespread in N. Hemisphere. Winters to Colombia, Africa. **Mexico:** Widespread in winter.

CANVASBACK *Aythya valisineria* See E, W, or T
Memo: White body, rusty head, long profile (♂).
Range: Western N. America. In winter, south to cen. Mexico (Michoacán, Federal Dist., Veracruz); rarely Guatemala.

REDHEAD *Aythya americana* See E, W, or T
Memo: Gray; black chest, round rufous head (♂).
Range: Western N. America. Winters through Mexico and Guatemala.

RING-NECKED DUCK *Aythya collaris* See E, W, or T
Memo: Black back, white mark before wing (♂).
Range: Canada, n. U.S. Winters through Mexico to Panamá.

LESSER SCAUP *Aythya affinis* See E, W, or T
Memo: Like preceding but head with purple gloss (♂).
Range: Western N. America. Winters to Colombia and W. Indies. **Mexico:** Winters throughout. Occasional in summer.

GREATER SCAUP *Aythya marila* See E, W, or T
Memo: Black chest, black head (green gloss), blue bill (♂).
Range: Alaska, nw. Canada, Iceland, n. Eurasia. Winters to nw. Mexico (very rarely), W. Indies, Mediterranean, India.

WOOD DUCK *Aix sponsa* See E, W, or T
Memo: Highly colored, crested; white face stripes (♂).
Range: S. Canada, nw. and e. U.S., and Cuba. Winters to

Mexico. **Mexico:** Recorded in Sinaloa, Valley of Mexico, San Luis Potosí, Tamaulipas.

MUSCOVY   *Cairina moschata*   ♂ 30–35, ♀ 25
  Field marks: A large, clumsy, black, gooselike duck with white wing patches and underwing coverts. Male has a *bare, knobby, red face.* Female is duller, may lack facial caruncles (knobs). Perches in forest trees. Domesticated Muscovy may be white, black, or patched; some individuals may become semiwild.
  Similar species: See Black-bellied Tree-Duck (p. 19).
  Range: Mexico to n. Argentina. **Mexico:** Coastal slopes from Sinaloa to Chiapas in west; Nuevo León and Tamaulipas to Yucatán Pen. (local) in east. **Habitat:** Wooded streams.

MUSCOVY

WHITE-WINGED SCOTER   See E, W, or T
Melanitta deglandi
  Memo: Black; white wing patch (♂).
  Range: W. Canada. Winters to s. U.S., nw. Mexico. **Mexico:** Coast of nw. Baja California, rarely Gulf of California.

SURF SCOTER   *Melanitta perspicillata*   See E, W, or T
  Memo: Black; white head patches (♂).
  Range: Nw. Canada. Winters to s. U.S., nw. Mexico. **Mexico:** Winters on coasts of Baja California, Sonora, Nayarit (rarely).

BLACK (COMMON) SCOTER   See E, W, or T
Melanitta nigra
  Memo: Plumage all black, yellow-orange base of bill (♂).

Range: Alaska, Iceland, n. Eurasia. Winters to s. U.S., Mediterranean. **Mexico:** Casual n. Baja California.

OLDSQUAW   *Clangula hyemalis*   **See E, W, or T**
Memo: Pied pattern, solid dark wings, needle tail.
Range: Arctic; circumpolar. Winters to s. U.S., cen. Eurasia.
Mexico: Accidental; reported Gulf of California.

COMMON GOLDENEYE   **See E, W, or T**
Bucephala clangula
Memo: Round white spot before eye (♂).
Range: Northern parts of N. Hemisphere. Winters to Gulf of
Mexico, s. Eurasia. **Mexico:** Rare; recorded Baja California,
Sonora, Sinaloa, Durango, Tamaulipas.

BUFFLEHEAD   *Bucephala albeola*   **See E, W, or T**
Memo: Large white head patch, white sides (♂).
Range: Nw. N. America. Winters to Florida and n. Mexico.
Mexico: Winters on coasts of Baja California, Sonora, Sinaloa,
Tamaulipas; rarely in highlands to cen. Mexico; rarely Yucatán.

HOODED MERGANSER   **See E, W, or T**
Lophodytes cucullatus
Memo: White crest, dark sides (♂).
Range: S. Canada, n. U.S. In winter to s. U.S.; rarely to Mexico. Recorded Baja California, Tamaulipas, Veracruz, Michoacán, Valley of Mexico.

COMMON MERGANSER (GOOSANDER)   **See E, W, or T**
Mergus merganser
Memo: Long whitish body, dark head (♂).
Range: Northern parts of N. Hemisphere. Winters to s. Eurasia, n. Mexico, and Gulf states. **Mexico:** Winters occasionally in
northern border states; casual in State of México.

RED-BREASTED MERGANSER   **See E, W, or T**
Mergus serrator
Memo: White collar, wispy crest (♂).
Range: Northern parts of N. Hemisphere. Winters to n. Africa,
s. China, n. Mexico, Gulf states. **Mexico:** Winters mainly on
coasts of Baja California, Sonora, Sinaloa; also Chihuahua, Tamaulipas.

RUDDY DUCK   *Oxyura jamaicensis*   **See E, W, or T**
Memo: Rufous with white cheek (♂ summer); gray with white
cheek (♂ winter).
Range: W. Canada, south locally to Colombia (closely related
forms to Argentina). **Mexico:** Breeds locally in fresh marshes of

Baja California and central uplands. More widespread in winter, especially along coasts.

MASKED DUCK *Oxyura dominica* **See W or T**
Memo: Ruddy color; black face, white wing patch (♂).
Range: S. Texas and W. Indies to n. Argentina. **Mexico:** Rare, local and elusive. Recorded Nayarit, Sinaloa, Jalisco, Colima, Tamaulipas, Veracruz. Recorded also B. Honduras, Guatemala.

New World Vultures: Cathartidae

BLACKISH eagle-like scavengers, often seen soaring high on thermals; often called "buzzards." Heads small, naked; feet weak. Sexes alike. **Food:** Carrion. **Range:** S. Canada to Tierra del Fuego. **No. of species:** World, 7; Mexico, 4 (+1 formerly).

TURKEY VULTURE *Cathartes aura* **See E, W, or T**
Memo: 2-toned dark wings, small red head, longish tail.
Range: S. Canada to Tierra del Fuego. **Mexico:** Throughout.
Habitat: Open country; sea level to high mts.; wilderness areas as well as farms, etc.

LESSER YELLOW-HEADED (SAVANNA) VULTURE
Cathartes burrovianus 28 **Pl. 4**
Field marks: Similar to Turkey Vulture but smaller; shows more contrast; blacker above, with silvery undersurface of wings; often with a whitish patch above, suggestive of Black Vulture. Note the *orange-yellow* face and neck and *blue or blue-gray* crown. Legs whitish, not pink. Immature has dusky head with whitish nape.
Range: S. Mexico; locally from Cen. America to n. Argentina.
Mexico: Reported locally in savannas near coast of s. Tamaulipas, Veracruz, Tabasco, Campeche, Oaxaca. Not reported Guatemala. **Habitat:** Damp grasslands, marshes, savannas, broken patches of woods near water.

BLACK VULTURE *Coragyps atratus* **See E, W, or T**
Memo: Black; stubby tail, whitish wing patch.
Range: S. U.S. south to n. Chile, n. Argentina. **Mexico:** Widespread except Baja California. **Habitat:** Coasts, forest edges, farms, villages, cities, open country; less frequent at high elevations.

KING VULTURE *Sarcoramphus papa* 32 **Pl. 4**
Field marks: A whitish vulture with black flight feathers and tail. Naked head and neck, displaying much bright orange and

black; warty orange wattles above orange bill. Back and wing
coverts whitish washed with warm buff; blackish ruff around
base of neck. Flight silhouette similar to Black Vulture's. *Immature:* Blackish with bare orange neck and blackish head.
Young in transition may show white patches.
Range: S. Mexico, Cen. and S. America to n. Argentina. **Mexico:** From Isthmus of Tehuantepec east through Chiapas and
lower part of Yucatán Pen. Rarely north to Sinaloa, Puebla,
and Veracruz. **Habitat:** Tropical lowlands up to 3000–4000 ft.

CALIFORNIA CONDOR *Gymnogyps californianus*   **See W**
  Memo: Great size, white wing linings.
  Range: California; very rare, local. **Mexico:** Formerly in mts.
  of n. Baja California. Now presumably extirpated; a recent unconfirmed sight record.

Ospreys: Pandionidae

A LARGE fish-eating hawk; plunges feetfirst for fish. **Range:**
Nearly cosmopolitan. **No. of species:** World, 1; Mexico, 1.

OSPREY *Pandion haliaetus*   **See E, W, or T**
  Memo: Clear-white underparts. Black "wrist" marks in flight.
  Range: Eurasia and N. America. Winters to n. Chile, n. Argentina. **Mexico:** Breeds on coasts of Baja California, Sonora, Sinaloa; locally coastal Quintana Roo; also B. Honduras. Occasional nonbreeders elsewhere in summer. In winter
  widespread.

Kites, Hawks, Harriers, Eagles: Accipitridae

DIURNAL birds of prey with hooked beaks, hooked claws. Divided
into several subfamilies, which are discussed separately in the
other *Field Guides* (East, West, or Texas); but see special note on
Mexican kites, below. **Food:** Small mammals, birds, reptiles,
large insects, carrion. **Range:** Almost worldwide. **No. of species:**
World, 208; Mexico, 38.

KITES: Elaninae, etc.
  Note: Kites fall into 3 field categories in Mexico.
  A. Falconlike shape (pointed wings): (1) White-tailed Kite, (2)
Swallow-tailed Kite, (3) Mississippi Kite, and (4) Plumbeous
Kite.

B. Buteolike or oval-winged shape (rounded wings, rather broad tail): (1) Gray-headed Kite, (2) Hook-billed Kite, (3) Snail Kite.

C. Accipiterlike shape (short, rounded wings, long tail): Double-toothed Kite.

GRAY-HEADED (CAYENNE) KITE   Pl. 2
Leptodon cayanensis   18–20

Field marks: *Adult:* Note the *gray head.* Upperparts blackish, contrasting strikingly with white underparts. Tail with 2 or 3 narrow whitish bands. In flight overhead, buteolike in shape but tail longer. In typical adult *black* wing linings contrast with white body (wing linings white in subadults). Primaries barred black and white; tail boldly banded. *Immature, light phase:* Back, wings, and tail brownish black (tail with broad light bars); underparts (incl. underwing coverts) white. Head white; dark patch on crown; small area around eye black. *Immature, dark phase:* Head blackish; underparts very heavily streaked. There may be intermediates.

Similar species: (1) Adult Black-and-White Hawk-Eagle (similar to pale phase of immature Gray-headed Kite) is larger, has black feathers of rear crown *crested;* conspicuous *black patch* (lores) before eye. Legs feathered to toes. (2) Collared Forest-Falcon might be mistaken for pale phase of young Gray-headed Kite, but see Plate 3 (lacks white eyebrow stripe and has black on sides of face).

Voice: A catlike *myow;* a ringing cry suggestive of hawk-eagle (Slud). A far-carrying *kek-kek-kek-kek* (Wetmore).

Range: E. Mexico, Cen. America to Bolivia, n. Argentina. **Mexico:** Lowlands; s. Tamaulipas through Chiapas (including Pacific coast) and Yucatán Pen. Uncommon. **Habitat:** Swamp forests, marsh edges, savannas.

HOOK-BILLED KITE   Pl. 2
Chondrohierax uncinatus   15–17

Field marks: Note the long hook on the bill, the best giveaway. A rather oval-winged kite; tail longish; variable, with several basic color patterns. (1) *Adult male, "normal":* Dark gray with gray or closely gray-barred underparts. (2) *Adult female, "normal":* Dark brown, underparts coarsely barred with rufous; tawny collar. (3) *Black phase, adult:* Solid black; tail crossed by 1 broad white bar. Sexes alike. (4) *Immature, light phase:* White cheeks, collar, and underparts; bars on breast, thighs, and tail. (5) *Immature, black phase:* Brownish black throughout.

Similar species: (1) Snail Kite, which also has a long hook, has red or orange-yellow legs, white upper tail coverts (lacking in black phase of this species). (2) Dark phase might also be confused with other dark buteolike hawks (see Plate 5). (3) Col-

lared Forest-Falcon has a pattern similar to the immature (light phase) Hook-billed Kite.
Voice: A musical oriole-like whistle; a shrill scream.
Range: Mexico, Grenada south to n. Argentina. **Mexico:** Lowlands, foothills; s. Sinaloa and Tamaulipas south and east.
Habitat: Forests, plantations, swamps, savannas.

SWALLOW-TAILED KITE   See E or T
Elanoides forficatus
Memo: Black above, white below; long forked tail.
Range: Se. U.S.; s. Mexico, Cen. America to Bolivia, n. Argentina. **Mexico:** Summer resident locally in Chiapas, Campeche, Quintana Roo; rare migrant in e. Mexico. **Habitat:** Swamp forests; in Chiapas also mt. pine forests.

WHITE-TAILED KITE   *Elanus leucurus*   See E, W, or T
Memo: Falcon-shaped with white tail (adult).
Range: California, s. Texas, Mid. and S. America to n. Chile, Argentina. **Mexico:** Lowlands from Tamaulipas south and east to Oaxaca, Chiapas, Campeche, Quintana Roo; also w. Baja California (local). Extending range and increasing.

SNAIL (EVERGLADE) KITE   Pl. 5
Rostrhamus sociabilis   17–19
Field marks: *Male:* Completely black except for white at base of square tail; long red or orange-yellow legs. Slender hook on bill. *Female:* Heavily streaked with dark on buffy body; white line over eye and white tail patch.
Similar species: (1) Suggests Marsh Hawk at any distance, but without wavering, tilting flight. (2) See other black birds of prey on Plate 5, especially Bay-winged Hawk.
Range: Florida, Cuba; e. Mexico, Cen. and S. America to Argentina. **Mexico:** Locally common in eastern and southern lowlands from Veracruz, Oaxaca to Chiapas, Campeche, Quintana Roo. **Habitat:** Fresh marshes, open swamps, lakeshores.

DOUBLE-TOOTHED KITE   Pl. 2
Harpagus bidentatus   12–15
Field marks: Note the *black median throat stripe.* Like a small accipiter (short rounded wings, longish tail). Soars often, showing extensive, white, fluffy under tail coverts. *Adult:* Underparts heavily barred or washed with rufous; tail banded. *Immature:* Buffy white below, heavily streaked.
Similar species: See (1) Hook-billed Kite, (2) Sharp-shinned Hawk, and (3) Barred Forest-Falcon — all without median throat stripe.
Voice: A shrill *chiew-ip* (Laughlin); a thin *tsip-tsip-tsip-tsip-wheeeeeeooo;* also a thin, long-drawn *wheeeeoooo* (Eisenmann).

Range: S. Mexico to Bolivia, Brazil. **Mexico:** Uncommon from Guerrero, Veracruz, Oaxaca south and east. **Habitat:** Lowland rain forest and edge.

PLUMBEOUS KITE *Ictinia plumbea* 14–15   Pl. 2

Field marks: Note the *rufous primaries* and the *banded tail* in flight. Otherwise this gray falcon-shaped kite resembles the Mississippi Kite (next), a transient in Mexico. The young bird (inset, Plate 2) has lightly streaked white underparts and usually lacks rufous in wings.

Similar species: Mississippi Kite (a migrant only) lacks rufous in wings, lacks tailbands; has paler head and shows broad light band on rear of wing. Feet dusky, not orange-yellow. Young birds, although often more heavily striped below with rufous-brown than young Plumbeous Kites, show a similar banded tail pattern below and are rarely safely separated under field conditions.

Range: E. Mexico to Bolivia, n. Argentina. **Mexico:** Summer visitor and migrant; s. Tamaulipas south through n. Oaxaca, n. Chiapas, and east through Yucatán Pen. **Habitat:** Forests, river woods.

MISSISSIPPI KITE   Pl. 2; also E, W, or T
Ictinia misisippiensis

Memo: Falcon shape; black tail, no bands (see preceding species).

Range: S.-cen. and se. U.S. Winters apparently in southern subtropical S. America (Paraguay, n. Argentina). **Mexico:** Migrates in flocks through e. and s. Mexico (Tamaulipas, Veracruz, Oaxaca, Tabasco, Chiapas).

BALD EAGLE   *Haliaeetus leucocephalus*   See E, W, or T

Memo: White head, white tail. *Young:* White wing linings.

Range: Treeline Alaska, n. Canada to s. U.S., nw. Mexico. **Mexico:** Breeds Baja California; casual n. Gulf Coast.

CRANE HAWK   Pl. 5
Geranospiza caerulescens (nigra) 17–21

Field marks: Note the *very long orange legs* when perched. A lanky, relatively slim, blackish hawk with a long tail crossed by 2 broad white bands. A narrow whitish band across underwing. Eye *red.* The race in s. Sonora is larger and paler; deep gray rather than blackish. Young birds are finely barred with gray and white below; note the long legs, tail pattern.

Note: The *nigra* complex was formerly regarded as a separate species, "Black Crane Hawk."

Voice: A nasal whining whistle suggesting Roadside Hawk. A nasal *kaah* or *whaow* (Smithe).

Range: Mexico to Bolivia, n. Argentina. **Mexico:** Lowlands from s. Sonora (local), Tamaulipas south and east to Chiapas, Yucatán. **Habitat:** Lowland forests, wooded swamps.

MARSH HAWK (NORTHERN HARRIER)   See E, W, or T
Circus cyaneus
    Memo: ♂ gray; white rump. ♀ brown; white rump.
    Range: Eurasia; N. America to nw. Mexico. Winters to Colombia. **Mexico:** Breeds n. Baja California. Winters throughout.

NORTHERN GOSHAWK   *Accipiter gentilis*   See E, W, or T
    Memo: Very large accipiter; pale pearl-gray breast (adult).
    Range: Eurasia and N. America. **Mexico:** Resident in mt. forests of nw. Mexico (not Baja California).

SHARP-SHINNED HAWK   See E, W, or T
Accipiter striatus
    Memo: Small accipiter; tail square or notched.
    Note: The resident Mexican races are washed with rufous below, almost obscuring the barring; thighs rufous (no bars).
    Range: From tree limit in N. America to Mexico; W. Indies.
    Mexico: Breeds in highlands from Chihuahua and Nuevo León to Michoacán. The northern race (Canada, U.S.) migrates and winters through much of Mexico to w. Panamá. Closely related forms are found from Chiapas to Nicaragua (see next "species"); also Colombia, Venezuela to Paraguay, n. Argentina.

WHITE-BREASTED HAWK   Pl. 2
Accipiter chionogaster   10–14
    Field marks: Similar in size and shape to Sharp-shinned Hawk (treated as conspecific by Brown and Amadon and by Storer) but *immaculate white* below; thighs *buff;* uniform slaty above.
    Range: S. Mexico (Chiapas), Guatemala, Honduras, El Salvador, Nicaragua. **Habitat:** Mt. forests; pine and oak woods.

COOPER'S HAWK   *Accipiter cooperii*   See E, W, or T
    Memo: An accipiter near size of a crow; rounded tail.
    Range: S. Canada to n. Mexico. Winters rarely to Mid. America. **Mexico:** Breeds Baja California and in northern states east to Nuevo León and south in uplands to Michoacán. Winters also cen. and s. Mexico; casual Yucatán.

WHITE HAWK   *Leucopternis albicollis*   19–22   Pl. 3
    Field marks: A large *very white* buteolike hawk with some black barring on wings and a black subterminal band on tail.
    Voice: A harsh buteolike scream, *sheeeer* (Amadon).

Range: S. Mexico to Bolivia, s. Brazil. **Mexico:** Oaxaca, s. Veracruz through Chiapas. **Habitat:** Forests, edges, clearings.

BICOLORED HAWK   *Accipiter bicolor*   14–18   **Pl. 2**
Field marks: Resembles a smallish Cooper's Hawk in shape (short rounded wings, long rounded tail) but underparts *pale gray* without bars; thighs *rufous. Immature:* Brownish black above; white, pale buff, or tawny below. May have buff collar.
Similar species: (1) Collared Forest-Falcon has similar pattern and shape of young of this species but is considerably larger (20–24 in.). (2) See also Barred Forest-Falcon (p. 38).
Voice: ♂ has a soft clear whistle; ♀ (near nest?) a loud *cac cac cac* (Amadon).
Range: Se. Mexico through Cen. and S. America to Tierra del Fuego. **Mexico:** S. Tamaulipas south to Chiapas and east to Yucatán Pen. **Habitat:** Humid woodlands, forest edges.

COMMON (LESSER) BLACK HAWK   **Pl. 5**
Buteogallus anthracinus   18–22
Field marks: A stocky black hawk with very broad wings (suggesting Black Vulture), long chickenlike yellow legs, and 1 broad *white band* midtail. In flight overhead, a whitish spot at base of primaries. Lacks white rump of next species but might show white tipping on upper tail coverts.
Note: B. L. Monroe, Jr., considers birds of the Pacific mangrove coast from Chiapas and Guatemala to nw. Peru a distinct species, *B. subtilis,* Mangrove Black Hawk.
Similar species: (1) Great Black Hawk (similar in size or larger) has white upper tail coverts and usually 2 white bands across tail. (2) Solitary Eagle is much larger (26–28 in.), with shorter tail and no white spot on underwing.
Voice: A nasal squealing whistle; also a harsh *haaaah;* a high 3-syllabled whistle (RTP).
Range: U.S. Mexican border to Ecuador, n. Venezuela, St. Vincent. **Mexico:** Lowlands, foothills; Sonora, Chihuahua, and Tamaulipas south and east through Chiapas, Yucatán Pen. **Habitat:** Wooded streams, ponds, mangroves.

GREAT BLACK HAWK   **Pl. 5**
Buteogallus (Hypomorphnus) urubitinga   20–24
Field marks: Similar to Common Black Hawk (which see) but with *white rump* and usually 2 white bands subdividing tail (upper band not always visible). Light spot at base of primaries more grayish, less extensive. Legs longer and heavier. White barrings on "trousers" and underwing coverts. Skin area before eye, dark — not yellow (but cere is yellow in both species).
Similar species: (1) Common Black Hawk has *black* upper tail coverts; only 1 white band across tail; whiter wing spot. (2)

Solitary Eagle is larger, slightly crested; broader-winged, shorter-tailed. No white spot on underwing.
Voice: A longish whistled *wheeeeeeer;* in aerial display, *keek-keek-keek-keek* (Eisenmann).
Range: Mexico to Bolivia, n. Argentina, Uruguay. **Mexico:** Lowlands, foothills from Sonora, s. Tamaulipas south and east. **Habitat:** Wooded streams; near fresh water in arid or humid country; mangroves.

SOLITARY EAGLE *Harpyhaliaetus solitarius* 26–28 **Pl. 5**
Field marks: Similar to Great Black Hawk but larger, with relatively broader wings, much darker upper tail coverts, shorter tail; slightly crested (bushy). In flight overhead shows broad white median tailband; no white wing spot. Immature lacks any distinct tailbars.
Similar species: See above (1) Common Black Hawk and (2) Great Black Hawk.
Voice: Very unlike that of Great Black Hawk. An arresting *yeep-yeep-yeep-yeep;* also *pipipipipip* (Slud).
Range: Mexico, through Cen. America to Venezuela, Peru. **Mexico:** Very rare, local; w. and s. Mexico, recorded se. Sonora to Chiapas. **Habitat:** Forested mt. slopes, pines.

BLACK-COLLARED HAWK (FISHING BUZZARD)   **Pl. 2**
Busarellus nigricollis 20–22
Field marks: *Bright chestnut* with a *whitish head* and a *black chest patch.* At a distance this chunky hawk appears vulture-like. Very wide-winged, with cinnamon wing linings contrasting with black flight feathers. Tail *very short* with a wide black band. Young birds are similar, but darker, streaked on light head and breast. Note *black band* across chest.
Voice: An almost jaylike *ya ya ya ya ya;* a nasal gutteral *whaaaaa* or *whag* (Chalif).
Range: Local; s. Mexico through Cen. and S. America to n. Argentina. **Mexico:** Lowlands; from Sinaloa south locally along Pacific; Veracruz to Campeche along Gulf Coast. Casual Yucatán Pen. **Habitat:** Marshes, swamps, estuaries.

BAY-WINGED (HARRIS') HAWK   **Pl. 5; also W or T**
Parabuteo unicinctus 19–22
Field marks: A black buteo with a flashy *white rump* and a *white band* at tip of tail. Note the *chestnut- or rufous-colored areas* on thighs and wings — a mark distinguishing it from other black buteos. Immature has light, streaked underparts and *rusty shoulders;* might be confused with Red-shouldered Hawk but more slender, with conspicuous white at base of tail.
Similar species: Immature might be mistaken for (1) Red-shouldered Hawk (below) or (2) ♀ or young Marsh Hawk (p. 30).

Voice: A harsh *karrr* (RTP).
Range: Sw. U.S., south locally to cen. Chile, Argentina. **Mexico:** Lowlands, foothills from Baja California and northern edge of Mexico south to Veracruz, Chiapas. **Habitat:** Savannas, brush, sparse woods, semidesert.

GRAY HAWK   *Buteo nitidus*   **Pl. 3**
Field marks: Buteo proportions (stocky; wide wings, wide tail), gray back, gray and white barred underparts, white rump, and wide tailbands (similar to Broad-winged Hawk's). Immature has narrow-barred tail, striped buffy underparts; darker, more heavily marked than young of Broad-winged or Roadside Hawk.
Voice: A loud plaintive *cree-eer* (RTP).
Range: U.S.–Mexican border to n. Argentina. **Mexico:** Mainly lowlands; Sonora and Tamaulipas south and east. **Habitat:** Wood edges, riverine forests, semi-arid groves.

ROADSIDE HAWK   *Buteo magnirostris*   14–16   **Pl. 3**
Field marks: A smallish gray-brown buteo (wide wings, wide tail) with rufous barring on underparts. *Rufous primaries* conspicuous in flight. Tail banded with pale gray and dark brown. Some races in Mexico are grayer, especially on head, with lower abdomen mainly white. Immature is browner, streaked on whitish breast, barred with rufous on abdomen.
Similar species: (1) Adult Broad-winged Hawk is darker above; tailbands boldly black and white, ruddier on breast. Young Broad-winged and (2) Gray Hawks are less rufous and are less barred below, more streaked than young of this species.
Voice: A querulous *heyaaa;* a hoarse whistling *seeuu* (Chalif). A buzzy or hissing squeal, *kzweeeooo* (Eisenmann).
Range: Cen. Mexico, Cen. and S. America to n. Argentina. **Mexico:** Resident from Jalisco and cen. Tamaulipas south and east, including Yucatán Pen. **Habitat:** Roadsides, woodland borders, open woods, plantations, clearings, savannas; mainly lower elevations.

RED-SHOULDERED HAWK   See E, W, or T
Buteo lineatus
Memo: Rufous shoulders and underparts (adult).
Range: Se. Canada, e. U.S., California, Mexico. **Mexico:** Rare resident, ne. Baja California. Winters rarely to Sinaloa; in east from Río Grande delta to Valley of Mexico, Veracruz.

BROAD-WINGED HAWK   See E, W, or T
Buteo platypterus
Memo: Wide white bands on tail; rusty underparts (adult).
Range: E. and cen. N. America. Winters mainly in s. Mid. America and n. S. America south to Peru, Bolivia, n. Brazil.

Mexico: Migrant, often in large loose flocks through ne. and s. Mexico (except Yucatán Pen.) A few may winter.

SHORT-TAILED HAWK   *Buteo brachyurus*   **Pl. 5; also E**
Memo: *Dark phase:* Black body, pale banded tail. *Light phase:* Clear white belly and wing linings.
Range: S. Florida, Mexico to Chile, Bolivia, ne. Argentina.
Mexico: Rare, local; lowlands from cen. Sinaloa, Veracruz to Chiapas, Yucatán Pen. **Habitat:** Forests, borders, savannas.

SWAINSON'S HAWK   *Buteo swainsoni*   **See E, W, or T**
Memo: Heavy dark breastband (typical adult).
Range: Alaska, w. Canada to nw. Mexico. Winters mainly in S. America to cen. Argentina (a few in s. Florida, Panamá, etc.).
Mexico: Breeds Baja California and northwestern states east to Coahuila. Migrates in loose flocks through Mexico (except Yucatán Pen.) and Cen. America.

WHITE-TAILED HAWK   *Buteo albicaudatus*   23–24   **Pl. 3**
Field marks: *Adult:* Note the white tail with a narrow black band near tip. A long-winged, short-tailed buteo with clear white underparts. Upperparts dark gray, shoulders rufous. *Immature:* May be quite blackish below, or may have dark throat, light chest, and heavily marked underparts. In flight overhead has a whitish tail and blackish wing linings, light primaries.
Voice: A repeated *ke-ke-ke-ke-ke-ke;* also *cut-a, cut-a,* etc. (RTP).
Range: S. Texas to n. Patagonia. **Mexico:** Sonora and Tamaulipas south; local. Absent north-central highlands and Baja California. **Habitat:** Brushy prairies, open country, eroded land.

ZONE-TAILED HAWK   *Buteo albonotatus*   18½–21½   **Pl. 5**
Field marks: A dull black hawk that "mimics" Turkey Vulture (note the longish wings for a buteo and *bicolored wing effect*), but hawk head and tailbands identify the adult. Immature has narrower tailbanding and a scattering of *small white spots* on its black underparts.
Similar species: Compare other black or blackish species on Plate 5, especially Black Hawk-Eagle (broader wings, more checkered effect).
Voice: A squealing whistle, suggesting Red-tail's (RTP).
Range: Sw. U.S. to Bolivia, Paraguay, Brazil. **Mexico:** Mountains of Baja California, northern states, locally to cen. and s. Mexico; lower levels in winter. **Habitat:** Breeds in pine-oak belt of mts. Winters in lowlands.

RED-TAILED HAWK   *Buteo jamaicensis*   **See E, W, or T**
Memo: Reddish tail (adult).

Range: S. Alaska, treeline in Canada to w. Panamá. **Mexico:** Baja California across to Tamaulipas in north; south locally in pine forests of uplands through Chiapas. Northern migrants may occur elsewhere; absent in Yucatán Pen.

ROUGH-LEGGED HAWK *Buteo lagopus*   **See E, W, or T**
   Memo: *Light phase:* Dark belly, black "wrist" marks under wing. Whitish tail with broad dark terminal band.
   Range: Subarctic; circumpolar. Winters to s. U.S., cen. Eurasia. **Mexico:** Occasional extreme northern edge.

FERRUGINOUS HAWK *Buteo regalis*   **See W or T**
   Memo: Rufous upperparts and "trousers"; white or rusty tail.
   Range: Plains of w. N. America. **Mexico:** Winters occasionally in arid highlands to cen. Mexico.

HARPY EAGLE *Harpia harpyja* 34–36   **Pl. 4**
   Field marks: A *huge,* robust, black and white eagle with a conspicuous *2-part crest.* Note the *broad black chestband* separating the *gray head* from the white underparts. Upperparts black; tail gray with broad black bands; thighs barred. Feet very powerful (for catching monkeys, sloths). Young birds lack the broad black chestband and have an *immaculate white crested head* and underbody; upperparts dark.
   Voice: A wailing *wheeeeoooooo.*
   Range: S. Mexico to Bolivia, nw. Argentina, s. Brazil. **Mexico:** Very rare; reported Veracruz, Chiapas, Campeche. Also B. Honduras, Guatemala. **Habitat:** Tropical forests.

GOLDEN EAGLE *Aquila chrysaetos*   **See E, W, or T**
   Memo: Dark; dark wing linings, golden nape. *Young:* Ringed tail, white wing patches.
   Range: Eurasia, N. America. **Mexico:** N. Baja California; Sonora east to Nuevo León and south to cen. Mexico.

BLACK-AND-WHITE HAWK-EAGLE   **Pl. 4**
Spizastur melanoleucus 22–24
   Field marks: A striking black and white bird of prey. Upperparts black; underparts immaculate white. Head *white* with a short *black crown-crest.* Conspicuous *black* patch before and *encircling eye.* Tail rather short, barred with black and gray. *Immature:* Similar but browner above.
   Similar species: See (1) immature Ornate Hawk-Eagle (below) and (2) immature Gray-headed Kite (pale phase), p. 27.
   Range: S. Mexico through Cen. and S. America to Paraguay, n. Argentina. **Mexico:** Rare resident in Veracruz, Oaxaca, Chiapas; casual Yucatán. **Habitat:** Lowland forests, wooded rivers.

BLACK HAWK-EAGLE   **Pls. 4, 5**
Spizaetus tyrannus   25–28
   Field marks: Largely black with some white checking on
   lower underparts. Note the short *erectile black and white crest.*
   In flight overhead tail is long, broad, and rounded, crossed by 4
   whitish bands; wings rounded, underside *boldly checkered* with
   black and white on flight feathers. *Immature:* Brown above,
   heavily streaked below. Cheek *dark;* eyebrow stripe and throat
   white.
   Voice: A ringing call, *whut, whut, whut-eeeeeeer, whut-eeeer*
   (Willis). Calls constantly when soaring; a liquid, loud, melancholy phrase, *oolee'oo* or *tleewee'oo* or *kweeoo;* sometimes *kee
   keek leeweeoo* (Eisenmann). *Ka reee oh* (Alden).
   Range: S. Mexico through Cen. and S. America to Paraguay,
   ne. Argentina. **Mexico:** Rare resident of Gulf slope from s. Tamaulipas to Campeche; occasional Yucatán Pen. **Habitat:**
   Dense rain forest of lowlands; cloud forest of lower mts.

ORNATE HAWK-EAGLE   *Spizaetus ornatus*   23–25   **Pl. 4**
   Field marks: Note the long spiky *black crest, bright cinnamon* cheeks and neck, and narrow black whisker outlining the
   white throat. Upperparts black; underparts boldly barred with
   black and white. In flight, tail is long, wings short and rounded.
   Immature: Note the *white head* with long *black and white
   crest.* Dark brown above; underparts white; flanks *barred.*
   Similar species: (1) Black-and-White Hawk-Eagle is similar
   to immature of this species (white head, black crest) but back is
   blacker, crest and tail are short, and flanks are not barred. Note
   the greater amount of black before eye. (2)See also immature
   Black Hawk-Eagle (preceding).
   Voice: Call, *whee whee wee wee wheet* (Alden).
   Range: S. Mexico, Cen. and S. America to Bolivia, Paraguay,
   n. Argentina. **Mexico:** Gulf slope; s. Tamaulipas, Veracruz
   through n. Oaxaca, n. Chiapas; occasional Yucatán Pen. **Habitat:** Heavy forest of humid lowlands, lower mts.

Caracaras, Forest-Falcons, and
Falcons: Falconidae

CARACARAS are largish long-legged birds of prey with naked faces.
FOREST-FALCONS have rounded wings, longish tails, accipiterlike
appearance. FALCONS are streamlined birds of prey with long
pointed wings, longish tails. **Food:** Some caracaras prefer carrion,
others eat wasp larvae. Forest-falcons and falcons eat birds, rodents, insects, sometimes bats and snakes. **Range:** Caracaras from

s. U.S. to s. Argentina. Forest-falcons live in tropical American forests; falcons are almost cosmopolitan. **No. of species:** World, 58; Mexico, 12 (+ 1 recently extinct).

RED-THROATED CARACARA   Pls. 4, 5
Daptrius americanus   20–23

Field marks: A distinctive glossy-black bird of prey with a *bare red face and throat,* yellow bill. Belly, thighs, and under tail coverts *immaculate white,* sharply separated from the black breast — the only black bird of prey so patterned. Legs orange-red. Wanders about in noisy groups.

Similar species: Most likely to be mistaken for a guan!

Voice: A loud harsh *cacao* or *ca-ca-ca-ca-caw,* from which it derives its Spanish name, "Comecacao" (Land).

Range: S. Mexico, Guatemala, to Peru, s. Brazil. **Mexico:** Locally, s. Veracruz, n. Chiapas. **Habitat:** Lowland humid forests, borders. Feeds largely on wasp larvae.

GUADALUPE CARACARA   *Polyborus lutosus*   Not illus.
Extinct. Closely related to next species. A brown-barred, yellow-faced species (or race) formerly found only on Guadalupe I. off Baja California. Extinct since 1900.

CRESTED CARACARA   *Caracara plancus*   Pls. 4, 5
Field marks: This large, long-legged, long-necked dark bird of prey is often seen feeding with vultures, where its *black crest* and red face are its outstanding features. In flight, its underbody presents alternating areas of light and dark — whitish throat and breast, black belly, and white, dark-tipped tail. *Whitish patches* near tips of dark wings are conspicuous. These are determinative when seen in conjunction with the white chest. Young birds are browner, streaked on breast, not barred.

Voice: Harsh grating calls, *trak-trak-trak.* Also *quick-quick-quick-querr,* last note delivered with toss of head (Amadon and Brown).

Range: Florida, Texas, and Arizona to Tierra del Fuego (the northern group of forms has been called *P. cheriway*). **Mexico:** Baja California and most of mainland from U.S. border south; most common in lowlands, dry open country, wet savannas.

LAUGHING FALCON   Pl. 3
Herpetotheres cachinnans   18–22

Field marks: A large, big-headed, pale buff and dark brown falcon; unfalconlike in flight. Note the *black face mask* on the pale cream-colored or buff head. Crown, hindneck, and underparts pale buff; upperparts deep brown; tail banded buff and black. In flight shows buffy patch on primaries.

Voice: Very much like a human laugh; a loud shrill *ha ha ha* repeated up to 14 times (Grossman). A rather fast *hah, hah, hah-hah-hahahahah,* somewhat accelerating and falling slightly in pitch (Eisenmann).
Range: Mexico to Bolivia, Paraguay, nw. Argentina. **Mexico:** Pacific slope from Sinaloa (rarely Sonora) south; east slope from Tamaulipas through Yucatán Pen. Very local in interior. **Habitat:** Forest borders, semi-open land; most common in humid areas; also dry forest; perches in open.

BARRED FOREST-FALCON   Pl. 3
Micrastur ruficollis 13–15

Field marks: Small, *accipiterlike* (long tail, short rounded wings). Note the *finely barred* or vermiculated underparts, *yellow* cere and loral area. *Male:* Slaty-backed; gray barring below. *Female:* Similar but browner, more coarsely barred. *Immature:* Dark-backed, incompletely barred below, with buff collar (sometimes hidden); often shows conspicuous ruff. Breast may be washed with tawny; variable.
Similar species: See (1) Collared Forest-Falcon (much larger), next, and (2) Bicolored Hawk (lacks barring), p. 31.
Voice: One to several distinctly separated barking sounds, much like those of a small dog (Slud).
Range: S. Mexico to n. Argentina. **Mexico:** From Puebla, Veracruz south and east through Chiapas, and southern part of Yucatán Pen. **Habitat:** Lowland forests, forest edges. Perches low in dense growth; hard to see.

COLLARED FOREST-FALCON   Pl. 3
Micrastur semitorquatus 19–24

Field marks: Large, slender; shaped much more like an accipiter than a falcon (small head, short rounded wings, long rounded tail). Crescentic stripe on side of face helps indicate a forest-falcon. *Adult, light phase:* Blackish above with narrow white collar; cheeks and underparts immaculate white; tail black, narrowly banded with white. *Tawny phase:* Similar but white replaced by pale tawny or buff. *Black phase:* Blackish throughout, but note slender accipitrine shape, long rounded tail with narrow gray bars. *Immature:* Patterned like adult but browner above; barred below with brown and washed with cinnamon on breast and collar.
Similar species: See (1) immature Barred Forest-Falcon (preceding) and (2) Bicolored Hawk (p. 31).
Voice: A loud *hah hah hah,* etc., suggesting Laughing Falcon.
Range: Mexico to Paraguay, n. Argentina. **Mexico:** Both coastal slopes; Sinaloa and s. Tamaulipas south and east through Chiapas, Yucatán Pen. **Habitat:** Heavy forest; lowlands and lower mt. slopes. Usually perches below canopy.

AMERICAN KESTREL (SPARROW HAWK)
Falco sparverius   **See E, W, or T**
Memo: Small falcon; rufous back, rufous tail.
Range: Breeds from treeline Alaska, Canada south to Nicaragua, W. Indies. Also S. America locally to Tierra del Fuego.
Mexico: Resident in Baja California and w. Mexico south to Guerrero; also Chiapas. Winters nearly throughout.

MERLIN (PIGEON HAWK)   **See E, W, or T**
Falco columbarius
Memo: Small falcon; slaty back, banded gray tail.
Range: Northern parts of N. Hemisphere. Migrates and winters to Mid. America, n. S. America, n. Africa, India. **Mexico:** Migrant and winter visitor, mainly near coasts.

BAT FALCON   *Falco rufigularis*   9–11   **Pl. 3**
Field marks: A small black falcon with a conspicuous *whitish throat* (sometimes tinged with rusty). Blue-black above; underparts extensively black, very narrowly barred with whitish. Lower belly, thighs, and under tail coverts rufous. *Immature:* Similar; abdomen sooty brown.
Similar species: (1) Orange-breasted Falcon is larger; note orange chest. (2) See Aplomado Falcon (larger, paler, different head pattern). (3) See also White-collared Swift (p. 92).
Voice: A thin querulous *krree krree krree kree*, etc., or *peel peel* (5–8 times), suggesting Kestrel (Chalif).
Range: Mexico to Bolivia, Paraguay, n. Argentina. **Mexico:** Pacific slope (rare), se. Sonora through Chiapas; Gulf slope, s. Tamaulipas through Yucatán Pen. **Habitat:** Woodland borders, clearings; perches conspicuously on dead trees.

APLOMADO FALCON   *Falco femoralis*   15–18   **Pl. 3**
Field marks: Gray-backed with a black cummerbund. Note the *head pattern* with black mustache and buff stripe behind eye. Relatively slender.
Similar species: (1) Bat Falcon and (2) Orange-breasted Falcon have head entirely black except for white throat.
Range: Sw. U.S. locally through Mid. and S. America to Tierra del Fuego. **Mexico:** Coastal scrub, arid country from Sinaloa, Chihuahua, Tamaulipas to Chiapas, Yucatán. Very local; now rare in north and west. **Habitat:** Open country, plains, short-grass savannas.

PRAIRIE FALCON   *Falco mexicanus*   **See W or T**
Memo: Pale, sandy; dark axillars (in wingpits).
Range: Sw. Canada to s. Mexico. **Mexico:** Breeds locally in Baja California. Winters to cen. Mexico; rarely Oaxaca.

ORANGE-BREASTED FALCON   **Pl. 3**
Falco deiroleucus   13–15
   Field marks: A rare falcon, like a large, *big-footed,* heavy-billed version of the Bat Falcon. The bright orange breast below the white throat identifies it.
   Similar species: (1) Bat Falcon is smaller (9–11 in.) and lacks the broad orange band across chest. (2) Aplomado Falcon is larger (15–18 in.), much paler, with very different head pattern.
   Voice: Like a peregrine's; a rasping *aczeek-aczeek* (Amadon and Brown).
   Range: S. Mexico to Peru, n. Argentina. **Mexico:** Rare; recorded Veracruz, nw. Chiapas. **Habitat:** Lowland forests, edges.

PEREGRINE FALCON   *Falco peregrinus*   **See E, W, or T**
   Memo: Slate above, pale below; heavy black mustache.
   Range: Nearly worldwide. **Mexico:** Breeds Baja California and locally islands in Gulf of California; possibly in mts. Migrant and winter visitor elsewhere, mainly coasts.

Chachalacas, Guans, Curassows: Cracidae

FOWL-LIKE birds of forests, woodlands; mainly arboreal. Nest in trees. Long-tailed, strong-legged; most species crested, bill hen-like. Relatively long hind toe assists in perching. **Food:** Fruit, seeds, leaves, insects. **Range:** Neotropical; s. Texas to Paraguay. **No. of species:** World, 39; Mexico, 7.

PLAIN (EASTERN) CHACHALACA   **Pl. 6**
Ortalis vetula   20–24
   Field marks: A large olive-brown bird shaped somewhat like a half-grown turkey with a small head; long, rounded, pale-tipped tail, bare red throat. Difficult to observe; best found in morning when calling raucously from treetops.
   Note: The 3 similar species of Mexican Chachalacas separate out by range except in a limited area (Pijijiapan) in the Isthmus of Tehuantepec, where they slightly overlap. Plain Chachalaca is eastern; West Mexican Chachalaca (incl. rufous-bellied form) replaces it on Pacific slope; White-bellied Chachalaca occurs in s. Chiapas only.
   Similar species: See (1) roadrunners (p. 80) and (2) other chachalacas.
   Voice: Alarm, a harsh chickenlike cackle. Characteristic call, a raucous 3-syllabled *cha-ca-lac,* repeated in chorus from treetops, especially in morning and evening. Dr. A. A. Allen described a chorus as *keep'-it-up, keep'-it-up, keep'-it-up,* etc., answered by a lower *cut-it-out, cut-it-out.*

Range: See map. Lower Río Grande Valley, Texas, to nw. Costa Rica. **Mexico:** Gulf slope from n. Tamaulipas to n. and cen. Chiapas, Yucatán. **Habitat:** Woodlands, tall brush.

WEST MEXICAN CHACHALACA   Pl. 6
Ortalis poliocephala   25–27
(including Rufous-bellied or Wagler's Chachalaca)

Field marks: Similar to Plain Chachalaca but larger and with a more noticeable tuft or crest on forehead. Resident in w. Mexico (see map). The northern population (Sonora south to Jalisco), formerly regarded as a distinct species, Rufous-bellied Chachalaca, *O. wagleri*, is *deep rufous or chestnut* on belly, under tail coverts, and tail tips. It intergrades in Jalisco and Colima with the nominate form, which is paler but almost indistinguishable in the field from the Plain Chachalaca except, apparently, by voice (Davis).

Voice: Similar to Plain Chachalaca's but 4-syllabled.

Similar species: (1) Plain Chachalaca replaces it on Gulf slope (overlaps slightly or meets it in Isthmus of Tehuantepec and in s. Chiapas); has different voice. (2) See White-bellied Chachalaca (Chiapas), next.

Range: See map. Resident w. Mexico only, from s. Sonora (Alamos) south to sw. Chiapas (Pijijiapan). **Habitat:** Lowland thickets; wooded mt. slopes.

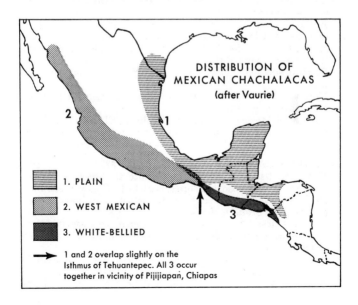

DISTRIBUTION OF
MEXICAN CHACHALACAS
(after Vaurie)

2

1

1. PLAIN

2. WEST MEXICAN

3. WHITE-BELLIED

3

1 and 2 overlap slightly on the
Isthmus of Tehuantepec. All 3 occur
together in vicinity of Pijijiapan, Chiapas

WHITE-BELLIED CHACHALACA *Ortalis leucogastra* **Pl. 6**
Field marks: Similar to the other 2 chachalacas but quite *white* on the abdomen, with gray scaling on breast. Tail tipped with pure white.
Voice: Call 4-syllabled, similar to West Mexican Chachalaca's but "less burry, with closer intervals" (Vaurie).
Range: Pacific slope of s. Mexico, Guatemala, El Salvador, Honduras, nw. Nicaragua. **Mexico:** S. Chiapas only, where it meets ranges of other 2 chachalacas in vicinity of Pijijiapan.
Habitat: Similar to that of other chachalacas.

CRESTED GUAN *Penelope purpurascens* 34–36   **Pl. 6**
Field marks: Size of a small turkey, but with a rather small body, long tail. Dusky olive-brown; feathers of underparts edged with white. Throat *red,* loose-skinned, bristly. Head with a short bushy crest (not recurved as in Great Curassow). Legs magenta-red. Eye-ring bluish. Sexes alike.
Similar species: See below (1) ♀ Great Curassow and (2) ♀ Black Penelopina.
Voice: Harsh throaty cackles; honking sounds. "A loud metallic *kwank* or *kwink* repeated many times" (Chalif).
Range: Mexico to Ecuador, Venezuela. **Mexico:** Coastal slopes from Sinaloa and s. Tamaulipas south. **Habitat:** Arboreal. Forests, second growth; sea level to 6000 ft.

BLACK PENELOPINA (BLACK CHACHALACA)   **Pl. 6**
Penelopina nigra 21–25
Field marks: Not a true chachalaca, but size and shape of one. *Male:* Glossy black with a long tail, *bright red dewlap,* scarlet legs. *Female:* Brown, heavily barred above and on tail; legs *scarlet;* bare red throat.
Similar species: Chachalacas lack barring of ♀, have blackish legs.
Voice: A long whistle, steady in volume but rising in pitch over a 2-octave range (Land).
Range: S. Mexico, Guatemala, Honduras, El Salvador, Nicaragua. **Mexico:** Mts. of e. Oaxaca, Chiapas. **Habitat:** Cloud forest, pine-oak woods; 3000–10,000 ft.

HORNED GUAN *Oreophasis derbianus* 32–36   **Pl. 7**
Field marks: Size of a turkey. Note the erect *red* casque ("horn") on the head and bright red feet. Glossy green-black above, with a finely streaked white breast. Tail black, crossed midway by a *broad white band.*
Voice: A deep low 3- or 4-note *oo-oo-oo,* repeated several times and having a soft mooing quality. Also mandible-clacking and croaking (Andrle).
Range: Sierra Madre of extreme se. Mexico and s. Guatemala; historically reported from 24 localities (Andrle). Now much endangered. **Mexico:** Now restricted mainly to 2 or 3 volcanic

peaks in se. Chiapas (esp. Tacaná and El Triunfo). **Habitat:** In Guatemala, probably most frequent in Volcán Tajamulco. Humid, evergreen broadleaf forests on volcanic mt. tops; 7000–11,000 ft.

GREAT CURASSOW *Crax rubra* 30–38   **Pl. 6**
   Field marks: Fowl-like, size of a turkey, with a *curly crest.* *Male:* Glossy black with a white abdomen. Note frilly crest and bulbous *yellow knob* above bill. *Female:* Somewhat smaller; bright rufous, shading to black on tail; paler below. Wings and tail mottled or barred; variable. Head, neck, and recurved crest checkered black and white.
   Similar species: See Crested Guan (above).
   Voice: ♂ has a high, thin, whistled *wheeeoo* and *wheep;* also *whee, whee, whee.* A squeaky *weeyp.* Sometimes combined as *wheeyp wheeeeeee* (rising in pitch). During display, a low-pitched hooting ending in a boom — *whoooo-hoo-hoo; boom.* ♀ a soft *hmmm;* also a *hoot-hoot* (Eisenmann).
   Range: Mexico to Colombia. **Mexico:** Lowlands to 3000 ft.; Tamaulipas, San Luis Potosí south to Chiapas, Yucatán Pen. **Habitat:** Undisturbed humid forests.

Wood-Partridges, Quails, etc.: Phasianidae

Scratching, chickenlike birds, majority smaller than grouse. Wood-partridges (or "tree-quails") are a bit larger than other quails and have much longer tails. Pheasants (larger) also belong to this family but occur in Mexico in only 1 locality (introduced). Sexes usually unlike except in neotropical species. **Food:** Insects, seeds, buds, berries. **Range:** Nearly worldwide except for colder regions. **No. of species:** World, 174; Mexico, 15 (+2 introduced and 1 in Guatemala).

BEARDED WOOD-PARTRIDGE   **Pl. 8**
Dendrortyx barbatus 10–12
   Field marks: This rare and local "tree-quail" can be distinguished from the next by its *gray* throat and brownish to cinnamon breast and belly.
   Similar species: Long-tailed Wood-Partridge, which overlaps locally in cen. Veracruz, has a conspicuous black throat.
   Range: Mexico. Rare and local in mts. of San Luis Potosí and Veracruz (Cofre de Perote, Pico de Orizaba, Jalapa, Jico, etc.). **Habitat:** Cloud forest.

LONG-TAILED WOOD-PARTRIDGE   **Pl. 8**
Dendrortyx macroura 9–11
   Field marks: Wood-partridges, also known as "tree-quails," are larger and *longer-tailed* than other quails, giving them a

more chickenlike aspect. This species is identified by its *black throat.* Legs, bill, and eye *red.* Short crest.
Similar species: Bearded Wood-Partridge overlaps range of this species in cen. Veracruz.
Range: Mexico only. Higher ridges and volcanoes from Jalisco across to cen. Veracruz and south to Guerrero, Oaxaca. **Habitat:** Mostly cloud forest; also pine-oak zone.

BUFFY-CROWNED (HIGHLAND) WOOD-PARTRIDGE
Dendrortyx leucophrys   12–14   **Pl. 8**
Field marks: Note the *buffy* forehead, *whitish* throat, *black* bill. Otherwise similar to other wood-partridges.
Similar species: No other wood-partridge in Chiapas.
Range: S. Mexico to Costa Rica. **Mexico:** Se. Chiapas only.
Habitat: Mt. forests; oak-pine and cloud forests with grassy or brushy floor.

MOUNTAIN QUAIL   *Oreortyx picta*   **Pl. 9; also W**
Memo: Long straight head plume; white bars on sides.
Range: W. U.S. from n. Washington, n. Idaho south through Pacific states. **Mexico:** Resident in Sierra Juárez and Sierra San Pedro Mártir in n. Baja California. **Habitat:** Conifer forests in summer; to oak-chaparral zone in winter.

SCALED QUAIL   *Callipepla squamata*   **Pl. 9; also W or T**
Memo: Pale gray, scaly; "cotton top."
Range: Sw. U.S. to cen. Mexico. **Mexico:** Ne. Sonora across to n. Tamaulipas and south in the arid interior to Valley of Mexico and Morelos.

CALIFORNIA QUAIL   *Lophortyx californica*   **Pl. 9; also W**
Memo: Curved head plume, scaled belly.
Range: Oregon, California, Baja California. **Mexico:** Throughout Baja California except for northeastern corner (Colorado drainage), where replaced by next species.

GAMBEL'S QUAIL   *Lophortyx gambelii*   **Pl. 9; also W or T**
Memo: Curved head plume, rufous crown, black patch on belly.
Range: Deserts of sw. U.S., nw. Mexico. **Mexico:** Northeastern corner of Baja California (Colorado drainage), where it replaces California Quail; Sonora, nw. Sinaloa, northern edge of Chihuahua.

ELEGANT QUAIL   *Lophortyx douglasii*   8–10   **Pl. 9**
Field marks: *Male:* Note the *speckled throat* and elegant *tawny crest* on its pepper-and-salt-colored head. Body gray, with round white spots on underparts; much rufous in wings. *Female:* Crest shorter, darker; bird browner.

Similar species: Most other Mexican quails have a scalloped effect on underparts; this species has round white spots.
Range: W. Mexico from cen. Sonora and w. Chihuahua south on Pacific slope through Sinaloa, Nayarit, Jalisco to Colima.
Habitat: Brush, second growth of cutover forests.

BANDED QUAIL *Philortyx fasciatus* 7–8½ **Pl. 8**
Field marks: A small quail. Note the heavy *black and white barring* on underparts and *straight slender crest* (black tipped with rufous). Back heavily scaled with dark. Sexes similar. *Immature* (Nov. to Jan.): *Black face and throat;* otherwise banded like adult.
Voice: A squeal when flushed.
Range: S.-cen. Mexico only. Pacific slope from s. Jalisco to Guerrero; inland through Michoacán to Puebla. **Habitat:** Dense weed patches, farmland, open bushy slopes.

COMMON BOBWHITE *Colinus virginianus* 8½–10½ **Pl. 9**
Field marks: The most variable bird in Mexico, ranging from the typical white-breasted form found in the U.S. to black-throated, black-chested birds. They interbreed freely and are regarded as conspecific. All whistle the familiar *bob-white!* On Plate 9 we show males of 5 basic types (females have buff throats and look quite alike): (a) typical; white throat, barred whitish belly (ne. Mexico); (b) white throat, rufous underparts (cen.-w. Mexico); (c) white throat, black chest, rufous belly (s. Mexico); (d) "Masked" Bobwhite; black throat, white brow, rufous underparts (Sonora only; rare); (e) black head (eyebrow stripe indistinct or lacking) underparts cinnamon barred with black (s. Chiapas, w. Guatemala).
Similar species: In Yucatán see Black-throated Bobwhite.
Voice: A clearly whistled *bob-white!* or *poor, bob-whoit!* Covey call, *ka-loi-kee?* answered by *whoil-kee* (RTP).
Range: E. and cen. U.S. to Mexico, Guatemala, Cuba. **Mexico:** Sonora (masked race); also from lower Río Grande in ne. Mexico south along Gulf slope and through s. Mexico to Tabasco, Chiapas; also across cen. Mexico to Pacific slope in Nayarit, Jalisco. Absent from Baja California, n.-cen. Mexico, most of w. Mexico, Yucatán Pen. **Habitat:** Agricultural land; weedy, brushy open country, edges, roadsides.

BLACK-THROATED (YUCATAN) BOBWHITE **Pl. 9**
Colinus nigrogularis 7–8
Field marks: Note the *boldly scalloped* pattern of breast and upper belly. Throat black; white stripe above and *below* eye. Allopatric, it replaces Common Bobwhite in Yucatán Pen. *Female:* Similar to female Common Bobwhite.
Voice: Practically indistinguishable from Common Bobwhite's.

Range: Nw. Yucatán Pen. (Campeche, Yucatán), B. Honduras, n. Guatemala (local), e. Honduras, Nicaragua (local). **Habitat:** Fields, clearings, pine savannas, plantations.

SPOT-BELLIED BOBWHITE   Pl. 8
Colinus leucopogon   7–8

Field marks: A small bobwhite with numerous *round white spots* on the belly. In northern race (Guatemala) the throat and breast are *white*.
Voice: Similar to Common Bobwhite's.
Range: Arid interior and Pacific lowlands of s. Guatemala, Honduras, El Salvador, Nicaragua to cen. Costa Rica. Not in Mexico. **Habitat:** Fields, brush, wood edges.

SPOTTED WOOD-QUAIL   Pl. 8
Odontophorus guttatus   10–12

Field marks: Note the *orangish crest.* A dark quail. Back olive or reddish brown. Underparts chocolate with *white spots.* Throat black with narrow white streaks.
Voice: Loud; a low-high-low combination: *grouww-chow-lo* or *hrook-chou-low,* repeated (Chalif). An excited, ringing *whipa-whipee'o;* repeated, musical (Eisenmann).
Range: Se. Mexico to sw. Panamá. **Mexico:** Cen. Veracruz, e. Oaxaca east through Chiapas, Campeche, Quintana Roo. **Habitat:** Understory of humid forests, cloud forest, edges.

SINGING QUAIL   *Dactylortyx thoracicus*   8–9   Pl. 8
Field marks: A dark brown quail with a very stubby tail. *Male:* Note the rich *tawny-orange* throat and eyebrow stripe. *Female:* Dull grayish or whitish on face and throat; bright tawny buff below, paler on abdomen.
Voice: Loud clear whistles, beginning with 4 whistles increasing in volume (but decreasing in interval), then 3 to 6 repeated phrases. Call note, *pitter pititit* (Chalif).
Range: Mexico, Guatemala, El Salvador, Honduras. **Mexico:** Range discontinuous, in 5 areas — (1) nw. Jalisco (San Sebastián), (2) cen. Guerrero, (3) eastern escarpment from cen. Tamaulipas, e. San Luis Potosí to cen. Veracruz, (4) highlands of Chiapas, (5) cen. and w. Yucatán Pen. **Habitat:** Highlands; cloud forest, oak-sweetgum forests, humid canyons; in Yucatán, lowland scrub.

MONTEZUMA (HARLEQUIN) QUAIL   Pl. 8
Cyrtonyx montezumae   7–9½

Field marks: Note the oddly striped clown's face, pale bushy crest (not always erected), and speckled body of male. Females are brown, with less obvious facial stripings. Tame.
Note: The ♂ shown on Plate 8 is typical of the north; in s.

Mexico ♂ has the spots on the lower sides purplish brown, not white; somewhat intermediate between the northern form and the next species.
Similar species: See Ocellated Quail (next).
Voice: A soft whinnying or quavering whistle. Ventriloquial (vaguely suggests Common Screech-Owl).
Range: Arizona, New Mexico to s. Mexico. **Mexico:** Highlands from n. Sonora, w. Chihuahua, n. Coahuila, Tamaulipas (local) south to Oaxaca. **Habitat:** Oak-pine zone of mts.; grassy canyons, wooded slopes with bunchgrass.

OCELLATED QUAIL   *Cyrtonyx ocellatus*   8–10   **Pl. 8**
Field marks: Like a washed-out version of the Montezuma Quail and possibly should be regarded as a race of that bird. *Male:* Head pattern similar to Montezuma Quail's; chest buff, breast and flanks chestnut with black barring.
Range: S. Mexico to Nicaragua. **Mexico:** E. Oaxaca, Chiapas.
Habitat: Pine-oak zone of highlands.

CHUKAR PARTRIDGE   *Alectoris chukar*   **See W or T**
Memo: Striped flanks, black "necklace"; rusty tail, red legs. Sometimes regarded as conspecific with *A. graeca* (Rock Partridge) of cen. and s. Europe.
Range: Asia, se. Europe; introduced w. N. America. **Mexico:** Introduced successfully in mts. of n. Baja California.

COMMON (RING-NECKED) PHEASANT   **See E, W, or T**
Phasianus colchicus
Memo: *Male:* White neck-ring, long pointed tail. *Female:* Brown; long pointed tail.
Range: Asia, se. Europe. Introduced widely in Europe, temperate N. America, and elsewhere. **Mexico:** Established in Mexicali valley in extreme ne. Baja California.

Turkeys: Meleagrididae

VERY LARGE fowl-like birds; highly iridescent, naked-headed. Males with large tails erected fanwise in display. **Food:** Berries, acorns, nuts, other seeds, insects. **Range:** E. and s. U.S. to s. Mexico. **No. of species:** World, 2; Mexico, 2.

COMMON TURKEY   *Meleagris gallopavo*   **See E, W, or T**
Memo: Streamlined version of the barnyard turkey.
Range: E. and sw. U.S.; n. Mexico. Domesticated worldwide.
Mexico: In west, uplands of Sonora, w. Chihuahua south locally to Michoacán; in east, locally in Coahuila, s. Nuevo León, Tamaulipas, e. San Luis Potosí; formerly more widespread.

Habitat: Mostly pine-oak zone in mts., and (in Tamaulipas) adjacent coastal plain.

OCELLATED TURKEY   *Agriocharis ocellata*   32–40   **Pl. 7**
Field marks: *Male:* Note the fleshy *orange-red knob* and wartlike tubercles on the bare blue head; also the blue-green *eye spots* on the *grayish* tail. Lacks chest "beard" of Common Turkey. Plumage dark, glossed with blue-green and bronze. Wings with broad white on secondaries; flight feathers barred black and white. *Female:* Duller, lacking warts.
Voice: Gobbling utterly unlike that of *Meleagris* and may be written as *ting-ting-ting-co-on-cot-zitl-glung,* the last note having a bell-like quality (Leopold).
Range: Yucatán Pen. and adjacent parts of Guatemala, B. Honduras. **Mexico:** S. Tabasco, se. Campeche, extreme ne. Chiapas, e. Yucatán, Quintana Roo. **Habitat:** Second-growth scrub, abandoned cornfields, wood edges, savannas.

Cranes: Gruidae

LARGE, long-legged birds superficially like large herons; bare red skin about face (in some), and elongated inner secondary feathers that curl over ends of wings. Sexes alike. Neck extended in flight. Trumpetlike calls. **Food:** Omnivorous. **Range:** N. America, Africa, Eurasia, Australia. **No. of species:** World, 14; Mexico, 1 (+ 1 formerly).

WHOOPING CRANE   *Grus americana*   **See E, W, or T**
Memo: Very large, white; red face, black primaries.
Range: Breeds nw. Canada. Winters coastal Texas. Now rare and local. **Mexico:** Former winter visitor to n. Mexico; vagrants should be looked for in Tamaulipas.

SANDHILL CRANE   *Grus canadensis*   **See E, W, or T**
Memo: Large, gray; red crown, tufted rear.
Range: Ne. Siberia; nw., w., and se. N. America; Cuba. In winter to Mexico. **Mexico:** Winters in northern states and south in interior to Jalisco and Puebla (occasionally to Yucatán Pen).

Limpkins: Aramidae

LONG-LEGGED marsh birds; a monotypic family related to cranes and rails. **Food:** Freshwater snails; also frogs, reptiles, etc. Tropical America. **No. of species:** World, 1; Mexico, 1.

LIMPKIN   *Aramus guarauna*   **See E or T**
Memo: Brown, spotted; long decurved bill.
Range: Se. U.S., Mexico, W. Indies to Argentina. **Mexico:** Gulf lowlands: Veracruz, Oaxaca, Chiapas, Campeche, Quintana Roo. **Habitat:** Swamps, marshes; adjacent brush.

Rails, Gallinules, and Coots: Rallidae

RAILS are compact, rather chicken-shaped marsh birds, more often heard than seen. Wings short and rounded; tails short. Gallinules and coots swim; resemble ducks except for smaller heads, forehead shields and henlike bills. **Food:** Aquatic plants, insects, frogs, crustaceans, mollusks, seeds, buds. **Range:** Worldwide, except in colder regions, some deserts. **No. of species:** World, 119; Mexico, 15 (+ 1 in B. Honduras).

KING RAIL   *Rallus elegans*   **See E or T**
Memo: Large, rusty brown; slender bill, barred flanks.
Note: A tawny race of the Clapper Rail (next), inhabiting the fresh marshes of the Federal Dist., México (Río Lerma), and Tlaxcala, is sometimes considered a race of the King Rail.
Range: Eastern N. America; Cuba. **Mexico:** Casual. Reported Tamaulipas (?), Guanajuato, Veracruz.

CLAPPER RAIL   *Rallus longirostris*   **See E, W, or T**
Memo: Large; gray and tawny, slender bill.
Note: The various populations of Clapper Rails in Mexico are a subject of taxonomic dispute. The Pacific Coast birds were formerly regarded as a separate species (Western Rail, *R. obso-letus*). The isolated fresh-marsh birds of cen. Mexico are so tawny as to suggest the King Rail *(R. elegans)* and are sometimes lumped with that species.
Range: Coasts of e. and s. U.S., California, Mexico, B. Honduras; W. Indies, also n. S. America south to Peru, Brazil. **Mexico:** Discontinuous in 4 areas — (1) west; coastal marshes and mangroves from California south to s. Baja California, Nayarit; (2) northeast (probably Tamaulipas); (3) east, very local on islands off Yucatán, Quintana Roo; (4) interior; fresh marshes of Federal Dist., Río Lerma, Tlaxcala.

VIRGINIA RAIL   *Rallus limicola*   **See E, W, or T**
Memo: Small, rusty; gray cheeks, slender bill.
Range: S. Canada south locally to cen. Mexico; very locally in w. S. America. Winters to Guatemala. **Mexico:** Local; breeds Baja California, Sonora (?), Federal Dist. Winters elsewhere locally.

SPOTTED RAIL   *Pardirallus maculatus*   9½–11   **Pl.10**
   Field marks: Strikingly patterned with black and white —
   bars and spots; back and wings deep brownish. Bill yellow-
   green with red spot at base. Feet red.
   Voice: A deep, chesty grunting; also a clucking *tuk-tuk-tuk,*
   etc., gradually accelerating (Bond).
   Range: Cuba; Mid. and S. America. Extremely rare in Mexico
   (Veracruz, Chiapas) and B. Honduras. **Habitat:** Marshes.

UNIFORM CRAKE   *Amaurolimnas concolor*   8–8½   **Pl. 10**
   Field marks: A small reddish rail; like a smaller edition of
   Rufous-necked Wood-Rail, but more uniform in color. Lacks
   the gray upper back and blackish tail. Bill greenish, legs red, as
   in wood-rails.
   Range: S. Mexico, locally to e. Peru, e. Bolivia, Brazil; formerly
   Jamaica. **Mexico:** Very rare. Reported Oaxaca, Veracruz,
   Chiapas. **Habitat:** Swampy lowland woods.

GRAY-NECKED WOOD-RAIL   **Pl. 10**
Aramides cajanea   14–17
   Field Marks: Size of a chicken; not as secretive as most other
   rails. Note combination of *gray* head and neck, *cinnamon* sides
   and upper abdomen, and *black* lower undersides and tail. Legs
   and eyes red; bill yellow-green, red at base.
   Voice: A striking cry, heard most often at dawn or dusk; a
   repeated chickenlike cackle: *pop-tiyi pop-tiyi co-co-co-co-co* or
   chittyco chittyco caw-caw-caw (Slud).
   Range: Mexico to Bolivia, n. Argentina. **Mexico:** S. Tamaulipas south through e., cen., and s. Mexico to Chiapas and
   Yucatán Pen. **Habitat:** Swamps, swampy forests, mangroves.

RUFOUS-NECKED WOOD-RAIL   **Pl. 10**
Aramides axillaris   12
   Field marks: This rare rail is similar to the Gray-necked
   Wood-Rail but is somewhat smaller, with a rufous head and
   neck. Upper back and lower underparts gray.
   Similar species: See above (1) Gray-necked Wood-Rail and
   (2) Uniform Crake.
   Range: Mexico (not Guatemala), locally through Cen. and S.
   America to w. Ecuador, Surinam. **Mexico:** Pacific Coast; re-
   corded Sinaloa, Nayarit, Guerrero; also locally Yucatán Pen.
   Habitat: Coastal; mangrove swamps. Rare.

SORA   *Porzana carolina*   **See E, W, or T**
   Memo: Small, gray and brown; short yellow bill.
   Range: Canada, n. and w. U.S. In winter to Peru, Guyana.
   Mexico: Has bred nw. Baja California (San Antonio del Mar).
   Winters (probably widely) in marshes, mangroves.

YELLOW-BREASTED CRAKE   **Pl. 10**
Porzana flaviventer   5-6
   Field marks: A tiny rail with a *pale creamy* breast, black
   stripe through eye, *white stripe* above eye. Strongly barred on
   sides. Bill, *blue-black;* legs pale cream-yellow.
   Similar species: (1) Yellow Rail has *yellow* bill, *white* wing
   patches. (2) Immature Sora is larger (8-9½ in.), grayer, with a
   thicker *yellow* bill, *greenish* legs.
   Range: Mexico (very local), Greater Antilles, locally to Argentina. **Mexico:** Reported only from Veracruz and Guatemalan
   border of Chiapas (Lagartero River). **Habitat:** Marshy edges of
   rivers, streams, ponds.

BLACK RAIL (CRAKE)   **See E, W, or T**
Laterallus jamaicensis
   Memo: Tiny; slaty with dark rusty nape, black bill.
   Similar species: See similar Gray-breasted Crake (next).
   Range: U.S. (local), nw. Mexico, Jamaica, Galápagos Is., Peru,
   Chile. Winters to Honduras. **Mexico:** Resident only in nw.
   Baja California (San Quintín, San Ramón).

GRAY-BREASTED CRAKE *Laterallus exilis*   **Not illus.**
   Field marks: Similar to Black Rail but paler, especially on
   breast; lacks white marks on upper back. Bill partly green.
   Range: Honduras, Nicaragua, Panamá, n. S. America.
   Reported B. Honduras but not in Mexico or Guatemala.

RUDDY CRAKE (RED RAIL) *Laterallus ruber* 5-6 **Pl. 10**
   Field marks: A small deep rufous rail, paler below, with a
   blackish head; bill black, legs greenish.
   Voice: A churring whinny (Slud).
   Range: E. Mexico to Costa Rica. **Mexico:** Gulf slope from s.
   Tamaulipas south and east to Yucatán Pen. **Habitat:** Marshes,
   brushy edges, wet fields, high grass.

YELLOW RAIL (CRAKE)   **See E, W, or T**
Coturnicops noveboracensis
   Memo: Small, buffy; striped back, white wing patch.
   Range: Mainly cen.-s. Canada; local n. U.S., cen. Mexico.
   Winters s. U.S. **Mexico:** Resident Río Lerma marshes, State of
   México.

COMMON GALLINULE *Gallinula chloropus* **See E, W, or T**
   Memo: Ducklike, dark; red bill, white side stripe.
   Range: Se. Canada, U.S. to n. Chile, Argentina; Eurasia,
   Africa, miscellaneous oceanic islands. **Mexico:** Local resident
   or transient in marshes nearly throughout.

PURPLE GALLINULE   *Porphyrula martinica*   **See E or T**
   Memo: Purple neck, blue frontal shield, red bill.
   Range: Se. U.S. to n. Chile, n. Argentina. **Mexico:** Fresh
   marshes, ponds, and lakes locally from Sonora, Tamaulipas,
   south and east to Chiapas, Quintana Roo.

AMERICAN COOT   *Fulica americana*   **See E, W, or T**
   Memo: Ducklike, blackish; white bill.
   Range: Canada, U.S., locally to Chile, w. Argentina; Hawaii.
   Mexico: Breeds very locally (particularly in Baja California
   and in volcanic cordillera). Winters along both coasts and lo-
   cally in interior, throughout.

Finfoots: Heliornithidae

SOLITARY aquatic birds with slender necks, pointed bills, rather
long stiff tails. Legs very short; cootlike lobes on toes. They swim
(often half-submerged) and dive, grebelike. **Food:** Crustaceans,
mollusks, fish, insects. **Range:** Tropical America, Africa, se. Asia.
No. of species: World, 3; Mexico, 1.

SUNGREBE (AMERICAN FINFOOT)   **Pl. 10**
Heliornis fulica   11–12
   Field marks: This slender stream-dweller suggests a small cormorant when swimming. It is olive-brown above, with a buffy
   breast, white belly, and stiff black tail with a white tip. Note the
   bold pattern of *black and white stripes* on the head and neck.
   Cheeks cinnamon in female, white in male. Legs short; toes
   lobed, yellow banded with black.
   Similar species: Sunbittern is much larger (18–20 in.), has
   much longer *red* legs, longer neck, longer tail; does not swim.
   Voice: A peculiar bark of 1–3 notes (Chalif). Note, *Kow,* given
   once or repeated; suggests Pied)billed Grebe (Wetmore).
   Range: S. Mexico to Bolivia, Paraguay, ne. Argentina. **Mex-
   ico:** E. San Luis Potosí, Veracruz south through Oaxaca,
   Chiapas, Campeche. **Habitat:** Secluded forest lakes, streams.
   Sungrebes hug heavily vegetated banks when swimming.

Sunbitterns: Eurypygidae

SLENDER, somewhat heronlike or rail-like wading birds with a
very slender neck, slender bill. Wings and tail broad and strikingly
patterned. **Food:** Crustaceans, insects. **Range:** Tropical
America. **No. of species:** World, 1; Mexico, 1.

SUNBITTERN   *Eurypyga helias*   18–20   **Pl. 10**
Field marks: Unlike the Sungrebe, the Sunbittern is a stalker and a wader, not a swimmer, flying into trees when alarmed. Sometimes spreads its broad wings, patterned in a spectacular sunburst of black, chestnut, yellow, gray, and white. At rest, body is held horizontal, rear part often weaving uncannily. Neck very slender, erect. Legs red.
Similar species: Sungrebe is smaller, usually seen swimming.
Voice: A mournful, dragging tinamoulike whistle (RTP). A reedy trill; a plaintive piping.
Range: S. Mexico to Peru, Bolivia, Brazil. **Mexico:** Gulf lowlands of Tabasco, n. Chiapas; local. **Habitat:** Wooded swamps, forested tropical streams, lake borders.

Jacanas: Jacanidae

SLENDER marsh birds with a spur on the wing and extremely long toes for walking on floating plants. Also called "lily-trotters" and "lotus birds." **Food:** Mollusks, small fish, insects, aquatic seeds. **Range:** Tropical America, Africa, India, se. Asia, Australasia. **No. of species:** World, 7; Mexico, 1.

NORTHERN JACANA   *Jacana spinosa*   8–9   **Pl. 10**
Field marks: Note the *extremely long toes. Adult:* Head and neck blackish, rest of body deep chestnut. The best field marks are the *yellow forehead shield* and extensive *pale greenish-yellow wing patches. Immature:* Gray-brown above, whitish below; white stripe over eye. Extremely long toes, yellow wing patches, rail-like flight, notes, habitat, distinguish it.
Voice: A sharp cackle, especially in flight. Also rasping, chattering, and clacking notes.
Range: S. Texas (rarely) to w. Panamá; W. Indies. A closely related species, Panamá to Argentina. **Mexico:** Gulf slope from Tamaulipas to Yucatán Pen.; Pacific slope from cen. Sinaloa south. **Habitat:** Roadside ponds, marshes, riverbeds.

Oystercatchers: Haematopodidae

LARGE WADERS with long, laterally flattened, chisel-tipped, red bills. Sexes alike. **Food:** Bivalves, oysters, crabs, etc. **Range:** Widespread on coasts of world. **No. of species:** World, 6 (or 4); Mexico, 2.

AMERICAN OYSTERCATCHER   **See E or T**
Haematopus palliatus
  Memo: Large; dark head and chest, white belly, red bill.
  Range: E. U.S., nw. Mexico to Chile, Argentina. **Mexico:** Both
  coasts, including islands in Gulf of California and off w. Mexico;
  very local on east coast.

BLACK OYSTERCATCHER *Haematopus bachmani* **See W**
  Memo: Large, all black; large red bill, pale legs.
  Range: Pacific Coast of N. America; resident from w. Aleutians
  south to cen. Baja California (Pacific side).

Plovers, etc.: Charadriidae

WADING birds, more compactly built, thicker-necked than most
sandpipers, with shorter, pigeonlike bills, larger eyes. Unlike sandpipers, plovers run in short stops and starts. Sexes alike. **Food:**
Small marine life, insects, etc. **Range:** Worldwide. **No. of species:** World, 60; Mexico, 9.

BLACK-BELLIED PLOVER   **See E, W, or T**
Pluvialis (Squatarola) squatarola
  Memo: *Spring:* Black below, pale above. *Winter:* Gray; black
  axillars.
  Range: Arctic; circumpolar. Winters coastal U.S., s. Eurasia to
  S. Hemisphere. **Mexico:** Migrant and winter visitor to both
  coasts; occasional inland.

AMERICAN GOLDEN PLOVER   **See E, W, or T**
Pluvialis (Squatarola) dominica
  Memo: *Spring:* Brown, black below. *Winter:* Brown, brown
  tail.
  Range: Siberia, arctic America. Winters to Argentina, Hawaii,
  s. Asia, Australia. **Mexico:** Noted rarely in migration; coasts
  and interior.

SEMIPALMATED PLOVER   **See E, W, or T**
Charadrius semipalmatus
  Memo: Mud-brown back; ringed chest. Orange or yellow legs.
  Range: Arctic America. Winters to Chile, Argentina. **Mexico:**
  Migrates and winters along both coasts.

PIPING PLOVER *Charadrius melodus*   **See E or T**
  Memo: Pale; ringed chest, yellow legs.
  Range: Eastern N. America. Winters to s. U.S., ne. Mexico, W.
  Indies. **Mexico:** Winters south to coast of Tamaulipas.

SNOWY PLOVER *Charadrius alexandrinus* **See E, W, or T**
   Memo: Pale; *dark* legs, dark ear patch, *slender* black bill.
   Range: Widespread; s. and w. U.S., n. Mexico, W. Indies; coastal Peru and Chile, s. Eurasia, Australia, Africa. **Mexico:** Breeds Baja California; probably ne. Tamaulipas. In winter, elsewhere on coasts.

COLLARED PLOVER *Charadrius collaris* 5–6   **Pl. 10**
   Field marks: A bit smaller and darker than Snowy Plover. Differs in having a *complete* breastband, *cinnamon* on head and neck, and pale yellowish or flesh (not black) legs.
   Voice: Note, a sharp metallic *tsee;* also a slightly rolling *tur-r-r* (Wetmore).
   Similar species: See (1) Wilson's and (2) Snowy Plovers.
   Range: Mexico to Argentina. **Mexico:** Sinaloa in west and San Luis Potosí, Veracruz in east, south to Chiapas, Tabasco; local. **Habitat:** Coastal beaches; also exposed bars of lowland rivers.

KILLDEER *Charadrius vociferus*   **See E, W, or T**
   Memo: 2 breast rings, long tawny tail.
   Range: S. Canada to cen. Mexico, W. Indies; also coastal Peru. Winters to n. S. America. **Mexico:** Breeds locally south to Guerrero in west, Guanajuato in cen. Mexico, Tamaulipas in east. Winters widely elsewhere.

WILSON'S PLOVER *Charadrius wilsonia*   **See E or T**
   Memo: Breastband, heavy black bill, flesh-gray legs.
   Range: New Jersey to Guyana and nw. Peru. Winters to ne. Brazil. **Mexico:** Resident coast of Baja California, Sonora, Sinaloa, Nayarit. Winters locally along east coast.

MOUNTAIN PLOVER *Charadrius montanus*   **See W or T**
   Memo: White eyebrow stripe, no breast-ring.
   Range: Plains, plateaus of w. U.S. In winter to grassy plains of n. Mexico.

Sandpipers, Snipe, etc.: Scolopacidae

A VARIED family of small to medium-sized wading birds. Legs slender; bills more slender than those of plovers. Chiefly gregarious. Sexes alike in most species. Many migrant shorebirds remain throughout the summer in coastal Mexico but are not known to breed. **Food:** Insects, small crustaceans, mollusks, worms; sometimes seeds, berries. **Range:** Almost cosmopolitan. **No. of species:** World, 75; Mexico, 30.

GREATER YELLOWLEGS   See E, W, or T
Tringa (Totanus) melanoleuca
   Memo: Yellow legs, slightly upturned bill. 3-note whistle.
   Range: Alaska, Canada. Winters from coasts of U.S. to Tierra
   del Fuego. **Mexico:** Migrates and winters in coastal lowlands;
   migrant in interior.

LESSER YELLOWLEGS   See E, W, or T
Tringa (Totanus) flavipes
   Memo: Yellow legs, slim bill. 1- or 2-note whistle.
   Range: Alaska, Canada. Winters from Gulf states to Argen-
   tina. **Mexico:** Migrates and winters along east and south
   coasts; scarcer in northwest. Also regular migrant in interior.

SOLITARY SANDPIPER *Tringa solitaria*   See E, W, or T
   Memo: All-dark wings, barred tail, eye-ring, dark legs.
   Range: Alaska, Canada. Winters to cen. Argentina. **Mexico:**
   Migrant locally throughout; some winter.

WILLET *Catoptrophorus semipalmatus*   See E, W, or T
   Memo: Gray; stocky bill, bold black and white wing pattern.
   Range: S. Canada to Gulf of Mexico, W. Indies. Winters s. U.S.
   to Peru, Brazil. **Mexico:** Breeds n. Tamaulipas. Winters along
   coasts, mainly on Pacific side.

SPOTTED SANDPIPER *Actitis macularia*   See E, W, or T
   Memo: Teeters. Breast spots (summer); shoulder mark, no
   spots (winter).
   Range: Alaska, Canada to cen. U.S. Winters s. U.S. to Chile,
   n. Argentina. **Mexico:** Migrant throughout. Winters on coasts
   and low altitudes inland.

WANDERING TATTLER *Heteroscelus incanus*   See W
   Memo: Grayish, lacking pattern; yellow legs (winter).
   Range: Alaska, nw. Canada. Winters coastally to Peru, Pacific
   islands. **Mexico:** Winters mainly along Pacific side of Baja
   California, offshore islands; recorded also west coast from So-
   nora to Guerrero.

RUDDY TURNSTONE *Arenaria interpres*   See E, W, or T
   Memo: Rusty back, harlequin face pattern (summer). In
   winter, dark breast, orange legs; bold flight pattern.
   Range: Arctic, Subarctic; circumpolar. Winters s. U.S., s.
   Eurasia to S. Hemisphere, including many oceanic islands.
   Mexico: Migrates and winters on both coasts.

BLACK TURNSTONE *Arenaria melanocephala*   See W
   Memo: Dark; dark legs. Turnstone shape and flight pattern.
   Range: Breeds along coasts of w. and s. Alaska. Winters along

Pacific Coast from se. Alaska to nw. Mexico. **Mexico:** Winters on coasts of Baja California, Sonora.

SURFBIRD *Aphriza virgata* **See W**
  Memo: Slaty (winter); black-tipped white tail, yellowish legs.
  Range: Breeds in mts. of s.-cen. Alaska. Winters from se. Alaska south along coast to Tierra del Fuego. **Mexico:** Winters along Pacific Coast, especially outer Baja California.

RED KNOT *Calidris canutus* **See E, W, or T**
  Memo: Chunky. Rusty breast, short bill (summer). Gray, short bill, scaly back (winter).
  Range: Greenland, Siberia, nw. Alaska, Arctic islands. Winters chiefly S. Hemisphere. **Mexico:** Irregular migrant; local on both coasts but not often reported.

LEAST SANDPIPER **See E, W, or T**
Calidris (Erolia) minutilla
  Memo: Very small; slim bill, yellowish-green legs.
  Range: Alaska, n. Canada. Winters s. U.S. to n. Chile, Brazil.
  Mexico: Winters on both coasts; local migrant inland.

BAIRD'S SANDPIPER **See E, W, or T**
Calidris (Erolia) bairdii
  Memo: Small; buffy breast, scaly back, dark legs.
  Range: Ne. Siberia, N. American arctic. Winters chiefly in Andes from Ecuador to s. Argentina. **Mexico:** Migrant chiefly through interior (locally on lakes in high mts. and plateaus). Less frequent on coasts. Avoids Yucatán Pen.

WHITE-RUMPED SANDPIPER **See E, W, or T**
Calidris (Erolia) fuscicollis
  Memo: Small, brown (summer) or gray (winter); white rump.
  Range: Arctic America. Winters from Brazil to Tierra del Fuego. **Mexico:** To be expected in migration (probably overlooked). Recorded Yucatán, Cozumel I., B. Honduras.

PECTORAL SANDPIPER **See E, W, or T**
Calidris (Erolia) melanotos
  Memo: Sharp division of breast and belly; striped back.
  Range: Ne. Siberia, American arctic. Winters south to Chile, Argentina. **Mexico:** Migrant, coastal lowlands and interior; absent Yucatán Pen.

DUNLIN *Calidris (Erolia) alpina* **See E, W, or T**
  Memo: Rusty back, black belly (summer). Gray; droop at tip of bill (winter).
  Range: Arctic; circumpolar. Winters from coasts of U.S., s. Eurasia to Mexico, n. Africa, India. **Mexico:** Winters on coasts of Baja California, Sonora, Tamaulipas.

ROCK SANDPIPER   *Calidris (Erolia) ptilocnemis*   **See W**
  Memo: Slaty; dull yellowish legs, eye-ring. Sea rocks.
  Range: Siberia and Alaska. Winters to ne. Asia, s. California.
  Mexico: Sight reports from nw. Baja California.

SEMIPALMATED SANDPIPER   **See E, W, or T**
Calidris (Ereunetes) pusilla
  Memo: Small; bill shorter than Western's, straight.
  Range: American arctic. Winters se. U.S. to n. Chile, n. Argentina. **Mexico:** Presumably winters along east coast.

WESTERN SANDPIPER   **See E, W, T**
Calidris (Ereunetes) mauri
  Memo: Small; bill longer than Semipalmated's; droop at tip.
  Range: Alaska. Winters s. U.S. to Peru. **Mexico:** Migrates and winters on both coasts.

SANDERLING   *Calidris (Crocethia) alba*   **See E, W, or T**
  Memo: Whitish (winter); stout bill, strong bold wing stripe.
  Range: Arctic; circumpolar. Winters from U.S., Britain, China to S. Hemisphere. **Mexico:** Winters both coasts.

STILT SANDPIPER   **See E, W, or T**
Micropalama himantopus
  Memo: Barred below; rusty ear patch (summer). Gray; white rump, greenish legs (winter).
  Range: American arctic. Winters in Bolivia, Brazil, n. Argentina. **Mexico:** Migrant, reported occasionally in e. and s. Mexico (probably overlooked); recorded also B. Honduras, Guatemala.

BUFF-BREASTED SANDPIPER   **See E, W, or T**
Tryngites rubruficollis
  Memo: Buffy underparts, white underwing, yellowish legs.
  Range: N. American arctic. Winters in Argentina. **Mexico:** Migrant, but rarely recorded. Look on prairies, fields.

UPLAND SANDPIPER (UPLAND PLOVER)
Bartramia longicauda   **See E, W, or T**
  Memo: Small head, short bill, thin neck, long tail.
  Range: Canada, n. U.S. Winters in s. Brazil and on pampas of Paraguay, Argentina. **Mexico:** Spring and fall migrant; absent from Baja California, northwestern states, Yucatán Pen.

LONG-BILLED CURLEW   **See E, W, or T**
Numenius americanus
  Memo: Large, buffy; very long curved bill, no head stripes.
  Range: Breeds on plains, plateaus of sw. Canada, w. U.S.
  Mexico: Winters on both coasts; locally inland to Guatemala.

WHIMBREL   *Numenius phaeopus*   **See E, W, or T**
Memo: Decurved bill; gray-brown, striped crown.
Range: Arctic and Subarctic; circumpolar. Winters to s. S.
America, s. Africa. **Mexico:** Migrant and winter visitor on Pa-
cific Coast; seldom reported on Atlantic Coast (although com-
mon in Texas).

ESKIMO CURLEW   *Numenius borealis*   **See E or T**
Memo: Half bulk of Whimbrel. Bill short, slightly curved.
Range: Near extinction. Formerly bred in w. Canadian arctic,
wintering s. Brazil to s. Argentina. **Mexico:** Some migrants formerly passed nonstop over Mexico (few records). To be looked
for (recent sightings in coastal Texas).

HUDSONIAN GODWIT   *Limosa haemastica* **See E, W, or T**
Memo: Long upturned bill, ringed tail, blackish underwing.
Range: Arctic Canada; migrates to s. S. America via Carib-
bean. **Mexico:** Some may pass through unobserved (regular in
Texas; esp. in spring). Recorded Veracruz, Oaxaca (Pacific
Coast); also B. Honduras.

MARBLED GODWIT   *Limosa fedoa*   **See E, W, or T**
Memo: Large, tawny brown; long upturned bill.
Range: Breeds n. Great Plains of N. America. Winters to n.
Chile. **Mexico:** Winters on both coasts; casual inland.

LONG-BILLED DOWITCHER   **See E, W, or T**
Limnodromus scolopaceus
Memo: Differs from next by voice (1-note, not 3-note call).
Range: Ne. Siberia, n. Alaska, nw. Canada. Winters s. U.S.,
Mexico, Cen. Ameria; casually to S. America. **Mexico:** Winters
mainly on Pacific Coast but also locally inland.

COMMON (SHORT-BILLED) DOWITCHER **See E, W, or T**
Limnodromus griseus
Memo: Snipe bill; rusty breast (summer). Gray breast
(winter).
Range: S. Alaska, Canada. Winters s. U.S. to Peru, Brazil.
Mexico: Winters both coasts.

COMMON SNIPE   **See E, W, or T**
Gallinago [Capella] gallinago
Memo: Very long bill, orange tail, zigzag flight.
Range: N. Eurasia, n. N. America. Winters to cen. Africa, Brazil. Closely related forms in S. America. **Mexico:** Reported to
have bred Jalisco, Guanajuato; possibly mts. of n. Baja California. Winters except in arid areas, casual Yucatán.

Stilts and Avocets: Recurvirostridae

WADING BIRDS with very long legs and very slender bills (bent upward in avocets). Sexes alike. **Food:** Insects, crustaceans, other small aquatic life. **Range:** U.S., Mid. and S. America, Africa, s. Europe, Asia, Australia, Pacific region. **No. of species:** World, 7; Mexico, 2.

BLACK-NECKED STILT   See E, W, or T
Himantopus mexicanus
    Memo: Black above, white below; very long red legs.
    Range: W. and se. U.S. to Bolivia, Argentina; closely related forms in Old World (may be conspecific). **Mexico:** Lowlands of both coasts; local in interior.

AMERICAN AVOCET   See E, W, or T
Recurvirostra americana
    Memo: Long upturned bill; black and white back pattern.
    Range: Sw. Canada to n. Mexico. **Mexico:** Has bred San Luis Potosí. Winters locally to Guatemala; not Yucatán Pen.

Phalaropes: Phalaropodidae

SMALL sandpiperlike birds with lobed toes. They wade and swim; when feeding they often spin like tops on the water. Females are larger, more colorful. **Food:** Plankton, marine invertebrates, mosquito larvae, other insects. **Range:** Arctic and Subarctic (circumpolar) and N. American plains; migrate to S. Hemisphere. Two species, Northern and Red, are oceanic much of year. **No. of species:** World, 3; Mexico, 3.

WILSON'S PHALAROPE   See E, W, or T
Steganopus tricolor
    Memo: Dark neck stripe (summer). White rump, needle bill, no wing stripe (winter).
    Range: W. and cen. N. America. Winters to Argentina. **Mexico:** Migrates mainly through w. Mexico; coast and inland.

NORTHERN PHALAROPE   See E, W, or T
Lobipes lobatus
    Memo: Rusty neck, white throat (summer). Striped back, bold wingbar, needle bill (winter).
    Range: Circumboreal. Winters at sea, mainly in S. Hemisphere. **Mexico:** Migrates off Pacific Coast and in Gulf of California; casual inland.

RED PHALAROPE   *Phalaropus fulicarius*   **See E, W, or T**
  Memo: Deep rusty, white cheek (summer). Sanderlinglike with
  less contrasty wing stripe (winter). Thicker bill than Northern's.
  Range: Circumboreal, wintering at sea mainly in S. Hemisphere. Migrant off Pacific Coast of Baja California; casual
  elsewhere in w. Mexico.

Thick-knees: Burhinidae

LARGE, brown, ploverlike birds with very large eyes, conspicuous
wing pattern. Legs moderately long with rather thickened joints.
Range: Eurasia, Africa, Australasia, tropical America. **Food:**
Worms, insects, crustaceans, mollusks, frogs. **No. of species:**
World, 9; Mexico, 1.

DOUBLE-STRIPED THICK-KNEE   **Pl. 10**
(MEXICAN STONE CURLEW)   *Burhinus bistriatus*   18–20
  Field marks: A large ploverlike bird of dry semi-open country
  that would rather run than fly. Note the large-eyed look and
  white eyebrow stripe. In flight shows a Willetlike striped wing
  pattern and a Mourning Dove-like pattern on its graduated tail.
  Most active at dusk and at night.
  Voice: Very noisy at night. "A long-continued *prrrip prrrip*
  prrrip pip pip pip pipipipipipipipip" (Slud).
  Range: S. Mexico to Costa Rica; Colombia, Venezuela to n.
  Brazil; also Hispaniola. **Mexico:** Local; Veracruz, Tabasco,
  Oaxaca, Chiapas. **Habitat:** Savannas, dry semi-open land.

Jaegers and Skuas: Stercorariidae

DARK falconlike seabirds with narrow wings showing a white flash
and a pronounced angle; bill slightly hooked. Adults have 2 elongated central tail feathers. Piratical, they harass gulls, terns, force
them to disgorge. **Food:** Food taken from other birds or from the
sea. **Range:** Seas of world, breeding near polar regions. **No. of
species:** World, 4 or 5; Mexico, 3.

POMARINE JAEGER   **See E, W, or T**
Stercorarius pomarinus
  Memo: Blunt (partially twisted) central tail feathers.
  Range: Arctic; circumpolar. Winters at sea from latitude of s.
  U.S. to S. Hemisphere. **Mexico:** Regular off west coast; seen off
  Quintana Roo (Contoy I.); possibly regular off Yucatán and
  elsewhere off continental shelf of e. Mexico.

PARASITIC JAEGER   See E, W, or T
Stercorarius parasiticus
  Memo: Pointed central tail feathers (moderate length).
  Range: Arctic; circumpolar. Winters at sea as far south as s.
  Chile, s. Australia. **Mexico:** Recorded at sea off Baja California
  (probably regular); probably occurs off continental shelf of e.
  Mexico.

LONG-TAILED JAEGER   See E or W
Stercorarius longicaudus
  Memo: Very long, flexible, pointed central tail feathers.
  Range: Arctic; circumpolar. Winters at sea in S. Hemisphere.
  Mexico: Recorded casually (Clarión I.), but should be regular
  far off west coast.

Gulls and Terns: Laridae

LONG-WINGED water birds with superb flight. Gulls are more robust, usually longer-legged than terns; bills slightly hooked (terns,
sharp-pointed); tails square-tipped or rounded (terns, usually
forked). Gulls seldom dive (terns hover, plunge headfirst); they
swim (terns seldom do). Sexes alike. **Food:** Gulls are omnivorous;
terns eat fish, small marine life, some insects. **Range:** Nearly
worldwide. **No. of species:** World, 78; Mexico, 24 (+3 accidental
and 1 extralimital).

HEERMANN'S GULL   *Larus heermanni*   See W
  Memo: Dark with black tail, whitish head, red bill.
  Range: Breeds locally on islands off Pacific Coast from cen.
  Baja California (both coasts) to Jalisco; wanders north regu-
  larly to Puget Sound and south rarely to Guatemala.

RING-BILLED GULL   *Larus delawarensis*   See E, W, or T
  Memo: Black ring on bill, yellowish legs.
  Range: Canada, n. U.S. In winter to Mid. America, Panamá,
  W. Indies. **Mexico:** Winter visitor mainly to west coast; also
  upper Gulf Coast; locally inland.

HERRING GULL   *Larus argentatus*   See E, W, or T
  Memo: Black wing tips with "mirrors"; pink or flesh legs.
  Range: Northern parts of N. Hemisphere. In winter to coasts
  of Mid. America, Panamá, Africa, India. **Mexico:** Winters both
  coasts; most frequent on Gulf Coast; occasional inland.

CALIFORNIA GULL   *Larus californicus*   See W or T
  Memo: Red or red and black spot on bill; greenish legs.
  Range: Western N. America. South in winter to Pacific Gua-

temala. **Mexico:** Winters mainly on Pacific Coast; casual inland and on east coast to Veracruz.

WESTERN GULL *Larus occidentalis* **See W**
Memo: Blackish or slaty mantle; flesh or yellow legs. The race in the Gulf of California, *L. o. livens,* has yellowish (not flesh) legs and is sometimes called Yellow-legged Gull.
Range: Coast of w. U.S. and nw. Mexico. Winters to Nayarit.

GLAUCOUS-WINGED GULL *Larus glaucescens* **See W**
Memo: Gray primaries with white "mirrors."
Range: Bering Sea to Washington. In winter, south to n. Japan and Baja California; casual Sonora.

GLAUCOUS GULL *Larus hyperboreus* **See E or W**
Memo: Large; white or whitish primaries (no gray spots).
Range: Arctic; circumpolar. In west, winters south to California. **Mexico:** Accidental Baja California.

BLACK-HEADED GULL *Larus ridibundus* **See E**
Memo: Like large Bonaparte's Gull; bill red.
Range: Eurasia; regular in small numbers on east coast of N. America. **Mexico:** Accidental Veracruz.

LAUGHING GULL *Larus atricilla* **See E, W, or T**
Memo: Small size, dark wings with white trailing edge.
Range: Nova Scotia to s. Caribbean on Atlantic side; locally in s. California, w. Mexico. In winter through Mid. and S. America to Peru, Brazil. **Mexico:** Breeds locally in Sinaloa, Campeche, Yucatán. In winter, both coasts; casual inland.

FRANKLIN'S GULL *Larus pipixcan* **See E, W, or T**
Memo: White "windows" separate black from gray on wings.
Range: Prairies of Canada, n.-cen. U.S. Winters chiefly along Pacific Coast from Panamá and Colombia to Chile. **Mexico:** Migrant. Main fall route down Gulf slope to Isthmus of Tehuantepec, then across to Pacific; reversed in spring.

BONAPARTE'S GULL *Larus philadelphia* **See E, W, or T**
Memo: Long wedge of white in primaries.
Range: Alaska, w. Canada. Winters to W. Indies, n. Mexico (coasts of Baja California, Sonora, Sinaloa; casual northeastern coast).

BLACK-LEGGED KITTIWAKE **See E or W**
Rissa tridactyla
Memo: Solid "dipped in ink" wing tips, black legs.
Range: Oceans in northern part of N. Hemisphere. Winters to U.S., Mediterranean, Japan. **Mexico:** Winters to nw. Baja California.

SABINE'S GULL *Xema sabini*   See E or W
Memo: Black outer primaries, white triangle, forked tail.
Range: Arctic; circumpolar. Winters in Pacific to Peru, Chile; local in Atlantic. **Mexico:** Migrant off Pacific Coast.

BLACK TERN *Chlidonias niger*   See E, W, or T
Memo: Black body (summer). Pied head, dark back, gray tail (winter).
Range: Temperate N. America, Eurasia. Winters mainly Panamá, S. America, Africa. **Mexico:** Migrant on coasts; local inland.

GULL-BILLED TERN   See E, W, or T
Gelochelidon nilotica
Memo: Stout gull-like black bill.
Range: Breeds locally, wanders widely in many parts of world.
Mexico: Local resident in Baja California, Sonora, Sinaloa; also Tamaulipas, Veracruz (breeds?); local migrant elsewhere.

CASPIAN TERN *Hydroprogne caspia*   See E, W, or T
Memo: Very large; large red bill, slightly forked tail.
Range: Breeds locally, wanders widely around world. **Mexico:** Breeds locally in Baja California, Sinaloa, Tamaulipas; rare coastal transient.

COMMON TERN *Sterna hirundo*   See E, W, or T
Memo: Dusky primaries; orange-red bill, black tip.
Range: Temperate zone of N. Hemisphere. Winters to S. Hemisphere. **Mexico:** Migrates and winters both coasts.

FORSTER'S TERN *Sterna forsteri*   See E, W, or T
Memo: Pale primaries; orange bill with black tip.
Range: Breeds from w. Canada, cen. Atlantic Coast of U.S. to Tamaulipas. Winters along Pacific Coast of Mexico to Guatemala; Atlantic Coast to n. Veracruz.

ROSEATE TERN *Sterna dougallii*   See E or T
Memo: Pale; very long tail feathers, blackish bill.
Range: Breeds locally, wanders widely in many parts of world.
Mexico: Accidental. Breeds in B. Honduras.

BRIDLED TERN *Sterna anaethetus*   See E
Memo: Like Sooty Tern, but grayer, with light nape collar.
Range: Pan-tropical oceans of the world. **Mexico:** Reported off Guerrero. Has bred B. Honduras.

SOOTY TERN *Sterna fuscata*   See E, W, or T
Memo: Black above, white below; thin black bill.

Range: Pan-tropical oceans of the world. **Mexico:** Colonies on Revilla Gigedo Is., Tres Marías Is., and Isabela I., Nayarit; also off Yucatán, B. Honduras.

LEAST TERN *Sterna albifrons* **See E, W, or T**
Memo: Small size, yellow bill.
Range: Widespread but local in temperate and tropical regions of world. **Mexico:** Migrant (and may breed) on both coasts. Breeds in Baja California and perhaps Sonora, Sinaloa, Chiapas, etc.

ROYAL TERN *Thalasseus maximus* **See E, W, or T**
Memo: Large; orange bill, tufted crest, well-forked tail.
Range: Breeds s. U.S., Mexico, W. Indies, Venezuela, Argentina; also w. Africa. Winters along both coasts from s. U.S. to Peru, Argentina. **Mexico:** Resident both coasts.

ELEGANT TERN *Thalasseus elegans* **See W**
Memo: Slender yellow-orange bill, long crest.
Range: Breeds on islands off west coast from Baja California to Nayarit. Winters from sw. Ecuador to Chile; wanders north along coasts to cen. California (has bred s. California).

SANDWICH TERN *Thalasseus sandvicensis* **See E or T**
Memo: Slender black bill, yellow tip.
Range: Virginia south to Gulf of Mexico, Caribbean region, wintering to Argentina. Also Eurasia, n. Africa. **Mexico:** Occurs along Gulf Coast and locally Pacific Coast (Tehuantepec). Breeds on islands off Yucatán Pen.; also B. Honduras.

BROWN NODDY *Anous stolidus* **See E or W**
Memo: Brown body, whitish crown, rounded black tail.
Range: Tropical oceans. **Mexico:** In west, breeds on islands off Nayarit and Jalisco (Revilla Gigedo, Tres Marías, Isabela, Tres Marietas Is., etc.). In east, islands off coast of Yucatán, Quintana Roo; also B. Honduras.

WHITE-CAPPED (BLACK or LESSER) NODDY **See W**
Anous minutus (tenuirostris)
Memo: Smaller than Brown Noddy; cap whiter, tail gray.
Range: Islands in tropical Atlantic and Pacific. **Mexico:** No definite record. Recorded Clipperton I. (French) far out in Pacific; also B. Honduras.

WHITE TERN *Gygis alba* **See W**
Memo: Snow-white; black ring around dark eye.
Range: Tropical oceans. **Mexico:** O'Neal Rock near Socorro.

Skimmers: Rynchopidae

RELATIVES of gulls and terns with a knifelike red bill, jutting lower mandible. **Food:** Small fish, crustaceans. **Range:** E. U.S. to S. America. Closely related forms in s. Asia, Africa. **No. of species:** World, 3; Mexico, 1.

BLACK SKIMMER   *Rynchops nigra*   **See E or T**
     Memo: Black above, white below; long unequal red bill.
     Range: E. U.S. to Chile, Argentina. **Mexico:** Coastal, breeding locally. In west, from Sonora south; in east, Tamaulipas to Yucatán Pen.

Auks, etc.: Alcidae

BLACK and white diving seabirds, the northern counterpart of the penguins, but they can fly. Short necks and pointed, stubby or deep and laterally compressed bills. Swim and dive expertly. Sexes alike. **Food:** Fish, crustaceans, mollusks. **Range:** Northern oceans. **No. of species:** World, 19; Mexico, 4 (+1 accidental).

XANTUS' MURRELET   *Endomychura hypoleuca*   **See W**
     Memo: Small; solid black above, white below; small bill.
     Note: The race *E. h. craverii,* "Craveri's Murrelet" (or species, as designated in the 1957 A.O.U. *Check-List*), breeds on islands in the Gulf of California and is separable *in the hand* by its *grayish* instead of immaculate wing linings.
     Range: Baja California and Gulf of California, breeding locally on offshore islands; also Guadalupe I.

ANCIENT MURRELET   *Synthliboramphus antiguus*   **See W**
     Memo: Small; black cap, gray back, white underparts.
     Range: Bering Sea and northern parts of N. Pacific (both coasts). Winters south to n. Baja California (casual).

CASSIN'S AUKLET   *Ptychoramphus aleuticus*   **See W**
     Memo: Very small, dark; light spot on bill.
     Range: Pacific Coast from Alaska to cen. Baja California.

RHINOCEROS AUKLET   *Cerorhinca monocerata*   **See W**
     Memo: Yellow bill, thin white head plumes (may be absent).
     Range: Northern N. Pacific (both sides). **Mexico:** Winters rarely to nw. Baja California.

COMMON MURRE   *Uria aalge*   **See E or W**
     Memo: Black above, white below; slender pointed bill.
     Range: Northern parts of N. Pacific and N. Atlantic. **Mexico:**

Accidental. Photographed off nw. Baja California (Coronados Is.).

Pigeons and Doves: Columbidae

PLUMP, fast-flying birds with small heads, low cooing voices. Most have pink or red legs. Two main types: (1) large, with fanlike tails (pigeons) and (2) smaller, with rounded or pointed tails (doves). The names "pigeon" and "dove" are somewhat arbitrary. Sexes similar. **Food:** Seeds, fruits, insects. **Range:** Nearly worldwide in temperate and tropical regions. **No. of species:** World, 285; Mexico, 23 (+1 introduced).

ROCK DOVE (DOMESTIC PIGEON)   See W or T
Columba livia
    Memo: White rump, black wingbars. Many color forms.
    Range: Old World origin; worldwide in domestication. **Mexico:** Sustains self in a feral or semiferal state around many towns (and possibly in some canyons, cliffs).

WHITE-CROWNED PIGEON   Pl. 12
Columba leucocephala   13½
    Field marks: Stocky; all dark except for *snow-white crown.*
    Voice: A low owl-like *wof, wof, wo, co-woo* (Maynard).
    Range: Florida Keys, W. Indies, locally Caribbean islands. **Mexico:** Islands off coasts of Quintana Roo, Cozumel I.; also B. Honduras. **Habitat:** Mangrove keys, wooded islands.

RED-BILLED PIGEON   *Columba flavirostris*   13–14   Pl. 11
    Field marks: A large dark pigeon with a broad tail, *red* on bill. In good light, deep maroon on foreparts. Arboreal.
    Similar species: (1) Pale-vented Pigeon has black bill, pale abdomen. (2) Short-billed Pigeon is smaller, with black bill.
    Voice: Cooing more drawn out than White-winged Dove's: *who who wooooooo,* long note swelling (RTP).
    Range: S. Texas through Mid. America to cen. Costa Rica. **Mexico:** Mainly lowlands; Gulf slope from n. Tamaulipas through Yucatán Pen.; Pacific slope from cen. Sonora south. **Habitat:** Semi-arid woodlands, river woods, tall brush.

PALE-VENTED (RUFOUS) PIGEON   Pl. 11
Columba cayennensis   12–14
    Field marks: Dark; resembles Red-billed Pigeon but prefers more humid habitat. Note *black* bill and pale or *whitish* abdomen. Foreparts dark maroon-brown in good light; tail paling to brown. Arboreal, rare.
    Similar species: (1) Red-billed Pigeon (preceding) and (2) Short-billed Pigeon (p. 68).

Voice: Sounds like "Santa Cruz"; 1st 2 notes (San-ta) short and musical, last note (Cruz) a long *cooooouu* (Chalif). *Coo'oo, ruk-tu-coo'oo* or *ruk-tu-coo'oo* (Eisenmann).
Range: S. Mexico to n. Argentina. **Mexico:** Lowlands of s. Veracruz, Tabasco, Campeche, e. Chiapas. **Habitat:** Wooded swamps, humid forests or wood edges, plantations.

BAND-TAILED PIGEON   Pl. 11; also W or T
Columba fasciata
Memo: White crescent on nape; dark band midtail.
Range: Sw. B. Columbia to nw. Argentina. **Mexico:** Widespread in pine-oak highlands throughout.

SCALED PIGEON   *Columba speciosa*   11–13   Pl. 12
Field marks: Note the heavy dark *scaling* (or white spotting) on the neck and breast of this large dark pigeon. Back rufous. Bill and area around eye red. Female duller. Arboreal.
Voice: A fairly loud *hoo-oo'-hoo;* slightly resonant (Andrle).
Range: S. Mexico to Bolivia, ne. Argentina. **Mexico:** N. Oaxaca, s. Veracruz east through Chiapas, Yucatán Pen. **Habitat:** Dense forests; sits quietly in bare treetops.

SHORT-BILLED PIGEON   Pl. 11
Columba nigrirostris   10–12
Field marks: An all-dark pigeon, about Mourning Dove size, with rounded tail; no white. Bill black, feet red. Arboreal.
Similar species: (1) Red-billed Pigeon is larger, with gray rump, red bill. (2) Pale-vented Pigeon is larger, more maroon; pale or whitish on abdomen and under tail coverts.
Voice: *Ooo,* then *oo-coo-hooooo,* descending on a long drawn note (Chalif). A melancholy, drawn-out *hoo, cu-cu-coo'oo,* sometimes shortened to *cook, cuckoo'oo* (Eisenmann).
Range: S. Mexico to Panamá. **Mexico:** N. Oaxaca, s. Veracruz east to n. Chiapas, s. Yucatán Pen. (rarely). **Habitat:** Humid lowland forests, forest interiors.

MOURNING DOVE   Pl. 11; also E, W, or T
Zenaida (Zenaidura) macroura
Memo: Pointed tail with white sides.
Range: Se. Alaska, s. Canada, to Panamá. **Mexico:** Widespread south to Isthmus of Tehuantepec, breeding mainly in central and western sections; rarer in Chiapas; casual in Yucatán.

SOCORRO DOVE   Pl. 11
Zenaida (Zenaidura) graysoni   12
Field marks: Resembles Mourning Dove, but underparts *rufous.*
Range: Socorro I. in Revilla Gigedo Is. off w. Mexico.

ZENAIDA DOVE *Zenaida aurita* 10–11 **Pl. 11**
Field marks: Similar to Mourning Dove but with a squarish
tail tipped with pearl-gray. Note the *broad white stripe* on rear
edge of wing.
Similar species: (1) White-winged Dove has diagonal white
patch on wing, *white* tail corners. (2) White-tipped Dove has no
white in wing.
Voice: A mournful *cuacoo-coo-coo* like a Mourning Dove but
slightly more curtailed; also a short *ooa-oo* (Bond).
Range: W. Indies and Yucatán Pen. **Mexico:** Tip of Yucatán
Pen.; Cozumel I. **Habitat:** Arid coastal scrub.

WHITE-WINGED DOVE *Zenaida asiatica* 11–12½ **Pl. 11**
Field marks: Note the *white patch* diagonally across the
wing. Tail rounded, with white corners.
Similar species: See White-tipped Dove (p. 71).
Voice: A harsh cooing, *who cooks for you?;* also, *ooo-uh-
cuck'oo.* Sounds vaguely like crowing of young rooster (RTP).
Range: Sw. U.S. through Mid. America to w. Panamá; W.
Indies; S. America from sw. Ecuador to n. Chile. **Mexico:**
Throughout except rain forest and higher mts. **Habitat:** Scrub,
dry woods, mesquite, hedgerows, towns.

INCA DOVE *Scardafella inca* 7–9 **Pl. 12**
Field marks: A small, slender dove with a pale *scaly appearance* (above and below). Differs from Common Ground-Dove
by comparatively *slender* square-ended tail (looks pointed when
folded, *white sides* when spread). Both show rufous in wings.
Similar species: Ground-Dove has short dark tail.
Voice: 2 notes on same pitch, *coo-hoo* or *"no hope"* (RTP).
Range: Sw. U.S. to nw. Costa Rica. **Mexico:** Nearly countrywide except Yucatán Pen. **Habitat:** Towns, farms, scrub.

COMMON GROUND-DOVE **Pl. 12**
Columbina passerina 6–6¾
Field marks: A near-sparrow-sized dove. Note the *stubby
black tail* and rounded wings that flash *rufous* in flight. Breast
scaly or spotted. Feet yellow; bill pink or reddish.
Similar species: Plain-breasted Ground-Dove lacks breast-
spotting, has blackish bill.
Voice: A soft monotonously repeated *woo-oo.* In distance
sounds monosyllabic: *wooo,* with rising inflection (RTP).
Range: S. U.S. to Costa Rica; n. S. America. **Mexico:** Widespread. **Habitat:** Farms, villages, roadsides, arid country.

PLAIN-BREASTED GROUND-DOVE **Pl. 12**
Columbina minuta 5–6
Field marks: Similar to Common Ground-Dove but breast
plain, lacking scaly or spotted appearance; bill *gray or black.*

Similar species: (1) Common Ground-Dove has spots on breast, pink or reddish bill. (2) See ♀ Ruddy Ground-Dove.
Voice: A rather fast *whoop-whoop-whoop,* etc., 10–30 times, often given without pause; speed varies (Eisenmann).
Range: S. Mexico to Bolivia, n. Paraguay, ne. Argentina.
Mexico: Lowlands of s. Veracruz, Tabasco, Chiapas. **Habitat:** Open savannas, grasslands, farms.

RUDDY GROUND-DOVE   Pl. 12
Columbina talpacoti   6–7

Field marks: Male, a small *reddish-looking* dove with a light *blue-gray* crown. Black underwing coverts. The dull gray-brown female resembles the Plain-breasted Ground-Dove but is a bit larger, browner, more extensively rufous in wings.
Similar species: (1) Ruddy Quail-Dove, a forest bird, is larger, lacks gray crown, black tail; note the distinctive face pattern. (2) Plain-breasted Ground-Dove closely resembles ♀ Ruddy Ground-Dove, but is smaller, less brown, less rufous in wings, has white corners in tail.
Voice: *Whoop* or *per-woop,* repeated 2–24 times (Chalif).
Range: Mexico to Bolivia, n. Argentina. **Mexico:** Pacific slope, from s. Sinaloa south; Gulf slope from Tamaulipas south and east through Chiapas, Yucatán Pen. **Habitat:** Open country, brushy savannas, clearings, fields, towns.

BLUE GROUND-DOVE   *Claravis pretiosa*   7–8   Pl. 12
Field marks: *Male:* A *powdery-blue* ground-dove; paler on the face and underparts. *Female:* Brown with a *rusty tail,* chestnut wingbars.
Similar species: Maroon-chested Ground-Dove has deep maroon chest, white sides on tail.
Voice: A single *woop* or sometimes *poooop,* repeated after a pause (Eisenmann). A single deep *hawp* or *hoop* (Slud).
Range: E. Mexico to Bolivia, n. Argentina. **Mexico:** Mainly lowlands of Gulf slope, from s. Tamaulipas and San Luis Potosí to Puebla, Oaxaca, Chiapas, and Yucatán Pen. **Habitat:** Humid forest edges, clearings, undergrowth, mangroves; in trees or on woodland floor.

MAROON-CHESTED GROUND-DOVE   Pl. 12
Claravis mondetoura   8–9

Field marks: A dark gray ground-dove with a *maroon chest.* Forehead and throat whitish. Sides of tail white.
Similar species: Blue Ground-Dove (mainly lowlands).
Voice: A deep *woop-woop-woop,* etc., similar to that of Blue Ground-Dove, but much shorter intervals (Eisenmann).
Range: S. Mexico locally to Bolivia. **Mexico:** High mts. of Veracruz, se. Chiapas. Very rare. **Habitat:** Ground and undergrowth of mt. forests to 7000 + ft.

WHITE-TIPPED (WHITE-FRONTED) DOVE   Pl. 11
Leptotila verreauxi   10–12
Field marks: Size of Mourning Dove but with a *rounded* tail (note conspicuous white corners). Belly whitish.
Similar species: (1) White-winged and (2) Zenaida Doves both have white in the wing. (3) Gray-headed and (4) Gray-chested Doves are very similar (see accounts below).
Voice: A low, soft, ghostly *oo-whooooooo;* at a distance only the hollow long-drawn *whooooooo* is audible (RTP).
Range: S. Texas to Argentina. **Mexico:** From s. Sonora on Pacific slope and n. Tamaulipas on Gulf slope south and east through Chiapas, Yucatán Pen. **Habitat:** Terrestrial. Dry woodlands, dense second growth, river thickets.

CARIBBEAN (WHITE-BELLIED) DOVE   Pl. 11
Leptotila jamaicensis   12–13
Field marks: Similar to White-tipped Dove, but white face and underparts are distinctive. No black or white in wings.
Similar species: (1) White-tipped Dove has pinkish-brown breast. (2) Zenaida Dove has brownish underparts, black and white areas on wing.
Voice: A plaintive *cu-cu-cu-oooo* (Bond).
Range: Jamaica, Grand Cayman, St. Andrew; also locally n. Yucatán Pen. and adjacent islands; Honduras (Bay Is.). **Habitat:** Terrestrial. Deciduous forests, also humid forests.

GRAY-HEADED DOVE   *Leptotila plumbeiceps*   9–11   Pl. 11
Field marks: Very similar to White-tipped Dove but crown *lead-gray,* cheeks buff, forehead pale gray (not buff); no iridescence on neck; orbital skin *red.*
Similar species: (1) White-tipped Dove has olive-brown crown, pale buff forehead, iridescent neck, blue orbital skin. (2) Gray-chested Dove has chocolate-brown crown, darker gray chest.
Voice: A short, hollow *cooooo* (Smithe).
Range: E. Mexico to Colombia. **Mexico:** Mostly eastern lowlands from extreme s. Tamaulipas, e. San Luis Potosí south and east to Oaxaca, n. Chiapas, s. Quintana Roo. **Habitat:** Terrestrial. Humid forests, dense undergrowth, and woodland borders.

GRAY-CHESTED (CASSIN'S) DOVE   Pl. 11
Leptotila cassinii   9½–11
Field marks: Very similar to White-tipped and Gray-headed Doves but darker than either, with a brown crown, markedly *gray* chest, *brownish* flanks. No neck iridescence. Like the Gray-headed it has *red* orbital skin (White-tipped has blue).
Similar species: (1) White-tipped and (2) Gray-headed Doves.
Voice: A sorrowful *oooo,* almost on 1 pitch (Chalif).
Range: Se. Mexico to n. Colombia. **Mexico:** S. Tabasco, n. and e. Chiapas; local. **Habitat:** Mainly humid lowland forests.

PURPLISH-BACKED QUAIL-DOVE   **Pl. 12**
Geotrygon lawrencii   10
  Field marks: This stocky gray-chested, purplish-backed dove
  is best identified by the conspicuous *black facial stripe* that separates cheek from throat.
  Voice: A fairly soft, low-pitched *who-who'-oo,* last syllable
  slurred downward (Andrle).
  Range: Local. Se. Mexico; hill country Costa Rica to Panamá. **Mexico:** Se. Veracruz (Cerro de Tuxtla, Volcán San
  Martín). **Habitat:** Terrestrial. Very humid, densely shaded
  forests on ridges and lower mt. slopes (1500–3500 ft.).

RUDDY QUAIL-DOVE   *Geotrygon montana*   8–10   **Pl. 12**
  Field marks: A shy, stocky, *completely reddish* dove; more
  purplish-brown above, pinkish below. Note *dark facial stripe*
  outlining cheek. Bill red. Immatures resemble females but have
  cinnamon spotting, dusky barring, dusky bill.
  Similar species: Ruddy Ground-Dove (open areas) is smaller,
  with black tail feathers, black bill, blue-gray crown.
  Voice: A low humming *mmmm,* at ½-second intervals (Eisenmann); a prolonged, booming note, suggesting fog buoy (Bond).
  Range: W. Indies; Mexico to Paraguay, s. Brazil. **Mexico:**
  Mainly coastal lowlands and foothills from s. Sinaloa and cen.
  Tamaulipas south. **Habitat:** Terrestrial. Humid forests and
  woodlands, plantations with heavy undergrowth.

WHITE-FACED QUAIL-DOVE   **Pl. 12**
Geotrygon albifacies (linearis)   11–13
  Field marks: Note the *scaly* or lined appearance of the neck.
  Face pale, underparts *cinnamon,* back deep purplish.
  Voice: Deep and very loud notes heard at rare intervals
  (Dickey and van Rossem). A booming *whoo-oooo* (Parker).
  Range: S. Mexico to n. Nicaragua. **Mexico:** Mts. of cen. Guer-
  rero, s. San Luis Potosí, cen. Veracruz, n. Oaxaca, Chiapas.
  Habitat: Terrestrial. Dense undergrowth of cloud forest.

Macaws, Parakeets, Parrots:
Psittacidae

COMPACT, short-necked birds with stout hooked bills. Feet zygodactyl (2 toes fore, 2 aft). Noisy and gaudily colored. Most Mexican species are largely green and fall into 3 basic categories: (1)
macaws; large with very long slender tails; (2) parakeets (or paro-
quets); small with pointed or wedge-shaped tails, pointed wings;
and (3) true parrots; stocky with short squarish tails. The *Ama-*

zona group in our area all show a red patch on the secondaries and
fly with shallow ducklike wingbeats, usually in pairs. **Food:** Fruit,
nuts, seeds, nectar. **Range:** Most of S. Hemisphere; also tropics
and subtropics of N. Hemisphere. **No. of species:** World, 317;
Mexico, 19.

MILITARY MACAW *Ara militaris* 27–30   **Pl. 13**
　　Field marks: A very large parrot with a long pointed tail; the
　　only widespread macaw in Mexico. Flies with slow heronlike
　　wingbeats. Green, with red face and tail; flight feathers and
　　rump blue. Brassy yellow under wings and tail. Usually seen
　　flying in flocks, calling loudly.
　　Similar species: See Thick-billed Parrot (below).
　　Voice: Loud raucous cries.
　　Range: Mexico; also S. America from n. Venezuela to nw. Ar-
　　gentina. **Mexico:** In west, from se. Sonora, sw. Chihuahua to
　　Isthmus of Tehuantepec. Also cen. Mexico from Zacatecas, s.
　　Nuevo León, and Tamaulipas to State of México. **Habitat:** De-
　　ciduous forests of mts. and semi-arid areas; treetops, cliffs.

SCARLET MACAW *Ara macao* 34–38   **Pl. 13**
　　Field marks: Unmistakable; a very large long-tailed *scarlet*
　　parrot, exhibiting a wing pattern of red, yellow, and blue.
　　Voice: Harsh calls — *rrraaaa* (Haverschmidt).
　　Range: E. Mexico to Bolivia, Brazil. **Mexico:** Tropical low-
　　lands of s. Veracruz, Oaxaca, Chiapas; rare, local. Recorded also
　　s. Tamaulipas, s. Campeche. **Habitat:** Tall deciduous trees of
　　lowland forests, savannas, and watercourses.

GREEN PARAKEET *Aratinga holochlora* 10–12   **Pl. 14**
　　Field marks: *Aratinga* parakeets have long pointed tails and
　　so are readily separable from the chunkier square-tailed parrots.
　　This, the largest (size of Mourning Dove), has *no blue* in wing.
　　It is green above, yellow-green below, and comes in 2 basic
　　forms: (1) all green, including throat (*holochlora* group of Pa-
　　cific slope), and (2) adults with *red throat (A. h. rubritorquis)* of
　　Gulf slope from e. Guatemala to Nicaragua; once regarded as a
　　distinct species (immatures lack red throat). Flight not as er-
　　ratic as that of most other parakeets.
　　Similar species: (1) Aztec Parakeet has olive-brown throat
　　and breast, blue in wing. (2) Orange-fronted Parakeet has
　　orange forehead, blue in wing.
　　Voice: Sharp, squeaky notes, shrill noisy chatter.
　　Range: Tropical Mexico to s. Nicaragua. **Mexico:** Local in
　　northwest (s. Sonora, ne. Sinaloa, sw. Chihuahua); Socorro I.; in
　　east from Nuevo León, Tamaulipas south to Oaxaca, Chiapas.
　　Habitat: Foothills, mts. (3000–7000 ft.); woodlands, scrub,
　　plantations; not in humid rain forest.

AZTEC (OLIVE-THROATED) PARAKEET   Pl. 14
Aratinga astec   9–10
Field marks: Note the dingy *olive-brown* throat and breast. *Blue* in the wing and darker underparts distinguish this parakeet from the preceding.
Similar species: (1) Orange-fronted Parakeet has orange patch on forehead. (2) Green Parakeet has no blue in wing.
Voice: Noisy, shrieking chatter.
Range: E. Mexico to w. Panamá. **Mexico:** Eastern lowlands from cen. Tamaulipas south and east through Veracruz, n. Oaxaca, n. Chiapas, Yucatán Pen. **Habitat:** Forest edges, brush, plantations, cornfields.

ORANGE-FRONTED PARAKEET   Pl. 14
Aratinga canicularis   9–10
Field marks: Note *orange patch* on the forehead (young birds may have this patch much reduced). Also shows blue on crown, broad yellow eye-ring. Extensive blue in wing; throat and breast washed with olive-brown.
Similar species: Aztec Parakeet (more extensively dusky below) has merest trace of orange at edge of forehead (seldom noticed), but ranges of two species do not overlap.
Voice: Raucous, screechy; *can-can-can* or *ca-ca-ca* (Slud).
Range: W. Mexico to nw. Costa Rica. **Mexico:** Pacific slope from Sinaloa and w. Durango south. **Habitat:** Dry woodlands, heavy forests and edges, scrub, plantations.

THICK-BILLED PARROT   Pl. 13
Rhynchopsitta pachyrhyncha   15–16
Field marks: A heavily built green parrot with a long *pointed* or wedge-shaped tail, a very heavy *black* bill, red forehead, and red bend of wing. In flight, shows a bright *yellow stripe* on underwing. Rare and local; decreasing.
Similar species: See (1) Maroon-fronted Parrot (next) and (2) Military Macaw (larger, long red tail, blue in wing).
Voice: Squawks, screeches. Audible more than mile (Wetmore).
Range: Mts. of nw. Mexico (Sierra Madre Occidental), wandering south over central plateau to Michoacán; formerly sporadic to s. Arizona. **Habitat:** Highland pine forests.

MAROON-FRONTED PARROT   Pl. 13
Rhynchopsitta terrisi   16–17
Field marks: Very similar to Thick-billed Parrot (and possibly conspecific), replacing it locally in mts. of ne. Mexico. Differs in having a deep maroon (almost blackish) forehead; it also lacks the yellow underwing patch.
Range: Rare and very local in mts. of Nuevo León and Tamaulipas. **Habitat:** Highland pine forests.

BARRED PARAKEET *Bolborhynchus lineola* 6–7 **Pl. 14**
   Field marks: A sparrow-sized, wedge-tailed parakeet; entirely green, with *black barring*. Wings with bold black bars; shoulder with a black patch (not always visible).
   Voice: In flight, cries suggestive of small songbirds (Slud).
   Range: Mts. of s. Mexico, Guatemala, Honduras, Costa Rica, w. Panamá; also Andes of nw. Venezuela, Colombia, cen. Peru.
   Mexico: Mts. of Veracruz, Guerrero, Chiapas; local and rare.
   Habitat: Open forests of high mts.; tall trees, pines; usually seen in high, rapid flight.

BLUE-RUMPED (MEXICAN) PARROTLET   **Pl. 14**
Forpus cyanopygius 5–5½
   Field marks: A tiny, stubby green parrot with a relatively short wedge-shaped tail and bright *cerulean-blue rump* (in males). Also blue greater wing coverts and underwing coverts. Females and young show little or no blue; they are recognized by their pygmy size. Usually in very dense flocks.
   Voice: Constant chattering in flight, quiet when perched.
   Range: W. Mexico only; lowlands, foothills from s. Sonora to Colima and east to Durango, Zacatecas. Also Tres Marías Is.
   Habitat: Semi-open countryside, weedy fields, forest edges.

ORANGE-CHINNED (TOVI) PARAKEET   **Pl. 14**
Brotogeris jugularis 6–7
   Field marks: A short-tailed, green, sparrow-sized parakeet with a *spot of orange* on chin, *brown* shoulders. Note *bright yellow* wing linings in flight.
   Similar species: Orange-fronted Parakeet has much longer tail.
   Voice: In flight, a shrill noisy chattering. A scratchy *ra-a-a-a-a-a* or *ack-ack-ack,* etc. (Slud). A semimusical *week, week, kweekee'roo, kee'roo, kee'roo,* etc. (Eisenmann).
   Range: S. Mexico to n. Colombia, n. Venezuela. **Mexico:** Pacific lowlands of Guerrero, Oaxaca, Chiapas. **Habitat:** Semi-arid country, semi-open woods, edges, scrub.

BROWN-HOODED PARROT   **Pl. 14**
Pionopsitta haematotis 8–9
   Field marks: A stocky, short-tailed parrot, readily identified flying overhead by the red wingpits; also shows red in tail (so does next species). At rest the *dusky hood* with its small red ear spot is diagnostic. Breast brownish olive; wings largely blue. Flight erratic like a parakeet's.
   Similar species: White-crowned Parrot also shows red in tail.
   Voice: High-pitched, including a thin, unparrotlike *tseek,* and a *cheek-cheek* varied to *check-check* (Eisenmann).
   Range: S. Mexico to Colombia, Venezuela. **Mexico:** Gulf low-

lands (to 3000 ft.); Veracruz to n. Chiapas, Campeche. **Habitat:** Humid forests and edges, treetops.

WHITE-CROWNED PARROT *Pionus senilis* 9–10   **Pl. 14**
Field marks: Chunky, medium-sized; *purplish blue* with a *white crown and throat.* Red at tail base, none in wings.
Similar species: (1) White-fronted and (2) Yellow-lored Parrots also have white on forecrown but are predominantly green and have large red wing patches.
Voice: Noisy, screeching calls.
Range: S. Mexico to w. Panamá. **Mexico:** Eastern lowlands from San Luis Potosí, s. Tamaulipas through e. and s. Mexico to Oaxaca, Chiapas and southern parts of Yucatán Pen. **Habitat:** Humid forests, wood edges.

YELLOW-LORED (YUCATAN) PARROT   **Pl. 13**
Amazona xantholora 9–10
Field marks: *Male:* Similar to the White-fronted Parrot (white forehead, red patch around eye), but lores (area before eye) *yellow.* Note also the *dusky ear patch.* Otherwise largely green, heavily scaled with black. Bright red patch in wing, some red in tail (basally). *Female:* Red on head and wings lacking; forecrown *blue* (not white); ear patch less conspicuous; note the *blue crown, yellow lores.*
Similar species: White-fronted Parrot has red lores; lacks ear patch, is less heavily scaled.
Range: Yucatán Pen., n. B. Honduras, Honduras (Roatán I.).
Habitat: Pinelands, deciduous forests; light humid forests.

WHITE-FRONTED PARROT   **Pl. 13**
Amazona albifrons 9–10
Field marks: A green Amazon parrot with a *white forecrown,* red wing patch. Distinguished from Yellow-lored Parrot by *red lores.* Greener; lacks dark ear patch. Female shows some white on forehead, red lores; almost no red in wing.
Similar species: See above (1) Yellow-lored Parrot (Yucatán Pen., B. Honduras) and (2) White-crowned Parrot (dark blue).
Voice: A noisy yapping, *ak-ak-ak* or *yap-yap-yap.*
Range: Mexico to Costa Rica. **Mexico:** Pacific slope, foothills from s. Sonora to Chiapas; Gulf lowlands from se. Veracruz east through lower Yucatán Pen. **Habitat:** Dry country, open woodlands, scrub; also border of humid forests in lower Yucatán Pen.

RED-CROWNED PARROT   **Pl. 13**
Amazona viridigenalis 12
Field marks: A stocky, square-tailed parrot with *entire crown red.* Square red patch on secondaries of wing. Female has less

red on head. Amazon parrots have quick shallow wingbeats, usually fly in pairs.
Similar species: No other in its area.
Voice: A harsh *kree-o, krak-krak-krak* (RTP).
Range: Ne. Mexico only; lowlands, foothills of s. Nuevo León, s. Tamaulipas, e. San Luis Potosí, n. Veracruz. **Habitat:** Arid country, streams, brush.

LILAC-CROWNED (PACIFIC) PARROT   Pl. 13
Amazona finschi   11–13
   Field marks: An Amazon parrot with a dark dull red forehead; remainder of crown *lilac* or *powder-blue.* Separated from next species by *green* cheeks and by range.
   Similar species: See Red-lored Parrot (e. Mexico), next.
   Range: W. Mexico only; so. Sonora, sw. Chihuahua to Oaxaca.
   Habitat: Wooded foothills and mts., sometimes to coast.

RED-LORED (YELLOW-CHEEKED) PARROT   Pl. 13
Amazona autumnalis   12–13
   Field marks: A stocky Amazon parrot with a red forehead and *bright yellow cheeks* (sometimes mixed with red). Crown powder-blue, scaled, similar to that of Lilac-crowned Parrot. May have red on chin. Young birds lack the yellow cheeks and have less red on the forehead.
   Similar species: See Lilac-crowned Parrot (w. Mexico).
   Voice: Noisy; *kyake kyake kyake,* etc., or *yoik yoik yoik,* etc.; *ack-ack* or *eck-eck,* etc. (Slud).
   Range: E. Mexico to w. Ecuador, n. Brazil. **Mexico:** Eastern and southern lowlands from s. Tamaulipas and e. San Luis Potosí south and east to Oaxaca, Chiapas, s. Campeche, extreme s. Quintana Roo. **Habitat:** Humid forests, moist second growth.

YELLOW-HEADED PARROT   Pl. 13
Amazona ochrocephala   12–15
   Field marks: Adults are of 2 basic types that may prove to be specifically distinct: (1) northern birds with the *head entirely yellow* when fully adult; (2) southern birds (s. Oaxaca, Chiapas, Guatemala) with *yellow forehead and nape.* Like other Amazons, this species is stocky, short-tailed, with a square red patch on the secondaries. Also red on shoulders. Young birds are entirely green, without yellow or red.
   Voice: Raucous cries; often with a human quality.
   Range: Mexico south to e. Peru, Brazil. **Mexico:** Pacific slope from Colima south; also Tres Marías Is.; Gulf slope from s. Nuevo León and cen. Tamaulipas south. Not in Yucatán Pen.
   Habitat: Dry open woods, edges, savannas.

MEALY (BLUE-CROWNED) PARROT   **Pl. 13**
Amazona farinosa   14–16
   Field marks: The largest and dullest green of the square-tailed
   Amazon parrots, recognized by absence of red on the head and
   (in its Mexican form) by its *light blue* crown. Tail broadly
   tipped with yellowish. Like other Amazons, it has a red patch
   on the secondaries.
   Similar species: (1) Lilac-crowned and (2) Red-lored Parrots
   have red on forehead.
   Voice: Noisy; a rolling *krrrillik, krrrillik,* etc., and a raucous
   chowk, chowk, etc. (RTP). Flight calls usually include a *chop-
   chop* phrase (Schwartz) or *kyup-kyup* (Eisenmann).
   Range: S. Mexico to Bolivia, Brazil. **Mexico:** Lowlands of
   Veracruz, Oaxaca, Chiapas, southern parts of Yucatán Pen.
   Habitat: Humid forests, woodlands, forest borders.

Cuckoos, Anis, Roadrunners: Cuculidae

SLENDER, long-tailed birds. Feet zygodactyl (2 toes forward, 2
aft). Sexes usually similar. Mexican cuckoos are slim, various
shades of brown above, light below. Two species (Striped and
Pheasant Cuckoos) are parasitic. Anis are loose-jointed, slender,
coal-black, with deep, high-ridged bills. Roadrunners are large
streaked ground-cuckoos. **Food:** Caterpillars, other insects. Anis
eat seeds, fruits, grasshoppers; roadrunners eat insects, reptiles,
etc. **Range:** Nearly all warm and temperate parts of world. **No.
of species:** World, 125; Mexico, 11.

BLACK-BILLED CUCKOO   See E, W, or T
Coccyzus erythropthalmus
   Memo: Black bill, red eye-ring, small tail spots.
   Range: S. Canada, cen. and ne. U.S. Winters from Colombia
   to n. Peru. **Mexico:** Migrant through e. and cen. Mexico.

YELLOW-BILLED CUCKOO   See E, W, or T
Coccyzus americanus
   Memo: Yellow bill, rufous in wings, large white tail spots.
   Range: S. Canada to Mexico, W. Indies. Winters south to Ar-
   gentina. **Mexico:** Breeds locally in nw. Mexico (Baja Califor-
   nia, Sonora, Sinaloa, Chihuahua) and e. Mexico (Tamaulipas,
   Veracruz, Yucatán). Migrant elsewhere.

MANGROVE CUCKOO *Coccyzus minor* 11–13   **Pl. 15**
   Field marks: Similar to Yellow-billed Cuckoo, but underparts
   strong *yellowish buff* or *pale cinnamon;* no rufous in wing. A
   black ear patch or mask extends behind the eye.

Voice: A deep throaty, rather deliberately uttered *gaw-gaw-gaw,* etc. (Bond). Call of Yellow-bill is faster.
Range: S. Florida, W. Indies, Mid. America to Guianas, n. Brazil. **Mexico:** Pacific slope from s. Sonora south; also Tres Marías Is.; Gulf lowlands from Tamaulipas to Chiapas, Yucatán. **Habitat:** Mangrove swamps; also dry thickets in tropical deciduous forests well inland (to 3000 ft.).

SQUIRREL CUCKOO *Piaya cayana* 17–19   **Pl. 15**
Field marks: A very slim, *bright cinnamon* cuckoo with *pale gray* belly; tail very long, graduated, with broad white tips.
Voice: A series of 5–10 slow whistling *yeep*'s; also *yah-aaa,* (Chalif). *Geep-kareer,* suggestive of call of Kiskadee; also a loud clear series *whep, whep, whep,* etc. (Eisenmann).
Range: Mexico to w. Peru, n. Argentina. **Mexico:** S. Sonora, Chihuahua, Tamaulipas south and east through Chiapas, Yucatán Pen. **Habitat:** Dry woodlands, humid forests, thickets; sea level to 7000 ft.

SMOOTH-BILLED ANI *Crotophaga ani*   **Pl. 15; also E**
Memo: See Groove-billed Ani (below) under **Similar species.**
Range: S. Florida, W. Indies, Mid. America to n. Argentina.
Mexico: Recorded Holbox and Cozumel Is. off Quintana Roo.

GROOVE-BILLED ANI *Crotophaga sulcirostris* 13   **Pl. 15**
Field marks: Note the deep-grooved bill with its *curved ridge,* giving a puffinlike profile. A coal-black, cuckoolike bird, with a loose-jointed tail, short rounded wings. It has a weak flight and alternately flaps and sails.
Similar species: (1) Great-tailed Grackle has a slender, pointed bill. (2) Smooth-billed Ani, which occurs with Groovebill on Cozumel I. off Yucatán Pen., has an ungrooved, highly arched bill with a more noticeable bump near its base. Voice of Smooth-bill a long-drawn whining whistle, *ooeeeee.*
Voice: A repeated *whee-o* or *tee-ho* (1st note slurring up and thin, 2nd lower); in flight a low chuckling note (RTP).
Range: S. Texas through Mid. and S. America to Peru, n. Argentina. **Mexico:** Nearly countrywide at lower altitudes except Baja California and northwest. **Habitat:** Forest edges, savannas, agricultural land, roadsides.

STRIPED CUCKOO *Tapera naevia* 11–12   **Pl. 15**
Field marks: No other cuckoo in Mexico (other than the roadrunners) has a *striped back.* Bill relatively short, head crested; light stripe behind eye.
Voice: A high clear 2-note whistle, *feen-feeen* (2nd note half a tone higher), repeated at steady intervals (Chalif). A melancholy, repeated *puu-peee,* etc. (Eisenmann). Also a melancholy

series of 4 short whistles, last lower in pitch (Land). The bird responds to an imitation of its call.

Range: S. Mexico south to Bolivia, Argentina. **Mexico:** Veracruz, Tabasco, Oaxaca, Chiapas, s. Quintana Roo. **Habitat:** Semi-open brushy country, scrubby fields, thickets.

PHEASANT CUCKOO   Pl. 15
Dromococcyx phasianellus   14–15

Field marks: A crested cuckoo with a *broad fanlike tail.* Note the buffy eye stripe, *lightly spotted breast,* and *heavy dark patches* on sides of throat and breast. Upperparts very dark, with scaly pattern; lower underparts white.

Similar species: See (1) roadrunners and (2) Striped Cuckoo.

Voice: Resembles 2-note whistle of Striped Cuckoo, but with a 3rd trilled note, *puu, peee, pr'r'r'r* (Eisenmann). A 3-note whistle, *whoo-hee-wer'r'r'r'r,* the 2nd higher, the 3rd with a tinamoulike quaver (Willis).

Range: S. Mexico to Paraguay. **Mexico:** Veracruz, Oaxaca, Chiapas and Yucatán Pen. **Habitat:** Thickets, tangles, thick cover in shady second growth. Terrestrial.

LESSER GROUND-CUCKOO   Pl. 15
Morococcyx erythropygus   10–11

Field marks: Resembles Mangrove Cuckoo (underparts tawny or cinnamon-buff), but note buffy-white stripe over and behind eye, and black stripe through it. Rump tinged *rufous.*

Similar species: Mangrove Cuckoo lacks whitish eye stripe.

Voice: A series of short burbling whistles, suggestive of a referee's whistle: *prrr-prrr-prrr-prrrr,* etc.; series dropping slightly in pitch and slowing in interval (RTP).

Range: W. Mexico to w. Costa Rica. **Mexico:** Pacific lowlands and arid foothills from s. Sinaloa south. **Habitat:** Thickets, second growth in arid country. Terrestrial.

GREATER ROADRUNNER   Pl. 15; also E, W, or T
Geococcyx californianus

Memo: Streaked; long tail, strong legs, ragged crest.

Range: Sw. U.S. to Peru. **Mexico:** U.S. border south to s. Baja California, and south on central plateau to cen. Mexico (Michoacán, México, Hidalgo, Veracruz).

LESSER ROADRUNNER   *Geococcyx velox*   17–20   Pl. 15

Field marks: Similar to Greater Roadrunner but smaller; foreneck and chest *unstreaked.*

Voice: Softer than Greater Roadrunner's; a soft mournful *coo* given 4 times in descending scale (Chalif).

Range: W. Mexico to Nicaragua. **Mexico:** Pacific slope and foothills from extreme s. Sonora south; also locally across lower parts of central plateau, Veracruz (Mt. Orizaba), n. Yucatán, e. Chiapas, etc. **Habitat:** Arid scrub, farmlands. Terrestrial, elusive.

Owls: Tytonidae (Barn Owls) and Strigidae (True Owls)

LARGELY NOCTURNAL birds of prey, with large heads, flattened faces forming facial disks, and large forward-facing eyes. Hooked bills, hooked claws; usually feathered feet (outer toe reversible). Flight noiseless, mothlike. Some species have feather tufts ("horns" or "ears"). Sexes similar; females larger. **Food:** Rodents, birds, reptiles, fish, large insects. **Range:** Nearly cosmopolitan. **No. of species:** World, 131 (barn owls, 11; other owls, 120); Mexico, 27 (barn owls, 1; other owls, 26).

BARN OWL *Tyto alba*   **See E, W, or T**
Memo: Whitish heart face or monkey face; pale breast.
Range: Nearly worldwide in tropical and temperate regions; in New World from s. Canada, U.S. through W. Indies, Mid. and S. America to Tierra del Fuego. **Mexico:** Probably nearly throughout, including some Pacific islands; often overlooked.

FLAMMULATED OWL *Otus flammeolus*   **See W or T**
Memo: The only small highland owl with brown eyes; ear tufts rudimentary compared to those of related screech-owls. Voice, a mellow *hoot* (or *hoo-hoot*).
Range: Mts. of w. U.S., Mexico, and Guatemala. **Mexico:** High mts. of cen. Mexico and probably elsewhere. Rare; undoubtedly overlooked. **Habitat:** Pine forests of mts.

COMMON SCREECH-OWL *Otus asio*   **See E, W, or T**
Memo: Small, with conspicuous "ears." See **Note.**
Note: The various screech-owls of Mexico are almost indistinguishable under field conditions, but may be separated up to a point by voice, habitat, and range. The eastern type of the Common Screech-Owl (red and gray color phases, with whinnying diminuendo call) is found only in ne. Mexico. In the rest of the Mexican range birds are of the western type (mainly grayish with 1-pitch, "bouncing ball" voice, becoming gruffer to the southward). All the closely related screech-owls of the Pacific Coast, including Vinaceous Screech-Owl *(O. vinaceus),* Balsas Screech-Owl *(O. seductus),* and Pacific Screech-Owl *(O. cooperi),* treated separately in the following accounts, fall into a consistent color cline, with a finer pattern as one goes south. However, the Balsas Screech-Owl has *brown* eyes, not yellow. Joe T.

Marshall, Jr., the authority on this subtly complex group, now regards them as conspecific, all forms of *O. asio,* the Common Screech-Owl.

Range: Se. Alaska, s. Canada, U.S. to cen. Mexico. **Mexico:** Baja California; also n. Mexico and south on central plateau to Jalisco and Hidalgo. If closely related forms are included, the range is also along Pacific Coast to Costa Rica.

VINACEOUS SCREECH-OWL   Not illus.
Otus vinaceus (or *O. asio* in part)

Field marks: May be part of the Common (or Northern) Screech-Owl species complex *(O. asio)* and indistinguishable under field conditions. Very finely textured with gray on back, overlaid with reddish wine color.

Range: Pacific Coast of Mexico only. S. Sonora and w.-cen. Chihuahua south along coastal plain to Sinaloa. Similar forms or incipient species range south to Colima and Guerrero *(seductus)* and Oaxaca *(cooperi)*. **Habitat:** Hills, plains; tropical deciduous woods, cardon cactus, mesquite, streamside woods.

BALSAS SCREECH-OWL   Not illus.
Otus seductus (or *O. asio* in part)

Field marks: Similar to Common Screech-Owl and may be a race of that bird but *eyes brown.* No red phase.

Voice: Similar to "bouncing ball" song of Common Screech-Owl of w. U.S., but much louder, with a gruff threatening quality. Also a trill or double trill (Marshall).

Range: Pacific slope of w. Mexico, from Colima south to lower Río de las Balsas drainage in Michoacán and Guerrero. **Habitat:** Tropical deciduous woods with giant cardon; edges of milpas, mesquite.

PACIFIC SCREECH-OWL   Not illus.
Otus cooperi (or *O. asio* in part)

Field marks: Very similar to Common Screech-Owl and may be an incipient species or a race of that bird (Marshall, 1967). The only screech-owl in its range.

Voice: A series of 13–15 short notes rising in pitch then dropping to the starting pitch. A loud, gruff, slow trill of threatening quality; the notes sound like *pup-pup-pup,* etc. (Marshall).

Range: Pacific slope; s. Mexico to nw. Costa Rica. **Mexico:** Arid Pacific lowlands of Chiapas. **Habitat:** Water's edge, woodlands, mangroves, palms, giant cardon.

WHISKERED (SPOTTED) SCREECH-OWL   Pl. 16
Otus trichopsis   6½–8

Field marks: Virtually identical in appearance with Common Screech-Owl. Distinguished *in the hand* by much smaller feet,

absence of white bars on inner web of outermost primary,
coarser black markings on underparts, and much longer facial
bristles. More easily identified by voice; readily attracted by
imitation.

Voice: *Boobooboo-boo, boobooboo-boo,* etc. (3 *boo*'s, a pause
and a *boo*); the arrangement of this "code" may vary. At times
a repeated 4-syllabled *chooyoo-coocooo,* vaguely suggestive of
White-winged Dove; also a rapid series on 1 pitch, *boo boo boo
boo boo boo boo boo,* usually slowing toward end (RTP). A
syncopated duetting of short and long notes like Morse code, all
on same pitch. Usual phrase, 2 "dots" and 3 "dashes" delivered
thrice and terminated with an extra "dash" (Marshall).

Range: Se. Arizona to Honduras, El Salvador. **Mexico:** Resident in highlands from n. Sonora, Chihuahua, Nuevo León
south to Oaxaca, Veracruz. Also s.-cen. Guatemala. **Habitat:**
Mainly pine-oak forests in mts.

BEARDED (BRIDLED) SCREECH-OWL   Not illus.
Otus barbarus 6½

Field marks: Quite unlike any other screech-owl in our area;
smaller, spotted in tricolor (brown, white, and black), with a
broad white bridle on face and neck (Marshall). Bristly tips to
facial feathers greatly developed, somewhat like Whiskered
Screech-Owl's. Toes and lower part of rear tarsus naked; feet
large. Brown and rufous color phases.

Voice: A short trill like a cricket. Very faint. Also little, single,
inflected, plaintive whistles (Marshall).

Range: Rare; very local in highlands of cen. Guatemala. Recorded s. Chiapas. **Habitat:** Open woods (4400–6000 ft.).

VERMICULATED (GUATEMALAN) SCREECH-OWL
Otus guatemalae 8–9   **Pl. 16**

Field marks: Similar to other screech-owls but toes completely bare (not a field character). Lacks strong vertical shaft
pattern of other screech-owls and shows more numerous fine
crossbars. Less distinct facial rim; less distinct white eyebrows.

Voice: A tremulous series of quavering notes rising to a cres-
cendo, then cutting off sharply. Suggests call of eastern form of
Common Screech-Owl (Land). Song, a long trill on 1 pitch, like
a spadefoot toad, starting softly, gradually swelling, then it cuts
off abruptly (Marshall).

Range: Cen. Mexico to Bolivia. **Mexico:** Pacific slope; local in
arid country from s. Sonora, Sinaloa, Durango to Jalisco; Gulf
slope; Tamaulipas to Veracruz, n. Chiapas. Also Yucatán Pen.
(the only screech-owl). **Habitat:** Dense tropical woods from deciduous woods of lowlands to oak woodlands of mts. (1000–5000
ft.).

CRESTED OWL *Lophostrix cristata* 16–17 **Pl. 16**
Field marks: The only large brown owl with *white or buffy-white ear tufts.* Also broad white eyebrows, rufous facial disks. Underparts light tawny, very finely marked with darker vermiculations. Wings spotted with white.
Similar species: Spectacled Owl lacks ear tufts. No other tufted owl has plain-appearing underparts.
Voice: A peculiar growling, somewhat froglike *k'k'k'k'-krrrrrr;* or at a distance, *grrrrrr* (Eisenmann).
Range: S. Mexico to Bolivia, nw. Argentina. **Mexico:** Lowlands of Veracruz, Oaxaca, Chiapas; local, rare. **Habitat:** Humid forests, river groves; lowlands, foothills.

GREAT HORNED OWL *Bubo virginianus* **See E, W, or T**
Memo: Large size, "ears," white throat, barred underparts.
Range: Arctic N. America to Tierra del Fuego. **Mexico:** Widespread resident, mainly highlands; rare Yucatán Pen.

SPECTACLED OWL *Pulsatrix perspicillata* 17–20 **Pl. 16**
Field marks: A large, *tuftless,* dark chocolate-brown owl with *white eyebrows* and a broad dark chocolate breastband. Crescent-shaped white patch below bill. Buff belly.
Voice: A deep, abrupt *bu hu hu* or *bu hu hu hui,* easily imitated (Wetmore). A long-continued rapid series of chucks, similar to rapid tapping of a woodpecker (Anthony).
Range: S. Mexico to nw. Argentina and se. Brazil. **Mexico:** S. Veracruz, e. Oaxaca, Chiapas. **Habitat:** Humid tropical forests, river woods.

NORTHERN PYGMY-OWL *Glaucidium gnoma* **See W**
Memo: Small, earless; black neck patches, 5–7 white tailbars. See **Voice** under Least Pygmy-Owl (next).
Range: Se. Alaska, w. Canada, w. U.S., Mexico, and Guatemala to Honduras. **Mexico:** Pine-oak zone of higher mts.

LEAST PYGMY-OWL **Pl. 16**
Glaucidium minutissimum 5–6
Field marks: Similar to Ferruginous Pygmy-Owl but smaller; back and rump unspotted; tail short, with only 3–4 whitish or pale buff bars.
Similar species: (1) Ferruginous Pygmy-Owl (streaked crown in adults, spotted back, 6–8 rusty bars on tail). (2) See also Northern Pygmy-Owl (under Ferruginous Pygmy-Owl, next); voice described below.
Voice: Note is *poop,* whistled 1–12 times (Slud). Similar to voice of Northern Pygmy-Owl but notes higher-pitched, series shorter. Northern Pygmy-Owl gives a single *took* every 2–3 seconds; also a series: *too-too-too-too-too-too-too-too,* ending with

a slow *took, took, took.* Ferruginous Pygmy-Owl gives a more rapid *poop* or *purp* or *poip,* 2–3 per second, a great many times. **Range:** Mexico to Paraguay. **Mexico:** Pacific lowlands and foothills from Sinaloa to Guerrero; in east, locally from e. San Luis Potosí, sw. Tamaulipas to e. Oaxaca, Chiapas. **Habitat:** Forest undergrowth, woodland edges, plantations.

FERRUGINOUS PYGMY-OWL   Pl. 16
Glaucidium brasilianum   6½–7

Field marks: A very small, earless, gray-brown or rufous-brown owl (2 color phases); relatively small-headed, with a *black patch* on each side of hindneck, suggesting eyes on back of head. Crown finely *streaked* with buff (not readily noticeable). Breast striped with brown. Tail rusty, with 7–8 darker brown bars; often held at an angle.
Similar species: (1) Northern Pygmy-Owl, its high-mt. counterpart, has light *spots* (not streaks) on crown, and whitish spots on sides of breast; tail longer, with 5–7 narrow white bars. (2) See Least Pygmy-Owl (preceding) and (3) also Elf Owl (next).
Voice: A mellow staccato whistle, *poop* or *purp* or *poip,* often repeated rapidly and monotonously 2–3 times per second (RTP). Calls in daytime as well as at night.
Range: Resident from southwestern border of U.S. to Strait of Magellan. **Mexico:** Lowlands, foothills, below 4000 ft. Widespread; rare in central plateau; absent in Baja California. **Habitat:** Mesquite thickets, river woods, scrubby second growth, forest edges.

ELF OWL   *Microthene whitneyi*   5–6   Pl. 16

Field marks: A tiny, sparrow-sized, gray-brown, earless owl. Underparts softly striped with rusty; eyebrows white. Roosts in hole in saguaro or tree; found at night by calls.
Similar species: Pygmy-owls have longer tails, extending well beyond wing tips; have large black "eyes" on hindneck, more well-defined striping on underparts.
Voice: A rapid high-pitched *whi-whi-whi-whi-whi-whi* or *chewk-chewk-chewk-chewk,* etc., becoming higher, more yipping, puppylike, and chattering in middle of series (RTP).
Range: Sw. U.S. to cen. Mexico. **Mexico:** S. Baja California, Socorro I.; w. and cen. Mexico from Sonora to Puebla. **Habitat:** Saguaro deserts, oaks, arid wooded canyons.

BURROWING OWL   *Speotyto cunicularia*   See E, W, or T

Memo: Long legs, stubby tail. Open country.
Range: Sw. Canada, U.S., Mexico; Bahamas, Hispaniola. Migrates and winters into Mid. America. Also local resident S. America to Tierra del Fuego (formerly). **Mexico:** Widespread but local in suitable open country; casual Yucatán.

MOTTLED (WOOD) OWL *Ciccaba virgata* 12–15 **Pl. 16**
Field marks: This hornless forest owl appears uniformly dark brown above (fine mottlings show at close range). Underparts white or buff with dark brown streaks. Eyes *brown.*
Similar species: Barred Owl is heavily barred across chest and thickly patterned with large whitish spots on back.
Voice: *Waaa-a'-oooo;* harsh and mournful, increasing in pitch and volume, then decreasing. Also *boo, boo-ab, boo-ab, boo-ab, boo-ab, boo-ab* (Chalif). A downward modulated *hoot;* a semi-whistled screech; a gruff growl (Eisenmann).
Range: Mexico to Bolivia, Paraguay, ne. Argentina. **Mexico:** Pacific slope from s. Sonora, sw. Chihuahua south; Gulf slope from s. Nuevo León and Tamaulipas south through Chiapas and east through Yucatán Pen. **Habitat:** Forests of lowlands, foothills; trees in coffee plantations.

BLACK-AND-WHITE OWL **Pl. 16**
Ciccaba nigrolineata 15–16
Field marks: A rare black and white owl with black back, black cap, and black face. Underparts, eyebrows, and collar on back of neck *thickly barred* with black and white.
Voice: A loud, drawn-out, catlike *whee-u-u-u* (Ingles). A resonant, low-pitched *whoo, whoo, whoo* (Eisenmann).
Range: S. Mexico to w. Ecuador, ne. Peru. **Mexico:** Recorded s. Veracruz, Oaxaca, Chiapas. **Habitat:** Humid lowland forests.

SPOTTED OWL *Strix occidentalis* **See W or T**
Memo: Brown eyes; both breast and belly barred.
Range: Southern B. Columbia locally through w. U.S. to cen. Mexico. **Mexico:** Mts. of Sonora, Chihuahua, and Nuevo León south locally to cen. Mexico (e. Michoacán). Rare.

BARRED OWL *Strix varia* **See E, W, or T**
Memo: Large brown eyes, barred breast, streaked belly.
Range: Canada, U.S. (east of Rockies) to cen. Mexico. **Mexico:** Wooded mts. from Durango south to Oaxaca, Veracruz.

FULVOUS OWL *Strix fulvescens* 16–17 **Not illus.**
Field marks: Similar to Barred Owl (barred crosswise on breast, streaked lengthwise on belly), but much more rusty above and tawny below. Regarded by some as a smaller reddish race of the Barred Owl.
Similar species: Barred Owl, which may be conspecific, replaces Fulvous Owl north of Isthmus of Tehuantepec.
Voice: Hooting, similar to that of Barred Owl.
Range: S. Mexico (e. Oaxaca, Chiapas), Guatemala, Honduras, El Salvador. **Habitat:** Cloud forest, pine-oak zone of mts.

STRIPED OWL *Rhinoptynx clamator* 13–15   **Pl. 16**
Field marks: Size and shape of Long-eared Owl, but face disks *whitish;* underparts white or buff with narrow dark streaks, no bars. Eyes *brown.* Juvenile bird has cinnamon face.
Similar species: (1) Long-eared Owl has rufous face, yellow eyes. (2) Stygian Owl has dusky face, yellow eyes.
Voice: A barking hoot, *ow, ow, ow, ow,* often increasing in loudness. A loud, penetrating *keeeeeeyou* (Eisenmann).
Range: Se. Mexico to Bolivia, Paraguay, n. Argentina. **Mexico:** Very rare; reported s. Veracruz, Chiapas. **Habitat:** Savannas, grassy clearings, marshes, scrub.

LONG-EARED OWL *Asio otus*   **See E, W, or T**
Memo: Told from Horned Owl by streaked belly, closer ears.
Range: Canada to Mexico; Eurasia, n. Africa. **Mexico:** Resident nw. Baja California. Winters south to cen. Mexico (Puebla).

STYGIAN OWL *Asio stygius* 15–17   **Pl. 16**
Field marks: A very dark owl, with blackish face and "horns." The very dark general appearance, like a dusky Long-eared Owl, identifies it. Back blackish, marked with buff; underparts heavily striped. Feet naked, eyes yellow.
Similar species: (1) Long-eared Owl has a rufous face. (2) Striped Owl has a whitish face, whitish underparts, dark eyes. Both have feathered feet.
Voice: A loud *hu* or *hu-hu* (Bond).
Range: Mexico to Nicaragua; W. Indies; Colombia to Paraguay, n. Argentina. **Mexico:** Very rare. Reported ne. Sinaloa, nw. Durango, Veracruz, Chiapas. Recorded also B. Honduras, Guatemala. **Habitat:** Mt. forests.

SHORT-EARED OWL *Asio flammeus*   **See E, W, or T**
Memo: Medium-sized; buffy-brown, streaked breast; marshes.
Range: Eurasia, N. America, Greater Antilles, S. America.
Mexico: Winters Baja California, offshore islands, and elsewhere in open marshes, grasslands to cen. Mexico; seldom below Isthmus of Tehuantepec; rarely Guatemala.

NORTHERN SAW-WHET OWL   **See E, W, or T**
Aegolius acadicus
Memo: Small, earless; broad brown streaks below. Immature chocolate-brown above, cinnamon-buff below; white eyebrows.
Range: Se. Alaska, Canada, w. and ne. U.S.; mts. of n. and cen. Mexico (south to Oaxaca, Veracruz).

UNSPOTTED SAW-WHET OWL   **Pl. 16**
Aegolius ridgwayi 7–7½
Field marks: A small tuftless owl, differing from the Northern

Saw-whet and all other small earless owls by complete lack of light spots. Typical specimens (presumably adult) closely resemble the immature plumage of the Northern Saw-whet, being buff on the belly, darkening to cinnamon-buff across the breast and with conspicuous white eyebrows.

Voice: A series of 10 mellow whistles, each distinct, but not staccato. Much softer than whistle of Ferruginous Pygmy-Owl (Marshall).

Range: Local; s. Mexico, Guatemala, El Salvador, Costa Rica, w. Panamá. **Mexico:** Reported from Chiapas (Volcán Tacaná).

Habitat: Cloud forest, clearings (4500–8000 ft.).

Potoos: Nyctibiidae

SOLITARY nocturnal birds similar to goatsuckers, but they perch in an upright position, simulating a broken tree stub. Bill small; gape huge, but without bristles. Legs very short, claws much curved. Sexes alike. **Food:** Nocturnal insects caught by hawking. **Range:** Tropical Mid. and S. America. **No. of species:** World, 5; Mexico, 1 (+ 1 in Guatemala).

GREAT POTOO *Nyctibius grandis* 18½   **Not illus.**
  Field marks: Much larger than Common Potoo; size of a large owl. Underparts appear much whiter than Common Potoo's.
  Voice: A harsh, uncouth, grating sound, *wah-h-h oo-oo-oo,* strongly guttural; unbirdlike (Wetmore).
  Range: Guatemala (local in lowlands) to e. Peru, Brazil. Not in Mexico. **Habitat:** Woods by day, open land at night.

COMMON POTOO *Nyctibius griseus* 14–17   **Pl. 15**
  Field marks: Resembles a very large Whip-poor-will, but when seen by day it will be perched upright, eyes closed, on a stick or stump so as to seem part of it; head appears small, bill points up. At night looks large-headed, and round eyes reflect beam of flashlight.
  Similar species: (1) See Great Potoo (preceding). (2) All nightjars (whip-poor-wills, etc.) perch horizontally.
  Voice: A guttural *ho-wow;* also a hoarse *waark-cucu* (Bond). Also a series of loud, sustained notes becoming slightly softer at the end, *wah-wah-wah-wah-wu-wu-susu;* something between a wail and a laugh (Chalif). Birds from sw. Costa Rica to S. America utter extremely sweet plaintive whistles dropping in pitch *(poor-me-one);* not recorded in our area.
  Range: Mexico to n. Argentina; Jamaica, Hispaniola. **Mexico:**

Lowlands; in west, from Sinaloa south; in east, from s. Tamaulipas, e. San Luis Potosí south and east through Yucatán Pen. **Habitat:** Woodlands during day; open terrain at night.

Nightjars (Goatsuckers): Caprimulgidae

NOCTURNAL birds with ample tails, large eyes, tiny bills, huge gapes with long bristles, tiny legs. By day they rest horizontally on limbs or on ground, camouflaged by "dead leaf" pattern. Best identified at night by voice. Nighthawks are aberrant nightjars, often abroad by day. **Food:** Mainly nocturnal insects. **Range:** Nearly worldwide in temperate and tropical land regions. **No. of species:** World, 69; Mexico, 11 (or 12).

COMMON NIGHTHAWK *Chordeiles minor* **See E, W, or T**
Memo: High flier; pointed wing with white bar.
Range: Canada to Panamá. Winters in S. America south to cen. Argentina. **Mexico:** Breeds locally in northwest (Sonora, Chihuahua, Durango), northeast (n. Tamaulipas), and southeast (Chiapas); also B. Honduras, possibly Guatemala. Probably migrant throughout except Baja California; rare Yucatán Pen.

LESSER NIGHTHAWK *Chordeiles acutipennis* **See W or T**
Memo: Low flier; white bar nearer wing tip.
Range: Sw. U.S. to Peru, n. Bolivia, Paraguay. **Mexico:** Nearly throughout, withdrawing in winter from northern half.

PAURAQUE *Nyctidromus albicollis* 11–12 **Pl. 15**
Field marks: A common large nightjar, similar to Whip-poor-will and Chuck-will's-widow but with a *white band* across wing (reduced in female). Note also the chestnut ear patch.
Similar species: Nighthawks also have white in the wing, but lack the large tail patches (note shape of wings, tail).
Voice: At night, a hoarse whistle, *pur-we'eeeeer;* sometimes with 1 or 2 preliminary notes *(pup pup pur-we'eeeeer).* At a distance only the breezy *we'eeeeer* is heard (RTP).
Range: S. Texas to s. Brazil, ne. Argentina. **Mexico:** Lowlands, foothills; in west, from Sinaloa south; in east, from lower Río Grande south through Chiapas and Yucatán Pen. Also Tres Marías Is., Cozumel I. **Habitat:** Woodlands, brush, river thickets; at night, open places, roadsides.

COMMON POORWILL   **See W or T**
Phalaenoptilus nuttallii
    Memo: Small, gray; small white tail corners (♂).
    Range: Sw. Canada through w. U.S. to cen. Mexico. **Mexico:** Resident Baja California and n. Mexico (east to Coahuila); occurs south to cen. Mexico (Guanajuato).

EARED POORWILL   *Otophanes mcleodii*   7½–8   **Not illus.**
    Field marks: A very rare and little-known nightjar differing from the Common Poorwill in being more brownish and having distinct erectile ear tufts (formed by long lateral feathers of crown) and a distinct flap or "apron" extending from chest. Female similar but more rufous-brown.
    Range: W. Mexico only; recorded s. Sonora, sw. Chihuahua, Jalisco, Guerrero.

YUCATAN POORWILL   **Not illus.**
Otophanes yucatanicus   7½–8
    Field marks: A small nightjar, no white in wing; often heard but seldom observed because of arboreal habits. More reddish than other poorwills (female more rufous than male). It has a "flap" on chest as in Eared Poorwill, but no ear tufts. Only poorwill in Yucatán Pen.
    Similar species: The other resident nightjars of Yucatán (Parauque and Tawny-collared Nightjar) are considerably larger, less arboreal.
    Voice: *Ree'-o-ree'*, rising in intensity on 1st and last syllables, dropping abruptly on middle syllable. Produced rapidly and several times in succession (Paynter).
    Range: Yucatán Pen., n. B. Honduras, n. Guatemala (n. Petén). **Habitat:** Deciduous forests, scrub.

CHUCK-WILL'S-WIDOW   **See E or T**
Caprimulgus carolinensis
    Memo: Like large Whip-poor-will; brown throat, buffy tail.
    Range: Se. U.S. Migrates through Mid. America to Colombia. **Mexico:** Migrant through eastern sections; may winter.

WHIP-POOR-WILL   *Caprimulgus vociferus*   **See E, W, or T**
    Memo: Dead-leaf look, white tail patches (♂), black throat.
    Range: Cen. and e. Canada to Honduras. In winter to Costa Rica. **Mexico:** Widespread except Baja California and Yucatán Pen., breeding locally in highlands.

TAWNY-COLLARED NIGHTJAR (CHIP-WILLOW)   **Pl. 15**
Caprimulgus salvini   10
    Field marks: There are 3 or 4 Mexican nightjars with rufous or buffy collars on the hindneck. This is the largest; collar is

rufous. The white tail tips have an oblique forward edge. Females have buff tail tips.

Note: Yucatán birds on basis of vocal studies by L. Irby Davis may be specifically distinct ("Will," *C. badius*). They also show much more white in the tail from below (more than half), are grayer above, blacker below. The tawny collar is wider.

Similar species: (1) Buff-collared Nightjar (w. Mexico) is grayer; collar is buffy; tail white-tipped but not oblique. (2) Spot-tailed Nightjar (Chiapas and neighboring e. Oaxaca, s. Veracruz) is smaller, has a blackish head, conspicuous white spots on blackish chest, no white or buff throat patch.

Voice: Somewhat similar to that of Common Poorwill. A rapidly repeated *chuck-will* (Chalif) or *chip-willow* (Sutton). Yucatán birds utter a single vibrato *will* in series (Davis).

Range: Lowlands of e. Mexico (Nuevo León, Tamaulipas, San Luis Potosí, Veracruz). Also Yucatán, B. Honduras, n. Guatemala, n. Nicaragua *(C. badius)*. **Habitat:** Forest edges.

BUFF-COLLARED NIGHTJAR (COOKACHEEA)   Pl. 15
Caprimulgus ridgwayi   8½–9

Field marks: A gray-brown, round-winged nightjar, similar to Whip-poor-will, but with a buff or tawny collar on hindneck, and a very different voice.

Similar species: (1) Tawny-collared Nightjar and (2) Spot-tailed Nightjar are eastern.

Voice: Unbirdlike. A rapid, staccato, insectlike series, ending on an emphatic phrase in a higher pitch: *cuk-cuk-cuk-cuk-cuk-cuk-cuk-cukacheea* (Davis).

Range: W. Mexico, Guatemala, Honduras. Recorded se. Arizona. **Mexico:** Mainly western lowlands and foothills from Sonora south to Chiapas; east to Durango and southern parts of central plateau. **Habitat:** Brushy hills, scrub, rocky slopes.

SPOT-TAILED NIGHTJAR (PIT-SWEET)   Pl. 15
Caprimulgus maculicaudus   7–7½

Field marks: The smallest of the nightjars possessing rufous or tawny collars. The crown, cheeks, and malar area are blackish; the breast is blackish with large white spots; no white throatband as in similar species. Tail has narrow white corners (in males) and concealed oval white spots (evident below in specimens). Females lack white in tail.

Similar species: (1) Tawny-collared Nightjar is much larger (see its range). (2) Buff-collared Nightjar is western.

Voice: A loud, high-pitched passerine-like *pit-sweet* or *spit-sweet* (Zimmerman).

Range: S. Mexico (recorded e. Oaxaca, s. Veracruz, Tabasco, n. Chiapas); also S. America, from Colombia to n. Bolivia. **Habitat:** Wood borders, scrub by day; open savannas at night.

Swifts: Apodidae

SWALLOWLIKE in appearance and behavior, but with longer, more scythelike wings. Structurally distinct, with flat skulls, and all 4 toes pointing forward (hallux reversible). Flight very rapid, twinkling, sailing between spurts; wings often stiffly *bowed*. **Food:** Flying insects. **Range:** Nearly cosmopolitan. **No. of species:** World, 65; Mexico, 9 (+1 B. Honduras).

WHITE-COLLARED SWIFT   **Pl. 17**
Streptoprocne zonaris 8–8½
   Field marks: A very large swift with a *complete white collar* encircling chest and hindneck. Tail slightly forked. Flight very rapid; often seen high in air in wheeling flocks. Immature has little white on foreneck and chest.
   Similar species: (1) Swallow-tailed swifts have white throats, more deeply forked tails. (2) White-naped Swift has white on hindneck only (true also of immature White-collared Swift). (3) See also Bat Falcon (may mimic this swift), p. 39.
   Voice: A shrill *screee-screee,* reminiscent of European Swift (Bond). A loud explosive *cheeach* (Chalif).
   Range: W. Indies, Mexico, Cen. America to Bolivia, n. Argentina. **Mexico:** From Guerrero, San Luis Potosí, s. Tamaulipas south to Chiapas, Tabasco. **Habitat:** Breeds in mt. cliffs, ravines; wanders widely, high in air, to lowlands.

WHITE-NAPED SWIFT   **Pl. 17**
Streptoprocne semicollaris 9–9½
   Field marks: A large blackish swift with a white half-collar on nape only (difficult to see from below). Tail lacks notch of White-collared Swift.
   Similar species: (1) Black Swift lacks white nape (often hard to determine from below), is blacker on head and chest. (2) Immature White-collared may lack full collar; head blacker.
   Range: Mexico only; mts. of western and central parts from Sinaloa, Chihuahua to México, Hidalgo, Chiapas. Fairly common on Popocatepetl. **Habitat:** Aerial; highland canyons, but large flocks may also descend to sea level.

CHESTNUT-COLLARED SWIFT   **Pl. 17**
Cypseloides rutilus 5–5½
   Field marks: A small blackish swift; male with a partial *chestnut collar.* Females are uniformly dark, or sometimes with a trace of the male's chestnut pattern, but duller.
   Similar species: All-dark females may be mistaken for (1) Vaux's or (2) Chimney Swifts, but are much darker on underparts. See also (3) Black Swift (below).
   Range: Cen. Mexico to n. S. America. **Mexico:** In west, mts. of Durango, Nayarit, Zacatecas, Jalisco; ranging east to south-

ern parts of central plateau; also se. Chiapas. **Habitat:** Highlands; aerial, ranging widely.

WHITE-CHINNED SWIFT
Not illus.

Cypseloides cryptus 6
Field marks: Resembles Black Swift, but tail very short, not forked; a whitish or buffy spot on chin.
Range: Recorded B. Honduras, Honduras, Nicaragua, Costa Rica, Panamá; also S. America from Colombia to Guyana and e. Peru. Not recorded Mexico or Guatemala but to be expected.

BLACK SWIFT *Cypseloides niger*
See W

Memo: Large, all black; white forehead spot, notched tail.
Range: Se. Alaska, sw. Canada to Costa Rica; also Cuba to Guyana. **Mexico:** Migrates or winters in west and south; breeds locally in Durango, Nayarit, Puebla, Veracruz, Chiapas.

CHIMNEY SWIFT *Chaetura pelagica*
See E or T

Memo: Small (5 in.); sooty; a "cigar with wings."
Range: Cen. and e. Canada to Gulf states. Winters in upper Amazon basin of Peru. **Mexico:** Migrant through east slope.

VAUX'S SWIFT *Chaetura vauxi*
See W

Memo: Smaller than Chimney Swift (4¼ in.), with paler throat.
Note: Mexican breeding birds are sometimes rated as 2 distinct species: "Yucatán Swift," *C. gaumeri* (Yucatán Pen.), and "Richmond's Swift," *C. richmondi* (rest of Mid. America).
Range: Se. Alaska locally through w. N. America and Mid. America to Colombia, n. Venezuela. **Mexico:** Breeds locally in eastern and southern parts (San Luis Potosí, Tamaulipas to Chiapas, Yucatán Pen., Cozumel I.). Migrant in west. Winters s. Mexico.

WHITE-THROATED SWIFT
See W or T

Aeronautes saxatalis
Memo: Underparts white with black side patches.
Range: Southern B. Columbia, w. U.S. to Honduras, El Salvador. **Mexico:** Migrates or winters in highlands nearly throughout (including Baja California), breeding locally.

GREAT SWALLOW-TAILED (GERONIMO) SWIFT Pl. 17

Panyptila sanctihieronymi 7-8
Field marks: This and the next species are the only swifts with *deeply forked,* Barn Swallow-like tails. Usually the forked tail is closed, giving the appearance of a single long point. Black with a white throat and collar, line of white on trailing edge of wing.
Similar species: (1) Lesser Swallow-tailed Swift is almost identical, but only half the size and shows less white edging on

rear of wing. (2) White-throated Swift has white belly stripe, only moderately notched tail.

Range: Highlands of s. Mexico to Honduras. **Mexico:** Michoacán, Guerrero, Chiapas (Tuxtla Gutiérrez). **Habitat:** Aerial; nests in rocky ravines in mts.

LESSER SWALLOW-TAILED SWIFT Pl. 17
Panyptila cayennensis 5

Field marks: A small black swift with a *white throat* and collar, white spot on flanks, and *deeply forked,* Barn Swallow-like tail (usually folded in a single long point).

Similar species: (1) Great Swallow-tailed Swift is twice the size. (2) White-throated Swift has white belly stripe, moderately notched tail.

Voice: Call, a low chatter (Wetmore), *dzip-dzip-dzip.*

Range: S. Mexico to Peru, Brazil. **Mexico:** Very local; s. Veracruz to Chiapas. **Habitat:** Aerial; usually at lower altitudes than for preceding species. In Panamá the bird nests on trees, buildings, constructs a large tube.

Hummingbirds: Trochilidae

THE SMALLEST of all birds are in this family. Usually iridescent, with needlelike bills for sipping nectar. The wing motion, often causing a buzz, is so rapid that wings in most species appear blurred. Hover when feeding. Pugnacious. Jewel-like, glittering throat feathers (gorgets) adorn adult males of most species. (*Note:* Iridescence can vary, depending on age, individual variation, angle of light, etc.) Females usually lack gorgets. Some females and immatures of allied species are not safely separable under field conditions even for experts. **Food:** Nectar of flowers (red flowers often favored; so are century plants); also aphids, small insects, spiders. **Range:** W. Hemisphere; majority in tropical latitudes. **No. of species:** World, 320; Mexico, 50 (+4 in Guatemala).

BAND-TAILED BARBTHROAT Not illus.
Threnetes ruckeri 4½

Field marks: Long decurved bill and facial pattern suggest the hermits (next 2 species). Tail broadly banded and tipped with white; not elongated. Throat rufous; breast gray, becoming tawny on belly.

Range: Caribbean lowlands; B. Honduras, Guatemala to nw. S. America. Not in Mexico. **Habitat:** Humid forests, shady woodlands and edges.

LONG-TAILED HERMIT Pl. 20
Phaethornis superciliosus 6–6½

Field marks: Note the *2 elongated white central tail feathers* and the very long curved bill; easy to identify. Underparts, including throat, dull buff. Face strongly striped. Sexes alike. Tail hangs vertically when hovering.

Similar species: Little Hermit has shorter bill and tail.

Voice: Rapid twitters. Song, a single squeaky *sree* repeated monotonously (Skutch).

Range: S. Mexico to Amazon drainage. **Mexico:** Pacific slope from Nayarit south; Gulf lowlands from Veracruz south, excluding Yucatán Pen. **Habitat:** Lowland forests, wooded water courses, humid second growth. Feeds on *Heliconia*.

LITTLE HERMIT *Phaethornis longuemareus* 3½ **Pl. 20**

Field marks: Similar to Long-tailed Hermit (strong face pattern, buff belly) but much smaller, with shorter bill, shorter tail (central feathers have tawny or whitish tips).

Similar species: Long-tailed Hermit is larger, with 2 much-extended white central tail feathers.

Voice: Squeaky. Song, a deliberate *chip-chip-chip-chip* followed by a rapid higher-pitched *do-da-do-a-da* (Smithe).

Range: S. Mexico to cen. Peru, cen. Amazon region. **Mexico:** Gulf lowlands from cen. Veracruz, cen. Oaxaca east through southern parts of Yucatán Pen. **Habitat:** Lowland forests, undergrowth, brushy edges. Keeps low.

SCALY-BREASTED HUMMINGBIRD **Pl. 18**

Phaeochroa cuvierii 4½–5½

Field marks: A largely green hummer with a scaly dull greenish throat and breast shading to brownish on belly (whitish in female). Both sexes have broad, glossy, green and black tails with large white corners.

Similar species: ♀ White-necked Jacobin is even more scaly-breasted, has much less white in tail corners. See also other green-throated hummers.

Voice: High-pitched squeaks and rattles. Song, a musical trill: *chee-twee-twee-twee-twee-twee-trill-chup-chup* (Skutch); or *stchip-stchip-stchip sku'r wee* (Slud).

Range: Lowlands of n. and e. Guatemala to n. Colombia. Not in Mexico (except possibly extreme e. Chiapas). **Habitat:** Forest edges, thickets, scrub, clearings.

WEDGE-TAILED SABREWING **Pl. 20**

Campylopterus curvipennis 5–5½

Field marks: A very large hummer with a violet-blue crown (not always noticeable), small all-white spot behind eye, *plain light gray* underparts, large wedge-shaped tail. Sexes similar, but female has duller crown, whitish tail spots.

Similar species: None with such a large wedge-shaped tail.

Voice: Spirited, chippering squeals, squeaks (Sutton).

Range: E. Mexico, Guatemala to Honduras. **Mexico:** Lowlands; Gulf slope from Tamaulipas through n. Chiapas and Yucatán Pen. **Habitat:** Humid forests, open woods.

RUFOUS SABREWING *Campylopterus rufus* 5½ **Pl. 20**
Field marks: A very large bronzy-green hummer with *rufous-cinnamon* underparts. Sides and tip of tail rufous with a *broad black bar.* Sexes similar.
Similar species: Cinnamon Hummingbird is smaller, deeper rufous below; tail completely rusty; bill *red* (black at tip).
Range: Highlands of s. Mexico (e. Chiapas), s. Guatemala, El Salvador; local. **Habitat:** Banana and coffee plantations, second growth, brushy fields.

VIOLET SABREWING **Pl. 19**
Campylopterus hemileucurus 5½
Field marks: *Male:* A large dark violet hummer (may appear black) with *very conspicuous white tips* on 3 outer tail feathers. Bill *strongly curved* and black. *Female:* Upperparts metallic green; 3 outer tail feathers white-tipped as in male; underparts grayish, with *violet* throat patch.
Similar species: ♂ Blue-throated Hummingbird somewhat resembles ♀ of this species but has a shorter, straighter bill, blue throat, blue-black tail.
Voice: Song weak, unmelodious: *tsee tsee, tuc see, tu wit see* in slow tempo, squeaky voice (Skutch).
Range: S. Mexico to w. Panamá. **Mexico:** Highlands and foothills; Guerrero, Veracruz, Oaxaca, Tabasco, Chiapas. **Habitat:** Humid mt. forests, openings, edges; locally to sea level.

WHITE-NECKED JACOBIN **Pls. 19, 20**
Florisuga mellivora 4½–5
Field marks: *Male:* Note the *white tail,* entirely *blue-black head,* and *white crescent* at back of neck. Back metallic green, belly white. *Female:* Underparts *heavily scaled* or spotted with gray-green (some females resemble males or are intermediate).
Similar species: See (1) Scaly-breasted Hummingbird (above) and (2) Purple-crowned Fairy (p. 104).
Voice: Squeaky "tsitting" notes (Slud).
Range: S. Mexico to Bolivia, Brazil. **Mexico:** Veracruz, Oaxaca, Chiapas. **Habitat:** Lowland forests, wooded streams, plantations.

BROWN VIOLET-EAR *Colibri delphinae* 4–4½ **Not illus.**
Field marks: A medium-sized *dark brown* hummer with *violet-blue ear patches.* A white stripe below the cheek borders a *narrow green-blue-violet throat patch.* The greenish-bronze tail is crossed by a wide dark subterminal band.

Range: Cen. Guatemala (rare and local) to Bolivia, Brazil. Not in Mexico. Habitat: Woodland edges in highlands.

GREEN VIOLET-EAR   *Colibri thalassinus*   4½   Pl. 18
Field marks: An all-green hummer with *violet ear patches,* some violet-blue on the chest. Tail bluish with a broad *black subterminal band.* Sexes similar, but female duller.
Voice: Loud double note given often while perched (Alden).
Range: Mexico to Bolivia. Mexico: Highlands from Jalisco, San Luis Potosí south. Habitat: Oak woods, clearings.

GREEN-BREASTED (PREVOST'S) MANGO   Pl. 19
Anthracothorax prevostii   4½
Field marks: *Male:* A dark hummer with a *purple tail.* Throat *velvety black* bordered by metallic emerald-green. Center of belly deep blue-green. White tufts on legs conspicuous. *Female:* Median underparts white with an irregular *dark stripe* from throat to belly. Dusky tail.
Similar species: No other Mexican hummer has purple tail.
Range: E. Mexico to Costa Rica; w. Colombia to n. Peru.
Mexico: Gulf slope; s. Tamaulipas to Chiapas, Yucatán Pen.
Habitat: Forest edges, clearings, roadsides.

EMERALD-CHINNED HUMMINGBIRD   Pl. 18
Abeillia abeillei   3
Field marks: A tiny green hummer with a small *emerald-green gorget* and *blackish breast.* Bill *very short.* Tail greenish black. *Female:* Dusky gray below, lighter on throat.
Similar species: (1) Fork-tailed Emerald (deeply forked tail) and (2) Blue-tailed Hummingbird (blue-black tail) have no color separation between green of gorget and breast.
Range: Se. Mexico to n. Nicaragua. Mexico: Highlands of Veracruz, Oaxaca, Chiapas. Habitat: Cloud forest.

RUFOUS-CRESTED COQUETTE   Pls. 18, 20
Lophornis delattrei   2½
Field marks: *Male:* A tiny hummer with a wispy *rufous crest,* emerald-green gorget, reddish-brown tail. Note also the white bar across rump. Bill tiny, reddish with dark tip. *Female:* Lacks crest, but *crown rufous.* Throat speckled with rufous. Note the whitish or buffy bar on rump.
Similar species: Black-crested Coquette has black crest.
Range: Costa Rica to e. Peru, n. Bolivia. Mexico: Accidental (?) sw. Guerrero (alt. 1500 ft.).

BLACK-CRESTED COQUETTE   Pls. 18, 20
Paphosia helenae   2½
Field marks: A tiny bronzy-green hummer. *Male:* Note the

wispy black hairlike crest and long *buff side whiskers.* Tail rufous; throat emerald-green bordered by a black beard; bill red. Note also *white bar* across rump and *bronze spots* on abdomen. *Female:* Similar, with white bar on rump, but lacks crest. Throat buff; belly spotted as in male.

Similar species: See Rufous-crested Coquette (very rare).

Range: S. Mexico to Costa Rica. **Mexico:** S. Veracruz, e. Oaxaca, Chiapas. **Habitat:** Humid lowlands, plantations, clearings, roadsides.

FORK-TAILED EMERALD   Pls. 18, 20
Chlorostilbon canivetii 3–3½

Field marks: *Male:* A small green hummer, glittering on underparts; tail blue-black, *deeply forked* (appears long and very narrow when closed). Bill red with a dark tip. *Female:* Tail not as deeply forked; lateral feathers with a black band, pale gray tips. Underparts pale greenish gray. Face has masked effect.

Similar species: (1) Common Woodnymph is blacker, has black bill, slightly notched tail. See below (2) Broad-billed Hummingbird and (3) Blue-tailed Hummingbird (p. 101).

Voice: An endlessly repeated wiry *tseee-tseeree* (Slud).

Range: Cen. Mexico to Costa Rica. **Mexico:** Lowlands and foothills from Sinaloa, San Luis Potosí, and s. Tamaulipas south and east, including Yucatán Pen. **Habitat:** Woodland openings, shrubby edges, scrub.

DUSKY HUMMINGBIRD *Cynanthus sordidus* 3½–4 Pl. 20

Field marks: A very drab hummingbird; dull bronzy green above, mouse-gray below, with a reddish dark-tipped bill. Like a number of other hummers, it has a whitish mark behind eye (accentuating dark face mask). Sexes similar, but in female, lateral tail feathers have a dark band, pale tips.

Similar species: ♀ Broad-billed Hummingbird has a blue-black (not banded) tail.

Range: W. and cen. Mexico; Jalisco south to Guerrero and east to Hidalgo, Puebla. **Habitat:** Roadsides, agaves, gardens.

BROAD-BILLED HUMMINGBIRD   Pls. 19, 20
Cynanthus latirostris 3¼–4

Field marks: *Male:* Dark green above and below with a *blue throat* (looks all black at a distance). Bill bright red with black tip. *Female:* Note combination of red bill and unspotted pearly-gray throat and underparts. Tail blue-black.

Similar species: (1) Dusky Hummingbird resembles ♀ Broad-bill but has a dull olive-green (not blue-black) tail. (2) ♀ White-eared Hummingbird has a bit more white behind eye, a spotted throat, mottled sides.

Voice: A chatter. In aerial display, hum of ♂ is high-pitched; has "zing of rifle bullet" (Willard).

Range: Border of sw. U.S. (s. Arizona, sw. N. Mexico, w. Texas) and Mexico. **Mexico:** Mainly northern and central parts; from Sonora, Chihuahua, Nuevo León, and Tamaulipas south to Veracruz, Oaxaca. **Habitat:** Favors arid country from sea level to mts.; desert canyons, rocky slopes, agaves, mesquite; also wet forests and riversides in west.

COMMON WOODNYMPH   *Thalurania furcata*   4   Pl. 18
(including Mexican Woodnymph, *T. ridgwayi,* and Honduras Woodnymph, *T. townsendi*)

Field marks: *Male:* A very dark, almost black hummer with a glittering green throat and upper breast. Belly black or greenish black in Mexican birds, green in Guatemalan birds. Tail blue-black, notched. *Female:* Green above, grayish below. Tail greenish, outer feathers tipped with white.
Similar species: (1) ♂ Magnificent Hummingbird (higher mts.) is larger, longer-billed, with green confined to gorget, not extending onto upper breast. (2) See Fork-tailed Hummingbird (above).
Voice: Weak chipping, tsitting, and ticking notes.
Range: The woodnymph complex may represent 1 or several species, ranging from w. Mexico and e. Guatemala to n. Argentina. **Mexico:** Wet barrancas of Nayarit, w. Jalisco, Colima *(T. ridgwayi).* Birds of the Caribbean lowlands of e. Guatemala and Honduras are of the green-bellied race or species *(T. townsendi).*
Habitat: In w. Mexico, wet barrancas, ravines; in e. Guatemala humid forests, edges, plantations, streamsides.

BLACK-FRONTED (XANTUS') HUMMINGBIRD
Hylocharis xantusii   3½   **Pls. 18, 20**

Field marks: *Male:* Resembles male White-eared Hummingbird (white post-eye stripe, green throat, red bill), but violet on face replaced by *black;* belly *cinnamon,* tail *chestnut* (not green-black). *Female:* Lacks green throat of male; underparts *cinnamon-buff,* lateral tail feathers rufous; bill reddish below, post-eye stripe white.
Similar species: White-eared Hummingbird is not found in Baja California.
Range: Confined to southern half of Baja California.

WHITE-EARED HUMMINGBIRD   **Pls. 18, 20**
Hylocharis leucotis   3½

Field marks: *Male:* Note the conspicuous *white stripe behind eye.* Bill *red* with black tip; underparts green (gorget *emerald*); forehead and chin metallic *violet. Female:* Has red bill, strong white stripe behind eye but throat and median underparts whitish. Note the small *spots* on throat, green-barred sides.
Similar species: See (1) Black-fronted Hummingbird (s. Baja

California only), preceding. (2) ♂ Broad-bill has a blacker tail, blue throat, and only a small white spot behind eye; ♀ Broad-bill may be mistaken for ♀ White-eared, but throat and underparts are evenly gray.

Voice: A low, clear *tink, tink, tink,* sounding like a small bell (Skutch). A metallic rattle; various other notes.

Range: Arizona border to Nicaragua. **Mexico:** Highlands; Sonora, Chihuahua, San Luis Potosí, Tamaulipas south to Chiapas. **Habitat:** Pine-oak woods near streams.

BLUE-THROATED GOLDENTAIL   Pl. 19
Hylocharis eliciae 3¼

Field marks: Note the *burnished green-gold tail,* copper rump, and metallic blue-violet throat. Bill red with black tip. Underparts largely green. Sexes similar, but female has more restricted gorget, is more tawny on belly.

Similar species: No other hummer matches green-gold tail.

Voice: A warblerlike song of usually 4 two-syllabled notes: *see-bit see-bit see-bit see-bit.* Also *tsit* notes (Slud).

Range: S. Mexico to Panamá. **Mexico:** Lowlands of Veracruz, Chiapas; local, rare. **Habitat:** Broken forests, edges, shady streams.

WHITE-BELLIED EMERALD   Pl. 18
Amazilia candida 3½

Field marks: A rather plain green hummer; clean white on throat, median underparts, and under tail coverts. Tail gray-green with a darker subterminal band on lateral feathers. Lower mandible *pink.* Sexes alike.

Similar species: Other white-throated amazilias (Red-billed Azurecrown, Violet-crowned Hummingbird, and Green-fronted Hummingbird) have chestnut or bronzy tails, are larger, with longer bills. Females of certain U.S. migrants may be similar but lack pink on bill.

Voice: Song, a series of 2–3 lisping squeaks, *tsk-see-seet-seet-seet* (Willis).

Range: Mexico to Costa Rica. **Mexico:** Lowlands, foothills of Gulf slope from s. San Luis Potosí, Veracruz, south to Oaxaca, Chiapas, and east through Yucatán Pen. **Habitat:** Forest edges, coffee plantations, clearings.

RED-BILLED AZURECROWN   Pl. 18
Amazilia cyanocephala 4

Field marks: Note the combination of *iridescent violet-blue crown* and *white throat.* Sides and flanks greenish; tail olive or greenish bronze. Red on lower mandible. Sexes alike.

Similar species: (1) White-bellied Emerald lacks violet-blue crown, has gray-green tail. (2) Violet-crowned Hummingbird

has rufous tail, more extensive white on underparts. (3) See Green-fronted Hummingbird (p. 102).
Range: E. Mexico to Nicaragua. **Mexico:** Mts. of Tamaulipas, San Luis Potosí, Veracruz, Oaxaca, Chiapas. **Habitat:** Pine-oak forests, brush.

BERYLLINE HUMMINGBIRD   Pl. 18
Amazilia beryllina 3½
   Field marks: *Male:* Glittering green on underparts. Rump and tail purplish chestnut; much *chestnut in wings.* Bill red below. *Female:* Duller; belly may be gray or brownish.
   Similar species: (1) Fawn-breasted Hummingbird (green throat, rusty tail) is more eastern, has *buff* belly, *notched* tail. (2) Rufous-tailed Hummingbird (green throat, rufous tail) has gray abdomen, lacks chestnut in wings; (3) Blue-tailed Hummingbird (all green below) has *blue-black* tail.
   Range: W. and s. Mexico, Guatemala, Honduras, El Salvador. **Mexico:** Lowlands and mts.; s. Sonora, s. Chihuahua east to Veracruz and south to Chiapas. Not on Yucatán Pen. **Habitat:** Forest edges, coffee fincas, banana groves.

BLUE-TAILED HUMMINGBIRD   Pl. 18
Amazilia cyanura 3¾
   Field marks: Underparts entirely emerald-green (except under tail coverts); tail *blue-black,* slightly notched; rump dark violet. May show chestnut patch on wing. Sexes similar.
   Similar species: (1) Fork-tailed Emerald (also emerald-green below) has *deeply forked* tail. (2) See Berylline Hummingbird (preceding).
   Range: S. Mexico to Costa Rica. **Mexico:** Pacific slope of Chiapas. **Habitat:** Lowlands, foothills; arid woods, scrub.

CINNAMON HUMMINGBIRD *Amazilia rutila* 4   Pl. 20
   Field marks: Entire underparts *cinnamon;* tail rufous; much red on bill.
   Similar species: Rufous Sabrewing (larger; higher altitude).
   Voice: A descending "tsittering" trill similar to that of Rufous-tailed Hummingbird (Slud).
   Range: W. and s. Mexico to cen. Costa Rica. **Mexico:** Arid lowlands of Pacific slope from Sinaloa to Chiapas; Tres Marías Is.; also coastal Yucatán, Quintana Roo. **Habitat:** Arid scrub, pastures, brushy forest edges.

FAWN-BREASTED (BUFF-BELLIED) HUMMINGBIRD
Amazilia yucatanensis 4–4½   Pl. 18
   Field marks: A rather large green hummer with a red bill, glittering green throat, *buff to tawny* belly and *slightly forked* rufous tail. Sexes similar.

Similar species: Rufous-tailed Hummingbird has a gray belly and lacks fork or notch in tail.
Voice: Shrill, squeaky notes.
Range: S. Texas, Mexico, B. Honduras, Guatemala. **Mexico:** Semi-arid lowlands of Atlantic slope from Coahuila, Tamaulipas to Yucatán Pen. **Habitat:** Woods, scrub, flowering shrubs, citrus groves.

RUFOUS-TAILED HUMMINGBIRD   Pl. 18
Amazilia tzacatl   3½–4

Field marks: Similar to Fawn-breasted Hummingbird but abdomen gray, tail not notched, bill with less red.
Similar species: Fawn-breasted Hummingbird has buff belly, well-notched or forked tail.
Voice: A descending trill of rapidly given *ts* notes. Song, 2–4 sibilant, piercing accented *tss* notes (Slud).
Range: E. Mexico to Ecuador. **Mexico:** S. Tamaulipas south to Chiapas and east to Yucatán Pen. **Habitat:** Humid lowlands, foothills; forest edges, clearings, farms, gardens.

VIOLET-CROWNED HUMMINGBIRD   Pl. 18
Amazilia violiceps (verticalis)   4

Field marks: A rather large hummer with immaculate white underparts, including throat. Note the male's *blue-violet crown* (dull greenish blue in female and immature). Tail bronzy chestnut. Bill red with black tip.
Similar species: See (1) Green-fronted Hummingbird (next) and (2) Red-billed Azurecrown (p. 100).
Range: Se. Arizona (local) to s. Mexico. **Mexico:** E. Sonora, Chihuahua, south to Chiapas in foothills and mts. **Habitat:** Riparian groves in canyons; sycamores, agaves, scrub, forest edge, plantations.

GREEN-FRONTED HUMMINGBIRD   Pl. 18
Amazilia viridifrons   4

Field marks: Very similar to Violet-crowned Hummingbird but crown and forehead dull blackish glossed with dark green. Back bronzy; tail burnished chestnut or rufous, bill red with black tip. Sexes similar.
Note: Status as a valid species has been questioned.
Similar species: (1) Violet-crowned Hummingbird has iridescent blue-violet crown. (2) Red-billed Azurecrown (e. Mexico) has blue crown, olive-green flanks and sides.
Range: Mexico only; cen. Guerrero, cen. Oaxaca to Chiapas.

STRIPE-TAILED HUMMINGBIRD   Pls. 18, 20
Eupherusa eximia   3½

Field marks: Unmistakable. Note the conspicuous *rufous or*

cinnamon patch on the wing. Tail blackish, outer 2 feathers with *white inner webs*. Male has glittering emerald-green throat and breast. Female is pinkish gray on underparts (note the wing patch).
Note: Some authorities believe 2 distinct species must be recognized in Mexico, and designate the birds of the mountainous Pacific slope of Oaxaca as the Blue-capped (or Oaxaca) Hummingbird, *E. cyanophrys.* ♂ has *blue* on crown.
Voice: A pebbly "tsitting" (Slud).
Range: S. Mexico to Panamá. **Mexico:** Guerrero, Veracruz, Oaxaca, Chiapas; local. **Habitat:** Humid lower mt. slopes; rain forest. Arboreal.

BLUE-THROATED HUMMINGBIRD   Pls. 19, 20
Lampornis clemenciae 4½–5¼
   Field marks: Note the big blue-black tail with its *large white patches. Male:* A very large hummingbird with black and white streaks around eye, *bright blue throat. Female:* Large, with *evenly gray* underparts and big blue-black tail with large white corners as in male.
   Similar species: See (1) Amethyst-throated Hummingbird (next), (2) ♀ Violet Sabrewing (p. 96), and (3) ♀ Magnificent Hummingbird (p. 104).
   Voice: A squeaking *seek* (RTP).
   Range: Sw. border of U.S. to s. Mexico. **Mexico:** Highlands and central plateau south to Oaxaca, rarely Chiapas. **Habitat:** Wooded streams in canyons of mts.

AMETHYST-THROATED HUMMINGBIRD   Pls. 19, 20
Lampornis amethystinus 4½–5
   Field marks: A large dark hummingbird, male with a metallic *purplish-red throat, sooty underparts.* Gray spots in tail. Throat of female tawny brown.
   Similar species: (1) Garnet-throated Hummingbird has rufous wings. (2) Starthroats are usually found at lower levels, have longer bills, lighter underparts, white in tail.
   Range: Cen. and s. Mexico, Guatemala, Honduras, El Salvador. **Mexico:** Mts. from Nayarit, San Luis Potosí, s. Tamaulipas south. **Habitat:** Cloud forest, pine-oak zone.

GREEN-THROATED MOUNTAIN-GEM   Pl. 18
Lampornis viridipallens 4–4½
   Field marks: A dark green hummer; male with a green gorget scaled with white, giving a spotted look. Chest and median underparts white, *contrasting* with green gorget and sides. Tail black. Female has buffy-white throat, dark tail with *light gray sides.*
   Similar species: This is the only green-throated hummer in

Mexico with a contrasting white chest. See ♀ White-necked Jacobin (p. 96).
Range: S. Mexico to Nicaragua. **Mexico:** Highlands of Chiapas. **Habitat:** Pine-oak zone of mts., thickets.

GARNET-THROATED HUMMINGBIRD   Pl. 19
Lamprolaima rhami   4½–5
Field marks: One of the most beautiful hummers. Note the *bright rufous wings* and deep *violet-purple tail*. Male has a *garnet-red* throat patch surrounded by velvety black; chest iridescent violet, abdomen sooty black; back glittering emerald. Female lacks garnet throat and is dark sooty below, but note *rufous wings,* glossy purple-black tail.
Range: S. Mexico, Guatemala, Honduras, El Salvador. **Mexico:** Mts. of Guerrero, Mexico, Veracruz, Oaxaca, Chiapas. **Habitat:** Cloud forest, pine-oak zone, openings, edges.

MAGNIFICENT (RIVOLI'S) HUMMINGBIRD   Pls. 18, 20
Eugenes fulgens   4½–5
Field marks: A very large hummingbird with *blackish underparts, glittering green throat* and *violet-purple* crown. Looks all-black at a distance. *Female:* Large; greenish above, heavily washed with greenish or gray below. Known from female Bluethroated Hummingbird by more mottled underparts, spotted throat, dark greenish tail.
Similar species: (1) ♀ Blue-throated is uniformly gray below; tail blue-black. (2) ♀ Fork-tailed Emerald (mainly lowlands) is smaller, has forked tail.
Voice: Note, a thin sharp *chip.*
Range: Sw. U.S. through mts. of Mid. America to w. Panamá. **Mexico:** Mts. from n. Mexico through Chiapas (not in Baja California). **Habitat:** High altitudes; pine-oak zone, cloud forest; lower levels in winter.

PURPLE-CROWNED FAIRY   *Heliothrix barroti*   4½   Pl.18
Field marks: A large, exquisite hummer with emerald-green back, black eye patch, immaculate white underparts, and long, *graduated blue-black and white tail.* Male has violet crown and glittering *green malar stripe,* which female lacks. Feeds high in trees.
Voice: A weak *tsir* or *tsup* (Slud).
Range: S. Mexico, Guatemala to sw. Ecuador. **Mexico:** N. Chiapas (common at Palenque); noted, Tabasco; to be expected e. Chiapas. **Habitat:** Dense lowland rain forest and edge.

PLAIN-CAPPED STARTHROAT   Pl. 19
Heliomaster constantii   4½
Field marks: The 2 starthroats have *very long,* rather straight

bills and a *streak of white on the rump*. Both have glittering *red* gorgets bordered by a conspicuous *white malar stripe*. This species has a *dull crown*. From below shows white tail with black band. Sexes similar, but red of throat more restricted or lacking in female.

Similar species: Long-billed Starthroat prefers more humid country; has a glittering blue crown. From below, tail and coverts largely *black*.

Range: W. Mexico to Costa Rica. **Mexico:** Pacific slope from s. Sonora south. **Habitat:** Arid lowlands, foothills, dry woods, scrub, farms. Often hovers for insects over roads.

LONG-BILLED STARTHROAT   Pls. 19, 20
Heliomaster longirostris   5
Field marks: Similar to Plain-capped Starthroat but male with an *iridescent blue crown,* less white behind eye. Tail mostly black below, with white corners. Females lack the iridescent crown and throat patches. Note under-tail pattern, olive-green wash on sides.

Similar species: Plain-capped Starthroat prefers more arid country; from below shows white tail with black band.

Range: S. Mexico to Bolivia, Brazil. **Mexico:** Guerrero, Veracruz, Tabasco, Oaxaca, Chiapas. **Habitat:** Humid lowlands; forest clearings, edges, plantations.

SLENDER SHEARTAIL   Pls. 19, 20
Doricha enicura   ♂ 4½, ♀ 3
Field marks: A tiny, slender, green hummer, male with a *very long, deeply forked* black tail (as in Barn Swallow), an iridescent *violet-purple* gorget, and a broad crescent of buffy white across chest; sides bronzy green. Female has tail only moderately forked and is tawny buff below. This small species is "slow in flight, looking like a big parasitic wasp" (Land).

Range: S. Mexico to Honduras. **Mexico:** Highlands of Chiapas. **Habitat:** Second-growth, brushy edges.

MEXICAN SHEARTAIL   *Doricha eliza*   3½   Pls. 19, 20
Field marks: A tiny bronzy-green hummer, male with an iridescent *rose-red* gorget and a long curved bill. Note the long deeply forked tail, outer feathers of which are black with inner webs broadly margined with *pale cinnamon,* giving spotted effect. Female lacks gorget; is very bronzy above; tail relatively short, tawny at base of outer feathers, these with a broad black subterminal band, white tips.

Similar species: (1) Slender Sheartail has different range. (2) ♀ Fork-tailed Emerald and (3) ♀ Ruby-throat overlap in habitat and can be confused, but in ♀ of this species look for deeply curved bill and the tail pattern.

Range: Mexico only; cen. Veracruz (rare); coastal Yucatán and Quintana Roo. **Habitat:** Coastal scrub.

SPARKLING-TAILED (DUPONT'S) HUMMINGBIRD
Tilmatura dupontii ♂ 3½, ♀ 2½ **Pls. 19, 20**

Field marks: *Male:* A tiny green hummer with a *white spot* on each side of lower back, a *violet-blue gorget,* and a long scissorlike tail, broadly *banded with white.* Bill relatively short. Chest white, contrasting with dark green of lower underparts. Tail cocked up while feeding. *Female:* Very tiny, with a short blackish, white-tipped tail; underparts bright *cinnamon or rufous.* Has the 2 diagnostic *white back spots.*

Similar species: White bands on long tail of ♂ are unique.

Range: S. Mexico to n. Nicaragua; Costa Rica (?). **Mexico:** Highlands from Jalisco, México, Veracruz south to Chiapas. **Habitat:** Open woods, thickets.

LUCIFER HUMMINGBIRD **Pls. 19, 20**
Calothorax lucifer 3¾

Field marks: *Male:* Elongated purple gorget, no purple on crown; tail deeply forked with *sharp-pointed* outer feathers; sides rusty; bill decurved. *Female:* Uniformly buff underparts; tawny at base of tail; bill decurved.

Similar species: (1) ♂ Costa's Hummingbird has *purple crown;* bill is straighter, sides green, tail not deeply forked. (2) See Beautiful Hummingbird (more southern), next.

Range: W. Texas, Mexico. **Mexico:** Highlands; mainly eastern and central sections; occurs west to Durango, Sinaloa, Jalisco; east to Nuevo León, San Luis Potosí, Veracruz; south at least to Guanajuato. Migratory in north, some birds moving as far south as s.-cen. Mexico. **Habitat:** Arid slopes, agaves.

BEAUTIFUL HUMMINGBIRD **Pl. 19**
Calothorax pulcher 3¾

Field marks: Very similar to Lucifer Hummingbird (perhaps conspecific), replacing it in s. Mexico. Differences are slight and of almost no use in the field. Diagnostic is the tail, with outer feathers *rounded* at the tip (not sharp-pointed), an "in-the-hand" character. For practical field purposes, assume that northern birds are *lucifer,* southern resident birds *pulcher,* except in the nonbreeding season — when migrant *lucifer*s from the north might overlap the range of this species.

Similar species: See Lucifer Hummingbird (more northern).

Range: S. Mexico only. Recorded Guerrero, Morelos, Puebla, Oaxaca, Chiapas. **Habitat:** Arid brush, open country.

RUBY-THROATED HUMMINGBIRD **See E, W, or T**
Archilochus colubris

Memo: ♂ fire-red throat, forked black tail.

Range: S. Canada to Gulf states. Winters to Panamá. **Mexico:** Migrant and winter visitor except in northwest and Baja California.

BLACK-CHINNED HUMMINGBIRD See W or T
Archilochus alexandri
   Memo: ♂ black chin, blue-violet throat.
   Range: Breeds se. B. Columbia (rare), w. U.S., nw. Mexico.
   Mexico: Breeds in n. Baja California, Sonora, nw. Chihuahua.
   In winter to s.-cen. Mexico (Michoacán, Federal Dist.).

ANNA'S HUMMINGBIRD *Calypte anna* See W
   Memo: ♂ rose-red gorget and crown.
   Range: Resident in California, nw. Baja California. **Mexico:**
   Breeds nw. Baja California, Guadalupe I. Winters in Baja California and on offshore islands; also n. Sonora.

COSTA'S HUMMINGBIRD *Calypte costae* See W
   Memo: ♂ purple gorget (projecting at sides), purple crown.
   Range: Sw. U.S., nw. Mexico. **Mexico:** Resident Baja California, Sonora, Sinaloa, and nearby islands.

CALLIOPE HUMMINGBIRD *Stellula calliope* See W
   Memo: ♂ gorget with red rays on white ground.
   Range: Breeds sw. Canada, w. U.S., n. Baja California. **Mexico:** Breeds in Sierra San Pedro Mártir of n. Baja California.
   Winters in w. Mexico south to Guerrero.

BUMBLEBEE (HELOISE'S) HUMMINGBIRD Pl. 19
Atthis heloisa 2¾
   Field marks: Tiny; similar to Calliope Hummingbird but (1) throat and *elongated gorget* of male is not streaked with white but is *solid* iridescent reddish purple and (2) tail is rounded, not notched, and pattern is different (outer feathers *cinnamon* at base, with broad black subterminal band and *white tips*). Female very much like female Calliope but tips of outer tail feathers usually buffy.
   Similar species: (1) Wine-throated Hummingbird is its Chiapas counterpart. (2) See Calliope Hummingbird (in Western *Field Guide* for illustration).
   Range: Mexico only. Mts. from sw. Chihuahua, Nuevo León, and Tamaulipas south to Veracruz, Oaxaca. **Habitat:** Cloud forest, pine or pine-oak woodlands.

WINE-THROATED HUMMINGBIRD Not illus.
Atthis ellioti 2½–2¾
   Field marks: Almost identical in the field with Bumblebee Hummingbird (and may be conspecific), but male has more red-

dish gorget, smaller bill; it replaces that bird below Isthmus of Tehuantepec.
Range: Se. Mexico to Honduras. **Mexico:** Mts. of Chiapas.

BROAD-TAILED HUMMINGBIRD   See W or T
Selasphorus platycercus
   Memo: ♂ rose-red throat; tail not forked; wings "trill."
   Range: W. U.S. to Guatemala. **Mexico:** Breeds south in highlands (7000–12,000 ft.) to s.-cen. Mexico (Guanajuato, México, Federal Dist.); also Chiapas and w. Guatemala.

RUFOUS HUMMINGBIRD   *Selasphorus rufus*   See W or T
   Memo: ♂ fire-red throat, rufous back and tail.
   Range: Se. Alaska, s. Yukon south to nw. U.S. Winters in Mexico south to Guerrero, México, Veracruz.

ALLEN'S HUMMINGBIRD   *Selasphorus sasin*   See W
   Memo: ♂ like Rufous Hummingbird but upper back green.
   Range: Breeds on coast of n. California. **Mexico:** Winters mainly in west (recorded Baja California, Sinaloa south to Federal Dist.).

Trogons: Trogonidae

BRIGHTLY-COLORED, often metallic, forest birds with short necks, broad stubby bills, long and truncate or square-tipped tails (in Quetzal, long streaming tail coverts far exceed blunt tail). Feet very small, heterodactyl (1st and 2nd toes turned backward). Solitary, quiet, erect, when perched; flutter in air when plucking small fruit. **Food:** Small fruits, insects. **Range:** Mainly tropical parts of world. **No. of species:** World, 35; Mexico, 8.

RESPLENDENT QUETZAL   Pl. 21
Pharomachrus mocinno   14–15 (+24 in. for plumes of ♂)
   Field marks: The most spectacular bird in the New World. *Male:* Intense emerald and golden green with red belly and under tail coverts. Tail from below almost wholly *white;* concealed from above by the *extremely long green upper tail coverts,* which give the appearance of a tail. Head with a short rounded crest, stubby yellow bill. *Female:* Lacks crest and elongated plumes. Chest green, rest of underparts gray except for crimson lower underparts. Green upper tail coverts reach only tip of barred tail. Bill black.
   Voice: A repetitious 2-note call (1st note high, 2nd low), Chalif. 2 calls: a low double note, *wahco, wahco,* etc., and a whistled *whee'oo* (Eisenmann).

Range: Mts. from s. Mexico (Chiapas), Guatemala to w. Panamá. **Habitat:** Cloud forest.

EARED TROGON *Euptilotis neoxenus* 13½ **Pl. 21**
Field marks: The *ear tufts* of this trogon are unique but not easily seen. Other points that separate the male from similar red-bellied trogons are: (1) *black bill;* (2) much more white in tail, presenting a distinctive aspect from beneath; (3) no pepper-and-salt effect on wing coverts. *Female:* Head and chest dark gray. Tail pattern much as in male.
Similar species: Males of other red-bellied trogons have yellow or orange bills, different tail patterns.
Range: Mts. of w. Mexico only; Chihuahua, Sinaloa, Durango, Nayarit, Zacatecas, Michoacán. Rare. **Habitat:** Pine forests, 6000–10,000 ft.

SLATY-TAILED (MASSENA) TROGON **Pl. 21**
Trogon massena 12½–14
Field marks: Note the *all-black tail* below (bronzy green above); *no white.* One of the red-bellied trogons; *no white band* across breast. Bill salmon or orange. *Female:* Slaty on head and chest; tail and abdomen as in male.
Similar species: Other Mexican trogons have white in tail.
Voice: A rather slow deliberate series, *cow, cow, cow,* etc., or *cuk, cuk,* etc. Also a *kereek, kereek, kereek* (Eisenmann).
Range: S. Mexico to nw. Ecuador. **Mexico:** Atlantic slope of Veracruz, Oaxaca, Chiapas, Tabasco, Campeche, Quintana Roo. **Habitat:** Humid lowland forests, coffee fincas.

CITREOLINE TROGON *Trogon citreolus* 10–11 **Pl. 21**
(including "Black-headed" Trogon)
Field marks: A *yellow-bellied* trogon with a blackish head and chest. Viewed from beneath, the tail shows much white and lacks the narrowly barred effect of Violaceous Trogon. Females are duller above. From below their white tail tips do not overlap, but are broadly separated by black.
Note: 2 strikingly different forms occur in our area: (1) *yellow-eyed* (Pacific slope) and (2) *dark-eyed* with *blue eye-ring* (Gulf slope). The latter has been regarded by some as specifically distinct ("Black-headed" Trogon, *T. melanocephalus*).
Similar species: See Violaceous Trogon (below).
Voice: *Cow, cow, cow, cow-cow-cow-cowcow,* the 1st 3 or 4 given slowly, then faster toward the end (Chalif). A harsh clucking, accelerating into a chatter (Skutch).
Range: Mexico to Costa Rica. **Mexico:** Coastal lowlands and foothills; Pacific slope from Sinaloa south to s.-cen. Chiapas; Gulf slope from s. Tamaulipas south through n. Oaxaca, n. Chiapas and east through Yucatán Pen. **Habitat:** Open forests, wood edges, plantations.

MOUNTAIN (MEXICAN) TROGON Pl. 21
Trogon mexicanus 12

Field marks: Of the various red-bellied trogons, 3 (both males and females) have a narrow white band across the breast. These are further separated by tail patterns when viewed from below. This one (male) has 3 broad white bands on black. Males of all 3 are glossy greenish above with black faces and throats. Females have these parts dark brown. Note tail patterns.

Similar species: (1) ♂ Collared and (2) ♂ Elegant Trogons have differing and distinctive tail patterns (see Plate 21) and so do females. In addition, ♀ Elegant has a white ear spot, yellow bill.

Voice: While perched, *tucka-tucka-tucka.* Also a slow *cowh,* repeated 4–6 times. Alarm, a low sharp *tuck* or *cut.* In flight, a rapid low *cut-a-cut-cut* (Chalif).

Range: Highlands of Mexico, Guatemala, Honduras. **Mexico:** Mts. from Chihuahua, Tamaulipas to Chiapas (4000–10,000 ft.).

Habitat: Pine or pine-oak woodlands, cloud forest.

ELEGANT (COPPERY-TAILED) TROGON Pl. 21
Trogon elegans 11–12

Field marks: Observe the erect posture; stub-billed profile and geranium-red belly; one of several similar species. *Male:* Head, back, and chest dark glossy green, separated from the red belly by a narrow white band across the breast. Note under-tail pattern; either finely vermiculated or narrowly barred, interrupted by 3 broad white bands. (Birds of Guatemala and south have stronger barring on under tail.) *Female:* Head and upperparts brown; much less red on underparts; *white spot* on ear, *yellow* bill.

Similar species: See (1) Mountain and (2) Collared Trogons.

Voice: A series of low, coarse notes, slightly bisyllabic: *kowm kowm kowm kowm kowm kowm* or *koa, koa,* etc. (RTP).

Range: S. Arizona to nw. Costa Rica. **Mexico:** Lowlands, foothills and mts. from n. Mexico south to Veracruz, Oaxaca; also Tres Marías Is. **Habitat:** Scrubby woodlands, dry mt. forests, pine-oak or sycamore canyons.

COLLARED TROGON *Trogon collaris* 9½–10 Pl. 21

Field marks: *Male:* Very similar to males of the other 2 red-bellied, white-ringed species but differs in having the undertail evenly barred with *narrow black bars* interrupted by 3 slightly wider white ones. *Female:* Similar to females of the other 2 white-ringed species but more extensively red below; lacks broad white tips on outer tail feathers.

Similar species: (1) Mountain Trogon and (2) Elegant Trogon have broad white tips on tail feathers. ♀ Elegant has white ear spot, yellow bill.

Voice: A guttural *kwa kwa kwa kwa kwa kwa;* also *choi choi choi choi choi choi* or *cow cow,* etc. (Chalif).
Range: E. Mexico to n. Bolivia, Brazil. **Mexico:** Eastern slope from San Luis Potosí, Veracruz south through Oaxaca, Chiapas; sparingly Yucatán Pen. **Habitat:** Humid forests, forest edges, plantations, foothills to 5000+ ft.

VIOLACEOUS TROGON *Trogon violaceus* 9–9½ **Pl. 21**
Field marks: A yellow-bellied trogon, similar to Citreoline Trogon but smaller and tail narrowly barred. The male has a yellow eye-ring and is glossed with violet on chest; both sexes have a fine-barred pepper-and-salt effect on wing coverts. Female lacks violet gloss on chest.
Similar species: Citreoline Trogon is larger, lacks narrow tailbars and pepper-and-salt effect on wing coverts; eye-ring blue.
Voice: A soft, sweet, pleasant, *cow-cow-cow,* etc., incessantly repeated (Skutch).
Range: Mexico to w. Ecuador, n. Bolivia, Brazil. **Mexico:** Eastern slope from e. San Luis Potosí, s. Tamaulipas south through Oaxaca, Chiapas, Yucatán Pen. **Habitat:** Forest edges, clearings, plantations; lowlands, foothills to 5000+ ft.

Kingfishers: Alcedinidae

SOLITARY fish-eaters with large heads, straight daggerlike bills, small weak syndactyl feet (2 toes joined for part of length). Mexican species (except Pygmy) are mainly fish-eaters, fishing from a perch above water, or they may hover and plunge headlong.
Range: Almost worldwide. **No. of species:** World, 86; Mexico, 5.

RINGED KINGFISHER *Megaceryle torquata* 15–16 **Pl. 22**
Field marks: A *very large* blue-gray-backed kingfisher with extensively rufous underparts. Females have a broad gray band across chest; rest of underparts rufous.
Similar species: (1) Belted Kingfisher is smaller, without reddish belly (but ♀ has rusty band). (2) Amazon Kingfisher is smaller, with a dark green back; ♂ has reddish on chest only.
Voice: A rusty *cla-ack* or *wa-ak* (Webster).
Range: S. Texas (rarely), Lesser Antilles to Tierra del Fuego.
Mexico: Pacific slope from s. Sinaloa south; Gulf slope from lower Río Grande south and east. **Habitat:** Rivers, streams, lakes.

BELTED KINGFISHER *Megaceryle alcyon* **See E, W, or T**
Memo: Blue-gray, crested; bands (♂ 1, ♀ 2) across white chest.
Range: Alaska, Canada to s. U.S. Winters to n. S. America (rarely). **Mexico:** Widespread in winter throughout.

AMAZON KINGFISHER   *Chloroceryle amazona*   11   **Pl. 22**
Field marks: The largest of the 3 green-backed kingfishers and
only one with a crest. Chest rufous in male, sides striped. In
female, rufous is replaced by an incomplete greenish band.
Similar species: Green Kingfisher is half the bulk, lacks crest,
and shows much more white spotting on wings and tail.
Voice: A short harsh *chert* (Chalif); sometimes repeated in a
rattle.
Range: Mexico to cen. Argentina. **Mexico:** Lowlands from s.
Sinaloa, s. Tamaulipas south; absent from most of Yucatán
Pen. **Habitat:** Rivers, streams.

GREEN KINGFISHER   *Chloroceryle americana*   8   **Pl. 22**
Field marks: A small kingfisher; deep oily green above with a
white collar and some *white spots* on wings. In flight the *largely
white outer tail feathers* are a good field mark. Male has rufous
breast, green-spotted sides. Female lacks rufous breastband, has
1 or 2 greenish bands.
Similar species: (1) Amazon Kingfisher is twice the bulk and
has very little white spotting in wings and tail. (2) Pygmy
Kingfisher lacks collar, is more extensively rufous below.
Voice: A sharp *tick tick tick;* also a sharp squeak (RTP).
Range: S. Texas to Argentina. **Mexico:** Lowlands (and to 7000
ft.) from n. Sonora, n. Tamaulipas south through Chiapas, Yucatán Pen. **Habitat:** Rivers, streams, ponds, swamps.

PYGMY KINGFISHER   *Chloroceryle aenea*   5½   **Pl. 22**
Field marks: This, the tiniest kingfisher, lacks the conspicuous
white throat and collar of its larger relatives. Underparts extensively rufous; upperparts greenish black. Female has a narrow
green band across breast.
Voice: A scratchy *tsweek;* creaking notes (Slud).
Range: S. Mexico to Bolivia, s. Brazil. **Mexico:** S. Oaxaca,
Veracruz south and east. **Habitat:** Swampy woods, lowland
streams, mangroves. Catches insects as well as small fish.

Motmots: Momotidae

SOLITARY forest birds adorned in green, blue, black, and brown;
usually with a single black spot in center of breast, and a black ear
patch. Bill strong, decurved. In all but 2 of the Mexican species
the 2 long central tail feathers are stripped of their webbing (by
the bird itself), for an inch or two, forming *racket-shaped* tips.
Feet syndactyl (toes 3 and 4 joined for part of length). Perch
upright, sometimes swinging tail slowly from side to side like a
pendulum. Nest in holes in banks. **Food:** Flying insects, small

fruits. **Range:** Mexico to ne. Argentina. **No. of species:** World, 8; Mexico, 6.

TODY MOTMOT *Hylomanes momotula*   6½–7   **Pl. 22**
  Field marks: This, the smallest motmot, differs from the others in having no dark tuft or spot on the chest; it also differs from all other Mexican motmots but the Blue-throated in not developing rackets on the tail. Tail relatively *short;* crown and nape *rufous.* Note also *white stripes* on sides of neck and cheek. Phlegmatic; secretive.
  Similar species: Blue-throated Motmot also lacks rackets (and so might others when tail is newly molted).
  Voice: A rapid screech-owl-like quavering *cooooooo-o-o-o-oh;* also a low continued *hoot-hoot-hoot,* etc. (Willis).
  Range: S. Mexico, Cen. America to nw. Colombia. **Mexico:** Lowlands of Veracruz, n. Oaxaca, Chiapas, Tabasco, s. Quintana Roo. **Habitat:** Heavy undergrowth in humid forests.

BLUE-THROATED MOTMOT   **Pl. 22**
Aspatha gularis   10–11
  Field marks: The only one of the larger Mid. American motmots that does not acquire racket-shaped tail tips. The *blue throat, green crown* (without blue eyebrow stripe) are also determinative. Area around eye *tan.* Secretive.
  Voice: A ringing *oot-oot-oot* at 5-second intervals (Parker).
  Range: S. Mexico, Guatemala, El Salvador, Honduras. **Mexico:** Chiapas. **Habitat:** Mt. woods; cloud forest.

KEEL-BILLED MOTMOT   **Pl. 22**
Electron carinatum   13–15
  Field marks: Note the *broad* decidedly curved bill with its keel-like ridges, and the rufous forehead. No throat patch; crown dark green.
  Similar species: Other green-capped motmots (Blue-throated and Turquoise-browed) have conspicuous throat patches.
  Voice: A loud far-reaching *cut-cut-cakock',* strikingly like the cackle of a hen (Lowery and Dalquest).
  Range: S. Mexico to Costa Rica. **Mexico:** Lowlands of s. Veracruz, Tabasco, e. Chiapas. **Habitat:** Humid forests.

TURQUOISE-BROWED MOTMOT   **Pl. 22**
Eumomota superciliosa   13
  Field marks: Note the *triangular blue-bordered black patch* from chin to breast, and the *broad turquoise eyebrow stripe.* Crown green. Underparts dull cinnamon. Typical racket tail.
  Similar species: Blue-browed forms of Blue-crowned Motmot have black (not green) crowns.
  Voice: A guttural froglike cry. Also *ka-wock kawock* and a chickenlike *awk awk* (Slud).

Range: S. Mexico, Guatemala (but not B. Honduras) to Costa Rica. **Mexico:** Veracruz south to Oaxaca, Chiapas and east to Yucatán Pen. **Habitat:** Semi-arid country, deciduous forests, scrub, plantations, roadsides.

RUSSET-CROWNED MOTMOT
Pl. 22

Momotus mexicanus 11–13

Field marks: A largish motmot with entire crown *rufous* as well as upper back. Underparts pale bluish green.

Similar species: Tody Motmot has a partially rufous crown but is small (7 in.) and short-tailed.

Voice: A low *krrrooop* (Chalif).

Range: W. Mexico and Guatemala. **Mexico:** Pacific slope; lowlands, foothills from s. Sonora, sw. Chihuahua south. **Habitat:** Arid country, dry woodlands, scrub.

BLUE-CROWNED MOTMOT
Pl. 22

Momotus momota 15½–17

Field marks: The largest motmot. Note the *all-blue* or largely *black* crown bordered by blue. Birds of ne. and cen. Mexico (south to Puebla, n. Veracruz) have crown wholly blue; those of s. Mexico and Guatemala have crown black (bordered by blue forehead and eyebrow stripe), and were formerly known as Lesson's Motmot, *M. lessonii.*

Similar species: Turquoise-browed Motmot has a green cap.

Voice: A very low resonant, owl-like *hoot-hoot* or *oot-boot,* often given before daybreak (RTP).

Range: E. Mexico to nw. Argentina, Paraguay. **Mexico:** Mainly lowlands, foothills, from Nuevo León, cen. Tamaulipas south to Oaxaca, Chiapas and east through Yucatán Pen. **Habitat:** Humid woodlands, second growth, clearings, plantations.

Jacamars: Galbulidae

ALTHOUGH related to woodpeckers, these long-billed metallic-colored birds of the tropical forests resemble giant hummingbirds. Solitary, they nest in holes in banks. **Food:** Butterflies, other flying insects. **Range:** Mexico to s. Brazil. **No. of Species:** World, 15; Mexico, 1.

RUFOUS-TAILED (BLACK-CHINNED) JACAMAR
Pl. 22

Galbula ruficauda 10

Field marks: This slender metallic-green bird with its long *needlelike bill* suggests an oversized hummingbird (or attenuated kingfisher). Throat white (male) or tawny (female); chest green, belly and sides of tail *rufous.* Perches upright, bill pointed up; makes flycatcherlike sallies, sometimes for butterflies.

Note: The Mid. American form *(G. r. melanogenia)* may be entitled to specific rank (Black-chinned Jacamar).
Voice: A nasal *peet.* A variety of calls, including a succession of short clear notes running up or down scale (Chalif).
Range: S. Mexico to n. Bolivia, Paraguay, ne. Argentina.
Mexico: Lowlands of Veracruz, e. Oaxaca, Chiapas, s. Campeche, s. Quintana Roo. **Habitat:** Humid forests and woodlands, edges, wooded streams, cut banks.

Puffbirds: Bucconidae

LARGE-HEADED forest birds that perch quietly in erect flycatcherlike posture, darting out occasionally to catch insects. Solitary; easily overlooked. Nest in holes in banks, termite nests.
Food: Insects. **Range:** S. Mexico to Paraguay, s. Brazil. **No. of species:** World, 30; Mexico, 2.

WHITE-NECKED PUFFBIRD   **Pl. 22**
Notharchus macrorhynchos   9–10
   Field marks: This chunky, large-headed, large-billed black and white bird is often overlooked as it sits quietly, flycatcher fashion, in high trees. The broad black chestband and white collar are the best field marks.
   Voice: A thin, high, reedy twitter (Eisenmann).
   Range: S. Mexico to Paraguay, ne. Argentina. **Mexico:** Lowlands of Oaxaca, Chiapas, s. Campeche, s. Quintana Roo. **Habitat:** Humid forests, edges, open woods, second growth, treetops.

WHITE-WHISKERED (BROWN) PUFFBIRD   **Pl. 22**
Malacoptila panamensis   8
   Field marks: Note the shaggy *white whiskers* and long bristles around the bill. Cinnamon-brown, paler below, with soft streaks. Eye red. Stance like flycatchers; sits quietly, perches low.
   Voice: Seldom heard; a high-pitched *peep;* a long-drawn plaintive *tzeeee* (Skutch).
   Range: S. Mexico to w. Ecuador. **Mexico:** Lowlands of Tabasco, Chiapas; local. **Habitat:** Undergrowth in humid forests.

Toucans: Ramphastidae

LARGISH "banana-billed" birds of the forest crown. The great canoe-shaped, colorful bills are structurally porous and very light in weight; function is mysterious. Gregarious, often moving in groups in forest canopy. Nest in tree cavities, woodpecker holes.

Food: Mainly fruit; sometimes eggs, young birds, lizards, insects.
Range: Mexico to s. Brazil, n. Argentina. **No. of species:** World,
37; Mexico, 3.

KEEL-BILLED TOUCAN   Pl. 22
Ramphastos sulfuratus 20

Field marks: This, the largest Mexican toucan, can be told by
its *bright yellow cheeks and chest* and *huge brightly colored bill*
(green, blue, red, and orange), which has given it the nickname
"banana bill." Rump *white;* under tail coverts scarlet. Flight,
2 labored flaps and a glide.
Similar species: Collared Araçari is smaller, has a solid-black
head, red rump, and a smaller, less colorful bill.
Voice: A monotonously repeated scratchy *krrrk* or *grrik;* very
froglike (RTP). A very often repeated *gaab* (Chalif).
Range: S. Mexico to n. Colombia, nw. Venezuela. **Mexico:**
From Oaxaca, Puebla, Veracruz south and east. **Habitat:** Lowland forests and forest borders to 2000 ft.

EMERALD TOUCANET   Pl. 22
Aulacorhynchus prasinus 13

Field marks: A small *bright green* toucan with a whitish
throat and rufous under tail coverts. The canoe-shaped bill is
bicolored: yellowish above and black below. Small groups fly
follow-the-leader, alternately flapping and swooping.
Voice: Low nasal barking notes; repetitious froglike calls, etc.
Said to mimic other birds.
Range: Cen. Mexico through Cen. America to Panamá, also
Andes of Colombia, w. Venezuela, Ecuador, Peru. (Birds of
Costa Rica to Panamá and those of S. America often regarded
as a separate species.) **Mexico:** E.-central and southern mts.;
local resident in highlands of e. San Luis Potosí, Veracruz, Hi-
dalgo, Puebla, Guerrero, Oaxaca, Chiapas; also Quintana Roo.
Habitat: Cloud forest of higher mts.; clearings with trees;
sometimes lower foothills and partially deforested lands.

COLLARED ARAÇARI (TOUCAN)   Pl. 22
Pteroglossus torquatus 15–16

Field marks: A slim *black-headed* toucan with a *red* rump.
Underparts yellow with a black chest spot and *red and black*
belly band. Bill bicolored: ivory above, black below. Araçaris
fly with steady beats on a level course. Gregarious.
Voice: A squeaky, repeated *we-chip, we-chip, we-chip,* etc.
(RTP). A repeated *ksee-yik* (Eisenmann).
Range: S. Mexico to Colombia, Venezuela. **Mexico:** Veracruz
east to Yucatán, Quintana Roo; Oaxaca through Chiapas.
Habitat: Forests, wood edges, coffee plantations, etc.; sea level
to 4000 + ft.

Woodpeckers: Picidae

CHISEL-BILLED tree-climbing birds with strong zygodactyl feet (usually 2 toes front, 2 rear), remarkably long tongues, and stiff, spiny tails that act as props when climbing. Most males have some red on head. **Food:** Tree-boring insects; some eat ants, flying insects, berries, acorns, sap. **Range:** Mainly wooded parts of world but absent in Australian region, Madagascar, most oceanic islands. **No. of species:** World, 209 (incl. piculets); Mexico, 25 (or 27) +1 piculet in Guatemala.

OLIVACEOUS PICULET   *Picumnus olivaceus*   3¾
  Field marks: A tiny nuthatchlike woodpecker. Piculets do not use the stubby tail as a brace; often perch like a songbird. Upperparts olive-brown with a touch of yellowish in wings and tail. Underparts dull yellow, darkest on chest. Forehead spotted with red in male, nape dotted with white; female lacks red.
  Similar species: There are no nuthatches in Guatemala.
  Voice: A laughing rattle; a sharp little *pss pss* (Slud).
  Range: Caribbean lowlands of e. Guatemala to w. Ecuador. Not in Mexico or B. Honduras. **Habitat:** Forest edges, thickets.

OLIVACEOUS PICULET

YELLOW-SHAFTED FLICKER   See E, W, or T
Colaptes auratus
  Memo: Yellow wing and tail linings; black mustache (♂). All flickers have brown, barred backs, white rumps.
  Range: Treeline in Alaska and Canada south to Gulf states of U.S. **Mexico:** Casual; recorded Sonora, Tamaulipas.

RED-SHAFTED FLICKER   *Colaptes cafer*   See W or T
  Memo: Red wing and tail linings; red mustache (♂).
  Note: Flickers as a group are highly variable and complex. The Yellow-shafted Flicker (preceding) of e. N. America, Red-shafted Flicker, and Gilded Flicker (next) should perhaps be regarded as a single species, Common Flicker, *C. auratus*. There

is some evidence that another near-species may be involved below the Isthmus of Tehuantepec. Thus, the "Guatemalan Flicker," the *mexicanoides* group of Chiapas southward, differs in minor ways, notably in having more orange, less pink, wing and tail linings; red and black whiskers in males, rufous in females.

Range: Se. Alaska, sw. Canada to n. Nicaragua. **Mexico:** Wooded highlands of Baja California and mainland. Not in Yucatán Pen. or B. Honduras.

GILDED FLICKER   *Colaptes chrysoides*   See W

Memo: Brown crown, gray cheek, yellow wing linings.

Range: Resident in deserts of se. California, s. Arizona, Baja California, Sonora, n. Sinaloa.

GRAY-CROWNED WOODPECKER   Pl. 23
Piculus auricularis   8–8½

Field marks: The only greenish-backed woodpecker in w. Mexico. Underparts thickly barred. Crown uniformly gray. *Male:* Note the red mustache; no red on nape or crown. *Female:* Lacks red mustache.

Similar species: (1) Bronze-winged and (2) Golden-olive Woodpeckers do not occur in w. Mexico; males of both have red on nape and sides of crown.

Range: W. Mexico only. Pacific slope from se. Sonora to Guerrero. **Habitat:** Broadleaf forests of lowlands and foothills, high, moist barranca forests, wet pine-oak woods.

BRONZE-WINGED WOODPECKER   Pl. 23
Piculus aeruginosus   9–10

Field marks: A greenish woodpecker with *bronzy* wings that in flight flash *yellow* below. Underparts thickly barred. Crown gray, bordered with red *behind eye* in male. Male also has red mustache, red nape; female has red nape only. Probably conspecific with Golden-olive Woodpecker (next).

Similar species: See (1) Gray-crowned Woodpecker (west only) and (2) Golden-olive Woodpecker (south; see **Range**).

Range: Ne. Mexico from s. Nuevo León, s. Tamaulipas south to Puebla, n. Veracruz. **Habitat:** Lowlands, foothills to 6000 ft.

GOLDEN-OLIVE WOODPECKER   Pl. 23
Piculus rubiginosus   8–9

Field marks: Very similar to the Bronze-winged Woodpecker (which may be merely a well-marked northern subspecies) but the male of this bird has more red on back of head and a border of red *completely enclosing* the gray crown. Immature has unbarred light olive-yellow underparts.

Similar species: Bronze-winged Woodpecker is more northern.

Voice: A repeated *keek* or *keer* (Eisenmann). Also a series resembling Downy Woodpecker but not dropping (Land).
Range: S. Mexico to nw. Argentina. **Mexico:** S. Veracruz south through Chiapas and east through Yucatán Pen. **Habitat:** Humid lowland forests; also foothills, mts.

CHESTNUT-COLORED WOODPECKER   Pl. 23
Celeus castaneus 9
Field marks: A *chestnut-colored* woodpecker with a paler *tawny* head and *crest*. Bill yellow. Male has broad red mustache and some red on cheek. Female lacks red on face.
Voice: A low *kwar* (Wetmore). A great variety of squeaks, a nasal *skahr* followed by a lower, weaker *heh-heh-heh* (Slud).
Range: Se. Mexico to Panamá. **Mexico:** Eastern lowlands from Veracruz through n. Oaxaca, n. Chiapas, lower Yucatán Pen. **Habitat:** Humid forests and woodlands.

LINEATED WOODPECKER   *Dryocopus lineatus* 12   Pl. 23
Field marks: A rather large black and white woodpecker with a *flaming red crest*. Note the *black ear patch*. Underparts heavily barred. Male has a red mustache stripe. Female has a black mustache stripe, black forehead.
Similar species: Pale-billed Woodpecker has more extensive red on the head, and lacks the white stripe on face.
Voice: A high *peek* and a lower *cuchrrrrrrr*. Suggests a flicker (Chalif). *Wicka, wicka, wicka* (Eisenmann).
Range: Mexico to n. Argentina. **Mexico:** In west, from s. Sonora south; in east from Tamaulipas through Yucatán Pen. **Habitat:** Lowland and foothill forests, open woods, clearings; humid forests to dry scrub.

LEWIS'S WOODPECKER   See W or T
Melanerpes (Asyndesmus) lewis
Memo: Pink belly, black back.
Range: Breeds sw. Canada, w. U.S. **Mexico:** In winter to n. Baja California; casual n. Sonora.

ACORN WOODPECKER   See W or T
Melanerpes formicivorus
Memo: Black, white, and red head pattern; black back.
Range: Sw. U.S. to w. Panamá, Colombia. **Mexico:** Pine-oak zone of highlands generally (Baja California and mainland); also stands of dead trees in lowlands of Tabasco, n. Chiapas, etc.

GOLDEN-CHEEKED WOODPECKER   Pl. 23
Centurus (Tripsurus) chrysogenys 8–8¾
Field marks: "Zebra-backed" with a *black eye patch* and wash of dull yellow on cheeks. Red crown of male merges into golden-yellow on nape (female lacks red). Rump barred.

Similar species: See (1) Gila Woodpecker (no eye patch, no yellow on nape), (2) Gray-breasted Woodpecker (black around eye indistinct, no yellow on nape), and (3) Golden-fronted Woodpecker (no eye patch, no bars on rump).
Voice: A loud *cheek-oo, cheek-oo, cheek-oo* (Alden).
Range: W. and cen. Mexico only; s. Sinaloa south to Oaxaca.
Habitat: Heavy forests, light woodlands, towns.

BLACK-CHEEKED WOODPECKER   Pl. 23
Centurus (Tripsurus) pucherani 7½
Field marks: A small woodpecker with a barred back and broad *black mask* from lores to neck; red patch on belly. Male has red crown; female has black crown and red nape.
Similar species: See (1) Ladder-backed Woodpecker of drier scrub (black face triangle), (2) Golden-cheeked Woodpecker.
Voice: *Churrr, churrr, churrr;* also a higher, sharp *chirriree* or *keereereek* (Eisenmann).
Range: Se. Mexico to w. Colombia, Ecuador. **Mexico:** Gulf slope; Puebla and s. Veracruz to Tabasco, n. Chiapas. **Habitat:** Lowlands, foothills; humid forests, borders, clearings.

GILA WOODPECKER   *Centurus uropygialis* 8–10   Pl. 23
Field marks: *Male:* Note the *round red cap.* A "zebra-backed" woodpecker showing in flight a white wing patch; head and underparts gray-brown. *Female:* Similar, without red cap.
Similar species: See (1) Gray-breasted Woodpecker (the two may be conspecific) and (2) Golden-fronted Woodpecker.
Voice: A rolling *churr* and a sharp *pit* or *yip* (RTP).
Range: Sw. U.S., w. Mexico. **Mexico:** Deserts of Baja California; Pacific lowlands from Sonora south to Jalisco. **Habitat:** Deserts or semidesert lowlands, towns, river groves, saguaros.

GRAY-BREASTED WOODPECKER   Pl. 23
Centurus hypopolius 8–9
Field marks: Of the various red-capped, "zebra-backed" woodpeckers, only this and the Gila *lack color* (red, yellow, or orange) *on the nape.* The two may be conspecific, but this southern form is *very much darker* on head and underparts, and quite *blackish around eye.* Small red spot below eye.
Similar species: See Gila Woodpecker (more northern).
Range: Sw. Mexico only; Guerrero, México, Morelos, Puebla, Oaxaca. **Habitat:** Deserts; large cacti, river groves.

GOLDEN-FRONTED WOODPECKER   Pl. 23
Centurus aurifrons 8½–10½
Field marks: A "zebra-backed" woodpecker with plain underparts and white rump. A white wing patch in flight. 2 basic types: (a) broad-barred, male with *separated* head patches (red on center of crown, orange-yellow on nape); the form found in

Texas and ne. and cen. Mexico, except where following occurs;
(b) narrow-barred, male with undivided red crown and nape
(giving appearance of Red-bellied Woodpecker of e. U.S.); extreme s. Tamaulipas east through Yucatán Pen.; also Pacific
Coast of Chiapas, Guatemala, etc. Females of both have orange
or red on nape only.
Similar species: (1) In Yucatán Pen. see Red-vented Woodpecker (a smaller sibling species). (2) In arid west see Gila
Woodpecker (no nape patch).
Voice: A tremulous rolling *churrrr.* A flickerlike *kek-kek-kek-
kek,* etc. (RTP).
Range: Sw. Oklahoma, Texas to Nicaragua. **Mexico:** See
under **Field marks. Habitat:** Open woodland, scattered trees,
roadsides, river woods.

RED-VENTED (YUCATAN) WOODPECKER   Pl. 23
Centurus pygmaeus 6
Field marks: A small "zebra-backed" woodpecker, very simi-
lar to the narrow-barred form of the Golden-fronted Woodpecker (extensive red crown) but yellow usually encircling base
of bill; white on forehead more extensive.
Similar species: The very similar and more numerous
Golden-fronted Woodpecker (narrow-barred form) coexists with
this species in the Yucatán Pen. but is larger (8½–10), with a
longer bill. It prefers higher forest.
Range: E. Mexico, B. Honduras, Honduras (Bay Is.). **Mexico:**
Yucatán Pen. and Cozumel I. **Habitat:** Deciduous forests, second growth, coastal scrub.

YELLOW-BELLIED SAPSUCKER   See E, W, or T
Sphyrapicus varius (in part)
Memo: Long white wing patch, barred back, black chest patch.
Range: Canada to s. U.S. in Rocky Mts., Appalachians.
Winters through Mid. America to cen. Panamá, W. Indies.
Mexico: Winters widely throughout; rare in Yucatán Pen. See
red-breasted form (next).

RED-BREASTED SAPSUCKER   See W
Sphyrapicus varius (in part)
Memo: Red head and breast, long white shoulder patch.
Note: Regarded by some authors as entitled to specific rank.
Range: Se. Alaska, w. B. Columbia, Pacific states of U.S.
Mexico: Winters in n. Baja California.

WILLIAMSON'S SAPSUCKER   See W or T
Sphyrapicus thyroideus
Memo: ♂ long white wing patch, black back, white face
stripes. ♀ brown; "zebra" back, barred sides.

Range: Se. B. Columbia, w. U.S. Winters to w. Mexico. **Mexico:** Winters in n. Baja California and from Sonora, Chihuahua, south to Jalisco.

SMOKY-BROWN WOODPECKER   Pl. 23
Veniliornis fumigatus   6–6½
   Field marks: A small drab woodpecker, uniformly *smoky brown* with a paler ear patch. Underwings show broad bars of white. Crown of male red with dark streaks; female lacks red.
   Voice: A rapid harsh rasping *zur-zur-zur-zur,* etc. (Slud).
   Range: E. Mexico to Bolivia, nw. Argentina. **Mexico:** Eastern lowlands and lower mts. from San Luis Potosí, n. Veracruz south and east through Chiapas and Yucatán Pen. **Habitat:** Humid forest borders, thickets, wooded streams, plantations.

HAIRY WOODPECKER   See E, W, or T
Dendrocopos villosus
   Memo: White back, black- and white-striped face.
   Note: Hairy Woodpeckers of Mid. America become progressively browner below (less white) and smaller to the south. Those in s. Mexico and Guatemala are no larger than Downy Woodpeckers (Downy does not occur south of U.S.).
   Range: Alaska, Canada, U.S., Mid. America to w. Panamá. **Mexico:** Wooded highlands (pine-oak, etc.) from northern tier of states south to Chiapas.

NUTTALL'S WOODPECKER   *Dendrocopos nuttallii*   See W
   Memo: Similar to Ladder-back (next) but black malar stripe joined to black on nape.
   Range: Resident in California and nw. Baja California.

LADDER-BACKED WOODPECKER   Pl. 23
Dendrocopos scalaris   5½–7½
   Field marks: A black and white "zebra-backed" woodpecker of arid country with *black face stripes* forming a *triangle.* Male has a red cap; female, a black cap.
   Similar species: Nuttall's Woodpecker (nw. Baja California) avoids desert; black malar stripe joins black on nape.
   Voice: A rattling series: *chikikikikikikikik,* diminishing. Note, a sharp *pick* or *chik* (RTP).
   Range: Resident sw. U.S., Mexico; locally in B. Honduras, Honduras, ne. Nicaragua. Not known from Guatemala. **Mexico:** Arid country nearly throughout. **Habitat:** Deserts, canyons, cottonwoods, arid brush, groves, woodlands.

BROWN-BACKED (ARIZONA) WOODPECKER   Pl. 23
Dendrocopos arizonae   7–8
   Field marks: A dark, uniformly *brown-backed* woodpecker

with a *white-striped* face; spotted and barred below. Male has a red nape patch.
Similar species: (1) Brown-barred Woodpecker (may be conspecific) has a brown and white *barred* back; different range. (2) Smoky-brown Woodpecker, the only other Mexican woodpecker with an unbarred brown back, lacks facial stripes.
Voice: A sharp *spik* or *tseek,* sharper than notes of Ladder-backed Woodpecker. A hoarse whinny (RTP).
Range: Mts. of se. Arizona and w. Mexico. **Mexico:** Ne. Sonora, n. Chihuahua south to s.-cen. Mexico (Michoacán). **Habitat:** Oaks in mts., pine-oak canyons.

BROWN-BARRED WOODPECKER   Pl. 23
Dendrocopos stricklandi   7–7½
   Field marks: Very similar to Brown-backed Woodpecker (preceding), and may be conspecific, but back *barred* with brown and white; red on back of head of male more extensive. Replaces Brown-backed Woodpecker in range given below.
   Range: High mts. of s.-cen. Mexico (Michoacán, México, Federal Dist., Morelos, Puebla, Veracruz); rare. **Habitat:** Mt. forests, 8000–13,000 ft.

PALE-BILLED (FLINT-BILLED) WOODPECKER   Pl. 23
(GUATEMALAN IVORYBILL)
Campephilus (Phloeoceastes) guatemalensis   13–14
   Field marks: A large, red-crested, black and white woodpecker, similar to the smaller Lineated Woodpecker, but *side of face entirely red,* lacking the black and white facial stripes. White stripes running down each side of neck join on the back to make or almost make a V. Female has a black forehead and throat. All the large crested woodpeckers in Mexico have pale whitish or yellowish bills.
   Similar species: Lineated Woodpecker has a voice more like a flicker's; white stripe crosses face.
   Voice: *Ka ka ka ka ka kay.* Call suggests a nuthatch (Chalif). Has a distinctive double rap when it drums.
   Range: S. Mexico to w. Panamá. **Mexico:** In west, from Sonora south; in east, from Tamaulipas south to n. Chiapas and east to Yucatán Pen. Absent from central plateau. **Habitat:** Heavily forested lowlands, foothills to 6000+ ft.; clearings, edges.

IMPERIAL WOODPECKER   Pl. 23
Campephilus imperialis   20–22
   Field marks: A very big woodpecker, the world's largest. The male is blue-black with a pointed flaming crest on an otherwise black head; has a powerful ivory-colored bill, a *large white patch* on each wing, and a white V on the back. Female lacks

red crest; her *black crest* curls forward.
Similar species: (1) Lineated and (2) Pale-billed Woodpeckers
are much smaller; both have heavily barred underparts.
Range: Formerly pine forests of Sierra Madre in Sonora, Chihuahua, Durango, Nayarit, Zacatecas, Jalisco, Michoacán. Very
close to extinction. Not recorded recently.

Woodcreepers (Woodhewers):
Dendrocolaptidae

BROWN tree-climbing birds of the American tropics, suggesting
large editions of the familiar but unrelated Brown Creeper both in
shape (often with slender and decurved bill) and actions (hugging
tree trunk, hitching upward, dropping to base of next tree). Tail
feathers, like those of woodpeckers, are stiff-pointed for support
when climbing, but feet are like those of passeriform (perching)
birds (3 toes forward, 1 back). All Mexican woodcreepers have
rufous on wings and tail. Identification often difficult under forest
conditions. Note especially the bill shape and extent or absence of
barring or pale streaking or spotting. **Food:** Insects, spiders, small
frogs, etc. **Range:** New World tropics; Mexico to n. Argentina.
No. of species: World, 47; Mexico, 12 (+ 1 Guatemala).

TAWNY-WINGED WOODCREEPER   Pl. 24
Dendrocincla anabatina   7–7½
  Field marks: A plain-breasted woodcreeper (without conspicuous bars, streaks, or spots). Olive-brown above and below with
  a creamy-buff throat. Note the *2-toned wing pattern* (tawny-rufous primaries and secondaries, dull brown coverts), especially
  noticeable in flight.
  Similar species: (1) Ruddy Woodcreeper is more rufescent
  throughout, especially on wings, without 2-toned contrast. (2)
  See Olivaceous Woodcreeper (gray head and underparts).
  Voice: Uusual note a reedy, sometimes quavering *squirp;* call
  a long-drawn softened rattle (Slud).
  Range: S. Mexico to Panamá. **Mexico:** Gulf lowlands from s.
  Veracruz, n. Oaxaca through n. Chiapas, Tabasco, Yucatán
  Pen. **Habitat:** Dense rain forest, tangles, mangroves.

RUDDY WOODCREEPER   Pl. 24
Dendrocincla homochroa   7½
  Field marks: Ruddy throughout, especially bright on head,
  wings, and tail; throat paler. *No* bars, streaks or spots. Very
  secretive.
  Similar species: See Tawny-winged Woodcreeper (preceding).

Voice: Reedy, scratchy, or squeaky notes; a chattering and a churring *rattle,* and a grating-pulley sound (Slud).
Range: Se. Mexico to n. Colombia, nw. Venezuela. **Mexico:** Mainly Yucatán Pen. Recorded also in adjacent n. Chiapas and rarely n. Oaxaca. **Habitat:** Humid forests, high deciduous forests; mainly lowlands.

OLIVACEOUS WOODCREEPER   Pl. 24
Sittasomus griseicapillus   6–6½
Field marks: The *olive-gray head and underparts* contrasting with the brown back and rufous wings and tail, *without any spotting* on the underparts, identify this small woodcreeper. Bill relatively short.
Similar species: (1) Wedge-bill has an even shorter bill (note shape) but has buff spots on throat and chest. (2) See Tawny-winged Woodcreeper (above).
Voice: A dry rattle or twitter on descending scale (Chalif). Also described as a watch spring suddenly running down, a forced buzz, rising in pitch, then descending rapidly.
Range: S. Mexico to nw. Argentina, e. Paraguay. **Mexico:** Lowlands; Jalisco to Oaxaca. Also e. San Luis Potosí, s. Tamaulipas south and east to Chiapas, Yucatán Pen. **Habitat:** Wet or open forests, woodlands, borders, clearings.

WEDGE-BILLED WOODCREEPER   Pl. 24
Glyphorhynchus spirurus   5¾–6
Field marks: A small woodcreeper with a *short bill* that is not decurved. Rather, it is slightly *upturned* at the tip. Throat and breast spotted with buff; buff eyestripe. In flight, wing shows patch of ocher-buff.
Similar species: See (1) Olivaceous Woodcreeper (preceding) and (2) Plain Xenops (p. 129). Neither has spotted breast.
Voice: A fine *chip;* may be rapidly repeated. Song, a rapid warblerlike trill that tapers off sharply (Skutch).
Range: S. Mexico to Bolivia, Brazil. **Mexico:** Lowlands of Veracruz, n. Oaxaca, n. Chiapas. **Habitat:** Humid forests.

STRONG-BILLED WOODCREEPER   Pl. 24
Xiphocolaptes promeropirhynchus   12
Field marks: The largest Mexican woodcreeper (1 ft. long with 2-in. bill). The very large, heavy bill and fine light shaft streaks (not bold spots or stripes) identify this woodcreeper of the mts.
Similar species: Several other woodcreepers have heavily streaked or spotted breasts. In this species the light shaft streaks are finely etched on an otherwise plain breast.
Voice: A loud rough *schifferty-schifferty-schifferty-schiff;* also call notes, *yip-yip-yip* and *pee-yub* (Willis).
Range: Mexico to Bolivia. **Mexico:** Guerrero, San Luis Potosí

south to Chiapas. **Habitat:** Foothills, mts. to 10,000 ft. Humid pine-oak forests, cloud forest edge.

BARRED WOODCREEPER   Pl. 24
Dendrocolaptes certhia   10–11½
> **Field marks:** Thickly *barred* on head, back, and underparts; the only Mexican woodcreeper so marked. Some populations of this species have ivory-colored bills.
> **Similar species:** Black-banded Woodcreeper (next) has narrow black barring on lower underparts but head and upper breast are predominantly spotted and streaked with buff, not barred.
> **Voice:** A loud *tew'-wee, tew'wee, tew'wee* (Howell). A slow *oi-ink,* repeated 2–3 times (Slud).
> **Range:** Se. Mexico to Bolivia. **Mexico:** Gulf slope from cen. Veracruz through n. Oaxaca, n. Chiapas, s. Campeche, s. Quintana Roo. **Habitat:** Dense humid forests in lowlands.

BLACK-BANDED WOODCREEPER   Pl. 24
Dendrocolaptes picumnus   10–11
> **Field marks:** Note the *barring on lower underparts.* Unlike the preceding species, which it resembles, it lacks barring on head and back, instead the head is spotted and streaked with buff. Bill paler.
> **Similar species:** See Barred Woodcreeper (preceding), which it replaces in higher altitudes.
> **Range:** Highlands from se. Mexico to nw. Argentina. **Mexico:** Chiapas. **Habitat:** Cloud forest, edges, pine-oak zone.

BUFF-THROATED WOODCREEPER   Not illus.
Xiphorhynchus guttatus   8½–9
> **Field marks:** A medium-sized woodcreeper with a conspicuous buff throat and some light streaking on breast. Head and upper back lightly spotted or streaked with buff. Wings and tail reddish brown.
> **Voice:** Noisy. Call, a descending series of plaintive *wick*'s, each gradually losing intensity (Slud).
> **Range:** Extreme e. Guatemala (lower Motagua valley; rare) south to n. Bolivia, Amazonian Brazil. Not in Mexico. **Habitat:** In Guatemala, edges of lowland woods, forests.

IVORY-BILLED WOODCREEPER   Pl. 24
Xiphorhynchus flavigaster   9–9½
> **Field marks:** Note the light buff throat and *strongly streaked back.* The droplet-shaped spots on back and breast have been likened to "loose strings of beads" (Smithe). A well-defined dark *malar stripe* borders buff throat.
> **Similar species:** (1) Spot-crowned Woodcreeper has similar

breast streaks and a buff throat but lacks strong streaks on back. (2) Streak-headed Woodcreeper has streaked back but is smaller and lacks dark malar mark on side of buff throat. Both (below) have more slender bills.

Voice: A rapid, whistled series *whi whi whi whi,* etc., running down the scale; or may end with a bright *whee-whee* (RTP).

Range: Mexico to Costa Rica. **Mexico:** Lowlands, foothills; Pacific slope from s. Sonora south; Gulf slope from e. San Luis Potosí, s. Tamaulipas, through Yucatán Pen. **Habitat:** Open woodlands, edges, clearings, plantations.

SPOTTED WOODCREEPER   Pl. 24
Xiphorhynchus erythropygius 8–8½
Field marks: The only woodcreeper in our area patterned with *roundish spots* (incl. back) instead of streaks.
Voice: 2 or more sad "desolately whistled sighs" that taper downward and are successively lower (Slud).
Range: Cen. Mexico south to w. Ecuador. **Mexico:** San Luis Potosí, Veracruz, Guerrero, Oaxaca, Chiapas. **Habitat:** Foothills and mts.; humid and cloud forests, pines.

WHITE-STRIPED WOODCREEPER   Pl. 24
Lepidocolaptes leucogaster 9
Field marks: The immaculate *white throat and lower cheeks,* white postocular stripe, and creamy-white underparts *boldly scalloped with black* easily distinguish this strictly Mexican woodcreeper.
Similar species: See Spot-crowned Woodcreeper (*buff* throat).
Range: W. and cen. Mexico only; s. Sonora and s. Chihuahua south to Oaxaca, Veracruz. **Habitat:** Arid tropics to high mts.; dry woods, river groves, pine-oaks, firs.

STREAK-HEADED WOODCREEPER   Pl. 24
Lepidocolaptes souleyetti 7½–8
Field marks: Similar to its highland counterpart, the Spot-crowned Woodcreeper (next) but back strongly *streaked with buff;* buff throat lacks dark malar mark at edge. Found at lower altitudes.
Similar species: (1) Spot-crowned Woodcreeper (highlands) lacks streaks on back. (2) Ivory-billed Woodcreeper (streaked back) is larger, with larger bill; note dark malar streak.
Voice: A series of fast even notes, *chichichichi,* etc., on same pitch or rising and falling in pitch (Chalif).
Range: S. Mexico to nw. Peru, n. Brazil. **Mexico:** Mainly lowlands, foothills; Veracruz, Tabasco, sw. Campeche, Guerrero, Oaxaca, Chiapas. **Habitat:** Humid semi-open woods, deciduous forests, edges, plantations, shade trees.

SPOT-CROWNED WOODCREEPER   **Pl. 24**
Lepidocolaptes affinis   7½–8
   Field marks: Similar to Ivory-billed Woodcreeper (*buff throat
   with dark malar mark,* heavily buff-streaked underparts) but
   back mostly *plain,* without conspicuous streaks.
   Similar species: (1) Streak-headed Woodcreeper (lowlands)
   and (2) Ivory-billed Woodcreeper have strong buff streaks on
   back.
   Voice: A low *tseeyup* or *cheeyup* (Chalif). A 3-note set of reedy
   squeaks (Slud).
   Range: E. Mexico to Bolivia. **Mexico:** Eastern and southern
   highlands; San Luis Potosí, w. Tamaulipas, Hidalgo, Veracruz,
   Puebla, México, Guerrero, Oaxaca, Chiapas. **Habitat:** Highland
   forests (to 9500 ft.); forest clearings, pines, oaks, parklike groves.

Ovenbirds (Horneros) and Allies: Furnariidae

UNRELATED to the North American ovenbird, which is a wood-
warbler, this large family of Middle and South American birds is
so various in appearance and habits that it is difficult to generalize
except that almost all species are colored modestly in shades of
brown, rufous, gray, and black. A few are crested. Bills are
slender, usually (but not always) slightly curved. Sexes alike.
Food: Mainly insects and spiders; some eat seeds. **Range:** S.
Mexico to southern tip of S. America. **No. of species:** World, 215
(mostly in S. America); Mexico, 7.

RUFOUS-BREASTED SPINETAIL   **Pl. 25**
Synallaxis erythrothorax   5¾–6
   Field marks: A brownish wrenlike bird with a *rufous breast*
   and long, spiny-tipped, *frayed-looking,* dark rufous tail. Wings
   with much rufous. Throat finely streaked with dusky, termi-
   nating in a *slaty or blackish band* above red breast.
   Voice: Song, 3 or 4 emphatic notes ascending in pitch, and
   dropping on last note: *wit-wit-wit-tew* or *pit-peet-peechew*
   (RTP). *Zhee-zhee-zhee-zhoo* (Monroe).
   Range: S. Mexico, B. Honduras, Guatemala, Honduras, El Sal-
   vador. **Mexico:** Gulf lowlands from s. Veracruz east through
   Yucatán Pen.; also Pacific lowlands of Chiapas. **Habitat:**
   Humid thickets, brush, woodland undergrowth.

SCALY-THROATED FOLIAGE-GLEANER   **Pl. 25**
Anabacerthia variegaticeps   6–6½
   Field marks: This bird feeds around the tips of twigs in an
   acrobatic manner much like a Plain Xenops or a chickadee.
   Note *buff eyebrow stripe* (above and behind eye), buff eye-ring,

and *scaling* on throat. Upperparts rufous-brown, crown dusky; underparts paler olive-brown, lightly streaked with white on chest.

Similar species: (1) Buff-throated Foliage-gleaner (mainly lowlands) has bright buff throat and cheeks; broad buff eyebrow stripe starts from bill, not eye; throat not noticeably scaly. (2) Scaly-throated Leafscraper is much darker and lacks buff eyebrow stripe. (3) See Plain Xenops (below).

Voice: A harsh *nye-wee'yo* (Eisenmann).

Range: S. Mexico to w. Panamá. **Mexico:** Highlands from Guerrero, s. Veracruz south through Oaxaca, Chiapas. **Habitat:** Humid mt. forests (3000–6500 ft.). Arboreal; often travels with mixed bands of other birds.

RUDDY FOLIAGE-GLEANER   Pl. 25
Automolus rubiginosus   7½–8¼

Field marks: Dark chestnut-brown above, lightening to tawny and rufous on throat and underparts; no distinguishing marks other than rich ruddy color. Secretive.

Similar species: See (1) Tawny-throated Leafscraper (p. 130), (2) ♀ Bare-crowned Antbird (p. 133), and (3) ♀ Dusky Antbird (p. 133).

Voice: 3 or 4 long inflected whistles much like a human whistle (Marshall). A clear 2-note call (Rowley).

Range: Cen. Mexico to Bolivia. **Mexico:** Highlands of San Luis Potosí, Veracruz, Guerrero, Oaxaca, Chiapas. **Habitat:** Undergrowth, ravines of humid mt. forests to 7500 + ft.; cloud forest, oaks, brush; close to ground.

BUFF-THROATED FOLIAGE-GLEANER   Pl. 25
Automolus ochrolaemus   7–7½

Field marks: A shy dark brown bird of the forest undergrowth and low tangles. Note the unspotted buff throat and cheeks; also buff eyebrow stripe.

Similar species: Scaly-throated Foliage-gleaner (smaller) has a whitish, noticeably scaled throat. The buff eyebrow stripe starts from the eye. It is more strictly arboreal, acrobatic, less secretive; occurs in mt. country.

Voice: A snorting *churr* or nasal roll. Also a low, harsh, frog-like "crecking" *churr* (Slud).

Range: S. Mexico to Bolivia, cen. Brazil. **Mexico:** Mainly Gulf lowlands; s. Veracruz, Tabasco, n. Oaxaca, n. Chiapas. **Habitat:** Low undergrowth, dense tangles of rain forest; also leaf clusters in midtree levels.

PLAIN (LITTLE) XENOPS   *Xenops minutus*   4½–4¾   Pl. 25

Field marks: This tiny brown bird has a bill that appears *up-turned.* Note this wedge-shaped bill, the *silvery white crescent* on the *lower cheek.* Black feathers in the rufous tail may give the tail a striped effect. Very active, often hangs upside down from twigs like a chickadee.

Similar species: (1) Scaly-throated Foliage-gleaner, similarly acrobatic, is much bigger and lacks the white cheek mark. (2) See Wedge-billed Woodcreeper (p. 125).

Voice: A fine, sharp, very rapid trill (Skutch). A high thin *tsiss;* other hisslike notes (Slud).

Range: S. Mexico to Bolivia, ne. Argentina. **Mexico:** Gulf lowlands from cen. Veracruz, n. Oaxaca through Tabasco, n. Chiapas, and lower parts of Yucatán Pen. **Habitat:** Humid forests and woodlands.

TAWNY-THROATED LEAFSCRAPER   Pl. 25
Sclerurus mexicanus   6–6½

> **Field marks:** A dark brown, *ruddy-breasted* bird resembling the Ruddy Foliage-gleaner but with a longer, narrower, more curved bill. Lower underparts *dusky;* rump *chestnut.* Tail short, blackish terminally. Note also the *light cheeks.*
>
> **Similar species:** See (1) Ruddy Foliage-gleaner (p. 129) and (2) ♀ Bare-crowned Antbird (p. 133).
>
> **Voice:** A series of sharp descending *squee's* (Slud).
>
> **Range:** S. Mexico to n. Bolivia, Brazil. **Mexico:** Mainly lowlands; recorded Veracruz, Puebla, n. Chiapas. Rare, local. **Habitat:** Floor of humid lowland and hill forests, cloud forest.

SCALY-THROATED LEAFSCRAPER   Pl. 25
Sclerurus guatemalensis   6½–7

> **Field marks:** A dusky bird of the forest floor. When it allows a glimpse, the *scaled whitish throat* and obscurely scaled breast are determinative. Bill straighter than that of preceding leaf-scraper. Secretive.
>
> **Similar species:** See (1) Buff-throated Foliage-gleaner (p. 129) and (2) Scaly-throated Foliage-gleaner (p. 128).
>
> **Voice:** Song, *pwik-wik-wik-wik-wik-wik-wik-wik;* rises and speeds in middle, then slows somewhat (Slud).
>
> **Range:** S. Mexico to Ecuador. **Mexico:** Gulf lowlands; Veracruz, Tabasco, n. Chiapas, Quintana Roo. Rare. **Habitat:** Floor and undergrowth of humid forests and second growth.

Antbirds: Formicariidae

A VERY large family of neotropical birds found mainly in wood-land and brushland. A few species (but not most) regularly follow army ants to prey on other disturbed insects and invertebrates. Antbirds have radiated so as to emulate birds of many other groups; thus we have antshrikes, antvireos, antwrens, antthrushes, antpittas, etc. Terrestrial species have longer legs than arboreal

species. Bills strong, often slightly hooked. Sexes unlike in most
species. **Food:** Chiefly insects and other arthropods. **Range:** S.
Mexico to cen. Argentina. **No. of species:** World, 224; Mexico, 9
(+ 2 in Guatemala).

GREAT ANTSHRIKE *Taraba major* 7½–8   **Pl. 25**
 Field marks: A somewhat crested shrikelike bird with a heavy
 hook-tipped bill, bright red eyes. *Male:* Upperparts black with
 white wingbars (often concealed). Throat and underparts immaculate white except for dark under tail coverts and lower
 flanks. Immature male lacks wingbars. *Female:* Black replaced
 by rufous; no wingbars.
 Voice: An accelerating series of hoots, suggesting a trogon;
 often terminated by a nasal snarl (Eisenmann).
 Range: Se. Mexico to Argentina. **Mexico:** Gulf lowlands; s.
 Veracruz, Tabasco, n. Oaxaca, n. Chiapas. **Habitat:** Shady
 humid woodlands, second growth, within thickets near ground,
 dense brush, cane, bamboo.

BARRED ANTSHRIKE   **Pl. 25**
Thamnophilus doliatus 6–6½
 Field marks: The *transversely barred* black and white male is
 unmistakable. The female is strikingly different: bright cinnamon above, tawny below with strong *black streaks on buff
 cheeks and neck collar.* Eyes of both sexes pale yellow or white.
 Juvenal male barred with dark brown and buff.
 Voice: A rapid, accelerating roll or rattle, *kuk-kuk-kuk-uk-uk-
 uk-k-k-k-kkkkkkk,* ending with an emphatic *wek* (RTP).
 Range: Mexico to n. Argentina. **Mexico:** Gulf slope from s.
 Tamaulipas, e. San Luis Potosí through Yucatán Pen. Also Pacific slope of Oaxaca, Chiapas. **Habitat:** Low second-growth
 thickets; scrub, hedges, clearings; near ground.

SLATY ANTSHRIKE   **Pl. 25**
Thamnophilus punctatus 5½–6
 Field marks: *Male:* Slaty gray, paler below, with a *black cap,*
 blackish wings and tail. Wings show 2 or 3 broken white bars.
 Tail spotted and tipped with white. Bill strong, hooked. *Fe-
 male:* Olive-brown, paler below; wingbars buff or white. Tail
 tipped with pale buff.
 Voice: Resembles that of Barred Antshrike (Land).
 Range: Caribbean lowlands of B. Honduras, e. Guatemala to n.
 Bolivia, Brazil. Not in Mexico. **Habitat:** Lower growth of
 humid lowland forests, woodlands, and borders.

RUSSET (TAWNY) ANTSHRIKE   **Pl. 25**
Thamnistes anabatinus 5½–6
 Field marks: This small brown antbird may be known as an

antshrike by its rather hook-tipped bill. Lower mandible appears *swollen*. *Male:* May be identified with certainty by a small orange-brown patch on lower back (usually concealed, except in social display). Eyebrow stripe, cheeks, and underparts pale yellowish-brown; wings and tail, rufous. *Female:* Lacks orange patch of male (which is usually concealed anyway).
Similar species: Buff-throated Foliage-gleaner (p. 129) is larger, has longer bill, brighter throat.
Voice: Song, a measured series of *tswit's*, intensifying, then falling. Call notes, *switsit* or *weesawisst* (Slud).
Range: Se. Mexico to Bolivia. **Mexico:** Rare; reported in Tabasco and in Caribbean lowland of Guatemala. **Habitat:** Humid forests; often with mixed bands of birds.

PLAIN ANTVIREO *Dysithamnus mentalis* 4¼   **Pl. 25**
  Field marks: *Male:* A small gray antbird, darkest on crown, paler on underparts; belly whitish, flanks *olive;* 2 narrow whitish wingbars. *Female:* Gray-olive above, with *rufous crown,* 2 narrow buff wingbars; throat whitish, sides olive-gray, belly pale yellow.
  Similar species: See Slaty Antshrike (above).
  Voice: Song excellent, suggests certain antshrikes, but higher-pitched, faster: *hee, hee, hee-hee-hee-heeheeheehee.* Call, a nasal *nyoot, nyoot* (Eisenmann).
  Range: Se. Mexico, B. Honduras, Guatemala to Bolivia, ne. Argentina. **Mexico:** Very rare; recorded n. Chiapas, Campeche.
  Habitat: Usually at 5–15 ft. in heavy humid forests.

SLATY ANTWREN *Myrmotherula schisticolor* 4   **Pl. 25**
  Field marks: *Male:* A small, short tailed, *slate-gray* bird with a shieldlike *black throat and chest.* Black wing coverts spotted with white, forming bars. *Female:* Olive-brown above with darker wings and tail; buffy or tawny below, darker across breast and on flanks. Note *stubby tail* in both sexes. Often hangs upside down, chickadeelike.
  Similar species: (1) Dot-winged Antwren is blacker; tail longer, with white outer tips. (2) See Dusky Antbird (below).
  Voice: Song, *t'weet t'weet t'weet, t'weet weet weet weet weet,* in very low soft tones (Skutch). Call, a nasal, whining *nyeeah;* also a sharp *pseeyt* (Eisenmann).
  Range: S. Mexico to Peru. **Mexico:** Foothills of e. Chiapas.
  Habitat: Lower and mid-level of humid forests, chiefly in foothills to cloud forest; travels with other birds.

DOT-WINGED ANTWREN   **Pl. 25**
Microrhopias quixensis 4½
  Field marks: *Male:* Similar to Slaty Antwren but wholly

black. 1 strong wingbar; wing coverts with small white dots. Tail longer, with conspicuous white tips on outer feathers. White patch on back (usually concealed); white underwing coverts. *Female:* Slaty above, *rufous below;* wing, tail, and white underwing coverts as in male. Searches for insects in low trees, warbler fashion.

Similar species: See (1) Slaty Antwren, (2) Dusky Antbird.

Voice: Song, 6 weak ascending notes, followed by a falling rattle: *chee chee chee chee chee chee chr′r′r′r′r′r* (Skutch). Calls, *wit-wit; tit-tit; cheet, cheet,* etc. (Eisenmann).

Range: S. Mexico to Bolivia, Amazonian Brazil. **Mexico:** Gulf lowlands of Veracruz, n. Oaxaca, Tabasco, s. Quintana Roo. **Habitat:** Humid woodlands, thickets, low trees bordering humid forests; travels with other species.

DUSKY ANTBIRD *Cercomacra tyrannina* 5¼–6   **Pl. 25**
  Field marks: *Male:* A slaty-black wrenlike bird with mere dots of white on wing coverts; a concealed white patch on back; tail narrowly tipped with white. *Female:* Dark olive-brown above and bright tawny below, lightest on throat.

  Similar species: (1) Dot-winged Antwren is smaller, arboreal; ♂ has stronger wingbar, more white in tail tips; ♀ is distinctive. (2) Ruddy Foliage-gleaner is larger, more ruddy than ♀ Dusky Antbird; a highland forest bird. (3) See also Slaty Antwren (stubby tail, etc.), above.

  Voice: Song, 5–8 piping whistles rising irregularly in pitch, *pu, pu, pipipee* and *pu, peh, pi′pipipeepee* (Eisenmann).

  Range: Se. Mexico to Amazonian Brazil. **Mexico:** Gulf lowlands of s. Veracruz, Tabasco, n. Oaxaca, n. Chiapas, sw. Campeche, s. Quintana Roo. **Habitat:** Thickets at edge of forests.

BARE-CROWNED ANTBIRD   **Pl. 25**
Gymnocichla nudiceps 6–6½
  Field marks: *Male:* Note the bare area of *bright blue* on the crown and encircling eye. Otherwise a larger, blacker edition of several other blackish antbirds, antwrens, etc. (but white on wing more conspicuous). *Female:* Brown, deep rufous below; rufous or tawny wingbars; tail tipped with pale rusty; bare blue restricted to area around eye.

  Similar species: Ruddy Foliage-gleaner (p. 129) is similar to ♀ of this species but lacks blue area around eye and pale tail tipping. Compare other similar species on Plate 25.

  Voice: Song, about 8 loud, rich *cheep*'s, the last few speeded up; suggests Dusky Antbird (Slud).

  Range: B. Honduras, Guatemala (Caribbean lowland) to n. Colombia. Not in Mexico. **Habitat:** Humid lowlands, dense tangles, thickets at edge of forests. Keeps low; follows army ants.

BLACK-FACED ANTTHRUSH   Pl. 25
Formicarius analis 7

Field marks: This dark antthrush does not seem thrushlike. Rather, it acts like a small rail as it furtively *walks* on the forest floor with *cocked-up tail.* Little patches of *pale blue* skin around eye are striking. Note also *black throat and face* bordered by rufous. Warm brown above, dark gray below. Sexes alike.

Voice: A rapid series of mellow whistles on an even pitch, starting with 1 deliberate note: *whew, hew-hew-hew-hew-hew-hew-hew-hew* (RTP).

Range: Se. Mexico to Amazonia. **Mexico:** Gulf slope; mainly lowlands, foothills, from s. Veracruz, n. Oaxaca through n. Chiapas, Tabasco, Yucatán Pen. **Habitat:** Floor of humid lowland forests, second growth. Terrestrial.

SCALED ANTPITTA *Grallaria guatimalensis* 7½   Pl. 25

Field marks: A rotund, large-headed, long-legged, *almost tailless* bird of the forest floor, shaped like a ball on 2 sticks. Hops over ground and flicks leaves with bill. Note scaly pattern above, buff throat, cinnamon underparts. Terrestrial, secretive.

Similar species: Black-faced Antthrush walks, does not hop.

Voice: A hollow, repeated whistle, accelerating, then slowing: *cow, cow, cow-cow-cowcowcowcow, cow* (Skutch).

Range: Cen. Mexico to Peru. **Mexico:** Mainly mts. (to 11,500 ft.); Jalisco, México, Veracruz south through Chiapas. **Habitat:** Humid highland forest floor; sometimes foothills.

Manakins: Pipridae

SMALL chubby birds, most with stubby tails (some have elongated central feathers). Bill short, broad, slightly hooked; wings short and rounded; legs short. Males often colorful; females usually olive-green. Males of many species indulge in unusual group dance displays, wing-snapping, etc. **Food:** Fruit, insects. **Range:** American tropics (Mexico to Paraguay). **No. of species:** World, 61; Mexico, 4 (+ 1 in Guatemala).

GRAY-HEADED MANAKIN   Not. illus.
Piprites griseiceps 4½

Field marks: Known as a manakin by its small chubby appearance, short tail, stubby bill. Dull greenish above, yellower below. Note *white eye-ring,* gray head, yellow throat. Sexes alike.

Similar species: Greenish females of other manakins lack bright yellow throat and white eye-ring.

Voice: A prolonged *wip-pip-pipürürürürürr-pprürr* (Slud).
Range: Caribbean slope; extreme e. Guatemala (1 specimen),
Honduras, Nicaragua, Costa Rica. Not in Mexico or B. Honduras. **Habitat:** Humid lowland forests, vine-tangled second
growth.

RED-CAPPED MANAKIN   *Pipra mentalis* 4   **Pl. 26**
Field marks: *Male:* The *flame-colored head* and hindneck
make this little stumpy-tailed black bird unmistakable. Chin,
"trousers," wing linings, and bill *yellow;* eye white. *Female:*
Dull olive-green or olive-gray, paler on throat and belly; legs
dark. Note manakin shape.
Similar species: ♀ White-collared Manakin is darker on
throat, yellower on belly than ♀ of this species; has *orange* legs.
Voice: Male in display flicks wings and gives a rough, flat buzz
("Bronx cheer" or "raspberry"). Also light *tsit* notes. When
leaving perch, male makes a dry snap (RTP).
Range: Se. Mexico to w. Ecuador. **Mexico:** Gulf lowlands
from s. Veracruz, n. Oaxaca through Yucatán Pen. **Habitat:**
Understory of humid lowland forests, shady second growth.

LONG-TAILED MANAKIN   **Pl. 26**
Chiroxiphia linearis 4 (+ long central tail feathers)
Field marks: *Male:* Unique; *wire-thin* central tail feathers ex-
tend 5 in. beyond the stubby tail, more than doubling the bird's
length. *Scarlet caplike* crest, *cerulean-blue* back, and orange
legs are in striking contrast to jet-black of rest of bird. *Female:*
Dull olive, much like other female manakins but central tail
feathers extend prominently; legs orange. Immature male may
be dull olive with blackish head, red crest.
Voice: A mournful, whistled *teoo-ho,* the *teoo* slurred, *ho* lower
(RTP).
Range: Pacific slope; s. Mexico to nw. Costa Rica. **Mexico:**
Pacific slope of Oaxaca, Chiapas. **Habitat:** Mainly lowlands;
woodland borders, thickets, brush.

WHITE-COLLARED MANAKIN   **Pl. 26**
Manacus candei 4½
Field marks: *Male:* Strikingly patterned; *white foreparts,
black cap,* wings, midback, and tail; yellow abdomen. Legs
salmon-orange. *Female:* Dull olive underparts, throat and
breast, brightening to yellow on belly. Legs *orange.*
Similar species: ♀ Red-capped Manakin lacks bright yellow
on belly, has dull-colored legs.
Voice: In display dance, wing-snapping, terminating in a short
buzz (Land).
Range: Se. Mexico to e. Costa Rica. **Mexico:** Gulf lowlands

from s. Veracruz, n. Oaxaca east through lower parts of Yucatán Pen. **Habitat:** Lowlands; humid semi-open forests, thickets, brushy edges.

THRUSHLIKE MANAKIN   Pl. 26
Schiffornis turdinus   6½

Field marks: A nondescript, big-eyed, olive-brown bird; slightly more russet-brown on wings and tail, more olive below. No really distinguishing marks. Looks more like a dull, dark thrush than a manakin (voice suggests a mourner). Traditional status as a manakin is dubious.

Similar species: See thrushes (pp. 183–89).

Voice: A 3-part whistle, pensive and restrained – 1st part ascending, 2nd very short, 3rd ascending (Skutch). *Ho-wee'-pee* (Smith).

Range: S. Mexico to Bolivia, se. Brazil. **Mexico:** Gulf lowlands from s. Veracruz south and east through Tabasco, n. Chiapas and base of Yucatán Pen. (rarely). **Habitat:** Understory within humid forests and shady tall second growth.

Cotingas: Cotingidae

A TROPICAL family, much varied in color, pattern, size (kinglet-sized to crow-sized), and behavior; includes such spectacular South American birds as umbrellabirds, bellbirds, and cocks-of-the-rock (sometimes put in a separate family). In Mexico, the family includes only 1 brilliantly colored member, the Lovely Cotinga; most others (attilas, becards, mourners, pihas, and tityras) are more modestly garbed in brown, gray, etc., and somewhat resemble tyrant flycatchers (to which they are closely related). **Food:** Insects, berries. **Range:** Tropical America, from extreme southern border of U.S. to w. Argentina. **No. of species:** World, 91; Mexico, 10 (+1 in Guatemala).

LOVELY COTINGA   *Cotinga amabilis*   7½   Pl. 26
Field marks: *Male: Intense glossy blue* with a triangular patch of *rich purple* on the abdomen and another on the throat, separated by a blue breastband. Wings and tail black marked with blue. *Female:* A big-eyed, gray-brown bird *thickly dappled* or speckled above and below (whitish speckles on dark ground above, bold dark spots on white ground below).

Voice: In flight, males make a sound intermediate between a rapid tinkle and a rattle (Skutch).

Range: Se. Mexico to Costa Rica. **Mexico:** Gulf lowlands of s. Veracruz, n. Oaxaca, n. Chiapas. **Habitat:** High trees of humid forests in lowlands and foothills, cloud forest.

BRIGHT-RUMPED ATTILA   *Attila spadiceus*   7–8½   **Pl. 26**
Field marks: Looks like a flycatcher (and may be one). Rich streaked brown above with a rufous tail and *bright tawny-yellow rump*. Variable; underparts may be largely whitish or strongly yellowish to cinnamon on breast and sides; soft dusky streaks on throat and chest. Bill strong, noticeably hook-tipped.
Similar species: See Streaked Flycatcher (p. 143).
Voice: A musical *weeba weeba weeba weeba* (Chalif). A flycatcherlike *wheet, wheet — wheet — wheeto, wheeto* (RTP).
Range: S. and w. Mexico to Bolivia, Brazil. **Mexico:** Lowlands; in west from s. Sonora, Chihuahua south; in east, from Veracruz south through Gulf lowlands and Yucatán Pen., including Cozumel I. **Habitat:** Forest borders, tall second growth.

SPECKLED MOURNER   *Laniocera rufescens*   8   **Not illus.**
Field marks: Similar to Rufous Mourner but indistinctly scalloped, with darker on breast and back of head. A *yellow patch* may or may not show on each side of breast when wings are lifted. Rufous speckling on wing coverts.
Similar species: See Rufous Mourner (next).
Voice: A loud, clear, deliberate *tee', deh* (almost half second between notes; sometimes *tee'-dee-deh* (Eisenmann).
Range: Se. Mexico to nw. Ecuador. **Mexico:** Rare. Gulf lowlands; s. Veracruz, n. Oaxaca, n. Chiapas; also B. Honduras and Guatemala. **Habitat:** Humid forests, usually near streams. Arboreal.

RUFOUS MOURNER   *Rhytipterna holerythra*   8–8½   **Pl. 26**
Field marks: There are 4 similar rufous-brown members of the family. The Rufous Mourner is middle in size, with head about same color as back; underparts, including throat, almost uniformly rufous, lighter than back.
Similar species: (1) Rufous Piha is larger and is paler on throat. (2) Cinnamon Becard is much smaller; darker crown contrasts with much lighter throat; lores blackish. (3) See also Speckled Mourner (rare); similar in size; indistinctly scalloped with dusky on head and breast.
Voice: A minor-keyed 2-note "wolf whistle." Also a sad *weep* (Slud). An emphatic mournful *so-dear* (Eisenmann).
Range: Se. Mexico to n. Colombia, nw. Ecuador. **Mexico:** Gulf slope of s. Veracruz, n. Oaxaca, n. Chiapas. **Habitat:** Humid forests in lowlands to lower cloud forest.

RUFOUS PIHA   *Lipaugus unirufus*   9–9½   **Pl. 26**
Field marks: The largest of the 4 similar rufous cotingids of humid forests. Rufous-brown above; paler below, especially on throat and belly. Sexes alike.
Similar species: Rufous Mourner (smaller) is not as pale on throat, is more uniformly colored below.

Plate 1

LONG-LEGGED WADING BIRDS

CHESTNUT-BELLIED (AGAMI) HERON *Agamia agami* p. 14
    Adult: Chestnut belly, green-black back, very long bill.
    Immature: Similar, but belly striped.

RUFESCENT (LINEATED) TIGER-HERON p. 15
Tigrisoma lineatum (doubtful in our area)
    Adult: Chestnut head and neck, striped belly.
    Immature: Tawny; boldly banded and spotted (lacks bare yellow throat of Bare-throated Tiger-Heron).

PINNATED BITTERN *Botaurus pinnatus* p. 16
    Tawny; striped breast, barred and spotted above.

BARE-THROATED TIGER-HERON (TIGER-BITTERN) p. 16
Tigrisoma mexicanum
    Adult: Black crown, yellow throat, finely barred gray neck.
    Immature: Bare yellow throat, coarsely barred neck and breast.

BOAT-BILLED HERON *Cochlearius cochlearius* p. 17
    Adult: Broad, slipperlike bill; night-heron aspect.
    Immature: Slipperlike bill; browner than adult.

JABIRU *Jabiru mycteria* p. 17
    Large, white; red neck collar, black head, huge bill.
    Immature (not shown): Gray-brown to whitish. Note bill.

1

immature
RUFESCENT
TIGER-HERON

immature

adult

CHESTNUT-
BELLIED
HERON

adult

PINNATED
BITTERN

BARE-THROATED
TIGER-HERON

immature

adult

BOAT-
BILLED
HERON

adult

immature

JABIRU

Plate 2

BIRDS OF PREY:
KITES, ACCIPITERS, BLACK-COLLARED HAWK

GRAY-HEADED (CAYENNE) KITE *Leptodon cayanensis* p. 27
  Adult: Black above, white below; gray head.
  Immature, light phase: White head with black cap.
  Immature, dark phase: Head blackish; heavy streaks below.

HOOK-BILLED KITE *Chondrohierax uncinatus* p. 27
  Long hooked beak in all plumages.
  Adult ♂: Closely gray-barred underparts.
  Adult ♀: Rufous-barred underparts.
  Black phase: Solid black; tail with 1 broad white bar.
  Immature light phase: White collar and underparts; black cap
  and back.

DOUBLE-TOOTHED KITE *Harpagus bidentatus* p. 28
  Black center stripe on throat.

PLUMBEOUS KITE *Ictinia plumbea* p. 29
  Adult: Rufous in pointed wings; tail banded from below.
  Immature: Usually lacks rufous in wings. Note shape.

MISSISSIPPI KITE *Ictinia misisippiensis* p. 29
  No rufous in pointed wings; tail solid black from below.

BICOLORED HAWK *Accipiter bicolor* p. 31
  Adult: Pale gray below with rufous thighs.
  Immature: White, pale buff, or tawny rufous below.

WHITE-BREASTED HAWK *Accipiter chionogaster* p. 30
  Like Sharp-shinned Hawk but white below; thighs pale buff.

BLACK-COLLARED HAWK (FISHING BUZZARD) p. 32
Busarellus nigricollis
  Chestnut and black; whitish head, black frontal collar.

2

GRAY-HEADED KITE

adult

immature, light phase

immature, dark phase

HOOK-BILLED KITE

♂

♀

black phase

immature

DOUBLE-TOOTHED KITE

adult

immature

PLUMBEOUS KITE

MISSISSIPPI KITE

PLUMBEOUS KITE

adult

immature

BLACK-COLLARED HAWK

BICOLORED HAWK

adult

immature

immature

WHITE-BREASTED HAWK

Plate 3

BIRDS OF PREY:
FALCONS, FOREST-FALCONS, BUTEONINE HAWKS

APLOMADO FALCON *Falco femoralis*   p. 39
Black cummerbund, striped head.

BAT FALCON *Falco rufigularis*   p. 39
Small; black on underparts; whitish throat.

ORANGE-BREASTED FALCON *Falco deiroleucus*   p. 40
Larger than Bat Falcon; orange band across chest, very large feet.

LAUGHING FALCON *Herpetotheres cachinnans*   p. 37
Buff head and underparts; black face mask.

COLLARED FOREST-FALCON *Micrastur semitorquatus*   p. 38
Small-headed, short-winged, long-tailed.
Adult: White or tawny below with light collar.
Black phase: All black; gray tailbars. Note shape.
Immature: Similar to adult but barred below.

BARRED FOREST-FALCON *Micrastur ruficollis*   p. 38
Accipitrine shape (short wings, long tail); yellow loral area.
♂ Slaty-backed; closely barred breast.
♀ Dark brown above, coarsely barred below.
Immature: Incompletely barred, buff collar.

WHITE HAWK *Leucopternis albicollis*   p. 30
White; black barring on wings, band on tail.

ROADSIDE HAWK *Buteo magnirostris*   p. 33
Closely barred with red-brown below; dull gray-brown above.
Some Mexican races are much grayer.

GRAY HAWK *Buteo nitidus*   p. 33
Stocky buteo proportions; finely gray-barred underparts.

WHITE-TAILED HAWK *Buteo albicaudatus*   p. 34
White below, gray above; white tail with black band.

3

APLOMADO FALCON

ORANGE-BREASTED FALCON

BAT FALCON

adult

imm.

black phase

LAUGHING FALCON

adult

COLLARED FOREST-FALCON

♂

imm.

♀

BARRED FOREST-FALCON

WHITE HAWK

ROADSIDE HAWK

WHITE-TAILED HAWK

GRAY HAWK

Plate 4

LARGE BIRDS OF PREY

1. HARPY EAGLE   *Harpia harpyja*   p. 35
   a. *Adult:* Huge; crested gray head, broad black chestband.
   b. *Immature:* White below, dark back; crested white head.

2. BLACK HAWK-EAGLE   *Spizaetus tyrannus*   p. 36
   a. *Adult:* Black; erectile black and white crest.
   b. *Immature:* Brown; streaked below; dark cheek, white eyebrow stripe.
   See also Plate 5.

3. ORNATE HAWK-EAGLE   *Spizaetus ornatus*   p. 36
   a. *Adult:* Long black crest, cinnamon cheeks and neck.
   b. *Immature:* Head white, with long black and white crest.

4. BLACK-AND-WHITE HAWK-EAGLE   p. 35
   Spizastur melanoleucus
   Black above, white below; head white with short black crest.

5. CRESTED CARACARA   *Polyborus plancus*   p. 37
   Crested black cap, red face; barred back and breast. See also
   Plate 5.

6. RED-THROATED CARACARA   *Daptrius americanus*   p. 37
   Black with white belly, red face and throat. See also Plate 5.

7. KING VULTURE   *Sarcoramphus papa*   p. 25
   Buff-white and black; colorful head, orange wattles.

8. LESSER YELLOW-HEADED (SAVANNA) VULTURE   p. 25
   Cathartes burrovianus
   Orange-yellow on head, bluish midcrown.

Plate 5
BLACK BIRDS OF PREY OVERHEAD

SNAIL (EVERGLADE) KITE *Rostrhamus sociabilis* p. 28
Square tail with white at base and with a broad subterminal band.

BAY-WINGED (HARRIS') HAWK *Parabuteo unicinctus* p. 32
Chestnut wing linings and thighs; broad black tailband.

ZONE-TAILED HAWK *Buteo albonotatus* p. 34
Wings 2-toned; tail slender, 3–4 bands.
Immature: Narrower tailbanding.

BLACK HAWK-EAGLE *Spizaetus tyrannus* p. 36
Checkered wings; 4 or 5 tailbands. See also Plate 4.

COMMON BLACK HAWK *Buteogallus anthracinus* p. 31
1 broad white band across tail; small white wing spot. Upperside shows black upper tail coverts.

GREAT BLACK HAWK p. 31
Buteogallus (Hypomorphnus) urubitinga
2 white bands across tail. Upperside shows white upper tail coverts.

SOLITARY EAGLE *Harpyhaliaetus solitarius* p. 32
Large; 1 broad white tailband; no white spot on underwing.

CRANE HAWK *Geranospiza caerulescens (nigra)* p. 29
Whitish bar across primaries, long red legs; 2 white tailbands.

CRESTED CARACARA *Polyborus plancus* p. 37
Whitish chest, white patches at wing ends. See also Plate 4.

RED-THROATED CARACARA *Daptrius americanus* p. 37
White belly, red throat. See also Plate 4.

SHORT-TAILED HAWK *Buteo brachyurus* p. 34
Small; short tail, 2-toned wings.

5

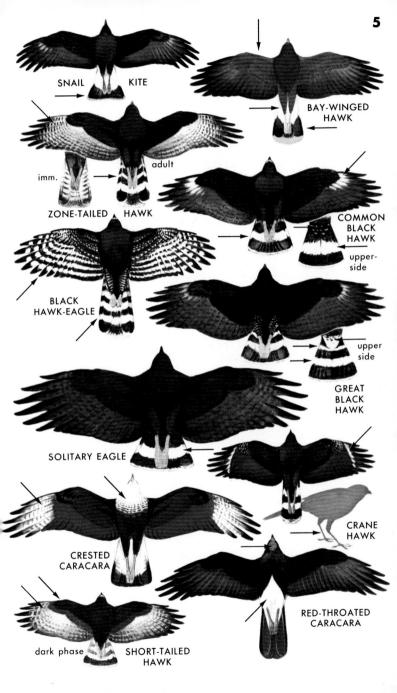

SNAIL KITE

BAY-WINGED HAWK

imm.   adult

ZONE-TAILED HAWK

COMMON BLACK HAWK

upper-side

BLACK HAWK-EAGLE

GREAT BLACK HAWK

upper side

SOLITARY EAGLE

CRANE HAWK

CRESTED CARACARA

RED-THROATED CARACARA

dark phase   SHORT-TAILED HAWK

Plate 6
GUANS, CURASSOWS, CHACHALACAS

CRESTED GUAN *Penelope purpurascens* p. 42
Both sexes: Large, brown; bushy crest, bare red throat.

GREAT CURASSOW *Crax rubra* p. 43
♂ Large, black; curly crest, yellow knob above bill.
♀ Rufous; checkered head and neck, curly crest.

BLACK PENELOPINA (BLACK CHACHALACA) p. 42
Penelopina nigra
♂ Black; red dewlap, red legs.
♀ Brown, heavily barred; red legs.

WEST MEXICAN CHACHALACA *Ortalis poliocephala* p. 41
Small head, bare throat; long, dark, buff-tipped or chestnut-tipped tail.
Southern form: Pale belly. See map, p. 41.
Northern form: Rufous belly and tail tips. See map, p. 41.

PLAIN (EASTERN) CHACHALACA *Ortalis vetula* p. 40
Similar to preceding (northern form) but inhabits Gulf slope.
See map, p. 41.

WHITE-BELLIED CHACHALACA *Ortalis leucogastra* p. 42
Whiter belly than preceding. S. Chiapas south. See map, p. 41.

6

CRESTED GUAN

GREAT CURASSOW

♂

♀

BLACK PENELOPINA

♂

♀

WHITE-BELLIED CHACHALACA

PLAIN CHACHALACA

WEST MEXICAN CHACHALACA
southern form

northern form

WEST MEXICAN CHACHALACA

Plate 7

TINAMOUS, HORNED GUAN, AND OCELLATED TURKEY

Note: Tinamous are fowl-like birds of almost tailless aspect with short legs, slender necks, and slightly decurved bills.

THICKET (RUFESCENT) TINAMOU   p. 2
Crypturellus cinnamomeus
  Conspicuous barring, bright red legs.

SLATY-BREASTED (BOUCARD'S) TINAMOU   p. 1
Crypturellus boucardi
  Dark slaty coloration, bright orange or red legs.

LITTLE TINAMOU   *Crypturellus soui*   p. 1
  Very small, rusty underparts, greenish legs.

GREAT TINAMOU   *Tinamus major*   p. 1
  Large; barred flanks, grayish legs.

HORNED GUAN   *Oreophasis derbianus*   p. 42
  Erect red "horn," white breast and tailband, bright red feet.

OCELLATED TURKEY   *Agriocharis ocellata*   p. 48
  ♂ Blue head with red warts; "eyed" tail feathers.
  ♀ (not shown) Duller, without warts.

7

THICKET
TINAMOU

SLATY-BREASTED
TINAMOU

LITTLE
TINAMOU

GREAT
TINAMOU

HORNED
GUAN

OCELLATED
TURKEY

♂

Plate 8

QUAILS AND WOOD-PARTRIDGES

Note: Birds on the page opposite are males (♂).
Females (♀), when they differ, are described in the text.

MONTEZUMA (HARLEQUIN) QUAIL   p. 46
Cyrtonyx montezumae
  Spotted below; harlequin face.

OCELLATED QUAIL   *Cyrtonyx ocellatus*   p. 47
  Like washed-out version of Montezuma Quail; barred flanks.

BANDED QUAIL   *Philortyx fasciatus*   p. 45
  Heavy black banding below, straight crest.

SINGING QUAIL   *Dactylortyx thoracicus*   p. 46
  Stubby tail, tawny-orange throat.

SPOT-BELLIED BOBWHITE   *Colinus leucopogon*   p. 46
  Small; numerous white spots on belly; white chest.

SPOTTED WOOD-QUAIL   *Odontophorus guttatus*   p. 46
  Orangish crest, small white spots.

LONG-TAILED WOOD-PARTRIDGE   p. 43
Dendrortyx macroura
  Long tail, black throat, red bill.

BEARDED WOOD-PARTRIDGE   *Dendrortyx barbatus*   p. 43
  Gray throat, cinnamon breast, red bill.

BUFFY-CROWNED (HIGHLAND) WOOD-PARTRIDGE   p. 44
Dendrortyx leucophrys
  Buffy forehead, whitish throat, black bill.

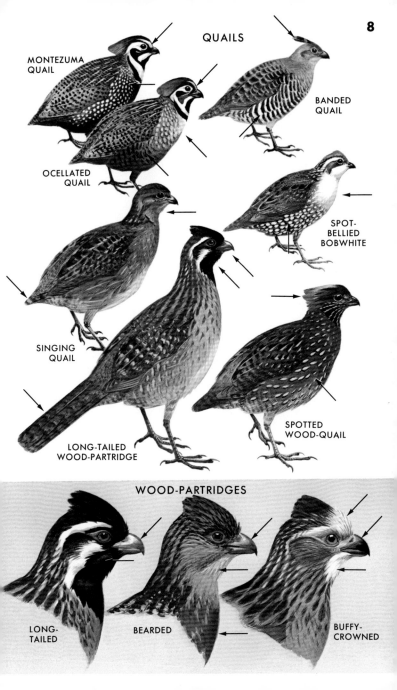

8

QUAILS

MONTEZUMA QUAIL

BANDED QUAIL

OCELLATED QUAIL

SPOT-BELLIED BOBWHITE

SINGING QUAIL

LONG-TAILED WOOD-PARTRIDGE

SPOTTED WOOD-QUAIL

WOOD-PARTRIDGES

LONG-TAILED

BEARDED

BUFFY-CROWNED

Plate 9

QUAILS

Note: Birds on the page opposite are males (♂).
Females (♀), when they differ, are described in the text.

CALIFORNIA QUAIL   *Lophortyx californica*   p. 44
  Curved head plume, scaled belly.

GAMBEL'S QUAIL   *Lophortyx gambelii*   p. 44
  Curved plume, rufous crown, black patch on unscaled belly.

ELEGANT QUAIL   *Lophortyx douglasii*   p. 44
  Tawny head plume, streaked head and throat.

MOUNTAIN QUAIL   *Oreortyx picta*   p. 44
  Long straight head plume; white bars on sides.

SCALED QUAIL   *Callipepla squamata*   p. 44
  Pale gray, scaly; "cotton top."

BLACK-THROATED (YUCATAN) BOBWHITE   p. 45
Colinus nigrogularis
  Black throat, heavily scaled underparts.

COMMON BOBWHITE   *Colinus virginianus*   p. 45
  Highly variable, interbreeding freely. Red-brown, usually with
  white eyebrow stripe. All whistle the familiar *bob-white!* Males
  of 5 basic types are shown opposite.

  a. "Typical" northern form; barred whitish belly (ne. Mexico).

  b. White-throated, red-chested (cen.-w. Mexico).

  c. White-throated, black-chested (s. Mexico).

  d. Black-throated, red-chested (Sonora only).

  e. Black-throated, black-chested (s. Chiapas, w. Guatemala).

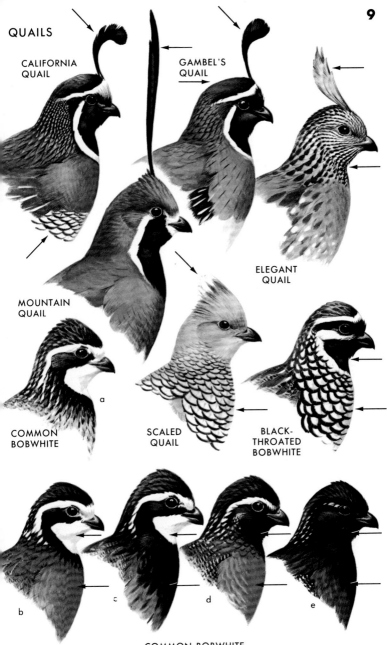

9

QUAILS

CALIFORNIA QUAIL

GAMBEL'S QUAIL

ELEGANT QUAIL

MOUNTAIN QUAIL

COMMON BOBWHITE

a

SCALED QUAIL

BLACK-THROATED BOBWHITE

b

c

d

e

COMMON BOBWHITE

Plate 10

RAILS, SUNBITTERN, SUNGREBE, WADERS, ETC.

GRAY-NECKED WOOD-RAIL *Aramides cajanea*   p. 50
Gray head and neck, cinnamon sides, black belly and tail.

RUDDY CRAKE (RED RAIL) *Laterallus ruber*   p. 51
Small; rufous body, blackish head.

RUFOUS-NECKED WOOD-RAIL *Aramides axillaris*   p. 50
Rufous head and neck, gray upper back, green bill.

YELLOW-BREASTED CRAKE *Porzana flaviventer*   p. 51
Small; creamy-buff breast, barred sides, black bill.

UNIFORM CRAKE *Amaurolimnas concolor*   p. 50
Red-brown nearly throughout, green bill.

SPOTTED RAIL *Pardirallus maculatus*   p. 50
Boldly barred and spotted.

SUNBITTERN *Eurypyga helias*   p. 53
Slender bill, red legs; spectacular wing pattern.

SUNGREBE (AMERICAN FINFOOT) *Heliornis fulica*   p. 52
Striped head and neck; a swimming bird.

DOUBLE-STRIPED THICK-KNEE   p. 61
(MEXICAN STONE CURLEW) *Burhinus bistriatus*
Large, ploverlike; light eyebrow stripe, large eye. Willetlike
wing pattern in flight.

COLLARED PLOVER *Charadrius collaris*   p. 55
Heavy breastband, cinnamon on head and neck, pale legs.

NORTHERN JACANA *Jacana spinosa*   p. 53
Greenish-yellow wing patches; extremely long toes.
Adult: Chestnut body, black head and neck.
Immature: White eyebrow stripe and underparts.

10

GRAY-NECKED WOOD-RAIL

RUDDY CRAKE

center
RUFOUS-NECKED WOOD-RAIL

YELLOW-BREASTED CRAKE

SPOTTED RAIL

UNIFORM CRAKE

SUN-GREBE

SUNBITTERN

DOUBLE-STRIPED THICK-KNEE

immature

COLLARED PLOVER

adult

NORTHERN JACANA

Plate 11

PIGEONS AND DOVES

RED-BILLED PIGEON *Columba flavirostris* p. 67
All dark (including abdomen); bill red.

PALE-VENTED (RUFOUS) PIGEON p. 67
Columba cayennensis
Similar to preceding but abdomen whitish, bill black.

SHORT-BILLED PIGEON *Columba nigrirostris* p. 68
All dark; smaller than above 2; abdomen not white, bill black.

MOURNING DOVE *Zenaida macroura* p. 68
Pointed tail with white sides.

SOCORRO DOVE *Zenaida graysoni* p. 68
A rufous version of Mourning Dove.

BAND-TAILED PIGEON *Columba fasciata* p. 68
White crescent on nape; pale band at tail tip.

WHITE-TIPPED (WHITE-FRONTED) DOVE p. 71
Leptotila verreauxi
Light underparts, rounded tail with white tips; no white in wing.

WHITE-WINGED DOVE *Zenaida asiatica* p. 69
White wing patch.

ZENAIDA DOVE *Zenaida aurita* p. 69
White stripe on secondaries, gray tail tips.

GRAY-CHESTED (CASSIN'S) DOVE *Leptotila cassinii* p. 71
Similar to White-tipped Dove but chest gray, crown brown.

GRAY-HEADED DOVE *Leptotila plumbeiceps* p. 71
Similar to the White-tipped and Gray-chested Doves but cheeks
buff, crown gray.

CARIBBEAN DOVE *Leptotila jamaicensis* p. 71
White face and underparts, iridescent neck; no white in wings.

11

RED-BILLED PIGEON

PALE-VENTED PIGEON

MOURNING DOVE

SHORT-BILLED PIGEON

SOCORRO DOVE

BAND-TAILED PIGEON

WHITE-TIPPED DOVE

WHITE-WINGED DOVE

ZENAIDA DOVE

WHITE-TIPPED

GRAY-CHESTED

GRAY-HEADED

Leptotila doves

CARIBBEAN

Plate 12

PIGEONS AND DOVES

BLUE GROUND-DOVE *Claravis pretiosa*　　　　　　p. 70
Blue-gray with black in wings and tail.

RUDDY GROUND-DOVE *Columbina talpacoti*　　　　p. 70
Ruddy with blue-gray crown; black in tail.

PLAIN-BREASTED GROUND-DOVE *Columbina minuta*　p. 69
Similar to Common Ground-Dove but smaller, breast unspotted, bill black.

COMMON GROUND-DOVE *Columbina passerina*　　p. 69
Rufous in wings; short black tail; scaled or spotted breast.

INCA DOVE *Scardafella inca*　　　　　　　　p. 69
Scaly; rufous wings, slender tail with white sides.

MAROON-CHESTED GROUND-DOVE　　　　　　p. 70
Claravis mondetoura
Blue-gray with maroon chest; sides of tail white.

RUDDY QUAIL-DOVE *Geotrygon montana*　　　　p. 72
Ruddy; no black in tail; note face pattern.

WHITE-FACED QUAIL-DOVE *Geotrygon albifacies*　p. 72
Scaly neck, pale face, cinnamon underparts.

WHITE-CROWNED PIGEON *Columba leucocephala*　p. 67
Dark gray body, snow-white crown.

SCALED PIGEON *Columba speciosa*　　　　　　p. 68
Large, dark; back rufous, neck heavily scaled.

PURPLISH-BACKED QUAIL-DOVE *Geotrygon lawrencii*　p. 72
Gray chest, purplish back; black facial stripe.

PLAIN-BREASTED

COMMON

RUDDY

BLUE

GROUND-DOVES

INCA DOVE

BLUE GROUND-DOVE

PLAIN-BREASTED GROUND-DOVE

COMMON GROUND-DOVE

INCA DOVE

MAROON-CHESTED GROUND-DOVE

RUDDY QUAIL-DOVE

RUDDY GROUND-DOVE

WHITE-FACED QUAIL-DOVE

RUDDY QUAIL-DOVE

WHITE-CROWNED PIGEON

SCALED PIGEON

PURPLISH-BACKED QUAIL-DOVE

Plate 13

MACAWS AND PARROTS

SCARLET MACAW *Ara macao*   p. 73
  Scarlet; long scarlet tail; red, yellow, and blue wings.

MILITARY MACAW *Ara militaris*   p. 73
  Green; red face, long red tail.

THICK-BILLED PARROT *Rhynchopsitta pachyrhyncha*   p. 74
  Green; pointed tail, thick black bill, yellow underwing stripe.

MAROON-FRONTED PARROT *Rhynchopsitta terrisi*   p. 74
  Similar to Thick-bill, but forehead darker, no underwing stripe.

RED-CROWNED PARROT *Amazona viridigenalis*   p. 76
  Red crown.

LILAC-CROWNED (PACIFIC) PARROT *Amazona finschi*   p. 77
  Red forehead, lilac crown, green cheeks.

WHITE-FRONTED PARROT *Amazona albifrons*   p. 76
  White forehead; red completely surrounding eye.

YELLOW-LORED (YUCATAN) PARROT   p. 76
Amazona xantholora
  Similar to White-front, but lores (before eye) yellow.

RED-LORED (YELLOW-CHEEKED) PARROT   p. 77
Amazona autumnalis
  Similar to Lilac-crown, but cheeks yellow.

YELLOW-HEADED PARROT *Amazona ochrocephala*   p. 77
  Northern type: Yellow head.
  Southern type: Yellow forehead and nape.

MEALY (BLUE-CROWNED) PARROT *Amazona farinosa*   p. 78
  Blue crown.

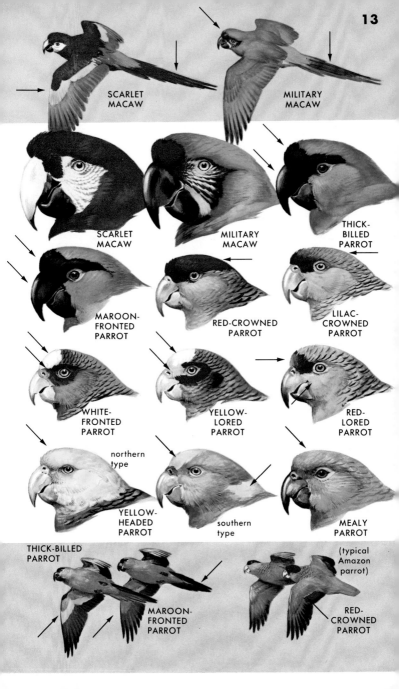

SCARLET MACAW

MILITARY MACAW

SCARLET MACAW

MILITARY MACAW

THICK-BILLED PARROT

MAROON-FRONTED PARROT

RED-CROWNED PARROT

LILAC-CROWNED PARROT

WHITE-FRONTED PARROT

YELLOW-LORED PARROT

RED-LORED PARROT

northern type

YELLOW-HEADED PARROT

southern type

MEALY PARROT

THICK-BILLED PARROT

MAROON-FRONTED PARROT

(typical Amazon parrot)

RED-CROWNED PARROT

Plate 14

PARAKEETS AND SMALL PARROTS
Parakeets have pointed tails.

BARRED PARAKEET *Bolborhynchus lineola* p. 75
Sparrow-sized, black barring.

BLUE-RUMPED (MEXICAN) PARROTLET p. 75
Forpus cyanopygius
Tiny, short-tailed; blue rump, blue wing linings.

WHITE-CROWNED PARROT *Pionus senilis* p. 76
White crown and throat; red tail patch.

ORANGE-CHINNED (TOVI) PARAKEET p. 75
Brotogeris jugularis
Sparrow-sized; orange chin spot, yellow wing linings.

BROWN-HOODED PARROT *Pionopsitta haematotis* p. 75
Dark brown head, red ear spot; red wingpits.

GREEN PARAKEET *Aratinga holochlora* p. 73
Red-throated form: Red throat (e. Guatemala south).
Northern form: All green; slender pointed tail.

ORANGE-FRONTED PARAKEET *Aratinga canicularis* p. 74
Orange forehead; much blue in wings.

AZTEC (OLIVE-THROATED) PARAKEET *Aratinga astec* p. 74
Olive-brown throat and breast.

14

BARRED
PARAKEET

BLUE-RUMPED
PARROTLET

WHITE-CROWNED
PARROT

ORANGE-CHINNED
PARAKEET

BROWN-HOODED
PARROT

GREEN
PARAKEET

GREEN
PARAKEET

red-throated
form

northern
form

ORANGE-FRONTED
PARAKEET

AZTEC
PARAKEET

Plate 15

CUCKOOS, NIGHTJARS, POTOOS

SMOOTH-BILLED ANI *Crotophaga ani* p. 79
Puffinlike profile (note hump on bill ridge). Coal-black, with long, loose-jointed tail.

GROOVE-BILLED ANI *Crotophaga sulcirostris* p. 79
Similar to above; bill grooved, ridge lacks distinct hump.

LESSER GROUND-CUCKOO *Morococcyx erythropygus* p. 80
Whitish eye stripe, tawny or cinnamon-buff underparts.

MANGROVE CUCKOO *Coccyzus minor* p. 78
Dark mask, buff underparts.

STRIPED CUCKOO *Tapera naevia* p. 79
Striped back; crest.

PHEASANT CUCKOO *Dromococcyx phasianellus* p. 80
Long fanlike tail; crested; dark patch on side of breast.

SQUIRREL CUCKOO *Piaya cayana* p. 79
Very slender; cinnamon; pale gray abdomen.

GREATER ROADRUNNER *Geococcyx californianus* p. 80
Long tail, streaked chest, ragged crest; runs.

LESSER ROADRUNNER *Geococcyx velox* p. 80
Similar to preceding, but foreneck and forechest unstreaked.

SPOT-TAILED NIGHTJAR (PIT-SWEET) p. 91
Caprimulgus maculicaudus
Small; with collar; breast blackish with white spots. Tail (not shown) has concealed oval white spots.
Voice: A high-pitched passerine-like *pit-sweet.*

BUFF-COLLARED NIGHTJAR (COOKACHEEA) p. 91
Caprimulgus ridgwayi
Similar to Whip-poor-will but with buff collar.
Voice: A staccato, insectlike series, ending on higher pitch.

TAWNY-COLLARED NIGHTJAR (CHIP-WILLOW) p. 90
Caprimulgus salvini
Tawny collar. White tail spots have oblique forward edge (♂). Yucatán form has more white in tail (see text).
Voice: An oft-repeated *chuck-will* or *chip-willow* (nominate form) or *will* (Yucatán form).

PAURAQUE *Nyctidromus albicollis* p. 89
White patches in wings and tail; chestnut ear patch.
Voice: A hoarse whistle, *pur-we'eeeeer.*

COMMON POTOO *Nyctibius griseus* p. 88
Camouflaged; perches upright, simulating tree stub.

15

LESSER
GROUND-CUCKOO

SMOOTH-
BILLED
ANI

GROOVE-
BILLED
ANI

MANGROVE
CUCKOO

STRIPED
CUCKOO

PHEASANT
CUCKOO

SQUIRREL
CUCKOO

GREATER
ROADRUNNER

LESSER
ROADRUNNER

SPOT-TAILED
NIGHTJAR

BUFF-COLL.
NIGHTJAR

TAWNY-
COLL. N.

COMMON
POTOO

PAURAQUE

Plate 16

OWLS

STRIPED OWL *Rhinoptynx clamator* p. 87
Eared; face disks pale, underparts striped.

CRESTED OWL *Lophostrix cristata* p. 84
Dark; white or buffy-white ear tufts and eyebrows.

SPECTACLED OWL *Pulsatrix perspicillata* p. 84
Dark chocolate-brown with white eyebrows and throatband;
dark chestband; no ear tufts.

STYGIAN OWL *Asio stygius* p. 87
Very dark; face disks and "horns" dusky.

WHISKERED SCREECH-OWL *Otus trichopsis* p. 82
Similar to Common Screech-Owl; facial bristles much longer,
feet smaller (not field characters). Identify by voice (see text).

VERMICULATED (GUATEMALAN) SCREECH-OWL p. 83
Otus guatemalae
Lacks strong vertical shaft pattern below of other screech-owls;
shows more numerous crossbars.

FERRUGINOUS PYGMY-OWL *Glaucidium brasilianum* p. 85
Small; black patch on hindneck. Tail with 7–8 bars.

LEAST PYGMY-OWL *Glaucidium minutissimum* p. 84
Smaller than Ferruginous Pygmy-Owl; back and rump unspotted. Tail with 3–4 bars.

MOTTLED (WOOD) OWL *Ciccaba virgata* p. 86
Dark brown above, streaked below. No ear tufts. Eyes brown.

ELF OWL *Micrathene whitneyi* p. 85
Tiny; gray-brown with white eyebrows. Softly streaked below.
No eye patches on hindneck.

UNSPOTTED SAW-WHET OWL *Aegolius ridgwayi* p. 87
Dark brown above, lacking light spots; tawny-buff below.
Tuftless; conspicuous white eyebrows.

BLACK-AND-WHITE OWL *Ciccaba nigrolineata* p. 86
Black back, cap, and face disks. Underparts barred.

OWLS

16

STRIPED

CRESTED

SPECTACLED

STYGIAN

below
VERMICULATED
SCREECH-

WHISKERED SCREECH-

FERRUGINOUS
PYGMY-

LEAST PYGMY-

ELF

MOTTLED

UNSPOTTED
SAW-WHET

BLACK-AND-WHITE

Plate 17

SWIFTS AND SWALLOWS

WHITE-NAPED SWIFT   *Streptoprocne semicollaris*   p. 92
  Large; white nape (often hard to see).

WHITE-COLLARED SWIFT   *Streptoprocne zonaris*   p. 92
  Large; complete white collar, black throat.

GREAT SWALLOW-TAILED (GERONIMO) SWIFT   p. 93
Panyptila sanctihieronymi
  Large; complete white collar, white throat; deeply forked tail
  (usually folded in a single long point).

LESSER SWALLOW-TAILED SWIFT   p. 94
Panyptila cayennensis
  Half size of preceding; tail shorter, less deeply forked.

CHESTNUT-COLLARED SWIFT   *Cypseloides rutilus*   p. 92
  Partial chestnut collar.

CAVE SWALLOW   *Petrochelidon fulva*   p. 161
  Similar to Cliff Swallow (pale rusty rump) but throat pale, forehead dark chestnut.

BLACK-CAPPED SWALLOW   *Notiochelidon pileata*   p. 159
  Black cap, sooty-brown back and wings.

MANGROVE SWALLOW   *Tachycineta albilinea*   p. 159
  White rump.

SNOWY-BELLIED MARTIN   *Progne dominicensis*   p. 160
  Large. ♂ resembles Purple Martin but has broad median area
  of white on underparts; sides blue-black.

GRAY-BREASTED MARTIN   *Progne chalybea*   p. 160
  Large. Resembles ♀ Purple Martin (dusky breast) but lacks
  grayish collar and light forehead patch.

WHITE-NAPED SWIFT

GREAT SWALLOW-TAILED SWIFT

WHITE-COLLARED SWIFT

LESSER SWALLOW-TAILED SWIFT

CAVE SWALLOW

above
CHESTNUT-COLLARED SWIFT

MANGROVE SWALLOW

BLACK-CAPPED SWALLOW

SNOWY-BELLIED MARTIN

GRAY-BREASTED MARTIN

17

Plate 18

HUMMINGBIRDS

Males (♂) unless indicated otherwise.
See Plate 20 for additional females (♀).

1. **GREEN-THROATED MOUNTAIN-GEM**   p. 103
   Lampornis viridipallens
   Scaly green gorget, white post-eye line, white chest.
2. **MAGNIFICENT (RIVOLI'S) HUMMINGBIRD**   p. 104
   Eugenes fulgens
   Large, blackish; green throat, violet crown.
3. **COMMON WOODNYMPH**   *Thalurania furcata*   p. 99
   Green throat and chest; blackish or greenish abdomen.
4. **GREEN VIOLET-EAR**   *Colibri thalassinus*   p. 97
   Both sexes: Violet ear patch; bluish tail, black band.
5. **STRIPE-TAILED HUMMINGBIRD**   *Eupherusa eximia*   p. 102
   Cinnamon wing patch, black and white tail pattern.
6. **WHITE-EARED HUMMINGBIRD**   *Hylocharis leucotis*   p. 99
   White post-eye stripe, red bill, green throat.
7. **BLACK-FRONTED HUMMINGBIRD**   *Hylocharis xantusii*   p. 99
   Similar to No. 6 but belly cinnamon, tail chestnut.
8. **BLUE-TAILED HUMMINGBIRD**   *Amazilia cyanura*   p. 101
   All-green body, notched blue-black tail. Sexes similar.
9. **EMERALD-CHINNED HUMMINGBIRD**   *Abeillia abeillei*   p. 97
   Short bill, green throat, blackish chest.
10. **RUFOUS-CRESTED COQUETTE**   *Lophornis delattrei*   p. 97
    Rufous crest, green gorget, white rump patch.
11. **BLACK-CRESTED COQUETTE**   *Paphosia helenae*   p. 97
    Black crest, spotted belly, tricolored gorget, white rump patch.
12. **SCALY-BREASTED HUMMINGBIRD**   *Phaeochroa cuvierii*   p. 95
    Scaly dull green underparts; white tail spots.
13. **FORK-TAILED EMERALD**   *Chlorostilbon canivetii*   p. 98
    Green underparts, deeply forked black tail.
14. **PURPLE-CROWNED FAIRY**   *Heliothrix barroti*   p. 104
    Black mask, white underparts, black and white tail. ♂ with violet
    crown, green malar stripe (♀ without it).
15. **FAWN-BREASTED (BUFF-BELLIED) HUMMINGBIRD**   p. 101
    Amazilia yucatanensis
    Both sexes: Green throat, buff belly, notched rufous tail.
16. **RUFOUS-TAILED HUMMINGBIRD**   *Amazilia tzacatl*   p. 102
    Both sexes: Similar to No. 15; tail not notched, belly grayish.
17. **BERYLLINE HUMMINGBIRD**   *Amazilia beryllina*   p. 101
    ♂ All green below, rufous wings and tail.
    ♀ (not shown) Duller; may be gray or brown below.
18. **WHITE-BELLIED EMERALD**   *Amazilia candida*   p. 100
    Both sexes: White underparts; tail gray-green with dark band.
19. **RED-BILLED AZURECROWN**   *Amazilia cyanocephala*   p. 100
    Both sexes: White throat, greenish sides, violet-blue crown, olive tail.
20. **GREEN-FRONTED HUMMINGBIRD**   *Amazilia viridifrons*   p. 102
    Both sexes: White underparts, red bill, rufous tail.
21. **VIOLET-CROWNED HUMMINGBIRD**   *Amazilia violiceps*   p. 102
    Both sexes: Similar to No. 20 but crown blue-violet, sides whiter.

18

Plate 19

HUMMINGBIRDS

Males (♂) unless indicated otherwise.
See Plate 20 for additional females (♀).

1. **PLAIN-CAPPED STARTHROAT** *Heliomaster constantii* p. 104
   Red throat, long bill, white face stripes, white rump patch.
2. **LONG-BILLED STARTHROAT** *Heliomaster longirostris* p. 105
   Red throat, long bill, blue crown, green sides.
3. **AMETHYST-THROATED HUMMINGBIRD** p. 103
   Lampornis amethystinus
   Red throat, blackish underparts and tail.
4. **BUMBLEBEE HUMMINGBIRD** *Atthis heloisa* p. 107
   Tiny; elongated rose gorget; cinnamon in tail.
   Wine-throated Hummingbird, *A. ellioti* (not shown), is similar.
5. **SPARKLING-TAILED (DUPONT'S) HUMMINGBIRD** p. 106
   Tilmatura dupontii
   Tail forked, banded; blue throat, 2 white patches on back.
6. **SLENDER SHEARTAIL** *Doricha enicura* p. 105
   Very long, deeply forked tail; violet-purple gorget.
7. **BEAUTIFUL HUMMINGBIRD** *Calothorax pulcher* p. 106
   Deeply forked tail, long purple gorget.
8. **LUCIFER HUMMINGBIRD** *Calothorax lucifer* p. 106
   Very similar to No. 7. See text.
9. **MEXICAN SHEARTAIL** *Doricha eliza* p. 105
   Forked black and buff tail, rose-red gorget.
10. **VIOLET SABREWING** *Campylopterus hemileucurus* p. 96
    Violet-black; curved bill; large white tail patches.
11. **GARNET-THROATED HUMMINGBIRD** p. 104
    Lamprolaima rhami
    ♀ Rufous wings, dusky underparts.
    ♂ Rufous wings, garnet throat, black underparts.
12. **VIOLET SABREWING** *Campylopterus hemileucurus* p. 96
    ♀ Violet throat, gray underparts, white tail patches, curved bill.
13. **BLUE-THROATED HUMMINGBIRD** p. 103
    Lampornis clemenciae
    Blue throat, white eye line; black tail with white patches.
14. **BLUE-THROATED GOLDENTAIL** *Hylocharis eliciae* p. 100
    Blue-violet throat, bronzy or green-gold tail, red bill.
15. **BROAD-BILLED HUMMINGBIRD** p. 98
    Cynanthus latirostris
    Blue throat, red bill, notched blue-black tail.
16. **GREEN-BREASTED MANGO** *Anthracothorax prevostii* p. 97
    ♀ Dark median stripe on throat and breast.
    ♂ Purple tail, glittering green malar stripe.
17. **WHITE-NECKED JACOBIN** *Florisuga mellivora* p. 96
    Deep blue head, white hindneck, white tail.

19

1 ♂ 2 ♂ 3 ♂ 4 ♂

5 ♂ 6 7 ♂ 8 ♂ 9 ♂

10 ♂ 11 ♀ 11 ♂

12 ♀ 13 ♂ 14 ♂ 15 ♂

16 ♀ 16 ♂ 17 ♂

Plate 20

HUMMINGBIRDS

Females (♀) shown except for Nos. 1, 2, 5, 7, and 8,
where sexes are similar. See Plates 18, 19 for males (♂).

1. **RUFOUS SABREWING** *Campylopterus rufus*   p. 96
   Both sexes: Rufous-cinnamon on underparts and sides of tail.
2. **WEDGE-TAILED SABREWING** *Campylopterus curvipennis*   p. 95
   Both sexes: Violet crown, gray underparts, large wedge-shaped tail.
3. **DUSKY HUMMINGBIRD** *Cynanthus sordidus*   p. 98
   Both sexes: Dull gray below, reddish bill, white eye stripe. ♂ lacks
   white spots in tail.
4. **FORK-TAILED EMERALD** *Chlorostilbon canivetii*   p. 98
   Forked tail, black tailband, white eye stripe, dark mask.
5. **CINNAMON HUMMINGBIRD** *Amazilia rutila*   p. 101
   Both sexes: Underparts cinnamon, tail rufous, bill red.
6. **LUCIFER HUMMINGBIRD** *Calothorax lucifer*   p. 106
   Buff underparts, tawny base of tail.
   Beautiful Hummingbird, *C. pulcher (*♀ not shown here), is more
   southern and almost identical. ♂ Plate 19.
7. **LONG-TAILED HERMIT** *Phaethornis superciliosus*   p. 94
   Both sexes: Long white central tail feathers; striped face.
8. **LITTLE HERMIT** *Phaethornis longuemareus*   p. 95
   Both sexes: Smaller than Long-tail; smaller bill and tail.
9. **RUFOUS-CRESTED COQUETTE** *Lophornis delattrei*   p. 97
   Rufous crown, white or buffy bar on rump.
10. **BLACK-FRONTED HUMMINGBIRD** *Hylocharis xantusii*   p. 99
    Buff underparts, rusty sides of tail, white eye stripe.
11. **SLENDER SHEARTAIL** *Doricha enicura*   p. 105
    Forked tail; tawny-buff underparts.
12. **MEXICAN SHEARTAIL** *Doricha eliza*   p. 105
    Tail tawny with black subterminal band; bill curved.
13. **SPARKLING-TAILED (DUPONT'S) HUMMINGBIRD**   p. 106
    Tilmatura dupontii
    Tiny; bright rufous-cinnamon below; white back spots.
14. **BLACK-CRESTED COQUETTE** *Paphosia helenae*   p. 97
    White bar on rump; spotted underparts.
15. **MAGNIFICENT (RIVOLI'S) HUMMINGBIRD** *Eugenes fulgens*   p. 104
    Large; mottled underparts, spotted throat, greenish tail.
16. **BLUE-THROATED HUMMINGBIRD** *Lampornis clemenciae*   p. 103
    Large, evenly gray below; blue-black tail, white corners.
17. **BROAD-BILLED HUMMINGBIRD** *Cynanthus latirostris*   p. 98
    Unspotted gray underparts, red bill, blue-black tail.
18. **AMETHYST-THROATED HUMMINGBIRD**   p. 103
    Lampornis amethystinus
    Tawny-brown throat, sooty-gray breast and belly.
19. **LONG-BILLED STARTHROAT** *Heliomaster longirostris*   p. 105
    Long bill; throat patch restricted or lacking; see text.
20. **STRIPE-TAILED HUMMINGBIRD** *Eupherusa eximia*   p. 102
    Gray below; white outer tail feathers, rusty wing patch.
21. **WHITE-EARED HUMMINGBIRD** *Hylocharis leucotis*   p. 99
    Red bill, white eye stripe, spotted throat.
22. **WHITE-NECKED JACOBIN** *Florisuga mellivora*   p. 96
    Heavily scaled or spotted below.

20

Plate 21

TROGONS

Medium-sized forest birds, most with long square-ended tails;
metallic green backs (males) and either red or yellow bellies.
Note the tail patterns.

Red-bellied Species
A. Without white breastbands

SLATY-TAILED (MASSENA) TROGON   *Trogon massena*   p. 109
Tail solid dark below (both sexes); orange bill.

EARED TROGON   *Euptilotis neoxenus*   p. 109
Tail largely white below, black at base and tip.
"Ears" on ♂ inconspicuous; bill black.

RESPLENDENT QUETZAL   *Pharomachrus mocinno*   p. 108
♂ Long sweeping plumes, largely white tail.
♀ Belly gray, tail barred, plumes lacking.

B. With white breastbands

MOUNTAIN (MEXICAN) TROGON   *Trogon mexicanus*   p. 110
♂ Tail with bold pattern below.
♀ Strong tail pattern; no white ear spot.

COLLARED TROGON   *Trogon collaris*   p. 110
♂ Tail with narrow black bars below.
♀ Tail obscurely marked below; no white ear spot.

ELEGANT (COPPERY-TAILED) TROGON   *Trogon elegans*   p. 110
♂ Tail marbled below, coppery above.
♀ White ear spot.

Yellow-bellied Species

CITREOLINE TROGON   *Trogon citreolus*   p. 109
Yellow-eyed form (Pacific slope): Wide white breastband.
Dark-eyed form (Gulf slope): Blue eye-ring, narrower white
breastband.

VIOLACEOUS TROGON   *Trogon violaceus*   p. 111
♂ Yellow eye-ring; violaceous breast; tail barred below.
♀ Note tail pattern.

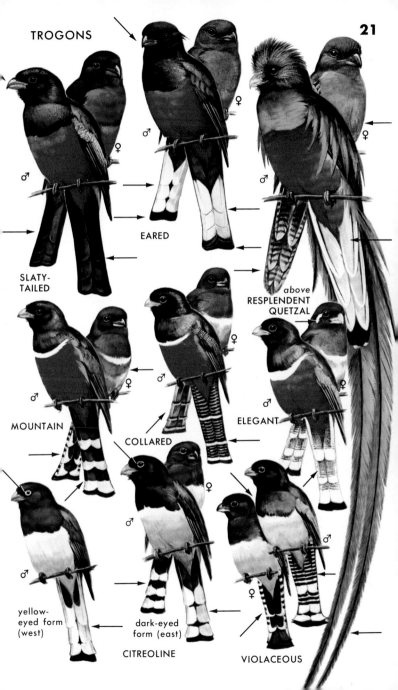

21

TROGONS

EARED

SLATY-
TAILED

above
RESPLENDENT
QUETZAL

MOUNTAIN

COLLARED

ELEGANT

yellow-
eyed form
(west)

dark-eyed
form (east)

CITREOLINE

VIOLACEOUS

Plate 22

TOUCANS, MOTMOTS, PUFFBIRDS, JACAMAR, KINGFISHERS

TOUCANS: Note the huge, canoe-shaped bills.

1. **KEEL-BILLED TOUCAN** *Ramphastos sulfuratus*   p. 116
   Yellow cheeks and breast; scarlet under tail coverts, colorful bill.
2. **COLLARED ARAÇARI (TOUCAN)** *Pteroglossus torquatus*   p. 116
   Solid-black head, variegated underparts.
3. **EMERALD TOUCANET** *Aulacorhynchus prasinus*   p. 116
   Green body, black and yellow bill.

MOTMOTS: See No. 9 for general appearance. All except Nos. 7 and 8 have racket-tipped tails.

4. **RUSSET-CROWNED MOTMOT** *Momotus mexicanus*   p. 114
   Tawny-rufous crown.
5. **BLUE-CROWNED MOTMOT** *Momotus momota*   p. 114
   a. Blue-crowned form (ne. and cen. Mexico).
   b. Black-crowned form (s. Mexico, Guatemala).
6. **KEEL-BILLED MOTMOT** *Electron carinatum*   p. 113
   Broad keeled bill (inset), rufous forehead.
7. **BLUE-THROATED MOTMOT** *Aspatha gularis*   p. 113
   Completely blue throat, no tail rackets.
8. **TODY MOTMOT** *Hylomanes momotula*   p. 113
   Small size, no tail rackets, rufous nape.
9. **TURQUOISE-BROWED MOTMOT** *Eumomota superciliosa*   p. 113
   Black throat bordered by turquoise.

PUFFBIRDS: Large-headed; flycatcherlike.

10. **WHITE-NECKED PUFFBIRD** *Notharcus macrorhynchos*   p. 115
    Black and white; black cap and chestband.
11. **WHITE-WHISKERED (BROWN) PUFFBIRD**   p. 115
    Malacoptila panamensis
    Warm brown, streaked; white whiskers.

JACAMARS: Note slender shape, needlelike bill.

12. **RUFOUS-TAILED JACAMAR** *Galbula ruficauda*   p. 114
    Metallic green; rufous belly and outer tail feathers. ♂ has white throat, ♀ cinnamon-buff.

KINGFISHERS: Males shown here; females differ — see text.

13. **RINGED KINGFISHER** *Ceryle torquata*   p. 111
    Very large, crested; blue-gray above, extensive rufous below. ♀ has gray band across upper breast.
14. **AMAZON KINGFISHER** *Chloroceryle amazona*   p. 112
    Dark green above, noticeable crest. ♀ lacks rufous on chest, has incomplete greenish band.
15. **GREEN KINGFISHER** *Chloroceryle americana*   p. 112
    Smaller than Amazon; less crest; more white in wings, tail. ♀ has 1 or 2 greenish chestbands.
16. **PYGMY KINGFISHER** *Chloroceryle aenea*   p. 112
    Tiny; sides and flanks rufous, no white collar. ♀ has narrow green band across chest; throat rusty.

22

TOUCANS

1

2

3

5a 5b

4 6

7 8

MOTMOTS

9

10 11 ♂ 12 ♂

JACAMAR

PUFFBIRDS

13 ♂

14 ♂ 15 ♂ 16 ♂

KINGFISHERS

Plate 23

WOODPECKERS
The birds shown are males (♂) unless noted otherwise.

Zebra-backed Species (black and white bars)

1. **LADDER-BACKED WOODPECKER** *Dendrocopus scalaris* p. 122
Black face stripes form triangle.

2. **GOLDEN-CHEEKED WOODPECKER** *Centurus chrysogenys* p. 119
Black eye patch; dull yellow on cheeks.

3. **GILA WOODPECKER** *Centurus uropygialis* p. 120
Round red crown patch, pale brown head and chest.

4. **GRAY-BREASTED WOODPECKER** *Centurus hypopolius* p. 120
Similar to No. 3 but dark head and chest.

5. **BLACK-CHEEKED WOODPECKER** *Centurus pucherani* p. 120
Black cheeks, red crown.

6. **GOLDEN-FRONTED WOODPECKER** *Centurus aurifrons* p. 120
a. *Broad-barred form:* Separated head and nape patches.
b. *Narrow-barred form:* Undivided crown and nape.
Note: Females of both forms have nape patch only.

7. **RED-VENTED (YUCATAN) WOODPECKER** *Centurus pygmaeus* p. 121
A small version of 6b; smaller bill. Yucatán, B. Honduras.

Green- or Brown-backed Species (see also No. 14)

8. **GOLDEN-OLIVE WOODPECKER** *Piculus rubiginosus* p. 118
Red completely enclosing gray cap; south.

9. **BRONZE-WINGED WOODPECKER** *Piculus aeruginosus* p. 118
Bronzy wings, no red before eye; east.

10. **GRAY-CROWNED WOODPECKER** *Piculus auricularis* p. 118
Red mustache, but no red on nape or crown; west.

11. **SMOKY-BROWN WOODPECKER** *Veniliornis fumigatus* p. 122
Dark brown with pale ear patch.

12. **BROWN-BACKED WOODPECKER** *Dendrocopos arizonae* p. 122
Dark brown back (unbarred); striped face.

13. **BROWN-BARRED WOODPECKER** *Dendrocopos stricklandi* p. 123
Similar to No. 12 but white bars on lower back.

Crested Species

14. **CHESTNUT-COLORED WOODPECKER** *Celeus castaneus* p. 119
Chestnut body, tawny head and crest.

15. **PALE-BILLED WOODPECKER** *Campephilus guatemalensis* p. 123
Red head, including cheeks; barred underparts. ♀ has black forehead.

16. **LINEATED WOODPECKER** *Dryocopus lineatus* p. 119
Similar to No. 15 but note black ear patch. ♀ (not shown) has black mustache and forehead.

17. **IMPERIAL WOODPECKER** *Campephilus imperialis* p. 123
Very large, with crest (♀ recurved), large white wing patch.

Plate 24

WOODCREEPERS

BARRED WOODCREEPER *Dendrocolaptes certhia*   p. 126
 Thickly barred on head, back, underparts.

BLACK-BANDED WOODCREEPER   p. 126
Dendrocolaptes picumnus
 Bars on lower underparts; spotted throat.

IVORY-BILLED WOODCREEPER   p. 126
Xiphorhynchus flavigaster
 Striped back; dark malar stripe.

WHITE-STRIPED WOODCREEPER   p. 127
Lepidocolaptes leucogaster
 Boldly scalloped below; white throat, eye stripe.

SPOT-CROWNED WOODCREEPER   p. 128
Lepidocolaptes affinis
 Mostly plain back; dark malar mark.

STREAK-HEADED WOODCREEPER   p. 127
Lepidocolaptes souleyetti
 Well-streaked back; no malar mark.

SPOTTED WOODCREEPER   p. 127
Xiphorhynchus erythropygius
 Spotted back and underparts.

STRONG-BILLED WOODCREEPER   p. 125
Xiphocolaptes promeropirhynchus
 Very large; large, heavy bill.

WEDGE-BILLED WOODCREEPER   p. 125
Glyphorhynchus spirurus
 Short, wedge-tipped bill.

RUDDY WOODCREEPER *Dendrocincla homochroa*   p. 124
 Ruddy throughout; no streaks or spots.

TAWNY-WINGED WOODCREEPER   p. 124
Dendrocincla anabatina
 2-toned wing pattern; plain breast.

OLIVACEOUS WOODCREEPER   p. 125
Sittasomus griseicapillus
 Olive-gray head and underparts; rufous wings and tail.

BARRED

BLACK-
BANDED

IVORY-
BILLED

WHITE-
STRIPED

SPOT-
CROWNED

STREAK-
HEADED

STRONG-
BILLED

SPOTTED

WEDGE-BILLED

RUDDY

TAWNY-
WINGED

OLIVACEOUS

Plate 25

ANTBIRDS; OVENBIRDS AND ALLIES

1. **GREAT ANTSHRIKE** *Taraba major* p. 131
   ♂ Black and white, crested; shrikelike bill, red eye.
   ♀ Similar, but red-brown and white.

2. **BARRED ANTSHRIKE** *Thamnophilus doliatus* p. 131
   ♂ Black and white bars above and below.
   ♀ Cinnamon; black streaks on cheeks and collar.

3. **DOT-WINGED ANTWREN** *Microrhopias quixensis* p. 132
   ♂ Black; white tail corners, dotted wings.
   ♀ Similar but underparts rufous.

4. **SLATY ANTWREN** *Myrmotherula schisticolor* p. 132
   ♂ Slaty; short tail, black chest, white wingbars.
   ♀ Olive-brown above, tawny below; short tail.

5. **BARE-CROWNED ANTBIRD** *Gymnocichla nudiceps* p. 133
   ♂ Black; bright blue face, barred wings.
   ♀ Deep rufous; touch of blue around eye.

6. **SLATY ANTSHRIKE** *Thamnophilus punctatus* p. 131
   ♂ Slaty; black cap, dotted wings.
   ♀ Brown; buff-spotted wings.

7. **RUSSET (TAWNY) ANTSHRIKE** *Thamnistes anabatinus* p. 131
   Swollen bill, rufous wings; orange spot on back (♂).

8. **PLAIN ANTVIREO** *Dysithamnus mentalis* p. 132
   ♂ Gray; sides olive, belly white; 2 narrow wingbars.
   ♀ Gray-olive; rufous crown, buff wingbars.

9. **DUSKY ANTBIRD** *Cercomacra tyrannina* p. 133
   ♂ Slaty; wing dots much reduced.
   ♀ Dark brown; tawny underparts.

10. **TAWNY-THROATED LEAFSCRAPER** *Sclerurus mexicanus* p. 130
    Ruddy breast, light cheeks, long curved bill.

11. **BUFF-THROATED FOLIAGE-GLEANER** p. 129
    Automolus ochrolaemus
    Unspotted buff throat, buff eyebrow stripe.

12. **RUDDY FOLIAGE-GLEANER** *Automolus rubiginosus* p. 129
    Ruddy, lighter below; no distinguishing marks.

13. **SCALY-THROATED LEAFSCRAPER** p. 130
    Sclerurus guatemalensis
    Dark; scaly throat and breast.

14. **SCALY-THROATED FOLIAGE-GLEANER** p. 128
    Anabacerthia variegaticeps
    Buff eyebrow stripe and eye-ring, scaly throat.

15. **SCALED ANTPITTA** *Grallaria guatimalensis* p. 134
    Rotund, stub-tailed; scaly above, cinnamon below; striped buff throat.

16. **BLACK-FACED ANTTHRUSH** *Formicarius analis* p. 134
    Rail-like; black throat, rufous cheeks, bluish eye-ring.

17. **RUFOUS-BREASTED SPINETAIL** *Synallaxis erythrothorax* p. 128
    Black-streaked throat, rufous breast, spiny tail.

18. **PLAIN (LITTLE) XENOPS** *Xenops minutus* p. 129
    White mustache, upturned bill, striped tail.

Plate 26

MANAKINS AND COTINGAS

1. **RED-CAPPED MANAKIN** *Pipra mentalis*   p. 135
   ♂ Flame-colored head, yellow "trousers."
   ♀ Dull olive, paler on throat, abdomen.

2. **LONG-TAILED MANAKIN** *Chiroxiphia linearis*   p. 135
   ♂ 2 wiry tail feathers, blue back, scarlet rear cap.
   ♀ Similar to other manakins, but central tail feathers longer.

3. **WHITE-COLLARED MANAKIN** *Manacus candei*   p. 135
   ♂ White foreparts, black cap, yellow abdomen.
   ♀ Dull olive; legs bright orange.

4. **THRUSHLIKE MANAKIN** *Schiffornis turdinus*   p. 136
   Dark olive-brown; no distinguishing marks; thrushlike.

5. **LOVELY COTINGA** *Cotinga amabilis*   p. 136
   ♂ Glossy blue; large purple patches.
   ♀ Thickly dappled above and below.

6. **WHITE-WINGED BECARD**   p. 138
   Pachyramphus polychopterus
   ♂ Black above, slate below; much white in wings.
   ♀ Dull olive; cinnamon wingbars.

7. **MASKED TITYRA** *Tityra semifasciata*   p. 139
   ♂ Pale gray; black wings; face mask encloses red eye patch.
   ♀ Similar but back, cheeks, and crown brown.

8. **ROSE-THROATED BECARD** *Platypsaris aglaiae*   p. 139
   ♂ Blackish cap, rose throat. Southern birds darker.
   ♀ Brown, dark cap, buff collar.

9. **GRAY-COLLARED BECARD** *Pachyramphus major*   p. 138
   ♂ Black cap and back; gray collar and underparts.
   ♀ Cinnamon; blackish cap, buff collar. See No. 8 (♀).

10. **BLACK-CROWNED TITYRA** *Tityra inquisitor*   p. 139
    ♂ Similar to No. 7 but black cap, all-black bill.
    ♀ Black cap, rufous cheeks, all-black bill.

11. **BRIGHT-RUMPED ATTILA** *Attila spadiceus*   p. 137
    Tawny-yellow rump, rufous tail, streaked throat and chest.
    Quite variable.

12. **CINNAMON BECARD** *Pachyramphus cinnamomeus*   p. 138
    Rufous, crown darker; black eye line; small.

13. **RUFOUS MOURNER** *Rhytipterna holerythra*   p. 137
    Rufous, paler on underbody; middle-sized.

14. **RUFOUS PIHA** *Lipaugus unirufus*   p. 137
    Rufous-brown, paler on throat, belly; large.

26

Plate 27

FLYCATCHERS

KINGBIRDS: Dark tails, yellow bellies (except No. 4). Uppersides of tail shown in Nos. 1, 2, 3.

1. WESTERN KINGBIRD *Tyrannus verticalis*   p. 141
White sides on black tail.

2. CASSIN'S KINGBIRD *Tyrannus vociferans*   p. 141
Dark breast; tail not notched, pale edging at tip.

3. TROPICAL KINGBIRD *Tyrannus melancholicus*   p. 142
Notched brownish tail.

4. THICK-BILLED KINGBIRD *Tyrannus crassirostris*   p. 142
Whitish underparts, thick bill, no tailband.

MYIARCHUS FLYCATCHERS: Rusty tails (except No. 6); pale yellowish bellies. Outer 3 tail feathers shown (Nos. 6–11).

5. FLAMMULATED FLYCATCHER *Deltarhynchus flammulatus* p. 147
Like a small *Myiarchus,* but note short bill, light breast streaks.

6. DUSKY-CAPPED (OLIVACEOUS) FLYCATCHER   p. 147
Myiarchus tuberculifer
Small, little or no rufous in tail; see **Voice, Range.**

7. YUCATAN FLYCATCHER *Myiarchus yucatanensis*   p. 146
Similar to No. 6, but some rufous in tail; Yucatán.

8. ASH-THROATED FLYCATCHER *Myiarchus cinerascens*   p. 145
Medium-sized, pale breast; see **Voice, Range.**

9. NUTTING'S (PALE-THROATED) FLYCATCHER   p. 145
Myiarchus nuttingi
Similar to No. 8 on Pacific slope; see **Voice.**

10. BROWN-CRESTED (WIED'S) FLYCATCHER   p. 146
Myiarchus tyrannulus
Large; widespread resident; see text.

11. GREAT-CRESTED FLYCATCHER *Myiarchus crinitus*   p. 145
Similar to No. 10; migrant; see text. Both sides of tail shown.

STRIPED FLYCATCHERS

12. STREAKED FLYCATCHER *Myiodynastes maculatus*   p. 143
Similar to No. 13; eye stripe yellowish, underparts whitish.

13. SULPHUR-BELLIED FLYCATCHER *Myiodynastes luteiventris* p. 143
Reddish tail; striped yellowish underparts.

14. PIRATIC FLYCATCHER *Legatus leucophaius*   p. 143
Small; short bill, plain back, dark tail.

KISKADEELIKE FLYCATCHERS: Striped heads, yellow bellies.

15. GREAT KISKADEE *Pitangus sulphuratus*   p. 144
Striped head, yellow underparts; rufous wings and tail.

16. BOAT-BILLED FLYCATCHER *Megarynchus pitangua*   p. 144
Similar to No. 15; bill broad; wings and tail dull brown.

17. SOCIAL FLYCATCHER *Myiozetetes similis*   p. 144
Small; short bill.

27

Plate 28

FLYCATCHERS

1. **YELLOW-OLIVE FLYCATCHER**   p. 153
   Tolmomyias sulphurescens
   Gray head, bright olive-green back, whitish eye.

2. **SEPIA-CAPPED FLYCATCHER**   p. 157
   Leptopogon amaurocephalus
   Dark brown cap, ochre-buff wingbars.

3. **PILEATED FLYCATCHER**   *Aechmolophus mexicanus*   p. 152
   Prominent crest; grayish chest.

4. **EYE-RINGED FLATBILL**   *Rhynchocyclus brevirostris*   p. 154
   Greenish; prominent eye-ring, very broad bill (inset).

5. **GREENISH ELAENIA**   *Myiopagis viridicata*   p. 156
   Yellow crown (often concealed), yellow belly, no wingbars.

6. **YELLOW-BELLIED ELAENIA**   *Elaenia flavogaster*   p. 155
   White crown patch, yellowish belly.

7. **CARIBBEAN ELAENIA**   *Elaenia martinica*   p. 155
   Similar to No. 6 but lacks eye-ring and strong yellowish belly.

8. **MOUNTAIN ELAENIA**   *Elaenia frantzii*   p. 156
   Similar to Nos. 6 and 7 but lacks crown patch; see text.

9. **TROPICAL PEWEE**   *Contopus cinereus*   p. 148
   Like Eastern Wood-Pewee (wingbars, no eye-ring); see text.

10. **WHITE-THROATED FLYCATCHER**   p. 149
    Empidonax albigularis
    White throat, dusky chest.

11. **YELLOWISH FLYCATCHER**   *Empidonax flavescens*   p. 151
    Yellow throat and belly; see text.

12. **PINE FLYCATCHER**   *Empidonax affinis*   p. 150
    Resident in pines of highlands and plateaus; see text.

13. **RUDDY-TAILED FLYCATCHER**   p. 152
    Terenotriccus erythrurus
    Rufous wings and tail; tawny underparts.

14. **TUFTED FLYCATCHER**   *Mitrephanes phaeocercus*   p. 148
    Tufted crest, cinnamon-brown underparts.

15. **BELTED FLYCATCHER**   *Xenotriccus callizonus*   p. 152
    Pointed crest, orange-brown breastband.

16. **BUFF-BREASTED FLYCATCHER**   *Empidonax fulvifrons*   p. 151
    Rich buff breast; white eye-ring and wingbars.

17. **SULPHUR-RUMPED FLYCATCHER**   p. 152
    Myiobius sulphureipygius
    Sulphur-yellow rump.

28

Plate 29

FLYCATCHERS

FORK-TAILED FLYCATCHER p. 141
Muscivora tyrannus [= *Tyrannus savana*]
  Adult: Long scissorlike black tail, black cap.
  Immature: Shorter, notched tail.

NORTHERN ROYAL-FLYCATCHER p. 153
Onychorhynchus mexicanus
  Usual appearance: Folded crest; tawny rump and tail.
  In display: Fanlike crest (seldom observed).

VERMILION FLYCATCHER *Pyrocephalus rubinus* p. 140
  ♂ Vermilion underparts, crown; blackish back.
  ♀ Streaked pinkish or yellowish belly.

YELLOW-BELLIED TYRANNULET *Ornithion semiflavum* p. 157
  Stubby tail, white eyebrow stripe, yellow underparts.

COMMON TODY-FLYCATCHER *Todirostrum cinereum* p. 154
  Blackish face and cap, pale to dark eyes, yellow underparts.

SLATE-HEADED TODY-FLYCATCHER *Todirostrum sylvia* p. 154
  Similar to preceding but head and chest gray; belly whitish.

NORTHERN BENTBILL *Oncostoma cinereigulare* p. 155
  Bill bent at tip; white eye.

PALTRY TYRANNULET *Tyranniscus vilissimus* p. 157
  Slaty crown, whitish eyebrow stripe. Eye pale to dark.

OCHRE-BELLIED FLYCATCHER *Pipromorpha oleaginea* p. 157
  Gray breast, pale ochre belly.

NORTHERN BEARDLESS TYRANNULET p. 156
(BEARDLESS FLYCATCHER) *Camptostoma imberbe*
  Small; light brownish wingbars; see text.

WHITE-THROATED SPADEBILL *Platyrinchus mystaceus* p. 153
  Stubby tail, broad flat bill; ear patch.

29

FORK-TAILED FLYCATCHER

immature

adult

crest
expanded
in display

usual
appearance

NORTHERN
ROYAL-
FLYCATCHER

♀

VERMILION
FLYCATCHER

♂

YELLOW-
BELLIED
TYRANNULET

COMMON
TODY-
FLYCATCHER

SLATE-
HEADED
TODY-
FLYCATCHER

NORTHERN
BENTBILL

PALTRY
TYRANNULET

OCHRE-BELLIED
FLYCATCHER

N. BEARDLESS
TYRANNULET

WHITE-THROATED
SPADEBILL

Plate 30

JAYS

MAGPIE JAY *Calocitta formosa*   p. 163
Long pointed crest; very long sweeping tail.
Black-throated form: Nw. Mexico.
White-throated form: Cen. and s. Mexico and south.

MEXICAN CROW *Corvus imparatus*   p. 162
Relatively small; all black; see text.

TUFTED JAY *Cyanocorax dickeyi*   p. 164
Bristly black crest, bicolored tail.

GREEN JAY *Cyanocorax yncas*   p. 164
Green body, yellow outer tail feathers.

BROWN JAY *Psilorhinus morio*   p. 163
Sooty brown, pale abdomen; bill black (adult) or yellow (immature).
Plain-tailed form: Ne. Mexico.
White-tipped form: Se. Mexico and south. Both forms occur together in intermediate zone (cen. Veracruz to Tabasco).

30

black-throated form

MEXICAN CROW

MAGPIE JAY

white-throated form

TUFTED JAY

GREEN JAY

adults

white-tipped form

plain-tailed form

BROWN JAY

immature

Plate 31

JAYS

WHITE-THROATED (OMILTEME) JAY　　　　　　　p. 165
Cyanolyca mirabilis
　White throat, black and white face pattern.

DWARF JAY　*Cyanolyca nana*　　　　　　　　　p. 166
　Black face mask, pale bluish-white throat.

PURPLISH-BACKED (BEECHEY'S) JAY　　　　　　p. 165
Cissilopha beecheii
　Purplish back, yellow or white eye. Nw. Mexico.

BLACK-THROATED JAY　*Cyanolyca pumilo*　　　p. 166
　Small, all dark; faintly outlined black face.

YUCATAN JAY　*Cissilopha yucatanica*　　　　　p. 164
　Only *blue* jay in Yucatán Pen. Similar to San Blas Jay but
　lacks frontal crest. *Juvenal:* Head and underparts white.

AZURE-HOODED JAY　*Cyanolyca cucullata*　　　p. 165
　Azure crown; white ear stripe.

BUSHY-CRESTED JAY　*Cissilopha melanocyanea*　p. 165
　Similar to Yucatán Jay but eye yellow, head with bushy crest.
　Guatemala.

SAN BLAS (BLACK-AND-BLUE) JAY　　　　　　　p. 164
Cissilopha sanblasiana
　Erectile frontal crest (not always noticeable). Eye yellow in full
　adult (subadult shown). W. Mexico.

UNICOLORED JAY　*Aphelocoma unicolor*　　　　p. 166
　Uniformly slaty blue; no distinctive marks.

STELLER'S JAY　*Cyanocitta stelleri*　　　　　　p. 167
　Black and blue; crest, white eye spots.
　Typical form has pointed crest.
　Southern form (Chiapas) shorter crest.

GRAY-BREASTED (MEXICAN) JAY　　　　　　　　p. 166
Aphelocoma ultramarina
　Underparts grayish, without streaks.

SCRUB JAY　*Aphelocoma coerulescens*　　　　　p. 166
　Necklace of dark streaks on upper breast.

JAYS

31

PURPLISH-
BACKED

WHITE-
THROATED

DWARF

YUCATAN

BLACK-
THROATED

adult

AZURE-
HOODED

immature

adult

BUSHY-
CRESTED

imm.

UNICOLORED

adult

SAN
BLAS

YUCATAN

juvenal

southern
form

STELLER'S

typical
form

GRAY-
BREASTED

SCRUB

Plate 32

WRENS

SOUTHERN HOUSE-WREN *Troglodytes musculus* p. 176
Similar to N. House-Wren; browner, washed with cinnamon.

BROWN-THROATED WREN *Troglodytes aedon* (in part) p. 176
Browner than N. House-Wren; throat buffier, flanks barred.

RUFOUS-BROWED WREN *Troglodytes rufociliatus* p. 176
A reddish-brown house-wren; rufous eyebrow stripe.

CLARION ISLAND WREN *Troglodytes tanneri* p. 175
A large house-wren; Clarión I. (Revilla Gigedo group).

SOCORRO WREN *Thryomanes sissonii* p. 175
Between House- and Bewick's Wrens in aspect. Socorro I.

BEWICK'S WREN *Thryomanes bewickii* p. 175
Whitish underparts, eyebrow stripe; dark tail with white
corners.

WHITE-BELLIED WREN *Uropsila leucogastra* p. 177
Stub tail, whitish breast, no cheek stripes.

GRAY-BREASTED WOOD-WREN p. 177
Henicorhina leucophrys
Stub tail, striped cheeks, gray breast.

WHITE-BREASTED WOOD-WREN p. 177
Henicorhina leucosticta
Stub tail, striped cheeks, white breast.

PLAIN WREN *Thryothorus modestus* p. 173
White brow, bright rump, buffy-cinnamon abdomen.

HAPPY WREN *Thryothorus felix* p. 174
Ochre-buff underparts; eyebrow stripe, striped cheeks.

CAROLINA WREN *Thryothorus ludovicianus* p. 173
Northeastern form (not shown): Rusty color, whitish eyebrow
stripe.
Yucatán form (White-browed Wren): Largely whitish underparts.

RUFOUS-AND-WHITE WREN *Thryothorus rufalbus* p. 174
Bright rufous upperparts, striped cheeks.

ROCK WREN *Salpinctes obsoletus* p. 178
Grayish; light breast streaks, rusty rump, buff tail corners.

BAR-VENTED (SINALOA) WREN *Thryothorus sinaloa* p. 174
Rusty tail, striped cheeks, white underparts, barred vent.

CANYON WREN *Catherpes mexicanus* p. 178
White throat, dark cheeks, dark belly.

SPOT-BREASTED WREN *Thryothorus maculipectus* p. 175
Thickly spotted and scaled underparts, plain wings.

BANDED WREN *Thryothorus pleurostictus* p. 174
Black bars on sides and flanks.

32

WRENS

BROWN-
THROATED

RUFOUS-
BROWED

SOUTHERN HOUSE-

CLARION
ISLAND

SOCORRO

BEWICK'S

WHITE-
BELLIED

GRAY-
BREASTED
WOOD-

PLAIN

WHITE-
BREASTED
WOOD-

HAPPY

CAROLINA
Yucatán
form

RUFOUS-
AND-
WHITE

ROCK

BAR-VENTED

CANYON

SPOT-
BREASTED

BANDED

Plate 33

WRENS, GNATCATCHERS, GNATWREN

GIANT WREN *Campylorhynchus chiapensis* p. 171
Large; rufous above, white below; black and white eye stripes.

CACTUS WREN *Campylorhynchus brunneicapillus* p. 172
Streaked back; heavy cluster of spots on upper breast.

RUFOUS-NAPED WREN *Campylorhynchus rufinucha* p. 171
Smaller than Giant Wren; spotting on lower back.
Rufous-backed form: S. Chiapas, Guatemala.
Rufous-naped form: Oaxaca and north.

BAND-BACKED WREN *Campylorhynchus zonatus* p. 171
Back banded, lower underparts bright buff.

GRAY-BARRED (GRAY) WREN p. 170
Campylorhynchus megalopterus
Gray-looking; barred on back and sides.

SPOTTED WREN *Campylorhynchus gularis* p. 172
Adult: White throat, black mustache; thrushlike spots below.
Immature: Unspotted below; note mustache mark.

NIGHTINGALE WREN *Microcerculus marginatus* p. 178
Small, stub-tailed, dark; indistinct scallops below.

SLENDER-BILLED WREN *Hylorchilus sumichrasti* p. 178
Dark, short-tailed; long bill, light throat.

TROPICAL GNATCATCHER *Polioptila plumbea* p. 190
♂ Black and white tail, black crown, white superciliary.

BLACK-CAPPED GNATCATCHER *Polioptila nigriceps* p. 190
♂ Similar to preceding, but solid black cap (in summer).

LONG-BILLED GNATWREN *Ramphocaenus rufiventris* p. 191
Very long bill, striped throat.

HEADS OF GNATCATCHERS, *Polioptila* (see text)

1.	**TROPICAL**	*P. plumbea*	♂	p. 190
2.	**TROPICAL**	*P. plumbea*	♀	p. 190
3.	**WHITE-LORED**	*P. albiloris*	♂ winter	p. 189
4.	**WHITE-LORED**	*P. albiloris*	♀	p. 189
5.	**WHITE-LORED**	*P. albiloris*	♂ summer	p. 189
6.	**BLACK-TAILED**	*P. melanura*	♂ (dark form)	p. 190
7.	**BLACK-CAPPED**	*P. nigriceps*	♂ summer	p. 190
8.	**BLACK-CAPPED**	*P. nigriceps*	♂ winter	p. 190
9.	**BLUE-GRAY**	*P. caerulea*	♂	p. 189
10.	**BLUE-GRAY**	*P. caerulea*	♀	p. 189

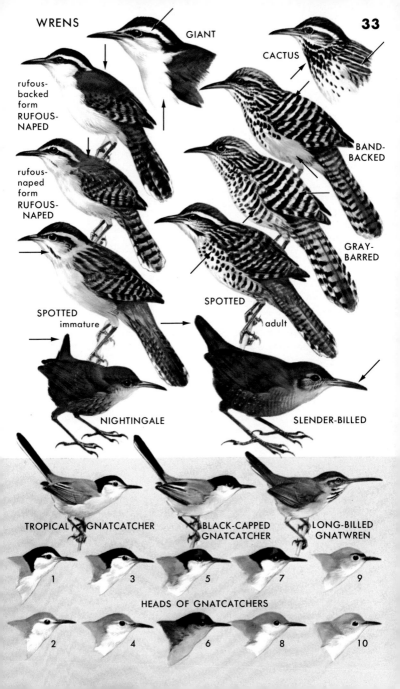

WRENS

33

GIANT

CACTUS

rufous-backed form RUFOUS-NAPED

rufous-naped form RUFOUS-NAPED

BAND-BACKED

GRAY-BARRED

SPOTTED

SPOTTED immature

SPOTTED adult

NIGHTINGALE

SLENDER-BILLED

TROPICAL GNATCATCHER

BLACK-CAPPED GNATCATCHER

LONG-BILLED GNATWREN

HEADS OF GNATCATCHERS

1 3 5 7 9

2 4 6 8 10

Plate 34

MIMIC-THRUSHES, SILKY-FLYCATCHERS

LONG-BILLED THRASHER *Toxostoma longirostre* p. 179
Heavily striped below, longish bill and tail.

COZUMEL THRASHER *Toxostoma guttatum* p. 179
Similar to Long-billed; smaller; Cozumel I. only.

OCELLATED THRASHER *Toxostoma ocellatum* p. 180
Roundish black breast spots, well-curved bill.

GRAY THRASHER *Toxostoma cinereum* p. 180
Tear-shaped breast spots. Baja California only.

CURVE-BILLED THRASHER *Toxostoma curvirostre* p. 180
Indistinctly spotted breast.

SOCORRO THRASHER *Mimodes graysoni* p. 181
Short thrushlike bill, plain breast. Socorro I.

✳ **BLUE MOCKINGBIRD** *Melanotis caerulescens* p. 181
Wholly dull gray-blue; black mask, red eye.

BLUE-AND-WHITE MOCKINGBIRD *Melanotis hypoleucus* p. 182
Dull gray-blue above, white below; black mask, red eye.

BLACK CATBIRD *Melanoptila glabrirostris* p. 182
Glossy blue-black. Coast of Yucatán Pen. and islands.

TROPICAL MOCKINGBIRD *Mimus gilvus* p. 182
Similar to Northern Mockingbird. Lacks large white wing
patches. South of Isthmus of Tehuantepec.

PHAINOPEPLA *Phainopepla nitens* p. 192
♂ Glossy black; slender crest, white wing patches.
♀ Dark gray; crest, light gray wing patches.

GRAY SILKY-FLYCATCHER *Ptiligonys cinereus* p. 193
♂ Gray, crested; long black and white tail, yellow crissum.
♀ Similar to ♂ but brown, not gray.

34

COZUMEL THRASHER

LONG-BILLED THRASHER

GRAY THRASHER

OCELLATED THRASHER

SOCORRO THRASHER

CURVE-BILLED THRASHER

BLUE-AND-WHITE MOCKINGBIRD

BLUE MOCKINGBIRD

BLACK CATBIRD

TROPICAL MOCKINGBIRD

GRAY SILKY-FLYCATCHER

♂

♀

♂

PHAINOPEPLA

♀

Plate 35

THRUSHES

AZTEC THRUSH *Ridgwayia pinicola* p. 185
   ♂ Dark hood, white belly; striking white wing patches.
   ♀ Similar to ♂ but brown.

BLACK ROBIN *Turdus infuscatus* p. 184
   ♂ All black; bright yellow bill and legs.
   ♀ Dusky brown, buff throat; dull yellow bill, legs.

RUFOUS-BACKED ROBIN *Turdus rufopalliatus* p. 183
   Rufous back; robinlike appearance.

RUFOUS-COLLARED ROBIN *Turdus rufitorques* p. 183
   Rufous collar, black belly.

WHITE-THROATED ROBIN *Turdus assimilis* p. 184
   White crescent below streaked throat.

CLAY-COLORED ROBIN *Turdus grayi* p. 184
   Brown with light tawny or cinnamon-buff belly.

SAN LUCAS ROBIN *Turdus confinis* p. 183
   Pale creamy-buff underparts.

MOUNTAIN ROBIN *Turdus plebejus* p. 184
   Dusky, with streaked throat, blackish bill.

SLATE-COLORED SOLITAIRE *Myadestes unicolor* p. 186
   Slaty; white eye-ring, white outer tail tips.

BROWN-BACKED SOLITAIRE *Myadestes obscurus* p. 185
   Similar to preceding but wings rusty.

SPOTTED NIGHTINGALE-THRUSH *Catharus dryas* p. 187
   Black head, spotted breast, orange bill and legs.

BLACK-HEADED NIGHTINGALE-THRUSH p. 187
Catharus mexicanus
   Black cap, unspotted olive chest, orange or yellow bill.

RUSSET NIGHTINGALE-THRUSH *Catharus occidentalis* p. 187
   Russet upperparts, grayish breast; lower mandible orangish, with
   dark tip.

ORANGE-BILLED NIGHTINGALE-THRUSH p. 188
Catharus aurantiirostris
   Similar to preceding, but entire bill bright orange.

RUDDY-CAPPED NIGHTINGALE-THRUSH (not shown) p. 188
Catharus frantzii
   Similar to Russet Nightingale-Thrush but lacks buff patch
   across spread wing. Lower mandible orange, lacking dark tip.

♀

♂

35

AZTEC
THRUSH

RUFOUS-
COLLARED
ROBIN

♀

BLACK
ROBIN

♂

RUFOUS-
BACKED
ROBIN

♂

CLAY-
COLORED
ROBIN

SAN
LUCAS
ROBIN

WHITE-
THROATED
ROBIN

BROWN-
BACKED
SOLITAIRE

SLATE-
COLORED
SOLITAIRE

MOUNTAIN
ROBIN

♂

SPOTTED

ORANGE-
BILLED

BLACK-
HEADED

RUSSET

NIGHTINGALE-THRUSHES

Plate 36

VIREOS AND ALLIES

YELLOW-GREEN VIREO *Vireo flavoviridis* p. 198
No wingbars; gray cap, yellow under tail coverts.

COZUMEL VIREO *Vireo bairdi* p. 195
Wingbars; cinnamon sides and cheeks. Cozumel I.

YUCATAN VIREO *Vireo magister* p. 198
Similar to Yellow-green Vireo but lacking yellow-green tones.
Yucatán Pen.

MANGROVE VIREO *Vireo pallens* p. 196
Wingbars; dingy yellow below. Mangroves. Pacific Coast birds
are dark-eyed, eastern birds pale-eyed.

GOLDEN VIREO *Vireo hypochryseus* p. 196
Entirely bright yellow below; yellow eyebrow.

BROWN-CAPPED VIREO *Vireo leucophrys* p. 199
No wingbars; brown crown, white eyebrow stripe.

SLATY VIREO *Neochloe brevipennis* p. 199
Slaty gray; white chin, olive-green crown and wings.

TAWNY-CROWNED GREENLET *Hylophilus ochraceiceps* p. 200
Tawny golden crown, pale yellow-buff underparts.

LESSER (GRAY-HEADED) GREENLET p. 200
Hylophilus decurtatus
Gray head, whitish eye-ring, olive-green back.

RUFOUS-BROWED PEPPERSHRIKE *Cyclarhis gujanensis* p. 194
Rufous eyebrow, gray cap and cheeks, yellow underparts. Cozumel I. race has whitish lower underparts.

GREEN SHRIKE-VIREO *Smaragdolanius pulchellus* p. 195
Bright green; blue crown, yellow throat.

CHESTNUT-SIDED SHRIKE-VIREO p. 194
Vireolanius melitophrys
Chestnut sides and chestband; yellow eyebrow, black whisker.

36

YELLOW-GREEN VIREO

COZUMEL VIREO

YUCATAN VIREO

MANGROVE VIREO

GOLDEN VIREO

BROWN-CAPPED VIREO

SLATY VIREO

LESSER GREENLET

RUFOUS-BROWED PEPPERSHRIKE

TAWNY-CROWNED GREENLET

GREEN SHRIKE-VIREO

CHESTNUT-SIDED SHRIKE-VIREO

Plate 37

HONEYCREEPERS AND WARBLERS

BANANAQUIT *Coereba flaveola* p. 202
White eyebrow stripe, gray throat, yellow breast. Cozumel I. race has white throat.

CINNAMON FLOWER-PIERCER *Diglossa baritula* p. 200
♂ Gray hood, cinnamon belly, upturned bill.
♀ Brown, paler below; note upturned bill.

GREEN HONEYCREEPER *Chlorophanes spiza* p. 201
♂ Deep brilliant green, black head.
♀ Grass-green, paler below, curved bill.

RED-LEGGED (BLUE) HONEYCREEPER *Cyanerpes cyaneus* p. 201
♂ Violet and black, has red legs.
♀ Dull green, whitish throat; obscure streaking.

SHINING HONEYCREEPER *Cyanerpes lucidus* p. 201
♂ Violet and black; black throat, yellow legs.
♀ Greenish; buffy-yellow throat, strong streaking.

RED WARBLER *Ergaticus ruber* p. 214
Red; white (usually) cheek patch.

PINK-HEADED WARBLER *Ergaticus versicolor* p. 214
Dark red; pink head.

RED-FACED WARBLER *Cardellina rubrifrons* p. 213
Red and black face pattern; white rump.

PAINTED REDSTART *Myioborus picta* p. 213
Red breast, white wing patch.

SLATE-THROATED REDSTART *Myioborus miniatus* p. 214
♂ Orange-red breast, no white on wing.
♀ Salmon-pink on breast.

RED-BREASTED CHAT *Granatellus venustus* p. 212
♂ Red breast, white throat, black chestband.
♀ Buff eye stripe; tail as in ♂.

GRAY-THROATED CHAT *Granatellus sallaei* p. 212
♂ Similar to preceding but gray head; no black chestband.

BANANAQUIT

CINNAMON
FLOWER-PIERCER

♀

♂

GREEN
HONEYCREEPER

♀

♂

♀

♂

RED-LEGGED
HONEYCREEPER

♀

♂

SHINING
HONEYCREEPER

RED-FACED
WARBLER

RED
WARBLER

PINK-HEADED WARBLER

PAINTED
REDSTART

♀

♂

SLATE-THROATED
REDSTART

♀

♂

RED-BREASTED
CHAT

♂

GRAY-THROATED
CHAT

Plate 38

WARBLERS

TROPICAL PARULA *Parula pitiayumi* p. 204
Black face, bluish head, yellow throat, white wingbars.

CRESCENT-CHESTED WARBLER *Vermivora superciliosa* p. 204
Chestnut crescent on yellow breast; white eyebrow stripe.

GOLDEN-BROWED WARBLER *Basileuterus belli* p. 215
Yellow eyebrow stripe, chestnut crown and cheeks.

RUFOUS-CAPPED WARBLER *Basileuterus rufifrons* p. 215
White eyebrow stripe, chestnut crown and cheeks.

CHESTNUT-CAPPED WARBLER *Basileuterus delattrii* p. 216
Similar to Rufous-capped but more extensively yellow below;
white malar streak; see text.

GOLDEN-CROWNED WARBLER *Basileuterus culicivorus* p. 215
2 black crown stripes; yellow median stripe.

GOLDEN WARBLER *Dendroica petechia* (in part) p. 205
♂ Like typical Yellow Warbler but crown chestnut. Cozumel I.

MANGROVE WARBLER p. 205
Dendroica erithacorides (or *D. petechia* in part)
♂ Like typical Yellow Warbler but entire head chestnut.

GRAY-CROWNED YELLOWTHROAT p. 211
Geothlypis (Chamaethlypis) poliocephala
♂ Black face, yellow throat; no wingbars.
♀ Similar to ♂; eye-ring; see text.

FAN-TAILED WARBLER *Euthlypis lachrymosa* p. 214
White-tipped fan tail; yellow crown spot, tawny-orange breast.

YELLOW-CROWNED YELLOWTHROAT p. 210
Geothlypis flavovelata
♂ Similar to Peninsular Yellowthroat but much more yellow
across crown above mask. Ne. Mexico only.

PENINSULAR YELLOWTHROAT *Geothlypis beldingi* p. 210
♂ Differs from Common Yellowthroat by yellow over mask.
Baja California only.
♀ See text.

BLACK-POLLED YELLOWTHROAT *Geothlypis speciosa* p. 211
♂ No white or yellow band above mask. Black forehead blends
into dusky crown.

HOODED YELLOWTHROAT *Geothlypis nelsoni* p. 211
♂ Mask bordered above with grayish.

TROPICAL PARULA

CRESCENT-CHESTED WARBLER

GOLDEN-BROWED WARBLER

RUFOUS-CAPPED WARBLER

CHESTNUT-CAPPED WARBLER

GOLDEN-CROWNED WARBLER

GOLDEN WARBLER

♂ MANGROVE WARBLER

♀ GRAY-CROWNED YELLOWTHROAT

♂ FAN-TAILED WARBLER

♂ ♂ inset (above) YELLOW-CROWNED YELLOWTHROAT

♀ ♂ PENINSULAR YELLOWTHROAT

above right BLACK-POLLED YELLOWTHROAT
above left HOODED YELLOWTHROAT

Plate 39

OROPENDOLAS, CACIQUES, BLACKBIRDS, ETC.

CHESTNUT-HEADED (WAGLER'S) OROPENDOLA   p. 217
Zarhynchus wagleri
 Often seen around stockinglike nests of colonies.
 Yellow and black tail, black wings, pale yellowish-green bill.

MONTEZUMA OROPENDOLA   *Gymnostinops montezuma*   p. 217
 Yellow and black tail, chestnut back and wings, bicolored bill,
 pale cheek patches. Nest colonies similar to above.

GIANT COWBIRD   *Scaphidura oryzivora*   p. 218
 Often seen around oropendola colonies.
  ♂ Large size; swollen neck ruff, red eye.
  ♀ Smaller, duller; lacks ruff.
 Immature: Pale eye, flesh-yellow bill.

YELLOW-WINGED (MEXICAN) CACIQUE   p. 217
Cassiculus melanicterus
 Yellow patch on wings, rump, tail; crested.
  ♂ Black.
  ♀ Smoky brown.

MELODIOUS (SINGING) BLACKBIRD   *Dives dives*   p. 220
  ♂ All black, dark eye, dark bill.
  ♀ (not shown) Similar; smaller, duller.

YELLOW-BILLED CACIQUE   *Amblycercus holosericeus*   p. 218
 All black; pale greenish-yellow bill, yellow eye.

39

GIANT
COWBIRD
♀

CHESTNUT-
HEADED
OROPENDOLA

MONTEZUMA
OROPENDOLA

GIANT
COWBIRD

♂

imm.

YELLOW-WINGED
CACIQUE

♂

♀

MELODIOUS
BLACKBIRD

♂

YELLOW-BILLED
CACIQUE

Plate 40

ORIOLES

Orange or Yellow-backed Species
(see also Shrike-Tanager, Plate 42)

ORANGE ORIOLE *Icterus auratus*   p. 225
Orange back; some white in wing.
♀ (not shown) See text.

YELLOW-BACKED ORIOLE *Icterus chrysater*   p. 223
Deep yellow back; black forehead, no white in wing.

BLACK-HEADED ORIOLE *Icterus graduacauda*   p. 223
Combination of ragged black hood, dull olive-yellow back.

Black-headed, Black-backed Species

BAR-WINGED ORIOLE *Icterus maculialatus*   p. 222
♂ Similar to Scott's, but tail all black. White wingbars.
♀ (not shown) See text.

BLACK-VENTED (WAGLER'S) ORIOLE *Icterus wagleri*   p. 221
Adult: Orange and black; no wingbars; black crissum.
Immature: Orangish below; no strong wingbars; black breast patch.

BLACK-COWLED ORIOLE *Icterus prosthemelas*   p. 221
Adult: Similar to Scott's but no white in wings or yellow in tail.
Immature: Greenish with blackish wings (no bars); black throat.

SCOTT'S ORIOLE *Icterus parisorum*   p. 221
♂ Yellow and black; white wingbar, yellow tail patches (at base).
♀ Dull greenish; 2 white wingbars.
Immature: Similar to ♀, but with black throat.

BALTIMORE ORIOLE *Icterus galbula*   p. 224
♂ Orange and black; orange tail patches (at tip).
♀ More orange than in similar females; see text.

ORIOLES

40

ORANGE ♂

YELLOW-BACKED

♂

BAR-WINGED

BLACK-HEADED

immature
BLACK-VENTED

adult
BLACK-VENTED

immature
BLACK-COWLED

adult
BLACK-COWLED

♀

imm. ♂

SCOTT'S

SCOTT'S ♂

♀

BALTIMORE

♂

Plate 41

ORIOLES

Black-throated, Orange-cheeked Species

STREAK-BACKED ORIOLE *Icterus sclateri*   p. 225
  Striped back.

SPOT-BREASTED ORIOLE *Icterus pectoralis*   p. 223
  Spots on sides of breast.

YELLOW-TAILED ORIOLE *Icterus mesomelas*   p. 222
  Yellow outer tail feathers.

ALTAMIRA (BLACK-THROATED) ORIOLE *Icterus gularis* p. 224
  Large; single white wingbar.

HOODED ORIOLE *Icterus cucullatus*   p. 222
  ♂ Similar to above but smaller; 2 white wingbars.
  ♀ Dull orangish below, dusky above, 2 white wingbars.
  Immature ♂ Similar to ♀ but with black throat.

BULLOCK'S ORIOLE *Icterus bullockii*   p. 224
  ♂ Black crown, white wing patch.
  ♀ Dull orange breast, whitish belly.

BLACK-BACKED (ABEILLE'S) ORIOLE *Icterus abeillei* p. 225
  ♂ Similar to Bullock's, but cheeks and sides black.

Ochre or Chestnut Species

OCHRE (FUERTES') ORIOLE *Icterus fuertesi*   p. 221
  ♂ Similar to Orchard, but paler (ochre).

ORCHARD ORIOLE *Icterus spurius*   p. 220
  ♂ Rich chestnut and black.
  ♀ Dull greenish, 2 narrow wingbars.
  Immature ♂ Similar to ♀ but with black throat.

ORIOLES

41

SPOT-BREASTED

STREAK-BACKED

YELLOW-TAILED

ALTAMIRA

♀

imm. ♂
HOODED

HOODED

♂

BULLOCK'S

♂

BLACK-BACKED

♂

BULLOCK'S

♀

OCHRE

♂

ORCHARD

♀

imm. ♂

ORCHARD

♂

Plate 42

TANAGERS

YELLOW-THROATED EUPHONIA   p. 229
Euphonia hirundinacea [= *lauta*]
   ♂ Blue-black above; yellow forecrown, throat, and underbelly.
   ♀ Olive, lighter below; some white on throat, belly.

OLIVE-BACKED EUPHONIA *Euphonia gouldi*   p. 229
   ♂ Olive; yellow forehead, rufous belly.
   ♀ Olive; dull rufous forehead.

SCRUB EUPHONIA *Euphonia affinis*   p. 229
   ♂ Similar to Yellow-throated Euphonia, but throat blue-black.
   ♀ Olive, lightening to yellow on throat and belly.

GRAY-HEADED TANAGER *Eucometis penicillata*   p. 234
Gray head, olive back, yellow underbody.

BLACK-THROATED SHRIKE-TANAGER *Lanio aurantius* p. 234
   ♂ Black head, yellow back; hooked bill (see orioles).
   ♀ Similar to Gray-headed Tanager; note tawny rump (not visible here), hooked bill.

STRIPE-HEADED TANAGER *Spindalis zena*   p. 231
   ♂ Striped head; chestnut and yellow breast, patterned wings.
   ♀ Olive-brown with a hint of male's wing pattern.

COMMON BUSH-TANAGER *Chlorospingus opthalmicus* p. 235
Plain drab coloration; white stripe above and below ear patch.

42

YELLOW-THROATED
EUPHONIA

OLIVE-BACKED
EUPHONIA

SCRUB
EUPHONIA

GRAY-HEADED
TANAGER

BLACK-THROATED
SHRIKE-TANAGER

STRIPE-HEADED TANAGER

COMMON
BUSH-TANAGER

Plate 43

TANAGERS

ROSE-THROATED TANAGER   *Piranga roseogularis*   p. 232
   ♂ Rose-pink throat; red crown, wings, and tail.
   ♀ Olive; gray chest, yellow throat, buff belly.

WHITE-WINGED TANAGER   *Piranga leucoptera*   p. 233
   ♂ Scarlet; black wings with 2 white bars.
   ♀ Olive; dark wings with 2 white bars.

BLUE-CROWNED CHLOROPHONIA   p. 227
Chlorophonia occipitalis
   ♂ Parrot-green, yellow underbody.
   ♀ Similar, but less yellow.

RED-HEADED TANAGER   *Piranga erythrocephala*   p. 233
   ♂ Olive and yellow; red head.
   ♀ Olive, brightening to yellow on throat.

MASKED TANAGER   *Tangara larvata*   p. 230
   Black, with golden head, dark mask, blue rump.

BLUE-HOODED EUPHONIA   *Euphonia elegantissima*   p. 228
   ♂ Blue crown and nape, cinnamon underbody.
   ♀ Olive-green; blue crown, cinnamon throat.

BLUE-GRAY TANAGER   *Thraupis episcopus*   p. 230
   Blue-gray; brighter blue on wings and tail.

YELLOW-WINGED TANAGER   *Thraupis abbas*   p. 231
   Lavender-gray head; yellow wing patches.

ROSE-THROATED
TANAGER

WHITE-WINGED
TANAGER

♀

♂

RED-HEADED
TANAGER

♀

♂

BLUE-CROWNED
CHLOROPHONIA

♀

♂

MASKED
TANAGER

♀

♂

BLUE-HOODED
EUPHONIA

YELLOW-WINGED
TANAGER

BLUE-GRAY
TANAGER

Plate 44

TANAGERS

SCARLET-RUMPED TANAGER   *Ramphocelus passerinii*   p. 231
  ♂ Black; scarlet rump, blue beak.
  ♀ Dark olive-brown; bluish beak.

CRIMSON-COLLARED TANAGER   p. 231
Phlogothraupis sanguinolenta
  Crimson crown, collar, and rump.

STRIPE-BACKED (FLAME-COLORED) TANAGER   p. 232
Piranga bidentata
  ♂ Fire-red; striped back, 2 whitish wingbars.
  ♀ Yellow-olive; striped back, 2 white wingbars.

RED-THROATED ANT-TANAGER   *Habia fuscicauda*   p. 234
  ♂ Similar to next species but red throat brighter, red crown less
  conspicuous.
  ♀ Brown, pale throat; no crown patch.

RED-CROWNED ANT-TANAGER   *Habia rubica*   p. 233
  ♂ Dusky red; red crown patch outlined by blackish.
  ♀ Similar to preceding species but orangish crown patch.

ROSY THRUSH-TANAGER   *Rhodinocichla rosea*   p. 235
  ♂ Sooty; rose breast and eye stripe.
  ♀ Russet breast, whitish post-eye stripe.

44

CRIMSON-COLLARED
TANAGER

SCARLET-RUMPED
TANAGER

♀

♂

STRIPE-BACKED
TANAGER

♀

♂

RED-THROATED
ANT-TANAGER

♂

♀

RED-CROWNED
ANT-TANAGER

♂

ROSY
THRUSH-TANAGER

♀

♂

Plate 45

FINCHES

ROSE-BELLIED (ROSITA'S) BUNTING *Passerina rositae*   p. 240
   ♂ Bright blue; rose-red belly.
   ♀ Brown with buff belly; tinge of blue on rump, tail.

ORANGE-BREASTED BUNTING *Passerina leclancherii*   p. 240
   ♂ Blue and yellow; green crown, orange breast.
   ♀ Gray-green, yellowish below; wings and tail tinged blue, eye-ring yellow.

YELLOW-THROATED BRUSH-FINCH *Atlapetes gutturalis*   p. 245
Similar to next species but yellow confined to throat.

WHITE-NAPED BRUSH-FINCH *Atlapetes albinucha*   p. 244
White crown stripe, black face, all-yellow underparts.

RUFOUS-CAPPED BRUSH-FINCH *Atlapetes pileatus*   p. 244
Rufous crown, yellow underparts.

BLACK-CAPPED SISKIN *Spinus atriceps*   p. 259
   ♂ Dark greenish; black cap, yellow wing patch.
   ♀ (not shown) Duller, with a dusky cap.

BLACK-HEADED SISKIN *Spinus notatus*   p. 259
   ♂ Black hood, yellow wing and tail patches.
   ♀ (not shown) Duller.
Immature: Lacks hood.

GRASSLAND YELLOW-FINCH *Sicalis luteola*   p. 244
   ♂ Yellowish, heavily streaked above.
   ♀ Similar, but mainly buff-brown.

CRIMSON-COLLARED GROSBEAK   p. 237
Rhodothraupis celaeno
   ♀ Dull olive-green; black on head and chest.
   ♂ See Plate 46.

YELLOW GROSBEAK *Pheucticus chrysopeplus*   p. 238
   ♂ Golden yellow and black; large triangular bill.
   ♀ Duller, streaked; large triangular bill.

BLACK-FACED GROSBEAK *Caryothraustes poliogaster*   p. 237
Black face and throat, golden forehead and cheeks.

HOODED GROSBEAK *Hesperiphona abeillei*   p. 258
   ♂ Black head, large pale bill, black and white wings.
   ♀ Duller; has dark cap, lacks hood.

45

ROSE-
BELLIED
BUNTING

♂   ♀

ORANGE-
BREASTED
BUNTING

♂   ♀

BLACK-
CAPPED
SISKIN

♂

YELLOW-
THROATED
BRUSH-FINCH

RUFOUS-
CAPPED
BRUSH-FINCH

♂

WHITE-NAPED
BRUSH-FINCH

immature
BLACK-HEADED
SISKIN

GRASSLAND
YELLOW-FINCH

♂   ♀

♂
YELLOW
GROSBEAK

♀

♀
above
CRIMSON-
COLLARED
GROSBEAK

BLACK-
FACED
GROSBEAK

♂   ♀
HOODED
GROSBEAK

Plate 46

FINCHES

PYRRHULOXIA *Pyrrhuloxia sinuata*   p. 237
  ♂ Gray; red down front, red crest; stubby yellow bill.
  ♀ Gray-brown; reddish crest, yellow bill.

VARIED BUNTING *Passerina versicolor*   p. 240
  ♂ Dark; red patch on nape.
  ♀ See text.

CRIMSON-COLLARED GROSBEAK   p. 237
Rhodothraupis celaeno
  ♂ Black hood, dark crimson collar and underbody.
  ♀ See Plate 45.

BLUE-BLACK GROSBEAK *Cyanocompsa cyanoides*   p. 239
  ♂ Blue-black; large grosbeak bill.
  ♀ Ruddy brown; large black bill.

THICK-BILLED SEED-FINCH *Oryzoborus funereus*   p. 242
  ♂ Similar to Variable Seedeater; bill deeper at base.
  ♀ Ruddy brown; note bill contour.

BLUE-BLACK GRASSQUIT *Volatinia jacarina*   p. 243
  ♂ Glossy blue-black, bill sharp-pointed.
  ♀ Streaked underparts.

BLUE BUNTING *Cyanocompsa parellina*   p. 239
  ♂ Deep blue, brighter on forehead, rump.
  ♀ Warm brown, paler below.

VARIABLE (BLACK) SEEDEATER   p. 242
Sporophila aurita (corvina)
  ♂ Black; white wing spot, stubby rounded bill.
  ♀ Olive-brown; note bill contour.
  Both sexes have white wing linings.

YELLOW-FACED GRASSQUIT *Tiaris olivacea*   p. 241
  ♂ Orange-yellow throat and eyebrow; black chest.
  ♀ Dull olive; dull spectacles, dusky chest.

WHITE-COLLARED SEEDEATER *Sporophila torqueola*   p. 241
  ♂ Variable; broad white collar or half-collar, black head, black or black-splotched chest, stubby bill.
  ♀ Olive-brown, buffy below; buff eye-ring and wingbar.

RUDDY-BREASTED SEEDEATER *Sporophila minuta*   p. 242
  ♂ Gray; rufous rump and underparts, white wing spot.
  ♀ Olive-brown; buffy underbody, pale wingbar.

46

PYRRHULOXIA

VARIED
BUNTING

CRIMSON-
COLLARED
GROSBEAK

BLUE-BLACK
GROSBEAK

THICK-BILLED
SEED-FINCH

BLUE-BLACK
GRASSQUIT

BLUE
BUNTING

VARIABLE
SEEDEATER

YELLOW-FACED
GRASSQUIT

RUDDY-
BREASTED
SEEDEATER

WHITE-
COLLARED SEEDEATER

Plate 47

FINCHES

thus ..

✳

BLACK-HEADED SALTATOR   *Saltator atriceps*   p. 236
   Olive back; white throat completely surrounded by black.

GRAYISH SALTATOR   *Saltator coerulescens*   p. 236
   Slaty; white eyebrow stripe and throat; no chestband.

BUFF-THROATED SALTATOR   *Saltator maximus*   p. 236
   Olive back; buff throat, black chestband.

BLACK-CHESTED SPARROW   *Aimophila humeralis*   p. 251
   Black chest belt, rufous back, black and white mustache. See
   also Plate 48.

GREEN-STRIPED BRUSH-FINCH   *Atlapetes virenticeps*   p. 245
   Green and black crown stripes.

ORANGE-BILLED SPARROW   *Arremon aurantiirostris*   p. 246
   Orange bill, black and white face, black chestband.

OLIVE SPARROW   *Arremonops rufivirgatus*   p. 246
   Olive back, 2 dull brown stripes on crown.

GREEN-BACKED SPARROW   *Arremonops chloronotus*   p. 246
   Similar to Olive Sparrow; back greener, head stripes black.

CHESTNUT-CAPPED BRUSH-FINCH   p. 245
Atlapetes brunneinucha
   Chestnut crown, black mask, white throat. See Collared
   Towhee.

WHITE-EARED GROUND-SPARROW   *Melozone leucotis*   p. 249
   White ear spot, ochre-yellow head stripe, black breast blotch.

OLIVE-BACKED TOWHEE   p. 247
Pipilo erythrophthalmus macronyx
   Rufous sides, spotted olive back.

COLLARED TOWHEE   *Pipilo ocai*   p. 247
   Similar to Chestnut-capped Brush-Finch (above), but note
   broad black chestband; may have white eyebrow stripe (as
   shown), gray eyebrow stripe, or none.

HYBRID TOWHEE   *Pipilo ocai × maculatus*   p. 247
   Collared and Rufous-sided Towhee hybrid; see text.

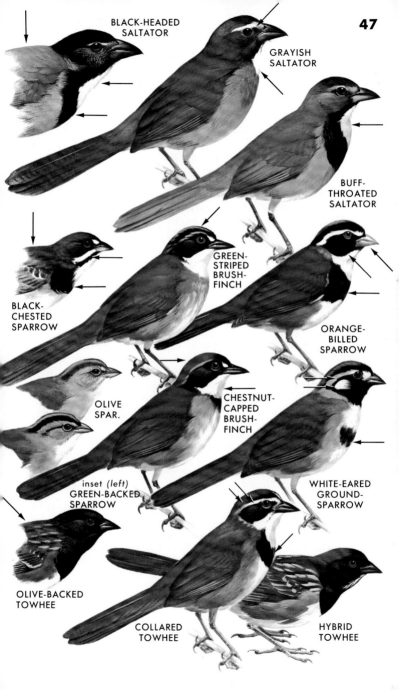

47

BLACK-HEADED SALTATOR

GRAYISH SALTATOR

BUFF-THROATED SALTATOR

BLACK-CHESTED SPARROW

GREEN-STRIPED BRUSH-FINCH

ORANGE-BILLED SPARROW

OLIVE SPAR.

CHESTNUT-CAPPED BRUSH-FINCH

WHITE-EARED GROUND-SPARROW

inset (left)
GREEN-BACKED SPARROW

OLIVE-BACKED TOWHEE

COLLARED TOWHEE

HYBRID TOWHEE

Plate 48

SPARROWS

BLACK-CHESTED SPARROW *Aimophila humeralis* p. 251
Rufous back, black chest belt, black and white mustache.

FIVE-STRIPED SPARROW *Aimophila quinquestriata* p. 250
5 throat stripes (3 white, 2 black); black breast spot.

RUSTY-CROWNED GROUND-SPARROW p. 248
Melozone kieneri
Rufous rear crown and nape; single breast spot.

WHITE-FACED GROUND-SPARROW p. 248
Melozone biarcuatum
Crescent-shaped ear patch on white face.

BRIDLED SPARROW *Aimophila mystacalis* p. 251
Dark; black throat, white mustache.

RUFOUS-COLLARED (ANDEAN) SPARROW p. 256
Zonotrichia capensis
Adult: Crest, rufous collar, black breast patches.
Immature: Streaked; note crest.

BOTTERI'S SPARROW *Aimophila botterii* p. 253
See text.

STRIPE-HEADED SPARROW *Aimophila ruficauda* p. 251
Black cheek patch, striped crown (white median stripe).

STRIPED SPARROW *Oriturus superciliosus* p. 249
Blackish cheek patch, all-black bill.

WORTHEN'S SPARROW *Spizella wortheni* p. 255
Like Field Sparrow; pink bill, eye-ring; rusty crown. See text.

CINNAMON-TAILED SPARROW *Aimophila sumichrasti* p. 252
2 short mustache stripes; tail light brown.

RUFOUS-WINGED SPARROW *Aimophila carpalis* p. 251
Small, pale; double mustache, reddish shoulder, pinkish bill,
light median crown stripe.

RUFOUS-CROWNED SPARROW *Aimophila ruficeps* p. 253
Solid rufous crown, black mustache.

RUSTY SPARROW *Aimophila rufescens* p. 252
2 rusty crown stripes, bold black mustache, all-black bill.

SIERRA MADRE SPARROW *Xenospiza baileyi* p. 250
Similar to Savannah Sparrow; lacks yellow on face. See text.

BROWN TOWHEE *Pipilo fuscus* p. 247
Brown; rusty cap, buff throat with short streaks.

WHITE-THROATED TOWHEE *Pipilo albicollis* p. 248
Similar to Brown Towhee; throat white bordered by dark
marks. Amounts of ochre in malar area variable.

YELLOW-EYED JUNCO *Junco phaeonotus* p. 257
Yellow eye, bicolored bill; white outer tail feathers.
a. *Mexican type:* Bright rusty back.
b. *Guatemalan type:* Dull brown back.

SPARROWS **48**

FIVE-STRIPED

WHITE-FACED GROUND-

BLACK-CHESTED

RUSTY-CROWNED GROUND-

BOTTERI'S

BRIDLED

imm.

adult RUFOUS-COLLARED

WORTHEN'S

STRIPE-HEADED

STRIPED

below RUSTY

CINNAMON-TAILED

SIERRA MADRE

RUFOUS-WINGED

RUFOUS-CROWNED

BROWN TOWHEE

b

a

left WHITE-THROATED TOWHEE

YELLOW-EYED JUNCO

Voice: A loud, emphatic whistled *choowee'oo,* sometimes *chee'oo* or *pee'a* or *whee'oo* (Eisenmann).
Range: S. Mexico to w. Ecuador. **Mexico:** Gulf lowlands; s. Veracruz, Tabasco, n. Oaxaca, n. Chiapas. **Habitat:** Humid forests.

CINNAMON BECARD   Pl. 26
Pachyramphus cinnamomeus 5½–6
Field marks: By far the smallest and stoutest of the rufous cotingids. Rufous crown *darker* than back; throat *pale,* almost whitish; a dark line between eye and bill and buff line above it. Sexes alike.
Similar species: Rufous Mourner of forest interior is larger, has rufous (not whitish) throat, lacks head contrast.
Voice: Song, a loud whistled trill, *tee-dee-dee-dee-dee-dee-dee.* Call, *tew-dee-dee* (Eisenmann).
Range: Se. Mexico to w. Ecuador. **Mexico:** Gulf lowlands of Tabasco, n. Oaxaca, n. Chiapas. **Habitat:** Humid forest borders, shade trees, plantations, roadside trees.

WHITE-WINGED BECARD   Pl. 26
Pachyramphus polychopterus 5–6
Field marks: *Male:* Black above, *dark gray* below and on rump. White on scapulars forms a broad *white stripe* on each side of black back. 2 white wingbars. *Female:* Dull olive, paler below; note 2 *buff wingbars.* Tail buff-tipped.
Similar species: ♂ Gray-collared Becard has light gray collar and much paler underparts. Females totally different.
Voice: Song, 6 or 7 quick liquid notes, each higher and weaker; sometimes at same pitch (Chalif). A rhythmic tittering series, *teet-teet-teet-teet-teet-teet* (Eisenmann).
Range: B. Honduras, Guatemala (Caribbean lowlands) to Paraguay, Uruguay. Not in Mexico. **Habitat:** Light woodlands, forest borders, plantations.

GRAY-COLLARED BECARD   Pl. 26
Pachyramphus major 5½–6
Field marks: *Male:* The *gray collar* that joins the gray underparts identifies this becard. Cap and back *black;* wings and tail strongly patterned with black and white. *Female:* Cinnamon above with a *blackish cap, buff collar.* Underparts dull buff-whitish; wings and tail strongly patterned with rufous and black.
Similar species: (1) ♂ White-winged Becard (a lowland bird of Guatemala) is darker below, lacks collar. (2) ♀ Rose-throated Becard is similar to this ♀ but lacks strong pattern of black in tail.
Voice: Song, a sweet repetitious, 2- or 3-note whistle, *sir-piti, sir-piti,* etc., with rising inflection (RTP).

Range: Mexico to e. Nicaragua. **Mexico:** Lowlands, foothills, mts. (to 8000 ft.). In west, from Sinaloa south; in east, from Nuevo León, Tamaulipas south to Oaxaca, Chiapas and east through Yucatán Pen. **Habitat:** Open deciduous woodlands; in mts., pine and oak woodlands, cloud forest.

ROSE-THROATED BECARD   Pl. 26
Platypsaris aglaiae   6–6½
Field marks: A big-headed, thick-billed bird, somewhat resembling a flycatcher. *Male:* Dark gray above, pale to dusky below, with a *blackish cap and cheeks* and *rose-colored throat* (some southern birds may show little or no red on throat). *Female:* Brown above with a *dark* cap, usually with a *buffy collar* around nape. Underparts washed with buff.
Similar species: ♀ Gray-collared Becard is similar to this ♀ but wings and tail show more contrast in pattern.
Voice: A thin 2-syllabled whistle, *swee-at* (Chalif).
Range: U.S. border of Arizona, Texas to n. Costa Rica. **Mexico:** Widespread except Baja California; sea level to 6000 ft.
Habitat: Wooded canyons, river groves, open woods, forest edges.

MASKED TITYRA   *Tityra semifasciata*   7½–8   Pl. 26
Field marks: *Male:* Stocky; pale gray with black wings, black forehead and *face mask* enclosing a *bare red eye patch.* Bill heavy, *bicolored* (red with black tip). Tail with broad black band. *Female:* Back, cheeks, and crown brown.
Similar species: ♂ Black-crowned Tityra is smaller, lacks black on cheeks and red around eye; bill all black. ♀ has rufous cheeks, black crown; bill all black.
Voice: Grunting notes. A dry *quert-quert* (Sutton). A nasal *quet, quet, quet,* varied to *quit, quit, quit* (Eisenmann).
Range: Mexico to Bolivia. **Mexico:** Pacific slope from Sonora south; Gulf slope from Tamaulipas south, including Yucatán Pen. **Habitat:** Dead treetops, forest and woodland borders, clearings, plantations.

BLACK-CROWNED TITYRA   Pl. 26
Tityra inquisitor   7–7½
Field marks: The black crown is the most obvious difference between this tityra and the last. Bill all black. *Female:* Crown black; rufous on sides of back. Bill all black.
Similar species: See Masked Tityra (preceding).
Voice: Call, a soft rattle; also a nasal *wuz wuz* or *swaz-waz* (Chalif). Notes less grunty than last species.
Range: E. Mexico to Paraguay, ne. Argentina. **Mexico:** Gulf slope from e. San Luis Potosí, Veracruz south to n. Oaxaca, n. Chiapas and east through Yucatán Pen. **Habitat:** Humid forests in lowlands to cloud forest, treetops, dead trees.

Tyrant Flycatchers: Tyrannidae

FLYCATCHERS usually perch quietly upright on exposed branches and sally forth to snap up passing insects. Bill rather flattened, with bristles at base in most species. Song not well developed, but many species have "dawn songs," seldom given at other times of day. **Food:** Mainly flying insects. In tropics many eat fruit, some small reptiles, etc. **Range:** New World; majority in tropics. **No. of species:** World, 365; Mexico, 63 (+1 accidental and 1 in Guatemala).

EASTERN PHOEBE   *Sayornis phoebe*   See E, W, or T
   Memo: No strong wingbars, no eye-ring; wags tail.
   Range: S. Canada, U.S., east of Rockies. Winters to e. Mexico.
   Mexico: Winters mainly cen. and e. Mexico south to Oaxaca, Veracruz; accidental Baja California, Quintana Roo.

BLACK PHOEBE   *Sayornis nigricans*   See W or T
   Memo: Only black-breasted flycatcher; belly white.
   Range: Resident sw. U.S. to Bolivia, n. Argentina. **Mexico:** Resident Baja California, w., cen., and s. Mexico; not on Gulf slope; favors rapid, rocky rivers.

SAY'S PHOEBE   *Sayornis saya*   See W or T
   Memo: Pale rusty underparts, black tail.
   Range: N.-cen. Alaska, nw. Canada, U.S. to s.-cen. Mexico.
   Mexico: Breeds in Baja California; also n. and cen. Mexico from Sonora east to San Luis Potosí and south to Oaxaca. Winters south to s. Baja California, Chiapas.

VERMILION FLYCATCHER   Pl. 29
Pyrocephalus rubinus   5–6
   Field marks: *Male:* Crown, underparts, vermilion; upperparts, ear patch, tail dusky brown to blackish. *Female and immature:* Gray-brown above, whitish below, narrowly streaked; lower underparts washed with pink or yellow.
   Similar species: Say's Phoebe might be confused with ♀.
   Voice: A slightly phoebelike *p-p-pit-zee* or *pit-a-zee;* elaborated during male's butterflylike hovering display flight (RTP).
   Range: Sw. U.S. to Argentina. **Mexico:** Semi-arid or arid country nearly throughout. **Habitat:** Near water in desert country; mesquite, willows, cottonwoods, open woods, lowland pine areas, open savannas, scrub.

SCISSOR-TAILED FLYCATCHER   See E, W, or T
Muscivora forficata
   Memo: Very long forked (mostly white) tail, pale head.

Range: S.-cen. U.S. Winters to cen. Panamá. **Mexico:** Transient mainly in eastern and southern sections. Winters in south.

FORK-TAILED FLYCATCHER Pl. 29
Muscivora tyrannus [= *Tyrannus savana*] ♂ 13–16, ♀ 10–12
Field marks: *Adult:* Note the *black cap* and long, flexible, *black scissorlike tail* (to 10 in.). A concealed yellow crown spot. Underparts immaculate white. *Immature:* May lack long tail (only slight fork) and yellow crown spot.
Similar species: Scissor-tailed Flycatcher lacks black on head, has a largely white tail.
Voice: A pebbly *krrrrrr;* a metallic *zlit;* a clicking sound produced by bill (Chalif).
Range: Se. Mexico to Patagonia. Northernmost and southernmost populations migratory. **Mexico:** Lowlands of Veracruz, Tabasco, n. Oaxaca, n. Chiapas, base of Yucatán Pen. **Habitat:** Savannas, semi-arid country, open brush, marshes.

EASTERN KINGBIRD *Tyrannus tyrannus* See E, W, or T
Memo: White band at tip of tail; white underparts.
Range: Cen. Canada to Gulf of Mexico. Winters Honduras to Bolivia. **Mexico:** Migrant through eastern and southern sections, including Yucatán Pen.

CASSIN'S KINGBIRD *Tyrannus vociferans* 8–9 Pl. 27
Field marks: Similar to Tropical Kingbird but darker, with a *darker gray breast;* tail *not notched,* may have a pale tip.
Similar species: See (1) Tropical Kingbird (p. 142) and (2) Western Kingbird (paler on breast, white sides on tail).
Voice: A low nasal *queer* or *chi-queer* or *ki-dear;* also an excited *ki-ki-ki-dear, ki-dear, ki-dear,* etc. (RTP).
Range: W. U.S., w. and cen. Mexico. Winters to Guatemala. **Mexico:** Breeds from n. Baja California east to Nuevo León and south to Michoacán and Guanajuato. Winters widely (east to cen. Tamaulipas and south to Chiapas). **Habitat:** Semi-open high country, scattered trees, pine-oak mts., ranch groves.

WESTERN KINGBIRD *Tyrannus verticalis* 8–9 Pl. 27
Field marks: Similar to Tropical Kingbird but paler on back and breast; tail not notched, *black with narrow white sides.*
Similar species: (1) Tropical Kingbird (notched brown tail). (2) Cassin's Kingbird (dark breast, lacks white tail sides).
Voice: Shrill bickering calls; a sharp *whit* or *whit-ker-whit* (RTP).
Range: Sw. Canada, w. and n.-cen. U.S., n. Mexico. Winters to Costa Rica. **Mexico:** Breeds n. Baja California, Sonora, Chi-

huahua. Migrant through western sections, wintering southward. **Habitat:** Open country with scattered trees, farms, roadsides.

TROPICAL KINGBIRD   Pl. 27
Tyrannus melancholicus 8–9
Field marks: The most widespread kingbird in the American
tropics; olive-backed, yellow-bellied, with a gray head and black
"domino" through the eyes. Note the well-notched brown to
dusky tail, a mark of distinction from similar kingbirds.
Technical note: The race *couchii,* of the Gulf slope from s.
Texas to n. Puebla, Veracruz, etc., has strikingly different vocal-
ization (*fide* L. Irby Davis and W. J. Smith) and may prove to
be specifically distinct.
Similar species: See above (1) Cassin's Kingbird and (2)
Western Kingbird. (3) The *Myiarchus* group of flycatchers
shown on Plate 27 have rufous tails.
Voice: *T. m. couchii,* a high nasal, slurred *queer* or *chi-queer* or
preer, resembling notes of Cassin's Kingbird but higher. Also
preer-tiwichew (RTP). A long-drawn *gereeeeeeer,* suggesting a
distant Pauraque (Kincaid). Voice of the more widespread Cen.
American form *(T. m. chloronotis)* is a high-pitched, rapid twittering *piriireeree;* also a loud clear *seet-teet-teet* (Eisenmann).
Range: S. Arizona, s. Texas to cen. Argentina. **Mexico:** Pacific
slope from Sonora south; Gulf slope from Tamaulipas south,
including Yucatán Pen. **Habitat:** River groves, scattered trees,
plantations, roadsides, towns.

THICK-BILLED KINGBIRD   Pl. 27
Tyrannus crassirostris 9
Field marks: Differs from similar Mexican kingbirds (Cas-
sin's, Western, Tropical) by its largely whitish underparts.
Throat white, breast grayish white, belly pale yellow (sometimes
almost white). Tail gray-brown.
Similar species: Large bill, bull-headed look suggest Gray
Kingbird of W. Indies (accidental off Yucatán Pen.).
Voice: *Brrr-zee* or *purr-eet* (Zimmerman).
Range: Mainly w. Mexico; local se. Arizona, sw. New Mexico.
Winters to Guatemala. **Mexico:** Pacific slope from n. Sonora
south at least to Guerrero; some winter farther south. **Habitat:**
Lowlands, foothills, semi-arid canyons.

GRAY KINGBIRD   *Tyrannus dominicensis*   See E
Memo: Gray above, white below; large bill, notched tail.
Range: S. Florida, W. Indies, Venezuela (?). Winters to Pan-
amá, n. S. America. **Mexico:** Casual off Yucatán Pen. (Cozumel
I. and Isla Cancum).

GIANT KINGBIRD   *Tyrannus cubensis*   10¼   **Not. illus.**
Field marks: Resembles Gray Kingbird (white below) but
much darker and browner above; crown dark sooty brown, back
gray-brown; bill very heavy.
Range: Cuba, Isle of Pines, Inagua I., Caicos Is. **Mexico:** Accidental; an old record on Mujeres I. off Quintana Roo.

PIRATIC FLYCATCHER   **Pl. 27**
Legatus leucophaius   5¾-6½
    Field marks: *Smallest* of the 3 similar striped flycatchers. Eye-
brow stripe and throat clean white. Differs from its larger look-
alikes in having a *stubby* black bill, *no streaks on back,* and
virtually *no rufous* in tail. Called Piratic because it takes over
nests of orioles, caciques, becards, etc.
    Similar species: (1) Sulphur-bellied and (2) Streaked Fly-
catchers are larger, with longer bills, bright rufous tails, and
streaked backs.
    Voice: A rising and falling *swee-el,* followed by *dididi* on level
pitch (Chalif). A partly trilled, complaining *wee'-yee* with an
added *piririree* (Eisenmann).
    Range: Se. Mexico to n. Argentina. **Mexico:** Gulf lowlands; e.
San Luis Potosí, s. Veracruz, Puebla, n. Oaxaca, Tabasco, n.
Chiapas; rarely Quintana Roo. **Habitat:** Humid lowlands,
plantations, open woods, river edges, exposed treetops.

SULPHUR-BELLIED FLYCATCHER   **Pl. 27**
Myiodynastes luteiventris   7½-8½
    Field marks: A large flycatcher with a bright rufous tail, dark
eye patch, and *white* stripe above it; dark mustache; underparts
yellowish with dark streaks. Among flycatchers only this species and Streaked Flycatcher are streaked *above and below.*
    Similar species: (1) Streaked Flycatcher has yellowish (not
white) eyebrow stripe and *whitish* underparts (with yellow
tinge); lacks dusky chin. (2) See Piratic Flycatcher (preceding).
    Voice: A high penetrating *kee-zee'-ik! kee-zee'-ik* given by
both ♂ and ♀, often in duet (Sutton).
    Range: Se. Arizona to Costa Rica. Winters in Peru, Bolivia.
Mexico: Summer resident from e. Sonora, Chihuahua, Nuevo
León, cen. Tamaulipas south, including Yucatán Pen. **Habitat:**
Sycamores in canyons, open woods and borders, plantations.

STREAKED FLYCATCHER   **Pl. 27**
Myiodynastes maculatus   8-8½
    Field marks: Very similar to Sulphur-bellied Flycatcher, but
note the *yellowish* (not white) eye stripe, and *whitish* underparts
with only a very light yellowish tinge. See **Voice.**
    Similar species: See Sulphur-bellied Flycatcher (preceding).
    Voice: *Sip sip sip seeyf* (rising on *seeyf*); *bap-bap-bap-bap,*

ending with *seeyf* (Chalif). A semiwhistled *chee'oo-reweep* or *wee'-a-roweep* often introduced by a *chup* (Eisenmann).

Range: Se. Mexico to Bolivia, n. Argentina. **Mexico:** Summer resident; Gulf slope from s. Tamaulipas, e. San Luis Potosí south through Veracruz, Puebla, n. Oaxaca, n. Chiapas and east through Tabasco and Yucatán Pen. **Habitat:** Open woodlands, plantations, second growth, edges.

BOAT-BILLED FLYCATCHER   Pl. 27
Megarynchus pitangua   8½–9½

Field marks: Superficially very similar to Great Kiskadee but note the *very wide,* thick bill (most evident from above or below). Wings and tail mostly *dull gray-brown* (not bright rufous). Yellow crown patch more restricted (often concealed).

Similar species: See Great Kiskadee (below).

Voice: A rough, rasping *khrrrrr;* also a loud repeated *chirrup,* suggestive of House Sparrow (RTP). *Kee'rrrrik,* vaguely suggesting Belted Kingfisher's rattle (Eisenmann).

Range: Mexico to Bolivia, Paraguay, Brazil. **Mexico:** Pacific slope from s. Sinaloa south; Gulf slope from s. Tamaulipas, e. San Luis Potosí through Yucatán Pen. **Habitat:** Sea level to 6000 ft.; high second growth, forest edges, plantations.

SOCIAL (VERMILION-CROWNED) FLYCATCHER   Pl. 27
Myiozetetes similis   7

Field marks: A *small* version of the Boat-billed Flycatcher; very similar in plumage but with a proportionately *much smaller bill.* Concealed crown patch vermilion, not yellow.

Similar species: (1) Boat-billed Flycatcher and (2) Great Kiskadee are much larger, with longer bills.

Voice: An excited *chee' cheechee' cheechee' cheechee'* (Slud). A loud harsh *kree'yoo;* also a rapid explosive *kee'yoo-kyi-kyi-kyi-kyi-kee* (Eisenmann).

Range: Mexico to Paraguay, ne. Argentina. **Mexico:** Pacific slope from s. Sonora south; Atlantic slope from s. Tamaulipas through Yucatán Pen. **Habitat:** Trees near water, open woods, semi-open land, plantations.

GREAT KISKADEE (KISKADEE FLYCATCHER)   Pl. 27
Pitangus sulphuratus   9–10

Field marks: A very large bull-headed flycatcher, suggesting a kingfisher (may even catch small fish). Bright yellow underparts and strikingly patterned black and white head distinguish it from all but Boat-billed and Social Flycatchers. Note *bright rufous* in wings and tail, absent in those species. Yellow crown spot more noticeable than in Boat-bill.

Similar species: (1) Boat-billed and (2) Social Flycatchers.

Voice: A loud *kis-ka-deer* or *ki-deer;* also *dzhee* or *queee*

(RTP). *Geep career, geep, geep career* (Sutton and Pettingill).
Range: S. Texas to Argentina. **Mexico:** Pacific slope from s.
Sonora south; Gulf slope from Río Grande south and east, including Yucatán Pen. **Habitat:** Sea level to 6000 ft.; semi-open
areas, streamside thickets, orchards, groves, woodland borders,
plantations, towns.

GREAT-CRESTED FLYCATCHER   Pl. 27
Myiarchus crinitus 8–9
    Field marks: This large rusty-tailed, yellow-bellied flycatcher
of e. and cen. N. America winters in Mexico and is very difficult
to separate from the similarly sized resident *Myiarchus,* the
Brown-crested Flycatcher, except by voice (but likely to be si-
lent), hence we treat it in full here. Subtle distinctions are: (1)
brown (not blackish) lower mandible; (2) more abrupt separation on underparts of gray (darker) and yellow (brighter); (3)
more extensive cinnamon on inner webs of tail feathers (see No.
11, Plate 27); (4) back slightly more greenish; (5) in hand, mouth
lining orange.
    Similar species: See Brown-crested Flycatcher (below).
    Voice: A loud whistled *wheeeep!* (rising inflection); a rolling
prrrrret! (RTP). Also *whoit-whoit-whoit* (Bent).
    Range: S. Canada to Gulf states. Winters e. Mexico to Colom-
bia. **Mexico:** Migrant and winter visitor in eastern and southern sections; rare Yucatán Pen. **Habitat:** Forests, plantations.

ASH-THROATED FLYCATCHER   Pl. 27
Myiarchus cinerascens 7½–8½
    Field marks: A medium-sized flycatcher typical of the rufous-
tailed *Myiarchus* group. Smaller than Brown-crested Flycatcher; throat whiter, yellow on belly very pale, back grayer,
less olive. In hand, mouth lining flesh color. These are subtle
distinctions; voice is a better clue.
    Similar species: See (1) Brown-crested Flycatcher (below)
and (2) Nutting's Flycatcher (next).
    Voice: *Pwit;* also a rolling *chi-beer* or *prit-wherr* (RTP). *Ka-
brick;* also *ha-whip* and *ha-wheer* (Lanyon).
    Range: W. U.S. to cen. Mexico. Winters to Costa Rica. **Mex-
ico:** Mainly arid country of Baja California and northern
states; breeds south in uplands locally to Guerrero, Morelos.
Winters widely to s. Mexico except Yucatán Pen. **Habitat:**
Semi-arid country, deserts, brush, mesquite, open woods.

NUTTING'S (PALE-THROATED) FLYCATCHER   Pl. 27
Myiarchus nuttingi 7
    Field marks: Very very similar to Ash-throated Flycatcher; a
shade smaller and a bit browner above. Perhaps not separable

in the field except by voice and breeding range. According to W. E. Lanyon the interior of the mouth is *orange* and the tail feathers usually have a broader dark shaft streak, seldom spreading into a dark tip.

Similar species: (1) See Ash-throated Flycatcher (preceding), which winters in range of this species. (2) Dusky-capped Flycatcher (below) has little or no rufous in tail.

Voice: A clear, penetrating, whistled *peer;* suggests voice of Dusky-capped Flycatcher, but higher, less plaintive.

Range: W. Mexico to w. Costa Rica. **Mexico:** Pacific slope from s. Sonora, s. Chihuahua south. **Habitat:** Semi-arid wooded slopes to about 5000 ft.

BROWN-CRESTED (WIED'S) FLYCATCHER Pl. 27
Myiarchus tyrannulus 9

Field marks: A kingbird-sized flycatcher with *cinnamon-rufous wings and tail,* pale gray throat and breast, pale yellow belly. Raises slight bushy brownish crest when excited. Paler below than Great-crested Flycatcher (a migrant).

Technical note: In hand, mouth lining pale ochre-buff; inner webs of tail feathers (except middle pair) always with a well-defined broad dusky shaft streak (Lanyon).

Similar species: See (1) Great-crested Flycatcher (above) and (2) Ash-throated Flycatcher (smaller, throat whiter, yellow paler).

Voice: A sharp *whit,* a short *prrrr,* and a rolling throaty *purreer.* Voice stronger than Ash-throated Flycatcher's (RTP).

Range: Sw. U.S. to n. Argentina. **Mexico:** In west, from Sonora, Chihuahua south; not in Baja California. In east, from Río Grande Valley south and east, including Yucatán Pen. Migrant in north. **Habitat:** Woodland clearings, second growth, river groves, plantations, dry country, saguaros.

YUCATAN FLYCATCHER Pl. 27
Myiarchus yucatanensis 7

Field marks: One of 2 small *Myiarchus* flycatchers of Yucatán, differing from its congener the Dusky-capped Flycatcher in having some rufous on inner webs of tail (not always easy to see and not a field mark); mouth lining orange. Voices are distinctive (see below).

Similar species: (1) Dusky-capped Flycatcher (Yucatán population) has *no rufous* in tail (except in immatures). (2) Brown-crested Flycatcher is much larger.

Voice: Call, a long whistled *wheeeeee* rising in pitch; also a shorter call rising, then dropping (Lanyon).

Range: Confined to Yucatán Pen. (incl. Campeche, Yucatán, Quintana Roo), B. Honduras, and n. Petén in Guatemala. **Habitat:** Woodlands.

DUSKY-CAPPED (OLIVACEOUS) FLYCATCHER   Pl. 27
Myiarchus tuberculifer   6–7

Field marks: Of the same type as the Ash-throated Fly-catcher, but considerably smaller, very little rufous in the tail (none in Yucatán population except in immatures); more deeply colored below, yellower on abdomen; grayish instead of white throat. In hand, mouth lining is flesh or ocher-buff. Voice is best field character.

Similar species: See (1) Ash-throated Flycatcher; in west see also (2) Nutting's Flycatcher and (3) Flammulated Flycatcher; in Yucatán see (4) Yucatán Flycatcher.

Voice: A mournful whistle, slurring down, *peeur* (RTP). A whistled *wheeew* and *wheeeep,* sometimes slurred (Eisenmann).

Range: Se. Arizona, sw. Texas to nw. Argentina. **Mexico:** Nearly countrywide except Baja California and northeastern corner. **Habitat:** Open woods, edges, scrubby slopes, pine-oak canyons, junipers, plantations; sea level to 8000 ft. in mts.

FLAMMULATED FLYCATCHER   Pl. 27
Deltarhynchus flammulatus   6

Field marks: This small flycatcher resembles a small *Myiarchus* (see preceding group). Note the *indistinct whitish streaking* on pale gray breast.

Similar species: See Dusky-capped Flycatcher (above).

Voice: Plaintive, suggesting Dusky-capped Flycatcher. Also a low bubbling or rolling *prrrreep.*

Range: Sw. and s. Mexico only; Pacific slope from Sinaloa to Chiapas. **Habitat:** Dry woods, scrub, semi-arid country.

OLIVE-SIDED FLYCATCHER   See E, W, or T
Contopus (Nuttallornis) borealis

Memo: Dark "vest," unbuttoned down front; white side tufts.

Range: Alaska, Canada, w. and ne. U.S., nw. Mexico. Winters Costa Rica to Peru. **Mexico:** Breeds in mts. of n. Baja California. Transient elsewhere except Yucatán Pen.

EASTERN WOOD-PEWEE   See E, W, or T
Contopus virens

Memo: 2 white wingbars, no eye-ring; lighter on breast than in next species. Plaintive song, *(pee-ur* and *pee-a-wee).*

Range: S. Canada, e. and cen. U.S. Winters Nicaragua to Peru. **Mexico:** Migrant through eastern and southern sections including Yucatán Pen. Often calls on migration.

WESTERN WOOD-PEWEE   See W or T
Contopus sordidulus

Memo: 2 white wingbars, no eye-ring; dark breast and sides. Nasal song *(peeyee* or *peeeer).*

Range: Breeds from cen. Alaska, w. Canada south to Costa Rica. Winters Panamá to Peru. **Mexico:** Breeds in mts. of Baja California and locally in highlands from northern states south to Chiapas. Widespread in migration except Yucatán Pen.

TROPICAL PEWEE *Contopus cinereus* 5–5½ **Pl. 28**
Field marks: During migration when the Eastern Wood-Pewee is present, this very similar species can only be separated in the field by its song (at other seasons it is the only pewee in its range). Closely resembles Eastern Wood-Pewee (wingbars, no eye-ring) but smaller, darker on crown.
Technical note: In the hand, 10th primary is shorter than 6th (about length of 5th). In other 2 wood-pewees, 10th is distinctly longer.
Similar species: (1) Eastern Wood-Pewee whistles a clear, drawling *pee-a-wee* (slurring down, then up); also *pee-wee'* and a downward slurred *pee-ur*. (2) Western Wood-Pewee has darker breast and sides; sings a nasal, burry *peeyee*.
Voice: A burred or slightly trilled *preeee;* a repeated *swee'rrip;* a *wheerrt* or *prrreet* (Eisenmann).
Range: Se. Mexico to Bolivia, Paraguay, n. Argentina. **Mexico:** Mainly lowlands from s. Veracruz, e. Oaxaca south and east to Chiapas, Yucatán Pen. **Habitat:** Open woodlands, plantations, clearings with scattered trees.

GREATER PEWEE (COUES' FLYCATCHER) **See W**
Contopus pertinax 7½
Memo: Similar to Olive-sided Flycatcher; more uniform gray, grayer throat. Song, a thin plaintive whistle, *ho-say, re-ah* or *ho-say, ma-re-ah* ("José María").
Range: Cen. and se. Arizona, sw. New Mexico south to Nicaragua. **Mexico:** Wooded highlands (3000–11,000 ft.) from n. Sonora, nw. Chihuahua, s. Coahuila, cen. Nuevo León, cen. Tamaulipas south. Winters to sea level. **Habitat:** Pine and pine-oak forests of mts., wooded canyons.

TUFTED FLYCATCHER *Mitrephanes phaeocercus* 5 **Pl. 28**
Field marks: The tufted *crest* and rich *cinnamon-brown underparts* identify this small mountain flycatcher. Wingbars buff; cheeks and eye-ring cinnamon.
Similar species: (1) Buff-breasted Flycatcher is paler, has no crest. (2) Belted Flycatcher has whitish throat, cinnamon belt.
Voice: *Che che che che tse tse tse tse* (Chalif). A fast piping *peepeepeepeepeepeepee* (Eisenmann), and a plaintive, rapidly given *turee-turee* (Parker).
Range: Nw. Mexico to Andes of Peru, Bolivia. **Mexico:** Highlands of w. and s. Mexico from ne. Sonora, Chihuahua south to Chiapas. Also locally in eastern mts. and south-central plateau

from sw. Tamaulipas to w.-cen. Veracruz, Oaxaca. **Habitat:** Pine-oak forests, cloud forest; usually perches fairly low.

YELLOW-BELLIED FLYCATCHER See E, W, or T
Empidonax flaviventris
Memo: Greenish above; yellowish underparts (incl. throat). Voice, a spiritless, rising *chur-wee.*
Range: Canada, ne. U.S. Winters to Panamá. **Mexico:** Migrant and winter visitor in eastern sections, except Yucatán Pen.

ACADIAN FLYCATCHER *Empidonax virescens* See E or T
Memo: Throat as well as abdomen may be yellow in fall and winter but color clearer than that of Yellow-bellied. Voice, a rising *spit-chee!* or a thin *peet.*
Range: E. U.S. Winters Costa Rica to Ecuador. **Mexico:** Transient through eastern and southern sections except Yucatán Pen. Recorded B. Honduras.

WILLOW (TRAILL'S) FLYCATCHER See E, W, or T
Empidonax traillii
Memo: Not recognizable in field except by voice, a sneezy *fitz-bew;* may call in winter.
Range: Alaska, Canada, to se. and e.-cen. U.S. Winters s. Mexico to Argentina. **Mexico:** Possibly breeds n. Baja California. Migrant and winter visitor, mainly lowlands, semi-open country, river woods, except Yucatán Pen.

ALDER FLYCATCHER *Empidonax alnorum*
Memo: This and Willow Flycatcher (preceding) were formerly regarded as conspecific. Not separable in field except by voice; this secies sings *zwee-bee'-o* or *fee-bee'-o.*
Range: Relative status of this and Willow Flycatcher still to be determined in Mexico.

WHITE-THROATED FLYCATCHER Pl. 28
Empidonax albigularis 4¾-5
Field marks: A small dull-brown *Empidonax* showing considerable contrast between white throat and dusky chest. Eye-ring and wingbars buff. Readily identified only in nesting season when northern migrants of similar species are not present.
Technical note: In hand, underwing coverts and thighs are buffy brown; 10th (outer) primary usually shorter than 5th, equal to 4th; 6th primary may be slightly emarginate (narrowed on outer web).
Similar species: (1) Willow Flycatcher and other migrant empidonaces from north may make identification inconclusive except in summer, when they are not present. See also (2) Pine Flycatcher (larger, less white on throat), below.

Voice: A sharp *buzzt* (Marshall). Song, an explosive, but not loud, *pseeyp* or *kzeeyip* (Eisenmann).
Range: Mexico to w. Panamá. **Mexico:** Mainly mts.; in west from s. Chihuahua south; in east from San Luis Potosí south. In winter to sea level. **Habitat:** Mainly highlands (3000–11,500 ft.); brush, semi-open growth, pastures, fields with scattered shrubs and small trees.

LEAST FLYCATCHER
Empidonax minimus
See E, W, or T

Memo: Gray; white eye-ring, 2 wingbars. Voice, *che-bek'*.
Range: Canada, east of Rockies; n.-cen. and ne. U.S. Winters Mexico to Panamá. **Mexico:** Migrant and winter visitor mainly in east and south, Yucatán Pen. and south-central plateau.

HAMMOND'S FLYCATCHER
Empidonax hammondi
See W or T

Memo: Certain field recognition almost impossible in winter.
Range: Breeds se. Alaska, w. Canada, w. U.S. Winters to Nicaragua; also Peru. **Mexico:** Migrant and winter visitor to highlands (both west and east) and central plateau.

DUSKY (formerly WRIGHT'S) FLYCATCHER
*Empidonax oberholseri (*formerly *wrightii)*
See W or T

Memo: Certain field recognition almost impossible in winter.
Range: Breeds se. Alaska, w. Canada, w. U.S. Winters in Mexico. **Mexico:** Transient and winter visitor in mts., plateaus (east and west) south to Chiapas.

GRAY FLYCATCHER
Empidonax wrightii (griseus)
See W or T

Memo: Back gray; no yellow below; lower mandible *flesh.*
Range: Breeds w. U.S. Winters mainly Mexico. **Mexico:** Winters Baja California; and from Sonora, cen. Chihuahua, s. Coahuila, Tamaulipas to s.-cen. Mexico.

PINE FLYCATCHER *Empidonax affinis* 5–5½ **Pl. 28**
Field marks: A small variable *Empidonax* flycatcher, very similar to the Dusky Flycatcher, which breeds in w. U.S., and probably not distinguished with certainty in the field from that and other similar species except during nesting season (the only one in pine-oak forests in summer).
Similar species: (1) Dusky and (2) Hammond's Flycatchers (above) of w. U.S. invade its Mexican range in migration and winter; (3) White-throated Flycatcher (different habitat) is smaller, has a more conspicuous white throat.
Range: Mexico; breeds in highlands and plateau area from Sinaloa, s. Chihuahua, s. Coahuila, sw. Tamaulipas south to

southern parts of central plateau (Guerrero, Puebla, w.-cen. Veracruz). Winters to Guatemala. **Habitat:** Pine forests.

WESTERN FLYCATCHER *Empidonax difficilis* **See W or T**
  Memo: Yellowish underparts, including throat. Note, a sharp *pseet* or *seest* (rising inflection). Dawn song (sometimes heard all day), 3 thin notes: *pseet-trip-seet!* Arangement varies (RTP).
  Range: Se. Alaska, w. Canada, w. U.S., w. and cen. Mexico; northern populations migratory. **Mexico:** Breeds in mts. of Baja California and highlands of w. Mexico and central plateau; also lowlands of w. Sinaloa, possibly to Nayarit; in winter, western lowlands south at least to Oaxaca. **Habitat:** Breeds in pine and oak woodlands of mts., especially in canyons and groves of arid tropical zone.

YELLOWISH FLYCATCHER   **Pl. 28**
Empidonax flavescens 5
  Field marks: Very similar to the more northern Western Flycatcher (and may be conspecific). Greenish olive above, yellowish below, washed on chest with olive to brownish; conspicuous eye-ring light yellowish, wingbars *buff*.
  Note: The taxonomy of this group is in dispute. Some authors treat the Yellowish Flycatcher complex as subspecies of the Western Flycatcher, *E. difficilis*. Others call all birds from s. Veracruz, Chiapas, and Guatemala south *E. flavescens*. This treatment is adopted here.
  Similar species: (1) Western Flycatcher is duller, more brownish above; wingbars and eye-ring whitish; may not be separable in field, especially when Yellowish Flycatcher is in worn plumage. (2) Yellow-bellied Flycatcher, a migrant and winter visitor, has whitish eye-ring and wingbars; in hand, 10th (outer) primary is equal to or longer than 5th (in both Yellowish and Western 10th is shorter than 5th).
  Voice: Dawn song, *seee seee chit,* sometimes *see chit see;* call, *tseeent* or *psink* (Skutch and Slud).
  Range: S. Mexico to w. Panamá. **Mexico:** Highlands of s. Veracruz (Sierra de Tuxtla) and Chiapas. **Habitat:** Cloud forest and borders.

BUFF-BREASTED FLYCATCHER   **Pl. 28**
Empidonax fulvifrons 4½–5
  Field marks: A very small *Empidonax* flycatcher with a conspicuous white eye-ring and wingbars. Distinguished from its confusing close relatives by the *rich buff breast*.
  Similar species: (1) Tufted Flycatcher has pointed crest, deep cinnamon-brown underparts. (2) Belted Flycatcher (highlands

of Chiapas, Guatemala) has pointed crest, dark cinnamon breastband.

Voice: *Chicky-whew* (Lusk); *chee-lick* (Brandt).

Range: Mts. of cen. and se. Arizona, cen.-w. New Mexico to Guatemala, Honduras. **Mexico:** Mts. of west, from ne. Sonora, n. Chihuahua south to central plateau (and east to w.-cen. Veracruz); highlands of Chiapas. Northern birds migrate southward. **Habitat:** Canyon groves, oak-pine forests, brush.

PILEATED FLYCATCHER   Pl. 28
Aechmolophus mexicanus   5½

Field marks: This small dull flycatcher with its 2 whitish wingbars might be taken for an *Empidonax* or a small pewee were it not for its *crest.* Underparts dingy yellowish white, with a grayish wash across breast. Rare.

Similar species: (1) Tufted Flycatcher (also crested) has rich cinnamon-brown underparts. (2) Belted Flycatcher has rusty breastband, different range.

Voice: Song, *ra-reee-e-e-e-reechoo* (Davis); *twheeyu, tr-r-r-eet-yu* (Edwards).

Range: Cen. Mexico only; Michoacán, México, Puebla to Oaxaca. **Habitat:** Oak-thorn scrub.

BELTED FLYCATCHER   *Xenotriccus callizonus*   5   Pl. 28

Field marks: The long *pointed crest* and *orange-brown breastband* are distinctive. Lower underparts pale yellowish, throat grayish white. Wingbars deep buff; eye-ring whitish.

Similar species: See (1) Pileated and (2) Tufted Flycatchers.

Voice: An excited *pic-pic-pweer* or *pic-pic-piweer* (RTP).

Range: Highlands of se. Mexico (Chiapas) and Guatemala. Local and rare. **Habitat:** Brushy growth near water.

RUDDY-TAILED FLYCATCHER   Pl. 28
Terenotriccus erythrurus   3½

Field marks: A very small flycatcher that rapidly flicks its wings. Cinnamon-tawny underparts and especially *rufous wings and tail* are distinctive. No noticeable wingbars.

Similar species: Other buff- or cinnamon-breasted flycatchers are larger, have strong wingbars, lack rufous tail.

Voice: A thin *tsee'oo-tee* or *seeoo-bzew* (Eisenmann). A high thin *chee'-twit* (Howell).

Range: Se. Mexico (Tabasco, e. Chiapas), Guatemala to Bolivia, Brazil. **Habitat:** Lowlands; humid forests and borders.

SULPHUR-RUMPED FLYCATCHER   Pl. 28
Myiobius sulphureipygius   5

Field marks: Note the *sulphur-yellow rump patch,* contrasting with blackish tail, the only Mexican flycatcher so adorned.

Chest and sides light brown; belly and under tail coverts light yellow. No wingbars. Often fans tail like Redstart.
Voice: Note, a sharp *psit.* Song, 5 high, sharp notes followed by about 5 warbled notes. Also *cheu cheu cheu cheu* in a pleasant voice (Skutch).
Range: Se. Mexico to w. Ecuador. **Mexico:** Gulf lowlands; cen. and s. Veracruz, n. Oaxaca, n. Chiapas, Tabasco, Campeche, Quintana Roo. **Habitat:** Humid forests and thickets.

NORTHERN ROYAL-FLYCATCHER   Pl. 29
Onychorhynchus mexicanus   6–7
Field marks: The extraordinary crest is very rarely seen in display unless the bird is wounded or taken by hand from a mist net. Then it is spread fully; the bird weaves its head back and forth in a slow reptilian movement, with open mouth, exhibiting the orange interior. Normally its crest lies flat, giving a hammerheaded look, betraying just a hint of color. Rump and much of tail *light tawny.*
Similar species: See Bright-rumped Attila (No. 11, Plate 26).
Voice: A loud, clear hollow-sounding whistle; also a higher, sharper, wiry note, repeated many times (Skutch).
Range: Se. Mexico to n. Colombia, nw. Venezuela. **Mexico:** Mainly Gulf lowlands from cen. and s. Veracruz, n. Oaxaca, east through n. Chiapas, Tabasco, and Yucatán Pen. **Habitat:** Understory of humid forests and borders.

WHITE-THROATED SPADEBILL   Pl. 29
Platyrinchus mystaceus   3½–4
Field marks: Note the *very broad flat bill,* large head, earspot, and stumpy tail of this stubby brown flycatcher. Males have a small concealed yellowish crown patch.
Voice: A nasal or reedy *tidit* or *ditarit* (Eisenmann). A frequently repeated buzzy, 2-noted call (Russell).
Range: Se. Mexico to Paraguay, ne. Argentina. **Mexico:** Gulf lowlands of s. Veracruz, n. Chiapas, Tabasco, and Yucatán Pen. **Habitat:** Understory of shady moist woodlands, swampy places; thickets in gallery forest.

YELLOW-OLIVE (WHITE-EYED) FLYCATCHER   Pl. 28
Tolmomyias sulphurescens   5–5½
Field marks: Note the combination of *gray* head and breast, bright *olive-green* back and *whitish* (or pale yellowish) eye that seems larger because of a white eye-ring. The broad bill is black above, whitish below. Immature may have dark eye.
Similar species: (1) Sepia-capped Flycatcher and (2) Eye-ringed Flatbill have dark eyes, lack gray head. See below also (3) Bentbill, (4) Paltry Tyrannulet, (5) White-eyed Vireo (p. 196).

Voice: A thin hissing whistle, insistent; suggests lisping call of Cedar Waxwing (Skutch); *ss-ss-ss-ss* (Slud).
Range: Se. Mexico to nw. Argentina, Brazil. **Mexico:** Mainly lowlands; cen. and s. Veracruz, Oaxaca, Chiapas, Tabasco, and Yucatán Pen. **Habitat:** Understory and borders of cutover humid forests, open deciduous woodlands, plantations.

EYE-RINGED FLATBILL   Pl. 28
Rhynchocyclus brevirostris   6
Field marks: A *greenish* flycatcher, with a *very broad bill;* similar to Yellow-olive Flycatcher but lacks whitish eye and clear gray of head and breast. Eye is dark with a very conspicuous white ring. No distinct wingbars.
Similar species: See (1) Yellow-olive Flycatcher (preceding) and (2) Yellowish Flycatcher (buff wingbars), p. 151.
Voice: Note, a weak, harsh, sputtering whistle (Skutch).
Range: S. Mexico to Ecuador. **Mexico:** S. Veracruz, Puebla, e. Oaxaca, Tabasco, Chiapas, Yucatán Pen. **Habitat:** Humid forests, tall second growth; sea level to 6000 + ft.

COMMON (NORTHERN) TODY-FLYCATCHER   Pl. 29
Todirostrum cinereum   4
Field marks: The tiny tody-flycatchers (2 species) have long, flat, narrow bills. This one is known by its *bright yellow* underparts and *blackish* face and cap. Eye may vary from pale to dark (age or sex?). Common Tody-Flycatchers are very active, cocking their tails and moving them *from side to side.*
Similar species: See Slate-headed Tody-Flycatcher (very shy), next.
Voice: *Ziziup, ziziup,* etc., repeated 3–5 times (Chalif). A resonant trill, *trrrrr,* repeated at intervals. Also a short *srrrr, atsip;* a series of high *tick* notes (Eisenmann).
Range: Se. Mexico to Bolivia, Brazil. **Mexico:** Chiefly Gulf lowlands; s. Veracruz, n. Oaxaca, n. Chiapas, Tabasco, Campeche, Quintana Roo. **Habitat:** Semi-open areas, wood borders, plantations, brushy pastures, savannas with large trees.

SLATE-HEADED TODY-FLYCATCHER   Pl. 29
Todirostrum sylvia   3¾
Field marks: Similar in shape and actions to preceding species but underparts *grayish* paling to whitish on throat and abdomen. Lacks the sharply capped look; has a white line from bill to eye. Eye color varies from white to brown. Very shy, hard to see well in low thickets.
Similar species: See (1) Common Tody-Flycatcher (yellow below, blackish cap), (2) Bentbill, (3) Paltry Tyrannulet.
Voice: Call, *tip-trrrr;* also *turp; trrrp-trrrp.* A rattling trill, *trrrrrrii* (Eisenmann).

Range: Mexico to n. Brazil. **Mexico:** Gulf lowlands; s. Veracruz, e. Oaxaca, Tabasco; casual cen. Quintana Roo. Much less frequent than the Common Tody-Flycatcher. **Habitat:** Low thickets, tangles, brush, dense second growth.

NORTHERN BENTBILL   Pl. 29
Oncostoma cinereigulare 4
Field marks: This very small olive-green flycatcher has a *much curved bill* and *white eyes.* Breast obscurely streaked with gray and white; belly yellowish.
Similar species: Slate-headed Tody-Flycatcher has a longer, *straight* bill, lacks yellow on belly.
Voice: A short trilled whistle, *wwwwwwwww,* given very softly; bird will respond to imitation (Chalif).
Range: Mexico to Canal Zone. **Mexico:** Mainly lowlands; cen. and s. Veracruz, e. Oaxaca, Tabasco, Chiapas, and Yucatán Pen.
Habitat: Forest edges, thickets, brushy trails.

YELLOW-BELLIED ELAENIA   Pl. 28
Elaenia flavogaster 6
Field marks: Elaenias are rather plain, peweelike flycatchers (usually with 2 wingbars). The 3 Mexican elaenias have a white or yellow patch usually concealed in center of crown. In excitement this species frequently erects a 2-part crest, revealing a white crown patch (young birds may lack this). Belly yellowish; 2 pale buff or whitish wingbars.
Similar species: (1) Caribbean Elaenia (islands off Yucatán Pen.) also has white crown spot. (2) Greenish Elaenia has yellow crown spot. See also (3) Dusky-capped Flycatcher (p. 147) and (4) *Myiarchus* group of flycatchers (pp. 145ff.).
Voice: A noisy *pweer* or *preeup.* Also *preeup preeup whi preeup,* repeated insistently (Chalif). A harsh grating *kreeo* or *kreeo wee kreeo;* also a burred *freeee* (Eisenmann).
Range: S. Mexico to n. Argentina. **Mexico:** Mainly lowlands; Gulf slope from Veracruz, n. Oaxaca, n. Chiapas east through Yucatán Pen.; also Pacific slope of Chiapas. **Habitat:** Savannas, open brush, old fields, plantations, parks.

CARIBBEAN ELAENIA   *Elaenia martinica* 6   Pl. 28
Field marks: Similar to Yellow-bellied Elaenia (white crown patch) but lacks conspicuous eye-ring and strong yellowish wash on belly. Erects crest less often. Immatures are so much smaller and shorter-tailed as to seem a different species.
Similar species: See Yellow-bellied Elaenia (preceding). Some individuals of the 2 species are closely similar.
Voice: A harsh *je eyup whe whe yup* (Chalif). *Che-eup,* often followed by *wi-wi-eup* (Bond).
Range: Lesser Antilles and islands off Yucatán Pen. **Mexico:**

Cozumel, Mujeres, and other islands off east coast of Quintana Roo; also off B. Honduras. **Habitat:** Mangroves.

MOUNTAIN ELAENIA *Elaenia frantzii* 6 **Pl. 28**
Field marks: This elaenia *lacks a crown patch* (so does young of Yellow-bellied Elaenia). It has the merest trace of *yellow on throat* and abdomen. Bill pinkish. Restricted to higher altitudes (3000–6300 ft.) than Yellow-bellied, but ranges overlap.
Similar species: See (1) Yellow-bellied Elaenia (above) and (2) Tropical Pewee (p. 148).
Voice: A burred, drawled peweelike *peeee-err* and a *peeoo,* varied to *wheeoo* and *whee* (Eisenmann).
Range: Mts. of Guatemala (local; common Antigua) south to Colombia. Not in Mexico or B. Honduras. **Habitat:** Subtropical slopes; woodland clearings, streams and borders, brush.

GREENISH ELAENIA *Myiopagis viridicata* 5½ **Pl. 28**
Field marks: This small olive-green elaenia differs from the others in having a *yellow crown patch* and *no wingbars.* Chest grayish, abdomen yellow. Behaves unlike other elaenias, gleaning among foliage and twigs; posture less erect.
Similar species: See Yellow-olive Flycatcher (p. 153).
Voice: Note, a buzzy *cheez* or *cheez weez* (Slud).
Range: Mexico to n. Argentina. **Mexico:** Pacific slope from Nayarit (incl. Tres Marías Is.) south to Guerrero; also se. Chiapas. Gulf slope from San Luis Potosí, s. Tamaulipas through Yucatán Pen. **Habitat:** Undergrowth, low trees of thin woods, plantations, brushy clearings, trails.

NORTHERN BEARDLESS TYRANNULET **Pl. 29**
(BEARDLESS FLYCATCHER) *Camptostoma imberbe* 4
Field marks: A very small nondescript flycatcher that may even suggest a kinglet, vireo, or immature Verdin. Upperparts olive-gray, underparts dingy white with grayish wash across breast. Dull buff wingbars and indistinct eye-ring. Distinguished from *Empidonax* flycatchers by smaller size, smaller head, different behavior, and very small bill.
Similar species: (1) Bell's Vireo (different voice) is a bit larger; slightly more yellowish on sides; wingbars whitish or gray (usually buff in Beardless). (2) Immature Verdin (very similar) has a distinctive voice and tends to be more pure gray above; no wingbars. (3) See Paltry Tyrannulet (next).
Voice: Call note, a thin *peeee-yuk* or *squee-up.* Also a series of fine gentle notes, *ee, ee, ee, ee,* increasing in volume toward middle of series (Sutton).
Range: Se. Arizona, s. Texas to Costa Rica. **Mexico:** Arid lowlands from Sonora and lower Río Grande south and east, including Yucatán Pen. **Habitat:** Low woods, mesquite, stream thickets, brush, lower canyons.

PALTRY TYRANNULET   Pl. 29
Tyranniscus vilissimus 4½
> **Field marks:** This tiny flycatcher suggests a vireo or a war-
> bler. Tail often half cocked. Note the *dark slaty crown* and
> *whitish eyebrow stripe.* Back olive-green, underparts whitish
> with a wash of gray across chest and vaguely streaked with olive
> on sides. No wingbars. Eyes pale to dark.
> **Similar species:** The even smaller Yellow-bellied Tyrannulet,
> which has a similar eyebrow stripe, is bright yellow below and
> has a very short tail (about 1 in.).
> **Voice:** A frequently uttered, semiwhistled *peeee yick* or *chee-*
> *yip;* also a short trill (Eisenmann).
> **Range:** S. Mexico (e. Chiapas), Guatemala to Colombia, Vene-
> zuela. **Habitat:** Highlands, woodland borders, plantations.

YELLOW-BELLIED TYRANNULET   Pl. 29
Ornithion semiflavum 3–3½
> **Field marks:** This tiny olive-green flycatcher has a small
> chickadeelike bill and *stubby tail.* The dark slaty cap and
> cheeks, contrasting with a *white eyebrow stripe* and *yellow un-*
> *derparts,* help identify it. No wingbars.
> **Similar species:** See Paltry Tyrannulet (preceding).
> **Voice:** A series of 3–5 *dee*'s, of about same pitch (Slud).
> **Range:** Se. Mexico to Costa Rica. **Mexico:** Gulf lowlands of s.
> Veracruz, n. Oaxaca, Tabasco, n. Chiapas. **Habitat:** Edges of
> humid forests, thickets.

SEPIA-CAPPED FLYCATCHER   Pl. 28
Leptopogon amaurocephalus 4½–5
> **Field marks:** The *dark brown crown and nape,* contrasting
> with the olive-green back, and the 2 ochre-buff wingbars will
> help identify this small flycatcher. Underparts dull yellow with
> an olive wash across chest, fading to pale grayish on throat. A
> narrow light eye-ring.
> **Similar species:** See Tropical Pewee (p. 148).
> **Voice:** Exceedingly loud and harsh, seeming to come from a
> bird 3 times its size (Moore).
> **Range:** Se. Mexico to n. Argentina. **Mexico:** Gulf lowlands of
> s. Veracruz, n. Oaxaca, Tabasco, n. Chiapas. **Habitat:** Shrubby
> understory and lower trees of humid forests.

OCHRE-BELLIED FLYCATCHER   Pl. 29
Pipromorpha oleaginea 4½–5
> **Field marks:** Note the distinctive combination of *gray* throat
> and breast blending into *ochre or tawny buff* on the belly. Back
> olive-green; narrow brown wingbars not conspicuous. No eye-
> ring. Twitches one wing at a time above back.
> **Similar species:** Sepia-capped Flycatcher (preceding).

Voice: Song, a monotonously repeated *twick-twick-twick,* etc. (3 per second), or a slower *tsyick-tsyick-tsyick* (Eisenmann). **Range:** Se. Mexico to Amazonia. **Mexico:** Mainly Gulf lowlands; e. Puebla, cen. and s. Veracruz, n. Oaxaca, Tabasco, Chiapas, and Yucatán Pen. **Habitat:** Humid forests and borders, deciduous woodlands, tall second growth, plantations.

Larks: Alaudidae

MOST larks are streaked, brown, terrestrial birds. Hind claw elongated, almost straight. Voices musical; birds may sing high in display flight. Often gregarious. Sexes usually similar. **Food:** Mainly seeds, insects. **Range:** Old World except for Horned Lark. **No. of species:** World, 75; Mexico, 1.

HORNED LARK   *Eremophila alpestris*   See E, W, or T
  Memo: "Horns"; black ear and breast patches.
  Range: Breeds widely in Eurasia; locally to n. Africa; N. America south to Mexico; n. S. America (highlands of Colombia). **Mexico:** Widespread in open grasslands (incl. Baja California) south to Isthmus of Tehuantepec (Oaxaca), breeding locally, mainly in west and in central plateau.

Swallows: Hirundinidae

SLIM streamlined form and graceful flight are characterstic. Tiny feet, long pointed wings, and short bills with very wide gapes. **Food:** Mainly insects caught in flight. **Range:** Nearly cosmopolitan, except polar regions and some islands. **No. of species:** World, 79; Mexico, 12 (+1 accidental, 1 in Guatemala).

VIOLET-GREEN SWALLOW   See W or T
Tachycineta thalassina
  Memo: White patches on sides of rump; white around eye.
  Range: Cen. Alaska, w. Canada, w. U.S. to s. Mexico. Winters to highlands of Honduras, casually to w. Panamá. **Mexico:** Breeds Baja California, coast of Sonora; and south in central plateau and mts. to Oaxaca, Veracruz. In migration and winter south along Pacific Coast.

TREE SWALLOW   See E, W, or T
Tachycineta (Iridoprocne) bicolor
  Memo: Back blue-black; underparts snow-white.
  Range: Alaska, Canada to California, cen.-e. U.S. Winters to

W. Indies and Mid. America; irregularly to Colombia, Guyana.
Mexico: Widespread transient, winter visitor.

MANGROVE SWALLOW   Pl. 17
Tachycineta (Iridoprocne) albilinea   5
    Field marks: White-breasted with a blue-green glossed black back, much like Tree Swallow, but with a *white rump* and an inconspicuous white line between bill and eye. Immature is dusky brown above with a dull whitish rump.
    Similar species: Violet-green Swallow has white on *each side* of rump; white on face partially encircles eye.
    Voice: *Chi-chi* or *jir jir jir* (Chalif).
    Range: Mexico to Panamá; also coastal Peru. **Mexico:** Mainly coastal, from s. Sonora and s. Tamaulipas south, including Yucatán Pen. **Habitat:** Mangroves, rivers, shores.

BLACK-CAPPED SWALLOW   Pl. 17
Notiochelidon pileata   5
    Field marks: A dusky brown-backed swallow superficially like a Bank Swallow or a Rough-wing, but with a *black cap* and more deeply forked tail. Underparts white with *black* under tail coverts and dusky spotting across lower throat.
    Similar species: See (1) Bank and (2) Rough-winged Swallows.
    Voice: A note that sounds like *zweep* (Chalif).
    Range: Highlands of se. Mexico (Chiapas only), Guatemala, El Salvador; wanders to w. Honduras. **Habitat:** Edges, open country. Nests in holes in banks, roadcuts, cliffs.

BLUE-AND-WHITE (PATAGONIAN) SWALLOW
Pygochelidon cyanoleuca patagonica   5   **Not illus.**
    Field marks: Very similar to Tree Swallow (steel-blue above, white below) but under tail coverts black (not white).
    Range: Highlands; Costa Rica to Tierra del Fuego; birds of southern form ("Patagonian Swallow"), sometimes regarded as a distinct species, migrate northward (casually to Cen. America). **Mexico:** Recorded once in Chiapas. Could be overlooked because of similarity to Tree Swallow.

PURPLE MARTIN   *Progne subis*   See E, W, or T
    Memo: Large (8 in.), ♂ all black; ♀ gray breast and collar.
    Range: S. Canada to n. Mexico, Gulf states. Winters Colombia to Brazil. **Mexico:** Breeds Baja California, Sonora; central plateau south to Michoacán, Guanajuato. Widespread migrant.

CUBAN MARTIN   *Progne cryptoleuca*   7½   **Not illus.**
    Field marks: *Male:* Violet-blue-black, similar to male Purple Martin but with a concealed area of white on abdomen. *Fe-*

male: Similar to female Gray-breasted Martin but shows more contrast below, although less than in Snowy-bellied Martin. May be a race of Purple Martin.

Similar species: See Snowy-bellied Martin (next).

Range: Cuba and Isle of Pines. Recorded casually or accidentally in Guatemala. Not in Mexico.

SNOWY-BELLIED MARTIN   Pl. 17

Progne dominicensis 7–7½
(including Sinaloa and Caribbean Martins)

Field marks: *Male:* Similar to Purple Martin (blue-black) but with a *broad white median area* running from lower breast to under tail coverts; sides blue-black. *Female:* Similar to female Gray-breasted Martin but more contrast between white of underparts and dark chest and sides. May be a race of Purple Martin.

Range: W. Indies (except Cuba and Isle of Pines), Tobago, w. Mexico. Recorded once in Guatemala (Petén). **Mexico:** Western slope of Sierra Madre Occidental (3500–7500 ft.) from Sonora, sw. Chihuahua to n. Nayarit. Migratory. **Habitat:** Pine-oak zone of mts., often in colonies.

GRAY-BREASTED MARTIN   Pl. 17

Progne chalybea 6½–7

Field marks: A rather large swallow, superficially resembling female Purple Martin (dusky throat and breast, whitish belly), but with a dark forehead and no grayish collar or partial collar. Male is glossy blue-black above; female browner.

Similar species: Purple Martin ♂ is glossy blue-black on underparts; ♀ has a lighter gray patch on forehead and an indistinct gray collar or partial collar.

Voice: A musical *chrrrr*. Song, a warbling, rather musical *churrr churrrche churrr,* etc. (Chalif).

Range: Se. Texas (rarely), Mexico to cen. Argentina. **Mexico:** Pacific slope from Nayarit south; Gulf slope from Tamaulipas south, including Yucatán Pen. Migratory in north. **Habitat:** Mainly lowlands, foothills; open country, clearings, towns; hawks insects in air and over water.

ROUGH-WINGED SWALLOW   See E, W, or T

Stelgidopteryx ruficollis 5–5¾

Memo: Brown back, dingy throat.

Note: The Yucatán Pen. race (black under tail coverts) was formerly regarded as a separate species, Ridgway's Swallow, *S. ridgwayi.*

Range: S. Canada to Argentina; northern populations winter from s. California, s. Texas south into S. America. **Mexico:** Resident nearly throughout. Populations from U.S. and n. Mexico migrate south through Mexico.

BANK SWALLOW   *Riparia riparia*   **See E, W, or T**
  Memo: Brown back, dark breastband.
  Range: Widespread in N. Hemisphere. Winters to nw. Argentina, Africa, s. Asia. **Mexico:** Migrant, mainly coastal.

BARN SWALLOW   *Hirundo rustica*   **See E, W, or T**
  Memo: Very deeply forked tail.
  Range: Breeds widely in N. Hemisphere. Winters Costa Rica to Argentina; also Africa, s. Asia. **Mexico:** Breeds nw. Baja California and from n. Sonora, Chihuahua, south in highlands to Michoacán, cen. Puebla, w. Veracruz. Widespread migrant.

CLIFF SWALLOW   **See E, W, or T**
Petrochelidon pyrrhonota
  Memo: Pale rusty rump, dark throat, light forehead (usually).
  Range: Alaska, Canada to s. Mexico. Winters s. Brazil to cen. Argentina. **Mexico:** Breeds n. Baja California and from U.S. border south along Pacific slope to Nayarit; on central plateau to Oaxaca. Migrant elsewhere except Yucatán Pen. (casual).

CAVE SWALLOW   *Petrochelidon fulva*   6–8   **Pl. 17**
  Field marks: Similar to Cliff Swallow (pale rusty rump) but throat *pale,* forehead dark chestnut.
  Note: Some Cliff Swallows have dark foreheads. They would be dark on *both* forehead and throat.
  Similar species: Cliff Swallow usually has head colors reversed: forehead pale buff, throat dark chestnut with black patch on lower throat (these points may be unreliable in fall migration).
  Voice: A clear *weet* or *cheweet;* a loud accented *chu, chu.* Song, a series of squeaks blending into a complex melodic warble; ending in double-toned notes (Selander and Baker).
  Range: Se. New Mexico, s.-cen. Texas, W. Indies, e. Mexico. Winter range unknown. **Mexico:** Northeastern part; Chihuahua, Coahuila, Tamaulipas, e. San Luis Potosí; also northern half of Yucatán Pen. and Chiapas (Tuxtla Gutiérrez). Migrant through s. Mexico.

Crows and Jays: Corvidae

LARGE passerine birds; longish strong bills with nostrils usually covered by forward-pointing bristles. Crows and ravens are very large, black. Jays are usually colorful (running mainly to blues). Sexes look alike. **Food:** Omnivorous. **Range:** Nearly cosmopolitan except s. S. America, some islands, polar regions. **No. of species:** World, 102; Mexico, 21 or 22 (+ 1 in Guatemala).

COMMON RAVEN   *Corvus corax*   **See E, W, or T**
Memo: Very large (22–27 in.); wedge-shaped tail.
Range: Widespread in N. America (Arctic to Nicaragua); also Greenland, Eurasia, n. Africa. **Mexico:** Resident of Baja California and islands in Gulf of Baja California; western and central parts of country from U.S. border south to Chiapas, Veracruz; Revilla Gigedo Is. Ranges from sea level to 18,250 ft. on Orizaba. Also Guatemala; not B. Honduras.

WHITE-NECKED RAVEN   **See W or T**
Corvus crypotoleucus
Memo: Size of Common Crow; ravenlike tail, flight.
Range: Sw. and w.-cen. U.S. to cen. Mexico. **Mexico:** Arid regions of northern tier of states (except Baja California) and south in interior to Guanajuato and México.

AMERICAN (COMMON) CROW   **See E, W, or T**
Corvus brachyrhynchos
Memo: All black (17–21 in.); tail not wedge-shaped.
Range: Canada, U.S., nw. Mexico. **Mexico:** Resident n. Baja California. In winter to coastal Sonora.

MEXICAN CROW   *Corvus imparatus*   14½–16   **Pl. 30**
(including "Tamaulipas" and "Sinaloa" Crows)
Field marks: A small, social crow, endemic to Mexico. L. Irby Davis has argued persuasively, largely on the basis of voice, that 2 species may be involved, one on each coast; he has described the Pacific bird. The Mexican Crow has been lumped by some with the slightly larger Fish Crow *(C. ossifragus)* of e. U.S., but this seems unlikely when one considers its curious voice and different habits.
Voice: Birds of the Gulf slope utter a surprisingly low, hoarse *craw* (Chalif) or *khurrr* (RTP). Birds of the Pacific slope have a higher voice; a shrill *creow* (Davis).
Range: Mexico only (except for recent visits to area of Brownsville, Texas). **Mexico:** Pacific slope from s. Sonora to Colima *(C. sinaloae,* "Sinaloa Crow"); Gulf slope of Nuevo León, Tamaulipas, San Luis Potosí, n. Veracruz *(C. imparatus,* "Tamaulipas Crow"). **Habitat:** Sea level to 3000 ft. in coastal regions; semi-arid brush, farming country.

CLARK'S NUTCRACKER   *Nucifraga columbiana*   **See W**
Memo: Gray; white patches in black wings and tail.
Range: Resident sw. Canada, w. U.S., nw. Mexico. **Mexico:** Breeds in conifers of high mts. (Sierra San Pedro Mártir) of n. Baja California. Casual Sonora and Nuevo León.

PINYON JAY   *Gymnorhinus cyanocephalus*   **See W or T**
Memo: Dull gray-blue throughout; short tail.
Range: Resident w. U.S., nw. Mexico; wanders widely. **Mex-

ico: Breeds in arid pine zone of mts. (Sierra Juárez and Sierra San Pedro Mártir) of n. Baja California. Casual Chihuahua.

BLACK-THROATED MAGPIE JAY   Pl. 30
Calocitta formosa colliei   25–28

Field marks: A magnificent bluish jay with an *extremely long* tail, a *long, pointed,* black crest, and white underparts. The 2 very different types (black-throated and white-throated) are so unlike in aspect that they were formerly regarded as distinct species. Birds of intermediate characters occur. The two are treated separately here for field purposes. This black-throated form is the more northern.

Similar form: See White-throated Magpie Jay (conspecific).

Voice: Noisy; a variety of jaylike sounds; a harsh reiterated *grah* or *khrah;* also a querulous, downward-slurring *kew, kew, kew,* or *kyoo, kyoo, kyoo, kyoo,* etc.; bubbling and stuttering sounds (RTP).

Range: Black-throated form resides in nw. Mexico; Pacific slope from s. Sonora, sw. Chihuahua south to Jalisco (White-throated form from Colima, Puebla south to Costa Rica). **Habitat:** Semi-arid lowlands, open woods, brush.

WHITE-THROATED MAGPIE JAY   Pl. 30
Calocitta formosa (in part)   20–22

Field marks: Similar to the more northern Black-throated Magpie Jay but about 6 in. shorter; throat and face *white;* a narrow black band crosses white breast (*formosa* complex).

Similar form: See Black-throated Magpie Jay (conspecific).

Voice: Similar to Black-throated Magpie Jay's.

Range: Pacific slope of sw. Mexico to nw. Costa Rica. **Mexico:** Pacific slope; Colima south through Chiapas. **Habitat:** Brushy cattle country, second growth, thin woods.

BROWN JAY   *Psilorhinus morio*   14–18   Pl. 30
Field marks: A large sooty-brown jay, darkest (almost blackish) on the head, paling to light brown or dull creamy white on the belly. Bill black or yellow (young). May or may not have broad white tips on outer tail feathers, a fact that led to their former separation as distinct species (called Plain-tailed Brown Jay, *P. morio,* and White-tipped Brown Jay, *P. mexicanus*). It is now conceded that they are partly localized color phases (morphs) of 1 species (Selander, *Auk,* 1959). North of cen. Veracruz birds are plain-tailed; from Yucatán Pen. through Guatemala to Panamá, white-tipped. In the intermediate zone (cen. Veracruz to n. Chiapas, Tabasco) they are polymorphic (both).

Voice: Similar to that of Blue Jay of N. America but more nasal; a harsh *thief! thief!* (Chalif). An excited *jhay! jhay jhay,* etc., higher in pitch than Blue Jay (RTP).

Range: E. Mexico through Caribbean slope of Cen. America to nw. Panamá. **Mexico:** Gulf slope from Nuevo León (Monterrey) and Tamaulipas through Yucatán Pen. **Habitat:** Humid lowlands, foothills; second growth, forest borders, open woodlands.

TUFTED JAY *Cyanocorax dickeyi* 14–15 **Pl. 30**
Field marks: One of the most stunning of the jays. Note particularly its *bristly black crest* and *bicolored tail.* Crest, face, and throat black; back, wings, and basal half of tail rich blueblack; underparts, back of head, adjacent collar, and terminal half of tail white. Local Mexican name is "Urruca Pinta" (painted jay). Social.
Voice: Highly variable; most common basic call, *rak* (varied to *ruk, rook, tuk,* or *pik*); also a low-intensity, nasal *aaagh* and a bell-like *ped-el* or *pid-it* (Crossin).
Range: W. Mexico only; Pacific slope of Sierra Madre Occidental at 4500–7000 ft. on borders of se. Sinaloa, sw. Durango, nw. Nayarit; very local, rare. **Habitat:** Dense wooded growth in mt. barrancas and adjacent pine-oak ridges.

GREEN JAY *Cyanocorax yncas* 10–12 **Pl. 30**
Field marks: The only *green* jay in Mexico. Throat patch black; crown violet-blue, sides of tail *yellow.*
Voice: A rapid *cheh cheh cheh cheh;* also a slower *cleep, cleep, cleep,* etc.; a dry throaty rattle; also other calls.
Range: S. Texas to Honduras; also Venezuela to n. Bolivia.
Mexico: Pacific slope from Nayarit south; Gulf slope from lower Río Grande Valley south and east through Yucatán Pen.
Habitat: Lowlands to lower humid highlands; deciduous forest, second growth, brush, edges, pine-oak woods.

SAN BLAS (BLACK-AND-BLUE) JAY **Pl. 31**
Cissilopha sanblasiana 12
Field marks: This jay has a short erectile frontal crest (not always noticeable but longer in immatures) and is black on foreparts and below. Dark blue on back, wings, tail, and under tail coverts. Adults have black bills, yellow eyes; immatures yellow bills, dark eyes.
Similar species: (1) Yucatán Jay (no crest) is sometimes regarded as conspecific. (2) In highlands see Steller's Jay (p. 167).
Range: W. Mexico only; Pacific slope from Nayarit to Guerrero. **Habitat:** Mangroves, coastal scrub, woodlands, foothills.

YUCATAN JAY *Cissilopha yucatanica* 12–13 **Pl. 31**
Field marks: The only *blue* jay in the Yucatán Pen. (Green and Brown Jays are also present.) Similar to the preceding (San Blas Jay of Pacific Coast) but lacks a developed frontal crest. By some the two are regarded as conspecific. In juvenal plumage this jay may have a *white head and underparts,* yellow bill, acquiring black later.

Similar species: No other in the Yucatán Pen.
Range: Se. Mexico (Tabasco, Yucatán Pen.); n. Guatemala (Petén) and B. Honduras. **Habitat:** Deciduous forest, coastal scrub.

PURPLISH-BACKED (BEECHEY'S) JAY   Pl. 31
Cissilopha beecheii   15½–16
    Field marks: Similar to San Blas Jay (replacing it farther north), but much larger, with no frontal crest. The back is of a more *purplish or violet* hue. Eye *yellow or white*. Bill of immature yellow; adult black.
    Similar species: See above San Blas Jay (more southern).
    Range: Nw. Mexico only; Pacific slope, s. Sonora to Nayarit.
    Habitat: Lowlands, foothills (to 1500 ft.); thorn forests.

BUSHY-CRESTED JAY   Pl. 31
Cissilopha melanocyanea   11–12
    Field marks: A contrasty black and blue jay, similar to Yucatán Jay (Caribbean slope of n. Guatemala) but differs in 3 ways: (1) can erect a *bushy crest;* (2) eye is *yellow;* and (3) lower underparts are dull blue (not blackish).
    Similar species: See Steller's Jay (southern form), p. 167.
    Range: Cen. and s. Guatemala to Nicaragua. Not Mexico or B. Honduras. **Habitat:** Sea level to 8000 ft., but mainly highlands; pine-oaks, open woods, borders, plantations.

AZURE-HOODED JAY *Cyanolyca cucullata* 11–12   Pl. 31
    Field marks: Note the *pale azure crown* edged in front and on sides with a white line (which curves around ear region). Otherwise all dark blue-black (black on foreparts blending into dull dark blue on wings, tail, and lower underparts).
    Voice: A loud excited "spinking," almost ringing *peenk peenk peenk peenk;* also a harsh *aaaa* (Slud).
    Range: Se. Mexico to w. Panamá. **Mexico:** Mt. forests of Gulf slope of extreme s. San Luis Potosí, Veracruz, and adjacent Oaxaca; also interior Chiapas. **Habitat:** Humid mt. forests and borders at medium levels (mainly 3000–6000 ft.).

WHITE-THROATED (OMILTEME) JAY   Pl. 31
Cyanolyca mirabilis   9–10
    Field marks: A white stripe extends across the forehead, behind the eye, and around the ear patch to join the white throat. Black crown, cheek, and chest; rest of bird dull slaty blue.
    Similar species: See Dwarf Jay (below).
    Range: Sw. Mexico only; mts. (Sierra Madre del Sur) of Guerrero and Oaxaca. Local, rare. **Habitat:** Highland oak-pine forests. To 11,500 ft. on Mt. Teotepec.

BLACK-THROATED JAY *Cyanolyca pumilo* 9½–10 **Pl. 31**
  Field marks: A small all-dark jay, slaty blue with a black face and throat. Black of face faintly outlined with white across forehead, over and behind eye.
  Voice: Suggests Scrub Jay; a rapid scolding *kwesh-kwesh-kwesh;* a soft querulous *shrreee* (Hardy).
  Range: Mts. of se. Mexico, Guatemala, Honduras, El Salvador. **Mexico:** Highlands of Chiapas. **Habitat:** Brush in oak woodlands, cloud forest (4000–10,000 ft.), ravines.

DWARF JAY *Cyanolyca nana* 8–9 **Pl. 31**
  Field marks: A small dull gray-blue jay with a well-defined *black facial mask* and a contrasting pale *bluish-white throat.*
  Similar species: White-throated Jay (Guerrero, Oaxaca) has bold white facial stripings.
  Voice: A doubly inflected, harsh, nasal, querulous *perzheeup,* singly or in groups. *Not* loud (Hardy).
  Range: S. Mexico only (México, Veracruz, Oaxaca). **Habitat:** Mts. above 5000 ft.; pine-oak forests, firs. Rare.

SCRUB JAY *Aphelocoma coerulescens* 11–13 **Pl. 31**
  Field marks: Similar to Gray-breasted (Mexican) Jay, but note the whiter throat defined by its "necklace" of dark streaks across the upper breast. Voice very different.
  Voice: Rough rasping notes, *kwesh – kwesh.* Also a harsh *check-check-check-check* and a rasping *shreek* or *shrink* (RTP).
  Range: W. U.S. to s. Mexico. Also cen. Florida. **Mexico:** Baja California; western mts. (Sierra Madre Occidental) south to Jalisco, Guanajuato; eastern mts. (Sierra Madre Oriental) south to Veracruz, Puebla, México; also locally in mts. of Guerrero, Oaxaca. **Habitat:** Foothills, mts.; oaks, brush, river woods, pine-oak forests.

GRAY-BREASTED (MEXICAN) JAY **Pl. 31**
Aphelocoma ultramarina 12–13
  Field marks: Dull blue above with a gray-brown suffusion on back; underparts *light grayish* washed with dull brownish on chest. Lacks Scrub Jay's "necklace" of dark streaks.
  Voice: A rough, querulous *wink? wink?* or *zhenk?* (RTP).
  Range: Mts. of cen. and se. Arizona, sw. New Mexico, w. Texas to cen. Mexico. **Mexico:** Widely distributed in mts. from northern tier of states (except Baja California) south to highlands of Michoacán, Morelos, Puebla, Veracruz. **Habitat:** Open oak forests, oak-pine, junipers, scrub.

UNICOLORED JAY *Aphelocoma unicolor* 12–13 **Pl. 31**
  Field marks: Uniformly dark slaty blue or dull purplish blue, blacker on the face. No distinctive marks.
  Similar species: See Black-throated Jay (much smaller).

Voice: Similar to Gray-breasted Jay's, more varied (Hardy).
Range: S. Mexico to Honduras. **Mexico:** Local; mts. of s.-cen.
Guerrero, Puebla, w.-cen. Veracruz, Oaxaca, Chiapas. **Habitat:**
Oak-pine zone of mts., cloud forest.

STELLER'S JAY *Cyanocitta stelleri* 11–13 **Pl. 31; also W**
Field marks: A large black and blue jay of the highlands with
a long *pointed crest.* Foreparts blackish; rear parts (wings, tail,
belly) deep blue. Southern birds (Chiapas, Guatemala) have
much shorter crests (see Plate 31).
Similar species: (1) San Blas Jay of coastal slope of w. Mexico
has short frontal crest. (2) Bushy-crested Jay of Chiapas and
Guatemala lacks white eye spots.
Voice: A loud *shook-shook-shook* or *shack-shack-shack* or
wheck-wek — wek — wek or *kwesh kwesh kwesh,* etc. (RTP).
Range: S. Alaska, sw. Canada, w. U.S. to Nicaragua. **Mexico:**
Higher mts. nearly throughout, except Baja California (casual).
Habitat: Conifer and pine-oak forests of mts. (3000–13,000 ft.).

Titmice, Verdins, and Bushtits: Paridae

SMALL, plump, small-billed birds, acrobatic when feeding. Sexes
usually alike. Often roam in little bands. *Note:* Some recent authors place the Verdin in the family Remizidae (Old World pen-
duline tits) and the Bushtit in the family Aegithalidae (Old World
long-tailed tits). **Food:** Insects; also seeds, berries. **Range:** Widespread in boreal and temperate N. America, Eurasia, Africa. **No.
of species:** World, 62; Mexico, 7.

GRAY-SIDED (MEXICAN) CHICKADEE   **See W**
Parus sclateri
   Memo: Only chickadee in mainland Mexico. Dark gray sides.
   Range: Se. Arizona, sw. New Mexico, south in mts. of w. Mex-
   ico to Oaxaca.

MOUNTAIN CHICKADEE *Parus gambeli*   **See W or T**
   Memo: Only chickadee in Baja California. Eyebrow stripe.
   Range: Sw. Canada, w. U.S., nw. Mexico. **Mexico:** High mts.
   of n. Baja California (Sierra San Pedro Mártir; Sierra Juárez).

BLACK-CRESTED TITMOUSE   **See W or T**
Parus atricristatus
   Memo: Gray; rusty flanks, black crest.
   Range: W. Oklahoma, w. and cen. Texas, ne. Mexico. **Mexico:**
   Coahuila, Nuevo León, Tamaulipas, San Luis Potosí, Hidalgo,
   n. Veracruz.

PLAIN TITMOUSE *Parus inornatus*   **See W or T**
Memo: Gray; very plain; small gray crest.
Range: W. U.S., nw. Mexico. **Mexico:** Baja California (mts. of northwest and Cape); extreme ne. Sonora.

BRIDLED TITMOUSE *Parus wollweberi*   **See W**
Memo: "Bridled" face, crest.
Range: Mts. from se. Arizona, sw. New Mexico to s. Mexico.
Mexico: Western mts. (Sierra Madre Occidental and central plateau south to Guerrero; east in highlands to w. Tamaulipas, San Luis Potosí, w. Veracruz, Oaxaca.

VERDIN *Auriparus flaviceps*   **See W or T**
Memo: Gray; yellowish head, rusty shoulder.
Range: Sw. U.S., n. and w. Mexico. **Mexico:** Deserts of Baja California and northern tier of states from Sonora east to Tamaulipas; south to Jalisco, Guanajuato, Hidalgo.

BUSHTIT *Psaltriparus minimus*   **See W or T**
Memo: Long tail, brown or black cheeks, tiny bill.
Note: The Black-eared Bushtit, *P. melanotis,* formerly called a distinct species, is now regarded as a partly localized color phase occurring widely from the U.S. border southward over the Mexican plateau and mts.
Range: Sw. B. Columbia, w. U.S., to Guatemala. **Mexico:** Baja California (northwestern part and mts. of Cape); mts. of northern tier of states south through central plateau to Oaxaca; also mts. of Chiapas and Guatemala.

Nuthatches: Sittidae

SMALL, stout tree climbers with strong woodpeckerlike bills, strong feet. Stubby tails not braced woodpeckerlike in climbing; habitually go down tree trunks headfirst. Sexes similar. **Food:** Bark insects; seeds, nuts. **Range:** Mostly N. Hemisphere. **No. of species:** World, 31; Mexico, 3.

WHITE-BREASTED NUTHATCH   **See E, W, or T**
Sitta carolinensis
Memo: Upside-down climber; black cap, no eye stripe.
Range: S. Canada to s. Mexico: **Mexico:** Mts. of Baja California (northern part and Cape); highlands from Sonora east to Nuevo León, sw. Tamaulipas; south to Oaxaca, cen. Veracruz.

RED-BREASTED NUTHATCH   **See E, W, or T**
Sitta canadensis
Memo: Black line through eye; rusty breast.

Range: Se. Alaska, Canada, w. and ne. U.S. Winters to s. U.S.
Mexico: Formerly Guadalupe I. off Baja California (extirpated?). Occasional in winter in northern border areas.

PYGMY NUTHATCH   *Sitta pygmaea*   **See W or T**
  Memo: Gray-brown cap to eye; pine forests.
  Range: Southern B. Columbia, w. U.S., w. and cen. Mexico.
  Mexico: Mts. of n. Baja California; pine forests of highlands
  from Sonora east to Coahuila, s. Nuevo León; south to Michoacán, México, Puebla, w.-cen. Veracruz.

Creepers: Certhiidae

SMALL, slender stiff-tailed birds having slender decurved bills with
which they probe bark. **Food:** Bark insects. **Range:** Cooler parts
of N. Hemisphere. **No. of species:** World, 6; Mexico, 1.

BROWN CREEPER   *Certhia familiaris*   **See E, W, or T**
  Memo: Small, brown; slender decurved bill, creeping posture.
  Range: Eurasia; s. Alaska, Canada to Nicaragua. **Mexico:**
  Higher mts. except Baja California; also mts. of Guatemala.

Wrentits: Chamaeidae

THE WRENTIT is usually placed in a family of its own, but some
authorities regard it as an isolate of the large Old World family of
babblers (Timaliidae; 258 species). **Food:** Insects, berries.
Range: Oregon to nw. Baja California. **No. of species:** World, 1;
Mexico, 1.

WRENTIT   *Chamaea fasciata*   **See W**
  Memo: Streaked brown breast; long cocked tail, pale eye.
  Range: Coastal Oregon, California, nw. Baja California (from
  U.S. border south to Lat. 30° N).

Dippers: Cinclidae

PLUMP, short-tailed birds; resemble large wrens. Solitary. Dive,
swim underwater, walk on bottom. **Food:** Insects, aquatic invertebrates, small fishes. **Range:** Eurasia, w. N. America, w. S.
America (Andes). **No. of species:** World, 4; Mexico, 1.

AMERICAN DIPPER (WATER OUZEL)   See W
Cinclus mexicanus
  Memo: Chunky, slate-colored, short-tailed; mt. streams.
  Range: Aleutians, w. Canada, w. U.S. to w. Panamá. **Mexico:**
  Mt. streams of western highlands from Chihuahua south to Mi-
  choacán and eastward in south-central highlands to Puebla, n.
  Oaxaca, w.-cen. Veracruz.

Wrens: Troglodytidae

MOST wrens are small brown birds, rather stumpy, with slender
slightly decurved bills; tails often cocked. Most are energetic;
some are gifted songsters. The so-called cactus wren group *(Campylorhynchus)* are somewhat larger, more slender; sometimes
travel in small flocks. The taxonomy of certain wrens of Middle
America is still in an uncertain state. Some are very close and
obviously of the same ancestral stock; full specific rank may be
disputed. **Food:** Insects, spiders, etc. **Range:** New World; especially Mid. and S. America; only 1 species (Winter Wren) in Old
World. **No. of species:** World, 59; Mexico, 30.

SHORT-BILLED MARSH (GRASS or SEDGE) WREN
Cistothorus platensis   See E, W, or T
  Memo: Small, buffy; streaked back, buff under tail coverts.
  Range: S. Canada to e. and cen. U.S.; also locally from cen.
  Mexico to w. Panamá; also S. America (where it may be specifi-
  cally distinct). **Mexico:** Local resident Nayarit to Morelos; also
  in s. Veracruz, Chiapas. Northern migrants winter occasionally
  in ne. Tamaulipas, San Luis Potosí.

LONG-BILLED MARSH WREN   See E, W, or T
Telmatodytes palustris
  Memo: White eye stripe, strongly striped back; marshes.
  Range: Breeds from s. Canada to n. Baja California, Gulf
  Coast of U.S. Winters south into Mexico. **Mexico:** Resident
  locally in n. Baja California; n. Sonora, México. Winters from
  U.S. south to s. Baja California, Nayarit, Michoacán, México,
  Veracruz.

GRAY-BARRED (GRAY) WREN   Pl. 33
Campylorhynchus megalopterus   6½–7¾
  Field marks: A bar-backed wren, similar to the next species
  but paler, barred above with *dark gray and whitish;* underparts
  dull *whitish,* entirely spotted and barred.
  Similar species: (1) See Band-backed Wren (next).
  Voice: Harsh chattering, similar to Band-backed Wren's (Hardy).

Range: Cen. Mexico only; mts. of southern part of Mexican plateau from s. Jalisco east to w. Veracruz, Oaxaca. **Habitat:** Conifer forests of high mts. (6500–9500 ft.).

BAND-BACKED WREN   Pl. 33
Campylorhynchus zonatus   7–7¾

Field marks: Similar to Gray-barred Wren (both have banded backs) but *browner* in appearance. Bands on back have *buff* (not white) bars in between. *Bright buff or cinnamon* on lower underparts; breast spotted.

Similar species: Gray-barred Wren has dark gray and whitish bars above, no strong buff or cinnamon on underparts.

Voice: Suggests a muted jay, *raha, raha, raha, raha* (Chalif). *Tsu-ka, tsu-ka,* etc. (Skutch).

Range: Mexico to Colombia, nw. Ecuador. **Mexico:** Gulf slope from e. San Luis Potosí, n. Veracruz to Campeche; Chiapas. **Habitat:** Lowlands to highlands; tropical broadleaf forests and borders, clearings, plantations, gardens, pine-oak zone of mts.

RUFOUS-NAPED WREN   Pl. 33
Campylorhynchus rufinucha   6–7

Field marks: A largish wren with a dark brown or black cap, broad white eyebrow stripe, and dark stripe through the eye. Underparts immaculate white or tinged with pale gray or pale buff; sometimes with fine spots on breast. Wings and tail strongly barred. Nape *bright rufous.*

Note: Southern birds (Pacific slope of Chiapas, Guatemala to nw. Costa Rica) are more extensively rufous above and have sometimes been regarded as a separate species, *C. capistratus,* Rufous-backed Wren.

Similar species: (1) Giant Wren (Chiapas) looks like a very large edition of the rufous-backed form *(capistratus)* of this species but has *no barring on wings.* (2) See Rufous-and-White Wren (p. 174).

Voice: Song, a jerky, chanting *howdiwit howdiwit howdiwit howdiwit;* also a repetitious *chi-i-up* 4–6 times (Chalif).

Range: S. Mexico to nw. Costa Rica. **Mexico:** Arid Pacific lowlands from Colima south; Gulf lowlands in arid zone of cen. Veracruz, ne. Oaxaca. **Habitat:** Arid lowlands, foothills; dry forest edges, thorn scrub, plantations, clearings.

GIANT WREN   *Campylorhynchus chiapensis*   8–8½   Pl. 33

Field marks: Similar to the southern, rufous-backed form of the Rufous-naped Wren (*bright rufous back,* black cap, black and white eye stripes), but *much larger,* with *little or no barring* on wings. Underparts immaculate white; may be tinged with buff on abdomen.

Similar species: Rufous-naped Wren (form *capistratus*) is smaller, with strong dark barring on wings.
Range: Se. Mexico only (s. Chiapas). **Habitat:** Lowlands; humid forests.

CACTUS WREN   Pl. 33
Campylorhynchus brunneicapillus   7–8¾
   Field marks: A very large wren of arid country. Distinguished by its large size and heavy spotting on the underparts, which in adults forms a *dark cluster* on the upper breast. Like other wrens of this genus it has a dark cap and white eyebrow stripe. Back *striped with white.*
   Voice: A low monotonous *chuh-chuh-chuh-chuh,* etc., or *chug-chug-chug-chug-chug,* on 1 pitch. Unbirdlike (RTP).
   Range: Sw. U.S. to cen. and ne. Mexico. **Mexico:** Widespread in arid country; Pacific Coast south to s. Baja California, n. Sinaloa; central plateau south to Michoacán, México, Hidalgo; also Gulf Coast of Tamaulipas. **Habitat:** Deserts, arid foothills; cactus, yucca, mesquite, arid brush.

YUCATAN WREN   Not illus.
Campylorhynchus yucatanicus   7
   Field marks: Similar to Cactus Wren (black and white streaks on back), but grayer; underparts more lightly marked, without heavy clustering of black spots on breast. Until recently, regarded as an isolated race of Cactus Wren.
   Voice: Song series more bisyllabic than that of Cactus Wren; a dry, rollicking *chortle-chortle-chortle* (Edwards).
   Range: N. Yucatán only. **Habitat:** Opuntia scrub, semi-open land, coastal scrub, brushy thickets.

SPOTTED WREN   *Campylorhynchus gularis*   7   Pl. 33
   Field marks: Similar to Cactus Wren but with an *unspotted* whitish throat bordered by a black mustache; underparts much like a Wood Thrush's. Immature may lack spotting on underparts, but note mustache.
   Note: Sometimes lumped with the next species.
   Similar species: See (1) Cactus Wren (deserts, etc.), above, and (2) Boucard's Wren (more southern), next.
   Range: Mexico only; foothills and highlands (1400–8000 ft.) from s. Sonora, s. Chihuahua, s. Tamaulipas south to México, Querétaro, n. Hidalgo. **Habitat:** Oak-pine woods, semi-open dry country.

BOUCARD'S WREN   *Campylorhynchus jocosus*   7 **Not illus.**
   Field marks: Very similar to Spotted Wren, but browner above; more heavily spotted below; more southern.
   Similar species: See Spotted Wren (preceding).

Range: S. Mexico only; southern and eastern borders of Mexican plateau; Guerrero, Morelos, Federal Dist., s. Puebla, w. and cen. Oaxaca. **Habitat:** Dry mts. (1000–8200 ft.); arid country, dry pine forests.

CAROLINA WREN   See E, W, or T
Thryothorus ludovicianus 5
(including White-browed Wren)
Field marks: Most races of the Carolina Wren (such as the one in ne. Mexico) are rusty above with a white eyebrow stripe and *cinnamon-buff underparts.* The form found in cen. Guatemala and Nicaragua is also cinnamon-brown on the entire underparts. On the other hand, the race *albinucha,* formerly regarded as a distinct species, White-browed Wren (the one shown on Plate 32), is less rufous above and largely *white* below, especially on the throat and breast. It is confined to the Yucatán Pen. and n. Guatemala (Petén).
Voice: A 2- or 3-syllabled whistled phrase, repeated usually 3 times in a rollicking chant. Variable.
Range: S. Ontario, e. and cen. U.S., e. Mexico, Guatemala, and Nicaragua. **Mexico:** Typical Carolina Wren with buff-cinnamon underparts is resident in northeastern section (Tamaulipas, Nuevo León, e. Coahuila, San Luis Potosí). White-browed Wren with white throat and breast is confined to Yucatán Pen. and n. Guatemala (Petén). A form with cinnamon-brown underparts also occurs locally in cen. Guatemala and Nicaragua. **Habitat:** Undergrowth of woods, thickets.

WHITE-BROWED WREN   Pl. 32
Thryothorus albinucha (or *T. ludovicianus* in part) 5
See Carolina Wren (preceding). Formerly regarded as a distinct species but recently lumped with *T. ludovicianus.*

PLAIN WREN   *Thryothorus modestus* 5–5½   Pl. 32
Field marks: One of the many white-eyebrowed wrens; dull brown, *brighter on rump* and tail; underparts whitish blending into *buffy cinnamon on abdomen.* Wings and tail indistinctly barred.
Similar species: See (1) White-browed Wren (Caribbean lowlands), preceding, and (2) Rufous-and-White Wren (p. 174).
Voice: 4 whistled notes, repeated 3–5 times (Chalif). A screechy trisyllabic *chin-cheer-gwee,* repeated 3 times, apparently in duet by 2 birds (*chin-cheer,* then a lower answering *gwee*), Skutch. *Cheen'-chiriguee'* (Eisenmann).
Range: Pacific slope and mts. from s. Mexico (Chiapas) and Guatemala to cen. Panamá. **Habitat:** Lowlands, mt. slopes (to 6000 ft.); thickets, weedy fields, brushy roadsides, scrub.

BAR-VENTED (SINALOA) WREN — Pl. 32
Thryothorus sinaloa 5–5½

Field marks: A wren with a white eyebrow stripe; similar to the Plain Wren (preceding) but living in the western part of Mexico. More uniformly brown above; under tail coverts barred; has heavier wing-barring than the Happy Wren.

Similar species: In its range see Happy Wren (below).

Range: W. Mexico only. Pacific slope from s. Sonora to Guerrero. **Habitat:** Open woodlands, brush, thickets, mangroves.

BANDED WREN *Thryothorus pleurostictus* 5–5½ — Pl. 32

Field marks: Similar to the preceding 4 wrens but the white underparts are marked with *black bars on sides and flanks* as well as on under tail coverts. Immature is white beneath with brownish sides and flanks, no barring.

Similar species: (1) Plain Wren and (2) Bar-vented Wren lack black barring on sides.

Voice: A succession of repetitious whistles on various pitch levels: *prrrrrr, chechecheche, wit-wit-wit-wit-wit;* or *wee, whe-whewhe, chur-chur, choochoochoochoo,* etc. (RTP).

Range: Sw. Mexico to nw. Costa Rica. **Mexico:** Lowlands, foothills of Pacific slope; Michoacán, Guerrero, Morelos, Oaxaca, Chiapas. **Habitat:** Dry thickets, brush, wood edges.

RUFOUS-AND-WHITE WREN — Pl. 32
Thryothorus rufalbus 5½

Field marks: The most *rufous-backed* of all the similar small eyebrowed wrens. Underparts white, shading to light brownish on sides and flanks. Face white with blackish streaks; under tail coverts barred with black.

Similar species: (1) Plain Wren is grayer; face streaks and wing-barring less distinct; no bars on under tail coverts. (2) See Rufous-naped Wren (rufous-backed form), p. 171.

Voice: Song, a repetitious series beginning and ending with a higher note: *twee-chachalahlahlahlahlahlah-twee* (Chalif). A rhythmic series of *hooting* notes starting and ending with a higher-pitched *whit!* (Eisenmann).

Range: S. Mexico to Colombia. **Mexico:** Pacific slope of s. Chiapas. **Habitat:** Woodland edges, clearings, brush, streamside vegetation.

HAPPY WREN *Thryothorus felix* 5¼ — Pl. 32

Field marks: A rusty-brown wren with *ochre-buff underparts.* Note the *black and white striped cheeks* and dark whisker mark outlining the *white throat.*

Similar species: See Bar-vented Wren (above).

Voice: A rising *whee,* followed by a descending and accelerating *whee whi chou chou chou chou* (3–5 *chou*'s), Chalif.

Range: W. Mexico only; Pacific slope from s. Sonora to Oaxaca. **Habitat:** Roadsides, brushy washes, river thickets, shrubs.

SPOT-BREASTED WREN   Pl. 32
Thryothorus maculipectus 5–5½

Field marks: This plain-winged brown wren is *thickly spotted* on its whitish underparts. Note also the white eyebrow stripe with a black line below it. Tail strongly barred.

Similar species: Other wrens with spotted breasts are larger, with barred or streaked backs.

Voice: Song variable. One version suggests White-eyed Vireo but more elaborate, *wheet-we-wi-we'yu-you* (Chalif). An ascending buzz or trill; also a repetitious chant, *swee-purpiyou, swee-purpiyou, swee-purpiyou* (RTP).

Range: E. Mexico to n. Costa Rica. **Mexico:** Gulf slope from e. Nuevo León, s. Tamaulipas through n. Oaxaca, n. Chiapas, and Yucatán Pen.; also Pacific Coast of Chiapas. **Habitat:** Lowlands, foothills; forest borders, thickets, brush.

BEWICK'S WREN   *Thryomanes bewickii* 5–5½   Pl. 32

Field marks: A gray-brown wren with very pale gray underparts and a whitish eyebrow stripe. Note the *relatively long dark tail* with much *white in the outer feathers*. Often wobbles tail from side to side.

Voice: Song variable; typically a thin trill, prefaced by 1 or 2 high burry notes, *swee, swee, cheeeeeeee.* May suggest Song Sparrow (RTP).

Range: Sw. B. Colombia, s. Ontario through middle and w. U.S. to s.-cen. Mexico. **Mexico:** Resident south to s. Baja California (formerly Guadalupe I.); widespread in highlands and plateau south to Oaxaca, cen. Veracruz; also Gulf slope in Nuevo León and Tamaulipas. **Habitat:** Thickets, underbrush, juniper, oaks, gardens, parks.

SOCORRO WREN   *Thryomanes sissonii* 5–5½   Pl. 32

Field marks: Similar to Bewick's Wren (and possibly a race of it) but tail lacks broad white outer tips; white eyebrow stripe less pronounced; underparts more buff.

Range: Only Socorro I. of Revilla Gigedo Is. off w. Mexico.

CLARION ISLAND WREN   *Troglodytes tanneri* 5¼   Pl. 32

Field marks: May be an isolated race of Northern House-Wren. Similar but larger, grayer above, buffier below; markings on wings and tail less distinct.

Range: Only Clarión I. of Revilla Gigedo Is. off w. Mexico.

NORTHERN HOUSE-WREN   See E, W, or T
Troglodytes aedon (in part)

Memo: Similar to Brown-throated Wren (conspecific) and Southern House-Wren (possibly conspecific) but grayer on back,

pale gray rather than buff below; lacks buff eyebrow line.
Range: S. Canada to Baja California, sw. U.S. and central parts of e. U.S. **Mexico:** Breeds in mts. of n. Baja California. Winters to s. Baja California and Isthmus of Tehuantepec.

BROWN-THROATED WREN Pl. 32
Troglodytes aedon in part (or *T. brunneicollis*) 4¾
Field marks: Very similar to the Northern House-Wren (which invades Mexico in winter) but browner on back, buffier on throat and underparts, and with a more distinct buffy eyebrow stripe. Barring on sides and flanks more distinct. The 2 birds are now usually lumped as 1 species.
Similar species: (1) U.S. races of House-Wren are grayer above, lack a distinct eyebrow stripe, are grayer, less brown, on breast. See also (2) Southern House-Wren (ranges touch only in Oaxaca), next.
Voice: Song similar in pattern to other races of *T. aedon.*
Range: Mts. of se. Arizona and higher mts. of Mexico south to Isthmus of Tehuantepec. **Habitat:** Highlands (3000–13,000 ft.); forests of pines, oaks, firs.

SOUTHERN (TROPICAL) HOUSE-WREN Pl. 32
Troglodytes musculus 4¾
(including Cozumel Wren)
Field marks: A faintly barred brownish wren with no really distinctive field marks. Very similar to Northern House-Wren but browner, washed with rusty or dull cinnamon on rump and lower underparts; also a somewhat more distinct *buffy* stripe over eye. Much more like Brown-throated Wren and may be conspecific with that bird and Northern House-Wren.
Note: The race of Cozumel I. is sometimes treated as a distinct species, *T. beani,* Cozumel Wren. It is larger, grayer, and the only wren on the island.
Similar forms: (1) Northern House-Wren (not found below Isthmus of Tehuantepec) is grayer above and below, has less of an eye line, and its barred under tail coverts are whitish. (2) Brown-throated Wren (mts. north of Isthmus of Tehuantepec), is darker buff-brown below, more barred on flanks.
Voice: Song strongly resembles bubbling or gurgling song of *eastern* populations of Northern House-Wren; also a loud, rapid musical *chwee-chwee-chwee-chwee-chwee* (Eisenmann).
Range: Se. Mexico to Tierra del Fuego, Falkland Is. **Mexico:** Gulf slope from Veracruz to Tabasco; also e. Oaxaca, Chiapas, Yucatán Pen., Cozumel I. **Habitat:** Lowlands to mts.; shrubbery, clearings, plantations, gardens, towns, farms.

RUFOUS-BROWED WREN Pl. 32
Troglodytes ruficiliatus 4
Field marks: A reddish-brown house-wren somewhat similar to Southern House-Wren but darker, with a broad *rufous eye-*

brow stripe. Underparts strong buff to tawny rufous, lightening on belly. Brownish sides and flanks heavily barred.
Similar species: See Southern House-Wren (preceding).
Voice: Loud and nasal; suggests Southern House-Wren but is said to lack cheerful vitality.
Range: Se. Mexico (Chiapas), Guatemala, Honduras, El Salvador. **Habitat:** High mts. (6000–11,000 ft.); cloud forest, pine-oak woods, brushy ravines.

WHITE-BREASTED (LOWLAND) WOOD-WREN   Pl. 32
Henicorhina leucosticta   3½–4
Field marks: The 2 wood-wrens are *stub-tailed* birds with *boldly striped black and white cheeks.* This, the wood-wren of the lowlands, is known from its highland counterpart by the *white* throat and breast. More often heard than seen.
Similar species: Gray-breasted Wood-Wren (higher altitudes) has *gray* throat and breast, less stubby tail.
Voice: Song, clear whistled phrases, repeated, *cheery-cheery-bee, cheery-cheery-bee,* etc. (RTP). *Churry-churry-cheeer,* etc., and also *chwee-teew-teew* (Eisenmann).
Range: S. Mexico to Amazonia. **Mexico:** Mainly Gulf drainage from e. San Luis Potosí south to Puebla, n. Oaxaca, Chiapas, and east to Tabasco, Campeche, Quintana Roo. Also Pacific slope of Chiapas. **Habitat:** Lowlands, lower mts. (to 4000 ft.); undergrowth of humid forests.

GRAY-BREASTED (HIGHLAND) WOOD-WREN   Pl. 32
Henicorhina leucophrys   3½–4
Field marks: Similar to White-breasted Wood-Wren but breast *gray;* throat streaked with gray. Otherwise it has the same stripe-cheeked, rather stub-tailed look. Replaces other wood-wrens in highlands (but some overlapping).
Similar species: See White-breasted Wood-Wren (lowlands).
Voice: A variety of ringing whistled phrases; a phrase may be repeated over and over before changing: *too-teeoo-weet',* etc.; *weetee, weetoo,* etc.; *wee-loo-weechee,* etc. (Eisenmann).
Range: S. Mexico to cen. Peru, n. Bolivia. **Mexico:** Mts. from Michoacán, e. San Luis Potosí, cen. Veracruz south through Chiapas. **Habitat:** Highlands (3000–8000 + ft.); dense undergrowth and borders of cloud forest; thickets.

WHITE-BELLIED WREN   *Uropsila leucogastra*   3¾   Pl. 32
Field marks: A small *stub-tailed* wren with *whitish underparts* (incl. belly), tan flanks, white eyebrow stripe, but no striped cheek pattern as in wood-wrens.
Similar species: White-breasted Wood-Wren is strongly bicolored below, has black and white stripes on cheeks.
Voice: Musical, rhythmic tinkling and bubbling; softly given, ventriloquial (Sutton).

Range: Mexico, B. Honduras, Guatemala, Honduras. **Mexico:** Gulf lowlands from s. Tamaulipas south to n. Chiapas and east through Yucatán Pen.; also Pacific lowlands of Colima, Michoacán, Guerrero. **Habitat:** Undergrowth of humid forests, humid thickets, coastal scrub.

ROCK WREN *Salpinctes obsoletus* 5–6¼ **Pl. 32**
Field marks: A rather *gray* wren with a *lightly streaked* breast, rusty rump, *light or buffy patches* in tail corners.
Similar species: Canyon Wren, which shares same rocky habitat, has dark belly, white throat.
Voice: Song, a varied chant, *tew, tew, tew, tew* or *chr-wee, chr-wee, chr-wee* or *che-poo, che-poo, che-poo,* etc. Call, a loud dry trill on 1 pitch; also a clear *ti-keer* (RTP).
Range: Sw. Canada, w. U.S. to Costa Rica. **Mexico:** Low deserts to arid uplands; Baja California, Sonora, and most islands of w. Mexico; also central plateau and eastern highlands south to Chiapas; not on Gulf plain or Yucatán Pen. **Habitat:** Rocky slopes, canyons, talus, rock walls.

CANYON WREN *Catherpes mexicanus* 5½–5¾ **Pl. 32**
Field marks: Note the white bib. Dark rusty wren with a dark reddish-brown belly, contrasting with *white breast and throat.*
Similar species: Rock Wren is grayish; white below, streaked.
Voice: A gushing cadence of clear curved notes tripping down the scale, sometimes picking up at the end: *te-you, te-you, te-you tew tew tew tew* or *tee tee tee tee tew tew tew tew* (RTP).
Range: Sw. Canada, w. U.S., Mexico. **Mexico:** Baja California and offshore islands; Pacific slope, rocky highlands and plateaus of w., cen., and s. Mexico to Chiapas. Not on Gulf coastal slope. **Habitat:** Cliffs, canyons, rockslides, stone buildings. Often nests under roof tiles in villages and even in Mexico City.

SLENDER-BILLED (SUMICHRAST'S) WREN **Pl. 33**
Hylorchilus sumichrasti 5½–6
Field marks: Resembles Canyon Wren but tail shorter; lacks the white bib; almost entirely brown below, paler on throat; sooty abdomen is obscurely dotted and barred.
Voice: A sharp *peenk,* often repeated (Crossin and Ely).
Range: Se. Mexico only; cen. Veracruz (near Presidio) and adjacent n. Oaxaca, n. Chiapas. Rare and local. **Habitat:** Undergrowth in rocky areas of humid forests, ravines (800–3000 ft.).

NIGHTINGALE WREN **Pl. 33**
Microcerculus marginatus [*philomela*] 4
Field marks: A dark stub-tailed wren, somewhat similar in shape to the wood-wrens, but longer-billed and lacking facial striping. Dark brown above *without evident barring* on wings or

tail; underparts paler, less rufescent, with a slightly scalloped effect. Teeters rear parts like a Spotted Sandpiper. Heard but rarely seen.

Similar species: Wood-wrens have strong facial stripes.

Voice: An often endless series of single whistled notes, each well separated and higher or lower than the next, the key seemingly picked at random (Alden).

Range: Se. Mexico to Amazonia (birds from s. Costa Rica south may be specifically distinct). **Mexico:** Gulf slope of n. Chiapas; local. Reported B. Honduras. **Habitat:** Undergrowth of tall humid forests; lowlands to 3500 ft.

Thrashers and Mockingbirds: Mimidae

"MIMIC-THRUSHES" are noted for their apparent powers of mimicry. Excellent songsters. Strong-legged; usually longer-tailed than true thrushes; bill usually more decurved. **Food:** Insects, fruits. **Range:** New World; most numerous in Mid. America. **No. of species:** World, 31; Mexico, 18.

BROWN THRASHER   *Toxostoma rufum*   **See E, W, or T**
   Memo: Rufous above, brown stripes below.
   Range: East of Rockies; s. Canada to Gulf states. **Mexico:** Reported casually wintering in ne. Mexico; also Sonora.

LONG-BILLED THRASHER   **Pl. 34**
Toxostoma longirostre   10–12
   Field marks: A well-striped thrasher similar to Brown Thrasher of U.S. but less rufous; streaks blackish (not brown); cheeks grayer; bill a bit longer, more decurved, blacker.
   Similar species: Brown Thrasher (more rufous) may occur casually in northeastern border states of Mexico.
   Voice: Notes and phrases of song similar to other thrashers'; some pairing as in Brown Thrasher's. Call, *too-ree* (RTP).
   Range: S. Texas, e. and s.-cen. Mexico. **Mexico:** Northeastern slope from e. Coahuila east to Tamaulipas and south to Hidalgo, ne. Puebla, cen. Veracruz. **Habitat:** Woodland undergrowth, thickets, mesquite.

COZUMEL THRASHER   *Toxostoma guttatum*   9–10   **Pl. 34**
   Field marks: Very much like the Long-billed Thrasher but smaller, cheeks browner; the only thrasher on Cozumel I. Regarded by some authorities as an isolated race of the Long-billed Thrasher, *T. longirostre*.

Range: Confined to Cozumel I. off Yucatán Pen. **Habitat:** Woodland borders, thickets, scrub.

OCELLATED THRASHER   Pl. 34
Toxostoma ocellatum   11

Field marks: This dark-backed endemic thrasher of the highlands may be readily identified by its profusion of *roundish black spots* on breast, sides, and flanks. Narrow white tips on outer tail feathers.

Similar species: See Long-billed Thrasher (striped), above.

Voice: Musical thrasherlike phrases, paired or in threes.

Range: Highlands of s.-cen. Mexico only (Guanajuato and Hidalgo to Oaxaca). **Habitat:** Oak and oak-pine woodlands of uplands (5000–9000 ft.).

GRAY THRASHER   *Toxostoma cinereum*   9–10   Pl. 34

Field marks: A slender gray-brown thrasher with tear-shaped black spots or streaks on the underparts. Outer tail feathers tipped with white. The only other spotted or streaked thrasher occurring in Baja California, the Sage Thrasher (winter), is smaller, with a shorter tail (also white-tipped) and a shorter, more thrushlike bill.

Similar species: See Sage Thrasher (below).

Range: Baja California only; from Cape north to Lat. 31° on west side and to 29° (Animas Bay) on east side of peninsula. **Habitat:** Desert scrub, mesquite.

BENDIRE'S THRASHER   *Toxostoma bendirei*   See W

Memo: Rather straight robinlike bill, soft breast spots.

Range: Deserts of sw. U.S., nw. Mexico. **Mexico:** Breeds Sonora. Winters south to s. Sinaloa.

CURVE-BILLED THRASHER   Pl. 34
Toxostoma curvirostre   9½–11½

Field marks: This widespread thrasher of the deserts can be told from the other thrashers that have *well-curved bills* by the *indistinctly spotted breast*. Some individuals have narrow white wingbars. Eye pale orange or reddish.

Similar species: (1) Bendire's Thrasher (similar breast-spotting) has a shorter, more robinlike bill, yellow eye. (2) Leconte's and (3) Crissal Thrashers lack breast-spotting.

Voice: Note, a sharp liquid *whit-wheet!* like a human whistle of attention. Song, a musical series of notes and phrases, almost grosbeaklike in quality. Not much repetition (RTP).

Range: Deserts of sw. U.S. to s. Mexico. **Mexico:** Resident across n. Mexico and south through central plateau to uplands of Oaxaca. **Habitat:** Deserts, arid brush, scrubby wood borders.

CALIFORNIA THRASHER   *Toxostoma redivivum*   **See W**
  Memo: Dark brown; pale cinnamon belly; deeply curved bill.
  Range: Resident in California, nw. Baja California (south to
  Lat. 30°).

LECONTE'S (DESERT) THRASHER   **See W**
Toxostoma lecontei
  Memo: Very pale, sandy; no streaks, dark eye.
  Range: Deserts of sw. U.S., nw. Mexico. **Mexico:** N. and cen.-
  w. Baja California; nw. Sonora.

CRISSAL THRASHER   *Toxostoma dorsale*   **See W or T**
  Memo: Sickle bill, plain breast, rufous patch under tail.
  Range: Desert scrub; sw. U.S. to cen. Mexico. **Mexico:** N.
  Baja California; n. Sonora, n. Chihuahua, nw. Coahuila and
  south irregularly on central plateau to Zacatecas, San Luis Po-
  tosí, Hidalgo.

SAGE THRASHER   *Oreoscoptes montanus*   **See W or T**
  Memo: Striped below; white tail corners; bill and tail relatively
  short.
  Range: Breeds s. B. Columbia, w. U.S. Winters sw. U.S., n.
  Mexico. **Mexico:** Winters to deserts of Baja California and arid
  country of northern states; south on central plateau to Guanajuato.

SOCORRO THRASHER   *Mimodes graysoni*   10–11   **Pl. 34**
  Field marks: A plain gray-brown thrasher endemic to Socorro
  I. It has a relatively short thrushlike bill for a thrasher. Under-
  parts white or buffy white; sides, flanks, and under tail coverts
  streaked sparsely with brownish.
  Similar species: None on Socorro I.
  Range: Confined to Socorro I. in Revilla Gigedo Is. far off Pa-
  cific Coast of Mexico.

BLUE MOCKINGBIRD   *Melanotis caerulescens*   10   **Pl. 34**
  Field marks: A *wholly dull gray-blue* mockingbird, darker on
  lower belly, with a *black mask,* red eye. The immature is more
  blackish, tinged with dull blue above.
  Similar species: Blue-and-White Mockingbird (regarded by
  some as conspecific) has white underparts; more southern.
  Voice: Song, varied phrases suggestive of Northern Mockingbird but lower in pitch, less repetitious (RTP).
  Range: Mexico only; lowlands and mt. slopes from s. Sonora,
  sw. Chihuahua, s. Tamaulipas south to Isthmus of Tehuantepec. **Habitat:** Sea level to 8000 ft.; woods, brush, second
  growth.

BLUE-AND-WHITE MOCKINGBIRD   **Pl. 34**
Melanotis hypoleucus
   Field marks: Similar to preceding species (dull gray-blue
   above, *black mask*) but largely *white* below. Eye red.
   Similar species: (1) See Blue Mockingbird. (2) Tropical
   Mockingbird lacks black mask, has white wingbars, white in tail.
   Voice: Similar to Blue Mockingbird's.
   Range: Se. Mexico (uplands of Chiapas), Guatemala, Hon-
   duras, El Salvador. **Habitat:** Second growth, brush (2000–9000
   ft.).

BLACK CATBIRD   *Melanoptila glabrirostris* 8   **Pl. 34**
   Field marks: An entirely *glossy blue-black* catbird. Size and
   shape of Gray Catbird, which invades range in winter.
   Range: E. Mexico, n. Guatemala (Petén), B. Honduras, nw.
   Honduras. **Mexico:** Coastal Yucatán, Quintana Roo, and offshore islands (most abundant on Cozumel I.). Local or rare on
   mainland. **Habitat:** Coastal scrub, brush, wood edges.

GRAY (NORTHERN) CATBIRD   **See E, W, or T**
Dumetella carolinensis
   Memo: Slaty; black crown, chestnut under tail coverts.
   Range: S. Canada to Gulf states. Winters se. U.S. to Panamá,
   W. Indies. **Mexico:** Migrant and winter visitor through eastern
   and southern sections, including Yucatán Pen.

NORTHERN (COMMON) MOCKINGBIRD   **See E, W, or T**
Mimus polyglottos
   Memo: Like Tropical Mockingbird but has large white wing
   patches.
   Range: Se. Canada to s. Mexico, W. Indies. **Mexico:** Baja California and from U.S. border south to Isthmus of Tehuantepec
   in Oaxaca and Veracruz. Sea level to 7000 ft.

TROPICAL MOCKINGBIRD *Mimus gilvus* 9–10   **Pl. 34**
   Field marks: Similar to Northern Mockingbird (and may be
   conspecific), replacing that bird below Isthmus of Tehuantepec.
   It lacks large white wing patches (has only wingbars) and shows
   less white in tail.
   Similar species: Northern Mockingbird (north of Isthmus)
   has large white wing patches, more white along sides of tail.
   Hybrids are reported from the Isthmus and Veracruz.
   Voice: Song similar to Northern Mockingbird's but more leisurely, not so loud; less repetition of phrases or none. Predomi-
   nant phrases are *churr, chweee,* and *chwee'oo* (Eisenmann).
   Range: S. Mexico locally to s. Brazil. **Mexico:** From Veracruz,
   Isthmus of Tehuantepec (Oaxaca) east through Yucatán Pen.
   and Chiapas. **Habitat:** Towns, grassy roadsides, lawns, parks,
   edges, brush; sea level to uplands.

Thrushes, Solitaires, Bluebirds: Turdidae

LARGE-EYED, slender-billed, usually stout-legged songbirds. "Robins" (of genus *Turdus*) vary from all black or smoky brown to tan; some patterned with rufous. Bluebirds are intense blue above. Most other thrushes are brown above, often spotted below. Juveniles are spotted below. Among the finest singers. **Food:** Insects, worms, snails, berries, fruits. **Range:** Nearly worldwide. **No. of species:** World, 300; Mexico, 25 or 26.

AMERICAN ROBIN *Turdus migratorius*   See E, W, or T
Memo: Brick-red breast, gray back, darker head and tail.
Range: Alaska, Canada to s. Mexico. Winters to Guatemala. **Mexico:** Breeds in highlands south to Oaxaca, w.-cen. Veracruz. More widespread in winter, reaching Baja California and rarely Yucatán Pen. and Guatemala.

SAN LUCAS ROBIN   Pl. 35
Turdus confinis (or *T. migratorius* in part)
Field marks: Similar to American Robin (and may be regarded as merely a pale race) but underparts *very pale creamy buff.* Male does not have a blackish head (it is gray like back).
Range: Mts. of Cape district of Baja California.

RUFOUS-COLLARED ROBIN   Pl. 35
Turdus rufitorques   9–10
Field marks: *Male:* A smartly patterned *black* robin with a broad *rufous collar,* rufous breast. *Female:* Brownish above, with duller collar and breast.
Voice: Song, typical American Robin-like phrases, caroling.
Range: S. Mexico, Guatemala, El Salvador, Honduras (casual). **Mexico:** Chiapas. **Habitat:** Mts. (5000–11,000 ft.); pine-oak woodlands, pastures, brushy borders, cloud forest.

RUFOUS-BACKED ROBIN *Turdus rufopalliatus* 9   **Pl. 35**
Field marks: Like a pale American Robin (extensive cinnamon underparts; grayish head, wings, and tail) but with a *rufous wash on back* and *no white* around eye. An arboreal fruit-eater.
Similar species: The conspicuous American Robin (gray back) favors higher altitudes, pines.
Voice: Typical robinlike phrases.
Range: W. and s. Mexico; occasional in se. Arizona in winter. Lowlands, foothills, and highland valleys of Pacific slope from s. Sonora south to Isthmus of Tehuantepec. Also Federal Dist. and Tres Marías Is. **Habitat:** Fruiting crowns of deciduous forest trees, dense shrubbery, parks, gardens.

WHITE-THROATED ROBIN   Pl. 35
Turdus assimilis 9–9½

Field marks: Note the *white crescent* on the lower throat. Otherwise a dull olive-brown robin with a heavily streaked (sometimes almost blackish) upper throat. Underparts whitish, darkening to olive-gray on chest.

Similar species: See Rufous-backed and Clay-colored Robins.

Voice: A splendid singer; lively, somewhat repetitious phrases (like a thrasher's) that follow one another in varying sequence; often *whoa* or *whoa-ah-ah* in midst of song (Chalif). Characteristic call, a froglike nasal croak, *yenk* or *urnk;* also a screechy *dzee'-yoo* (Eisenmann).

Range: Mexico to nw. Ecuador. **Mexico:** Lowlands (perhaps not breeding), foothills to high elevations of mts. (to 11,500 ft.); highlands from s. Sonora, s. Chihuahua south; Gulf slope from s. Tamaulipas south, excluding Yucatán Pen. **Habitat:** Humid forests and borders, second growth, scrubby ravines.

CLAY-COLORED ROBIN   *Turdus grayi* 9–9½   Pl. 35

Field marks: *Warm brown* above; dull tan on the chest, paling to *light tawny or cinnamon-buff* on the belly. Throat streaked with light brown, not black. The rather uniform underparts are distinctive.

Similar species: See ♀ Black Robin (below).

Voice: Song, similar to but mellower than American Robin's. Call note, *meoo* or *meow;* this often repeated (Chalif).

Range: Mexico to Colombia. **Mexico:** Gulf slope from Nuevo León, Tamaulipas south and east to Yucatán Pen.; also from Guerrero to Chiapas. **Habitat:** Mainly semi-open areas in lowlands, but following clearings to 7000 ft.; plantations, gardens, forest openings and borders.

MOUNTAIN ROBIN   *Turdus plebejus* 9–10   Pl. 35

Field marks: Sooty brown above, lighter below. Note the *blackish* bill on this very drab dark robin. Other robins have yellow or dull greenish bills in adults. (Immatures may have dark bills.)

Similar species: See (1) ♀ Black and (2) Clay-colored Robins.

Voice: Song, very inferior for a *Turdus* of the "robin" group; hurried and monotonous with repetitions of same note and few changes in pitch. Calls, *cack-cack-cack; kick-kick,* etc. Also a mournful *ooooooreee* (Eisenmann).

Range: Mts.; se. Mexico to w. Panamá. **Mexico:** Se. Chiapas (Mt. Ovando, Volcán Tacaná). **Habitat:** High mts. (6000–10,000 ft.); cloud forest, oaks, open woods.

BLACK ROBIN   *Turdus infuscatus* 8½–9   Pl. 35

Field marks: *Male:* An *entirely black* robin with a bright yel-

low bill and legs. *Female:* Dark brown, paler below, lightening
to buff on throat. Bill and legs dull yellow.
Similar species: (1) In Chiapas and Guatemala, Mountain
Robin (black bill) might be confused with ♀ Black Robin.
(2) Clay-colored Robin (favors lower altitudes) is warmer brown
than ♀ Black Robin and has pale cinnamon belly.
Voice: Similar to White-throated Robin's in repetition of phrases,
but louder, even more thrasherlike (Hardy).
Range: Mts. of Guatemala, Mexico, El Salvador, Honduras.
Mexico: Highlands of e. and s. Mexico (sw. Tamaulipas, e. San
Luis Potosí south to Guerrero, Oaxaca, Chiapas). **Habitat:** Mts.
(4000–11,000 + ft.). Cloud forest, forest borders, oaks.

VARIED THRUSH   *Ixoreus naevius*   **See W**
   Memo: Similar to American Robin but with black chestband,
orange wingbars and eye stripe.
   Range: Alaska, w. Canada, nw. U.S. Winters mainly Pacific
states of U.S. **Mexico:** Irregular winter visitor to n. Baja California. Recorded Guadalupe I.

AZTEC THRUSH   *Ridgwayia pinicola*   8½   **Pl. 35**
   Field marks: A *dark-hooded* robinlike thrush with a white
belly, white rump. Wings strikingly *patched with white.* Male
sooty on head, breast, and back; female browner.
   Voice: Soft churring notes and a nasal *wheer* (Parker).
   Range: Mexico only. W. and central mt. ranges from s. Chihuahua, Coahuila south to Oaxaca, Veracruz. **Habitat:** Forests
of oak, pine, and fir in high mts. (to 11,000 ft.).

TOWNSEND'S SOLITAIRE   **See W or T**
Myadestes townsendi
   Memo: Gray; white eye-ring and tail sides, buff wing patch.
Song warbled, suggests Black-headed Grosbeak's; more rapid.
   Range: Alaska, w. Canada, w. U.S., n. Mexico. **Mexico:** Breeds
in high mts. from Sonora, Coahuila to Jalisco. Recorded occa-
sionally in winter from n. Baja California, Guadalupe I.

BROWN-BACKED SOLITAIRE   **Pl. 35**
Myadestes obscurus   8
   Field marks: A slender, small-billed gray thrush with a
brownish back and *rusty wings;* suggests a flycatcher rather
than a typical thrush. There is a conspicuous white eye-ring and
dull whitish outer feathers on the longish tail.
   Similar species: (1) Slate-colored Solitaire (lower altitudes) is
smaller, slate-gray above, without rufous in wings. (2) Townsend's Solitaire (nw. Mexico only) lacks brownish upperparts
and shows a contrasting tawny wing patch.
   Voice: Call note, *weenk* or *wenk.* Song suggests cranking up of

an old-time motor car; it starts off with *wenk, wenk,* then
catches and takes off at a fast pace with flutelike notes, etc.
(Chalif). A fine singer.
Range: Mts. of Mexico, Guatemala, El Salvador, Honduras.
Mexico: Highlands; s. Sonora, s. Chihuahua, Nuevo León, s.
Tamaulipas south through mts. of s. Mexico; also Tres Marías
Is. Lower levels in winter. **Habitat:** Highlands (mainly 4000–
8500 ft.); cloud forest, pine-oak zone, ravines.

SLATE-COLORED SOLITAIRE   Pl. 35
Myadestes unicolor   7–7½
   Field marks: A bit smaller than Brown-backed Solitaire and
   lacking the brown and rufous on back and wings. Dark slate
   above, lighter below. Has white eye-ring and broad whitish tips
   on outer tail feathers.
   Similar species: See Brown-backed Solitaire (preceding).
   Voice: One of the world's finest bird singers. "Makes all other
   thrushes sound like amateurs" (Fisher). A succession of penetrating piccolo-like whistles of great virtuosity, varying in pitch,
   often ending on a loose trill (RTP).
   Range: Se. Mexico to n. Nicaragua. **Mexico:** Mainly Gulf
   slope; Hidalgo, Puebla, Veracruz, n. Oaxaca, n. Chiapas. **Habitat:** Subtropical and temperate woodlands, brush of lower
   slopes.

WOOD THRUSH   *Hylocichla mustelina*   See E or T
   Memo: Rufous head and shoulders; large round spots.
   Range: Se. Canada, cen. and e. U.S. Winters Mexico to Pan-
   amá. **Mexico:** Migrant and winter visitor mainly Gulf slope.

HERMIT THRUSH   *Catharus guttatus*   See E, W, or T
   Memo: Rufous tail, well-spotted breast.
   Range: Alaska, Canada, w. and ne. U.S. Winters U.S. to Gua-
   temala. **Mexico:** Widespread in migration and winter except
   Yucatán Pen.

SWAINSON'S THRUSH   See E, W, or T
Catharus ustulatus
   Memo: Spotted breast, buffy cheek, broad buff eye-ring.
   Range: Alaska, Canada, w. and ne. U.S. Winters s. Mexico to
   w. Argentina, Paraguay. **Mexico:** Widespread migrant but sel-
   dom reported Yucatán Pen. Winters in s. Mexico.

GRAY-CHEEKED THRUSH   See E, W, or T
Catharus minimus
   Memo: Spotted breast, gray cheek, inconspicuous eye-ring.
   Range: Ne. Siberia, Alaska, Canada, ne. U.S. Winters in W.
   Indies and in S. America east of Andes to Peru, n. Brazil. **Mex-

ico: Rare or casual transient on Yucatán Pen.; should occur elsewhere in east; probably overlooked.

VEERY *Catharus fuscescens*   **See E, W, or T**
Memo: Tawny above, relatively fine spotting on breast.
Range: S. Canada, n. and cen. U.S. Winters in e. S. America, Colombia to Brazil. **Mexico:** Probably transient in east; rarely reported (Veracruz, Yucatán Pen.); probably overlooked.

SPOTTED NIGHTINGALE-THRUSH   **Pl. 35**
Catharus dryas 7
Field marks: The combination of *black* head (with white throat), *spotted* breast, and *orange* bill and legs identifies this gray thrush. Breast washed with light apricot color in life (fades to whitish in specimens).
Similar species: See Black-headed Nightingale-Thrush (yellow bill and legs; no spots), next.
Voice: Rich liquid phrases very suggestive of Wood Thrush but less loud and full (Eisenmann).
Range: Mts. of se. Mexico, Guatemala, Honduras; also n. S. America to nw. Argentina. **Mexico:** Mts. of Oaxaca, Chiapas (6000–10,000 ft.); local. **Habitat:** Forest undergrowth, thickets.

BLACK-HEADED NIGHTINGALE-THRUSH   **Pl. 35**
Catharus mexicanus 6
Field marks: A black-capped thrush with an unspotted pale olive chest. Bill yellow; legs dull yellow. Female has dark olive-gray (not black) cap. Immature lacks black cap, has black bill.
Similar species: See Spotted Nightingale-Thrush (spots on pale apricot-colored breast; orange bill and legs).
Voice: Song suggestive of Hermit Thrush in quality and form. Call notes, a high-pitched *seent* and a low *twaa* (Chalif).
Range: Ne. Mexico to w. Panamá. **Mexico:** Highlands of e. Mexico (mainly Gulf slope) from s. Tamaulipas to Chiapas. **Habitat:** Undergrowth of humid forests.

RUSSET NIGHTINGALE-THRUSH   **Pl. 35**
Catharus occidentalis 6–6½
Field marks: A rusty-brown thrush, ruddier on the crown, with a dimly mottled grayish breast. Note *buff patch* across spread wing. Bill orangish, often dark above and always with dark tip on lower mandible.
Similar species: (1) Ruddy-capped Nightingale-Thrush lacks buff wing patch; has entirely orange lower mandible. (2) Orange-billed Nightingale-Thrust has completely orange bill and orange legs.
Voice: Resembles that of next species but thinner, less musical, less varied. Call nasal, suggesting Gray Catbird (Hardy).
Range: Mexico only; high mts. from n. Sinaloa, Chihuahua,

San Luis Potosí, s. Tamaulipas south to Oaxaca. **Habitat:** Highland forests of pine, oak, and fir; undergrowth, ravines.

RUDDY-CAPPED (HIGHLAND) NIGHTINGALE-THRUSH
Catharus frantzii 6–6½   **Not illus.**

Field marks: Differs from Russet Nightingale-Thrush in *lacking* buff patch across spread wing. Lower mandible is entirely *yellow or orange*, lacking dark tip.

Similar species: See (1) Russet Nightingale-Thrush (preceding) and (2) Orange-billed Nightingale-Thrush (next).

Voice: Song has pattern of Wood Thrush's and quality of Hermit Thrush's (Eisenmann and Hartshorne). 1–3 flutelike *eeoolay* phrases, followed by a much higher phrase (Slud).

Range: Mts. of Mexico to w. Panamá. **Mexico:** High mts. of Jalisco and San Luis Potosí to Oaxaca and Chiapas. **Habitat:** Broadleaf forests, cloud forest, undergrowth, ravines.

ORANGE-BILLED NIGHTINGALE-THRUSH   Pl. 35
Catharus aurantiirostris 6–7

Field marks: A brown-backed, gray-breasted thrush, similar to the preceding but with *bright orange bill and legs.*

Similar species: (1) Russet Nightingale-Thrush has dark legs, mostly dark bill. (2) Ruddy-capped Nightingale-Thrush has dark legs, dark upper mandible. (3) Spotted Nightingale-Thrush (orange bill and legs) has a black head, spotted breast.

Voice: Emphatic phrases, rather like those of White-eyed Vireo, often ending with a *chick* or *we-chik* (RTP). Song may be interpreted as *diver-chi-doski;* also *cher-che-witzee, witzchee witzchewezi-wezi,* etc. (Chalif).

Range: Mexico to w. Panamá; also Colombia, Venezuela, Trinidad. **Mexico:** Mt. forests from n. Sinaloa, Chihuahua, San Luis Potosí, sw. Tamaulipas south to Chiapas. **Habitat:** Woodland undergrowth, oak brush, forest edges, ravines, thickets.

EASTERN BLUEBIRD   *Sialia sialis*   See E, W, or T
Memo: Blue back, rusty breast and throat (♂).

Range: East of Rockies; s. Canada to Gulf states; also se. Arizona, Mexico to Nicaragua. **Mexico:** Pacific foothills, Sonora to Oaxaca; highlands generally south to Chiapas. Also Gulf slope of Tamaulipas, Veracruz. Spreads somewhat in winter.

WESTERN BLUEBIRD   *Sialia mexicana*   See W or T
Memo: Rusty patch on back (usually), blue throat (♂).

Range: Southern B. Columbia, w. U.S. to cen. Mexico. **Mexico:** Breeds mts. of n. Baja California; highlands generally south to Michoacán, Morelos, Puebla, w. Veracruz. Spreads to lower altitudes in winter.

MOUNTAIN BLUEBIRD   *Sialia currucoides*   **See W or T**
Memo: Turquoise-blue breast (♂).
Range: Cen. Alaska, w. Canada, w. U.S. Winters to n. Mexico.
Mexico: Winters n. Baja California and northern states (east to
Nuevo León); casually south to Michoacán, Guanajuato.

Gnatcatchers, Gnatwrens, Kinglets, etc.: Sylviidae

TINY, active birds with slender bills. Gnatcatchers have long mo-
bile tails. Gnatwrens are slender wrenlike birds with very long
straight bills and longish tails. Kinglets have short bills, bright
crowns (some authors place the kinglets in a separate family, Reg-
ulidae). Old World and Australian warblers (none in Mexico) also
belong to the Sylviidae, which are sometimes merged into a much
larger family, the Muscicapidae (which in addition includes the
thrushes, babblers, Old World flycatchers, etc.). **Food:** Mainly insects, insect eggs, larvae. **Range:** Most large forested areas of
world except lower S. America. **No. of species:** World, 414; Mexico, 8.

BLUE-GRAY GNATCATCHER   **Pl. 33**
Polioptila caerulea   4½
    Field marks: Gnatcatchers look like miniature mockingbirds;
    tiny slender mites, gray above, usually whitish below, with long
    black, white-sided tails. This species may be known by its nar-
    row *white eye-ring*. Male has a black line across forehead.
    Similar species: Compare series of heads on Plate 33.
    Voice: Note, a thin peevish *zpee* or *chee*. Song, a thin, squeaky,
    wheezy series of notes, easily overlooked (RTP).
    Range: S. Utah, s. Ontario to Mexico, Guatemala, Bahamas.
    Winters also to B. Honduras (possibly breeds) and Honduras.
    Mexico: Widespread resident (incl. Baja California, Yucatán
    Pen. and islands) but not northeastern sector, where present
    only in migration and winter. Winters throughout. **Habitat:**
    Open mixed woods, oaks, juniper, scrub.

WHITE-LORED GNATCATCHER   **Pl. 33**
Polioptila albiloris   4¼
    Field marks: *Male:* A gnatcatcher with a *solid black cap* in
    summer. In winter the cap is reduced by white lores and a nar-
    row white eyebrow line. *Female:* Lacks black cap; has white
    lores and eye line at all seasons.
    Similar species: (1) Blue-gray Gnatcatcher (both sexes) has
    gray cap at all seasons; note white eye-ring. See also (2) Black-
    capped Gnatcatcher and (3) Tropical Gnatcatcher.

Range: S. Mexico to nw. Costa Rica. **Mexico:** Pacific lowlands and interior of s. Mexico from Michoacán, Puebla south through Chiapas; also coastal Yucatán and Quintana Roo. **Habitat:** Wood edges; in Yucatán, coastal scrub.

BLACK-CAPPED GNATCATCHER   Pl. 33
Polioptila nigriceps 4½
  Field marks: *Male:* A black-capped gnatcatcher lacking white lores or eyebrow stripe. In winter the black cap is missing; no white eyebrow stripe. *Female:* Lacks black cap, never has a white eye stripe. This bird has been regarded as a race of the White-lored Gnatcatcher.
  Similar species: (1) ♂ White-lored Gnatcatcher is almost identical with ♂ of this species in summer when it lacks white lores and eyebrow stripe. In winter males are readily separable. Females separable at all seasons by white lores and eyebrow stripes. (2) Blue-gray Gnatcatcher has white eye-ring.
  Range: W. Mexico only; resident on Pacific slope from Sonora, w. Chihuahua south to Colima and Durango. **Habitat:** Arid country, scrubby woodlands and borders.

TROPICAL GNATCATCHER   Pl. 33
Polioptila plumbea 3¾
  Field marks: Note the *broad white eyebrow stripe* and lores. Males have a glossy black cap that is slate-gray in female.
  Similar species: (1) Blue-gray Gnatcatcher never has a black cap, lacks superciliary (eyebrow) stripe. (2) White-lored Gnatcatcher has only a narrow white line behind eye; ♂ lacks white lores and superciliaries in summer. (3) Black-capped Gnatcatcher lacks white superciliaries at all seasons.
  Voice: Song, a slow trill, high and thin at outset, fuller and slower toward end (Skutch).
  Range: Se. Mexico, Cen. America to Peru, Brazil. **Mexico:** Yucatán Pen. (Campeche, Quintana Roo); local. **Habitat:** Undergrowth, edge of rain forest.

BLACK-TAILED GNATCATCHER   Pl. 33
Polioptila melanura 4½
  Field marks: Similar to Blue-gray Gnatcatcher but breeding male has a black cap and much less white on sides of tail (outer web only). Winter ♂ (without cap) and ♀ are duller than Blue-gray Gnatcatcher. From *underside* tail is largely *black;* in Blue-gray, largely white. Some races have dull gray underparts.
  Voice: Note, a thin harsh *chee,* repeated 2–3 times, or *pee-ee-ee* (Blue-gray usually gives single note), RTP.
  Range: Sw. U.S., n. Mexico. **Mexico:** Baja California, Sonora, Chihuahua, Nuevo León south to Durango, Zacatecas, San Luis Potosí, Guanajuato. **Habitat:** Desert brush, ravines, dry washes, mesquite.

LONG-BILLED GNATWREN   **Pl. 33**
Ramphocaenus rufiventris 5
    Field marks: Note the *very slender, long, straight bill* on this
    brown wrenlike bird. Breast and cheeks buff or cinnamon. Tail
    black, tipped with white; often cocked.
    Voice: A trill, *ti-eeeeeeeeeeeeeeee,* seeming to rise toward end
    (Chalif). A soft trilled whistle on same key (Griscom). Also a
    rougher trill, dropping in pitch (RTP).
    Range: Se. Mexico to Colombia, Ecuador. **Mexico:** Gulf slope
    of s. Veracruz, n. Oaxaca, n. Chiapas, Tabasco, Yucatán Pen.;
    also Pacific slope of Chiapas. **Habitat:** Borders of humid forests
    and tall second growth.

GOLDEN-CROWNED KINGLET   **See E, W, or T**
Regulus satrapa
    Memo: Striped head; yellow or orange and yellow crown.
    Range: Breeds s. Alaska, cen. Canada, south locally in mts.
    (west) to Guatemala and (east) to N. Carolina. Winters to Gulf
    states, n. Mexico. **Mexico:** Resident in high mts. of s. Mexico
    from Michoacán, México, Hidalgo south locally to Chiapas.
    Winter visitant in highlands of n. Mexico east to Gulf slope of
    Tamaulipas.

RUBY-CROWNED KINGLET   **See E, W, or T**
Regulus calendula
    Memo: Broken eye-ring; red crown spot (♂).
    Range: Alaska, Canada, w. U.S. Winters to Guatemala. **Mex-
    ico:** Resident Guadalupe I. off Baja California. Widespread in
    winter except Yucatán Pen.; mainly highlands in south.

Wagtails and Pipits: Motacillidae

TERRESTRIAL birds, with long hind claws, thin bills. Tails bob almost constantly. Pipits are brown streaked birds with white outer
tail feathers. Wagtails are more slender, strongly patterned, with
long tails, slender legs. **Food:** Insects, spiders, seeds. **Range:**
Nearly cosmopolitan (most species in Old World). **No. of species:**
World, 53; Mexico, 2 (+2 accidental).

WHITE (PIED) WAGTAIL *Motacilla alba*   **See Europe**
    Memo: Black cap and bib, white cheeks; black and white tail.
    Range: Eurasia. A few breed in nw. Alaska. **Mexico:** Acci-
    dental, La Paz, Baja California (the ne. Siberian *M. a. ocularis*).

WATER PIPIT *Anthus spinoletta*   **See E, W, or T**
    Memo: Thin bill, white outer tail feathers; bobs tail.

Range: Colder parts and high mts. of N. Hemisphere. Winters to Guatemala, El Salvador, n. Africa, s. Asia. **Mexico:** Winter visitor in open country south to s. Baja California, Oaxaca, Veracruz; casual below Isthmus of Tehuantepec.

RED-THROATED PIPIT *Anthus cervinus*   **See Europe**
Memo: In winter, heavily streaked breast, back, and rump.
Range: Tundras n. Eurasia. Occasional nw. Alaska; has bred.
Mexico: Accidental in Baja California (San José del Cabo).

SPRAGUE'S PIPIT *Anthus spragueii*   **See E, W, or T**
Memo: Distinguished from Water Pipit by striped back, pale legs.
Range: Breeds from central parts of Canadian prairie provinces to n. Wyoming, N. Dakota, nw. Minnesota. Winters s. U.S., Mexico. **Mexico:** Winters from Sonora and n. Tamaulipas south to Guerrero, Puebla, Veracruz; mainly coastal lowlands.

Waxwings: Bombycillidae

SLEEK crested birds often with red waxy tips on secondary wing feathers. Gregarious. **Food:** Berries, insects. **Range:** N. Hemisphere. **No. of species:** World, 3; Mexico, 1.

CEDAR WAXWING *Bombycilla cedrorum*   **See E, W, or T**
Memo: Crest; yellow band on tail tip.
Range: Breeds se. Alaska, Canada, n. and cen. U.S. Winters irregularly through Mid. America to Panamá, W. Indies. **Mexico:** Widespread winter visitor; rare Yucatán Pen.

Silky-Flycatchers or Silkies: Ptilogonatidae

SLIM, crested, waxwinglike birds. **Food:** Berries, mistletoe, insects. **Range:** Sw. U.S. to Panamá. **No. of species:** World, 4; Mexico, 2.

PHAINOPEPLA *Phainopepla nitens* 7–7¾   **Pl. 34**
Field marks: *Male:* A slim, *glossy-black* bird with a *slender crest. White wing patches* are conspicuous in flight. *Female:* Dark gray with slender crest; wing patches light gray, not conspicuous. Has fly-catching habits.

Similar species: (1) Cedar Waxwing is much browner than ♀ Phainopepla, has yellow tailband. (2) Mockingbird (white wing patches) shows much white in tail.

Voice: Note, a soft low *wurp.* Song, a week, casual warble, wheezy and disconnected.

Range: Sw. U.S. to s.-cen. Mexico. **Mexico:** Baja California, deserts of nw. Mexico, and arid country of Mexican plateau south to Puebla, Veracruz. **Habitat:** Desert scrub, mesquite, oak foothills, mistletoe, pepper trees.

GRAY SILKY-FLYCATCHER (SILKY)   Pl. 34
Ptilogonys cinereus   7½–8½

Field marks: *Male:* A slim, *crested,* gray bird with a striking *black and white pattern on its longish tail* (noticeable in flight). Under tail coverts and flanks, *yellow. Female:* Similar to ♂ but brown, not gray. Waxwinglike in aspect.

Voice: Call note, *chelp* or *kelp* (Chalif). A 2-note call, 2nd note higher and accented (Land).

Range: N. Mexico to Guatemala. **Mexico:** High mts. from Sinaloa, Chihuahua, cen. Nuevo León, and sw. Tamaulipas south to Chiapas. **Habitat:** Open forests of pine-oak zone, exposed treetops.

Shrikes: Laniidae

SONGBIRDS with hook-tipped bills and often hawklike behavior. Prey sometimes impaled on thorns. **Food:** Insects, lizards, mice, small birds. **Range:** Widespread in Old World; 2 in N. America, none in S. America. **No. of species:** World, 74; Mexico, 1.

LOGGERHEAD SHRIKE   See E, W, or T
Lanius ludovicianus

Memo: Gray; black mask, black and white wings and tail.

Range: S. Canada to s. Mexico; partial migrant. **Mexico:** Baja California and from northern tier of states south to Oaxaca, Veracruz (Tehuantepec); northern birds winter to Oaxaca.

Starlings: Sturnidae

BLACKBIRDLIKE in appearance. Usually short-tailed, sharp-billed; gregarious. **Food:** Omnivorous; insects, berries, seeds. **Range:** Widespread in Old World; introduced elsewhere. **No. of species:** World, 107; Mexico, 1 (introduced via U.S.).

COMMON STARLING   *Sturnus vulgaris*   **See E, W, or T**
Memo: Blackish; tail short, bill sharp (yellow in spring).
Range: Eurasia, n. Africa. Introduced N. America. **Mexico:**
Has recently invaded Mexico at various points and has reached
Guanajuato, n. Veracruz, Yucatán. Still spreading.

Peppershrikes: Cyclarhidae

ARBOREAL birds closely allied to the vireos and often merged with
that family. **Range:** Mexico to Argentina. **No. of species:**
World, 2; Mexico, 1.

RUFOUS-BROWED PEPPERSHRIKE   Pl. 36
Cyclarhis gujanensis   6–6½
   Field marks: A chunky bird, vireolike in color (olive back, yellowish underparts) but with a heavier bill than a vireo's. Note
the *rufous stripe* across forehead and over eyes. Crown and
cheeks gray. Sexes alike.
   Note: The Cozumel I. race lacks yellow on underparts and is
whitish on abdomen.
   Voice: A short, pleasing warbled phrase, repeated at intervals,
then changing to another phrase, again repeated (RTP). A rising *witu witu whichu,* dropping on last syllable. Also *to-wish-
to-we-yo.* Also *cheeee che chrrr,* succeeding notes lower and
faster (Chalif).
   Range: E. Mexico to n. Argentina. **Mexico:** Eastern and
southern sections from s. Tamaulipas, San Luis Potosí south
through Chiapas (both slopes) and east through Yucatán Pen.,
Cozumel I. **Habitat:** Forest borders, brushy openings, open
woods.

Shrike-Vireos: Vireolaniidae

ARBOREAL; closely allied to vireos; often merged with that family.
Bills slightly heavier than vireos', more hooked at tip. **Range:**
Mexico to Amazonia. **No. of species:** World, 3; Mexico, 2.

CHESTNUT-SIDED (HIGHLAND) SHRIKE-VIREO   Pl. 36
Vireolanius melitophrys   6½–7
   Field marks: The *black and yellow eye stripes, chestnut sides*
and breastband identify this olive-backed vireolike bird. Look
also for the *black mustache line* dividing the white cheek and
throat. Eye whitish.
   Range: Mexico and Guatemala. **Mexico:** Highlands of cen.

Mexico; Jalisco, San Luis Potosí south to Chiapas; local, uncommon. **Habitat:** Oak forests (4000–10,000 ft.).

GREEN SHRIKE-VIREO   **Pl. 36**
Smaragdolanius pulchellus   5–6
   Field marks: An *emerald-green* bird with a *powder-blue* crown and hindneck; throat yellow shading into yellow-green below. More often heard than seen in treetops.
   Similar species: See (1) ♀ Green Honeycreeper (p. 201), (2) ♀ Blue-hooded Euphonia (p. 228), and (3) Blue-crowned Chlorophonia (p. 227).
   Voice: A repetitious chant, *tew-tew-tew-tew* on same pitch, repeated at intervals (RTP). Suggests Tufted Titmouse, a repetitious *peter-peter-peter-peter* (Alden).
   Range: Se. Mexico to Colombia, nw. Venezuela. **Mexico:** Gulf lowlands of s. Veracruz, n. Oaxaca, n. Chiapas; local, uncommon. **Habitat:** Arboreal. Treetops in humid forests.

Vireos: Vireonidae

SMALL olive- or gray-backed birds; resembling wood-warblers, but with somewhat heavier bills (with a more curved ridge and slight hook) than in most warblers. May be divided into 2 groups: (1) those with wingbars (and usually eye-rings); and (2) those without wingbars (these generally have eye stripes). Some of those with wingbars might be confused with *Empidonax* flycatchers, but they do not sit in the upright posture, and the light loral spot is more evident, giving the aspect of spectacles. Confusion is also possible with certain other small flycatchers and tyrannulets that do not sit upright. **Food:** Mostly insects. **Range:** Canada to Argentina. **No. of species:** World, 37; Mexico, 21.

BLACK-CAPPED VIREO   *Vireo atricapillus*   **See E, W, or T**
   Memo: Blackish cap, very conspicuous white spectacles.
   Range: Breeds from cen. Oklahoma to cen. Coahuila in n. Mexico. Winters mainly in w. Mexico from s. Sinaloa, Durango south to Michoacán; recorded also Tamaulipas, México.

COZUMEL VIREO   *Vireo bairdi*   4½   **Pl. 36**
   Field marks: A vireo with *cinnamon cheeks and sides* on Cozumel I. would be this species, which is found nowhere else. Brown above, white below, washed with cinnamon on sides; 2 conspicuous white or yellowish wingbars and white spectacles.
   Voice: Suggests White-eyed Vireo's in character.
   Range: Confined to Cozumel I., off coast of Quintana Roo.
   Habitat: Undergrowth, thickets in deciduous forests.

WHITE-EYED VIREO   *Vireo griseus*   **See E or T**
Memo: Yellowish spectacles, whitish throat, white eyes.
Note: The subspecies *V. g. perquisitor* of n.-cen. Veracruz and ne. Puebla has been regarded by some as a distinct species, named the Veracruz Vireo, *V. perquisitor.* It is dingy yellow below (not white with yellow wash on sides).
Range: E. and cen. U.S., ne. Mexico. Winters Gulf states through Mid. America to Nicaragua, Cuba. **Mexico:** Resident on Gulf slope from Texas border south to ne. Puebla, n.-cen. Veracruz. Widespread migrant and winter visitant on Gulf slope, including Yucatán Pen.

MANGROVE VIREO   *Vireo pallens*   4–4¾   **Pl. 36**
Field marks: Very similar to White-eyed Vireo, and regarded by some as conspecific, but song is basically very different. Eye color varies; dark on Pacific slope, whitish to light brown in Gulf and Caribbean lowlands. Dingier than White-eye, with a dull yellow eyebrow stripe instead of eye-ring.
Note: The population in the Atlantic lowlands has sometimes been called a distinct species, the Petén Vireo, *V. semiflavus.*
Similar species: White-eyed Vireo (a winter visitor in eastern range of Mangrove Vireo) has white eyes in adult, brown in young birds, leading to confusion. White-eyed Vireos have distinct spectacles, rather than an eyebrow stripe and are more contrastingly colored.
Voice: A loud repetitious *che-che-che-che-che,* etc., or *jeer-jeer-jeer-jeer,* etc.
Range: Mexico to nw. Costa Rica and ne. Nicaragua. **Mexico:** On Pacific Coast from s. Sonora south. In Atlantic lowlands from Campeche through Yucatán Pen. and south. **Habitat:** Mangroves and swamps on Pacific Coast; water borders, mangroves and second growth in Atlantic lowlands.

HUTTON'S VIREO   *Vireo huttoni*   **See W or T**
Memo: Suggests Kinglet; broken eye-ring, dingy underparts.
Range: Sw. B. Columbia, Pacific states, sw. U.S. to Guatemala. **Mexico:** Oak zone of mts. generally, from northern tier of states south to s. Baja California and Chiapas.

GOLDEN VIREO   *Vireo hypochryseus*   5–½   **Pl. 36**
Field marks: A bright-greenish vireo with a broad *bright yellow* eyebrow stripe, *entirely yellow* underparts. No strong wing-bars.
Similar species: No similar vireo in its area, but ♀ Wilson's Warbler is abundant in Golden Vireo's range in winter; it has a longer, thinner tail, smaller head and bill.
Voice: Song, a rapid, rather high *chu-chu-chu-chu-chu-chu-chu-chu* on 1 pitch (RTP).

Range: W. Mexico only; Pacific slope from s. Sonora to Oaxaca; Tres Marías Is. **Habitat:** Mainly foothills; brushy canyons, dry woods, stream groves.

GRAY VIREO   *Vireo vicinior*   **See W or T**
Memo: Very gray; faint eye-ring, 1 faint wingbar.
Range: Breeds mainly in sw. U.S. **Mexico:** Breeds nw. Baja California (south to Lat. 30°). Winters south to s. Baja California and in northwest from Sonora to n. Sinaloa, Durango.

DWARF VIREO   *Vireo nelsoni* 4   **Not illus.**
Field marks: A small version of the Gray Vireo but with 2 narrow wingbars and a light eye stripe ending a little behind the eye. Gray above, whitish below. Rare; little known.
Similar species: (1) Bell's Vireo (slightly larger) has a yellowish wash on sides. It is found at lower altitudes. (2) Gray Vireo occurs in nw. Mexico.
Range: S. Mexico only; reported from mts. of Michoacán, Guanajuato, Oaxaca, at altitudes of 5600–7150 ft. **Habitat:** Semi-open arid country, thickets, brush.

BELL'S VIREO   *Vireo bellii*   **See E, W, or T**
Memo: Gray; eye-ring and 2 wingbars not too prominent. Its voice a husky *cheedle cheedle chee? Cheedle cheedle chew!*
Range: Cen. and sw. U.S., n. Mexico. Winters to n. Nicaragua. **Mexico:** Breeds across northern tier of states from n. Baja California and Sonora to Tamaulipas; south to Coahuila and Durango. Winters southward except Yucatán Pen. **Habitat:** Streamsides, willows, mesquite.

YELLOW-THROATED VIREO   *Vireo flavifrons*   **See E or T**
Memo: Bright yellow throat and spectacles; 2 wingbars.
Range: S. Canada to Gulf states. Winters from s. Mexico to Colombia, Venezuela; W. Indies. **Mexico:** Migrant e. Mexico, wintering from Oaxaca, Veracruz and Yucatán Pen. south.

SOLITARY VIREO   *Vireo solitarius*   **See E, W, or T**
Memo: Blue-gray head, white spectacles, white throat.
Note: Migrants in e. Mexico are of the olive-backed eastern type; most highland and Pacific slope birds are the duller gray-backed western birds.
Range: Canada to El Salvador; northern birds winter to Nicaragua, Cuba. **Mexico:** Breeds mts. of Baja California and highlands generally. Migrant and winter visitor nearly throughout, except Yucatán Pen. (but reported B. Honduras).

RED-EYED VIREO   *Vireo olivaceus*   **See E, W, or T**
Memo: Gray crown, black and white eyebrow stripes.

Range: Canada to Gulf states. Winters from Colombia and Venezuela to Amazon basin. **Mexico:** Migrant chiefly through eastern sections from Tamaulipas and Coahuila to Chiapas, including Yucatán Pen.

YELLOW-GREEN VIREO   *Vireo flavoviridis*   5–6¾   **Pl. 36**
Field marks: Very similar to Red-eyed Vireo (both in behavior and voice) but with strong yellow tones. Sides washed with greenish yellow, under tail coverts *yellow* (Red-eye, white). Head stripes less distinct. Some authors lump the 2 species.
Technical note: In hand, outermost primary (9th) is usually shorter than 6th (in Red-eye, 9th is usually longer than 6th).
Similar species: (1) Red-eyed Vireo has white under tail coverts. (2) Philadelphia Vireo, a migrant, has a dark eye, yellowish across breast, whitish under tail coverts.
Voice: Song similar to Red-eyed Vireo's but phrases shorter; longer pauses between phrases.
Range: Río Grande delta, Texas (rare), n. Mexico south to Panamá. Winters in S. America to upper Amazon basin. **Mexico:** Summer resident, mainly lowlands, foothills, of Pacific slope from cen. Sonora south; Atlantic slope from Nuevo León, n. Tamaulipas south, including Yucatán Pen. **Habitat:** Woodlands, scrub, shade trees, plantations.

YUCATAN VIREO   *Vireo magister*   6   **Pl. 36**
Field marks: Similar to Yellow-green or Red-eyed Vireo in aspect (eye stripe, no wingbars) but crown same color as back, eyebrow stripe grayish buff. Underparts dull yellowish gray. Regarded by some as conspecific with Black-whiskered Vireo of W. Indies (but lacking whiskers).
Similar species: (1) Red-eyed Vireo has gray crown contrasting with olive back, white eyebrow stripe. (2) Yellow-green Vireo has white eye stripe, gray crown, strong yellow under tail coverts. (3) Philadelphia Vireo has dull whitish eye stripe.
Voice: Song much like Red-eyed Vireo's but phrases more abrupt. Phrases consist of 2 or 3 notes (Bond).
Range: Grand Cayman I., Yucatán Pen., coastal B. Honduras and Bay Is., Honduras. **Mexico:** Islands off coast of Quintana Roo and narrow belt of adjacent mainland. **Habitat:** Mangroves, low woods, gardens, groves.

BLACK-WHISKERED VIREO   *Vireo altiloquus*   **See E**
Memo: Black whisker; no wingbars.
Range: S. Florida, W. Indies. Winters to n. S. America. Accidental in B. Honduras (Half Moon Cay). Not recorded in Mexico but could occur in migration on islands off coast of Quintana Roo. Regarded by some as conspecific with Yucatán Vireo, which lacks dark whisker mark.

PHILADELPHIA VIREO   See E, W, or T
Vireo philadelphicus
Memo: Yellow below, no wingbars; light eyebrow, dark lores.
Range: S. Canada, northeastern edge of U.S. Winters through
Mid. America to Panamá. **Mexico:** Sparse migrant, occasion-
ally wintering, mainly in southeast; Veracruz to Chiapas, Yuca-
tán Pen.

WARBLING VIREO   *Vireo gilvus*   See E, W, or T
Memo: No wingbars; whitish or buffy breast, light eyebrow.
Range: Canada to s. U.S., Mexico. Winters to El Salvador.
Mexico: Breeds in mts. of Baja California and in highlands
from northern tier of states south to Morelos, Oaxaca; widespread migrant except Yucatán Pen. Winters mainly in southern sections.

BROWN-CAPPED VIREO   Pl. 36
Vireo leucophrys (or *V. gilvus* in part)   4½
Field marks: A brownish vireo that closely resembles the
Warbling Vireo in appearance and song and replaces that bird
in the mts. of se. Mexico. They may be conspecific. Browner on
back, yellower below than Warbling Vireo, with a noticeably
darker brown crown that contrasts with the white eyebrow
stripe.
Note: Birds of se. Mexico, Guatemala, and Honduras are regarded by some authors as more closely allied to Warbling Vireo
than to Brown-capped Vireo of Costa Rica, Panamá, and S.
America. Others would lump the whole complex.
Similar species: (1) Warbling Vireo is grayer above, has duller
eyebrow stripe, lacks noticeable brown crown. (2) Philadelphia
Vireo, a migrant, is also similar.
Voice: Song warbled as in Warbling Vireo, but shorter, less
varied: *cheerooroowee'chee-chee'weeroooweeche-cheereechee;*
also *twee'cheeweechee,* thrice repeated (Eisenmann).
Range: S. Mexico to Bolivia (including closely allied forms).
Mexico: Highlands of s. Veracruz and Chiapas; very local.
Habitat: Forest edges, borders of streams, cutover woods.

SLATY VIREO   *Neochloe brevipennis* 4½   Pl. 36
Field marks: A rare, distinctively patterned vireo. *Slate-gray*
with *bright olive-green* crown, wings, and tail. Chin, lower
breast, belly, and under tail coverts white. Eye white.
Voice: Song, 3–5 notes, suggesting White-eyed Vireo, emphasis
on 3rd or 4th note (Loetscher).
Range: S. Mexico only; local and rare. Mts. of s. Jalisco,
Morelos, cen. Guerrero, cen. Veracruz, w. and cen. Oaxaca.
Habitat: Scrub oaks, oak-pines, ravines; 4000–6000 ft.

TAWNY-CROWNED GREENLET   **Pl. 36**
Hylophilus ochraceiceps   4½
  Field marks: A small olive-brown vireo with an orangish-olive
  or golden-brown crown and rich russet-brown tail. No wingbars. Face and throat pale gray, underparts dull yellowish,
  darkest on chest. Eyes yellow.
  Similar species: See Lesser Greenlet (next).
  Voice: A constantly uttered *nya-nya* and a more nasal vireo-
  nine *weng* (Eisenmann). Song, an ascending trill followed by a
  single lower-pitched note (Edwards and Tashian).
  Range: Se. Mexico to w. Amazonian basin. **Mexico:** Gulf lowlands of s. Veracruz, ne. Oaxaca, n. Chiapas, Tabasco, Campeche, Quintana Roo. **Habitat:** Humid forests.

LESSER (GRAY-HEADED) GREENLET   **Pl. 36**
Hylophilus decurtatus   3½–4
  Field marks: A small yellowish olive-green vireo without
  wingbars. Note the *whitish eye-ring* and *gray head*. Underparts
  whitish tinged with yellow-olive on sides.
  Similar species: Tennessee Warbler (a migrant) has an eye
  stripe, not an eye-ring; tail longer.
  Voice: Song resembles a single repeated phrase of Red-eyed
  Vireo, but higher-pitched; phrases more widely spaced (Land).
  Usually a 3-note phrase repeated: *tsitseeweet* and *itsacheet,*
  sometimes *tsiweet* (Eisenmann).
  Range: Se. Mexico to cen. Panamá. **Mexico:** Gulf slope from
  se. San Luis Potosí, Veracruz south through Oaxaca, Chiapas,
  and east through Tabasco, Campeche, Quintana Roo. **Habitat:**
  Rain forest, forest edges.

Honeycreepers: Coerebidae

A VARIED composite group of small, slender-billed, nectar-feeding
tropical birds; some rather allied to tanagers, others (such as the
Bananaquit) somewhat resemble wood-warblers, others may be
related to finches. The validity of this assemblage as a family is
questionable. **Food:** Nectar, berries, insects. **Range:** New World
tropics; Mexico, W. Indies to n. Argentina. **No. of species:** World,
36; Mexico, 5.

CINNAMON FLOWER-PIERCER   **Pl. 37**
(HIGHLAND HONEYCREEPER) *Diglossa baritula* 4¼
  Field marks: Note the distinctly *upturned, hooked bill. Male:*
  A small *blackish* bird with *bright cinnamon* breast and under-
  parts that contrast sharply against the slaty throat. *Female:*
  Brown, more olive on back, lighter ochre below.

Range: Cen. and s. Mexico, Guatemala, El Salvador, Honduras. **Mexico:** Mts. from Jalisco, Guanajuato, México, Puebla, Veracruz south. **Habitat:** Cloud forest and pine-oak zone of mts.; forest borders; 5000–11,000 ft.

RED-LEGGED (BLUE) HONEYCREEPER   Pl. 37
Cyanerpes cyaneus 4–5
  Field marks: *Male:* A small *deep violet-blue* bird patterned with jet-black back, wings, and tail. Note the *light turquoise crown, scarlet legs. Yellow* wing linings. *Female:* Dull greenish, lighter on underparts, which are *indistinctly streaked with whitish. Immature and postnuptial male:* Similar to female but with black wings and tail.
  Similar species: (1) See Shining Honeycreeper (next). (2) ♀ Green Honeycreeper is brighter grass-green above and below; lacks streaks on underparts, has much shorter bill.
  Voice: A sharp *tswe* (Chalif). Song, a simple, deliberate and protracted *tsip-tsip-chaa-tsip-tsip-tsic-cha,* etc. Note, a weak, nasal *chaa,* suggestive of gnatcatcher (Bond).
  Range: Se. Mexico, Cuba to Amazonian Brazil. **Mexico:** Lowlands from Veracruz, Puebla south through Oaxaca, Chiapas, and east through Yucatán Pen. **Habitat:** Rain forest edge, flowering trees and shrubs, coffee plantations, parks.

SHINING HONEYCREEPER   Pl. 37
Cyanerpes lucidus 4–4½
  Field marks: *Male:* Similar to Red-legged Honeycreeper but note the *bright yellow legs* and *black throat.* It lacks the light turquoise crown and yellow wing linings. *Female:* Similar to ♀ Red-legged Honeycreeper but underparts *more strongly striped* (with bluish), throat *buffy yellow.*
  Similar species: See Red-legged Honeycreeper (preceding).
  Range: Se. Mexico, Guatemala to nw. Colombia. **Mexico:** Recorded e. Chiapas; local. **Habitat:** Lowland humid forests, treetops, flowering trees.

GREEN HONEYCREEPER   Pl. 37
Chlorophanes spiza 5–5½
  Field marks: A *bright green* bird with a strongly curved bill. *Male:* Brilliant *green* with dusky wings and tail (feathers margined with green), head (except throat) *jet-black,* eye *red. Female:* All green; dark grass-green above, yellow-green below; eye dark. Note the yellowish decurved bill.
  Similar species: See (1) ♀ tanagers (pp. 227–35). (2) ♀ Painted Bunting (p. 240), (3) ♀ of 2 preceding honeycreepers.
  Voice: A loud, strident *tswee tswee* (Chalif). Song a tirelessly repeated *tsip* given rapidly (Slud). A short nasal grunt, *uhr* (Eisenmann).

Range: Se. Mexico to Bolivia, Brazil. **Mexico:** Caribbean low-lands of ne. Oaxaca, n. Chiapas, Campeche; local. **Habitat:** Humid forests and borders, adjacent plantations.

BANANAQUIT   *Coereba flaveloa*   3¼–4   **Pl. 37**
Field marks: A small blackish-backed warblerlike bird, recognized by its *white eyebrow stripe* and *yellow underparts.* Note also the *gray throat,* white wing spot, dull yellowish rump. The Cozumel I. race has a white throat. *Immature:* Eyebrow stripe yellow, back more olive.
Voice: Song, lisping and wheezy, varying geographically. A rising *sisisisi;* also *wiz wiz wiz sisisisi* (Chalif).
Range: Se. Mexico, W. Indies to Paraguay, ne. Argentina. **Mexico:** Gulf lowlands of s. Veracruz, n. Oaxaca, n. Chiapas; also islands off Quintana Roo (Cozumel, Holbox, etc.). **Habitat:** Humid forest borders, plantations, clearings, towns, parks.

Wood-Warblers: Parulidae

BRIGHT-COLORED small birds, usually smaller than sparrows and with thin bills. The majority have some yellow. Vireos are similar, but their colors generally are duller and their bills heavier, less needle-pointed. **Food:** Mainly insects. **Range:** Alaska and Canada to Argentina. **No. of species:** World, approximately 113; Mexico, 63–69 (depending on taxonomy).

BLACK-AND-WHITE WARBLER   See E, W, or T
Mniotilta varia
  Memo: Black and white stripes on crown, back, etc.
  Range: Canada to Gulf states. Winters from s. U.S. to W. Indies, Ecuador. **Mexico:** Widespread migrant and winter visitor, most numerous in eastern ssctions.

PROTHONOTARY WARBLER   See E and T
Protonotaria citrea
  Memo: Golden head and breast; blue-gray wings, no bars.
  Range: Great Lakes area to Gulf states. Winters se. Mexico to Colombia, Venezuela. **Mexico:** Migrant and winter visitor in southern and southeastern sections (esp. Yucatán Pen.).

SWAINSON'S WARBLER   See E or T
Limnothlypis swainsonii
  Memo: Brown back; brown crown, white stripe over eye.
  Range: Se. U.S. Winters to W. Indies, Yucatán Pen., B. Honduras. **Mexico:** Rare migrant and winter visitor along Gulf Coast and Yucatán Pen.

WORM-EATING WARBLER
See E or T

Helmitheros vermivorus
Memo: Black stripes on buffy head.
Range: E. U.S. Winters s. Mexico and W. Indies to Panamá.
Mexico: Migrant and winter visitor mainly along Gulf slope
from Tamaulipas through Chiapas and Yucatán Pen.

GOLDEN-WINGED WARBLER
See E or T

Vermivora chrysoptera
Memo: Black bib and cheek, white belly, yellow wingbars.
Range: E. U.S. Winters Guatemala to Colombia. **Mexico:**
Rare migrant through eastern sections; apparently a trans-Gulf
migrant to Yucatán Pen.

BLUE-WINGED WARBLER
See E or T

Vermivora pinus
Memo: Black eye line, yellow face and underparts.
Range: E. U.S. Winters s. Mexico to Panamá. **Mexico:** Mi-
grant through eastern sections. Winters occasionally in south.

TENNESSEE WARBLER
See E, W, or T

Vermivora peregrina
Memo: *Spring:* ♂ gray crown, white eye stripe, white breast.
Winter: Yellow-olive; white crissum, trace of wingbars.
Note: Many observers have trouble with winter-plumaged
birds, yellowish below, olive above. They act like honeycreepers, occur in flocks in flowering trees (often acquiring
orange faces from nectar-feeding).
Range: Canada, northeastern edge of U.S. Winters to Venezuela. **Mexico:** Migrant mainly in eastern and southern parts,
wintering in s. Mexico.

ORANGE-CROWNED WARBLER
See E, W, or T

Vermivora celata
Memo: Dingy olive-green, faintly streaked, no wingbars.
Range: Alaska, Canada, w. U.S. Winters s. U.S. to Guate-
mala.
Mexico: Breeds nw. Baja California (Todos Santos I. and
Coronados Is.). Widespread migrant and winter visitor except
Yucatán Pen.

NASHVILLE WARBLER
See E, W, or T

Vermivora ruficapilla
Memo: Gray head, white eye-ring, yellow throat.
Range: S. Canada, w. and n. U.S. Winters s. U.S. to Guate-
mala. **Mexico:** Widespread in migration and winter except
Baja California (casual) and Yucatán Pen.

VIRGINIA'S WARBLER *Vermivora virginiae* **See W or T**
Memo: Gray above; yellowish rump, yellowish across breast.
Range: W. U.S. (Great Basin ranges, s. Rockies). Winters w.
Mexico. **Mexico:** Migrant in western highlands and central
plateau. Winters from n. Jalisco and Guanajuato to Oaxaca.

COLIMA WARBLER *Vermivora crissalis* **See W or T**
Memo: Like Virginia's, but larger; lacks yellow on breast.
Range: Breeds w. Texas (Chisos Mts.) to mts. of n.-cen. and ne.
Mexico. **Mexico:** Breeds in mts. (Sierra Madre Oriental) of
Coahuila, Nuevo León, sw. Tamaulipas. Winters on Pacific
slope from s. Sinaloa south to Guerrero.

LUCY'S WARBLER *Vermivora luciae* **See W or T**
Memo: Gray above, chestnut rump patch.
Range: Sw. U.S., nw. Mexico. **Mexico:** Breeds in deserts of ne.
Baja California, n. Sonora. Migrant along Pacific Coast of So-
nora. Winters along western coast from Sinaloa to w. Guerrero.

CRESCENT-CHESTED (SPOT-BREASTED) WARBLER
Vermivora superciliosa 4–4¾ **Pl. 38**
Field marks: Note the *rufous or chestnut crescent* across the
yellow chest and the broad *white eyebrow stripe* on the *gray*
head. Sometimes the crescent is reduced to a spot. Sexes similar.
Similar species: (1) Northern and (2) Tropical Parulas have
white wingbars, lack eye stripe. (3) Rufous-capped and (4)
Chestnut-capped Warblers have reddish caps and cheeks, lack
breast crescent.
Voice: An often repeated song, *tcherrrrrrrrr,* about 1 second
in length (Chalif).
Range: Mexico to Nicaragua. **Mexico:** High mts. from Chihuahua, Nuevo León, and Tamaulipas south. Winters in s.
Mexico. **Habitat:** Cloud forest and oak-pine forests.

NORTHERN PARULA *Parula americana* **See E or T**
Memo: Similar to next species but ♂ has dark breastband.
Range: Se. Canada, e. U.S. to Gulf states. Winters to W.
Indies, Nicaragua. **Mexico:** Winter visitor to e. and s. Mexico
(incl. Yucatán Pen. and Pacific slope of Oaxaca).

TROPICAL PARULA *Parula pitiayumi* 4½ **Pl. 38**
(including Socorro Warbler)
Field marks: *Male:* A small bluish warbler with a *yellow*
throat and breast; very similar to Northern Parula, but *lacks*
the white eye-ring and dark upper breastband. Note *black face,*
sharply separating yellow throat from blue crown. *Female:*
Similar; face pattern not so contrasting. General blue and yel-

low color distinguishes it from other warblers except Northern Parula; wingbars shorter.
Note: Birds of Socorro and Revilla Gigedo Is. are sometimes considered a distinct species, *P. graysoni,* Socorro Warbler.
Similar species: See Northern Parula (a migrant).
Voice: Nearly identical with Northern Parula's song.
Range: Southern tip of Texas to n. Argentina. **Mexico:** Resident Socorro I., s. Baja California, Tres Marías Is., and Pacific slope from Sonora to Oaxaca. Also Gulf slope from Tamaulipas, Nuevo León, San Luis Potosí to Veracruz, Puebla; also mts. of Chiapas. **Habitat:** Dry and wet tropical woodlands with or without Spanish moss.

OLIVE WARBLER *Peucedramus taeniatus* **See W**
  Memo: ♂ has tawny head, black ear patch; ♀ with olive crown, gray back, white wingbars, dusky ear patch.
  Range: Arizona, New Mexico to Nicaragua. **Mexico:** Pine forests of high mts. from n. Sonora, n. Chihuahua, n. Coahuila, sw. Tamaulipas south through Chiapas.

YELLOW WARBLER **See E, W, or T**
Dendroica petechia (in part); *aestiva* group
  Memo: Yellow below with rusty streaks (♂). Yellow tail spots.
  Range: Alaska, Canada to s.-cen. Mexico. Winters to n. S. America. **Mexico:** Breeds in interior from n. Sonora, n. Chihuahua south to Oaxaca. In winter also lowlands throughout.

GOLDEN WARBLER **Pl. 38**
Dendroica petechia (in part) 4½
  Field marks: *Male:* Similar to Yellow Warbler (largely yellow with reddish breast stripes) but note the *chestnut* crown. Females are much like other Yellow Warblers.
  Voice: Song, in W. Indies, a sprightly *wee-chee-wee-chee-chee-wur* with many variations (Bond). More full-voiced than N. American Yellow Warbler.
  Range: Florida Keys, W. Indies, Mexico (Cozumel I.), Costa Rica (Cocos I.), Galápagos Is., Pacific Coast of S. America (sw. Colombia to nw. Peru). **Mexico:** Confined to Cozumel I. off coast of Quintana Roo. Resident. **Habitat:** On Cozumel, bushes, small trees, not mangroves.

MANGROVE WARBLER **Pl. 38**
Dendroica erithachorides (or *D. petechia* in part) 4½
  Field marks: *Male:* Similar to Yellow Warbler and Golden Warbler but *entire head chestnut.* Immature males may have tinge of chestnut on head. *Female:* Similar to female Yellow Warbler (a migrant in its range) but much grayer.
  Range: Coastally from n. Mexico, Cen. America to Colombia.

Mexico: Pacific Coast from s. Baja California and Sonora south; Gulf Coast from s. Tamaulipas south and east, including Yucatán Pen. and many of its islands (except Cozumel). **Habitat:** Coastal mangroves and other saltwater growth.

MAGNOLIA WARBLER   See E, W, or T
Dendroica magnolia
 Memo: White band across tail. Yellow below; heavy stripes.
 Range: Cen. and e. Canada, ne. U.S. to mts. of w. Virginia. Winters Mexico, W. Indies to Panamá. **Mexico:** Migrant mainly through eastern and southern states (incl. Yucatán Pen.). Winters from San Luis Potosí south and east.

CAPE MAY WARBLER   *Dendroica tigrina*   See E, W, or T
 Memo: In winter, heavily striped below; yellowish neck spot.
 Range: Canada, northeastern edge of U.S. Winters W. Indies; casually Mid. America. **Mexico:** Casual in winter Yucatán Pen.

BLACK-THROATED BLUE WARBLER   See E or T
Dendroica caerulescens
 Memo: ♂ blue-gray back, black throat. ♀ white wing spot.
 Range: Canada, ne. U.S., south in mts. to Georgia. Winters mainly W. Indies. **Mexico:** Occasional in winter on Cozumel I. off Yucatán Pen.; casual Guatemala, B. Honduras.

MYRTLE WARBLER   *Dendroica coronata*   See E, W, or T
 Memo: Similar to next species (and may be conspecific) but has throat white.
 Range: Alaska, Canada, ne. U.S. Winters to Panamá. **Mexico:** Widespread in migration and winter; more numerous in east.

AUDUBON'S WARBLER   See W or T
Dendroica auduboni (or *D. coronata* in part)
 Memo: Yellow rump, yellow throat; white wing patch, black chest on breeding ♂.
 Note: Mexican birds are more extensively black across the front; those of Chiapas and Guatemala quite black on back as well.
 Range: Sw. Canada, w. U.S., nw. Mexico, Guatemala. Winters to Costa Rica. **Mexico:** Breeds in conifers of high mts. south to n. Baja California, and in Sierra Madre Occidental from n. Chihuahua at least to s. Durango. Also a large dark form in mts. of w. Guatemala and adjacent Chiapas (sometimes called "Goldman's Warbler"). Winters widely except Yucatán Pen.

BLACK-THROATED GRAY WARBLER   See W or T
Dendroica nigrescens
 Memo: ♂ gray and white; black crown, cheek patch, and throat.

Range: Sw. B. Columbia, w. U.S., nw. Mexico. Winters to Guatemala (casual). **Mexico:** Breeds n. Baja California, ne. Sonora. Migrates and winters through western parts and central plateau south to Oaxaca.

TOWNSEND'S WARBLER See W or T
Dendroica townsendi
    Memo: Pattern of Black-throated Gray but black on yellow.
    Range: Mts. of s. Alaska, w. Canada, nw. U.S. Winters from n.-cen. Mexico to Nicaragua. **Mexico:** Migrant in Baja California and through highlands generally. Winters in highlands from ne. Sinaloa and cen. Nuevo León south through Chiapas.

BLACK-THROATED GREEN WARBLER See E, W, or T
Dendroica virens
    Memo: ♂ yellow cheek, black throat, green back.
    Range: Canada, e. U.S. Winters to Colombia. **Mexico:** Winters in Atlantic lowlands (incl. Yucatán Pen.), and eastern and southern mts. Rare or casual in west.

GOLDEN-CHEEKED WARBLER See W or T
Dendroica chrysoparia
    Memo: ♂ yellow cheek; black bib, cap, and back.
    Range: Breeds only in Texas (mainly Edwards Plateau). Winters s. Mexico, Guatemala, Honduras to Nicaragua. **Mexico:** Migrant through eastern highlands; may winter southward.

HERMIT WARBLER *Dendroica occidentalis* See W or T
    Memo: ♂ yellow head, black throat, gray back.
    Range: W. U.S. (mainly Pacific states). Winters to Nicaragua. **Mexico:** Migrant mainly in western highlands; rare in western lowlands and eastern mts. Winters from Sinaloa, Durango south.

CERULEAN WARBLER *Dendroica cerulea* See E or T
    Memo: ♂ blue back, narrow black line across white breast.
    Range: E. U.S. Migrates through Mid. America. Winters Colombia to n. Bolivia. **Mexico:** Rarely recorded, but undoubtedly goes through e. Mexico. Accidental Baja California.

BLACKBURNIAN WARBLER See E, W, or T
Dendroica fusca
    Memo: Orange on throat and surrounding dark cheek patch.
    Range: Canada, e. U.S. Winters Costa Rica to Peru. **Mexico:** Migrant throughout e. Mexico, including Yucatán Pen.

YELLOW-THROATED WARBLER See E or T
Dendroica dominica
    Memo: Gray; yellow bib, black mustache and side stripes.

Range: E. U.S. Winters s. U.S., W. Indies, Mid. America to Costa Rica. **Mexico:** Migrant and winter visitant through e. and s. Mexico, including Yucatán Pen.

GRACE'S WARBLER *Dendroica graciae* **See W or T**
Memo: Gray; yellow throat, gray cheeks, striped sides.
Range: Sw. U.S., mts. of Mid. America to n. Nicaragua. **Mexico:** Resident from mts. of northwestern states south and east to s. Veracruz, Oaxaca, and Chiapas.

CHESTNUT-SIDED WARBLER **See E, W, or T**
Dendroica pensylvanica
Memo: In spring, chestnut sides, yellow crown. In fall, yellow-green above, white below, eye-ring, wingbars.
Range: S. Canada, e. U.S. Migrates through Mid. America. Winters Guatemala to Colombia (casual). **Mexico:** Migrant mainly through Atlantic lowlands, including Yucatán Pen.

BAY-BREASTED WARBLER **See E, W, or T**
Dendroica castanea
Memo: In spring, chestnut breast, pale neck spot; in fall, dull greenish with light streaks and wingbars, dark legs.
Range: Canada, northeastern edge of U.S. Winters Costa Rica to Venezuela. **Mexico:** Sparse migrant through e. Mexico, mainly trans-Gulf via Yucatán Pen.

BLACKPOLL WARBLER *Dendroica striata* **See E, W, or T**
Memo: Spring ♂ black cap and whisker, white cheek; fall, greenish, fine streaks, wingbars, pale legs.
Range: Alaska, Canada, ne. U.S. Migrant via W. Indies to e. Colombia, Venezuela, Guianas, Brazil. **Mexico:** Straggler; rarely reported (Chihuahua, Oaxaca).

PINE WARBLER *Dendroica pinus* **See E or T**
Memo: Dull streaks on yellow underparts, 2 wingbars, unstreaked olive back.
Range: Se. Canada, e. U.S., W. Indies. Migrant in north. **Mexico:** Winters south very occasionally to n. Tamaulipas.

PRAIRIE WARBLER *Dendroica discolor* **See E or T**
Memo: Black stripes on yellow cheeks and on sides; wags tail.
Range: Se. Canada, e. U.S., Bahamas. Winters Florida, W. Indies, Caribbean islands off Mid. America to Nicaragua. **Mexico:** Winters on islands off Quintana Roo (Cozumel, etc.).

PALM WARBLER *Dendroica palmarum* **See E, W, or T**
Memo: Brownish back; streaks on whitish or yellowish breast; wags tail. Rusty cap in spring.
Range: Canada, northeastern edge of U.S. Winters in s. U.S.,

W. Indies, islands and coasts of Mid. America. **Mexico:** Winters Yucatán and Quintana Roo, mainly along coast and islands.

OVENBIRD *Seiurus aurocapillus*   **See E, W, or T**
Memo: Like a small thrush; eye-ring, dull orange crown.
Range: S. Canada, e. and cen. U.S. Winters se. U.S., Mid. America to n. Venezuela, Lesser Antilles. **Mexico:** Migrant through eastern and southern sections, wintering from Veracruz, Yucatán south; also winter visitor on western slope from Sinaloa south.

LOUISIANA WATERTHRUSH   **See E or T**
Seiurus motacilla
Memo: White eye stripe, unstreaked throat; striped breast.
Range: E. U.S. Winters from Mexico, W. Indies to ne. Colombia, nw. Venezuela, Trinidad. **Mexico:** Migrant and winter visitor on Pacific slope (rare), central plateau and Atlantic coastal plain. Casual Yucatán Pen.

NORTHERN WATERTHRUSH   **See E, W, or T**
Seiurus noveboracensis
Memo: Yellowish eye stripe, streaked throat; striped breast.
Range: Alaska, Canada, northern edge of U.S. Winters from Mexico, W. Indies through Cen. and n. S. America to n. Peru. **Mexico:** Widespread migrant, wintering from s. Baja California, Sinaloa, Veracruz, and Yucatán Pen. south.

KENTUCKY WARBLER *Oporornis formosus*   **See E or T**
Memo: Yellow below; black "sideburns," yellow spectacles.
Range: E. and cen. U.S. Winters from s. Mexico through Mid. America to Colombia, nw. Venezuela. **Mexico:** Migrant through lowlands of Tamaulipas, wintering from s. Veracruz to Chiapas and across lower parts of Yucátán Pen.

CONNECTICUT WARBLER   **See E, W, or T**
Oporornis agilis
Memo: Gray hood, complete white eye-ring.
Range: Cen.-s. Canada, central-northern edge of U.S. Migrates mainly via W. Indies to e. Colombia, Venezuela, Brazil. **Mexico:** Sight report Cozumel I.; otherwise not reported, but should be looked for inasmuch as it is a rare migrant through Texas. A spring sight report for B. Honduras (Half Moon Cay).

MOURNING WARBLER   **See E, W, or T**
Oporornis philadelphia
Memo: Gray hood (♂ black throat), no eye-ring. In fall some may have incomplete eye-ring.
Range: Canada, ne. U.S. Migrates through Mid. America. Winters Nicaragua to e. Ecuador. **Mexico:** Migrant through

coastal plain, lowlands of Tamaulipas, Veracruz, Oaxaca, Chiapas.

MacGILLIVRAY'S WARBLER   See W or T
Oporornis tolmiei
    Memo: Gray hood (♂ blackish on throat); white eye-ring broken fore and aft.
    Range: Se. Alaska, w. Canada, w. U.S. Winters through Mid. America to Panamá. **Mexico:** Widespread in migration except Yucatán Pen.; most frequent in western states. Winters from s. Baja California, s. Sonora, Nuevo León south.

COMMON YELLOWTHROAT   See E, W, or T
Geothlypis trichas
    Memo: ♂ has yellow throat, black mask with white stripe above. ♀ with yellow throat, whitish belly; lacks mask.
    Note: See also Chapala Yellowthroat (probably a local yellow-browed race of this species), below.
    Range: Se. Alaska, Canada to s. Mexico. Winters s. U.S. to W. Indies and through Mid. America to Panamá. **Mexico:** Breeds in n. Baja California (south to Lat. 30°) and from northern states south on Pacific slope to Colima and locally in highlands of Oaxaca, Veracruz. Winters widely throughout, especially on coastal slopes.

PENINSULAR (BELDING'S) YELLOWTHROAT   Pl. 38
Geothlypis beldingi 5½
    Field marks: *Male:* Similar to male Common Yellowthroat but stripe above black mask *yellow* (not whitish); belly also yellow (not whitish). *Female:* Not safely separable in field from female of Common Yellowthroat.
    Similar species: Only resident yellowthroat in its range (although Common Yellowthroat breeds in n. Baja California and invades range of this bird in winter).
    Range: Baja California only. Resident from cen. Baja California (Lat. 28°) south to Cape district. **Habitat:** Coastal marshes, riparian growth.

YELLOW-CROWNED (ALTAMIRA) YELLOWTHROAT
Geothlypis flavovelata 5   Pl. 38
    Field marks: Similar to Peninsular Yellowthroat but male with much more yellow across the crown and above the mask. The two may be conspecific bu. are widely separated by range.
    Similar species: See (1) Peninsular Yellowthroat (preceding) and (2) Chapala Yellowthroat (next).
    Range: Ne. Mexico only; s. Tamaulipas, n. Veracruz. **Habitat:** Coastal marshes, salt lagoons.

CHAPALA YELLOWTHROAT   Not illus.
Geothlypis chapalensis (or *G. trichas* in part)   5½
   Field marks: Similar to the preceding 2 yellowthroats (male
   with yellow across crown and around mask), but this one lives
   in inland marshes.
   Note: It has been suggested that this and the preceding 2 forms
   may be conspecific, but this one is more probably a yellow-
   browed race of the Common Yellowthroat, *G. trichas.*
   Similar species: See above (1) Peninsular and (2) Yellow-
   crowned Yellowthroats (both are coastal).
   Range: Jalisco (lower Río Lerma and eastern side of Lake
   Chapala). **Habitat:** Freshwater marshes.

BLACK-POLLED YELLOWTHROAT   Pl. 38
Geothlypis speciosa 5
   Field marks: *Male:* Similar to other yellowthroats (black
   mask, etc.) but *without* a white or yellow band above the mask.
   Black of forehead *blends into dusky crown.* Underparts deeper
   yellow than in other yellowthroats. *Female:* Similar to other
   female yellowthroats.
   Similar species: See Hooded Yellowthroat (next).
   Range: Mexico only. Southern highlands (transverse range)
   from Michoacán east through México to Veracruz (Mt. Orizaba). **Habitat:** Upland marshes, wetlands.

HOODED YELLOWTHROAT   *Geothlypis nelsoni* 5   Pl. 38
   Field marks: *Male:* This yellowthroat has a broad black mask
   bordered above with *grayish,* which blends into the crown. *Fe-*
   male: Similar to other female yellowthroats.
   Similar species: See Black-polled Yellowthroat (preceding).
   Range: Mexico only. Eastern mts. (Sierra Madre Oriental)
   from Coahuila, Nuevo León south to Oaxaca. **Habitat:** Wet or
   dry spots, brushy places, in highlands (5000–10,000 ft.).

GRAY-CROWNED YELLOWTHROAT (GROUND-CHAT)
Geothlypis (Chamaethlypis) poliocephala 5–5½   **Pl. 38**
   Field marks: Slightly larger than Common Yellowthroat,
   with a more vireolike bill. *Male:* Recognized by *restricted black*
   face patch between eye and bill (unlike extensive mask of other
   yellowthroats); *gray cap, partial white eye-ring.* Bill black
   above, flesh below. *Female:* Similar to female Common Yellowthroat but with darker lores and more pronounced eye-ring,
   less white on belly. Often flicks tail.
   Voice: Song, a buntinglike *twe twe twe weechy weechy wit a*
   twit weechy a weeech (Chalif). Usual song, a number of undis-
   tinctive vireolike phrases strung together (Slud).
   Range: Mexico to w. Panamá. **Mexico:** Pacific slope from
   Sinaloa south. Gulf slope from Tamaulipas (formerly southern

tip of Texas) south, including Yucatán Pen. **Habitat:** Brushy or semi-open grassy fields, sugarcane fields, clearings.

YELLOW-BREASTED CHAT   See E, W, or T
Icteria virens
  Memo: Large; white spectacles, yellow throat and breast.
  Range: S. Canada, e. and cen. U.S. to cen. Mexico. Winters through Mid. America to Panamá. **Mexico:** Breeds from U.S. border south to cen. Baja California; on Pacific coastal plain south to Nayarit, in interior to Morelos, in east to s. Tamaulipas. Widespread in migration, wintering mainly in southern parts, including Yucatán Pen.

RED-BREASTED CHAT   Pl. 37
Granatellus venustus 6
  Field marks: *Male:* A bluish-gray bird with a *white throat* surrounded by black, forming a chestband above the *rose-red breast.* Broad white stripe behind eye. *Female:* Gray above, buffy white below (sometimes with hint of pink on chest), *buff eye stripe.* Tail black and white, as in male.
  Note: Males on Tres Marías Is. lack black chestband.
  Similar species: No other red-breasted warbler has a white throat. See Gray-throated Chat (next).
  Voice: Variations of *chee-a-weep, chee-a-weep, chee-a-weep, chink chink chink chink.* Or *chee-a-weep* (4 times), *zeep, zeep* (Chalif).
  Range: Mexico only; Pacific slope from n. Sinaloa south to Chiapas. **Habitat:** Second growth, heavy dry brush; foothills.

GRAY-THROATED CHAT   *Granatellus sallaei* 5   Pl. 37
  Field marks: *Male:* A pale gray version of the Red-breasted Chat lacking contrasting black and white head pattern. Throat *gray, no black band* separating red breast. *Female:* Similar to female Red-breasted Chat, gray above, pale cinnamon below, with buff eye stripe.
  Note: Family status of *Granatellus* uncertain (they may be tanagers).
  Similar species: Only red-breasted warbler in Gulf lowlands. In west see Red-breasted Chat (preceding).
  Voice: A buntinglike song (Land).
  Range: S. Mexico to n. Guatemala, B. Honduras. **Mexico:** Gulf lowlands from s. Veracruz, n. Chiapas through Yucatán Pen. **Habitat:** Second growth, brush.

HOODED WARBLER   *Wilsonia citrina*   See E or T
  Memo: ♂ black hood surrounding yellow face. ♀ no hood; yellow face and underparts, olive back, white tail spots.
  Range: E. and cen. U.S. Winters W. Indies and through Mid.

America to Panamá. **Mexico:** Winters mainly on Atlantic slope from s. Tamaulipas to Yucatán Pen.

WILSON'S WARBLER *Wilsonia pusilla* **See E, W, or T**
Memo: ♂ yellow below, olive above, round black cap. ♀ may lack cap; yellow and olive, no tail spots or wingbars.
Range: Alaska, Canada, w. U.S., n. New England. Winters through Mid. America to Panamá. **Mexico:** Widespread migrant except Yucatán Pen. Winters in central and southern parts from Sinaloa, Durango, Tamaulipas south.

CANADA WARBLER *Wilsonia canadensis* **See E, W, or T**
Memo: Necklace of stripes on yellow; spectacles, no wingbars.
Range: Canada, e. U.S. Migrates through Mid. America. Winters Colombia to Peru, Brazil. **Mexico:** Migrant through e. and s. Mexico; straggler Yucatán Pen.

RED-FACED WARBLER *Cardellina rubrifrons* 5 **Pl. 37**
Field marks: A gray-backed warbler with a *bright red face* and breast; black patch on head, white nape, white belly. Sexes similar.
Similar species: Painted Redstart has no red on face.
Voice: A clear sweet song similar to Yellow Warbler's (RTP).
Range: Breeds Arizona, sw. New Mexico, nw. Mexico. Winters to Guatemala. **Mexico:** Breeds in mts. of Sonora, Chihuahua, Sinaloa, Durango. Winters through mts. of s. Mexico. **Habitat:** Open pine-oak forests in high mts.

AMERICAN REDSTART *Setophaga ruticilla* **See E, W, or T**
Memo: ♂ orange wing and tail patches; ♀ yellow patches.
Range: Canada to se. U.S. Winters from cen. Mexico, W. Indies to Peru, n. Brazil. **Mexico:** Widespread in migration. Winters from s. Baja California and cen. Mexico (Sinaloa, Veracruz) southward, including Yucatán Pen.

PAINTED REDSTART *Myioborus picta* 5 **Pl. 37**
Field marks: This beautiful bird postures with half-spread wings and tail in redstart fashion. Black head and upperparts; *large white patches* in wing and on sides of tail; *large bright red patch* on lower breast. Sexes similar.
Similar species: Slate-throated Redstart lacks white wing patch, has less white in tail; underparts more orange-red.
Voice: Song, a repetitious *weeta weeta weeta wee* or *weeta weeta chilp chilp chilp*. Note, an unwarblerlike *clee-ip* (RTP).
Range: Sw. U.S. to Nicaragua. **Mexico:** Pine-oak highlands generally (except Baja California) from U.S. border south to Chiapas. Winters in most of range. **Habitat:** Oak canyons, mt. pine-oak forests.

SLATE-THROATED REDSTART
Myioborus miniatus 5   **Pl. 37**

Field marks: Very much like Painted Redstart, but darker-looking, without white wing-patch; more orange-red on breast. A close look may reveal a chestnut cap. Female is more orange-pink on breast. Fans tail like other redstarts.

Similar species: Painted Redstart has white wing patch, breast is blood-red rather than vermilion or orange.

Voice: Song, a series of rapid notes repeated 5–8 times: *chee chee chee chee chee chee.* Also *tsewe, tsewe, tsewe, chee chee chee.* Also a rising *whi-cha, whi-cha, whi-cha, whi-cha* (Chalif).

Range: Mexico through Cen. and S. America to Bolivia. **Mexico:** Resident in mts. from Sonora, Chihuahua, San Luis Potosí south. **Habitat:** Cloud forest, pines, oaks.

FAN-TAILED WARBLER
Euthlypis lachrymosa 5½–6   **Pl. 38**

Field marks: A large warbler with a *yellow crown spot or cap* and a white spot before the eye. Underparts yellow washed with *tawny orange across chest.* This warbler flicks its fan-shaped, white-tipped tail a great deal and this is often the first evidence one gets of the bird.

Voice: Call note, *tseeng.* Song, *we we we we whicha weest.* Also *we we whicha* (Chalif).

Range: Mts.; Mexico, Guatemala, Honduras, El Salvador, nw. Nicaragua. **Mexico:** Pacific slope from s. Sonora south to Chiapas. Also Gulf slope from sw. Tamaulipas to Veracruz, n. Oaxaca. **Habitat:** Thickets, understory in forests.

RED WARBLER *Ergaticus ruber* 5   **Pl. 37**

Field marks: A *nearly all red* warbler with a *silvery-white cheek patch* (sometimes gray or dusky cheek patch). Wing and tail feathers dusky edged with reddish. Sexes similar. Immature is cinnamon-brown with light gray cheek patch.

Similar species: See Pink-headed Warbler (Chiapas), next.

Voice: Note, *p-seet.* Song, *cha cha cha see see see cha cha cha see; cha's* on same pitch, *see's* higher (Chalif).

Range: Mexico only. High mts.; in west from s. Chihuahua, Sinaloa south to Oaxaca; in east from Hidalgo to w. Veracruz (Orizaba). **Habitat:** Pine forests.

PINK-HEADED WARBLER *Ergaticus versicolor* 5 **Pl. 37**

Field marks: Similar to Red Warbler (replacing it in Chiapas and Guatemala) but lacking clean-cut white cheek patch. Head dull silvery pink, decidedly paler than rest of bird.

Similar species: May be conspecific with Red Warbler.

Range: Se. Mexico (Chiapas) and Guatemala. **Habitat:** Pine and oak forests of high mts. (6000–11,000 ft.).

GOLDEN-CROWNED WARBLER   Pl. 38
Basileuterus culicivorus 4½–5

Field marks: An olive-gray warbler with a crown suggesting that of a Golden-crowned Kinglet, and with dull yellowish-green eye stripes. Yellowish underparts. No wingbars.

Voice: Song, about 6 clear whistled notes, first 3 on same pitch, the next higher, the next lower, the last note at original pitch:

twee twee twee   *twee*   *twee* (Chalif).
            twee

Range: Mexico through cen. and S. America to Argentina. **Mexico:** In west, local in hill forests of Nayarit, Jalisco. In east, from Nuevo León and Tamaulipas south on Gulf slope to Oaxaca, Chiapas; also extreme s. Quintana Roo. **Habitat:** Rain forest; cloud forest (sea level to 5000+ ft.).

GOLDEN-BROWED (BELL'S) WARBLER   Pl. 38
Basileuterus belli 5

Field marks: An olive-green warbler with *rufous or chestnut crown and cheeks*. Note the wide *yellow* eyebrow stripe ("golden-brow"). Underparts yellow. No wingbars. Sexes similar.

Similar species: See next 2 species (white eyebrow stripes).

Voice: Song, *wit-ah-wit-ah-weechy* (Chalif).

Range: Highlands; Mexico, Guatemala, El Salvador, Honduras. **Mexico:** Mts.; from se. Sinaloa, w. Durango, sw. Tamaulipas south through Chiapas. **Habitat:** Cloud forest, oak-pine forests of mts. (4000–11,500 ft.).

RUFOUS-CAPPED WARBLER   Pl. 38
Basileuterus rufifrons 4½–5

Field marks: Similar to Golden-browed Warbler (rufous or chestnut cap and cheeks, yellow breast) but eyebrow stripe *white*.

Note: In the race *B. r. salvini* (Gulf slope of n. Oaxaca, n. Chiapas, s. Veracruz, Tabasco, and n. Guatemala) underparts may be *all yellow* and face has a distinct white malar stripe. Typical birds of the highlands of Mexico and cen. Guatemala are *whitish* on belly and under tail coverts.

Similar species: See Chestnut-capped Warbler (next).

Voice: Note, *tzep*. Song rises from beginning and accelerates: *cheap cheap cheap chi-chi-chi-chi;* sometimes order reversed (Chalif). Song short and canarylike (Land).

Range: S. Mexico, B. Honduras to cen. Guatemala. **Mexico:** Coastal slopes and mts. from se. Sonora, w. Chihuahua, cen. Nuevo León, and cen.-w. Tamaulipas south through Chiapas, Tabasco. **Habitat:** Open woodlands, brushy hillsides, rarely forests; foothills into mts. (to 7000 ft.).

CHESTNUT-CAPPED (DELATTRE'S) WARBLER   **Pl. 38**
Basileuterus delattrii (or *B. rufifrons* in part)   4½–5
    Field marks: Probably conspecific with Rufous-capped Warbler and very difficult to separate in the field, but more extensively yellow below and with deeper chestnut crown than the adjacent population of *rufifrons* that is found in the mts. of cen. Guatemala. However, according to Burt Monroe, Jr. (1968), the 2 forms, though essentially allopatric, probably intergrade in e. Guatemala and Honduras. Therefore, he lumps them as 1 species. The 2 Guatemalan races of *rufifrons* differ more from each other than they do from this "species." If you wish to tick off the Chestnut-capped Warbler on your list go by locality (Pacific slope of s. Guatemala and from there south). An unsatisfactory "species."
    Voice: Song, *tsit-tsit, tseetweet;* also a dry *chit-cha-chup-chachaweep.* Also calls *zeep-zeep* and a rather dry trill *trrrrr* (Eisenmann).
    Range: S. Guatemala (Pacific slope) through Cen. America to Colombia, nw. Venezuela. **Mexico:** Recorded casually in s. Chiapas. **Habitat:** Lower levels of forests, brush edges, plantations (near sea level to 6000 ft.).

Weaver Finches, etc.: Ploceidae

A LARGE Old World family of which the House Sparrow is the best known example. **Food:** Mainly insects, seeds. **Range:** Widespread in Old World; most species in Africa. **No. of species:** World, 132 (35 sparrow-weavers); Mexico, 1 (introduced via U.S.)

HOUSE SPARROW   *Passer domesticus*   See E, W, or T
    Memo: ♂ black throat, gray crown. ♀ dull breast and eye stripe.
    Range: Native to Eurasia, n. Africa. Introduced widely in N. America, S. America, s. Africa, Australia, many oceanic islands. **Mexico:** Resident around cities, towns, farms; south locally to Chiapas and s. Guatemala (Chichicastenango — Alden). Still extending range (following Pan American Highway?).

Blackbirds, Orioles, Meadowlarks: Icteridae

A VARIED group possessing conical, sharp-pointed bills and rather flat profiles. Sexes usually unlike. **Food:** Insects, small fruits, seeds, waste grain, small aquatic life. **Range:**New World;

most species in tropics. **No. of species:** World, 88; Mexico, 30 to 33 (+ 2 accidental, 1 extinct).

CHESTNUT-HEADED (WAGLER'S) OROPENDOLA
Zarhynchus wagleri   ♂ 13–14, ♀ 9½–11   **Pl. 39**

Field marks: The pale *yellowish-green* bill, *dark chestnut-brown* head and chest and solid-black wings identify this oropendola. As in next species, sides of tail deep yellow. Sexes similar but female smaller. Often conspicuous because of colonies of long, pendent, baglike nests. Giant Cowbird, a brood parasite, is often active around colonies.

Similar species: Montezuma Oropendola (larger) has chestnut (not black) back and wings, black (not chestnut) head, 2-toned orange-tipped black bill, pale cheek patches.

Voice: An unmusical *jiva jiva jiva jura glu glu glom glom glom glu,* ending in a rattle (Chalif). A series of gurgling notes, *plup, plup, plup, plup-loo-u'poo* (Eisenmann).

Range: Mexico to w. Ecuador. **Mexico:** Locally on Gulf slope of Veracruz, n. Chiapas, and Tabasco. **Habitat:** Openings and borders of humid forests (to 3000 ft.), plantations, tall roadside trees, ceiba trees.

MONTEZUMA OROPENDOLA   **Pl. 39**
Gymnostinops montezuma   ♂ 20, ♀ 15

Field marks: This, the largest of its family, is often seen around the long baglike or stockinglike nests of its colonies, where the males display with deep upside-down bows and gurgling accompaniment. Black head, *deep ruddy back and wings,* pale *cheek patches,* and orange-tipped *black bill* separate it from its smaller relative, the Chestnut-headed Oropendola. Both have yellow and black tails (appearing all yellow from below).

Similar species: Chestnut-headed Oropendola has pale yellow-green bill, chestnut head, solid-black wings.

Voice: Song, during display, sounds like water pouring out of a bottle: 5–7 liquid *glub*'s or *gloob*'s, getting higher and faster (Chalif). *Khruk, khruk, glug, glug, glug-glug-gluglooglook-kacheer'* (RTP). Call note, *kzweck* (Eisenmann).

Range: Mexico to Panamá. **Mexico:** Gulf lowlands from s. Tamaulipas south and east through n. Oaxaca, n. Chiapas, Veracruz and lower part of Yucatán Pen. **Habitat:** Openings and borders of humid forests, ceiba trees, plantations.

YELLOW-WINGED (MEXICAN) CACIQUE   **Pl. 39**
Cassiculus melanicterus   11½

Field marks: *Male:* A slim *crested black and yellow* bird with a pale greenish-white bill. Wing patch, rump, under tail coverts, and much of tail bright yellow. Eye yellowish. *Female:* Smoky brown with dark or yellow eye, duller bill.

Similar species: Oropendolas have similar yellow and black tails but lack yellow wing patches.

Voice: Discordant, creaking: *kruk, kruk, ksh-shee-ah* or, by a stretch of the imagination, *ca-seek-eh* — Spanish pronunciation of "cacique" (RTP).

Range: Mexico only; Pacific lowlands from s. Sonora to Chiapas. **Habitat:** Arboreal; woods, villages, plantations.

YELLOW-BILLED CACIQUE   Pl. 39
Amblycercus holosericeus   7½–10

Field marks: An elusive black bird with a pointed *pale yellowish or greenish-white bill* and pale yellow eye.

Similar species: (1) Melodious Blackbird has dark bill, dark eye. (2) Immature Giant Cowbird has light eye, flesh-yellow bill, grayish area on face. (3) Brewer's Blackbird (yellow eye) has dark bill. (4) Great-tailed Grackle has longer, creased tail, dark bill.

Voice: Harsh notes, usually double: *wahk-wahk* or *wahk chowh-chowh* (♀?). Also whistling notes, perhaps given by ♂ (Chalif).

Range: E. Mexico to Bolivia. **Mexico:** Eastern lowlands, foothills from San Luis Potosí, Tamaulipas south through Oaxaca, Chiapas, and east through Yucatán Pen. **Habitat:** Brushy second growth, dense undergrowth of open woodlands, cane.

GIANT COWBIRD   Pl. 39
Scaphidura oryzivora ♂ 13½, ♀ 11½

Field marks: *Male:* A black grackle-like bird with a relatively smallish head and swollen neck ruff. Eye red. In display, male places head down with bill against chest, puffs up, and spreads ruff. *Female:* Smaller and duller, lacks ruff. *Immature:* Pale eye, pale flesh bill, gray about face.

Similar species: (1) Bronzed Cowbird also has red eye and ruff but is much smaller (6½ – 9 in.). (2) Great-tailed Grackle has longer, keeled (not flat) tail; eye yellow (♂) or brown (♀). (3) Melodious Blackbird lacks ruff, has dark eye.

Voice: A guttural *waird* accompanied by a very high-pitched *weessss* given 3–4 times (Chalif).

Range: Se. Mexico to s. Brazil, ne. Argentina. **Mexico:** Gulf slope from Puebla, Veracruz through n. Oaxaca, n. Chiapas to Tabasco; occasional Quintana Roo. **Habitat:** Open forests, plantations; feeds or displays on lawns, grassland, river borders. Often seen in vicinity of oropendola and cacique colonies, where it is a brood parasite.

BRONZED (RED-EYED) COWBIRD   See W or T
Molothrus (Tangavius) aeneus

Memo: Blackish, ruff on neck, red eye.

Range: Sw. U.S. through Mid. America to Panamá, Colombia.

Mexico: Widespread; from northern states to Chiapas, Yucatán Pen.; absent Baja California.

BROWN-HEADED COWBIRD   See E, W, or T
Molothrus ater
  Memo: ♂ black; brown head, short bill. ♀ gray; short bill.
  Range: S. Canada to n. Mexico. Migrant in north. **Mexico:** Breeds south to n. Baja California, Guerrero, Puebla, Veracruz. Winters to Isthmus of Tehuantepec. Casual Cozumel I.

COMMON GRACKLE   *Quiscalus quiscula*   See E, W, or T
  Memo: ♂ bronzy back, purple head; creased tail.
  Range: S. Canada, east of Rockies, south to Gulf states. Partially migratory. **Mexico:** Accidental; reported n. Tamaulipas (sight record of flock southeast of Matamoros).

GREAT-TAILED GRACKLE   Not illus.
Cassidix mexicanus   ♂ 17, ♀ 13
See also W or T (under Boat-tailed Grackle)
  Field marks: A very large iridescent blackbird with a long, wide *keel-shaped* tail. Eye yellow (♂). Females are brown, not black, and are *much* smaller than males; eye brown.
  Note: The closely related Boat-tailed Grackle, found coastally from Texas north to New Jersey, overlaps in Texas and is now regarded as specifically distinct.
  Similar species: See (1) Mexican Crow (short tail), p. 162, (2) Giant Cowbird (flat tail, red eye: ♂ has neck ruff), (3) Melodious Blackbird (dark eye in both sexes, tail shorter, not keep-shaped). (4) See also anis (high, ridged bills), p. 79.
  Voice: Various excited, shrill, discordant notes, including a high, rapid *kee-kee-kee-kee-kee,* etc., or *kik-kik-kik-kik,* etc.; a lower blackbird *check, check.* Also an upward slurring *ma-ree* (RTP).
  Range: Sw. U.S. through Mid. and nw. S. America to n. Peru. **Mexico:** Widespread except Baja California; sea level to 9000 ft. **Habitat:** Groves, thickets, farms, towns, village squares, city parks, mangroves, muddy beaches.

SLENDER-BILLED GRACKLE   Not illus.
Cassidix palustris   ♂ 14, ♀ 11½
  Field marks: Similar to Great-tailed Grackle but much smaller, with a smaller, thinner bill. A marsh species.
  Range: Formerly marshes at headwaters of Río Lerma near Mexico City. Apparently *extinct* (from loss of environment). **Habitat:** Headwaters of Río Lerma; fresh marshes and lake edges.

RUSTY BLACKBIRD   *Euphagus carolinus*   See E, W, or T
  Memo: Similar to Brewer's; in winter rusty, with barred breast.

Range: Alaska, Canada, northeastern edge of U.S. Winters to Gulf of Mexico. **Mexico:** Accidental Baja California.

BREWER'S BLACKBIRD   See E, W, or T
Euphagus cyanocephalus
Memo: Black; smaller than Grackle, tail shorter, not keeled; in winter may have touch of rusty. ♀ rusty.
Range: Sw. Canada, w. and n.-cen. U.S. Winters to se. U.S., s. Mexico. Casual Guatemala. **Mexico:** Breeds nw. Baja California. Widespread in winter to Isthmus of Tehuantepec.

MELODIOUS BLACKBIRD   *Dives dives*   10–11   **Pl. 39**
Field marks: A large blackbird with a dark eye (both sexes). Male is all black and slightly glossed; female is smaller and tends toward sooty brown.
Similar species: (1) Great-tailed Grackle (larger) has a longer, *keeled* tail and yellow eyes (♂). (2) ♂ Brewer's Blackbird (smaller) has white eye. (3) Giant Cowbird (larger) has red eye, ♂ has neck ruff.
Voice: A variety of whistles like *what cheer* (given 2 or 3 times). Also *to weer to weer; will you chow-how; one-year one-year* (Chalif). *Chuck, wheeeur chuck, wheeeur;* also a thin down-slurred *cheeurrr, cheeurrr*, etc. (RTP).
Range: E. Mexico to Nicaragua (also sw. Ecuador, w. Peru if *D. warsewicki* is lumped). **Mexico:** Mainly Gulf slope from s. Tamaulipas and San Luis Potosí south through Mexico, Puebla, Veracruz, n. Oaxaca, n. Chiapas and Yucatán Pen. **Habitat:** Open woods, edges, plantations, farmlands, settlements.

ORCHARD ORIOLE   *Icterus spurius*   6–7¼   **Pl. 41**
Field marks: An all-dark oriole; rump and underparts *deep chestnut.* Head, neck, back, wings, and tail black (see also next entry). *Female and young:* Olive-green above, yellow-green below, with 2 white wingbars. *Immature male:* Similar to female but with black throat patch.
Similar species: (1) See Ochre Oriole. (2) Compare ♀ and immature ♂ Scott's Oriole (similarly greenish).
Voice: Song, a fast-moving outburst of piping whistles, guttural notes; unlike abrupt piping of most orioles. A strident slurred *what-cheer* or *wheer,* at or near end (RTP).
Range: Se. Canada, e. and cen. U.S. to cen. Mexico. Winters through Mid. America to n. Colombia, nw. Venezuela. **Mexico:** Breeds from Chihuahua and Río Grande south to Michoacán, México. May breed on Pacific Coast from cen. Sinaloa to Nayarit. Widespread in southern and southeastern sections in winter (incl. Yucatán Pen.). **Habitat:** Second growth, wood borders, scrub, gardens with trees, plantations.

OCHRE (FUERTES') ORIOLE   **Pl. 41**
Icterus fuertesi (or *I. spurius* in part)   6–7
    Field marks: *Male:* Like a pale *ochre-colored* edition of Or-
    chard Oriole and may be a rather restricted local race of that
    bird. *Female:* Similar to Orchard Oriole.
    Range: Breeds in s. Tamaulipas, n. Veracruz; spreads south-
    ward somewhat in winter.

BLACK-COWLED ORIOLE *Icterus prosthemelas* 8 **Pl. 40**
    Field marks: *Adult:* A *black-hooded* oriole similar to Scott's
    Oriole (*clear yellow* rump and underparts) but *no white in wing,*
    no yellow patches in tail. Note touch of chestnut below hood.
    Immature: Olive-green above, yellow below, with a black throat
    and *solid-black wings* (except shoulders).
    Similar species: None in its lowland range. (1) ♂ Scott's
    Oriole lives in arid highlands. (2) Black-vented Oriole (high-
    lands) is similar in pattern, but *orange,* not clear yellow below.
    Voice: Song, a series of melodious whistles. Call suggestive of
    House Sparrow, rather nasal and monotonous (Eisenmann).
    Range: Se. Mexico to Panamá; a closely related form, *I. do-
    minicensis,* in W. Indies may be conspecific. **Mexico:** Gulf low-
    lands from s. Veracruz, n. Oaxaca, n. Chiapas, Tabasco through
    Yucatán Pen. **Habitat:** Second-growth rain forest, edges, plan-
    tations, semi-open land near water.

BLACK-VENTED (WAGLER'S) ORIOLE   **Pl. 40**
Icterus wagleri 7½–9
    Field marks: Similar to the Black-cowled Oriole, a lowland
    bird (black head, no wingbars), but adults differ in having
    orange, not clear yellow underparts. Note particularly the
    black under tail coverts or "vent."
    Similar species: Black-cowled Oriole (eastern lowlands) is
    clear yellow below, including under tail coverts.
    Range: Mexico to Nicaragua. **Mexico:** Sonora, Chihuahua,
    Coahuila, Nuevo León south on west coast to Nayarit and in
    highlands to Chiapas. **Habitat:** Second-growth woods, edges.

SCOTT'S ORIOLE *Icterus parisorum* 7¼–8¼   **Pl. 40**
    Field marks: *Male:* A *lemon-yellow* oriole with black back,
    head, wings and tail. A strong *white bar* across wing. *Yellow
    patches* in basal half of tail. *Female:* More greenish yellow be-
    neath than most other female orioles (except Orchard). *Imma-
    ture male:* Similar to female but with black throat.
    Similar species: (1) Bar-winged Oriole is found in Chiapas
    and Guatemala. (2) Black-cowled Oriole lacks white wingbar
    and yellow tail patches; often has narrow edge of chestnut below
    black chest. (3) Black-headed Oriole has *yellow* back. (4) Din-
    gier underparts, grayer back, more extensive black on face help

separate young ♂ from those of other species (Black-cowled, Orchard, Hooded, etc.).
Voice: Song, rich whistles; suggests Western Meadowlark (RTP).
Range: Sw. U.S., w. Mexico. **Mexico:** Baja California and highlands of western and central states from northern border south to Oaxaca. Winters except in northern part of range.
Habitat: Dry woods and scrub in arid or semi-arid mts.; yuccas, oak slopes, pinyons.

BAR-WINGED ORIOLE   *Icterus maculialatus*   8   **Pl. 40**
Field marks: *Male:* Similar to Scott's Oriole (yellow shoulder patch, 1 white wingbar), but tail *all black,* lacking yellow patches; range is more southern. *Female:* Olive greenish above, greenish yellow below, with blackish throat patch and front of face.
Similar species: (1) Scott's Oriole (north of Tehuantepec) has yellow patches in tail. (2) Black-cowled and (3) Black-vented Orioles have no wingbar.
Range: Chiapas, Guatemala, El Salvador; local. **Habitat:** Second-growth woods, mainly foothills.

HOODED ORIOLE   *Icterus cucullatus*   7–7¾   **Pl. 41**
Field marks: *Male:* An *orange-crowned, black-throated* oriole, one of several; the most widespread and the only one in which the sexes differ. 3 others also have black backs. This is the smallest and can be known by its *2 white wingbars.* *Female:* Back, olive-gray; head and tail more yellowish, underparts dull orangish yellow, wings with 2 white bars. *Immature male:* Resembles female but has *throat black.*
Similar species: (1) Altamira Oriole (both sexes) is much larger, with larger bill, only 1 white wingbar. See below also (2) Spot-breasted Oriole, (3) Yellow-tailed Oriole, and (4) ♀ Baltimore Oriole (a migrant).
Voice: Song, throaty notes and piping whistles: *chut chut chut whew whew.* Note, a sharp *eek* (RTP).
Range: Sw. U.S., Mexico, B. Honduras. **Mexico:** Breeds Baja California, Sonora, Chihuahua south to Guerrero; also on Gulf slope from Nuevo León and Tamaulipas south and east to n. Chiapas and Yucatán Pen. Also B. Honduras, but not Guatemala. Somewhat more widespread in winter except northern parts. **Habitat:** Open woods, thickets, palms, shade trees.

YELLOW-TAILED ORIOLE   *Icterus mesomelas*   8–9   **Pl. 41**
Field marks: *Adult:* A yellow-crowned oriole with the *3 outer tail feathers largely yellow.* Throat, back, wings (except coverts), and central tail feathers black. *Immature:* Similar to

adult but largely yellowish olive above, lemon-yellow below; may or may not have black bib.

Similar species: Other yellow or orange-crowned orioles have *all-black* tails.

Voice: A loud clear whistle of 2 phrases, repeated: *chee-wow, chee-wow* or *gee-wow, gee-wow* (Chalif). A loud repetitious chant: *wur-chip-chewoo, wur-chip-chewoo, wur-chip-chewoo,* etc. (RTP).

Range: Se. Mexico to w. Peru. **Mexico:** Gulf slope from s. Veracruz, n. Oaxaca through n. Chiapas, Tabasco, Yucatán Pen. **Habitat:** Second growth, humid forest borders.

YELLOW-BACKED ORIOLE   *Icterus chrysater*   8–9   **Pl. 40**
Field marks: *Adult:* The *golden-yellow back* and black forehead and throat identify this oriole. No white in wing. *Immature:* Duller; contrast of wings and back lessened by olive coloration. May or may not have some black on throat.

Similar species: Other yellow or orange-backed orioles: (1) Orange Oriole more orange, some white in wing, no black on forehead. (2) Black-headed Oriole is dull olive-yellow, entire head black. See also (3) Black-throated Shrike-tanager (Plate 42); black head, hooked bill.

Voice: Song (in Panamá), 6–14 loud clear whistles, moving irregularly up and down scale, giving impression of being off-key. A frequent call is *teea, cheep-cheep-cheep, tee;* 1st and last notes whistled, others nasal (Eisenmann).

Range: Se. Mexico to Nicaragua; cen. Panamá to Colombia, n. Venezuela. **Mexico:** S. Veracruz, Chiapas; also northern parts of Yucatán Pen. (rare). **Habitat:** Pine ridges, second growth, oaks, scrub.

BLACK-HEADED ORIOLE   *Icterus graduacauda*   9   **Pl. 40**
Field marks: The only black-headed oriole with a yellowish back. The dull olive-yellow body contrasts with the ragged black hood. Wings and tail black. Sexes similar.

Similar species: (1) Yellow-backed Oriole has orangish cheeks and crown. (2) Other black-headed orioles have black backs.

Voice: Song, low whistled notes of human quality, disjointed, with halftones; suggests a boy learning to whistle (RTP).

Range: S. Texas to s. Mexico and nw. Guatemala (?). **Mexico:** Eastern, south-central, and southern parts from lower Río Grande Valley and Nayarit south locally to Oaxaca, Chiapas. **Habitat:** Woodlands, thickets; to 6000+ ft.

SPOT-BREASTED ORIOLE   *Icterus pectoralis*   8–9   **Pl. 41**
Field marks: *Adult:* Note the *heavy black spotting* on the sides of the breast. Otherwise much like Hooded or Altamira

Orioles but with less white in wing. *Immature:* Duller, more olivaceous; lacks spots on breast.
Similar species: (1) Hooded and (2) Altamira Orioles lack
black spots, have white wingbars.
Range: Sw. Mexico to nw. Costa Rica. Recently established
(by introduction or escape) in s. Florida. **Mexico:** Arid Pacific
lowlands from Colima south through s. Chiapas. **Habitat:** Dry
scrub, brush, agricultural country, villages.

ALTAMIRA (BLACK-THROATED) ORIOLE   Pl. 41
Icterus gularis   8½–10
Field marks: Very similar to Hooded Oriole, but considerably
larger. Bill is much thicker at base and upper wingbar is *yellow
or orange,* not white. Sexes similar. The nest, a well-woven
stocking, is 2 ft. long, much larger than Hooded Oriole's.
Similar species: (1) Male Hooded Oriole is smaller, has
smaller bill, 2 white wingbars. (2) Spot-breasted Oriole has
black spots on sides of breast.
Voice: A harsh rasping "fuss" note, *ike-ike-ike* (Kincaid).
Song, disjointed whistled notes.
Range: Southern tip of Texas through Mid. America to Nicaragua. **Mexico:** From lower Río Grande Valley south on Gulf
slope through Yucatán Pen.; Pacific slope from Guerrero
through Chiapas. **Habitat:** Dry open woodlands, plantations,
low second growth, near villages.

BALTIMORE ORIOLE   *Icterus galbula* (in part)   7–8   Pl. 40
Field marks: *Male:* Bright orange with a solid-black head.
Note the large orange patches on *outer half* of tail. *Female:*
Warm olive-brown or orange-brown above, burnt yellow-orange
below; 2 white wingbars. Some females have black on head,
suggesting male's hood. Hybridizes with Bullock's Oriole in cen.
U.S. and now regarded as conspecific by A.O.U. *Check-List.*
Similar species: (1) ♀ Bullock's Oriole has grayer back, whit-
ish belly. (2) ♀ Hooded Oriole is greener on back and has a more
rounded tail.
Voice: Song, a series of rich, piping whistled notes. Note, a low
mellow whistled *hew-li* (RTP).
Range: Canada, e. and cen. U.S. Winters mainly s. Mexico to
n. Colombia, nw. Venezuela. **Mexico:** Migrant through eastern
and southern sections, wintering in south. Noted often in
Nayarit in April; rare Yucatán Pen.

BULLOCK'S ORIOLE   Pl. 41
Icterus bullockii (or *I. galbula* in part)   7–8½
Field marks: *Male:* The *black crown,* eye stripes, and large
white wing patch identify this bright orange and black oriole
(see also next species). *Female:* Olive-gray above, more yel-

lowish on tail; 2 white wingbars. Less extensively yellow below than other female orioles; usually *whitish on belly;* back decidedly grayer. Immature male resembles female but has a black throat. Now considered conspecific with Baltimore Oriole by A.O.U. *Check-List.*

Similar species: (1) See next species. (2) Other orange-cheeked orioles lack black crown.

Voice: A series of accented double notes with 1 or 2 piping notes. Note, a sharp *skip;* also a chatter (RTP).

Range: Sw. Canada, w. U.S. to Mexico. Winters to Guatemala. **Mexico:** Breeds n. Baja California and mainland of nw. Mexico from Sonora east to n. Durango and Coahuila. Widespread in migration and winter except east coast and Yucatán Pen. **Habitat:** River groves, open woods, towns, farms.

BLACK-BACKED (ABEILLE'S) ORIOLE   Pl. 41
Icterus abeillei (or *I. bullockii* or *I. galbula* in part)   7½

Field marks: *Male:* Differs markedly from nominate Bullock's Oriole in having the eye stripe, cheeks, sides, and rump *black,* replacing the orange of those parts. Dark-looking; otherwise has typical white wing patch of Bullock's Oriole. *Female:* Similar to female Bullock's Oriole.

Note: Formerly regarded as a distinct species. Inasmuch as the Black-backed Oriole (a rather poor name) intergrades with *bullockii* in Durango it is now regarded as conspecific. Using similar criteria, Baltimore and Bullock's Orioles, though strikingly different, should also be regarded as conspecific.

Range: Cen. Mexico; southern part of central plateau (Durango, Zacatecas, and s. Nuevo León south to Oaxaca, Veracruz).

ORANGE ORIOLE   *Icterus auratus*   6½   Pl. 40

Field marks: Note the *orange back. Male:* Similar to the larger Yellow-backed Oriole, but more *orange* in color; some *white* in wing, no black on forehead. *Female:* Duller, washed with olive; back may be streaked.

Similar species: (1) Yellow-backed Oriole is larger, more yellow, lacks white in wing, has black forehead. (2) Hooded Oriole has black back.

Range: Confined to Yucatán Pen. (Campeche, Yucatán, Quintana Roo). **Habitat:** Abandoned farmlands, second growth.

STREAK-BACKED ORIOLE   *Icterus sclateri*   8   Pl. 41

Field marks: The only adult oriole with a *streaked back.* Has more white in wing than similar orioles. Males are basically yellow-orange, heads becoming almost red in northwestern edge of range. Female duller than male; back more olivaceous, but still streaked with black. Immature resembles female, but lacks black throat.

Note: Birds north of Isthmus of Tehuantepec are sometimes treated as a separate species, Flame-headed Oriole, *Icterus pustulatus.* Southern birds are less orange and have more heavily streaked backs. The birds from Tres Marías Is. have also been considered specifically distinct as *I. graysoni,* Tres Marías Oriole.

Similar species: *Caution:* Some southern populations are so heavily streaked that they may appear to have black backs, thereby resembling Hooded Orioles.

Voice: A poor vocalist; oriole-like musical chirps; a wrenlike rattle, a rapid, dry meadowlarklike chatter (Slud).

Range: W. Mexico to Costa Rica; casual sw. U.S. **Mexico:** Pacific slope; lowlands, foothills from cen. Sonora, Chihuahua south to Chiapas. Also Tres Marías Is. **Habitat:** Dry country, wood edges, arid scrub.

TRICOLORED BLACKBIRD *Agelaius tricolor* **See W**
> **Memo:** Colonial; ♂ with *white* margin on red patch. Song more nasal than Red-wing's: *on-ke-kaaangh.*
> **Range:** S. Oregon through California to nw. Baja California (south to Lat. 30°). Winters through most of range.

RED-WINGED BLACKBIRD **See E, W, or T**
Agelaius phoeniceus
> **Memo:** ♂ black; red "epaulettes" with yellow or buff edge; ♀ heavily striped.
> **Note:** A local form of this bird, known as the Bicolored Blackbird *(A. gubernator),* has the "epaulettes" solid red without the yellow edge. It may or may not be conspecific. In some Mexican localities it lives in association with other Red-winged Blackbirds without interbreeding.
> **Range:** Canada to Bahamas, Cuba, Costa Rica. **Mexico:** Resident in n. Baja California and Pacific slope from Sonora to Nayarit; widespread elsewhere where marshes occur, including Yucatán Pen.

YELLOW-HEADED BLACKBIRD **See E, W, or T**
Xanthocephalus xanthocephalus
> **Memo:** ♂ black; yellow head. ♀ brown; yellow throat, breast.
> **Range:** S. Canada, w. U.S., upper Mississippi Valley, nw. Mexico. Winters sw. U.S., Mexico. **Mexico:** Breeds in marshes of Colorado River delta and n. Tamaulipas. Winters south to s. Baja California, Guerrero, Puebla.

EASTERN (COMMON) MEADOWLARK **See E, W, or T**
Sturnella magna
> **Memo:** Black V on yellow breast; white outer tail feathers.

Range: Se. Canada, U.S., Cuba, Mid. and n. S. America to n. Brazil. Partial migrant. **Mexico:** Resident in open country from northern border states (except Baja California) south on Pacific slope to Jalisco and in highlands to Chiapas; in Gulf lowlands from Río Grande to n. Chiapas, Tabasco. Also coastal scrub of n. Yucatán.

WESTERN MEADOWLARK   See E, W, or T
Sturnella neglecta
  Memo: Like E. Meadowlark, but song flutelike, gurgling, double-noted (song of E. Meadowlark, clear slurred whistles).
  Range: Sw. Canada, upper Mississippi Valley to cen. Mexico. Partial migrant. **Mexico:** Breeds in nw. Baja California and from U.S. border south to Durango, Zacatecas, cen. Nuevo León. Winters south to s. Baja California, Michoacán, México, n. Veracruz.

BOBOLINK   *Dolichonyx oryzivorus*   See E, W, or T
  Memo: Spring ♂, black below, white patches above. ♀ and autumn ♂, brown; striped crown, buffy breast.
  Range: S. Canada, n. U.S. Migrates mainly through e. U.S., W. Indies to winter in Bolivia, s. Brazil, n. Argentina. **Mexico:** Rare transient; recorded Yucatán, Cozumel I., B. Honduras.

Tanagers: Thraupidae

MALE tanagers (and some females) are usually brilliantly colored; females are often more modestly colored, suggesting large, thick-billed warblers or vireos; some may also be confused with female orioles, but the rather thick bills are usually notched or "toothed." The euphonias and chlorophonias are an almost finchlike group of tanagers with plump bodies and finchlike bills. The systematics of this family are still in dispute. Recent authors, probably correctly, include some of the honeycreepers (Coerebidae) among the tanagers and reduce the tanager complex to a subfamily of the Emberizidae. **Food:** Insects, small fruits, mistletoe berries. **Range:** New World; most species in tropics. **No. of species:** World, 191; Mexico, 27 (+1 in Guatemala).

BLUE-CROWNED CHLOROPHONIA   Pl. 43
Chlorophonia occipitalis   4½–5½
  Field marks: *Male:* A small, short-billed, *parrot-green* tanager with a *clear yellow breast* and *turquoise-blue crown* (not always easy to see against green of head). A narrow brown line separates green hood from yellow breast. *Female:* Similar; all green, with only a trace of the yellow and blue. Often travels in foraging bands.

Similar species: See Green Shrike-Vireo (p. 195).
Voice: Note (in Costa Rica), a mournful, short dovelike *oo,* often repeated one or more times; ventriloquial; sometimes given by two birds in duet. Also a short *ek* (Slud). In Panamá, a fast puppylike *enk-enk-enk-enk* (Eisenmann).
Range: Se. Mexico to w. Panamá. The population of Costa Rica and Panamá is often considered a distinct species, Golden-browed Chlorophonia *(C. callophrys).* **Mexico:** Subtropical mts. of s. Veracruz, n. Oaxaca, Chiapas. **Habitat:** Forest edges, openings in cloud forest (to 6000 + ft.).

BLUE-HOODED EUPHONIA   Pl. 43
Euphonia elegantissima   4–5
Field marks: *Male:* A short-billed, warbler-sized tanager; blue-black with bright *cinnamon underparts* and a bright *blue crown* and hindneck. A deep reddish spot on forehead (may look black). *Female:* Dull olive-green, paler below; blue crown and reddish forehead as in male, but throat dull cinnamon. Euphonias are often seen in mistletoe.
Voice: Call, *chup* or *dyewp.* Song, an irregular sputtering or twittering series with some musical undertones (Eisenmann). One song suggests complex song of Winter Wren (Graber).
Range: Mexico to w. Panamá. The Mid. American populations are often merged in the species *E. musica* of W. Indies, as are closely related S. American forms. **Mexico:** Foothills and mts.; from s. Sonora, sw. Chihuahua, s. Nuevo León, s. Tamaulipas south. **Habitat:** Semi-open deforested country, woodland edges, mistletoe, plantations (to 9000 + ft.).

WHITE-VENTED EUPHONIA   Not illus.
Euphonia minuta   3½–4
Field marks: *Male:* A small euphonia, very similar to Scrub Euphonia but center of belly and under tail coverts *white. Female:* Olive-green above and yellowish on breast, contrasting with *grayish throat* and whitish abdomen.
Similar species: (1) ♂ Scrub Euphonia has completely yellow belly and under tail coverts; ♀ is yellowish on throat and abdomen (not grayish or whitish). (2) Pale-vented race of Scrub Euphonia also has white or pale under tail coverts but lives in drier country of w. Mexico; ♀ has gray nape. (3) See also Yellow-throated Euphonia (below).
Voice: Calls, *wee'-chup;* also *weet-tsick* and *tsick-tsick* (Eisenmann).
Range: Se. Mexico, B. Honduras, and Guatemala (local and rare); Nicaragua to w. Ecuador, Amazonian Brazil. **Mexico:** Ne. Chiapas (Palenque). **Habitat:** Humid forests and borders, plantations, humid second growth.

SCRUB EUPHONIA *Euphonia affinis* 3½–4½ **Pl. 42**
Field marks: A tiny finchlike tanager. *Male:* Glossy *blue-black* with a *golden-yellow forecrown patch* and yellow underparts. Throat and bib *black*. Some white in tail. Pacific slope birds have a white crissum. *Female:* Dull olive, lighter below, brightening to yellow on throat and belly.
Similar species: (1) ♂ Yellow-throated Euphonia has *yellow* throat; ♀ has whitish on throat and belly. (2) See White-vented Euphonia (preceding).
Voice: A thin, musical 3-syllable whistle at a level pitch; a vireolike *wheet-chichi-chi-chih* (Slud); a high-pitched *see-see-see, dewd-see* (Sutton and Pettingill).
Range: Mexico to Costa Rica. **Mexico:** Gulf slope from s. Tamaulipas south to Oaxaca, Chiapas and east through Yucatán Pen.; also Pacific slope from s. Sonora south to Guerrero (a pale-vented form, formerly regarded as a distinct species, *E. godmani*). **Habitat:** Broadleaf deciduous forests (crowns of trees), scrub, brushy fields, agricultural areas. Prefers drier country.

YELLOW-THROATED EUPHONIA **Pl. 42**
Euphonia hirundinacea [= *lauta*] 4–4½
Field marks: *Male:* Similar to Scrub Euphonia but underparts *all yellow, including throat* (replacing black throat and bib of that bird). *Female:* Dark olive above, lighter yellow-olive on chest; throat and belly with some whitish.
Similar species: See above (1) Scrub Euphonia and (2) White-vented Euphonia.
Voice: A short whistle, rapidly repeated 2 or 3 times, sometimes clear and bell-like (Skutch).
Range: E. Mexico to sw. Panamá. **Mexico:** Gulf lowlands from Tamaulipas south through n. Oaxaca, n. Chiapas and east through Yucatán Pen.; also Pacific lowlands of Chiapas. **Habitat:** Trees in wet tropical forests and borders, plantations, gardens (to 4000 ft.).

OLIVE-BACKED EUPHONIA **Pl. 42**
Euphonia gouldi 3¾
Field marks: A tiny, finchlike, olive-green tanager. *Male:* Dark olive-green above, paler on breast. Note the *yellow forecrown patch, rufous belly and under tail coverts*. *Female:* Similar in general color to male but forehead *dull rufous;* no rufous on belly (but some on under tail coverts).
Similar species: See preceding 2 euphonias.
Voice: An unmusical jumble of sharp notes, including a soft trill (Slud).
Range: Se. Mexico to nw. Panamá. **Mexico:** Gulf slope; s. Veracruz, n. Oaxaca, n. Chiapas, Tabasco; also Quintana Roo.

MASKED TANAGER   *Tangara larvata*   4½–5¼   **Pl. 43**
   Field marks: A small *black and blue* tanager with a *light
   golden-brown head* and a black mask bordered in ear region
   with light blue. Rump bright turquoise-blue, 2 blue wingbars.
   Sexes similar.
   Voice: A weak trill (1 second), *tsiriririririririt,* weaker and
   shorter than trill of Chipping Sparrow (Eisenmann).
   Range: Se. Mexico to w. Ecuador. A similar bird, *T. nigri-
   cincta* (east of Andes in n. S. America) may be conspecific.
   Mexico: Gulf lowlands of n. Oaxaca, n. Chiapas, Tabasco.
   Habitat: Humid forest borders, plantations.

AZURE-RUMPED TANAGER   **Not illus.**
Tangara cabanisi   5¾
   Field marks: Extremely rare; only 2 specimens known. A
   green and blue bird; upper back *metallic grass-green,* lower
   back and rump *azure-blue,* abdomen whitish; wings, tail, and
   sides of chest blackish with blue feather edgings; crown dull
   blue.
   Voice: A series of metallic chipping notes (Parker).
   Range: Known only from mts. of Chiapas and sw. Guatemala.
   Habitat: Probably cloud forest edges.

RUFOUS-WINGED TANAGER   **Not illus.**
Tangara lavinia   5
   Field marks: *Male:* A bright *green* tanager with a *reddish-
   brown head* (except throat), *yellow collar* on hindneck, *rufous
   wings.* Upper back yellowish, chin and belly turquoise. *Female:*
   Duller, without bright rufous cap. *Immature:* Plain glossy
   green, paler below.
   Range: Extreme e. Guatemala (Santo Tomás) through Cen.
   America to w. Ecuador. Not in Mexico. Reported B. Honduras.
   Habitat: Humid foothill forests and edges.

BLUE-GRAY (BLUE) TANAGER   **Pl. 43**
Thraupis episcopus   5½–6½
   Field marks: A light gray-blue tanager, brighter green-blue on
   wings and tail. Shoulders violet-blue. Sexes similar.
   Similar species: In nw. Mexico see Mountain Bluebird (p.
   189).
   Voice: Song, varied and intricate phrases, but tone weak and
   squeaky (Skutch). Suggests one of songs of American Redstart
   (Sturgis). Calls, *chueep* and *seeee* (Eisenmann).
   Range: Se. Mexico to Amazonia. **Mexico:** Eastern parts,
   mainly lowlands; San Luis Potosí, Guanajuato south through
   Oaxaca, Veracruz, Chiapas, Tabasco; also s. Quintana Roo.
   Habitat: Woodland borders, plantations, semi-open country,
   towns.

YELLOW-WINGED TANAGER   Pl. 43
Thraupis abbas   6–7
   Field marks: The *yellow patches* in the blackish wing are the
best mark for this lavender-gray-headed, olive-gray tanager.
Back spotted with black. Sexes similar.
   Voice: A series of strong chips suggesting Chipping Sparrow;
very metallic and rapid: *chi-chi-chi,* etc., or *chill-chill-chill,* etc.
(Chalif). Call, a long *seeeeeet* (Willis).
   Range: E. Mexico to Nicaragua. **Mexico:** Mainly Gulf slope;
lowlands, subtropical zone of mts. from San Luis Potosí, s. Tamaulipas south through Oaxaca, Veracruz, Chiapas and east
through Yucatán Pen. **Habitat:** Borders of humid forests,
clearings, settlements, plantations, orchards.

STRIPE-HEADED TANAGER   *Spindalis zena*   6–8   Pl. 42
   Field marks: *Male:* Note the 2 *white stripes* on the side of the
black head, yellow throat patch, and dark rufous or *chestnut
collar and chest.* Breast yellow. Wings and tail strongly patterned with black and white. *Female:* A plain, olive-brown,
finchlike bird with some of male's wing pattern.
   Voice: Song, a prolonged but weak warble, seldom heard. Call
note, a drawn-out *seep* (Bond).
   Range: Mainly Bahamas, Greater Antilles. **Mexico:** Resident
only on Cozumel I. off Yucatán Pen.

SCARLET-RUMPED TANAGER   Pl. 44
Ramphocelus passerinii   6½
   Field marks: *Male:* Velvety black except for *bright red rump*
and upper tail coverts. Bill light blue at base; eye red. *Female:*
Dark olive-brown, lightening to golden brown on chest and
rump. Bill *bluish* as in male.
   Voice: Song, loosely connected robin- or vireolike inconse-
quential phrases. Notes, a confidential *hist,* and a throaty *churr*
(Slud).
   Range: Se. Mexico to w. Panamá. **Mexico:** Gulf lowlands of
s. Veracruz, n. Chiapas, Tabasco. **Habitat:** Woodland borders,
brush, clearings, plantations. Not arboreal; stays in bushes.

CRIMSON-COLLARED TANAGER   Pl. 44
Phlogothraupis sanguinolenta   6–7½
   Field marks: A black tanager with a *crimson-red hood* or cowl
surrounding a black face. Rump and lower tail coverts red. Bill
thick (suggesting a grosbeak), pale grayish blue.
   Similar species: Crimson-collared Grosbeak (Plate 46) has
entire head black, no red on rump; bill blackish.
   Voice: *Tze-tze-tsweze,* or *tswe-twe,* or *tswizee* (Chalif).
   Range: Se. Mexico to nw. Panamá. **Mexico:** Mainly Gulf low-
lands of s. Veracruz, n. Oaxaca, n. Chiapas, Tabasco; also s.
Quintana Roo. **Habitat:** Humid forest borders, second growth.

SUMMER TANAGER *Piranga rubra*   **See E, W, or T**
Memo: ♂ rose-red, pale bill. ♀ olive above, deep yellow below;
pale bill, no wingbars.
Range: Cen. and s. U.S. to n. Mexico. Winters Mexico to w.
Amazonia. **Mexico:** Breeds from U.S. border south to ne. Baja
California, Sinaloa, Durango, Nuevo León, Tamaulipas.
Winters mainly from cen. Mexico south, including Yucatán Pen.

HEPATIC TANAGER *Piranga flava*   **See W or T**
Memo: ♂ deep dull red, black bill. ♀ similar to ♀ Summer
Tanager but bill blackish, cheek gray.
Range: Breeds sw. U.S. through Mid. and S. America to n. Ar-
gentina. **Mexico:** Breeds in highlands from Sonora, Coahuila to
Chiapas. Migrant in north; lower altitudes in winter. Does not
occur Yucatán Pen. In Guatemala and B. Honduras breeds in
pine forest in mts. and pine savannas in lowland.

ROSE-THROATED TANAGER   **Pl. 43**
Piranga roseogularis 6
    Field marks: *Male:* A small *grayish* tanager with a *red crown,*
reddish wings and tail, *rose-pink throat* and under tail coverts.
Female: Red of male replaced by olive; chest and sides gray,
throat *yellow,* belly and under tail coverts buffy.
    Range: Se. Mexico, n. Guatemala (Petén). **Mexico:** Confined
to Yucatán Pen. (n. Campeche, Yucatán, nw. Quintana Roo,
Cozumel I.). **Habitat:** Deciduous forest edges.

SCARLET TANAGER *Piranga olivacea*   **See E, W, or T**
Memo: ♂ scarlet; black wings. ♀ yellow green; dusky wings.
Range: Se. Canada, e. U.S. Migrates mainly through W.
Indies. Winters Colombia to w. Amazonia; Brazil. **Mexico:**
Rare migrant along Gulf Coast, including Yucatán Pen. Also
rare migrant B. Honduras, n. Guatemala.

WESTERN TANAGER *Piranga ludoviciana* **See E, W, or T**
Memo: ♂ yellow and black; red face, wingbars. ♀ olive above,
yellow below; white wingbars.
Range: W. Canada, w. U.S., nw. Mexico. Winters to Costa
Rica. **Mexico:** Breeds n. Baja California, ne. Sonora. Migrant
elsewhere, except east coast (rare) and Yucatán Pen. Winters
from s. Baja California, cen. Mexico south, mainly in mts.

STRIPE-BACKED (FLAME-COLORED) TANAGER **Pl. 44**
Piranga bidentata 6–7½
    Field marks: The only Mexican tanager with a *striped back.*
Male: Flaming orange-red with dusky ear patches, dark wings
with 2 *whitish or orangish wingbars,* dark tail tipped with white
in outer corners. *Female:* Yellow-olive above and dull yellow
below. Note the wingbars and striped back.

Similar species: (1) White-winged Tanager is smaller, lacks stripes on back. (2) Western Tanager in winter plumage can be very similar to ♀ and immature ♂.

Voice: Song, vireolike with a burr in it. Call note, *purrrrrit* (Chalif). Song with short burry phrases similar to those of Scarlet or Western Tanagers (RTP).

Range: Mexico to Panamá. **Mexico:** Mts. from Sonora, Chihuahua, Nuevo León, Tamaulipas south. Also Tres Marías Is.

Habitat: Cloud forest, pines, oaks (2500–9000 ft.).

WHITE-WINGED TANAGER   Pl. 43
Piranga leucoptera 5–6

Field marks: *Male:* Like a Scarlet Tanager with a *black mask,* black bill, *2 white wingbars. Female:* Olive, brightening to yellow below. Wings and tail black, *2 white wingbars* as in male; bill *black.*

Similar species: (1) ♀ Western Tanager (wingbars) has *pale* bill, is paler yellow below. (2) In w. Mexico see Stripe-backed Tanager (preceding).

Voice: Call, *tsupeet-peet;* also *seetseesee* (Eisenmann).

Range: E. Mexico to Brazil, Bolivia. **Mexico:** Gulf slope of mts. from s. Tamaulipas, San Luis Potosí south through Veracruz, Puebla, Oaxaca, Chiapas (both slopes). **Habitat:** Humid mt. forests, edges (2500–6000 ft.).

RED-HEADED TANAGER   Pl. 43
Piranga erythrocephala 6

Field marks: A yellowish-olive tanager with a red head. Breast and belly yellow. No wingbars. *Female:* Yellowish olive above, yellowish below, brightest on throat, washed with brownish on sides and flanks. Under tail coverts buffy.

Similar species: (1) ♂ Western Tanager (red-headed) has 2 white wingbars, black back; ♀ also has wingbars. (2) ♀ Hepatic Tanager has a more orange-yellow throat.

Range: W. and s. Mexico only. Mts. from s. Sonora, s. Chihuahua south through western and central states to Oaxaca. **Habitat:** Mts. from 3500 to 8000 + ft.

RED-CROWNED ANT-TANAGER   Pl. 44
Habia rubica 6–7

Field marks: A dark sooty-red or red-brown tanager with a *bright red crown patch bordered with blackish.* Throat light red. *Female:* Brown, lighter on underparts; throat buff; note the *orangish crown patch.*

Similar species: ♂ Red-throated Ant-Tanager is very difficult to separate in field; crown patch not bordered with blackish, red throat brighter, song different; ♀ lacks crown patch.

Voice: Song, *chu - cheeah - chu - cheeah - chu - cheeah* (Chalif). *Cheer-cheer-cheer-cheer* or *purtee'-pirtee'-pirtee'-pirtee';* the 2

types sometimes combined (Willis). Short whistled phrases, *cheer chur, cheer chur* or *cheer chur-chur* (RTP).
Range: Mexico to ne. Argentina. **Mexico:** Pacific slope from Nayarit south to Chiapas; Gulf slope from s. Tamaulipas south to Veracruz, n. Chiapas and east through Yucatán Pen. **Habitat:** Underbrush of dense humid forests and borders.

RED-THROATED ANT-TANAGER   Pl. 44
Habia fuscicauda   7–8

Field marks: *Male:* Very similar to Red-crowned Ant-Tanager, but red crown patch less evident, *without blackish outline;* throat brighter. *Female:* Deep warm brown, lighter below, especially on throat (light ochre-yellow). *No crown patch.*
Similar species: See Red-crowned Ant-Tanager (preceding).
Voice: Song, a sequence of paired notes, rising in pitch with each couplet (Land). A robinlike *chew-chew,* given 1–4 times (Chalif).
Range: E. Mexico through Cen. America to n. Colombia. **Mexico:** Gulf slope from Tamaulipas south through Veracruz, n. Oaxaca, n. Chiapas, and Yucatán Pen. Also Pacific slope of Chiapas. **Habitat:** Undergrowth of humid forest borders and deciduous woodlands, second growth.

BLACK-THROATED SHRIKE-TANAGER   Pl. 42
Lanio aurantius   6½–8

Field marks: *Male:* More likely to be taken for an oriole than a tanager, but note the prominently *hooked* bill. Head, wings, and tail black; rump and underparts yellow. A touch of white on wing coverts. *Female:* Olive-brown above, with grayish face and throat, yellow belly. Note the *hooked beak* and *bright tawny rump.*
Similar species: (1) Black-headed Oriole of plateau country has similar pattern but bill is pointed. (2) Gray-headed Tanager is similar to ♀ but is more yellow on chest and lacks light tawny rump and hook on bill. (3) Coloration of ♀ may also suggest a *Myiarchus* flycatcher.
Voice: Noisy; *stchee,* followed by 4 rich descending *chee*'s, ending with several *chee*'s on a level (Slud).
Range: Se. Mexico to Honduras. **Mexico:** Gulf lowlands of s. Veracruz, ne. Oaxaca, n. Chiapas, Tabasco, Campeche; also Quintana Roo. **Habitat:** Humid forests at low and mid-levels.

GRAY-HEADED TANAGER   Pl. 42
Eucometis penicillata   6–7

Field marks: An olive-green or yellowish-olive tanager with a *gray head* and warm yellow breast and paler yellow belly. Head may appear to be slightly crested.
Similar species: See ♀ Black-throated Shrike-Tanager.

Voice: A gifted singer. Song sweet and appealing: *whichis whichis whicheery whichis whichu,* etc. (Skutch).
Range: Se. Mexico to Paraguay, ne. Argentina. **Mexico:** Gulf lowlands; s. Veracruz, ne. Oaxaca, n. Chiapas, Tabasco, Yucatán Pen. **Habitat:** Forest undergrowth, second growth, forest edges. Follows army ants.

ROSY (ROSE-BREASTED) THRUSH-TANAGER   Pl. 44
Rhodinocichla rosea   8
Field marks: More like a thrush in aspect than a tanager (note the thrushlike bill). *Male:* A furtive blackish ground-dwelling bird with *rose-red eye stripe, throat, and breast. Female:* Browner, with red replaced by russet, giving a more robinlike look. The eye stripe is rufous fore, *whitish aft.* Extremely elusive.
Voice: Song, wrenlike, 4-noted: *wee, choohoo chyo* or *chee chyo, choyo* (Slud).
Range: W. Mexico, Costa Rica, Panamá, Colombia, n. Venezuela. **Mexico:** Pacific lowlands; Sinaloa to Guerrero. **Habitat:** Woodland undergrowth, thickets. Terrestrial.

COMMON BUSH-TANAGER   Pl. 42
Chlorospingus ophthalmicus   5–5¾
Field marks: A small plain olive-gray vireolike bird best distinguished by the *white stripes* above and below the *dark ear patch.* Crown and upperparts dark; underparts pale gray, washed with olive-yellow across chest. Wings, when flicked, flash white undersurface. Flocks; feeds like a warbler.
Voice: Notes while feeding, thin, grasshopperlike (Alden).
Range: S. Mexico through Cen. and S. America to Bolivia, nw. Argentina. **Mexico:** Mts. of s. San Luis Potosí, Hidalgo, México, Guerrero, Puebla, Veracruz, Oaxaca, Chiapas. **Habitat:** Forest understory, cloud forest border (3000–11,500 ft.).

Grosbeaks, Buntings, Sparrows, and Finches: Fringillidae

THE obvious feature of this family is the bill, short and stout, adapted for seed cracking. There are 3 main types of bills: that of the grosbeaks, extremely large, thick at base, and a bit rounded in outline; the more canarylike bill of the finches, sparrows, and buntings; and that of the crossbills, with mandibles crossed at the tips. Many species are highly colored; the more modest sparrows are often brown and streaked. *Note:* Some recent authorities restrict the Fringillidae to the subfamily Carduelinae (goldfinches, siskins, crossbills, etc.) and the Old World Fringillinae (chaf-finches, etc.). They place the other New World finches in the family Emberizidae, which includes the subfamilies (1) Cardinal-inae (cardinals, grosbeaks, American buntings), (2) Emberizinae (most American finches, sparrows, seedeaters, etc.); and also (3) Thraupidae (tanagers). **Food:** Seeds, insects, small fruits. **Range:** Worldwide. **No. of species:** World, 422 +; Mexico, 97 or 98 (+2 accidental).

BLACK-HEADED SALTATOR *Saltator atriceps* 10 **Pl. 47**
Field marks: The *white throat* completely surrounded by black will identify this yellowish-green-backed saltator from the smaller but similar Buff-throated Saltator. Head blackish; under tail coverts *cinnamon.* A race in s. Veracruz has a brown-ish throat.
Similar species: Buff-throated Saltator has *buff* throat and under tail coverts, grayer head, broader breastband.
Voice: Note, *chib.* Song, a rapid *chib-che-wab-ah-wab-ah-wab-ah-wab* (Chalif). 1 or 2 deliberate smacking notes followed by a rapid, uneven, grating series, *chack, chack, tch-ch-ch-ch-ch-chur* (RTP).
Range: Mexico to Panamá. **Mexico:** Lowlands (both slopes) from cen. Guerrero and s. Tamaulipas south and east through Chiapas and Yucatán Pen. **Habitat:** Humid forest borders, brush, thickets, dense undergrowth.

BUFF-THROATED SALTATOR **Pl. 47**
Saltator maximus 7–8½
Field marks: Similar to the Black-headed Saltator but smaller, with a *buffy throat,* buffy under tail coverts, grayer head, broader breastband.
Similar species: See Black-headed Saltator (preceding).
Voice: Song often suggests some species of robin (Eisenmann). *Cheery cheery* answered by *cheer to you,* delivered with falling cadence. Also *trale le-e-le, trale'le-e-le,* etc. (Skutch).
Range: S. Mexico to Brazil. **Mexico:** Gulf slope from cen. Veracruz east through n. Chiapas, Tabasco, Campeche, Quin-tana Roo. **Habitat:** Forest clearings, brushy stream edges, sec-ond-growth thickets, plantations.

GRAYISH SALTATOR *Saltator coerulescens* 8 **Pl. 47**
Field marks: Note the *white eyebrow stripe* and restricted white throat on this large, dusky, heavy-billed finch. Differs from other saltators in having a *dark gray,* not golden-green back and *no black chestband.* Lower underparts buffy.
Similar species: Other saltators have golden-green backs, black chestbands.
Voice: Song, *chip, chup chup, woid* (*chip* is sometimes left out;

woid is drawn out and rises). Also *crrrrr cheechu cheechu chee-chuuu;* and *chip weed* (Chalif). A musical *chirp-wheee* (rising), often followed by an uneven *tsur-wewewewe-chew* (RTP). **Range:** Mexico to Costa Rica; Colombia to n. Argentina. **Mexico:** Pacific slope from Sinaloa, w. Durango south; Gulf slope from s. Tamaulipas, e. San Luis Potosí south and east through Yucatán Pen. **Habitat:** Semi-arid second growth, woodland edges, thickets, plantation undergrowth.

CRIMSON-COLLARED GROSBEAK   Pls. 45, 46
Rhodothraupis celaeno   8–8½

Field marks: A blackish grosbeak with a *dark red collar and underparts* (except throat and chest). Red areas often spotted or blotched with black. *Female and immature:* Similar to male but *yellowish-green* replaces red.
Similar species: Crimson-collared Tanager (p. 231) has red rump, black belly, pale bill; it is more southern.
Range: E. Mexico only. Gulf slope of s. Nuevo León, s. Tamaulipas, e. San Luis Potosí, ne. Puebla, n. Veracruz. **Habitat:** Brushy woods, second growth.

BLACK-FACED GROSBEAK   Pl. 45
Caryothraustes poliogaster   6½–8

Field marks: A *yellowish-green* grosbeak with a *black face and throat* sharply set off against the *golden* forehead, cheeks, and chest. Rump, belly, and under tail coverts gray.
Voice: A descending whistle, *chi-cha-cha* (Chalif). Call, a sharp, short *pwtst chirp-chirp-chirp.* Song, a musical *churtweet' churtweet' churtweet'* in a leisurely manner (Slud). A short buzz followed by a whistled *tweet tweet* (Russell).
Range: Se. Mexico to w. Panamá. **Mexico:** Gulf lowlands; s. Veracruz, n. Oaxaca, n. Chiapas, Tabasco, s. Campeche, s. Quintana Roo. **Habitat:** High trees in humid forests, borders.

RED (COMMON) CARDINAL   See E, W, or T
Cardinalis cardinalis

Memo: ♂ red; crest, black face. ♀ brown; red bill and crest.
Range: S. Ontario to Gulf states; sw. U.S. to B. Honduras, Guatemala (Petén). **Mexico:** Resident of cen. and s. Baja California; widespread from northern states south to Isthmus of Tehuantepec and east on Gulf slope through Yucatán Pen. Includes the form *carnea* of Pacific Coast from Colima to Oaxaca, sometimes treated as a distinct species known as Long-crested Cardinal.

PYRRHULOXIA   *Pyrrhuloxia sinuata*   7½–8¼   Pl. 46
Field marks: *Male:* A slender *gray and red* bird with a crest and a small, stubby, almost parrotlike bill. The rose-colored

breast and crest suggest the Cardinal, but the gray back and *yellow* bill set it apart. *Female:* Note the *yellow* bill. Gray back, buff breast; a touch of red in wings and crest.
Note: Sometimes placed in genus *Cardinalis.*
Similar species: ♀ Cardinal (browner) has reddish bill.
Voice: Song, a clear *quink quink quink, quink quink,* on 1 pitch; also a slurred, whistled *what-cheer, what-cheer,* etc., thinner and shorter than Cardinal's song (RTP).
Range: Sw. U.S. to cen. Mexico. **Mexico:** Resident of cen. and s. Baja California and from borders of Arizona, New Mexico, Texas south to Michoacán, Guanajuato, Querétaro. **Habitat:** Mesquite, thorn scrub, deserts.

YELLOW GROSBEAK *Pheucticus chrysopeplus* 8–9 **Pl. 45**
Field marks: *Male:* A large *golden-yellow* bird with an *extremely large triangular bill.* Black wings and tail boldly patterned with white. *Female and immature:* Similar to male but duller; upperparts olive streaked with blackish.
Similar species: Similarly colored orioles have narrow bills.
Voice: Song very much like that of a robin (Chalif). Suggests mellow rising and falling passages of Rose-breasted or Black-headed Grosbeak, but more rapid (RTP).
Range: W. Mexico, Guatemala; similar species (races?) from Costa Rica to w. Panamá; Venezuela and Colombia to Peru. **Mexico:** Pacific slope; s. Sonora, sw. Chihuahua, south to Chiapas. **Habitat:** Foothills, mts.; forest borders, cutover breaks, brushy woods, wooded canyons.

ROSE-BREASTED GROSBEAK   See E, W, or T
Pheucticus ludovicianus
Memo: ♂ rose breast patch. ♀ striped head, breast; big bill.
Range: S. Canada, e. U.S. Winters in W. Indies and from cen. Mexico through Cen. and S. America to Peru. **Mexico:** Migrant mainly in eastern states. Winters from central states (Michoacán, San Luis Potosí, Veracruz) south and east, including Yucatán Pen.

BLACK-HEADED GROSBEAK   See W or T
Pheucticus melanocephalus
Memo: ♂ black head, rusty breast, big bill. ♀ striped head, sparse streaks on pale brown breast.
Range: Sw. Canada, w. U.S. to s. Mexico. **Mexico:** Breeds in n. Baja California and widely in uplands from northern tier of states south to Oaxaca; in migration to Pacific lowlands. Winters from northern states to Oaxaca.

BLUE GROSBEAK *Guiraca caerulea*   See E, W, or T
Memo: ♂ blue, tan wingbars. ♀ brown; tan wingbars.
Range: Cen. and s. U.S. south to nw. Costa Rica. Winters

Cuba, Mexico to Panamá. **Mexico:** Breeds in n. Baja California and from northern tier of states south throughout except Yucatán Pen., where it is a winter visitor. Winters from s. Baja California, s. Sonora, Veracruz south and east.

BLUE BUNTING *Cyanocompsa parellina* 5 **Pl. 46**
  Field marks: *Male:* A deep blue, almost blackish bunting, *brighter blue* on forehead, cheeks, rump, and wing coverts. *Female:* Warm brown above, paling to cinnamon-brown below, especially on throat and belly.
  Similar species: (1) Blue-black Grosbeak is larger, with *much larger* bill· ♂ is blacker; ♀ more rufous. (2) Blue-black Grassquit is smaller, with smaller, sharper bill; ♂ is blacker, ♀ striped below. (3) ♂ Indigo Bunting is much brighter blue.
  Voice: Song (Honduras), a whistled *whreet-whreet-wheet-weet-weet* (Willis).
  Range: Mexico to Nicaragua. **Mexico:** Lowlands, foothills; Pacific slope from cen. Sinaloa south; Gulf slope from s. Nuevo León, cen. Tamaulipas south through Yucatán Pen. **Habitat:** Humid forest borders, thickets, roadsides, brushy fields.

BLUE-BLACK GROSBEAK **Pl. 46**
Cyanocompsa cyanoides 6–6½
  Field marks: *Male:* A rather large black finch with a dull bluish gloss in some lights. Note the *very large* triangular grosbeak bill. *Female:* Ruddy brown, somewhat lighter below. Note the very large black bill.
  Similar species: (1) Blue Grosbeak (both sexes) has tan wingbars. (2) See Blue Bunting (preceding).
  Voice: Note, *klick* or *klink.* Song variable; a loud series of about 7 clear whistled notes (1st low, next 5 starting high and descending, last note high), Chalif; 4–8 deliberate strong mellow whistles often followed by a softer, rapid, breezy flourish or twitter (Eisenmann).
  Range: Se. Mexico to Amazonia. **Mexico:** Atlantic lowlands of s. Veracruz, n. Oaxaca, Tabasco, n. Chiapas, s. Quintana Roo. **Habitat:** Humid forest undergrowth, wet thickets.

INDIGO BUNTING *Passerina cyanea* **See E, W, or T**
  Memo: ♂ all blue, no wingbars. ♀ brown; faint streaks.
  Range: Se. Canada to Gulf states. Winters W. Indies, cen. Mexico to Panamá. **Mexico:** Widespread migrant, most numerous east and south. Winters from Sinaloa, San Luis Potosí south and east, including Yucatán Pen.

LAZULI BUNTING *Passerina amoena* **See W or T**
  Memo: ♂ blue above; rusty breast, white wingbars. ♀ brown; wingbars, no streaks.

Range: Sw. Canada, w. U.S., nw. Mexico. Winters to s.-cen. Mexico. **Mexico:** Breeds nw. Baja California; possibly n. Sonora. Widespread migrant in western sections, wintering south to Guerrero, México, cen. Veracruz.

VARIED BUNTING *Passerina versicolor* 4½–5½ **Pl. 46**
Field marks: *Male:* A small dark finch with a plum-colored body (looks black at a distance or in poor light). Crown blue, with a *bright red patch on nape. Female:* A small plain *gray-brown* finch with lighter underparts. *No* wingbars, stripes, or distinctive marks of any kind.
Similar species: (1) ♂ Painted Bunting has a bright red breast; ♀ is green. (2) ♀ Indigo Bunting is browner with a hint of wingbars and faint breast streaks. (3) ♀ Lazuli Bunting and (4) ♀ Seedeater have strong wingbars. (5) ♀ Blue Bunting is larger, darker chocolate-brown; bill larger.
Voice: A thin bright finch song, more distinctly phrased and less warbled than Painted Bunting's; notes not so distinctly paired as in songs of Lazuli or Indigo Buntings (RTP).
Range: Southwestern border of U.S. to Guatemala. **Mexico:** Breeds from s. Baja California and U.S. border (locally) south to Oaxaca, Veracruz, and Pacific slope of Chiapas. Winters except in extreme north. **Habitat:** Semi-arid wood edges, roadsides, brush, streamside growth.

ROSE-BELLIED (ROSITA'S) BUNTING **Pl. 45**
Passerina rositae 5¼–5½
Field marks: *Male: Bright blue* except for lower breast, and under tail coverts, which are *rose-red. Female:* Brown, paling to buff on throat and belly; rump and tail tinged with blue. Eyering buff.
Similar species: ♀ is very similar to ♀ Indigo Bunting.
Range: S. Mexico only; Pacific slope of s. Oaxaca, Chiapas (vicinity of Isthmus of Tehuantepec). **Habitat:** Tropical deciduous woodlands, brush, especially in hilly country.

PAINTED BUNTING *Passerina ciris* **See E, W, or T**
Memo: ♂ red below; green back, violet head. ♀ all green.
Range: S. U.S., n. Mexico. Winters through Mid. America to cen. Panamá; Cuba. **Mexico:** Breeds in Chihuahua, Coahuila, n. Tamaulipas (Río Grande Valley). Widespread migrant and winter visitor at lower elevations except Baja California and Sonora.

ORANGE-BREASTED BUNTING **Pl. 45**
Passerina leclancherii 5
Field marks: *Male:* The *green crown* and *orange breast* will identify this brilliant bunting which is otherwise azure-blue

above, yellow below. *Female:* Gray-green above (wings and tail tinged with blue), yellowish below, paling on throat and belly. Both sexes have yellow eye-rings.
Similar species: ♀ Painted Bunting is much greener.
Voice: A clear *wheat-cheeweet-cheat* (rising on last note); or *wheat-cheeweet;* or *wheat-cheeweet-cheat-cheat* (Chalif).
Range: Sw. Mexico only; Pacific slope from Jalisco south to w. Chiapas. **Habitat:** Tropical deciduous woodlands, scrub, brush, abandoned fields.

YELLOW-FACED GRASSQUIT   Pl. 46
Tiaris olivacea 4–4½
   Field marks: *Male:* The *orange-yellow throat and eyebrow* will identify this small dark olive-green finch; breast black. *Female:* Dull olive, paler below; dull yellowish on throat and spectacles; breast may be dimly marked with dusky.
   Similar species: ♀ Variable Seedeater is browner, not greenish.
   Voice: Note, *tzzip.* Song, an insectlike buzz, *tsi-tsi-tsi-tsi-tsi* (Chalif); in W. Indies a weak, rapidly uttered trill, like that of a Worm-eating Warbler (Bond).
   Range: E. Mexico, W. Indies to w. Colombia, n. Venezuela. **Mexico:** Gulf slope from s. Tamaulipas south to n. Oaxaca, n. Chiapas and east through Yucatán Pen. **Habitat:** Brushy fields, grassy clearings, and roadsides.

DICKCISSEL   *Spiza americana*   See E, W, T
   Memo: ♂ "like a small meadowlark." ♀ sparrowlike.
   Range: S. Ontario; U.S. between Rockies and Appalachians. Winters through Mid. America to n. Colombia, n. Venezuela, Guyana. **Mexico:** Widespread migrant in open country but casual in Baja California and Yucatán Pen. Winters mainly from s. Mexico south. Often travels in dense flocks.

WHITE-COLLARED SEEDEATER   Pl. 46
Sporophila torqueola 4–4½
   Field marks: *Male:* This small, variable finch may be known by the *broad white collar* or *half-collar,* tawny or whitish rump; *black or blackish hood,* black or black-splotched chest, and stubby rounded bill. Races of this bird vary from cinnamon to dull whitish below and may be black-throated or pale-throated. *Female:* Brown, lightening to ochre on underparts. Buffy eye-ring and distinct buffy to whitish wingbars. The stubby rounded bill is a useful indicator.
   Similar species: (1) ♀ Ruddy-breasted Seedeater is smaller, lacks distinct wingbars. (2) ♀ Variable Seedeater is more olive, without wingbars. (3) See ♀ Varied Bunting (p. 240).
   Voice: A sweet, loud song; begins on several high repeated

notes and drops to several notes on a lower pitch: *sweet sweet sweet sweet, cheer cheer cheer cheer;* often only 2 *cheer*'s (RTP). A canarylike song often ending with *chip-chip-chip.* Variations include *chee-wee, che-wee, che-wee, wiz-wiz-wiz-wiz,* etc. (Chalif).

Range: S. Texas to Panamá. **Mexico:** Pacific slope from Sinaloa south; highlands from Guanajuato south; Gulf slope from cen. Nuevo León, n. Tamaulipas south and east through Yucatán Pen. **Habitat:** Weedy places, tall grass, low thickets, roadsides; sea level to 7000 + ft.

VARIABLE (BLACK) SEEDEATER   Pl. 46
Sporophila aurita (corvina)   4½–5

Field marks: *Male:* A small glossy-black finch with a *white spot* in midwing (not always easy to see) and a stubby rounded bill. Wing lining (beneath) *white. Female:* Olive-brown, paler below; no wingbars. Wing linings white. Note size and contour of bill. Rare.

Similar species: (1) ♂ Thick-billed Seed-Finch also has a white spot in the wing but may be known by its much thicker, less rounded bill; ♀ is more rufous-brown. (2) ♀ White-collared Seedeater is buffy brown and has wingbars. (3) ♂ Blue-black Grassquit has blue gloss, lacks white wing spot and white underwing lining; bill is straighter, sharper; ♀ is streaked below. (4) See ♀ Yellow-faced Grassquit (above).

Voice: Calls, a sweet *see'oo* or *sleeoo* and *tse'wee* and *tseeyp.* Song, a rapid hurried twittering (Eisenmann). Song disordered; very different from patterned song of White-collared Seedeater (Slud).

Range: Se. Mexico to w. Peru, Amazonian Brazil. **Mexico:** Gulf slope of s. Veracruz, n. Oaxaca, n. Chiapas, Tabasco. **Habitat:** Second growth, weedy grassland, brush, roadsides.

RUDDY-BREASTED SEEDEATER   Pl. 46
Sporophila minuta   3¼–4

Field marks: *Male:* A very small dark gray finch with *rufous rump and underparts.* A small white spot in wing. *Female:* Light brown, paler and buffier on rump and underparts.

Similar species: See White-collared Seedeater (above).

Voice: Song, canarylike, tinkling; sometimes ending with *buzz-zee.* Also *wheat-wheat-wheat-wheat,* etc. (4–7 times), often ending with *chee* (Chalif).

Range: W. Mexico to n. Argentina, Uruguay. **Mexico:** Arid Pacific lowlands from Nayarit south to Chiapas. **Habitat:** Weedy fields, open tall grassland, bushes in open savannas.

THICK-BILLED SEED-FINCH   Pl. 46
Oryzoborus funereus   4½–5¼

Field marks: *Male:* Similar to Variable Seedeater (black with white wing spot) but its black bill is much deeper at base, less curved in outline. *Female:* Ruddy brown, lighter below. Note thickness and contour of bill. Both sexes have white underwing coverts.

Note: Sometimes regarded as a northwestern race of *O. ango-lensis* (S. America, east of Andes to Paraguay), called Lesser Seed-Finch.

Similar species: (1) See Variable Seedeater. Wing linings are white in both species. (2) ♀ Blue Seedeater is smaller, with a much smaller bill, brown wing linings.

Voice: A fine, long-continued, buntinglike song (Eisenmann). Call note, *ik* or *ek* (Slud).

Range: Se. Mexico to w. Ecuador. **Mexico:** Gulf lowlands of cen. and s. Veracruz, n. Oaxaca, n. Chiapas, Tabasco. **Habitat:** Humid forest edges, thickets, clearings and savannas, bushy grassland.

BLUE SEEDEATER   *Amaurospiza concolor*   5¼   **Not illus.**
Field marks: Rare in Mexico; seldom reported. *Male:* Uniformly dull blue. *Female:* Uniformly tawny brown, paler beneath. Mexican birds north of Tehuantepec, duller and larger, have sometimes been regarded as specifically distinct (known as Slate-blue Seedeater, *A. relicta*).

Similar species: (1) ♂ Blue Bunting has blue in patches (crown, cheeks, rump), lacks uniformity. (2) ♂ Blue-black Grassquit is smaller, blacker. (3) ♂ Slaty Finch is slate, lacking bluish tone; bill more slender. (4) Thick-billed Seed-Finch has a very heavy bill; ♂ is black; ♀ has white underwing coverts.

Range: S. Mexico; Honduras to w. Ecuador. Not reported in B. Honduras or Guatemala. **Mexico:** Very rare and local; reported from mts. of Jalisco, Morelos, Guerrero, Oaxaca, and Chiapas. **Habitat:** Shrubs and bamboo thickets bordering cloud forest and humid mt. woodlands.

BLUE-BLACK GRASSQUIT   *Volatinia jacarina*   4   **Pl. 46**
Field marks: *Male:* A small glossy *all blue-black* finch with a *concealed* white spot at juncture of wing and body. Bill straight-edged and sharp-pointed. *Female:* Small, brownish, with dark brown stripes on light underparts (may become obsolete in worn birds).

Similar species: (1) ♂ Variable Seedeater and (2) ♂ Thick-billed Seed-Finch have thicker bills (more rounded in contour), white wing linings, white spot in midwing, and different type of song and display; ♀ is not streaked.

Voice: A very short song, *weezit,* given as the bird jumps a foot or two above perch and returns (Chalif).

Range: Mexico through Cen. and S. America to n. Argentina. **Mexico:** Pacific slope from s. Sonora (rare), Sinaloa south; Gulf slope from s. Tamaulipas and San Luis Potosí through n.

Chiapas and east through Yucatán Pen. **Habitat:** Weedy pastures, brushy fields, grassy roadsides and wood borders, gardens, grassy places in towns.

GRASSLAND YELLOW-FINCH *Sicalis luteola* 4½ **Pl. 45**

Field marks: *Male:* A *yellowish* finch, *heavily streaked* on upperparts, bright yellow on face and underparts; grayer on wings and tail. *Female:* Patterned like male, but basically buff-brown, paling to buffy yellow on belly.

Similar species: ♀ Yellow Grosbeak (woodlands) is much larger, with a huge bill.

Voice: Notes suggest Horned Lark, *tsi tsip tsi tsip* or *tsi silp tsi silp.* In flight adds a *bzzzzzzzzzz* (Chalif).

Range: Locally from s. Mexico and Guatemala through Cen. and S. America to s. Chile, s. Argentina. Introduced Lesser Antilles. **Mexico:** Pacific watershed in Morelos, Puebla; Gulf slope in Veracruz (Orizaba), n. Chiapas. **Habitat:** Open grassland.

SLATY FINCH **Not illus.**
Haplospiza (Spodiornis) rusticus 5

Field marks: *Male:* This very rare bird is uniform *slate-gray,* a bit paler beneath, suggesting a junco, but bill relatively slender, sharp-pointed. *Female:* Dark olive-brown above, buffy brown below, paling to whitish on midbelly; throat and breast indistinctly streaked.

Similar species: (1) Blue Seedeater (p. 243) is more bluish; bill shorter, more typically finchlike. (2) See juncos (pp. 256–57).

Range: S. Mexico locally to w. Panamá; Colombia to e. Peru, Bolivia. **Mexico:** Recorded from highlands of Veracruz (Jalapa), Chiapas (Volcán Tacaná). Not recorded in B. Honduras or Guatemala. **Habitat:** Humid highlands; brush of cutover forests, grassy clearings, forest borders.

RUFOUS-CAPPED BRUSH-FINCH **Pl. 45**
Atlapetes pileatus 5¾

Field marks: The combination of *rufous crown* and *yellow underparts* identify this olive-brown-backed finch.

Similar species: (1) Chestnut-capped Brush-Finch lacks yellow on underparts. (2) Yellow-throated and (3) White-naped Brush-Finches have black and white caps.

Voice: A clear whistled *soo-sweet, chip chip chip* (Chalif).

Range: Mexico only; mts. from cen. Chihuahua, cen. Nuevo León south to Oaxaca. **Habitat:** Brush and undergrowth of pine and oak forests (3000–11,500 ft.).

WHITE-NAPED BRUSH-FINCH **Pl. 45**
Atlapetes albinucha 7

Field marks: The *white crown stripe* on the black head, blackish back, and *completely yellow underparts* (from chin to under tail coverts) identify this rather large brush-inhabiting finch. *Immature:* Similar to adult but browner above; chest and breast heavily streaked.

Similar species: (1) Yellow-throated Brush-Finch (similar head pattern) has yellow confined to throat. (2) Rufous-capped Brush-Finch (yellow underparts) has rufous cap.

Range: E. Mexico only. Mts. (2000–7300 ft.) in San Luis Potosí, Puebla, Veracruz, n. Oaxaca, Chiapas. **Habitat:** Mt. thickets.

YELLOW-THROATED BRUSH-FINCH Pl. 45
Atlapetes gutturalis 6½–6¾

Field marks: Similar to the preceding species and considered by some authorities to be a subspecies, but *yellow confined to throat;* remaining underparts whitish.

Similar species: See White-naped Brush-Finch.

Range: Se. Mexico through Cen. America to Colombia. **Mexico:** Mts. of s. Chiapas. **Habitat:** Undergrowth, brushy edges of mt. forests (5000–10,000 ft.).

CHESTNUT-CAPPED BRUSH-FINCH Pl. 47
Atlapetes brunneinucha 7½

Field marks: Note the combination of chestnut crown, black mask and white throat. No white eye stripe (but white spot before eye). There is usually a spot or crescent of black on upper chest (absent in race *A. b. apertus* of s. Veracruz).

Similar species: Collared Towhee (p. 247) is very similar but may have a *white or gray eye stripe,* or may lack one; in all cases the black chestband is *much broader.*

Voice: Call, a high-pitched *zeet;* song, a series of high-pitched notes (Edwards and Tashian).

Range: Mexico through Cen. and nw. S. America to w. Ecuador. **Mexico:** Mts. from Guerrero and e. San Luis Potosí south through Chiapas. **Habitat:** Undergrowth of mt. forests (2000–11,500 ft.).

PLAIN-BREASTED (TUXTLA) BRUSH-FINCH Not illus.
Atlapetes apertus (or *A. brunneinucha* in part) 7

Field marks: Very similar to Chestnut-capped Brush-Finch and may be conspecific, but *lacks black band* across chest.

Range: Mts. of s.-cen. Veracruz only (Volcán San Martín and adjacent Cerro de Tuxtla). **Habitat:** Cloud forest.

GREEN-STRIPED BRUSH-FINCH Pl. 47
Atlapetes virenticeps 7½

Field marks: This olive-backed brush-finch may be known from the others by *3 yellow-green stripes* on its black crown (one above each eye, one midcrown). Throat and belly white; breast

and sides gray. *Immature:* Browner; head stripes duller; throat and belly streaked with olive-yellow.
Range: Cen. Mexico only; mts. of southern part of Mexican plateau from Sinaloa, s. Durango south to Michoacán, México, Morelos, w. Puebla. Often regarded as a disjunct population of Stripe-headed Brush-Finch, *A. torquata* (sw. Costa Rica to nw. Argentina). **Habitat:** Undergrowth of mt. forests.

ORANGE-BILLED SPARROW   Pl. 47
Arremon aurantiirostris   6–6½
   Field marks: Note the *bright orange bill* on this strongly patterned sparrow. Eye stripe, throat, and mid-abdomen white. Broad black chestband and black cheek patch. Crown black with a dull gray stripe in center. Yellow mark on bend of wing (not always visible). Extremely elusive.
   Voice: Song, a slow, very high-pitched thin *ts, ts, ts, ts, ts;* also *tsit, tseedeedsteetseet.* Note, *dzeet,* also a sharp *tzick* (Eisenmann).
   Range: Se. Mexico to n. Peru. **Mexico:** Gulf slope of s. Veracruz, n. Oaxaca, Tabasco, n. Chiapas. **Habitat:** Low undergrowth in humid forests; mainly lowlands.

OLIVE SPARROW   *Arremonops rufivirgatus*   5½–6   Pl. 47
   Field marks: Note the *2 broad dull brown stripes on the crown.* A plain *olive-backed* finch with no wingbars. Underparts lighter; a dingy wash across breast and along sides. The Yucatán Pen. race has more contrasting pattern (darker head stripes), white underparts.
   Similar species: See (1) Green-backed Sparrow (next). (2) Green-tailed Towhee (winter visitor) is larger, with a grayer breast, clear-cut white throat, solid-rufous crown.
   Voice: Song, a series of dry chips on 1 pitch, starting deliberately and accelerating into a rattle (RTP).
   Range: S. Texas, Mexico to w. Costa Rica. **Mexico:** Mainly brushy lowlands, foothills; Pacific slope from s. Sinaloa to Oaxaca. Gulf slope from Nuevo León, n. Tamaulipas south to Yucatán Pen. **Habitat:** Undergrowth, weedy thickets, brush.

GREEN-BACKED SPARROW   Pl. 47
Arremonops chloronotus   5½
   Field marks: Very similar to Olive Sparrow but back brighter olive-green; head stripes darker, on a *gray head.*
   Similar species: Olive Sparrow is very difficult to separate in field on basis of appearance alone, but prefers brushy second growth, old fields rather than humid forests.
   Voice: Song, a series of notes resembling *peter-peter-peter* of Tufted Titmouse, but trailing off at end (Land).
   Range: Se. Mexico, B. Honduras, Guatemala, n. Honduras.

Mexico: Gulf lowlands of n. Chiapas, Tabasco, Yucatán Pen. **Habitat:** Underbrush at borders of humid forests or in open forests.

GREEN-TAILED TOWHEE *Chlorura chlorura* **See W or T**
Memo: Greenish; rusty cap, white throat, gray breast.
Range: W. U.S. In winter to cen. Mexico. **Mexico:** Migrant and winter visitor from northern states south to s. Baja California, Jalisco, Guanajuato, Hidalgo; occasionally Oaxaca.

COLLARED TOWHEE *Pipilo ocai* 8–8½ **Pl. 47**
Field marks: An olive-backed, *rufous-crowned* towhee with a broad black mask and *black chestband.* Throat white (sometimes restricted). Eye stripe may be white, gray, or lacking.
Note: This species may hybridize with Rufous-sided Towhee, producing birds with spotted backs, reddish sides, similar to that shown on Plate 47 (hybrid towhee, *P. ocai* × *maculatus*).
Similar species: Chestnut-capped Brush-Finch is extraordinarily similar but has a very reduced amount of black on chest and always lacks the white eye stripe.
Range: Sw. Mexico only; mts. of Jalisco, Michoacán, Guerrero, Puebla, w. Veracruz, Oaxaca. **Habitat:** Brushy trailsides, thickets, edges, in conifer forest belt.

RUFOUS-SIDED (SPOTTED) TOWHEE **See W or T**
Pipilo erythrophthalmus
(including Spotted and Olive-backed Towhees)
Memo: Rufous sides, white tail patches, red eyes.
Note: The Rufous-sided Towhee complex has many and varied races that can be grouped into 4 types: (1) Eastern Towhee; *solid* black or brown backs (e. N. America; casual in winter in ne. Tamaulipas); (2) Spotted Towhee (*maculatus* group); black or brown backs spotted with white (sw. Canada, w. U.S., Mexico, Guatemala); (3) Olive-backed Towhee *(macronyx)* males (Plate 47) with olive backs marked with light spots (cen. Mexico only); (4) Socorro Towhee *(socorroensis)* of Socorro I., a small form that has been considered specifically distinct. Sexes almost identical. The 3 mainland types tend to hybridize and were formerly regarded as distinct species. There is also some hybridization with the Collared Towhee, *P. ocai,* producing a rufous-capped form (see hybrid towhee, Plate 47).
Range: S. Canada, U.S., Mexico, Guatemala. **Mexico:** Baja California and highlands of mainland from northern states south locally to Chiapas. Also Socorro I. of Revilla Gigedo Is.

BROWN TOWHEE *Pipilo fuscus* 7½–9½ **Pl. 48**
Field marks: A dull gray-brown bird with a moderately long dark tail; suggests a very plain overgrown sparrow. Note the

pale *rusty under tail coverts* and pale *buff throat* outlined with
dark spots. Crown may be tinged with rusty.
Similar species: See (1) White-throated Towhee (Puebla,
Oaxaca) and (2) Abert's Towhee (Colorado River delta).
Voice: Note, a metallic *chink.* Song, a rapid *chink-chink-ink-
ink-ink-ink-ink-ink,* on 1 pitch. Often ends in a trill. Sometimes
chilp-chilp-chilp-chilp-chilp-chilp; other variations (RTP).
Range: Sw. U.S. to s. Mexico. **Mexico:** Mainly deserts, arid
slopes and highlands from northern states south to s. Baja California, Oaxaca, w.-cen. Veracruz. **Habitat:** Brushy, stony areas;
open woods, canyons, juniper, desert scrub, mesquite.

WHITE-THROATED TOWHEE *Pipilo albicollis* 7½ **Pl. 48**
Field marks: Similar to Brown Towhee but throat largely
white (not buff), bordered by dark marks. Malar area *ochre*
(amount variable).
Similar species: May be conspecific with Brown Towhee.
Range: Mexico only; local, s. Puebla, Oaxaca; casual Guerrero.

ABERT'S TOWHEE *Pipilo aberti* **See W**
Memo: Tawny brown; black patch around base of bill.
Range: Deserts of sw. U.S., nw. Mexico. **Mexico:** Resident of
Colorado River delta in ne. Baja California, nw. Sonora.

RUSTY-CROWNED GROUND-SPARROW **Pl. 48**
Melozone kieneri 6–6½
Field marks: A plain-backed, gray-brown sparrow with a
rufous rear crown and nape. Underparts whitish with a *single
dark spot on breast.* Cheeks and forecrown dark gray; a large
white spot before eye.
Similar species: In Chiapas and Guatemala see (1) White-
faced Ground-Sparrow (next) and (2) Rufous-collared Sparrow
(p. 256).
Range: W. and sw. Mexico only; Pacific slope from extreme s.
Sonora, Durango south to w. Puebla, w. Oaxaca. **Habitat:**
Forest floor, brush, thickets, canyons, up to 6500 ft.

WHITE-FACED (PREVOST'S) GROUND-SPARROW
Melozone biarcuatum 6–6½ **Pl. 48**
Field marks: Note the face pattern. Similar to Rusty-
crowned Ground-Sparrow (formerly regarded as conspecific) but
broad area of white behind and below eye and broad chestnut
and black crescent on lower cheek. No breast spot.
Similar species: (1) North of Tehuantepec see Rusty-crowned
Ground-Sparrow. (2) Rufous-collared Sparrow has striped
back, black patches on sides of breast, broad gray head stripe.
Voice: A rapid series of chirping *chep*'s (Slud).
Range: Se. Mexico to Costa Rica. **Mexico:** Pacific slope and

highlands of Chiapas. **Habitat:** Brush, thickets, coffee plantations (lower slopes to 7000 ft.).

WHITE-EARED GROUND-SPARROW
Pl. 47

Melozone leucotis 6½–7

Field marks: Note the *white ear spot* on this boldly patterned, black-faced sparrow. Upperparts brown; eye stripe *ochreyellow;* throat, sides of crown, and *blotch on breast* black.

Voice: A sibilant note repeated 5–15 times in a series that begins weakly and fades as it ends (Slud).

Range: S. Mexico to cen. Costa Rica. **Mexico:** Pacific slope of Chiapas only. **Habitat:** Undergrowth of forest, forest border (1500 ft. into highlands).

STRIPED SPARROW *Oriturus superciliosus* 6–7 Pl. 48

Field marks: The broad white or pale buff eye stripe and *dusky cheek patch* help identify this large, conspicuous, gray-breasted, streak-backed sparrow. Crown rusty brown with some streaking. Bill *all black.* Immature birds are buffy white below with dusky streaks on breast.

Similar species: Stripe-headed Sparrow is redder, with a white median crown stripe; bill bicolored.

Range: Mts. of Mexican tableland only, from e. Sonora, Chihuahua south to Oaxaca, w. Veracruz. **Habitat:** Grassy openings, meadows, pine forests (5000–14,000 ft.).

LARK BUNTING *Calamospiza melanocorys* See E, W, or T

Memo: Spring ♂, black body, white wing patch. ♀ and winter ♂, streaked; some white in wing.

Range: Prairies of s. Canada, w.-cen. U.S. Winters from sw. U.S. to cen. Mexico. **Mexico:** In winter, open country of northern states south to s. Baja California, Sinaloa, and on central plateau to Jalisco, Guanajuato, Hidalgo. Accidental B. Honduras.

SAVANNAH SPARROW
See E, W, or T

Passerculus sandwichensis

Memo: Streaked breast, striped crown, short notched tail.

Range: Alaska, Canada, n. and w. U.S., Mexico, Guatemala (?). Winters to El Salvador, Honduras, W. Indies. **Mexico:** Resident in coastal marshes of Baja California, Sonora, n. and cen. Sinaloa; also central plateau from Chihuahua, Durango south locally to Puebla, Oaxaca. In winter, widespread in northern states; less so in southern parts (incl. Yucatán Pen.).

GRASSHOPPER SPARROW
See E, W, or T

Ammodramus savannarum

Memo: Small; clear buffy breast, striped crown.

Range: S. Canada to s. U.S., W. Indies; also s. Mexico locally through Cen. and S. America to Ecuador. Winters from s. U.S. south. **Mexico:** Breeds locally in n. Sonora, Zacatecas, and in grasslands of s. Mexico (México, Oaxaca, Veracruz, Chiapas). More widespread in migration and winter.

BAIRD'S SPARROW *Ammodramus bairdii* **See E, W, or T**
Memo: Ochre crown stripe, "necklace" of short streaks.
Range: N. Great Plains of N. America. Winters sw. U.S., n. Mexico. **Mexico:** Rare winter visitor in northern states (Sonora, Chihuahua, Coahuila, Durango).

SHARP-TAILED SPARROW **See E, W, or T**
Ammospiza caudacuta
Memo: Ochre face pattern, gray ear patch.
Range: Prairies of Canada; ne. Atlantic Coast of U.S. Winters to s. U.S. **Mexico:** Accidental, Baja California.

SIERRA MADRE SPARROW *Xenospiza baileyi* 5 **Pl. 48**
Field marks: Like a Savannah Sparrow but *without the yellowish* on the face. The whitish underparts and *rusty upperparts* are heavily streaked with blackish. There is a *yellow edge* on the bend of the wing (usually concealed).
Similar species: See (1) Savannah Sparrow (p. 249) and (2) Song Sparrow (p. 255).
Voice: Song, 7–8 short syllables followed by 2 melodic notes (Blake).
Range: Highlands of w.-cen. Mexico only; local, rare. S. Durango, n. Jalisco, Morelos, Federal Dist. **Habitat:** Marshes and grassy open places in pine regions of mts.

VESPER SPARROW *Pooecetes gramineus* **See E, W, or T**
Memo: Streaked breast, white outer tail feathers.
Range: Canada to s.-cen. U.S. Winters to s. Mexico. **Mexico:** Winters through deserts, uplands, and open country south to s. Baja California, Oaxaca, Veracruz; casual or accidental Yucatán Pen., Guatemala.

LARK SPARROW *Chondestes grammacus* **See E, W, or T**
Memo: "Quail" head pattern, breast spot, white tail corners.
Range: S. Canada south (west of Appalachians) to n. Mexico. Winters s. U.S., Mexico, Guatemala, Honduras, El Salvador. **Mexico:** Breeds locally in northern states (Sonora, Chihuahua, Coahuila, Tamaulipas, Zacatecas (and probably farther south). Widespread in winter except Yucatán Pen. (casual).

FIVE-STRIPED SPARROW **Pl. 48**
Aimophila quinquestriata 5½–5¾
Field marks: This gray-brown sparrow gets its name from the

5 white head stripes (2 above eye, 3 on throat) or, to put it differently, *5 throat stripes* (3 white, 2 black). A *black chest spot.*
Similar species: See (1) Bridled Sparrow (next) and (2) Black-chested Sparrow (below).
Voice: Variable; *slip-tip-tip* followed by chipping (Parker).
Range: Mts. of w. Mexico; ne. Sonora, through w. Durango, w. Chihuahua; south locally to Jalisco. Casual se. Arizona. **Habitat:** Grass and scrub; lower and mid-levels of mts.

BRIDLED SPARROW *Aimophila mystacalis* 6 **Pl. 48**
Field marks: The black throat, *white mustache,* and rufous rump are good marks by which to identify this dark, gray-headed, gray-breasted sparrow. Immature is streaked on underparts; throat is whitish with dusky marks in center.
Similar species: See (1) Five-striped Sparrow (preceding) and (2) Black-chested Sparrow (next).
Voice: An excited song, like 2 birds fighting (Chalif).
Range: Mexico only; southern edge of central plateau (e. México, s. Puebla, cen.-w. Veracruz, Oaxaca). **Habitat:** Thorn forests, cactus, scrub.

BLACK-CHESTED SPARROW **Pls. 47, 48**
Aimophila humeralis 6
Field marks: A *rufous-orange-backed* sparrow with a white mustache and white throat separated by a black stripe. Note the *broad black chest belt.*
Similar species: Five-striped Sparrow lacks black belt.
Voice: *Wheesk — wheesk, wheesk, wheesk* (Chalif).
Range: Sw. Mexico only; Jalisco south to Guerrero, s. Puebla.
Habitat: Scrub; lower and mid-levels of mts.

STRIPE-HEADED SPARROW **Pl. 48**
Aimophila ruficauda 6–7
Field marks: Note the blackish cheek patch and 2 black crown stripes (separating *white median stripe* and white stripe over each eye). Bill *bicolored* (light below). Colonial.
Similar species: (1) Striped Sparrow has all-black bill, lacks white median crown stripe. (2) White-crowned Sparrow lacks black cheek patch.
Voice: A hoarse chipping. Song, *zup-a-tzip-a-tzip-a-tzip-a* (Chalif).
Range: W. Mexico to nw. Costa Rica. **Mexico:** Arid Pacific slope from s. Durango, Nayarit south to sw. Chiapas. **Habitat:** Brush, thickets, scrub.

RUFOUS-WINGED SPARROW **Pl. 48**
Aimophila carpalis 5–5½
Field marks: A small pale sparrow suggesting Chipping Sparrow with its cinnamon crown bisected by a gray median stripe;

tail not notched. Note the *2 black mustache stripes* and pinkish bill. *Rufous shoulder,* a sure mark, not easily seen.

Similar species: (1) Cinnamon-tailed Sparrow also has double-mustached look but is more southern, larger, and lacks cinnamon crown. (2) Rufous-crowned Sparrow is much browner, with rufous cap; has brown (not black) streaks on back; inhabits rocky slopes. (3) Brewer's Sparrow lacks median crown stripe. (4) Botteri's Sparrow is darker, has buffier (less gray) breast, lacks median crown line; mustaches fainter. (5) See also Rusty Sparrow (below).

Voice: Song, a clear *chip chip chip* and then a short trill on a lower key (Chalif); 1 or 2 sweet introductory notes and a rapid series of musical chips on 1 pitch (RTP).

Range: Resident cen.-s. Arizona (local) and nw. Mexico (Sonora to Sinaloa). **Habitat:** Tall desert grass (tubosa), desert thorn brush.

CINNAMON-TAILED (SUMICHRAST'S) SPARROW
Aimophila sumichrasti 6¼–6½ **Pl. 48**

Field marks: Note the *2 short mustache stripes* extending from the lower mandible. Tail rather pale *cinnamon-brown* (most sparrows have dark tails). Conspicuous whitish eyebrow stripe; bill bicolored (light lower mandible).

Similar species: (1) Rufous-winged Sparrow (nw. Mexico) is much smaller. (2) Rusty Sparrow (also found in Oaxaca) has only 1 black whisker, an all-black bill, and less distinct back striping. (3) Oaxaca Sparrow (highlands of Oaxaca) has 1 black whisker, all-black bill and gray-brown tail.

Voice: A loud, penetrating squeaking and chipping (Chalif).

Range: Pacific slope of Isthmus of Tehuantepec (s. Oaxaca only). **Habitat:** Arid tropical zone.

OAXACA SPARROW *Aimophila notosticta* 6¼ **Not illus.**

Field marks: Similar to Rusty Sparrow (next) but restricted to Oaxaca; distinctly smaller; tail gray-brown (not rufous-chestnut).

Similar species: (1) See Rusty Sparrow. (2) Cinnamon-tailed Sparrow has 2 mustache marks, bicolored bill, cinnamon-brown (not gray-brown) tail.

Range: Highlands of cen. Oaxaca; rare, local. **Habitat:** Brushy hillsides, scrubby ravines, rocky slopes.

RUSTY SPARROW *Aimophila rufescens* 6¾–7½ **Pl. 48**

Field marks: A large rusty-colored sparrow with a bold black mustache stripe and black bill. Crown rusty, in 2 stripes, with a gray median stripe between.

Similar species: (1) Rufous-crowned Sparrow (smaller) lacks

median stripe on crown, is duller, less rusty, and less distinctly streaked on back. In Oaxaca see also (2) Cinnamon-tailed Sparrow and (3) Oaxaca Sparrow (both above).
Voice: Song, a bright, accented *chu-we, chip-chip;* also *chi-chip, ti-ti-ti-you* (RTP).
Range: N. Mexico to nw. Costa Rica. **Mexico:** Pacific slope from Sinaloa south; highlands from n. Sonora, n. Chihuahua, Tamaulipas south; Gulf slope from Veracruz, Puebla to n. Chiapas. Unrecorded in Yucatán Pen. though present in B. Honduras and Petén of Guatemala. **Habitat:** Mainly lower and mid-levels of mts. Dry stony brush, canyon oaks, pines, savannas, scrub, grassy areas in pineland.

RUFOUS-CROWNED SPARROW   Pl. 48
Aimophila ruficeps 5–6¼
Field marks: Note the *black mustache* line bordering the whitish throat, and the solid *rufous crown.* Dull brown above with a grayish face and breast.
Similar species: Rusty Sparrow is much larger, rustier above, with stronger stripes, gray line on crown, blacker bill.
Voice: Song, stuttering and gurgling, 1st part ascending slightly, last notes descending; suggests House-Wren. Note, a nasal *chur, chur, chur* or *dear, dear, dear* (RTP).
Range: Sw. U.S. to s. Mexico. **Mexico:** Foothills, mts., from northern states south locally to s. Baja California, Oaxaca, cen.-w. Veracruz. **Habitat:** Dry grassy or rocky slopes with sparse low bushes; open pine-oak woods, canyons.

BOTTERI'S SPARROW *Aimophila botterii* 5–6   Pl. 48
(including Yellow-carpalled or Petén Sparrow)
Field marks: A very nondescript brownish sparrow of dry open country with a plain buff-gray breast, brownish tail; carpals (bend of wing) yellow, but usually concealed. Best identified by voice.
Note: The small dark race *(petenica)* of the Gulf lowlands (n. Oaxaca, se. Veracruz, n. Chiapas, Yucatán, B. Honduras, Petén of Guatemala to Costa Rica) was formerly regarded as a distinct species, called Yellow-carpalled or Petén Sparrow.
Similar species: (1) Cassin's Sparrow (northern states) is very similar but grayer above (Botteri's has browner tail). Cassin's has a very different, quite sweet "skylarking" song, opening on 1 or 2 short notes followed by a high sweet trill, then 2 lower notes: *ti ti tseeeeee tay tay* (suggestive of Savannah Sparrow); often flutters into air, giving trill at climax (RTP). (2) Grasshopper Sparrow is browner, more contrastingly striped on back; has median crown stripe, buffier breast. (3) Brewer's Sparrow (wintering in northwest) is Chippylike (notched tail); striped buff and black above.

Voice: Song, a constant tinkling and "pitting," sometimes running into a dry rattle (RTP).
Range: Se. Arizona and s. Texas (very local) south to nw. Costa Rica. **Mexico:** Breeds from n. Sonora and n. Tamaulipas south locally in scrub and grass association to Chiapas, Yucatán. Also B. Honduras and Guatemala (rare; highlands and Petén). **Habitat:** Coarse desert grass (sacaton), tall grassy fields, brushy coastal prairies, savannas, arid scrub, low palmettos.

CASSIN'S SPARROW *Aimophila cassinii*   See W or T
Memo: Streaked crown with no center stripe; dull unmarked breast; "skylarking" song.
Range: Sw. U.S., n. Mexico. **Mexico:** Breeds in northern states (n. Chihuahua, Coahuila, San Luis Potosí, Tamaulipas). Winters south sparingly to s. Sinaloa, Guanajuato.

BLACK-THROATED SPARROW   See W or T
Amphispiza bilineata
Memo: Black throat, white face stripes.
Range: Deserts of w. U.S. to n. Mexico. **Mexico:** Resident Baja California and from northern tier of states south in coastal lowlands to n. Sinaloa and s. Tamaulipas; on central plateau south to Jalisco, Guanajuato, Hidalgo.

SAGE SPARROW *Amphispiza belli*   See W
Memo: White outlines gray cheek; dark center breast spot.
Range: W. U.S., Baja California. Winters sw. U.S., nw. Mexico. **Mexico:** Resident in n. and cen. Baja California (south to Lat. 26°). Winter visitor to n. Sonora, n. Chihuahua.

CHIPPING SPARROW *Spizella passerina*   See E, W, or T
Memo: Rusty cap, white eyebrow stripe, black eye line.
Range: Canada, U.S., Mid. America to Nicaragua. Migrant in north. **Mexico:** Breeds in pinelands of mts. of n. Baja California and from northwestern states south through mts. of central plateau to Chiapas. In winter also to s. Baja California and northeastern states.

CLAY-COLORED SPARROW   See E, W, or T
Spizella pallida
Memo: Striped crown, brown ear patch.
Range: W. Canada, n.-cen. U.S. Winters mainly in Mexico. Casual Guatemala. **Mexico:** Winters in s. Baja California, and from northern tier of states south in deserts and plains to Oaxaca, rarely Chiapas (absent Yucatán Pen.).

BREWER'S SPARROW *Spizella breweri*   See W
Memo: Pale; clear breast, dusky cheek; crown finely streaked.

Range: W. Canada, w. U.S. Winters sw. U.S., n. Mexico. **Mexico:** Winters in Baja California and in northwestern states east to Nueva León and south to Jalisco, Guanajuato.

FIELD SPARROW *Spizella pusilla* **See E, W, or T**
Memo: Rusty cap, pink bill.
Range: Se. Canada, U.S. (east of Rockies) to Gulf states. Winters in e. and cen. U.S., ne. Mexico. **Mexico:** Sparse winter visitor to Coahuila, Nuevo León, n. Tamaulipas.

WORTHEN'S SPARROW *Spizella wortheni* 5½ **Pl. 48**
Field marks: A rare and little-known sparrow closely resembling Field Sparrow (pink bill, rusty cap, plain breast) but rusty of crown less extensive, eye-ring more conspicuous; cheeks grayer with no noticeable stripe behind eye.
Similar species: See Field Sparrow (sparse winter visitor).
Range: Ne. Mexico. Accidental New Mexico. **Mexico:** recorded Coahuila, sw. Tamaulipas, w. Zacatecas, San Luis Potosí, Puebla, Veracruz (perhaps a migrant in last 2 areas). **Habitat:** Arid brush.

BLACK-CHINNED SPARROW **See W or T**
Spizella atrogularis
Memo: Gray head; black surrounding pink bill (♂).
Range: Sw. U.S. to s. Mexico. **Mexico:** Breeds n. Baja California (winters to Cape) and from e. Sonora and Coahuila south through semi-arid highlands of interior to Oaxaca.

FOX SPARROW *Passerella iliaca* **See E, W, or T**
Memo: Rusty tail, very heavily striped breast.
Range: Alaska, Canada, w. U.S. In winter to s. U.S., nw. Mexico. **Mexico:** Winters in n. Baja California.

LINCOLN'S SPARROW *Melospiza lincolnii* **See E, W, or T**
Memo: Like Song Sparrow but buff breast, finer streaks.
Range: Alaska, Canada, w. and ne. U.S. Winters s. U.S. to B. Honduras, Guatemala, Honduras, El Salvador. **Mexico:** Winter visitor nearly throughout, but scarce Yucatán Pen.

SWAMP SPARROW *Melospiza georgiana* **See E, W, or T**
Memo: Rusty cap, gray breast, white throat.
Range: Canada, ne. U.S. Winters chiefly to Gulf of Mexico. **Mexico:** Rare in winter to northern states; casually to Jalisco.

SONG SPARROW *Melospiza melodia* **See E, W, or T**
Memo: Streaked breast with large central spot.
Range: Alaska, Canada, to cen. Mexico. **Mexico:** Breeds south to s.-cen. Baja California, n. Sonora, and in highlands south lo-

cally to Michoacán, México, Puebla. Migrants from U.S. reach northern border states.

WHITE-CROWNED SPARROW See E, W, or T
Zonotrichia leucophrys
> **Memo:** Black-striped crown, grayish throat. Immature has brown head stripes, pink or yellow bill.
> **Range:** Alaska, Canada, w. U.S. Winters to Cuba, cen. Mexico. **Mexico:** Winters across northern states and south to s. Baja California, Michoacán, Guanajuato, Querétaro.

GOLDEN-CROWNED SPARROW See W
Zonotrichia atricapilla
> **Memo:** Yellow crown, bordered with black.
> **Range:** Alaska, w. Canada. Winters to nw. Mexico. **Mexico:** Winters to n. Baja California; rarely to Cape. Casual Sonora, n. Sinaloa.

WHITE-THROATED SPARROW See E, W, or T
Zonotrichia albicollis
> **Memo:** Striped crown, white throat.
> **Range:** Canada, ne. U.S. Winters mainly to s. U.S. **Mexico:** Rare winter visitor to northeastern border and Sonora.

RUFOUS-COLLARED (ANDEAN) SPARROW Pl. 48
Zonotrichia capensis 5–6
> **Field marks:** The *rufous collar* encircling the hindneck and *black patch* on each side of the chest (sometimes joined) identify this cheerful-sounding sparrow. It often raises a short but conspicuous *crest*. A broad gray superciliary stripe separates the dark cheek and black crown. Young birds are streaked above and below but show the telltale crest.
> **Similar species:** See Rusty-crowned Ground-Sparrow (p. 248).
> **Voice:** A cheerful whistled arrangement; one of the most characteristic bird songs of Mid. and S. America, often varying locally. "Suggests E. Meadowlark" (Chalif). In Guatemala a typical song consists of 3 whistled notes, the 1st short with a rising inflection, the 2nd longer and dropping, the 3rd like the 1st (Land). In Panamá song somewhat suggests E. Meadowlark, *tee'oo tee'a* and variations (Eisenmann).
> **Range:** Se. Mexico, Hispaniola to Tierra del Fuego. **Mexico:** Highlands of Chiapas (to 10,000+ ft.). **Habitat:** Cleared areas, gardens, farms, roadsides, open pinelands.

SLATE-COLORED JUNCO See E, W, or T
Junco hyemalis (in part)
> **Memo:** Gray hood, sides and back; white tail sides (all juncos).
> **Range:** Alaska, Canada; in eastern mts. to n. Georgia. Winters

to s. U.S., n. Mexico. **Mexico:** Rare winter visitor to northern states (Baja California, Sonora, Chihuahua); n. Tamaulipas?

OREGON JUNCO *Junco hyemalis* (in part) **See E, W, or T**
(including Guadalupe Junco)
  Memo: Rusty sides, brown back, gray or black hood.
  Note: The *oreganus* group of juncos was formerly regarded as a distinct species, but now is lumped with the other dark-eyed juncos under *J. hyemalis.* Usually separable in the field. The race on Guadalupe I. off Baja California was also formerly treated as a distinct species, *J. insularis.*
  Range: Se. coastal Alaska, sw. Canada, n. Rocky Mt. states, Pacific states. **Mexico:** Breeds in mts. of n. Baja California; also Guadalupe I. Winters into n. Mexico (except northeastern corner).

GRAY-HEADED JUNCO **See W or T**
Junco caniceps (or *J. hyemalis* in part)
  Memo: Gray head, rufous back; white tail sides.
  Note: The Gray-headed Junco has usually been treated as a separate species but some recent thinking has lumped it with all the others of the dark-eyed junco complex under *J. hyemalis.*
  Range: Mt. regions of w. U.S. **Mexico:** Winter visitor to northwestern states south to n. Sinaloa, Durango.

YELLOW-EYED JUNCO *Junco phaeonotus* 6-6½ **Pl. 48**
(incl. Mexican, Arizona, Baird's, Chiapas, Guatemalan Juncos)
  Field marks: The widespread Mexican junco, and the only one with *yellow eyes.* As in all other juncos, has *white outer tail feathers,* but unlike its northern relatives it lacks the hooded effect; throat may be whitish, breast pale. Back bright rusty in northern birds, dull brown in Guatemalan birds. Bill bicolored. Walks rather than hops.
  Similar species: All other juncos have brown or dark reddish eyes and have recently been lumped into 1 species complex under the name of *J. hyemalis,* Dark-eyed Junco.
  Voice: Song musical, unlike trill of other juncos, more complicated; 3-parted, often thus: *chip chip chip, wheedle wheedle, che che che che che* (RTP).
  Range: Resident in high mts. of se. Arizona, extreme sw. New Mexico to Guatemala. **Mexico:** High mts. from ne. Sonora, n. Chihuahua, Coahuila, Nuevo León south to Chiapas; also Victoria Mts. of Cape of Baja California. **Habitat:** Conifer forests, pine-oak woods, highland pastures (4000–14,000 ft.).

McCOWN'S LONGSPUR **See E, W, or T**
Rynchophanes mccownii
  Memo: Rusty shoulder, inverted black T on white tail.
  Range: Plains of w.-cen. Canada, n.-cen. U.S. Winters sw. U.S.

and nw. Mexico. **Mexico:** Winter visitor to deserts, plateaus of n. Sonora, Chihuahua, n. Durango.

LAPLAND LONGSPUR See E, W, or T
Calcarius lapponicus
Memo: Rusty nape (♂), smudge on breast (winter); white outer tail feathers.
Range: Arctic; circumpolar. Winters to s. U.S., cen. Eurasia. **Mexico:** Accidental, Baja California.

CHESTNUT-COLLARED LONGSPUR See E, W, or T
Calcarius ornatus
Memo: Triangle of black on white tail.
Range: Prairies of s.-cen. Canada, n.-cen. U.S. Winters sw. U.S. to n. Mexico. **Mexico:** Winter visitor mainly to plateaus of northwestern states (n. Sonora, Chihuahua, Durango) but also recorded in high open country south to Puebla, Veracruz (Orizaba).

EVENING GROSBEAK See E, W, or T
Hesperiphona vespertina
Memo: ♂ dull yellow; black and white wings, large pale bill. ♀ silver-gray and yellow, large bill.
Range: Canada, w. and ne. U.S., Mexico. Winters irregularly to Gulf states of U.S. **Mexico:** Resident in pine forests of high mts.; in western mts. from Chihuahua south to Michoacán; in se. mts. from Hidalgo to Oaxaca.

HOODED GROSBEAK *Hesperiphona abeillei* 6–7 **Pl. 45**
Field marks: *Male:* A dull golden-yellow grosbeak with an *all-black head* and *large pale bill.* Wings black with large *white patch* on secondaries; tail black. *Female:* Similar but duller, with blackish cap only; whitish on belly.
Similar species: ♂ Evening Grosbeak has broad yellow eye stripe, lacks well-defined hood; ♀ lacks definite cap.
Voice: Call, *beebink* or *bree-bink* or *bre-bruk* or *beet beet.* A variant is *bee-bink-beeaw* – 1st 2 notes on same pitch, 3rd note starting high and sliding down (Chalif).
Range: Nw. Mexico to Guatemala (local). **Mexico:** Northwestern mts. (Sierra Madre Occidental) in s. Chihuahua, Sinaloa, Durango; also eastern and southern mts. from sw. Tamaulipas, e. San Luis Potosí, Michoacán south and east to Oaxaca, se. Chiapas (local). **Habitat:** Mt. forests, cloud forest.

PURPLE FINCH *Carpodacus purpureus* See E, W, or T
Memo: ♂ rosy; size of House Sparrow, no side stripes. ♀ has light eyebrow stripe, dark jaw stripe or mustache.
Range: Canada, ne. U.S., Pacific states, nw. Mexico. Winters

to s. U.S. **Mexico:** Breeds in mts. of n. Baja California (Sierra Juárez). Winters nearby in nw. Baja California south to San Ramón.

CASSIN'S FINCH *Carpodacus cassinii* **See W or T**
Memo: ♂ paler rose than House Finch; red cap, larger bill. ♀ similar to ♀ House Finch but stronger face pattern, larger bill.
Range: Sw. Canada, w. U.S., nw. Mexico. Winters to cen. Mexico. **Mexico:** Breeds in mts. of n. Baja California (San Pedro Mártir; in winter to Sierra Juárez). Winters on Mexican plateau south to Zacatecas, San Luis Potosí (rarely farther).

HOUSE FINCH *Carpodacus mexicanus* **See W or T**
Memo: ♂ rosy; striped belly and sides. ♀ streaked; stubby bill, no strong face pattern.
Range: Southern B. Columbia, w. U.S., Mexico. *Introduced* in Hawaii, ne. U.S. **Mexico:** Resident Baja California (incl. offshore islands); western and central sections from northern tier of states (east to Nuevo León, s. Tamaulipas) south on Pacific slope to Nayarit and in highlands to cen. Oaxaca.

PINE SISKIN *Spinus pinus* **See E, W, or T**
Memo: Streaked, touch of yellow in wings and tail.
Range: S. Alaska, Canada to s. Mexico. Partially migratory.
Mexico: Resident in mts. of n. Baja California and from Sonora, Chihuahua south locally in highlands through western and southern states to Chiapas. In winter to coastal Sonora.

BLACK-CAPPED SISKIN *Spinus atriceps* 4½ **Pl. 45**
Field marks: *Male:* A small *dark greenish* finch with a *black cap.* Wings and tail have some restricted yellow, much as in Pine Siskin. *Female:* Similar to male but duller, with a dusky cap. Young birds streaked, very much like Pine Siskin.
Similar species: (1) Pine Siskin, in all plumages, is streaked. (2) Black-headed Siskin has entire head and much of chest black; more yellow on body, wings, and tail.
Voice: Very similar to Pine Siskin's (Chalif). Calls similar to those of American Goldfinch (Baepler).
Range: Se. Mexico, Guatemala. **Mexico:** Highlands of Chiapas (San Cristóbal). **Habitat:** Pine forests, alders.

BLACK-HEADED SISKIN *Spinus notatus* 4½ **Pl. 45**
Field marks: *Male:* The most brightly colored siskin. *Entire head* and much of chest black; underparts *bright yellow;* large yellow patches in wings and tail. *Female:* Duller, may or may not lack dark hood.
Similar species: See Black-capped Siskin (preceding).
Range: W. and s. Mexico to Nicaragua. **Mexico:** Mts. from s.

Sonora, s. Chihuahua, San Luis Potosí south to Chiapas. **Habitat:** Pine-oak zone of highlands, borders, ranging to lower levels.

AMERICAN GOLDFINCH *Spinus tristis* **See E, W, or T**
Memo: Spring ♂, yellow; black wings. ♀ and winter ♂, yellow-olive; blackish wings, whitish rump.
Range: S. Canada to s. U.S., n. Baja California. **Mexico:** Resident in nw. Baja California (Ensenada). Winter visitor to northern Pacific slope; also Gulf slope south to Veracruz.

DARK-BACKED (LESSER) GOLDFINCH **See W or T**
Spinus psaltria
Memo: ♂ black or dark olive above, yellow below. ♀ greener than American Goldfinch; dark rump.
Range: W. U.S. to Peru. Migratory in north. **Mexico:** Nearly countrywide.

LAWRENCE'S GOLDFINCH *Spinus lawrencei* **See W or T**
Memo: ♂ black face, gray head; yellow wingbars. ♀ gray head, yellow wingbars.
Range: California, n. Baja California. Winters sw. U.S., nw. Mexico. **Mexico:** Breeds in nw. Baja California (south to Lat. 30°). In winter to Colorado River delta and n. Sonora.

RED CROSSBILL *Loxia curvirostra* **See E, W, or T**
Memo: ♂ dull red; blackish wings, crossed bill. ♀ dull olive; dark wings.
Range: Conifer forests of N. Hemisphere. In w. N. America, south in mts. and pine savannas to n. Nicaragua. In e. N. America south locally to mts. of N. Carolina. **Mexico:** Resident in mts. of n. Baja California and in pine belt of high mts. (5000–13,000 ft.) from northern tier of states south locally through Chiapas.

Selected Bibliography

BELOW are listed only the major and most relevant books on the birds of Mexico and Middle America that will be of interest to the observer with the binocular. Many interesting technical papers and notes will be found in the pages of the ornithological journals, especially *The Auk, The Condor,* and *The Wilson Bulletin.* These are not listed here.

All of Middle America (including Mexico)

Davis, L. Irby. 1972. A Field Guide to the Birds of Mexico and Central America. Austin and London: University of Texas Press.

Eisenmann, Eugene. 1955. The Species of Middle American Birds. New York: Linnaean Society of New York. Transactions, Vol. 7.

Ridgway, Robert (and Herbert Friedmann, Parts 9–11), 1901–1950. The Birds of North and Middle America. Bull. U.S. Natl. Mus., Parts 1–11.

Mexico

Alden, Peter. 1969. Finding the Birds in Western Mexico [Sonora, Sinaloa, Nayarit]. Tucson: University of Arizona Press.

Alvarez del Toro, Miguel. 1971. Las Aves de Chiapas. Tuxtla Gutiérrez, Chiapas: Instituto de Ciencias y Artes de Chiapas.

Blake, Emmet R. 1953. Birds of Mexico: A Guide for Field Identification. Chicago: University of Chicago Press.

Davis, L. Irby. Mexican Bird Songs. A 12-inch LP record of the voices of 74 species, produced by the Cornell Laboratory of Ornithology. Boston: Houghton Mifflin Co. Sounds of Nature series.

Edwards, Ernest P. 1968. Finding Birds in Mexico. 2nd ed. Sweet Briar, Va.: E. P. Edwards.

_____. 1972. A Field Guide to the Birds of Mexico. Sweet Briar, Va.: E. P. Edwards.

Friedmann, Herbert, Ludlow Griscom, and Robert T. Moore (also Alden H. Miller in Part 2). 1950, 1957. Distributional Check-List of the Birds of Mexico. Parts 1 and 2. Berkeley: Cooper Ornithological Club. Pacific Coast Avifauna, Nos. 29 and 33.

Leopold, A. Starker. 1959. Wildlife of Mexico. Berkeley and Los Angeles: University of California Press.

Paynter, Raymond A., Jr. 1955. The Ornithogeography of the Yucatán Peninsula. New Haven: Peabody Museum of Natural History. Bull. 9.

Sutton, George M. 1951. Mexican Birds: First Impressions. Norman, Okla.: University of Oklahoma Press.
——. 1972. A Bend in a Mexican River. New York: Paul S. Eriksson, Inc.

South of Mexico

Dickey, D. R., and A. J. van Rossem. 1938. The Birds of El Salvador. Chicago: Field Museum of Natural History. Zoological Series Pub. 406, Vol. 23.

Land, Hugh C. 1970. Birds of Guatemala. Wynnewood, Pa.: Livingston Publishing Co.

Meyer de Schauensee, Rodolphe. 1970. A Guide to the Birds of South America. Wynnewood, Pa.: Livingston Publishing Co. for the Academy of Natural Sciences of Philadelphia.

Monroe, Burt L., Jr. 1968. A Distributional Survey of the Birds of Honduras. Lawrence, Kan.: Allen Press. American Ornithologists' Union, Monograph 7.

Russell, Stephen M. 1964. A Distributional Study of the Birds of British Honduras. Lawrence, Kan.: Allen Press. American Ornithologists' Union, Monograph 1.

Skutch, Alexander. 1954, 1960, 1967. Life Histories of Central American Birds. 3 vols. Berkeley: Cooper Ornithological Society. Pacific Coast Avifauna, Nos. 31, 34, and 35.

Slud, Paul. 1964. The Birds of Costa Rica. New York: American Museum of Natural History, Bull. 128.

Smithe, Frank B. 1966. The Birds of Tikal [Guatemala]. New York: Natural History Press.

North of the Border (North America)

A.O.U. Check-List Committee. 1957. Check-List of North American Birds. 5th edition. Baltimore: American Ornithologists' Union.

Peterson, Roger Tory. 1947. A Field Guide to the Birds [East].
——. 1961. A Field Guide to Western Birds.
——. 1963. A Field Guide to the Birds of Texas. All three guides, Boston: Houghton Mifflin Co.

Pough, Richard H. 1946. Audubon Bird Guide.
——. 1951. Audubon Water Bird Guide.
——. 1957. Audubon Western Bird Guide. All three guides, New York: Doubleday and Co., Inc. Illustrated by Don Eckelberry.

Robbins, Chandler S., Bertel Bruun, and Herbert S. Zim. 1966. Birds of North America: A Guide to Field Identification. New York: Golden Press. Illustrated by Arthur Singer.

West Indies

Bond, James, 1971. Birds of the West Indies. 2nd ed. Boston: Houghton Mifflin Co.

Index

IN THE FIELD, the reader will find it practical to go to the illustration; in most cases his problem will be settled there. References to illustrations are given in **boldface**. In this index they are placed only after the English names of species. Page numbers in lightface type refer to the text.

The English names used throughout the text are those selected by Eugene Eisenmann, with the collaboration of Emmet Blake and Edward Chalif (1955), in an attempt to bring consistency to the names of Mexican and Central American birds. These names have won wide acceptance among the ornithological fraternity and can now be regarded as standard. To minimize the confusion of readers who may encounter differing names in other publications, we have included all (or most) of these names in this index (for example: Flycatcher, Derby. *See* Kiskadee, Great). Other obsolete or little-used vernacular names are not listed.

Abeillia abeillei, 97
Accipiter bicolor, 31
   chionogaster, 30
   cooperii, 30
   gentilis, 30
   striatus, 30
Accipitridae, 26
Actitis macularia, 56
Aechmolophus mexicanus, 152
Aechmophorus occidentalis, 3
Aegolius acadicus, 87
   ridgwayi, 87
Aeronautes saxatalis, 93
Agamia agami, 14
Agelaius gubernator. See under
   A. phoeniceus, 226
   phoeniceus, 226
   tricolor, 226
Agriocharis ocellata, 48
Aimophila botterii, 253
   carpalis, 251
   cassinii, 254
   humeralis, 251
   mystacalis, 251
   notosticta, 252
   petenica. See under *A. botterii,*
    253
   quinquestriata, 250
   rufescens, 252

Aimophila (contd.)
   ruficauda, 251
   ruficeps, 253
   sumichrasti, 252
Aix sponsa, 22
Ajaia ajaja, 18
Alaudidae, 158
Albatross(es), 4
   Black-footed, 4
   Laysan, 5
   Short-tailed, 4
Alcedinidae, 111
Alcidae, 66
Alectoris chukar, 47
Amaurolimnas concolor, 50
Amaurospiza concolor, 243
   relicta. See under *A. concolor,*
    243
Amazilia beryllina, 101
   candida, 100
   cyanocephala, 100
   cyanura, 101
   rutila, 101
   tzacatl, 102
   verticalis. See *A. violiceps,* 102
   violiceps, 102
   viridifrons, 102
   yucatanensis, 101
Amazona albifrons, 76

Amazona (contd.)
  autumnalis, 77
  farinosa, 78
  finschi, 77
  ochrocephala, 77
  viridigenalis, 76
  xantholora, 76
Amblycercus holosericeus, 218
Ammodramus bairdii, 250
  savannarum, 249
Ammospiza caudacuta, 250
Amphispiza belli, 254
  bilineata, 254
Anabacerthia variegaticeps, 128
Anas acuta, 21
  americana, 21
  carolinensis, 21
  clypeata, 22
  cyanoptera, 22
  diazi, 21
  discors, 22
  fulvigula, 21
  penelope, 21
  platyrhynchos, 21
  strepera, 21
  wyvilliana, 21
Anatidae, 19
Anhinga, 12
Anhinga anhinga, 12
Anhingas. *See* Darters, 12
Anhingidae, 12
Ani(s), 78
  Groove-billed, 79, **Pl. 15**
  Smooth-billed, 79, **Pl. 15**
Anous minutus, 65
  stolidus, 65
  tenuirostris. See *A. minutus,* 65
Anser albifrons, 19
Antbird(s), 130
  Bare-crowned, 133, **Pl. 25**
  Bare-fronted. *See* Antbird,
    Bare-crowned, 133
  Dusky, 133, **Pl. 25**
Anthracothorax prevostii, 97
Anthus cervinus, 192
  spinoletta, 191
  spragueii, 192
Antpitta, Guatemalan. *See* Ant-
    pitta, Scaled, 134
  Scaled, 134, **Pl. 25**
Antshrike, Barred, 131, **Pl. 25**
  Great, 131, **Pl. 25**

Antshrike (contd.)
  Russet, 131, **Pl. 25**
  Slaty, 131, **Pl. 25**
  Tawny. See Antshrike, Russet,
    131
Ant-Tanager. *See* Tanager
Antthrush, Black-faced, 134, **Pl.
  25**
  Mexican. *See* Antthrush, Black-
    faced, 134
Antvireo, Plain, 132, **Pl. 25**
Antwren, Boucard's. *See* Ant-
    wren, Dot-winged, 132
  Dot-winged, 132, **Pl. 25**
  Long-billed. *See* Gnatwren,
    Long-billed, 191
  Slaty, 132, **Pl. 25**
  Tyrannine. *See* Antbird,
    Dusky, 133
Aphelocoma coerulescens, 166
  ultramarina, 166
  unicolor, 166
Aphriza virgata, 57
Apodidae, 92
Aquila chrysaetos, 35
Ara macao, 73
  militaris, 73
Araçari, Collared, 116, **Pl. 22**
Aramidae, 48
Aramides axillaris, 50
  cajanea, 50
Aramus guarauna, 49
Aratinga astec, 74
  canicularis, 74
  holochlora, 73
  holochlora rubritorquis, 73
Archilochus alexandri, 107
  colubris, 106
Ardea herodias, 13
  "*occidentalis,*" 14
Ardeidae, 13
Arenaria interpres, 56
  melanocephala, 56
Arremon aurantiirostris, 246
Arremonops chloronotus, 246
  rufivirgatus, 246
Asio flammeus, 87
  otus, 87
  stygius, 87
Aspatha gularis, 113
Asyndesmus. See *Melanerpes,*
  119

Atlapetes albinucha, 244
　apertus, 245
　brunneinucha, 245
　brunneinucha apertus, 245
　gutturalis, 245
　pileatus, 244
　torquata. See under *A. virenti-
　　ceps,* 245
　virenticeps, 245
Atlapetes, Chestnut-capped. *See*
　Finch, Chestnut-capped
　Brush-, 245
　Green-striped. *See* Finch,
　　Green-striped Brush-, 245
　Rufous-capped. *See* Finch,
　　Rufous-capped Brush-, 244
　San Martin. *See* Finch, Chest-
　　nut-capped Brush-, 245
　White-naped. *See* Finch,
　　White-naped Brush-, 244
　Yellow-throated. *See* Finch,
　　Yellow-throated Brush-, 245
Atthis ellioti, 107
　heloisa, 107
Attila, Bright-rumped, 137, **Pl. 26**
　Polymorphic. *See* Attila,
　　Bright-rumped, 137
Attila spadiceus, 137
Auklet, Cassin's, 66
　Rhinoceros, 66
Auks, 66
Aulacorhynchus prasinus, 116
Auriparus flaviceps, 168
Automolus, Buff-throated. *See*
　Foliage-gleaner, Buff-
　throated, 129
　Ruddy. *See* Foliage-gleaner,
　　Ruddy, 129
Automolus ochrolaemus, 129
　rubiginosus, 129
Avocet(s), 60
　American, 60
Aythya affinis, 22
　americana, 22
　collaris, 22
　marila, 22
　valisineria, 22
Azurecrown, Red-billed, 100, **Pl.
　18**

Baldpate. *See* Wigeon, American,
　21

Bananaquit, 202, **Pl. 37**
Barbthroat, Band-tailed, 94
Barn Owl(s), 81
Bartramia longicauda, 58
Basileuterus belli, 215
　culcivorus, 215
　delattrii, 216
　rufifrons, 215, 216
　rufifrons salvini, 215
Becard, Cinnamon, 138, **Pl. 26**
　Gray-collared, 138, **Pl. 26**
　Mexican. *See* Becard, Gray-
　　collared, 138
　Rose-throated, 139, **Pl. 26**
　White-winged, 138, **Pl. 26**
Bentbill, Gray-throated. *See* Bent-
　bill, Northern, 155
　Northern, 155, **Pl. 29**
Bittern(s), 13
　American, 16
　Least, 16
　Mexican Tiger-. *See* Heron,
　　Bare-throated Tiger-, 16
　Pinnated, 16, **Pl. 1**
　Tiger-. *See* Heron, Bare-
　　throated Tiger-, 16
Blackbird(s), 216
　Bicolored. *See under* Black-
　　bird, Red-winged, 226
　Brewer's, 220
　Melodious, 220, **Pl. 39**
　Red-winged, 226
　Rusty, 219
　Singing. *See* Blackbird, Melo-
　　dious, 220
　Sumichrast's. *See* Blackbird,
　　Melodious, 220
　Tricolored, 226
　Yellow-headed, 226
Bluebird(s), 183
　Common. *See* Bluebird, East-
　　ern, 188
　Eastern, 188
　Mexican. *See* Bluebird, West-
　　ern, 188
　Mountain, 189
　Western, 188
Bobolink, 227
Bobwhite, Black-headed. *See*
　Bobwhite, Common, 45
　Black-throated, 45, **Pl. 9**
　Common, 45, **Pl. 9**

Bobwhite (contd.)
"Masked." *See* Bobwhite, Common, 45
Northern. *See* Bobwhite, Common, 45
Rufous-bellied. *See* Bobwhite, Common, 45
Spot-bellied, 46, **Pl. 8**
White-breasted. *See* Bobwhite, Spot-bellied, 46
Yucatán. *See* Bobwhite, Black-throated, 45
Bolborhynchus lineola, 75
Bombycilla cedrorum, 192
Bombycillidae, 192
Booby(ies), 10
Blue-faced. *See* Booby, Masked, 11
Blue-footed, 11
Brown, 11
Masked, 11
Red-footed, 11
Botaurus lentiginosus, 16
pinnatus, 16
Brant, Black, 20
Branta canadensis, 20
canadensis hutchinsii, 20
canadensis leucopareia, 20
canadensis minima, 20
canadensis moffitti, 20
canadensis parvipes, 20
hutchinsii. See under *B. canadensis,* 20
nigricans, 20
Brotogeris jugularis, 75
Brush-Finch. *See* Finch
Bubo virginianus, 84
Bubulcus ibis, 14
Bucconidae, 115
Bucephala albeola, 24
clangula, 24
Bufflehead, 24
Bunting(s), 235
Blue, 239, **Pl. 46**
Indigo, 239
Lark, 249
Lazuli, 239
Leclancher's. *See* Bunting, Orange-breasted, 240
Orange-breasted, 240, **Pl. 45**
Painted, 240
Rose-bellied, 240, **Pl. 45**

Bunting (contd.)
Rosita's. *See* Bunting, Rose-bellied, 240
Varied, 240, **Pl. 46**
Burhinidae, 61
Burhinus bistriatus, 61
Busarellus nigricollis, 32
Bush-Tanager. *See* Tanager
Bushtit(s), 167, 168
Black-eared. *See* Bushtit, 168
Plain. *See* Bushtit, 168
Buteo albicaudatus, 34
albonotatus, 34
brachyurus, 34
jamaicensis, 34
lagopus, 35
lineatus, 33
magnirostris, 33
nitidus, 33
platypterus, 33
regalis, 35
swainsoni, 34
Buteogallus anthracinus, 31
subtilis. See under *B. anthracinus,* 31
urubitinga, 31
Butorides virescens, 15
Buzzard, Fishing. *See* Hawk, Black-collared, 32
"Buzzards." *See* Vultures, New World, 25

Cacique, Mexican. *See* Cacique, Yellow-winged, 217
Prevost. *See* Cacique, Yellow-billed, 218
Yellow-billed, 218, **Pl. 39**
Yellow-winged, 217, **Pl. 39**
Cactus-Wren. *See* Wren
Cairina moschata, 23
Calamospiza melanocorys, 249
Calcarius lapponicus, 258
ornatus, 258
Calidris alba, 58
alpina, 57
bairdii, 57
canutus, 57
fuscicollis, 57
mauri, 58
melanotos, 57
minutilla, 57
ptilocnemis, 58

Calidris (contd.)
  pusilla, 58
Callipepla squamata, 44
Calocitta formosa, 163
  formosa colliei, 163
Calothorax lucifer, 106
  pulcher, 106
Calypte anna, 107
  costae, 107
Campephilus guatemalensis, 123
  imperialis, 123
Camptostoma imberbe, 156
Campylopterus curvipennis, 95
  hemileucurus, 96
  rufus, 96
Campylorhynchus brunneica-
  pillus, 172
  chiapensis, 171
  gularis, 172
  jocosus, 172
  megalopterus, 170
  rufinucha, 171
  rufinucha capistratus, 171
  yucatanicus, 172
  zonatus, 171
Canvasback, 22
Capella. See *Gallinago*, 59
Caprimulgidae, 89
Caprimulgus badius. See under
  C. salvini, 90
  carolinensis, 90
  maculicaudus, 91
  ridgwayi, 91
  salvini, 90
  vociferus, 90
Caracara(s), 36
  Audubon's. *See* Caracara,
    Crested, 37
  Crested, 37, **Pls. 4, 5**
  Guadalupe, 37
  Red-throated, 37, **Pls. 4, 5**
Caracara plancus, 37
Cardellina rubrifrons, 213
Cardinal, Common. *See* Cardi-
  nal, Red, 237
  Long-crested. *See under* Cardi-
    nal, Red, 237
  Red, 237
Cardinalis cardinalis, 237
  carnea. See under *C. cardi-*
    nalis, 237
  sinuata. See *Pyrrhuloxia sin-*

Cardinals (contd.)
  uata, 237
Carpodacus cassinii, 259
  mexicanus, 259
  purpureus, 258
Caryothraustes poliogaster, 237
Casmerodius albus, 14
Cassiculus melanicterus, 217
Cassidix mexicanus, 219
  palustris, 219
Catbird, Black, 182, **Pl. 34**
  Gray, 182
  Northern. *See* Catbird, Gray,
    182
Cathartes aura, 25
  burrovianus, 25
Cathartidae, 25
Catharus aurantiirostris, 188
  dryas, 187
  frantzii, 188
  fuscescens, 187
  guttatus, 186
  mexicanus, 187
  minimus, 186
  occidentalis, 187
  ustulatus, 186
Catherpes mexicanus, 178
Catoptrophorus semipalmatus,
  56
Celeus castaneus, 119
Centurus aurifrons, 120
  chrysogenys, 119
  hypopolius, 120
  pucherani, 120
  pygmaeus, 121
  uropygialis, 120
Cercomacra tyrannina, 133
Cerorhinca monocerata, 66
Certhia familiaris, 169
Certhiidae, 169
Chachalaca(s), 40
  Black. *See* Penelopina, Black,
    42
  Eastern. *See* Chachalaca,
    Plain, 40
  Plain, 40, **Pl. 6**
  Rufous-bellied. *See* Chacha-
    laca, West Mexican, 41
  Wagler's. *See* Chachalaca,
    West Mexican, 41
  West Mexican, 41, **Pl. 6**
  White-bellied, 42, **Pl. 6**

Chaetura gaumeri. See under *C.*
  vauxi, 93
  pelagica, 93
  richmondi. See under *C. vauxi,*
    93
  vauxi, 93
Chamaea fasciata, 169
Chamaeidae, 169
Chamaethlypis. See *Geothlypis,*
  211
Charadriidae, 54
Charadrius alexandrinus, 55
  collaris, 55
  melodus, 54
  montanus, 55
  semipalmatus, 54
  vociferus, 55
  wilsonia, 55
Chat, Gray-throated, 212, **Pl. 37**
  Red-breasted, 212, **Pl. 37**
  Tres Marías. *See* Chat, Red-
    breasted, 212
  Yellow-breasted, 212
Chen caerulescens, 20
  "*hyperborea.*" See *C. caerules-*
    cens, 20
  rossii, 20
Chickadee, Gray-sided, 167
  Mexican. *See* Chickadee, Gray-
    sided, 167
  Mountain, 167
Chip-willow. *See* Nightjar,
  Tawny-collared, 90
Chiroxiphia linearis, 135
Chlidonias niger, 64
Chloroceryle aenea, 112
  amazona, 112
  americana, 112
Chlorophanes spiza, 201
Chlorophonia, Blue-crowned,
  227, **Pl. 43**
  Golden-browed. *See under*
    Chlorophonia, Blue-
    crowned, 227
Chlorophonia callophrys. See
  under *C. occipitalis,* 227
  occipitalis, 227
Chlorospingus, Brown-headed.
  See Tanager, Common
  Bush-, 235
  Dusky-headed. *See* Tanager,
    Common Bush-, 235

Chlorospingus (contd.)
  Dwight's. *See* Tanager, Com-
    mon Bush-, 235
  White-fronted. *See* Tanager,
    Common Bush-, 235
Chlorospingus ophthalmicus, 235
Chlorostilbon canivetii, 98
Chlorura chlorura, 247
Chondestes grammacus, 250
Chondrohierax uncinatus, 27
Chordeiles acutipennis, 89
  minor, 89
Chuck-will, Salvin's. *See* Night-
  jar, Tawny-collared, 90
Chuck-will's-widow, 90
Ciccaba nigrolineata, 86
  virgata, 86
Ciconiidae, 17
Cinclidae, 169
Cinclus mexicanus, 170
Circus cyaneus, 30
Cissilopha beecheii, 165
  melanocyanea, 165
  sanblasiana, 164
  yucatanica, 164
Cistothorus platensis, 170
Clangula hyemalis, 24
Claravis mondetoura, 70
  pretiosa, 70
Coccyzus americanus, 78
  erythropthalmus, 78
  minor, 78
Cochleariidae, 16
Cochlearius cochlearius, 17
Coereba flaveloa, 202
Coerebidae, 200
Colaptes auratus, 117
  cafer, 117
  cafer mexicanoides, 117
  chrysoides, 118
Colibri delphinae, 96
  thalassinus, 97
Colinus leucopogon, 46
  nigrogularis, 45
  virginianus, 45
Columba cayennensis, 67
  fasciata, 68
  flavirostris, 67
  leucocephala, 67
  livia, 67
  nigrirostris, 68
  speciosa, 68

Columbidae, 67
Columbina minuta, 69
  passerina, 69
  talpacoti, 70
Condor, California, 26
Contopus borealis, 147
  cinereus, 148
  pertinax, 148
  sordidulus, 147
  virens, 147
Cookacheea. *See* Nightjar, Buff-collared, 91
Coot(s), 49
  American, 52
Coquette, Black-crested, 97, **Pls. 18, 20**
  Delattre's. *See* Coquette, Rufous-crested, 97
  Helena's. *See* Coquette, Black-crested, 97
  Rufous-crested, 97, **Pls. 18, 20**
Coragyps atratus, 25
Cormorant(s), 11
  Brandt's, 12
  Double-crested, 12
  Mexican. *See* Cormorant, Neotropic, 12
  Neotropic, 12
  Olivaceous. *See* Cormorant, Neotropic, 12
  Pelagic, 12
Corvidae, 161
Corvus brachyrhynchos, 162
  corax, 162
  crypotoleucus, 162
  imparatus, 162
  ossifragus. See under *C. imparatus,* 162
  sinaloae. See under *C. imparatus,* 162
Cotinga(s), 136
  Cinnamon. *See* Becard, Cinnamon, 138
  Lovely, 136, **Pl. 26**
  Rose-throated. *See* Becard, Rose-throated, 139
  Streaked. *See* Attila, Bright-rumped, 137
  Whistling. *See* Piha, Rufous, 137
Cotinga amabilis, 136
Cotingidae, 136

Coturnicops noveboracensis, 51
Cowbird, Bronzed, 218
  Brown-headed, 219
  Giant, 218, **Pl. 39**
  Red-eyed. *See* Cowbird, Bronzed, 218
Cracidae, 40
Crake, Black. *See* Rail, Black, 51
  Gray-breasted, 51
  Ruddy, 51, **Pl. 10**
  Uniform, 50, **Pl. 10**
  Yellow. *See* Rail, Yellow, 51
  Yellow-breasted, 51, **Pl. 10**
Crane(s), 48
  Sandhill, 48
  Whooping, 48
Crane-Hawk. *See* Hawk, Crane, 29
Crax rubra, 43
Creeper(s), 169
  Brown, 169
  Giant. *See* Woodcreeper, Strong-billed, 125
  Laughing. *See* Woodcreeper, Ivory-billed, 126
  Souleyett's. *See* Woodcreeper, Streak-headed, 127
  See also Woodcreeper
Crocethia. See *Calidris,* 58
Crossbill, Red, 260
Crotophaga ani, 79
  sulcirostris, 79
Crow(s), 161
  American, 162
  Common. *See* Crow, American, 162
  Fish. *See under* Crow, Mexican, 162
  Mexican, 162, **Pl. 30**
  "Sinaloa." *See under* Crow, Mexican, 162
  "Tamaulipas." *See under* Crow, Mexican, 162
Crypturellus boucardi, 1
  cinnamomeus, 2
  soui, 1
Cuckoo(s), 78
  Black-billed, 78
  Lesser Ground-, 80, **Pl. 15**
  Mangrove, 78, **Pl. 15**
  Pheasant, 80, **Pl. 15**

Cuckoo (contd.)
  Rufous-rumped. *See* Cuckoo, Lesser Ground-, 80
  Squirrel, 79, **Pl. 15**
  Striped, 79, **Pl. 15**
  Yellow-billed, 78
Cuculidae, 78
Cuejo, White-collared. *See* Pauraque, 89
Curassow(s), 40
  Central American. *See* Curassow, Great, 43
  Great, 43, **Pl. 6**
Curlew, Eskimo, 59
  Long-billed, 58
  Mexican Stone. *See* Thick-knee, Double-striped, 61
Cyanerpes cyaneus, 201
  lucidus, 201
Cyanocitta stelleri, 167
Cyanocompsa cyanoides, 239
  parellina, 239
Cyanocorax dickeyi, 164
  yncas, 164
Cyanolyca cucullata, 165
  mirabilis, 165
  nana, 166
  pumilo, 166
Cyclarhidae, 194
Cyclarhis gujanensis, 194
Cygnus buccinator, 19
  columbianus, 19
Cynanthus latirostris, 98
  sordidus, 98
Cypseloides cryptus, 93
  niger, 93
  rutilus, 92
Crytonyx montezumae, 46
  ocellatus, 47

Dactylortyx thoracicus, 46
Daption capense, 5
Daptrius americanus, 37
Darters, 12
Deltarhynchus flammulatus, 147
Dendrocincla anabatina, 124
  homochroa, 124
Dendrocolaptes certhia, 126
  picumnus, 126
Dendrocolaptidae, 124
Dendrocopos arizonae, 122
  nuttallii, 122

Dendrocopos (contd.)
  scalaris, 122
  stricklandi, 123
  villosus, 122
Dendrocygna autumnalis, 19
  bicolor, 19
Dendroica aestiva. See *D. petechia,* 205
  auduboni, 206
  caerulescens, 206
  castanea, 208
  cerulea, 207
  chrysoparia, 207
  coronata, 206
  discolor, 208
  dominica, 207
  erithachorides, 205
  fusca, 207
  graciae, 208
  magnolia, 206
  nigrescens, 206
  occidentalis, 207
  palmarum, 208
  pensylvanica, 208
  petechia, 205
  pinus, 208
  striata, 208
  tigrina, 206
  townsendi, 207
  virens, 207
Dendrortyx barbatus, 43
  leucophrys, 44
  macroura, 43
Dichromanassa rufescens, 14
Dickcissel, 241
Diglossa baritula, 200
Diglossa, Mexican. *See* Flower-piercer, Cinnamon, 200
  Mountain. *See* Flower-piercer, Cinnamon, 200
Diomedea albatrus, 4
  immutabilis, 5
  nigripes, 4
Diomedeidae, 4
Dipper(s), 169
  American, 170
Dives dives, 220
Dolichonyx oryzivorus, 227
Doricha eliza, 105
  enicura, 105
Dove(s), 67
  Blue Ground-, 70, **Pl. 12**

Dove (contd.)
Caribbean, 71, **Pl. 11**
Cassin's. *See* Dove, Gray-chested, 71
Common Ground-, 69, **Pl. 12**
Gaumer. *See* Dove, Caribbean, 71
Gray-chested, 71, **Pl. 11**
Gray-headed, 71, **Pl. 11**
Inca, 69, **Pl. 12**
Little Ground-, *See* Dove, Plain-breasted Ground-, 69
Maroon-chested Ground-, 70, **Pl. 12**
Mondetour Ground-. *See* Dove, Maroon-chested Ground-, 70
Mourning, 68, **Pl. 11**
Plain-breasted Ground-, 69, **Pl. 12**
Purplish-backed Quail-, 72, **Pl. 12**
Rock, 67
Ruddy Ground-, 70, **Pl. 12**
Ruddy Quail-, 72, **Pl. 12**
Scaly Ground-. *See* Dove, Common Ground-, 69
Socorro, 68, **Pl. 11**
Verreaux's. *See* Dove, White-tipped, 71
White-bellied. *See* Dove, Caribbean, 71
White-faced Quail-, 72, **Pl. 12**
White-fronted. *See* Dove, White-tipped, 71
White-tipped, 71, **Pl. 11**
White-winged, 69, **Pl. 11**
Yucatán. *See* Dove, Zenaida, 69
Zenaida, 69, **Pl. 11**
Dowitcher, Common, 59
Long-billed, 59
Short-billed. *See* Dowitcher, Common, 59
Dromococcyx phasianellus, 80
Dryocopus lineatus, 119
Duck(s), 19
Black-bellied Tree-, 19
Fulvous Tree-, 19
Hawaiian, 21
Masked, 25
Mexican, 21
Mottled, 21

Duck (contd.)
Ring-necked, 22
Ruddy, 24
Wood, 22
Dumetella carolinensis, 182
Dunlin, 57
Dysithamnus mentalis, 132

Eagle(s), 26
Bald, 29
Black Hawk-, 36, **Pls. 4, 5**
Black-and-White Hawk-, 35, **Pl. 4**
Golden, 35
Harpy, 35, **Pl. 4**
Ornate Hawk-, 36, **Pl. 4**
Solitary, 32, **Pl. 5**
Tyrant Hawk-. *See* Eagle, Black Hawk-, 36
Egret, American. *See* Egret, Great, 14
Cattle, 14
Common. *See* Egret, Great, 14
Great, 14
Large. *See* Egret, Great, 14
Reddish, 14
Snowy, 14
Egretta thula, 14
Elaenia, Caribbean, 155, **Pl. 28**
Greenish, 156, **Pl. 28**
Lesser Antillean. *See* Elaenia, Caribbean, 155
Mountain, 156, **Pl. 28**
Yellow-bellied, 155, **Pl. 28**
Elaenia flavogaster, 155
frantzii, 156
martinica, 155
Elaninae, 26
Elanoides forficatus, 28
Elanus leucurus, 28
Electron carinatum, 113
Emerald, Canivett's. *See* Emerald, Fork-tailed, 98
Fork-tailed, 98, **Pls. 18, 20**
White-bellied, 100, **Pl. 18**
Empidonax affinis, 150
albigularis, 149
alnorum, 149
difficilis, 151
flavescens, 151
flaviventris, 149

Empidonax (contd.)
  fulvifrons, 151
  griseus. See *E. wrightii,* 150
  hammondi, 150
  minimus, 150
  oberholseri, 150
  traillii, 149
  virescens, 149
  wrightii, 150
Endomychura hypoleuca, 66
  hypoleuca craverii, 66
Eremophila alpestris, 158
Ereunetes. See *Calidris,* 58
Ergaticus ruber, 214
  versicolor, 214
Erolia. See *Calidris,* 57–58
Eucometis penicillata, 234
Eudocimus albus, 18
Eugenes fulgens, 104
Eumomota superciliosa, 113
Euphagus carolinus, 219
  cyanocephalus, 220
Eupherusa cyanophrys. See under *E. eximia,* 102
  eximia, 102
Euphonia, Blue-hooded, 228, **Pl. 43**
  Bonaparte's. *See* Euphonia, Yellow-throated, 229
  Godman's. *See* Euphonia, Scrub, 229
  Gould's. *See* Euphonia, Olive-backed, 229
  Lesson's. *See* Euphonia, scrub, 229
  Olive-backed, 229, **Pl. 42**
  Scrub, 229, **Pl. 42**
  White-vented, 228
  Yellow-throated, 229, **Pl. 42**
Euphonia affinis, 229
  elegantissima, 228
  godmani. See *E. affinis,* 229
  gouldi, 229
  hirundinacea, 229
  lauta. See *E. hirundinacea,* 229
  minuta, 228
  musica. See under *E. elegantissima,* 228
Euptilotis neoxenus, 109
Eurypyga helias, 53
Eurypygidae, 52
Euthlypis lachrymosa, 214

Fairy, Barrot's. *See* Fairy, Purple-crowned, 104
  Purple-crowned, 104, **Pl. 18**
Falco columbarius, 39
  deiroleucus, 40
  femoralis, 39
  mexicanus, 39
  peregrinus, 40
  rufigularis, 39
  sparverius, 39
Falcon(s), 36
  Aplomado, 39, **Pl. 3**
  Barred Forest-, 38, **Pl. 3**
  Bat, 39, **Pl. 3**
  Collared Forest-, 38, **Pl. 3**
  Laughing, 37, **Pl. 3**
  Orange-breasted, 40, **Pl. 3**
  Peregrine, 40
  Prairie, 39
  White-throated. *See* Falcon, Bat, 39
Falconidae, 36
Finch(es), 235
  Cassin's, 259
  Chestnut-capped Brush-, 245, **Pl. 47**
  Grassland Yellow-, 244, **Pl. 45**
  Green-striped Brush-, 245, **Pl. 47**
  House, 259
  Lesser Seed-. *See under* Finch, Thick-billed Seed-, 242
  Plain-breasted Brush-, 245
  Purple, 258
  Rufous-capped Brush-, 244, **Pl. 45**
  Slaty, 244
  Striped. *See* Finch, Green-striped Brush-, 245
  Stripe-headed Brush-. *See under* Finch. Green-striped Brush-, 245
  Thick-billed Seed-, 242, **Pl. 46**
  Tuxtla Brush-. *See* Finch, Plain-breasted Brush-, 245
  White-naped Brush-, 244, **Pl. 45**
  Yellow-throated Brush-, 245, **Pl. 45**
Finfoot(s), 52
  American. *See* Sungrebe, 52
Flamingo(s), 18

Flamingo (contd.)
American, 18
Flatbill, Eye-ringed, 154, **Pl. 28**
Gray-headed. *See* Flycatcher,
Yellow-olive, 153
Short-billed. *See* Flatbill, Eye-
ringed, 154
Flicker, Common. *See under*
Flicker, Red-shafted, 117
Gilded, 118
"Guatemalan." *See under*
Flicker, Red-shafted, 117
Mexican. *See* Flicker, Red-
shafted, 117
Red-shafted, 117
Yellow-shafted, 117
Florida caerulea, 14
Florisuga mellivora, 96
Flower-piercer, Cinnamon, 200,
Pl. 37
Flycatcher, Acadian, 149
Alder, 149
Ash-throated, 145, **Pl. 27**
Beardless. *See* Tyrannulet,
Northern Beardless, 156
Belted, 152, **Pl. 28**
Bent-billed. *See* Bentbill,
Northern, 155
Boat-billed, 144, **Pl. 27**
Brown-crested, 146, **Pl. 27**
Buff-breasted, 151, **Pl. 28**
Common Tody-, 154, **Pl. 29**
Coues'. *See* Pewee, Greater,
148
Crested. *See* Flycatcher,
Great-crested, 145
Derby. *See* Kiskadee, Great,
144
Dusky, 150
Dusky-capped, 147, **Pl. 27**
Flammulated, 147, **Pl. 27**
Fork-tailed, 141, **Pl. 29**
Giraud's. *See* Flycatcher, So-
cial, 144
Gray, 150
Great-crested, 145, **Pl. 27**
Hammond's, 150
Kiskadee. *See* Kiskadee, Great,
144
Least, 150
Mexican. *See* Flycatcher,
Brown-crested, 146

Flycatcher (contd.)
Mexican Royal-. *See* Fly-
catcher, Northern Royal-,
153
Northern Royal-, 153, **Pl. 29**
Northern Tody-. *See* Fly-
catcher, Common Tody-, 154
Nutting's, 145, **Pl. 27**
Ochre-bellied, 157, **Pl. 29**
Olivaceous. *See* Flycatcher,
Dusky-capped, 147
Olive-sided, 147
Pale-throated. *See* Flycatcher,
Nutting's, 145
Pileated, 152, **Pl. 28**
Pine, 150, **Pl. 28**
Piratic, 143, **Pl. 27**
Placid. *See* Elaenia, Greenish,
156
Royal. *See* Flycatcher, North-
ern Royal-, 153
Ruddy-tailed, 152, **Pl. 28**
Scissor-tailed, 140
Sepia-capped, 157, **Pl. 28**
Slate-headed Tody-, 154, **Pl.
29**
Social, 144, **Pl. 27**
Streaked, 143, **Pl. 27**
Striped. *See* Flycatcher, Pira-
tic, 143
Sulphur-bellied, 143, **Pl. 27**
Sulphur-rumped, 152, **Pl. 28**
Swallow-tailed. *See* Fly-
catcher, Fork-tailed, 141
Traill's. *See* Flycatcher, Wil-
low, 149
Tufted, 148, **Pl. 28**
Vermilion, 140, **Pl. 29**
Vermilion-crowned. *See* Fly-
catcher, Social, 144
Western, 151
White-eyed. *See* Flycatcher,
Yellow-olive, 153
White-throated, 149, **Pl. 28**
White-tipped Tody-. *See* Fly-
catcher, Common Tody-, 154
Wied's. *See* Flycatcher, Brown-
crested, 146
Willow, 149
Wright's. *See* Flycatcher,
Dusky, 150
Yellow-bellied, 149

Flycatcher (contd.)
  Yellowish, 151, **Pl. 28**
  Yellow-olive, 153, **Pl. 28**
  Yucatán, 146, **Pl. 27**
Flycatchers, Tyrant, 140
Foliage-gleaner, Buff-throated, 129, **Pl. 25**
  Ruddy, 129, **Pl. 25**
  Scaly. *See* Foliage-gleaner, Scaly-throated, 128
  Scaly-throated, 128, **Pl. 25**
Forest-Falcon. *See* Falcon
Formicariidae, 130
Formicarius analis, 134
Forpus cyanopygius, 75
Fregata magnificens, 13
  minor, 13
Fregatidae, 13
Frigatebird(s), 13
  Great, 13
  Magnificent, 13
  Minor. *See* Frigatebird, Great, 13
Fringillidae, 235
Fulica americana, 52
Fulmar, Antarctic. *See* Fulmar, Northern, 5
  Northern, 5
  Silver-gray. *See under* Fulmar, Northern, 5
  Southern. *See under* Fulmar, Northern, 5
Fulmaris glacialis, 5
  glacialoides. See under *F. glacialis,* 5
Furnariidae, 128

Gadwall, 21
Galbula ruficauda, 114
  ruficauda melanogenia, 114 (115)
Galbulidae, 114
Gallinago gallinago, 59
Gallinula chloropus, 51
Gallinule(s), 49
  Common, 51
  Florida. *See* Gallinule, Common, 51
  Purple, 52
Gannet(s), 10
  Northern, 11

Gavia adamsii, 3
  arctica, 2
  immer, 3
  stellata, 2
Gaviidae, 2
Geese, 19
Gelochelidon nilotica, 64
Geococcyx californianus, 80
  velox, 80
Geothlypis beldingi, 210
  chapalensis, 211
  flavovelata, 210
  nelsoni, 211
  poliocephala, 211
  speciosa, 211
  trichas, 210, 211
Geotrygon albifacies, 72
  lawrencii, 72
  linearis. See *G. albifacies,* 72
  montana, 72
Geranospiza caerulescens, 29
  nigra. See *G. caerulescens,* 29
Glaucidium brasilianum, 85
  gnoma, 84
  minutissimum, 84
Glyphorhynchus spirurus, 125
Gnatcatcher(s), 189
  Black-capped, 190, **Pl. 33**
  Black-tailed, 190, **Pl. 33**
  Blue-gray, 189, **Pl. 33**
  Plumbeous. *See* Gnatcatcher, Black-tailed, 190
  Tropical, 190, **Pl. 33**
  White-browed. *See* Gnatcatcher, Tropical, 190
  White-lored, 189, **Pl. 33**
  Yucatán. *See* Gnatcatcher, White-lored, 189
Gnatwren(s), 189
  Long-billed, 191, **Pl. 33**
Goatsuckers. *See* Nightjars, 89
Godwit, Hudsonian, 59
  Marbled, 59
Goldeneye, Common, 24
Goldentail, Blue-throated, 100, **Pl. 19**
Goldfinch, American, 260
  Dark-backed, 260
  Lawrence's, 260
  Lesser. *See* Goldfinch, Dark-backed, 260

Goosander. *See* Merganser, Common, 24
Goose, Blue, 20
　Cackling. *See under* Goose, Canada, 20
　Canada, 20
　Lesser Canada. *See under* Goose, Canada, 20
　Richardson's Canada. *See under* Goose, Canada, 20
　Ross', 20
　Snow, 20
　Tundra Canada. *See under* Goose, Canada, 20
　Western Canada. *See under* Goose, Canada, 20
　White-fronted, 19
Goshawk, Northern, 30
Grackle, Boat-tailed. *See under* Grackle, Great-tailed, 219
　Common, 219
　Great-tailed, 219
　Pacific. *See* Grackle, Great-tailed, 219
　Slender-billed, 219
Grallaria guatimalensis, 134
Granatellus sallaei, 212
　venustus, 212
Grassquit, Blue-black, 243, **Pl. 46**
　Olive. *See* Grassquit, Yellow-faced, 241
　Yellow-faced, 241, **Pl. 46**
Grebe(s), 3
　Atitlán, 4, **4**
　Black-necked. *See* Grebe, Eared, 3
　Eared, 3
　Horned, 3
　Least, 3
　Mexican. *See* Grebe, Least, 3
　Pied-billed, 4
　Western, 3
Green-Kingfisher. *See* Kingfisher
Greenlet, Gray-headed. *See* Greenlet, Lesser, 200
　Lesser, 200, **Pl. 36**
　Tawny-crowned, 200, **Pl. 36**
Grosbeak(s), 235
　Abeille's. *See* Grosbeak, Hooded, 258
　Bishop. *See* Grosbeak, Black-faced, 237

Grosbeak (contd.)
　Black-faced, 237, **Pl. 45**
　Black-headed, 238
　Blue, 238
　Blue-black, 239, **Pl. 46**
　Crimson-collared, 237, **Pls. 45, 46**
　Evening, 258
　Hooded, 258, **Pl. 45**
　Rose-breasted, 238
　Yellow, 238, **Pl. 45**
Ground-Chat. *See* Yellowthroat, Gray-crowned, 211
Ground-Cuckoo. *See* Cuckoo
Ground-Dove. *See* Dove
Ground-Sparrow. *See* Sparrow
Gruidae, 48
Grus americana, 48
　canadensis, 48
Guan(s), 40
　Crested, 42, **Pl. 6**
　Horned, 42, **Pl. 7**
　Little. *See* Penelopina, Black, 42
Guiraca caerulea, 238
Gull(s), 62
　Black-headed, 63
　Bonaparte's, 63
　California, 62
　Franklin's, 63
　Glaucous, 63
　Glaucous-winged, 63
　Heermann's, 62
　Herring, 62
　Laughing, 63
　Ring-billed, 62
　Sabine's, 64
　Western, 63
　Yellow-legged. *See under* Gull, Western, 63
Gygis alba, 65
Gymnocichla nudiceps, 133
Gymnogyps californianus, 26
Gymnorhinus cyanocephalus, 162
Gymnostinops montezuma, 217

Habia fuscicauda, 234
　rubica, 233
Haematopodidae, 53
Haematopus bachmani, 54
　palliatus, 54
Haliaeetus leucocephalus, 29

Halocyptena microsoma, 8
Haplospiza rusticus, 244
Harpagus bidentatus, 28
Harpia harpyja, 35
Harpyhaliaetus solitarius, 32
Harrier(s), 26
    Northern. *See* Hawk, Marsh, 30
Hawk(s), 26
    Barred Forest. *See* Falcon, Barred Forest-, 38
    Bay-winged, 32, **Pl. 5**
    Bicolored, 31, **Pl. 2**
    Black-collared, 32, **Pl. 2**
    Black Crab-. *See* Hawk, Common Black, 31
    "Black Crane." *See* Hawk, Crane, 29
    Broad-winged, 33
    Chestnut. *See* Hawk, Black-collared, 32
    Collared Forest. *See* Falcon, Collared Forest-, 38
    Common Black, 31, **Pl. 5**
    Cooper's, 30
    Crane, 29, **Pl. 5**
    Duck. *See* Falcon, Peregrine, 40
    Ferruginous, 35
    Gray, 33, **Pl. 3**
    Great Black, 31, **Pl. 5**
    Harris'. *See* Hawk, Bay-winged, 32
    Large-billed. *See* Hawk, Roadside, 33
    Lesser Black. *See* Hawk, Common Black, 31
    Mangrove Black. *See under* Hawk, Common Black, 31
    Marsh, 30
    Mexican Black. *See* Hawk, Common Black, 31
    Pacific Crab-. *See* Hawk, Common Black, 31
    Pigeon. *See* Merlin, 39
    Red-shouldered, 33
    Red-tailed, 34
    Ridgway's Black. *See* Hawk, Great Black, 31
    Roadside, 33, **Pl. 3**
    Rough-legged, 35
    Sharp-shinned, 30

Hawk (contd.)
    Short-tailed, 34, **Pl. 5**
    Sparrow. *See* Kestrel, American, 39
    Swainson's, 34
    White, 30, **Pl. 3**
    White-breasted, 30, **Pl. 2**
    White-tailed, 34, **Pl. 3**
    Zone-tailed, 34, **Pl. 5**
Hawk-Eagle. *See* Eagle
Heliomaster constantii, 104
    longirostris, 105
Heliornis fulica, 52
Heliornithidae, 52
Heliothrix barroti, 104
Helmitheros vermivorus, 203
Henicorhina leucophrys, 177
    leucosticta, 177
Hermit, Boucard's. *See* Hermit, Little, 95
    Little, 95, **Pl. 20**
    Long-billed. *See* Hermit, Long-tailed, 94
    Long-tailed, 94, **Pl. 20**
Heron, Agami. *See* Heron, Chestnut-bellied, 14
    Banded Tiger-. *See* Heron, Rufescent Tiger-, 15
    Bare-throated Tiger-, 16, **Pl. 1**
    Black-crowned Night-, 15
    Boat-billed, 17, **Pl. 1**
    Chestnut-bellied, 14, **Pl. 1**
    Great Blue, 13
    Great White, 14
    Green, 15
    Lineated Tiger-. *See* Heron, Rufescent Tiger-, 15
    Little Blue, 14
    Louisiana. *See* Heron, Tricolored, 14
    Rufescent Tiger-, 15, **Pl. 1**
    Tricolored, 14
    Yellow-crowned Night-, 15
Herons, 13
    Boat-billed, 16
Herpetotheres cachinnans, 37
Hesperiphona abeillei, 258
    vespertina, 258
Heteroscelus incanus, 56
Himantopus mexicanus, 60
Hirundinidae, 158
Hirundo rustica, 161

Honeycreeper(s), 200
  Blue. *See* Honeycreeper, Red-
    legged, 201
  Green, 201, **Pl. 37**
  Highland. *See* Flower-piercer,
    Cinnamon, 200
  Red-legged, 201, **Pl. 37**
  Shining, 201, **Pl. 37**
  Yellow-legged. *See* Honey-
    creeper, Shining, 201
Horneros. *See* Ovenbirds, 128
House-Wren. *See* Wren
Hummingbird(s), 92
  Abeille's. *See* Hummingbird,
    Emerald-chinned, 97
  Allen's, 108
  Amethyst-throated, 103, **Pls.
    19, 20**
  Anna's, 107
  Azure-crowned. *See* Azure-
    crown, Red-billed, 100
  Beautiful, 106, **Pl. 19**
  Berylline, 101, **Pl. 18**
  Black-chinned, 107
  Black-fronted, 99, **Pls. 18, 20**
  Blue-capped. *See under* Hum-
    mingbird, Stripe-tailed, 102
  Blue-tailed, 101, **Pl. 18**
  Blue-throated, 103, **Pls. 19, 20**
  Broad-billed, 98, **Pls. 19, 20**
  Broad-tailed, 108
  Buff-bellied. *See* Humming-
    bird, Fawn-breasted, 101
  Bumblebee, 107, **Pl. 19**
  Calliope, 107
  Cazique. *See* Hummingbird,
    Amethyst-throated, 103
  Cinnamon, 101, **Pl. 20**
  Costa's, 107
  Cuvier's. *See* Hummingbird,
    Scaly-breasted, 95
  Doubleday's. *See* Humming-
    bird, Broad-billed, 98
  Dupont's. *See* Hummingbird,
    Sparkling-tailed, 106
  Dusky, 98, **Pl. 20**
  Elicia's. *See* Hummingbird,
    Blue-throated, 103
  Elliot's. *See* Hummingbird,
    Wine-throated, 107
  Emerald-chinned, 97, **Pl. 18**
  Fawn-breasted, 101, **Pl. 18**

Hummingbird (contd.)
  Garnet-throated, 104, **Pl. 19**
  Green-fronted, 102, **Pl. 18**
  Heloise's. *See* Hummingbird,
    Bumblebee, 107
  Jacobin. *See* Jacobin, White-
    necked, 96
  Lucifer, 106, **Pls. 19, 20**
  Magnificent, 104, **Pls. 18, 20**
  Oaxaca. *See under* Humming-
    bird, Stripe-tailed, 102
  Reiffer's. *See* Hummingbird,
    Rufous-tailed, 102
  Rivoli's. *See* Hummingbird,
    Magnificent, 104
  Ruby-throated, 106
  Rufous, 108
  Rufous-tailed, 102, **Pl. 18**
  Scaly-breasted, 95, **Pl. 18**
  Sparkling-tailed, 106, **Pls. 19,
    20**
  Stripe-tailed, 102, **Pls. 18, 20**
  Violet-crowned, 102, **Pl. 18**
  White-eared, 99, **Pls. 18, 20**
  White-tailed. *See* Humming-
    bird, Stripe-tailed, 102
  Wine-throated, 107
  Xantus'. *See* Hummingbird,
    Black-fronted, 99
Hydranassa tricolor, 14
Hydrobatidae, 8
Hydroprogne caspia, 64
Hylocharis eliciae, 100
  leucotis, 99
  xantusii, 99
Hylocichla mustelina, 186
Hylomanes momotula, 113
Hylophilus decurtatus, 200
  ochraceiceps, 200
Hylophilus, Gray-headed. *See*
  Greenlet, Lesser, 200
  Tawny-crowned. *See* Greenlet,
    Tawny-crowned, 200
Hylorchilus sumichrasti, 178
Hypomorphnus. See *Buteogallus,*
  31

Ibis(es), 18
  American Wood-. *See* Stork,
    Wood, 17
  Glossy. *See under* Ibis, White-
    faced, 18

Ibis (contd.)
  White, 18
  White-faced, 18
Icteria virens, 212
Icteridae, 216
Icterus abeillei, 225
  auratus, 225
  bullockii, 224, 225
  chrysater, 223
  cucullatus, 222
  dominicensis. See under *I. prosthemelas*, 221
  fuertesi, 221
  galbula, 224, 225
  graduacuada, 223
  graysoni. See under *I. sclateri*, 225
  gularis, 224
  maculialatus, 222
  mesomelas, 222
  parisorum, 221
  pectoralis, 223
  prosthemelas, 221
  pustulatus. See under *I. sclateri*, 225
  sclateri, 225
  spurius, 220, 221
  wagleri, 221
Ictinia misisippiensis, 29
  plumbea, 29
Iridoprocne. See *Tachycineta*, 158–59
Ivorybill, Guatemalan. See Woodpecker, Pale-billed, 123
  Imperial. See Woodpecker, Imperial, 123
Ixobrychus exilis, 16
Ixoreus naevius, 185

Jabiru, 17, **Pl. 1**
Jabiru mycteria, 17
Jacamar(s), 114
  Black-chinned. See Jacamar, Rufous-tailed, 114
  Rufous-tailed, 114, **Pl. 22**
Jacana(s), 53
  American. See Jacana, Northern, 53
  Northern, 53, **Pl. 10**
Jacana spinosa, 53
Jacanidae, 53

Jacobin, White-necked, 96, **Pls. 19, 20**
Jaeger(s), 61
  Long-tailed, 62
  Parasitic, 62
  Pomarine, 61
Jay(s), 161
  Azure-hooded, 165, **Pl. 31**
  Beechey's. See Jay, Purplish-backed, 165
  Black-and-Blue. See Jay, San Blas, 164
  Black-throated, 166, **Pl. 31**
  Black-throated Magpie, 163, **Pl. 30**
  Brown, 163, **Pl. 30**
  Bushy-crested, 165, **Pl. 31**
  Dickey's. See Jay, Tufted, 164
  Dwarf, 166, **Pl. 31**
  Gray-breasted, 166, **Pl. 31**
  Green, 164, **Pl. 30**
  Hartlaub's. See Jay, Bushy-crested, 165
  Mexican. See Jay, Gray-breasted, 166
  Omilteme. See Jay, White-throated, 165
  Pinyon, 162
  Plain-tailed Brown. See under Jay, Brown, 163
  Purplish-backed, 165, **Pl. 31**
  San Blas, 164, **Pl. 31**
  Scrub, 166, **Pl. 31**
  Short-crested. See Jay, Steller's, 167
  Steller's, 167, **Pl. 31**
  Tufted, 164, **Pl. 30**
  Unicolored, 166, **Pl. 31**
  White-throated, 165, **Pl. 31**
  White-throated Magpie, 163, **Pl. 30**
  White-tipped Brown. See under Jay, Brown, 163
  Yucatán, 164, **Pl. 31**
Junco, Arizona. See Junco, Yellow-eyed, 257
  Baird's. See Junco, Yellow-eyed, 257
  Chiapas. See Junco, Yellow-eyed, 257
  Dark-eyed. See Junco, Oregon, 257. See also under Junco,

Junco, Dark-eyed (contd.)
  Yellow-eyed, 257
  Gray-headed, 257
  Guadalupe. *See* Junco, Oregon, 257
  Guatemalan. *See* Junco, Yellow-eyed, 257
  Mexican. *See* Junco, Yellow-eyed, 257
  Oregon, 257
  Red-backed. *See* Junco, Gray-headed, 257
  Slate-colored, 256
  Yellow-eyed, 257, **Pl. 48**
Junco caniceps, 257
  hyemalis, 256, 257
  hyemalis oreganus, 257
  insularis. See *J. hyemalis,* 257
  phaeonotus, 257

Kestrel, American, 39
Killdeer, 55
Kingbird, Arkansas. *See* Kingbird, Western, 141
  Cassin's, 141, **Pl. 27**
  Couch's. *See* Kingbird, Tropical, 142
  Eastern, 141
  Giant, 143
  Gray, 142
  Thick-billed, 142, **Pl. 27**
  Tropical, 142, **Pl. 27**
  Western, 141, **Pl. 27**
Kingfisher(s), 111
  Amazon, 112, **Pl. 22**
  Belted, 111
  Green, 112, **Pl. 22**
  Least Green-. *See* Kingfisher, Pygmy, 112
  Little Green-. *See* Kingfisher, Green, 112
  Pygmy, 112, **Pl. 22**
  Ringed, 111, **Pl. 22**
Kinglet(s), 189
  Golden-crowned, 191
  Ruby-crowned, 191
Kiskadee, Great, 144, **Pl. 27**
Kite(s), 26
  Cayenne. *See* Kite, Gray-headed, 27
  Double-toothed, 28, **Pl. 2**
  Everglade. *See* Kite, Snail, 28

Kite (contd.)
  Gray-headed, 27, **Pl. 2**
  Hook-billed, 27, **Pl. 2**
  Mississippi, 29, **Pl. 2**
  Plumbeous, 29, **Pl. 2**
  Snail, 28, **Pl. 5**
  Swallow-tailed, 28
  White-tailed, 28
Kittiwake, Black-legged, 63
Knot, Red, 57

Lampornis amethystinus, 103
  clemenciae, 103
  viridipallens, 103
Lamprolaima rhami, 104
Laniidae, 193
Lanio aurantius, 234
Laniocera rufescens, 137
Lanius ludovicianus, 193
Laridae, 62
Lark(s), 158
  Horned, 158
Larus argentatus, 62
  atricilla, 63
  californicus, 62
  delawarensis, 62
  glaucescens, 63
  heermanni, 62
  hyperboreus, 63
  occidentalis, 63
  occidentalis livens, 63
  philadelphia, 63
  pipixcan, 63
  ridibundus, 63
Laterallus exilis, 51
  jamaicensis, 51
  ruber, 51
Leafscraper, Guatemalan. *See* Leafscraper, Scaly-throated, 130
  Mexican. *See* Leafscraper, Tawny-throated, 130
  Scaly-throated, 130, **Pl. 25**
  Tawny-throated, 130, **Pl. 25**
Legatus leucophaius, 143
Lepidocolaptes affinis, 128
  leucogaster, 127
  souleyetti, 127
Leptodon cayanensis, 27
Leptogon, Brown-capped. *See* Flycatcher, Sepia-capped, 157

Leptopogon amaurocephalus, 157
Leptotila cassinii, 71
  jamaicensis, 71
  plumbeiceps, 71
  verreauxi, 71
Leucophoyx. See *Egretta,* 14
Leucopternis albicollis, 30
Limnodromus griseus, 59
  scolopaceus, 59
Limnothlypis swainsonii, 202
Limosa fedoa, 59
  haemastica, 59
Limpkin(s), 48, 49
Lipaugus unirufus, 137
Lobipes lobatus, 60
Longspur, Chestnut-collared, 258
  Lapland, 258
  McCown's, 257
Loon(s), 2
  Arctic, 2
  Black-throated. *See* Loon, Arctic, 2
  Common, 3
  Pacific. *See* Loon, Arctic, 2
  Red-throated, 2
  Yellow-billed, 3
Lophodytes cucullatus, 24
Lophornis delattrei, 97
Lophortyx californica, 44
  douglasii, 44
  gambelii, 44
Lophostrix cristata, 84
Loxia curvirostra, 260

Macaw(s), 72
  Military, 73, **Pl. 13**
  Scarlet, 73, **Pl. 13**
Macawlet, Maroon-fronted. *See* Parrot, Maroon-fronted, 74
  Thick-billed. *See* Parrot, Thick-billed, 74
Mallard, 21
Malacoptila panamensis, 115
Manacus candei, 135
Manakin(s), 134
  Cande's. *See* Manakin, White-collared, 135
  Gray-headed, 134
  Long-tailed, 135, **Pl. 26**
  Red-capped, 135, **Pl. 26**
  Thrushlike, 136, **Pl. 26**

Manakin (contd.)
  White-collared, 135, **Pl. 26**
  Yellow-thighed. *See* Manakin, Red-capped, 135
Mango, Green-breasted, 97, **Pl. 19**
  Prevost's. *See* Mango, Green-breasted, 97
Man-o'-War Birds. *See* Frigate-birds, 13
Martin, Caribbean. *See* Martin, Snowy-bellied, 160
  Cuban, 159
  Gray-breasted, 160, **Pl. 17**
  Purple, 159
  Sinaloa. *See* Martin, Snowy-bellied, 160
  Snowy-bellied, 160, **Pl. 17**
  White-bellied. *See* Martin, Snowy-bellied, 160
Meadowlark(s), 216
  Common. *See* Meadowlark, Eastern, 226
  Eastern, 226
  Western, 227
Megaceryle alcyon, 111
  torquata, 111
Megarynchus pitangua, 144
Melanerpes formicivorus, 119
  lewis, 119
Melanitta deglandi, 23
  nigra, 23
  perspicillata, 23
Melanoptila glabrirostris, 182
Melanotis caerulescens, 181
  hypoleucus, 182
Meleagrididae, 47
Meleagris gallopavo, 47
Melospiza georgiana, 255
  lincolnii, 255
  melodia, 255
Melozone biarcuatum, 248
  kieneri, 248
  leucotis, 249
Merganser, Common, 24
  Hooded, 24
  Red-breasted, 24
Mergus merganser, 24
  serrator, 24
Merlin, 39
Micrastur ruficollis, 38
  semitorquatus, 38
Micrathene whitneyi, 85

Microcerculus marginatus [*philomela*], 178
Micropalama himantopus, 58
Microrhopias quixensis, 132
"Mimic-thrushes." *See* Thrashers and Mockingbirds, 179
Mimidae, 179
Mimodes graysoni, 181
Mimus gilvus, 182
  polyglottos, 182
Mitrephanes phaeocercus, 148
Mniotilta varia, 202
Mockingbird(s), 179
  Blue, 181, **Pl. 34**
  Blue-and-White, 182, **Pl. 34**
  Common. *See* Mockingbird, Northern, 182
  Graceful. *See* Mockingbird, Tropical, 182
  Mexican Blue. *See* Mockingbird, Blue, 181
  Northern, 182
  Tropical, 182, **Pl. 34**
  White-breasted Blue. *See* Mockingbird, Blue-and-White, 182
Molothrus aeneus, 218
  ater, 219
Momotidae, 112
Momotus lessonii. See *M. momota,* 114
  mexicanus, 114
  momota, 114
Morococcyx erythropygus, 80
Morus bassanus, 11
Motacilla alba, 191
Motacillidae, 191
Motmot(s), 112
  Blue-crowned, 114, **Pl. 22**
  Blue-throated, 113, **Pl. 22**
  Chestnut-headed. *See* Motmot, Russet-crowned, 114
  Keel-billed, 113, **Pl. 22**
  Lesson's. *See* Motmot, Blue-crowned, 114
  Russet-crowned, 114, **Pl. 22**
  Tody, 113, **Pl. 22**
  Turquoise-browed, 113, **Pl. 22**
Mountain-gem, Green-throated, 103, **Pl. 18**
Mourner, Brown. *See* Manakin, Thrushlike, 136

Mourner (contd.)
  Rufous, 137, **Pl. 26**
  Speckled, 137
Murre, Common, 66
Murrelet, Ancient, 66
  "Craveri's." *See under* Murrelet, Xantus', 66
  Xantus', 66
Muscivora forficata, 140
  tyrannus, 141
Muscovy, 23, **23**
Myadestes obscurus, 185
  townsendi, 185
  unicolor, 186
Mycteria americana, 17
Myiarchus cinerascens, 145
  crinitus, 145
  nuttingi, 145
  tuberculifer, 147
  tyrannulus, 146
  yucatanensis, 146
Myiobius sulphureipygius, 152
Myiobius, Sulphur-rumped. *See* Flycatcher, Sulphur-rumped, 152
Myioborus miniatus, 214
  picta, 213
Myiodynastes luteiventris, 143
  maculatus, 143
Myiopagis viridicata, 156
Myiozetetes similis, 144
Myrmotherula schisticolor, 132

Neochloe brevipennis, 199
Nighthawk, Booming. *See* Nighthawk, Common, 89
  Common, 89
  Lesser, 89
  Trilling. *See* Nighthawk, Lesser, 89
Night-Heron. *See* Heron
Nightingale-Thrush. *See* Thrush
Nightjar(s), 89
  Buff-collared, 91, **Pl. 15**
  Spot-tailed, 91, **Pl. 15**
  Tawny-collared, 90, **Pl. 15**
Noddy, Black. *See* Noddy, White-capped, 65
  Brown, 65
  Lesser. *See* Noddy, White-capped, 65
  White-capped, 65

Notharchus macrorhynchos, 115
Notiochelidon pileata, 159
Nucifraga columbiana, 162
Numenius americanus, 58
  borealis, 59
  phaeopus, 59
Nutcracker, Clark's, 162
Nuthatch(es), 168
  Pygmy, 169
  Red-breasted, 168
  White-breasted, 168
Nuttallornis. See *Contopus,* 147
Nyctanassa violacea, 15
Nyctibiidae, 88
Nyctibius grandis, 88
  griseus, 88
Nycticorax nycticorax, 15
Nyctidromus albicollis, 89

Oceanites oceanicus, 8
Oceanodroma castro, 9
  homochroa, 9
  leucorhoa, 8
  leucorhoa chapmani, 8
  leucorhoa socorroensis, 8
  leucorhoa willetti, 8
  macrodactyla, 8
  markhami, 9
  melania, 9
  tethys, 9
Odontophorus guttatus, 46
Oldsquaw, 24
Oncostoma cinereigulare, 155
Onychorhynchus mexicanus, 153
Oporornis agilis, 209
  formosus, 209
  philadelphia, 209
  tolmiei, 210
Oreophasis derbianus, 42
Oreortyx picta, 44
Oreoscoptes montanus, 181
Oriole(s), 216
  Abeille's. *See* Oriole, Black-
    backed, 225
  Altamira, 224, **Pl. 41**
  Baltimore, 224, **Pl. 40**
  Bar-winged, 222, **Pl. 40**
  Black-backed, 225, **Pl. 41**
  Black-cowled, 221, **Pl. 40**
  Black-headed, 223, **Pl. 40**
  Black-throated. *See* Oriole, Al-
    tamira, 224

Oriole (contd.)
  Black-vented, 221, **Pl. 40**
  Bullock's, 224, **Pl. 41**
  Flame-headed.
    Oriole, Streak-backed, 225
  Fuertes'. *See* Oriole, Ochre, 221
  Hooded, 222, **Pl. 41**
  Lesson's. *See* Oriole, Black-
    cowled, 221
  Lichtenstein's. *See* Oriole, Al-
    tamira, 224
  Mayan. *See* Oriole, Yellow-
    backed, 223
  Ochre, 221, **Pl. 41**
  Orange, 225, **Pl. 40**
  Orchard, 220, **Pl. 41**
  Scarlet-headed. *See* Oriole,
    Streak-backed, 225
  Sclater's. *See* Oriole, Streak-
    backed, 225
  Scott's, 221, **Pl. 40**
  Spot-breasted, 223, **Pl. 41**
  Streak-backed, 225, **Pl. 41**
  Tres Marías. *See under* Oriole,
    Streak-backed, 225
  Underwood's. *See* Oriole, Yel-
    low-backed, 223
  Wagler's. *See* Oriole, Black-
    vented, 221
  Yellow-backed, 223, **Pl. 40**
  Yellow-tailed, 222, **Pl. 41**
Oriturus superciliosus, 249
Ornithion semiflavum, 157
Oropendola, Chestnut-headed,
    217, **Pl. 39**
  Montezuma, 217, **Pl. 39**
  Wagler's. *See* Oropendola,
    Chestnut-headed, 217
Ortalis leucogastra, 42
  poliocephala, 41
  vetula, 40
  wagleri. See under *O. polio-
    cephala,* 41
Oryzoborus angolensis. See
    under *O. funereus,* 242
  funereus, 242
Osprey(s), 26
Otophanes mcleodii, 90
  yucatanicus, 90
Otus asio, 81, 82
  barbarus, 83
  cooperi, 82

Otus (contd.)
  flammeolus, 81
  guatemalae, 83
  seductus, 82
  trichopsis, 82
  vinaceus, 82
Ouzel, Water. *See* Dipper, American, 170
Ovenbird(s), 128, 209
  Buff-throated. *See* Foliage-gleaner, Buff-throated, 129
  Least. *See* Xenops, Plain, 129
  Mountain. *See* Foliage-gleaner, Scaly-throated, 128
  Ruddy. *See* Foliage-gleaner, Ruddy, 129
  Scaly-throated. *See* Leaf-scraper, Scaly-throated, 130
  Tawny-throated. *See* Leaf-scraper, Tawny-throated, 130
Owl(s), 81
  Acadian Saw-whet. *See* Owl, Northern Saw-whet, 87
  Balsas Screech-, 82
  Barn, 81
  Barred, 86
  Bearded Screech-, 83
  Black-and-White, 86, **Pl. 16**
  Black-and-White Wood-. *See* Owl, Black-and-White, 86
  Bridled Screech-. *See* Owl, Bearded Screech-, 83
  Burrowing, 85
  Common Screech-, 81
  Cooper's. *See* Owl, Pacific Screech-, 82
  Crested, 84, **Pl. 16**
  Eastern Screech-. *See* Owl, Common Screech-, 81
  Elf, 85, **Pl. 16**
  Ferruginous Pygmy-, 85, **Pl. 16**
  Flammulated, 81
  Fulvous, 86
  Great Horned, 84
  Guatemalan Screech-. *See* Owl, Vermiculated Screech-, 83
  Least Pygmy-, 84, **Pl. 16**
  Long-eared, 87
  Mottled, 86, **Pl. 16**
  Mottled Wood-. *See* Owl, Mottled, 86

Owl (contd.)
  Northern Pygmy-, 84
  Northern Saw-whet, 87
  Pacific Screech-, 82
  Ridgway's Saw-whet. *See* Owl, Unspotted Saw-whet, 87
  Río Balsas Screech-. *See* Owl, Balsas Screech-, 82
  Scops. *See* Owl, Flammulated, 81
  Short-eared, 87
  Spectacled, 84, **Pl. 16**
  Spotted, 86
  Spotted Screech-. *See* Owl, Whiskered Screech-, 82
  Striped, 87, **Pl. 16**
  Stygian, 87, **Pl. 16**
  Unspotted Saw-whet, 87, **Pl. 16**
  Vermiculated Screech-, 83, **Pl. 16**
  Vinaceous Screech-, 82
  Western Screech-. *See* Owl, Common Screech-, 81
  Whiskered Screech-, 82, **Pl. 16**
  Wood. *See* Owl, Mottled, 86
Oxyura dominica, 25
  jamaicensis, 24
Oystercatcher(s), 53
  American, 54
  Black, 54

Pachyramphus cinnamomeus, 138
  major, 138
  polychopterus, 138
Pajuil, Black. *See* Penelopina, Black, 42
Pandion haliaetus, 26
Pandionidae, 26
Panyptila cayennensis, 94
  sanctihieronymi, 93
Paphosia helenae, 97
Parabuteo unicinctus, 32
Parakeet(s), 72
  Aztec, 74, **Pl. 14**
  Barred, 75, **Pl. 14**
  Green, 73, **Pl. 14**
  Olive-throated. *See* Parakeet, Aztec, 74
  Orange-chinned, 75, **Pl. 14**
  Orange-fronted, 74, **Pl. 14**
  Pacific. *See* Parakeet, Green, 73

Parakeet (contd.)
 Red-throated. *See* Parakeet, Green, 73
 Tovi. *See* Parakeet, Orange-chinned, 75
Pardirallus maculatus, 50
Paridae, 167
Parrot(s), 72
 Blue-crowned. *See* Parrot, Mealy, 78
 Brown-hooded, 75, **Pl. 14**
 Finsch's. *See* Parrot, Lilac-crowned, 77
 Lilac-crowned, 77, **Pl. 13**
 Maroon-fronted, 74, **Pl. 13**
 Mealy, 78, **Pl. 13**
 Pacific. *See* Parrot, Lilac-crowned, 77
 Red-crowned, 76, **Pl. 13**
 Red-eared. *See* Parrot, Brown-hooded, 75
 Red-lored, 77, **Pl. 13**
 Thick-billed, 74, **Pl. 13**
 White-crowned, 76, **Pl. 14**
 White-fronted, 76, **Pl. 13**
 Yellow-cheeked. *See* Parrot, Red-lored, 77
 Yellow-headed, 77, **Pl. 13**
 Yellow-lored, 76, **Pl. 13**
 Yucatán. *See* Parrot, Yellow-lored, 76
Parrotlet, Blue-rumped, 75, **Pl. 14**
 Mexican. *See* Parrotlet, Blue-rumped, 75
Partridge, Bearded Wood-, 43, **Pl. 8**
 Buffy-crowned Wood-, 44, **Pl. 8**
 Chukar, 47
 Highland. *See* Partridge, Buffy-crowned Wood-, 44
 Highland Wood-. *See* Partridge, Buffy-crowned Wood-, 44
 Long-tailed Wood-, 43, **Pl. 8**
 Long-toed. *See* Quail, Singing, 46
Partridges, Wood-, 43
Parula americana, 204
 graysoni. See under *P. pitiayumi,* 204
 pitiayumi, 204

Parula, Northern, 204
 Socorro. *See* Parula, Tropical, 204
 Tropical, 204, **Pl. 38**
Parulidae, 202
Parus atricristatus, 167
 gambeli, 167
 inornatus, 168
 sclateri, 167
 wollweberi, 168
Passer domesticus, 216
Passerculus sandwichensis, 249
Passerella iliaca, 255
Passerina amoena, 239
 ciris, 240
 cyanea, 239
 leclancherii, 240
 rositae, 240
 versicolor, 240
Pauraque, 89, **Pl. 15**
Pelecanidae, 10
Pelecanus erythrorhynchos, 10
 occidentalis, 10
Pelican(s), 10
 Brown, 10
 White, 10
Penelope purpurascens, 42
Penelopina, Black, 42, **Pl. 6**
Penelopina nigra, 42
Peppershrike(s), 194
 Cozumel. *See* Peppershrike, Rufous-browed, 194
 Mexican. *See* Peppershrike, Rufous-browed, 194
 Rufous-browed, 194, **Pl. 36**
 Yellow-breasted. *See* Peppershrike, Rufous-browed, 194
Petrel, Ashy Storm-, 9
 Band-rumped Storm-, 9
 Beal's Storm-. *See* Petrel, Leach's Storm-, 8
 Black Storm-, 9
 Blue-footed, 7
 Cape, 5
 Cook's. *See* Petrel, Blue-footed, 7
 Dark-rumped, 7
 Galápagos Storm-. *See* Petrel, Wedge-rumped Storm-, 9
 Guadalupe Storm-, 8
 Harcourt's Storm-. *See* Petrel, Band-rumped Storm-, 9

Kermadec. *See* Petrel, Variable, 7
Leach's Storm-, 8
Least Storm-, 8
Pintado. *See* Petrel, Cape, 5
San Benito Storm-. *See* Petrel, Leach's Storm-, 8
Socorro Storm-. *See* Petrel, Leach's Storm-, 8
Sooty Storm-, 9
Variable, 7
Wedge-rumped Storm-, 9
White-necked, 7
Wilson's Storm-, 8
Petrels, Large, 5
Storm-, 8
Petrochelidon fulva, 161
pyrrhonota, 161
Peucedramus taeniatus, 205
Pewee, Eastern Wood-, 147
Greater, 148
Short-legged. *See* Pewee, Tropical, 148
Tropical, 148, **Pl. 28**
Western Wood-, 147
Phaeochroa cuvierii, 95
Phaethon aethereus, 10
lepturus, 10
rubricauda, 10
Phaethontidae, 9
Phaethornis longuemareus, 95
superciliosus, 94
Phainopepla, 192, **Pl. 34**
Crested. *See* Phainopepla, 192
Phainopepla nitens, 192
Phalacrocoracidae, 11
Phalacrocorax auritus, 12
olivaceus, 12
pelagicus, 12
penicillatus, 12
Phalaenoptilus nuttallii, 90
Phalarope(s), 60
Northern, 60
Red, 61
Wilson's, 60
Phalaropodidae, 60
Phalaropus fulicarius, 61
Pharomachrus mocinno, 108
Phasianidae, 43
Phasianus colchicus, 47
Pheasant, Common, 47
Ring-necked. *See* Pheasant,

Pheasant, Ring-necked (contd.)
Common, 47
Pheucticus chrysopeplus, 238
ludovicianus, 238
melanocephalus, 238
Philortyx fasciatus, 45
Phloeoceastes. See *Campephilus,* 123
Phlogothraupis sanguinolenta, 231
Phoebe, Black, 140
Eastern, 140
Say's, 140
Phoenicopteridae, 18
Phoenicopterus ruber, 18
Piaya cayana, 79
Picidae, 117
Piculet, Olivaceous, 117, **117**
Piculus aeruginosus, 118
auricularis, 118
rubiginosus, 118
Picumnus olivaceus, 117
Pigeon(s), 67
Band-tailed, 68, **Pl. 11**
Cayenne. *See* Pigeon, Pale-vented, 67
Domestic. *See* Dove, Rock, 67
Pale-vented, 67, **Pl. 11**
Red-billed, 67, **Pl. 11**
Rufous. *See* Pigeon, Pale-vented, 67
Scaled, 68, **Pl. 12**
Short-billed, 68, **Pl. 11**
White-crowned, 67, **Pl. 12**
Piha, Rufous, 137, **Pl. 26**
Pintail, Northern, 21
Pionopsitta haematotis, 75
Pionus senilis, 76
Pipilo aberti, 248
albicollis, 248
erythrophthalmus, 247
erythrophthalmus macronyx, 247
erythrophthalmus maculatus, 247
erythrophthalmus socorro-ensis, 247
fuscus, 247
ocai, 247
ocai × maculatus, 247
Pipit(s), 191

Pipit (contd.)
American. *See* Pipit, Water, 191
Red-throated, 192
Sprague's, 192
Water, 191
Pipra mentalis, 135
Pipridae, 134
Piprites griseiceps, 134
Pipromorpha oleaginea, 157
Pipromorpha, Oleaginous. *See* Flycatcher, Ochre-bellied, 157
Piranga bidentata, 232
erythrocephala, 233
flava, 232
leucoptera, 233
ludoviciana, 232
olivacea, 232
roseogularis, 232
rubra, 232
Pitangus sulphuratus, 144
Pit-sweet. *See* Nightjar, Spot-tailed, 91
Platypsaris aglaiae, 139
Platyrinchus mystaceus, 153
Plegadis chihi, 18
falcinellus. See under *P. chihi,* 18
Ploceidae, 216
Plover(s), 54
American Golden, 54
Black-bellied, 54
Collared, 55, **Pl. 10**
Mountain, 55
Piping, 54
Ringed. *See* Plover, Semipalmated, 54
Semipalmated, 54
Snowy, 55
Upland. *See* Sandpiper, Upland, 58
Wilson's, 55
Pluvialis dominica, 54
squatarola, 54
Podiceps auritus, 3
dominicus, 3
nigricollis, 3
Podicipedidae, 3
Podilymbus gigas, 4
podiceps, 4
Polioptila albiloris, 189

Polioptila (contd.)
caerulea, 189
melanura, 190
nigriceps, 190
plumbea, 190
Polyborus lutosus, 37
Pooecetes gramineus, 250
Poorwill, Common, 90
Eared, 90
Yucatán, 90
Porphyrula martinica, 52
Porzana carolina, 50
flaviventer, 51
Potoo(s), 88
Common, 88, **Pl. 15**
Great, 88
Jamaican. *See* Potoo, Common, 88
Procellariidae, 5
Progne chalybea, 160
cryptoleuca, 159
dominicensis, 160
subis, 159
Protonotaria citrea, 202
Psaltriparus melanotis. See *P. minimus,* 168
minimus, 168
Psilorhinus mexicanus. See under *P. morio,* 163
morio, 163
Psittacidae, 72
Pterodroma cookii, 7
externa, 7
neglecta, 7
phaeopygia, 7
Pteroglossus torquatus, 116
Ptilogonatidae, 192
Ptilogonys cinereus, 193
Ptilogonys, Mexican. *See* Silky-Flycatcher, Gray, 193
Ptychoramphus aleuticus, 66
Puffbird(s), 115
Brown. *See* Puffbird, White-whiskered, 115
White-necked, 115, **Pl. 22**
White-whiskered, 115, **Pl. 22**
Puffinus auricularis, 6
bulleri, 6
creatopus, 5
gavia. See under *P. puffinus,* 6
griseus, 6

Puffinus (contd.)
  lherminieri, 7
  nativitatus, 6
  opisthomelas. See under *P.*
    puffinus, 6
  pacificus, 5
  puffinus, 6
  tenuirostris, 6
Pulsatrix perspicillata, 84
Pygmy-Owl. *See* Owl
Pygochelidon cyanoleuca pata-
  gonica, 159
Pyrocephalus rubinus, 140
Pyrrhuloxia, 237, **Pl. 46**
  Gray. *See* Pyrrhuloxia, 237
Pyrrhuloxia sinuata, 237

Quail(s), 43
  Banded, 45, **Pl. 8**
  Barred. *See* Quail, Banded, 45
  California, 44, **Pl. 9**
  Douglas. *See* Quail, Elegant, 44
  Elegant, 44, **Pl. 9**
  Gambel's, 44, **Pl. 9**
  Harlequin. *See* Quail, Monte-
    zuma, 46
  Montezuma, 46, **Pl. 8**
  Mountain, 44, **Pl. 9**
  Ocellated, 47, **Pl. 8**
  Salle's. *See* Quail, Montezuma,
    46
  Scaled, 44, **Pl. 9**
  Singing, 46, **Pl. 8**
  Spotted Wood-, 46, **Pl. 8**
Quail-Dove. *See* Dove
Quetzal, Guatemalan. *See* Quet-
  zal, Resplendent, 108
  Resplendent, 108, **Pl. 21**
Quiscalus quiscula, 219

Rail(s), 49
  Black, 51
  Cayenne Wood-. *See* Rail,
    Gray-necked Wood-, 50
  Clapper, 49
  Gray-necked Wood-, 50, **Pl.
    10**
  King, 49
  Mexican. *See* Rail, Clapper, 49
  Red. *See* Crake, Ruddy, 51
  Ruddy. *See* Crake, Ruddy, 51

Rail (contd.)
  Rufous-headed Wood-. *See*
    Rail, Rufous-necked Wood-,
    50
  Rufous-necked Wood-, 50, **Pl.
    10**
  Spotted, 50, **Pl. 10**
  Uniform. *See* Crake, Uniform,
    50
  Virginia, 49
  Western. *See* Rail, Clapper, 49
  White-banded Wood-. *See*
    Rail, Gray-necked Wood-, 50
  Yellow, 51
  Yellow-breasted. *See* Crake,
    Yellow-breasted, 51
Rallidae, 49
Rallus elegans, 49
  limicola, 49
  longirostris, 49
  obsoletus. See *R. longirostris,*
    49
Ramphastidae, 115
Ramphastos sulfuratus, 116
Ramphocaenus rufiventris, 191
Ramphocelus passerinii, 231
Raven, Common, 162
  White-necked, 162
Recurvirostra americana, 60
Recurvirostridae, 60
Redhead, 22
Redstart, American, 213
  Painted, 213, **Pl. 37**
  Red-bellied. *See* Redstart,
    Slate-throated, 214
  Slate-throated, 214, **Pl. 37**
Regulus calendula, 191
  satrapa, 191
Rhinoptynx clamator, 87
Rhodinocichla rosea, 235
Rhodothraupis celaeno, 237
Rhynchocyclus brevirostris, 154
Rhyncopsitta pachyrhyncha, 74
  terrisi, 74
Rhytipterna holerythra, 137
Ridgwayia pinicola, 185
Riparia riparia, 161
Rissa tridactyla, 63
Roadrunner(s), 78
  Greater, 80, **Pl. 15**
  Lesser, 80, **Pl. 15**
Robin, American, 183

Robin (contd.)
    Black, 184, **Pl. 35**
    Clay-colored, 184, **Pl. 35**
    Gray's. *See* Robin, Clay-colored, 184
    Mountain, 184, **Pl. 35**
    Rufous-backed, 183, **Pl. 35**
    Rufous-collared, 183, **Pl. 35**
    San Lucas, 183, **Pl. 35**
    White-throated, 184, **Pl. 35**
Rostrhamus sociabilis, 28
Royal-Flycatcher. *See* Flycatcher
Rynchophanes mccownii, 257
Rynchopidae, 66
Rynchops nigra, 66

Sabrewing, Rufous, 96, **Pl. 20**
    Violet, 96, **Pl. 19**
    Wedge-tailed, 95, **Pl. 20**
Salpinctes obsoletus, 178
Saltator, Black-headed, 236, **Pl. 47**
    Buff-throated, 236, **Pl. 47**
    Grayish, 236, **Pl. 47**
    Lichtenstein's. *See* Saltator, Grayish, 236
Saltator atriceps, 236
    coerulescens, 236
    maximus, 236
Sanderling, 58
Sandpiper(s), 55
    Baird's, 57
    Buff-breasted, 58
    Least, 57
    Pectoral, 57
    Red-backed. *See* Dunlin, 57
    Rock, 58
    Semipalmated, 58
    Solitary, 56
    Spotted, 56
    Stilt, 58
    Upland, 58
    Western, 58
    White-rumped, 57
Sapsucker, Red-breasted, 121
    Williamson's, 121
    Yellow-bellied, 121
Sarcoramphus papa, 25
Sayornis nigricans, 140
    phoebe, 140
    saya, 140
Scaphidura oryzivora, 218

Scardafella inca, 69
Scaup, Greater, 22
    Lesser, 22
Schiffornis turdinus, 136
Sclerurus guatemalensis, 130
    mexicanus, 130
Scolopacidae, 55
Scoter, Black, 23
    Common. *See* Scoter, Black, 23
    Surf, 23
    White-winged, 23
Screech-Owl. *See* Owl
Seedeater, Black. *See* Seedeater, Variable, 242
    Blue, 243
    Cinnamon-rumped. *See* Seedeater, White-collared, 241
    Guerrero. *See* Seedeater, Blue, 243
    Minute. *See* Seedeater, Ruddy-breasted, 242
    Morellet's. *See* Seedeater, White-collared, 241
    Ruddy-breasted, 242, **Pl. 46**
    Sharpe's. *See* Seedeater, White-collared, 241
    Slate-blue. *See under* Seedeater, Blue, 243
    Thick-billed. *See* Finch, Thick-billed Seed-, 242
    Variable, 242, **Pl. 46**
    White-collared, 241, **Pl. 46**
Seed-Finch. *See* Finch
Seiurus aurocapillus, 209
    motacilla, 209
    noveboracensis, 209
Selasphorus platycercus, 108
    rufus, 108
    sasin, 108
Setophaga ruticilla, 213
Sheartail, Mexican, 105, **Pls. 19, 20**
    Slender, 105, **Pls. 19, 20**
Shearwater(s), 5
    Audubon's. *See* Shearwater, Dusky-backed, 7
    Black-vented. *See under* Shearwater, Manx, 6
    Christmas Island, 6
    Common. *See* Shearwater, Manx, 6
    Dusky-backed, 7

Shearwater (contd.)
Fluttering. *See under* Shearwater, Manx, 6
Gray-backed, 6
Manx, 6
New Zealand. *See* Shearwater, Gray-backed, 6
Pacific. *See* Shearwater, Wedge-tailed, 5
Pink-footed, 5
Revilla Gigedo, 6
Short-tailed, 6
Slender-billed. *See* Shearwater, Short-tailed, 6
Sooty, 6
Townsend's. *See* Shearwater, Revilla Gigedo, 6
Wedge-tailed, 5
Shoveler, Northern, 22
Shrike(s), 193
Loggerhead, 193
Shrike-Tanager. *See* Tanager
Shrike-Vireo(s), 194
Chestnut-sided, 194, **Pl. 36**
Emerald. *See* Shrike-Vireo, Green, 195
Green, 195, **Pl. 36**
Highland. *See* Shrike-Vireo, Chestnut-sided, 194
Sialia currucoides, 189
mexicana, 188
sialis, 188
Sicalis luteola, 244
Silkies. *See* Silky-Flycatchers, 192
Silky. *See* Silky-Flycatcher, Gray, 193
Silky-Flycatcher(s), 192
Gray, 193, **Pl. 34**
Siskin, Black-capped, 259, **Pl. 45**
Black-headed, 259, **Pl. 45**
Guatemalan. *See* Siskin, Black-capped, 259
Pine, 259
Sitta canadensis, 168
carolinensis, 168
pygmaea, 169
Sittasomus griseicapillus, 125
Sittidae, 168
Skimmer(s), 66
Black, 66
Skuas, 61

Smaragdolanius pulchellus, 195
Snipe, 55
Common, 59
Softwing. *See* Puffbird, White-whiskered, 115
Solitaire(s), 183
Brown-backed, 185, **Pl. 35**
Slate-colored, 186, **Pl. 35**
Slaty. *See* Solitaire, Slate-colored, 186
Townsend's, 185
Sora, 50
Spadebill, Mexican. *See* Spadebill, White-throated, 153
White-throated, 153, **Pl. 29**
Sparrow(s), 235
Acapulco. *See* Sparrow, Olive, 246
Andean. *See* Sparrow, Rufous-collared, 256
Bailey's. *See* Sparrow, Sierra Madre, 250
Baird's, 250
Belding's. *See* Sparrow, Savannah, 249
Bell's. *See* Sparrow, Sage, 254
Belted. *See* Sparrow, Black-chested, 251
Black-chested, 251, **Pls. 47, 48**
Black-chinned, 255
Black-throated, 254
Botteri's, 253, **Pl. 48**
Brewer's, 254
Bridled, 251, **Pl. 48**
Cassin's, 254
Chiapas. *See* Sparrow, Rusty-crowned Ground-, 248
Chipping, 254
Cinnamon-tailed, 252, **Pl. 48**
Clay-colored, 254
Field, 255
Five-striped, 250, **Pl. 48**
Fox, 255
Golden-crowned, 256
Grasshopper, 249
Green-backed, 246, **Pl. 47**
House, 216
Kiener's Ground-. *See* Sparrow, Rusty-crowned Ground-, 248
Large-billed. *See* Sparrow, Savannah, 249

Sparrow (contd.)
Lark, 250
Lincoln's, 255
Oaxaca, 252
Olive, 246, **Pl. 47**
Orange-billed, 246, **Pl. 47**
Petén. *See under* Sparrow, Botteri's, 253
Prevost's Ground-. *See under* Sparrow, White-faced Ground, 248
Rufous-collared, 256, **Pl. 48**
Rufous-crowned, 253, **Pl. 48**
Rufous-tailed. *See* Sparrow, Stripe-headed, 251
Rufous-winged, 251, **Pl. 48**
Rusty, 252, **Pl. 48**
Rusty-crowned Ground-, 248, **Pl. 48**
Sage, 254
Salvin's Ground-. *See* Sparrow, White-eared Ground-, 249
Savannah, 249
Schott's. *See* Sparrow, Olive, 246
Sharp-tailed, 250
Sierra Madre, 250, **Pl. 48**
Slate-colored. *See* Finch, Slaty, 244
Song, 255
Striped, 249, **Pl. 48**
Stripe-headed, 251, **Pl. 48**
Sumichrast's. *See* Sparrow, Cinnamon-tailed, 252
Swamp, 255
Texas. *See* Sparrow, Olive, 246
Vesper, 250
White-crowned, 256
White-eared Ground-, 249, **Pl. 47**
White-faced Ground-, 248, **Pl. 48**
White-throated, 256
Worthen's, 255, **Pl. 48**
Yellow-carpalled. *See under* Sparrow, Botteri's, 253
Speotyto cunicularia, 85
Sphyrapicus thyroideus, 121
varius, 121
Spindalis, Cozumel. *See* Tanager, Stripe-headed, 231
Spindalis zena, 231

Spinetail, Rufous-breasted, 128, **Pl. 25**
Spinus atriceps, 259
lawrencei, 260
notatus, 259
pinus, 259
psaltria, 260
tristis, 260
Spiza americana, 241
Spizaetus ornatus, 36
tyrannus, 36
Spizastur melanoleucus, 35
Spizella atrogularis, 255
breweri, 254
pallida, 254
passerina, 254
pusilla, 255
wortheni, 255
Spodiornis. See *Haplospiza,* 244
Spoonbill(s), 18
Roseate, 18
Sporophila aurita, 242
corvina. See *S. aurita,* 242
minuta, 242
torqueola, 241
Squatarola. See *Pluvialis,* 54
Starling(s), 193
Common, 194
Starthroat, Constant's. *See* Starthroat, Plain-capped, 104
Long-billed, 105, **Pls. 19, 20**
Plain-capped, 104, **Pl. 19**
Steganopus tricolor, 60
Stelgidopteryx ridgwayi. See *S. ruficollis,* 160
ruficollis, 160
Stellula calliope, 107
Stercorariidae, 61
Stercorarius longicaudus, 62
parasiticus, 62
pomarinus, 61
Sterna albifrons, 65
anaethetus, 64
dougallii, 64
forsteri, 64
fuscata, 64
hirundo, 64
Stilt(s), 60
Black-necked, 60
Stork(s), 17
Wood, 17

Storm-Petrel. *See* Petrel
Streptoprocne semicollaris, 92
  zonaris, 92
Strigidae, 81
Strix fulvescens, 86
  occidentalis, 86
  varia, 86
Sturnella magna, 226
  neglecta, 227
Sturnidae, 193
Sturnus vulgaris, 194
Sula dactylatra, 11
  leucogaster, 11
  nebouxii, 11
  sula, 11
Sulidae, 10
Sunbittern(s), 52, 53, **Pl. 10**
  Greater. *See* Sunbittern, 53
Sungrebe, 52, **Pl. 10**
Surfbird, 57
Swallow(s), 158
  Bank, 161
  Barn, 161
  Black-capped, 159, **Pl. 17**
  Blue-and-White, 159
  Cave, 161, **Pl. 17**
  Cliff, 161
  Coban. *See* Swallow, Black-
    capped, 159
  Mangrove, 159, **Pl. 17**
  Patagonian. *See* Swallow,
    Blue-and-White, 159
  Ridgway's. *See* Swallow,
    Rough-winged, 160
  Rough-winged, 160
  Salvin's. *See* Swallow, Rough-
    winged, 160
  Tree, 158
  Violet-green, 158
Swan(s), 19
  Trumpeter, 19
  Whistling, 19
Swift(s), 92
  Black, 93
  Chestnut-collared, 92, **Pl. 17**
  Chimney, 93
  Gaumer's. *See* Swift, Vaux's,
    93
  Geronimo. *See* Swift, Great
    Swallow-tailed, 93
  Great Swallow-tailed, 93, **Pl.
    17**

Swift (contd.)
  Lesser Swallow-tailed, 94, **Pl.
    17**
  "Richmond's." *See under*
    Swift, Vaux's, 93
  Vaux's, 93
  White-chinned, 93
  White-collared, 92, **Pl. 17**
  White-naped, 92, **Pl. 17**
  White-throated, 93
  "Yucatán." *See under* Swift,
    Vaux's, 93
Sylviidae, 189
Synallaxis erythrothorax, 128
Synallaxis, Rufous-breasted. *See*
    Spinetail, Rufous-breasted,
    128
Synthliboramphus antiguus, 66

Tachycineta albilinea, 159
  bicolor, 158
  thalassina, 158
Tanager(s), 227
  Abbot. *See* Tanager, Yellow-
    winged, 231
  Asure-rumped, 230
  Black-throated Shrike-, 234,
    Pl. 42
  Blue. *See* Tanager, Blue-gray,
    230
  Blue-crowned. *See* Chloro-
    phonia, Blue-crowned, 227
  Blue-gray, 230, **Pl. 43**
  Cabanis. *See* Tanager, Azure-
    rumped, 230
  Common Bush-, 235, **Pl. 42**
  Crimson-collared, 231, **Pl. 44**
  Dusky-tailed Ant-. *See* Tan-
    ager, Red-throated Ant-, 234
  Flame-colored. *See* Tanager,
    Stripe-backed, 232
  Golden-masked. *See* Tanager,
    Masked, 230
  Gray-headed, 234, **Pl. 42**
  Hepatic, 232
  Jungle. *See* Tanager, Red-
    throated Ant-, 234
  Lavinia's. *See* Tanager,
    Rufous-winged, 230
  Masked, 230, **Pl. 43**
  Plush. *See* Tanager, Scarlet-
    rumped, 231

Tanager (contd.)
  Red-crowned Ant-, 233, **Pl. 44**
  Red-headed, 233, **Pl. 43**
  Red-throated, Ant-, 234, **Pl. 44**
  Rose-breasted Thrush-. *See*
    Tanager, Rosy Thrush-, 235
  Rose-throated, 232, **Pl. 43**
  Rosy Thrush, 235, **Pl. 44**
  Rufous-winged, 230
  Scarlet, 232
  Scarlet-rumped, 231, **Pl. 44**
  Song. *See* Tanager, Scarlet-
    rumped, 231
  Stripe-backed, 232, **Pl. 44**
  Striped. *See* Tanager, Stripe-
    backed, 232
  Stripe-headed, 231, **Pl. 42**
  Summer, 232
  Western, 232
  White-winged, 233, **Pl. 43**
  Yellow-winged, 231, **Pl. 43**
Tangara cabanisi, 230
  larvata, 230
  lavinia, 230
  nigricincta. See *T. larvata,* 230
Tangavius. See *Molothrus,* 218
Tapera naevia, 79
Taraba major, 131
Tattler, Wandering, 56
Teal, Blue-winged, 22
  Cinnamon, 22
  Common. *See* Teal, Green-
    winged, 21
  Green-winged, 21
Telmatodytes palustris, 170
Terenotriccus erythrurus, 152
Tern(s), 62
  Black, 64
  Bridled, 64
  Cabot's. *See* Tern, Sandwich,
    65
  Caspian, 64
  Common, 64
  Elegant, 65
  Forster's 64
  Gull-billed, 64
  Least, 65
  Roseate, 64
  Royal, 65
  Sandwich, 65
  Sooty, 64
  White, 65

Tern (contd.)
  Yellow-nibbed.   *See*   Tern,
    Sandwich, 65
Thalasseus elegans, 65
  maximus, 65
  sandvicensis, 65
Thalurania furcata, 99
  ridgwayi. See under *T. furcata,*
    99
  townsendi. See under *T. fur-
    cata,* 99
Thamnistes anabatinus, 131
Thamnophilus doliatus, 131
  punctatus, 131
Thick-knee(s), 61
  Double-striped, 61, **Pl. 10**
Thrasher(s), 179
  Bendire's, 180
  Brown, 179
  California, 181
  Cozumel, 179, **Pl. 34**
  Crissal, 181
  Curve-billed, 180, **Pl. 34**
  Desert. *See* Thrasher, Le-
    conte's, 181
  Gray, 180, **Pl. 34**
  Leconte's, 181
  Long-billed, 179, **Pl. 34**
  Ocellated, 180, **Pl. 34**
  Sage, 181
  Socorro, 181, **Pl. 34**
Thraupidae, 227
Thraupis abbas, 231
  episcopus, 230
Threnetes ruckeri, 94
Threskiornithidae, 18
Thrush(es), 183
  Aztec, 185, **Pl. 35**
  Black-headed   Nightingale-,
    187, **Pl. 35**
  Frantzius' Nightingale-. *See*
    Thrush,   Ruddy-capped
    Nightingale-. 188
  Gray-cheeked, 186
  Hermit, 186
  Highland. *See* Thrush, Ruddy-
    capped Nightingale-, 188
  Highland Nightingale-. *See*
    Thrush,   Ruddy-capped
    Nightingale-, 188
  Olive-backed.   *See*   Thrush,
    Swainson's, 186

Thrush (contd.)
Orange-billed Nightingale-, 188, **Pl. 35**
Ruddy-capped Nightingale-, 188
Russet Nightingale-, 187, **Pl. 35**
Spotted Nightingale-, 187, **Pl. 35**
Swainson's, 186
Varied, 185
Wilson's. *See* Veery, 187
Wood, 186
Thrush-Tanager. *See* Tanager
Thryomanes bewickii, 175
  sissonii, 175
Thryothorus albinucha, 173
  felix, 174
  ludovicianus, 173
  maculipectus, 175
  modestus, 173
  pleurostictus, 174
  rufalbus, 174
  sinaloa, 174
Tiaris olivacea, 241
Tiger-Bittern. *See* Heron, Bare-throated Tiger-, 16
Tiger-Heron. *See* Heron
Tigrisoma lineatum, 15
  mexicanum, 16
Tilmatura dupontii, 106
Tinamidae, 1
Tinamou(s), 1
Boucard's. *See* Tinamou, Slaty-breasted, 1
Great, 1, **Pl. 7**
Little, 1, **Pl. 7**
Rufescent. *See* Tinamou, Thicket, 2
Slaty-breasted, 1, **Pl. 7**
Thicket, 2, **Pl. 7**
Tinamus major, 1
Titmice, 167
Titmouse, Black-crested, 167
Bridled, 168
Plain, 168
Tityra, Black-crowned, 139, **Pl. 26**
Masked, 139, **Pl. 26**
White-collared. *See* Tityra, Black-crowned, 139
Tityra inquisitor, 139

Tityra (contd.)
  semifasciata, 139
Todirostrum cinereum, 154
  sylvia, 154
Tody-Flycatcher. *See* Flycatcher
Tolmomyias sulphurescens, 153
Totanus. See Tringa, 56
Toucan(s), 115
Keel-billed, 116, **Pl. 22**
Collared. *See* Araçari, Collared, 116
Toucanet, Emerald, 116, **Pl. 22**
Wagler's. *See* Toucanet, Emerald, 116
Towhee, Abert's, 248
Brown, 247, **Pl. 48**
California. *See* Towhee, Brown, 247
Canyon. *See* Towhee, Brown, 247
Collared, 247, **Pl. 47**
Green-tailed, 247
hybrid. *See under* Towhee, Rufous-sided, 247 *and* **Pl. 47**
Olive-backed. *See under* Towhee, Rufous-sided, 247
Rufous-sided, 247
San Lucas. *See* Towhee, Brown, 247
Socorro. *See under* Towhee, Rufous-sided, 247
Spotted. *See under* Towhee, – Rufous-sided, 247
White-throated, 248, **Pl. 48**
Toxostoma bendirei, 180
  cinereum, 180
  curvirostre, 180
  dorsale, 181
  guttatum, 179
  lecontei, 181
  longirostre, 179
  ocellatum, 180
  redivivum, 181
  rufum, 179
Tree-Duck. *See* Duck
"Tree-Quails." *See* Partridges, Wood-, 43
Tringa flavipes, 56
  melanoleuca, 56
  solitaria, 56
Tripsurus. See Centurus, 119–20
Trochilidae, 94

Troglodytes aedon, 175, 176
  beani. See under *T. musculus,*
    176
  brunneicollis. See *T. aedon,*
    176
  musculus, 176
  rufociliatus, 176
  tanneri, 175
Troglodytidae, 170
Trogon(s), 108
  Bar-tailed. *See* Trogon, Col-
    lared, 110
  "Black-headed." *See under*
    Trogon, Citreoline, 109
  Citreoline, 109, **Pl. 21**
  Collared, 110, **Pl. 21**
  Coppery-tailed. *See* Trogon,
    Elegant, 110
  Eared, 109, **Pl. 21**
  Elegant, 110, **Pl. 21**
  Gartered. *See* Trogon, Viola-
    ceous, 111
  Jalapa. *See* Trogon, Collared,
    110
  Massena. *See* Trogon, Slaty-
    tailed, 109
  Mexican. *See* Trogon, Moun-
    tain, 110
  Mountain, 110, **Pl. 21**
  Slaty-tailed, 109, **Pl. 21**
  Violaceous, 111, **Pl. 21**
Trogon citreolus, 109
  collaris, 110
  elegans, 110
  massena, 109
  melanocephalus. See under *T.
    citreolus,* 109
  mexicanus, 110
  violaceus, 111
Trogonidae, 108
Tropicbird(s), 9
  Red-billed, 10
  Red-tailed, 10
  White-tailed, 10
  Yellow-billed. *See* Tropicbird,
    White-tailed, 10
Tryngites rubruficollis, 58
Turdidae, 183
Turdus assimilis, 184
  confinis, 183
  grayi, 184
  infuscatus, 184

Turdus (contd.)
  migratorius, 183
  plebejus, 184
  rufitorques, 183
  rufopalliatus, 183
Turkey(s), 47
  Bronze. *See* Turkey, Common,
    47
  Common, 47
  Ocellated, 48, **Pl. 7**
Turnstone, Black, 56
  Ruddy, 56
Tyrannidae, 140
Tyranniscus vilissimus, 157
Tyrannulet, Northern Beardless,
  156, **Pl. 29**
  Paltry, 157, **Pl. 29**
  Yellow-bellied, 157, **Pl. 29**
Tyrannus crassirostris, 142
  cubensis, 143
  dominicensis, 142
  melancholicus, 142
  melancholicus chloronotis, 142
  melancholicus couchii, 142
  savana. See *Muscivora ty-
    rannus,* 141
  tyrannus, 141
  verticalis, 141
  vociferans, 141
Tyto alba, 81
Tytonidae, 81

Uria aalge, 66
Uropsila leucogastra, 177

Veery, 187
Veniliornis fumigatus, 122
Verdin(s), 167, 168
Vermivora celata, 203
  chrysoptera, 203
  crissalis, 204
  luciae, 204
  peregrina, 203
  pinus, 203
  ruficapilla, 203
  superciliosa, 204
  virginiae, 204
Violet-ear, Brown, 96
  Green, 97, **Pl. 18**
  Mexican. *See* Violet-ear,
    Green, 97

Vireo(s), 195
  Bell's, 197
  Black-capped, 195
  Black-whiskered, 198
  Blue-headed. *See* Vireo, Solitary
  Brown-capped, 199, **Pl. 36**
  Cozumel, 195, **Pl. 36**
  Dwarf, 197
  Golden, 196, **Pl. 36**
  Gray, 197
  Gray-headed, *See* Greenlet,
    Lesser, 200
  Green-winged. *See* Vireo,
    Slaty, 199
  Hutton's, 196
  Mangrove, 196, **Pl. 36**
  Pale. *See* Vireo, Mangrove, 196
  Petén. *See under* Vireo, Man-
    grove, 196
  Philadelphia, 199
  Red-eyed, 197
  Slaty, 199, **Pl. 36**
  Solitary, 197
  Tawny-crowned. *See* Greenlet,
    Tawny-crowned, 200
  Veracruz. *See under* Vireo,
    White-eyed, 196
  Warbling, 199
  White-eyed, 196
  Yellow-green, 198, **Pl. 36**
  Yellow-throated, 197
  Yucatán, 198, **Pl. 36**
  See also Shrike-Vireo
Vireo altiloquus, 198
  atricapillus, 195
  bairdi, 195
  bellii, 197
  flavifrons, 197
  flavoviridis, 198
  gilvus, 199
  griseus, 196
  griseus perquisitor, 196
  huttoni, 196
  hypochryseus, 196
  leucophrys, 199
  magister, 198
  nelsoni, 197
  olivaceus, 197
  pallens, 196
  perquisitor. See under *V. gris-
    eus,* 196
  philadelphicus, 199

Vireo (contd.)
  semiflavus. See under *V. pal-
    lens,* 196
  solitarius, 197
  vicinior, 197
Vireolaniidae, 194
Vireolanius melitophrys, 194
Vireonidae, 195
Volatinia jacarina, 243
Vulture, Black, 25
  King, 25, **Pl. 4**
  Lesser Yellow-headed, 25, **Pl. 4**
  Savanna. *See* Vulture, Lesser
    Yellow-headed, 25
  Turkey, 25
Vultures, New World, 25

Wagtail(s), 191
  Pied. *See* Wagtail, White, 191
  White, 191
Warbler, Audubon's, 206
  Bay-breasted, 208
  Bell's. *See* Warbler, Golden-
    browed, 215
  Black-and-White, 202
  Blackburnian, 207
  Blackpoll, 208
  Black-throated Blue, 206
  Black-throated Gray, 206
  Black-throated Green, 207
  Blue-winged, 203
  Brasher's. *See* Warbler,
    Golden-crowned, 215
  Canada, 213
  Cape May, 206
  Cerulean, 207
  Chestnut-capped, 216, **Pl. 38**
  Chestnut-crowned. *See* War-
    bler, Golden, 205
  Chestnut-sided, 208
  Chiriqui. *See* Parula, Tropical,
    204
  Colima, 204
  Connecticut, 209
  Crescent-chested, 204, **Pl. 38**
  Delattre's. *See* Warbler, Chest-
    nut-capped, 216
  Fan-tailed, 214, **Pl. 38**
  Golden, 205, **Pl. 38**
  Golden-browed, 215, **Pl. 38**
  Golden-cheeked, 207
  Golden-crowned, 215, **Pl. 38**

Warbler (contd.)
  Golden-winged, 203
  "Goldman's." *See under* War-
    bler, Audubon's, 206
  Grace's, 208
  Hartlaub's. *See* Warbler, Cres-
    cent-chested, 204
  Hermit, 207
  Hooded, 212
  Kentucky, 209
  Lichtenstein's. *See* Warbler,
    Golden-crowned, 215
  Lucy's, 204
  MacGillivray's, 210
  Magnolia, 206
  Mangrove, 205, **Pl. 38**
  Meadow. *See* Yellowthroat,
    Gray-crowned, 211
  Mourning, 209
  Myrtle, 206
  Nashville, 203
  Olive, 205
  Orange-crowned, 203
  Ovenbird. *See* Ovenbird, 209
  Palm, 208
  Parula. *See* Parula, Northern
    or Tropical, 204
  Pine, 208
  Pink-headed, 214, **Pl. 37**
  Prairie, 208
  Prothonotary, 202
  Red, 214, **Pl. 37**
  Red-faced, 213, **Pl. 37**
  Rufous-capped, 215, **Pl. 38**
  Salvin's. *See* Warbler, Rufous-
    capped, 215
  Socorro. *See under* Parula,
    Tropical, 204
  Spot-breasted. *See* Warbler,
    Crescent-chested, 204
  Swainson's, 202
  Tennessee, 203
  Townsend's, 207
  Virginia's, 204
  Wilson's, 213
  Worm-eating, 203
  Yellow, 205
  Yellow-throated, 207
Warblers, Wood-, 202
Water-Ouzel. *See* Dipper, Ameri-
  can, 170
Waterthrush, Louisiana, 209

Waterthrush (contd.)
  Northern, 209
Waxwing(s), 192
  Cedar, 192
Weaver Finches, 216
Whimbrel, 59
Whip-poor-will, 90
  Ridgway's. *See* Nightjar, Buff-
    collared, 91
Wigeon, American, 21
  European, 21
"Will." *See under* Nightjar,
    Tawny-collared, 90
Willet, 56
Wilsonia canadensis, 213
  citrina, 212
  pusilla, 213
Woodcreeper(s), 124
  Barred, 126, **Pl. 24**
  Black-banded, 126, **Pl. 24**
  Buff-throated, 126
  Ivory-billed, 126, **Pl. 24**
  Olivaceous, 125, **Pl. 24**
  Ruddy, 124, **Pl. 24**
  Spot-crowned, 128, **Pl. 24**
  Spotted, 127, **Pl. 24**
  Streak-headed, 127, **Pl. 24**
  Strong-billed, 125, **Pl. 24**
  Tawny-winged, 124, **Pl. 24**
  Wedge-billed, 125, **Pl. 24**
  White-striped, 127, **Pl. 24**
Woodhewer, Allied. *See* Wood-
    creeper, Spot-crowned, 128
  Guatemalan. *See* Wood-
    creeper, Strong-billed, 125
  Mexican. *See* Woodcreeper,
    Olivaceous, 125
  Thin-billed. *See* Woodcreeper,
    Streak-headed, 127
Woodnymph, Common, 99, **Pl.
    18**
  Honduras. *See* Woodnymph,
    Common, 99
  Mexican. *See* Woodnymph,
    Common, 99
Wood-Partridge. *See* Partridge
Woodpecker(s), 117
  Acorn, 119
  Arizona. *See* Woodpecker,
    Brown-backed, 122
  Balsas. *See* Woodpecker,
    Gray-breasted, 120

Woodpecker (contd.)
  Black-cheeked, 120, **Pl. 23**
  Bronze-winged, 118, **Pl. 23**
  Brown. *See* Woodpecker,
    Smoky-brown, 122
  Brown-backed, 122, **Pl. 23**
  Brown-barred, 123, **Pl. 23**
  Chestnut. *See* Woodpecker,
    Chestnut-colored, 119
  Chestnut-colored, 119, **Pl. 23**
  Flint-billed. *See* Woodpecker,
    Pale-billed, 123
  Gila, 120, **Pl. 23**
  Golden-cheeked, 119, **Pl. 23**
  Golden-fronted, 120, **Pl. 23**
  Golden-olive, 118, **Pl. 23**
  Gray-breasted, 120, **Pl. 23**
  Gray-crowned, 118, **Pl. 23**
  Hairy, 122
  Imperial, 123, **Pl. 23**
  Ladder-backed, 122, **Pl. 23**
  Lewis's, 119
  Lineated, 119, **Pl. 23**
  Nuttall's, 122
  Oaxaca. *See* Woodpecker,
    Golden-fronted, 120
  Pale-billed, 123, **Pl. 23**
  Pucheran's. *See* Woodpecker,
    Black-cheeked, 120
  Red-vented, 121, **Pl. 23**
  Santacruz. *See* Woodpecker,
    Golden-fronted, 120
  Smoky-brown, 122, **Pl. 23**
  Strickland's. *See* Woodpecker,
    Brown-barred, 123
  Yucatán. *See* Woodpecker,
    Red-vented, 121
Wood-Pewee. *See* Pewee
Wood-Quail. *See* Quail
Wood-Rail. *See* Rail
Wood-Warbler. *See* Warbler
Wood-Wren. *See* Wren
Wren(s), 170
  Band-backed, 171, **Pl. 33**
  Banded, 174, **Pl. 32**
  Banded Cactus-. *See* Wren,
    Band-backed, 171
  Barred. *See* Wren, Band-
    backed, 171
  Bar-vented, 174, **Pl. 32**
  Bewick's, 175, **Pl. 32**
  Boucard Cactus-. *See* Wren,

Wren, Boucard Cactus- (contd.)
  Spotted, 172
Boucard's, 172
Brown-throated, 176, **Pl. 32**
Cactus, 172, **Pl. 33**
Canyon, 178, **Pl. 32**
Carolina, 173
Chiapas. *See* Wren, Giant, 171
Clarión Island, 175, **Pl. 32**
Cozumel. *See under* Wren,
  Southern House-, 176
Cozumel House. *See* Wren,
  Southern House-, 176
Giant, 171, **Pl. 33**
Grass. *See* Wren, Short-billed
  Marsh, 170
Gray. *See* Wren, Gray-barred,
  170
Gray-barred, 170, **Pl. 33**
Gray-breasted Wood-, 177, **Pl.
  32**
Gray Cactus-. *See* Wren, Gray-
  barred, 170
Happy, 174, **Pl. 32**
Highland Wood-. *See* Wren,
  Gray-breasted Wood-, 177
Long-billed Marsh, 170
Lowland Wood-. *See* Wren,
  White-breasted Wood-, 177
Modest. *See* Wren, Plain, 173
Nightingale, 178, **Pl. 33**
Northern Cactus-. *See* Wren,
  Cactus, 172
Northern House-, 175
Plain, 173, **Pl. 32**
Rock, 178, **Pl. 32**
Rufous-and-White, 174, **Pl. 32**
Rufous-browed, 176, **Pl. 32**
Rufous-naped, 171, **Pl. 33**
Sclater's Cactus-. *See* Wren,
  Rufous-naped, 171
Sedge. *See* Wren, Short-billed
  Marsh, 170
Short-billed Marsh, 170
Sinaloa. *See* Wren, Bar-
  vented, 174
Slender-billed, 178, **Pl. 33**
Socorro, 175, **Pl. 32**
Southern House-, 176, **Pl. 32**
Spot-breasted, 175, **Pl. 32**
Spotted, 172, **Pl. 33**
Spotted Cactus-. *See* Wren,

Wren, Spotted Cactus- (contd.)
Spotted, 172
Sumichrast's. *See* Wren,
Slender-billed, 178
Tropical House-. *See* Wren,
Southern House, 176
White-bellied, 177, **Pl. 32**
White-breasted Wood-, 177, **Pl. 32**
White-browed, 173, **Pl. 32.**
See also Wren, Carolina, 173
Yucatán, 172
Yucatán Cactus-. *See* Wren,
Yucatán, 172
Wrentit(s), 169

Xanthocephalus xanthocephalus, 226
Xema sabini, 64
Xenops, Little. *See* Xenops,
Plain, 129
Plain, 129, **Pl. 25**
Xenops minutus, 129
Xenospiza baileyi, 250
Xenotriccus callizonus, 152
Xiphocolaptes promeropirhynchus, 125
Xiphorhynchus erythropygius, 127
flavigaster, 126
guttatus, 126

Yellow-Finch, Mexican. *See*

Yellow-Finch, Mexican (contd.)
Finch, Grassland Yellow-, 244
Yellowhead, Lesser. *See* Vulture,
Lesser Yellow-headed, 25
Yellowlegs, Greater, 56
Lesser, 56
Yellowthroat, Altamira. *See* Yellowthroat, Yellow-crowned, 210
Belding's. *See* Yellowthroat,
Peninsular, 210
Black-polled, 211, **Pl. 38**
Brush. *See* Yellowthroat,
Hooded, 211
Chapala, 211
Common, 210
Gray-crowned, 211, **Pl. 38**
Hooded, 211, **Pl. 38**
Orizaba. *See* Yellowthroat,
Black-polled, 211
Peninsular, 210, **Pl. 38**
Yellow-crowned, 210, **Pl. 38**

Zarhynchus wagleri, 217
Zenaida asiatica, 69
aurita, 69
graysoni, 68
macroura, 68
Zenaidura. See *Zenaida,* 68
Zonotrichia albicollis, 256
atricapilla, 256
capensis, 256
leucophrys, 256

BAJA CALIFORNIA

Gulf of California

Pacific slope
and plain

Gulf (Atlantic)
slope and plain

Highlands

Central plateau

Pacific

Ocean